You're Busy so We're Bite-Sized

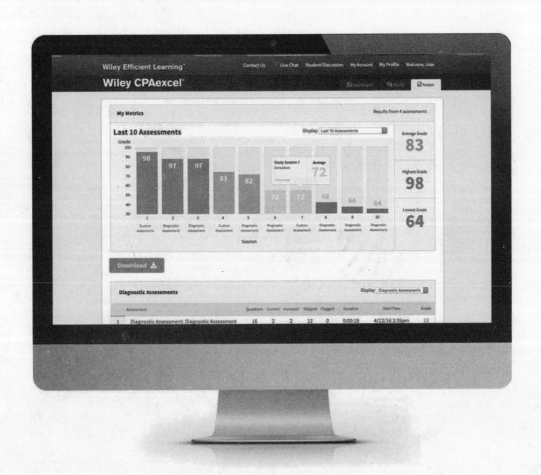

✓ **Complete Each Lesson in 30-45 minutes**

✓ **Video, Text, Assessment in Each Lesson**

✓ **Mobile App that Syncs Automatically with the Online Course**

✓ **Always Know Exactly Where You Stand**

✓ **Lesson Progress and Mastery Metrics**

Your Plan to Pass is Waiting

If you fail to plan, then plan to fail. Wiley's Exam Planner is at the heart of why 9 out of 10 pass using our system.

- ✓ **Enter Your Exam Date**
- ✓ **Enter Your Weekly Study Hours**
- ✓ **See 700 Lessons Scheduled to the Day**

You Can Do This!

efficientlearning.com/resources

Wiley CPAexcel® Exam Review

STUDY
GUIDE

JULY 2017

AUDITING AND ATTESTATION

Wiley CPAexcel® Exam Review

STUDY GUIDE

JULY 2017

Donald E. Tidrick, Ph.D., CPA, CMA, CIA
Robert A. Prentice, J.D.

Wiley Efficient Learning™

Cover image: © jeremykramerdesign/iStockphoto
Cover design: Wiley

ISBN 9781119429791

ISBN 9781119429784 (ebk); ISBN 9781119429777 (ebk)

Printed in the United States of America.

10 9 8 7 6 5 4 3 2 1

Contents

About the Authors

CPAexcel® content is authored by a team of accounting professors and CPA Exam experts from top accounting colleges such as the University of Texas at Austin (frequently ranked the #1 accounting school in the country), California State University at Sacramento, Northern Illinois University (frequently ranked in the top 10 in its peer group and top 20 overall), and the University of North Alabama.

Professor Craig Bain
CPAexcel® Mentor and Video Lecturer
Ph.D., CPA
Northern Arizona University: Franke College of Business, Professor and Accounting Area Coordinator

Professor Allen H. Bizzell
CPAexcel® Author, Mentor, and Video Lecturer
Ph.D., CPA (inactive)
Former Associate Dean and Accounting Faculty, University of Texas (Retired)
Associate Professor, Department of Accounting, Texas State University (Retired)

Professor Gregory Carnes
CPAexcel® Author and Video Lecturer
Ph.D., CPA
Raburn Eminent Scholar of Accounting, University of North Alabama
Former Dean, College of Business, Lipscomb University
Former Chair, Department of Accountancy, Northern Illinois University

Professor B. Douglas Clinton
CPAexcel® Author and Video Lecturer
Ph.D., CPA, CMA
Alta Via Consulting Professor of Management Accountancy, Department of Accountancy, Northern Illinois University

Professor Charles J. Davis
CPAexcel® Author
Ph.D., CPA
Professor of Accounting, Department of Accounting, College of Business Administration, California State University—Sacramento

Professor Donald R. Deis Jr.
CPAexcel® Author and Video Lecturer
Ph.D., CPA, CFE
TAMUS Regents Professor and Ennis & Virginia Joslin Endowed Chair in Accounting, College of Business,
   Texas A&M University—Corpus Christi
Former Director, School of Accountancy, University of Missouri—Columbia
Former Professor and Director, Accounting Ph.D. Program, Louisiana State University—Baton Rouge

Professor Emeritus Marianne M. Jennings
CPAexcel® Author and Video Lecturer
J.D.
Professor of Legal and Ethical Studies, W.P. Carey School of Business, Arizona State University

Professor Robert A. Prentice
CPAexcel® Author and Video Lecturer
J.D.
Ed and Molly Smith Centennial Professor In Business Law and Distinguished Teaching Professor, J.D.
   McCombs School of Business, University of Texas—Austin

Professor Pam Smith
CPAexcel® Author and Video Lecturer
Ph.D., MBA, CPA
KPMG Professor of Accountancy, Department of Accountancy, Northern Illinois University

Professor Dan N. Stone
CPAexcel® Author and Video Lecturer
Ph.D., MPA, CPA (inactive)
Gatton Endowed Chair, Von Allmen School of Accountancy, University of Kentucky

Professor Donald Tidrick
CPAexcel® Author and Video Lecturer
Ph.D., CPA, CMA, CIA
Deloitte Professor of Accountancy, Northern Illinois University
Former Associate Chairman, Department of Accounting, Director of Professional Program in Accounting and Director of the
   CPA Review Course, University of Texas at Austin

About the Auditing and Attestation Professors

Professor Donald E. Tidrick is currently Deloitte Professor of Accountancy in the Department of Accountancy at Northern Illinois University. From 1991 to 2000, Dr. Tidrick was on the faculty at the University of Texas at Austin, where he was Associate Chair of the Department of Accounting, Director of the Professional Program in Accounting and Director of UT's CPA Review Course. Among other professional distinctions, Dr. Tidrick serves on the Educators' Advisory Panel for the Comptroller General of the United States and he is a member of the Ethics Committee of the Illinois CPA Society.

Professor Robert A. Prentice is the Ed and Molly Smith Centennial Professor of Business Law at the University of Texas at Austin and has taught both UTs and other CPA courses for 15 years. He created a new course in accounting ethics and regulation that he has taught for the last decade. Professor Prentice has written several textbooks, many major law review articles on securities regulation and accountants' liability, and has won more than 30 teaching awards.

Welcome to Auditing and Attestation

Passing the Auditing and Attestation Part of the CPA Exam

Candidates sometimes have a misperception about the Auditing and Attestation part of the CPA examination, believing that auditing is primarily a practice-oriented part of the exam. They may believe that having had firsthand experience doing audit work is sufficient for success on this part, or that not having had such experience is insurmountable. Sometimes candidates have a false sense of security, expressing the view that "Auditing is just common sense!" However, their view often changes when they see the specificity of the CPA Exam questions that focus on the relevant concepts and the applicable professional standards. Passing the auditing part of the CPA examination is fundamentally an academic endeavor. I believe that everything you need to pass is contained in Wiley CPAexcel®—all that is required is your commitment to carefully study it.

AICPA Professional Standards

The Auditing and Attestation part of the CPA examination focuses heavily on candidates' familiarity with the applicable AICPA Professional Standards. Since the AICPA prepares the exam, it should not be surprising that they emphasize their professional literature. Indeed, a substantial majority of the points in auditing focuses on candidates' knowledge of the AICPA's Statements on Auditing Standards, the Statements on Standards for Attestation Engagements, the Statements on Standards for Accounting and Review Services, and, to a lesser extent, the Statements on Quality Control Standards. The entire set of AICPA Professional Standards tested in the Auditing and Attestation area has been outlined and addressed. Of course, the PCAOB auditing standards and IFAC's International Standards on Auditing are "fair game" for testing and are also appropriately covered in Wiley CPAexcel®. Fortunately, the AICPA's "clarified" auditing standards have now substantially reduced the significance of differences between the AICPA's Statements on Auditing Standards and the International Standards on Auditing.

Wiley CPAexcel® Materials

These materials strive to achieve an optimal balance between **technical depth**, covering the topics on the AICPA Content Specification Outlines, and **efficiency**, focusing on the task at hand without excess verbiage and unnecessary detail. The materials emphasize the professional standards and important concepts that are the primary object of testing in the Auditing and Attestation area.

I encourage you to review the study text basically in sequence, since auditing has something of a chronological order—including planning, evidence gathering, and reporting. Read the study text carefully, and very importantly, take the time to work on the proficiency questions, the multiple-choice questions, and task-based simulations that are integral to Wiley CPAexcel®'s successful approach.

Multiple-Choice Questions

Even though the number of professional standards has increased over the years, these standards often deal with only incremental changes to similar prior standards. In many cases, the underlying concepts have not changed very much. This part of the exam is not quantitative by nature, so questions cannot be updated by simply changing the "numbers." If you make a diligent effort studying these past exams' multiple-choice questions, you will very likely see some "old friends" on your examination, or, at the very least, some questions that are very similar to what you have practiced.

Final Review

In addition to diligently studying the study text and practicing proficiency questions and exam questions, candidates invariably benefit from an intensive final review. The study text is designed to facilitate an efficient review and I encourage you to spend a few days reviewing the study text from start to finish to refresh your memory of important concepts immediately prior to testing.

Work hard and enjoy the accomplishment of becoming a CPA for the rest of your life!

~ *Professor Donald Tidrick*

I am pleased to be responsible for teaching the Code of Professional Conduct in this material. Although much of the material in the Code relates directly to the public practice of auditors, hence its placement in AUD, there is much significant material here for accountants in any field of endeavor, including those who work for companies and even those who are between jobs or retired.

Although the material focuses primarily on the AICPA Code, auditors must be cognizant of the rules promulgated by the Securities and Exchange Commission (SEC), the Public Company Accounting Oversight Board (PCAOB) and, depending on the nature of their audit clients, the Government Accountability Office (GAO) and the Department of Labor (DOL).

Fortunately, although there are differing rules from agency to agency, the big picture is the same. If you master the AICPA's Code, you will be a long ways toward knowing how to apply the more specific rules of the SEC, PCAOB, GAO, and DOL. The AICPA Code should receive the bulk of your attention, though all sections are important.

~ Professor Robert Prentice

Ethics, Professional Responsibilities, and General Principles

AICPA Code of Professional Conduct

Introduction and Preface

> **After studying this lesson, you should be able to:**
>
> **1.** Understand the basic organizational structure of the new electronic version of the Code of Professional Conduct.
>
> **2.** Explain the six key principles on which the code is based.

I. Introduction

A. The AICPA dramatically reorganized the Code of Professional Conduct so that its new electronic format would be easily searchable by members who needed answers regarding their professional responsibilities. The code is available at: ****. While there were minor substantive changes, most of the changes were organizational. The following materials reflect the new electronic version of the code (which can now be easily updated). Most of the provisions are effective December 15, 2014. Some, mostly those dealing with the Conceptual Framework, are effective December 15, 2015.

B. Two major changes deserve mention in this introduction. First, the code now divides professional responsibilities in terms of the role that members play. Part 1 of the code sets out rules for members in public practice, such as independent auditors. This includes, of course, independence rules but also rules regarding integrity, objectivity, and discreditable acts. Part 2 of the code sets out rules for members in business, such as internal auditors at a corporation. They need not worry about independence rules, and many of the other rules for members in business are identical (or nearly so) to the nonindependence rules that apply to members in public practice. Part 3 sets out rules for other members, such as those who are unemployed or retired, who are expected to avoid discreditable acts.

C. Second, following the lead of the International Federation of Accountants, the AICPA has put into place (effective December 15, 2015), a Conceptual Framework for answering questions that arise that are not answered even by the many detailed code provisions and interpretations. In virtually every subject matter area of the entire code, if there is no clear answer, the Conceptual Framework should be applied.

II. Preface (Part 0)

A. Overview

   1. The code is divided into three main parts:

   a. Part 1 applies to members in public practice.

   b. Part 2 applies to members in business.

   c. Part 3 applies to other members.

   2. Members serving in multiple roles should choose the most restrictive applicable provisions.

B. Principles and rules of conduct contained in the code are supplemented by:

   1. Interpretations

   2. Definitions

   3. Applications

   4. Where applicable, standards promulgated by other bodies such as

   a. State certified public accounting (CPA) societies

   b. Securities and Exchange Commission

   c. Public Company Accounting Oversight Board

    d. Government Accountability Office

    e. Department of Labor

    f. Various taxing authorities

C. Principles of Professional Conduct

  1. By voluntarily joining the AICPA, members assume an obligation of self-discipline above and beyond legal requirements.

  2. The six major principles call for "an unswerving commitment to honorable behavior, even at the sacrifice of personal advantage":

    a. "Responsibilities principle. In carrying out their responsibilities as professionals, members should exercise sensitive professional and moral judgments in all their activities."

      i. This principle imposes a continuing responsibility on members to "cooperate with each other to:

        1. "improve the art of accounting,

        2. "maintain the public's confidence, and

        3. "carry out the profession's special responsibilities for self-governance."

    b. "Public Interest principle. Members should accept the obligation to act in a way that will serve the public interest, honor the public trust, and demonstrate a commitment to professionalism."

> **Note**
> *"A distinguishing mark of a profession is acceptance of its responsibility to the public."*

    c. "Integrity principle. To maintain and broaden public confidence, members should perform all professional responsibilities with the highest sense of integrity."

      i. "Integrity is measured in terms of what is right and just"; members should always ask "Am I doing what a person of integrity would do?"

    d. "Objectivity and Independence principle. A member should maintain objectivity and be free of conflicts of interest in discharging professional responsibilities. A member in public practice should be independent in fact and appearance when providing auditing and other attestation services."

      i. "Objectivity is a state of mind" that requires:

        1. impartiality,

        2. intellectual honesty, *and*

        3. freedom from conflicts of interest.

      ii. Only members in public practice must act with independence, but all members performing all services must act with objectivity and integrity.

    e. "Due care principle. A member should observe the profession's technical and ethical standards, strive continually to improve competence and the quality of services, *and* discharge professional responsibility to the best of the member's ability."

      i. Perfection is not required.

      ii. Competence requires a commitment to continued learning—hence, continuing professional education.

      iii. Members may derive competence from research or consultation with experts.

      iv. Due care entails

        1. Adequate planning of engagements

        2. Supervision of professional activities for which members are responsible

f. "Scope and nature of services principle. A member in public practice should observe the Principles of the Code of Professional Conduct in determining the scope and nature of services to be provided."

g. At a minimum, members should:

    i. Practice in firms that have good internal quality control procedures,

    ii. Use their individual judgments to determine whether the scope and nature of services provided to an audit client would create a conflict of interest, *and*

    iii. Individually assess whether a contemplated activity is consistent with their role as professionals.

	Audit	**Compilation**	**Tax**	**Consulting**
Integrity	Yes	Yes	Yes	Yes
Objectivity	Yes	Yes	Yes	Yes
Independence in Fact	Yes	No	No	No
Independence in Appearance	Yes	No	No	No

D. Definitions

1. Part 0 contains approximately 50 definitions, ranging from "Acceptable Level" to "Threats." This study guide sets out various definitions as they become relevant to the substantive provisions being discussed, but it couldn't hurt to read through the definitions.

> **Example**
> *Partner Equivalent*
> A professional employee who is not a partner of the firm but who either (a) has the ultimate responsibility for the conduct of an attest engagement, including the authority to sign or affix the firm's name to an attest report or issue, or authorize others to issue, an attest report on behalf of the firm without partner approval; or (b) has the authority to bind the firm to conduct an attest engagement without partner approval. For example, the professional employee has the authority to sign or affix the firm's name to an attest engagement letter or contract to conduct an attest engagement without partner approval.

Members in Public Practice

MIPPs Introduction and Conceptual Framework

After studying this lesson, you should be able to:

1. Apply the Conceptual Framework to answer questions of professional responsibility that are not clearly answered in the code itself.

I. Introduction

    A. Part 1 of the Code of Professional Conduct applies to members in public practice (MIPPs). Public practice consists of the performance of professional services (e.g., audit, tax, consulting) for a client by a member or the member's firm.

II. Conceptual Framework—Where the code's rules and interpretations do not provide a clear answer to a particular situation, members should always apply the threats-and-safeguards Conceptual Framework in order to determine whether threats to a member's compliance with the rules (independence and otherwise) can be reduced to an acceptable level (defined as "a level at which a reasonable and informed third party who is aware of the relevant information would be expected to conclude that a member's compliance with the rules is not compromised") by application of safeguards.

    A. There are three main steps to applying the Conceptual Framework:

        1. Identify threats.

        2. Evaluate the significance of the threats.

        3. Identify and apply safeguards.

    B. There are seven broad categories of threats:

        1. Adverse interest threats. Examples:

            a. Client sues or threatens to sue firm.

            b. Subrogee makes claim against firm to recover payments it made to client.

        2. Advocacy threats. Examples:

            a. Member provides forensic accounting services to client in lawsuit with third party.

            b. Firm acts as investment advisor, underwriter, promoter, or registered agent for a client.

        3. Familiarity threats. Examples:

            a. Member's spouse, parent, sibling, or close friend is employed by the client.

            b. Former firm partner joins client in a key position.

        4. Management participation threats. Example:

            a. Member takes on role of client management.

        5. Self-interest threats. Examples:

            a. Member has a financial interest in a client that may be affected by outcome of professional services the firm is providing.

            b. Firm relies excessively on revenue from a single client.

6. Self-review threats. Examples:

    a. Member relies on work product of own firm.

    b. Member does client's bookkeeping.

    c. Partner in firm was an officer or director of client.

7. Undue influence threats. Examples:

    a. Client threatens to fire firm or to withhold future business unless firm accedes to client's wishes.

    b. Client's major shareholder threatens to withdraw or terminate a professional service unless the member reaches desired conclusion.

C. Three kinds of safeguards exist:

1. Safeguards created by the profession, legislation, or regulation. Examples:

    a. Ethics education and training requirements, including continuing professional education (CPE)

    b. Professional standards and threat of discipline

    c. External reviews of a firm's quality controls

    d. Legislation regulating firm's professionals

    e. Licensure requirements

    f. Professional resources, such as ethics hotlines

2. Safeguards implemented by the client. The client has, for example:

    a. Knowledgeable and experienced managers

    b. Appropriate tone at the top regarding ethics and compliance

    c. Appropriate policies and procedures for compliance and fair reporting

    d. Appropriate ethics policies and procedures

    e. Appropriate governance structure, including an active audit committee

    f. Policies to prevent client from hiring a firm to provide services that would impair independence or objectivity

3. Safeguards implemented by the firm. Examples:

    a. Strong leadership emphasizing compliance and acting in the public interest

    b. Policies and procedures to implement and monitor engagement quality control

    c. Designation of qualified senior manager to oversee firm's quality control system

    d. An effective internal disciplinary system

    e. Rotation of engagement team senior personnel

    f. Policies precluding partners from being compensated for selling nonattest services to attest client

MIPPs Nonindependence Rules

Conflicts of Interest, Directorships, and Gifts

After studying this lesson, you should be able to:

1. Understand and be able to apply the Code of Professional Conduct's rules regarding: a) General conflicts of interest. b) Members serving on corporate boards. c) Gifts and entertainment (which can pose a threat to member integrity and objectivity).

I. **Conflicts of Interest**

    A. In evaluating possible conflicts of interest, members should ask: Would a *reasonable and informed third party* conclude that a conflict exists?

    B. There are two main types of conflicts:

        1. Between interests of two clients

        2. Between interests of client on one hand and firm and/or its members on the other.

 Examples

    1. Simultaneously advising two clients trying to acquire the same company

2. Preparing valuation of assets to two clients who are simultaneously the potential seller and the potential buyer of the same assets

3. Representing both a husband and a wife in a divorce proceeding

4. Advising a client to invest in a business owned by a member or member's relatives

5. Advising a client on acquisition of assets that the firm also seeks to acquire

6. Providing forensic accounting services to one client to assist it in deciding whether to sue another client

7. Providing personal financial planning services to several members of a family or group known to have conflicting interests

8. Referring a client to a service provider that, in turn, refers clients to member under an exclusive arrangement

---

    C. **Identification**—Before accepting an engagement, members should identify potential conflicts that threaten independence and objectivity, and should continue to monitor as engagement progresses.

        1. When **network firms** are involved, members are **not** required to take specific steps to identify conflicts of interest of other network firms but should apply the conceptual framework if they **know or have reason to know** that a conflict exists or might arise.

D. Evaluation—When an actual conflict is identified by any member, the Conceptual Framework should be applied and engagements should be refused or terminated if risk of violation is unacceptably high. Safeguards that might reduce threats to an acceptable level include:

1. Implementing mechanisms to prevent unauthorized disclosure of confidential information when providing services to multiple clients with conflicting interests, including use of:

   a. Separate engagement teams

   b. Policies and procedures to limit access to client files, confidentiality agreements and physical and electronic separation of confidential information

2. Regular review by a senior manager not involved in the engagement

3. Consulting with third parties, such as a professional body or legal counsel

E. Disclosure—Conflicts should be disclosed to clients and affected third parties, even if threats to compliance are at an acceptable level.

1. General disclosure (e.g., "We audit several firms in your industry sector") may suffice.

2. Specific disclosure (e.g., "We advise your closest competitor who would love to have access to your confidential information that we possess") may be needed, however.

F. Documenting the threat-reducing process is wise.

G. Members should always comply with federal (including Internal Revenue Service Circular 230), state, or local provisions that are more restrictive than the code.

II. Director Positions

A. Objectivity is threatened when a member serves as a client entity's director.

B. It is preferable to serve as a mere consultant to a client's board.

C. The Conceptual Framework should be applied to determine whether the threat to objectivity is unacceptably high.

III. Gifts and Entertainment

A. Objectivity and integrity are threatened if the client (including its officers, directors, and 10% shareholders) give gifts or entertainment to the firm or its members (or vice versa).

B. A violation is presumed if:

1. The member receives gifts or entertainment from a client that violate the member's or client's policies or applicable laws and regulations and

2. The member knows or is reckless in not knowing of the violation.

C. If no rules are violated, then there is no problem if the gifts or entertainment are "reasonable in the circumstances."

D. Factors in determining reasonableness include:

1. The nature of the gift or entertainment

2. The occasion giving rise to the gift

3. The cost or value of the gift or entertainment

4. The nature, frequency, and value of other gifts

5. Whether the entertainment was associated with active conduct of the business

Reporting Income and Subordination of Judgment

After studying this lesson, you should be able to:

1. Understand and be able to apply the new electronic Code of Professional Conduct's provisions regarding how to report income without violating the code.

2. Understand how to apply the rules and process governing how to avoid a subordination of judgment.

I. **Preparing and Reporting Income**

   A. Obviously there would be a violation of the Code if a member has:

      1. Made, permitted, or directed another to make materially false and misleading entries in an entity's financial statements or records,

      2. Failed to correct misstatements when having the authority to do so, *or*

      3. Signed, permitted, or directed another to sign misleading documents.

II. **Subordination of Judgment**

   A. Assume that members have a disagreement with a superior over how to record potential earnings (or some other issue). The members are not supposed to simply do what the superior wants and subordinate their judgment.

   B. The proper procedure is to:

      1. Evaluate whether the threat is at an **unacceptable level,** which occurs if the position taken would result in a material misrepresentation or legal violation. If the threat is **not significant**, then nothing further need be done.

      2. But if there is such a significant threat, the member should discuss the matter with the supervisor.

      3. If discussion with the supervisor does not resolve the difference of opinion, the member should go over the supervisor's head.

      4. If, after discussion with people up the chain, the member is still worried that the right thing is not going to be done, the member should, in no particular order, invoke the following safeguards:

         a. Determine whether the organization's policies and procedures have any additional requirements for reporting differences of opinion.

         b. Determine whether there is a duty to report to external authorities.

         c. Consult legal counsel.

         d. Fully document the situation.

      5. If the member ultimately concludes that the threat of misrepresentation or legal violation cannot be reduced to an acceptable level, he or she should consider quitting the firm and taking appropriate steps to eliminate his or her exposure to subordination of judgment.

      6. Although the code does not **require** the member to quit, only to consider it, it goes on to say that "nothing in this interpretation precludes a member from resigning from the organization at any time."

      7. Resigning from the firm would not necessarily discharge all obligations, such as to report to regulatory authorities or an external auditor.

Advocacy, Third-Party Service Providers (TSPs), General Standards, and Accounting Principles

After studying this lesson, you should be able to:

1. Explain and apply the Code of Professional Conducts rules regarding advocacy on behalf of clients and the outsourcing of work to third-party service providers.

2. Master the general standards that apply to members.

3. Understand members' responsibilities regarding basic accounting principles.

I. Client Advocacy

A. Members doing attest work may not advocate for their attest clients.

B. Members providing nonattest services may advocate for their clients, but should be careful and conservative so as to preserve credibility and avoid the "zealous" advocacy that lawyers often provide.

II. Use of a Third-Party Service Provider (TSP)

A. Outsourcing work to third-party service providers can threaten objectivity or integrity.

B. There is no problem if the third-party service provider provides only **administrative support** (e.g., record storage, software application hosting, authorized e-file transmittal services).

C. If substantive services are outsourced, clients should be notified, preferably in writing, before any confidential information is provided to the third-party service provider.

D. If the client objects, the member should:

1. Not outsource, *or*

2. Decline the engagement

III. General Standards

A. Members must follow rules set by appropriate bodies, meaning in part:

1. Take on jobs only if you can reasonably expect to complete them with **professional competence.**

2. You need not be perfect but should always exercise **due professional care** when providing all professional services

3. Always **adequately plan and supervise** your provision of professional services.

4. Never render conclusions or recommendations without **sufficient relevant data** to support them.

B. **Competence** means that the member or his/or her staff has appropriate technical qualifications and the member can supervise and evaluate quality of work performed.

1. Decline an engagement unless you have necessary knowledge or can acquire it through research or consultation with others.

2. If you employ a specialist to provide consulting services, you should have the ability to define the tasks and evaluate the results.

C. **Using Third-Party Service Providers**

1. Ensure any third-party service providers you use have the required professional qualifications, technical skills, and needed resources.

2. Adequately plan and supervise the third-party service providers' services and obtain the data needed to evaluate the job.

IV. Accounting Principles

A. Follow generally accepted accounting principles (GAAP) and other relevant accounting principles.

B. **Exceptions**—Departure from GAAP is appropriate if the member:

    1. Demonstrates that due to unusual circumstances, following GAAP would mislead

    2. Describes:

        a. The departure,

        b. Its approximate effects, and

        c. The reasons why compliance with GAAP would mislead.

C. Circumstances justifying departure include:

    1. New legislation

    2. Evolution of a new form of business

D. Circumstances **not** justifying departure include:

    1. An unusual degree of materiality

    2. Conflicting industry practice

E. Departure from GAAP is permitted when other accounting principles apply, such as:

    1. Financial reporting frameworks generally accepted in foreign country

    2. Frameworks prescribed by contract

    3. Other special-purpose frameworks required by a law or by a domestic or foreign regulatory agency

Discreditable Acts

This lesson mostly surveys the discreditable acts, some of which are covered in more detail elsewhere (such as the confidentiality duty). But it dives into detail regarding the fairly complicated rules regarding a member's obligation to produce accounting records pursuant to a client's request.

After studying this lesson, you should be able to:

1. Understand the (nonexclusive) list of acts that the Code of Professional Conduct deems to be discreditable acts by members in public practice.

I. **Discreditable Acts**—Members shall not commit discreditable acts, including:

   A. Discrimination and harassment in employment practices

   B. Solicitation or disclosure of CPA Exam questions and answers

   C. Failure to file a tax return (including one's one personal return or his or her firm's) or failure to pay a tax liability

   D. Negligence in the preparation of financial statements or records

   E. Material departure from the audit standards of government bodies, commissions, or other regulatory agencies

   F. Failure to follow additional government standards over and above generally accepted accounting standards where applicable

   G. Improper use of indemnification and limitation of liability provisions in violation of regulatory requirements

   H. Confidential information obtained from employment or volunteer activities (more detail in the "Advertising and Confidentiality" lesson)

   I. False, misleading, or deceptive acts in promoting or marketing professional services

   J. Use of the CPA credential in violation of rules and regulations

   K. Records requests (more detail below)

   L. Removing client files or proprietary information from a firm after termination

   M. Use of confidential information obtained from a prospective client or nonclient without consent

   N. **Records Requests**

      1. **Four categories of records**

         a. **Client-provided records** are records given by the client to the member.

         b. **Member-prepared records** are those the member was not specifically engaged to prepare and are not in the client's books and records, rendering the client's financial information incomplete. Example: adjusting, closing, combining, or consolidating journal entries and supporting schedules and documents that the member proposed or prepared as part of an engagement.

         c. **Member's work products** are deliverables set forth in the engagement letter, such as a tax return.

         d. **Working papers** are all other items prepared solely for purposes of the engagement, including items prepared by both the member (e.g., audit programs, analytical review schedules, and statistical sampling and analysis) and the client (e.g., papers prepared at the member's request and reflecting testing or other work done by the member).

2. **Proper treatment of requests from client**

   a. **Client-provided records** should be delivered to the client at the client's request, even if the client has not paid its bill to the member.

   b. **Member-prepared records** related to a completed and issued work product should be delivered to the client at the client's request, **except** that they may be withheld if fees are due for that specific work product.

   c. **Work products** should be delivered to the client at the client's request, except that they may be withheld under four circumstances:

      i. Fees are due for the specific work product.

      ii. The work product is incomplete.

      iii. To comply with professional standards (e.g., withholding an audit report because of unresolved audit issues).

      iv. If threatened or outstanding litigation exists concerning the engagement or the member's work.

   d. **Working papers** are the member's property and need not be provided to the client (unless some regulation or contractual provision requires production).

3. Members may charge a reasonable fee for the time and expense incurred in producing records.

4. Members need not convert records that are not in electronic format to electronic format.

5. Sometimes state laws are more demanding of accountants, and those laws must be followed.

6. Generally, client requests should be honored within **45 days**.

Fees

After studying this lesson, you should be able to:

1. Understand how members in public practice are supposed to handle contingent fees (mostly by avoiding them).

2. Understand how members in public practice are supposed to handle commissions and referral fees (mostly by avoiding them).

I. Contingent Fees

A. Members shall not receive contingent fees **for any service** performed for a client for whom he or she performs any of the following attest services:

    1. A financial statement audit or review,

    2. A financial statement compilation reasonably expected to be used by a third party that does not disclose a lack of independence, or

    3. An examination of prospective financial information.

B. Nor may a member prepare an original or amended tax return or claim for a tax refund for a contingent fee for **any client**, even nonattest clients.

C. The definition of a **contingent fee** ["a fee established for the performance of any service pursuant to an arrangement in which no fee will be charged unless a specified finding or result is attained, or in which the amount of the fee is otherwise dependent upon the finding or result of such service"] excludes fees "fixed by courts or other public authorities, or, in tax matters, if determined based on the results of judicial proceedings or the finding of government agencies."

D. A member may do tax work for nonattest clients in exchange for contingent fees if Internal Revenue Service rules are not to the contrary (which they sometimes are).

E. Examples of some permitted contingent fees in the tax area include:

    1. Representing a client before a revenue agent examining the client's income tax return

    2. Filing an amended federal or state income tax return claiming a refund based on a tax issue that is the subject of a test case involving a different taxpayer

    3. Filing an amended federal or state income tax return (or refund claim) claiming a tax refund in an amount that will be examined by a tax authority, such as the Joint Committee on Taxation

    4. Helping a client obtain a private letter ruling or influencing the drafting of a regulation or statute

F. Contingent fees are not permitted if a member prepared an amended return claiming a refund because of an error in the original return.

G. The code contains additional rules regarding services performed by a member's spouse for a contingent fee and contingent fees in connection with investment advisory services that are not covered here.

II. Commissions and Referral Fees

A. Referral fees and commissions are prohibited for attest clients.

B. For nonattest clients, they are permitted, but must be disclosed.

C. A member's spouse may receive a commission from the member's attest client, so long as the spouse's activities are separate from the member's practice and the member is not significantly involved in the spouse's activities.

D. Members taking title to a product and assuming risks of ownership may resell the product to a client at a profit without disclosure.

E. Similarly, members may subcontract services to third parties and mark up the cost of the services to the client without this being considered a commission.

Advertising and Confidentiality

After studying this lesson, you should be able to:

1. Explain and apply the relatively straightforward code restrictions on advertising.

2. Explain and apply the relatively more complicated rules on the confidentiality obligation that members in public practice owe to clients.

I. **Advertising**

   A. Members are responsible not only for their own promotional efforts, but also for those of third parties if they are asked to perform professional services for the client or customer of a third party.

   B. Promotional efforts are a discreditable act if they are false, misleading, or deceptive (i.e., if they contain any claim that would likely cause a reasonable person to be misled), which would be the case if they:

     1. Create false or unjustified expectations of favorable results

     2. Imply the ability to influence any court, tribunal, regulatory agency or similar body

     3. Contain a representation that the member will perform services for stated fees when it is likely at the time that the fees will be substantially increased

II. **Confidential Information**

   A. **General Rule**—A member in public practice shall not disclose confidential client information (defined as "any proprietary information pertaining to the employer or any organization for whom the member may work in a volunteer capacity that is not known to be available to the public and is obtained as a result of such relationships") without the specific consent of the client.

     1. It is a discreditable act to inappropriately disclose confidential client information.

     2. Members should take reasonable steps to ensure that staff members do not improperly disclose confidential information.

     3. The confidentiality duty survives the employment relationship.

   B. **Exceptions**—Disclosures allowed where:

     1. The client consents.

     2. Disclosure is permitted by law **and authorized by the employer**.

     3. Disclosure is **required by law**, for example, to:

       a. Comply with a validly issued and enforceable subpoena or summons

       b. Inform appropriate public authorities of violations of the law

     4. Members may have responsibility or right to disclose the information, when not prohibited by law, to:

       a. Initiate an ethics complaint with the American Institute of Certified Public Accountants (AICPA), a state board of accountancy, and so on

       b. Comply with professional standards and other ethics requirements

       c. Report potential concerns regarding questionable accounting, auditing, or other matters to the employer's confidential complaint hotline or those charged with governance

5. Disclosure is permitted on behalf of the employer to:

   a. Obtain financing from lenders

   b. Communicate with vendors, clients, and customers

   c. Communicate with the external accountant, attorneys, regulators, and others

6. Members should be sensitive to disclosing a client's confidential information when providing services to its competitors.

7. If taking on a new client would likely lead to disclosure of confidential information from an existing, identifiable client, the member should not take on new client without informed consent from the existing client.

8. When a member withdraws from an engagement due to, say, irregularities in a client's tax return, the member should, if contacted by a potential successor firm, suggest that the potential successor firm contact the client to ask permission to discuss all matters freely with the successor.

9. If a member prepares a tax return for a married couple, both are clients, so if during a divorce one spouse directs the member to withhold joint tax information from the other, the member may provide information to both spouses. When receiving conflicting directions from the spouses, the member should seek an attorney's advice.

10. When outsourcing work to a third-party service provider (TSP), a member should do one of the following **before** disclosing confidential information:

    1. Bind the third-party service provider contractually to maintain confidentiality and ensure that the third-party service provider has effective procedures in place.

    2. Obtain specific consent from the client.

11. Members involved in a peer review must keep information they receive confidential and not use it for their advantage.

12. If a third party, such as a trade association or member of academia, asks a member to disclose confidential information for purposes of publication or the like, the member should obtain the client's specific consent, preferably in writing, before disclosing.

13. Members who are directors of organizations must be cautious, because their fiduciary duty to the organization might conflict with their duty to clients who might, for example, be customers of the organization. The threats-and-safeguards conceptual framework should be utilized.

14. Disclosing clients' names is permissible, unless to do so discloses confidential information.

Example
Where the member does primarily bankruptcy work and disclosing clients' identities signals that clients are in financial difficulty.

Form of Organization and Names

After studying this lesson, you should be able to:

1. Explain and apply the code's rules regarding what form of organization members in public practice may practice in.

2. Explain what names they may use for denominating their firms.

I. Form of Organization

A. Basic Rules

1. Members in public practice may practice only in a form of organization permitted by law.

2. Members in public practice may not practice under misleading firm name.

3. Names of past owners may be included in the name of a successor firm.

4. A firm may not designate itself as "Members of the AICPA" unless all its CPA owners are members of the AICPA.

B. Ownership of a Separate Business

1. A member may own an interest in a separate business that performs accounting, tax, or consulting services, but if the member *controls* the separate business, then its owners and professional employees must comply with the code for issues such as commissions and referral fees. And regarding an attest client, independence rules would have to be complied with as well.

2. But if the member's interest is not a controlling one, then the code's provisions apply to him but not to the separate firm or its employees.

C. Partner Designation

1. Only members of a firm who are legally partners should use the designation "partner."

D. Responsibility for Nonmember Practitioners

1. If a member becomes an employee of a firm made up of one or more nonmembers, he or she still must comply with the code. And if the member is a partner in the firm, he or she is responsible for the firm's professional employees.

E. Attest Engagement Performed with a Former Partner

1. Two former partners may continue to jointly perform an attest engagement, but to make it clear that a partnership no longer exists, they should present their report on plain paper (with no letterhead).

F. Alternative Practice Structures

1. If a firm does attest work,

    a. CPAs must own a majority of its financial interests.

    b. CPAs must remain responsible, financially and otherwise, for a firm's attest work.

2. CPAs are responsible for compliance with laws and regulations, for enrollment in an AICPA-approved practice monitoring program, for compliance with independence rules, and for compliance with all other applicable standards within their firms.

II. Firm Name

A. If two firms merge, they may use in the newly formed firm's name the name of retired or other partners in either or both of the former firms.

B. A CPA member who is in partnership with non-CPAs may sign reports in the firm's name and also affix the designation "CPA" to his or her own signature if it is clear that the firm is not holding itself out as entirely comprised of CPAs.

C. No misleading name that causes confusion about the legal form of the firm or its owners' identities should be used.

D. Firms within a network may share a common brand or common initials as part of their firm name without misleading. To be part of a network, the firms should share one or more of the following with other network firms:

1. Common control among the firms

2. Profits or costs

3. Common business strategy

4. Significant portions of professional resources

5. Common quality control policies and procedures

MIPPs Independence Rules

Introduction to MIPPs Independence Rules

> **After studying this lesson, you should be able to:**
>
> 1. Understand the big picture regarding the independence obligations of members in public practice and be able to answer: a) What are the threats to independence? b) Who must comply with the rules? c) What time period is relevant?

I. Introduction

A. Members in public practice (MIPPs) shall be independent when performing attest services.

B. If the code and its interpretations do not resolve independence issues, **the Conceptual Framework should be applied.**

C. Threats and Safeguards

    1. The *threats* to independence detailed in the code are very much the same as the threats to integrity and objectivity discussed elsewhere in these materials: adverse interest threats, advocacy threats, familiarity threats, management participation threats, self-interest threats, self-review threats, and undue influence threats.

    2. The *safeguards* that may be applied to reduce the threats to independence come from the same three sources as those relevant to integrity and objectivity:

        a. The profession, legislation, or regulation

        b. The attest client

        c. The firm

D. The threats to independence (adverse interest, advocacy, etc.) are concentrated in four areas:

    1. Financial relationships—Example: An attest partner should not own stock in an audit client

    2. Employment relationships—Example: Attest partners should not be on an audit client's board of directors

    3. Family relationships—Example: An attest partner should not audit a client whose chief executive officer is the partner's spouse

    4. Consulting relationships—Example: An attest firm should not provide internal audit services to an attest client

E. Time Period—Independence rules must be followed when relationships exist during:

    1. The period covered by the financial statements

    2. The period of the professional engagement

F. Covered members must comply with the independence rules for financial interests (and many others):

    1. An individual on the attest engagement team (*team member*)

    2. An individual in a position to influence the attest engagement (PTI)

    3. A partner, partner equivalent (defined as "a person who is not a partner of the firm but either has the ultimate responsibility for the conduct of an attest engagement, or has the authority to bind the firm to conduct an attest engagement without partner approval"), or manager who provides more than 10 hours of nonattest services to the attest client within any fiscal year (*10-hour person*)

4. A partner or partner equivalent in the office in which the lead attest engagement partner or partner equivalent practices in connection with the attest engagement (*other partner in office*)

5. The firm, including the firm's employee benefit plans

6. An entity whose operating, financial, or accounting policies can be controlled by any of the individuals or entities described in items (1) through (5) or two or more such individuals or entities if they act together

Network Firms and Affiliates

After studying this lesson, you should be able to:

1. Understand and be able to apply the independence rules regarding network firms that band together to increase their competitiveness vis-à-vis the Big Four and other competitors.

2. Understand the rules regarding affiliates of clients. Obviously, if auditors cannot own a direct and material financial interest in an attest client, they also probably should not own a direct and material financial interest in a firm that controls the client or a firm controlled by the client.

3. Understand the rules regarding mergers and acquisitions of firms. If Firm A merges with Firm B, they may bring to the new consolidated firm sets of audit clients. Auditors at Firm A now have to worry about being independent of Firm B's clients and vice versa.

I. **Network Firms**

    A. Network firms are firms that cooperate to enhance their capabilities to provide professional services and share one or more of the following:

        1. A common brand name

        2. Common control

        3. Profits or costs

        4. A common business strategy

        5. Professional resources

        6. Common quality control policies and procedures

    B. Network firms must comply with the independence rules with respect to financial statement audit and review clients of other network firms *if* the use of the audit or review report for the client is not restricted.

    C. For all other attest clients, members should apply the Conceptual Framework to determine whether independence threats are at an unacceptable level.

II. **Alternative Practice Structures**

    A. The Code contains extremely complicated independence rules for firms operating in an APS environment that are not covered in these materials.

III. **Use of a Nonindependent Firm**

    A. If partners or professional employees of another, nonindependent firm participate on the attest engagement team, independence of the team would be impaired.

    B. Such members of another firm may work in a manner similar to internal auditors, however, without creating an independence problem so long as the firm complies with AU-C section 610 (which sets out the rules for the proper relationship between internal and external auditors).

IV. **Affiliates**

    A. Independence problems can obviously arise if covered members, while not having a financial, consulting, employment, etc. relationship with the attest client, have such a relationship with an "affiliate" of the client.

    B. The Code sets out numerous examples of such "affiliates," including:

        1. An entity that a client can control

        2. An entity in which a client has a direct and material financial interest

3. An entity that controls a client when the client is material to such entity

4. An entity with a direct and material financial interest in the client when that entity has significant influence over the client

5. A sister entity of a client if the client and sister entity are each material to the entity that controls both

6. A trustee that is deemed to control a trust financial statement attest client that is not an investment company

7. The sponsor of a single employer employee benefit plan financial statement attest client

C. Although there are significant exceptions (which we do not cover here), in general covered members must abide by independence rules for both their attest clients and their clients' affiliates. There are similar rules (and exceptions) when a firm audits some units, but not all, of related governmental agencies.

V. Mergers and Acquisitions

A. Independence issues can obviously arise if a member's firm acquires, is acquired by, or merges with another firm. The AICPA has recently issued detailed rules to cover such situations, focusing on (a) employment with an attest client and (b) provision of NAS.

B. Without covering those rules comprehensively, consider a situation where Maria, a partner of the ABC audit firm also works for DEF Co., which is an audit client of GHI audit firm. GHI proposes to purchase ABC. If the acquisition occurs, Maria may suddenly be an employee of her new firm's audit client. Independence should not be impaired so long as:

1. Maria terminates her relationship with DEF before the closing date of the acquisition;

2. Maria is not a team member or a PTI on the DEF audit if the engagement covers any period in which she worked for DEF;

3. Maria dissociates from DEF, including ceasing participation in its employee benefit plans if she is a covered member;

4. A responsible person within the new firm assesses Maria's prior relationship with DEF to ensure that any threats to independence are at a reasonable level. If Maria has any interaction with the attest engagement team or if the team evaluates any work done by Maria while she worked for DEF, an appropriate person within the firm should review the engagement prior to issuing the report to ensure that the team maintained integrity, objectivity, and professional skepticism; *and*

5. All safeguards should be discussed with DEF's management and the discussions should be documented.

C. Turning to NAS, the Code envisions two possibilities:

1. What if the ABC firm provides, say, internal audit services to LMN Corporation, which is audited by DEF firm? If ABC acquires DEF, ABC's independence is impaired with respect to LMN.

2. What if the ABC firm audits LMN Corporation and acquires DEF, which provides internal audit services to LMN Corporation? In this case, ABC's independence would be impaired unless all of the following conditions are met:

   a. DEF must terminate the prohibited NAS prior to the closing of the acquisition;

   b. Any individual who participated in the engagement to provide the NAS must not be on the LMN attest team or be a PTI; and

   c. An evaluation of the threats to independence must be conducted and it must be determined that by application of safeguards they have been reduced to an acceptable level. The evaluation must attribute the NAS to ABC in making the evaluation.

Reissues, Engagement Letters, ADR, and Unpaid Fees

> **After studying this lesson, you should be able to:**
>
> 1. Explain and apply rules regarding when no longer independent firms can put their names on a report that was signed when they were independent.
>
> 2. Explain and apply rules regarding what an engagement letter may contain without impairing independence.
>
> 3. Explain and apply rules regarding when an engagement letter properly mandates alternative dispute resolution.
>
> 4. Explain and apply rules regarding under what circumstances unpaid fees endanger independence.

I. Reissued Reports

A. Covered members or their firms that were independent when they first issued an audit report may reissue that report or consent to its incorporation by reference, even if they are no longer independent, so long as they do not perform new procedures that would require updating the date (or *dual dating*) of the original report.

B. In this connection, it is acceptable if necessary to assess the effect of recent facts on the original report to:

   1. Make inquiries of successor auditors

   2. Read subsequent financial statements

   3. Undertake similar procedures

II. Engagement Contractual Terms

A. Although the Securities and Exchange Commission (SEC) and other regulators disapprove of engagement contracts that indemnify auditors for the effects of their own mistakes, it is okay for an engagement letter to require an attest client to indemnify or hold harmless a member firm for liability and costs **resulting from knowing misrepresentations by the client's management.**

B. It would impair independence for a covered member to agree to indemnify an attest client for losses resulting from the client's own acts.

III. Alternative Dispute Resolution

A. Engagement letters may require use of alternative dispute resolution (ADR) to resolve disagreements with clients.

B. However, if alternative dispute resolution is initiated, binding arbitration is sufficiently similar to litigation that it could place the member in public practice and the client in positions of material adverse interests and thereby impair independence, so the Conceptual Framework should be applied.

IV. Unpaid Fees

A. A member in public practice (MIPP) may not sign a current-year audit report if it has unpaid fees from the client for services provided more than one year prior.

B. Fees are *unpaid* even if:

   1. They are unbilled.

   2. The client has issued to the firm a note receivable.

C. If the client is in bankruptcy, this rule does not apply.

Financial Interests

Overview and Unsolicited Financial Interests

After studying this lesson, you should be able to:

1. Recognize the terms that are important in understanding the financial interests that can cause independence problems for an attest firm.

2. Know that members in public practice may not own direct or material indirect interests in an attest client.

3. Explain and apply the rules that govern a situation where a financial interest unexpectedly comes the way of a member in public practice.

I. **Overview**—If a covered member has or is committed to acquire any direct (whether material or not) or any material indirect financial interest in an attest client, independence is impaired. Only if interests are both indirect and immaterial is independence not impaired.

II. **Definitions**

   A. **Financial Interest**—Includes ownership (or an obligation to obtain ownership) in equity, debt, or derivatives issued by an entity.

   B. **Direct Financial Interest**—An interest:

   1. Owned directly (even if managed by others)

   2. Under one's control (even if managed by others)

   3. Beneficially owned through an investment vehicle, estate, trust, or other intermediary when the beneficiary either:

   a. Controls the intermediary, or

   b. Has the authority to supervise or participate in the intermediary's investment decisions.

   C. **Indirect Financial Interest**—An interest beneficially owned through an investment vehicle, estate, trust, or other intermediary when the beneficiary neither:

   1. Controls the intermediary, nor

   2. Has the authority to supervise or participate in its investment decisions.

   D. **Beneficial Ownership**—Occurs when an individual or entity is not the record owner but has a right to some or all of the underlying benefits of ownership, such as to:

   1. Direct the voting

   2. Dispose of the interest

   3. Receive its economic benefits

III. **Financial Interests**—These rules about financial interests normally apply only to *covered members;* however, even if a partner or professional employee of a firm is not a covered member, that person (and his or her immediate family, or any group of such persons acting together) cannot own more than 5% of a client's ownership interests without impairing independence.

IV. Unsolicited Financial Interests

    A. If covered members receive or learn they will receive an unsolicited financial interest in an attest client (perhaps through gift or inheritance) that is either a direct interest or a material indirect interest, independence will not be impaired if they:

        1. Dispose of the interest as soon as practicable but not later than **30 days** after having both knowledge of the interest and gaining the right to dispose of it; and

        Do not participate on the attest engagement team after learning of the interest and before disposing of it.

Mutual Funds and Retirement Plans

After studying this lesson, you should be able to:

1. Understand the rules to avoid independence problems arising from personal investments in mutual funds retirement plans.

2. Apply those rules in order to avoid independence problems arising from personal investments in mutual funds retirement plans.

I. **Mutual Funds**

   A. A covered member who owns shares in a mutual fund has a direct financial interest in the fund itself.

   B. If the member owns 5% or less of the outstanding shares of a **diversified** mutual fund, the interest in the underlying investments of the fund is **indirect**. Immaterial and indirect interests do not impair independence.

   C. However, if the covered member owns more than 5% of a diversified fund's shares or owns a financial interest in an **undiversified** fund, then the member must evaluate the fund's underlying investments to determine whether he or she holds a material indirect financial interest in any of the underlying investments.

   D. **The code gives this illustration:**

   "If:

   a nondiversified mutual fund owns shares in attest client Company A,

   the mutual fund's net assets are $10,000,000,

   the covered member owns 1% of the outstanding shares of the mutual fund, having a value of $100,000, and

   the mutual fund has 10% of its assets invested in Company A,

   then the indirect financial interest of the covered member in Company A is $10,000 (10% × $100,000) and this amount should be measured against the covered member's net worth (including the net worth of his or her immediate family) to determine if it is material."

II. **Retirement, Savings, Compensation, or Similar Plans**

   A. If covered members or their immediate family members (IFMs) self-direct their investments into such a plan or have the ability to supervise or participate in the plan's investment decisions, then the financial interests held by the plan are direct financial interests that impair independence even if they are immaterial.

   B. Two examples:

      1. A covered member is trustee of a retirement plan and supervises its investments, which include shares of an attest client.

      2. A covered member participates in a retirement plan and has discretion to direct its investments, which include shares of an attest client.

   C. If covered members (or their immediate family members) do not self-direct or supervise or participate in a plan's investment decisions, the underlying investments are **indirect** and therefore do not create independence issues unless they are material.

D. When a **defined benefit plan** is involved, interests held by the plan are not interests held by the covered members unless the covered members (or their immediate family members) are trustees of the plan or otherwise have the ability to supervise or participate in the plan's investment decisions.

E. Allocated shares held in an employee stock option plan are beneficially owned by the covered members but are indirect interests **until** the members have the right to dispose of them. At that point, they become direct financial interests.

Partnerships, 529s, Trust and Estates, Employee Benefit Plans

> **After studying this lesson, you should be able to:**
>
> 1. Understand how to minimize problems in relation to investments in partnerships and limited liability corporations.
> 2. Understand how to minimize problems in 529 plans.
> 3. Understand how to minimize problems in employee benefit plans.
> 4. Understand how to minimize problems through trusts and estates.

I. **Partnerships and Limited Liability Corporations (LLCs)**

    A. **General Partnership**—A general partner (GP) has authority to influence investments, so a general partner's financial interests in both the partnership itself and its underlying investments are **direct**.

    B. **Limited Partnership**

        1. A general partner has authority to influence investments, so a general partner's financial interests in both the limited partnership itself and its underlying investments are **direct.**

        2. A limited partner's interest in the limited partnership is direct, but usually he or she will not have influence over its investments so this partner's financial interest in its underlying investments will be **indirect.**

            a. If the limited partner has authority to supervise or participate in investment decisions or the ability to replace the general partner(s), then his or her interest in the underlying investments will be direct.

    E. **Limited Liability Companies (LLCs)**

        1. If a limited liability company is member-managed, then it is sufficiently like a general partnership that members' interests in both the firm and its underlying investments are direct.

        2. If a limited liability company is agent-managed, then members are more like limited partners and their interests in the underlying investments are viewed as indirect unless the members have the authority to control the limited liability company or to supervise or participate in its investments.

II. **Section 529 Plans**

    A. **Prepaid Tuition Plans**—Owners of a 529 account used to prepay tuition have a direct interest in the plan but only an indirect interest in its underlying investments. Owners of such plans are essentially buying tuition credits. The state has an obligation to provide the education regardless of the investments' performance.

    B. **Savings Plans**—Owners of these accounts have a direct financial interest in both the plan and its investments because they may decide in which sponsor's 529 savings plan to invest and can determine before investing which firms the plan will invest in.

III. **Trusts and Estates**

    A. The fact that a covered member is asked to serve as trustee of a trust or executor of an estate does not by itself create an independence problem if an attest client's shares are owned by the trust or estate. However, there is a problem if:

        1. The covered member has the ability to make investment decisions for the trust or estate.

        2. The trust or estate owns or is committed to acquiring more than 10% of the attest client's ownership interests, *or*

        3. The value of the trust's or estate's ownership interest in the client exceeds 10% of its total assets.

B. Grantor—If a covered member acts as a grantor to set up a trust, its investments are **direct** financial interests if any of the following are true:

1. The covered member has the ability to amend or revoke the trust.

2. The covered member has authority to control the trust.

3. The covered member has the ability to supervise or participate in the trust's investment decisions.

4. The underlying trust investments ultimately will revert to the covered member as the grantor.

C. Beneficiary—If a covered member is a beneficiary of a trust, then the covered member's interest in it is direct and his or her interest in the trust's underlying investments is indirect, unless the covered member controls the trust or supervises or participates in its investment decisions, in which case the interest becomes direct.

D. Blind Trust—Because the investments ultimately will revert to the grantor who typically retains the right to amend or revoke, both a blind trust **and** its underlying investments are considered to be direct financial interests of the grantor.

IV. Participation in Employee Benefit Plans (EBP)

A. Independence is impaired if a covered member participates in an employee benefit plan that is an attest client or sponsored by one. Two exceptions apply:

1. When a covered member is an employee of a government organization that sponsors an employee benefit plan and the covered member is required by law to audit the plan, then it is acceptable to do so if all of the following safeguards are in place:

   a. The covered member is required to participate in the plan as a condition of employment.

   b. The plan is offered to all employees in comparable positions.

   c. The covered member is not a director, officer, employee, promoter, or the like of the plan.

   d. The covered member has no influence or control over the investment strategy, benefits, or other management activities of the plan.

2. When the covered member formerly was associated with an attest client but is no longer, then independence is not impaired.

Depository Accounts, Brokerage Accounts, and Insurance Policies

After studying this lesson, you should be able to:

1. Avoid independence problems that might arise from auditors using bank accounts and insurance policies.

2. Avoid independence problems that might arise from investing in the stock market using a stockbroker.

I. Depository Accounts

A. **Firm**—Firms may maintain depository accounts at a bank that is an attest client if they conclude that the likelihood is remote that the bank will experience financial difficulties.

B. **Individual**—Individual covered members may maintain such accounts if any of three conditions is met:

1. The balance in the depository account is fully insured, *or*

2. Any uninsured amounts were not material to the covered member's worth, *or*

3. If uninsured accounts are considered material, they are reduced to an immaterial amount within 30 days of becoming material.

II. Brokerage Accounts

A. A covered member's brokerage account at an attest client broker-dealer would not impair independence only if **both** of the following apply:

1. The attest client's services were rendered under the attest client's normal terms, procedures, and requirements.

2. Any covered member's assets subject to the risk of loss are immaterial to the covered member's net worth.

    a. In determining risk of loss, the question is not whether the assets' market value might decline but whether the client might become insolvent or commit fraud. Protection by regulators and insurance are relevant factors in determining risk of loss.

III. Insurance Policies

A. An insurance policy is not a financial interest unless it offers an investment option.

B. If there is an investment option, there would still not be an independence problem if the covered member bought the policy under normal terms and conditions, unless the covered member had either:

1. The ability to select the policy's underlying investments or

2. The authority to supervise or participate in the investment decision and the covered member invested in an attest client.

Loans, Leases, and Business Relationships

After studying this lesson, you should be able to:

1. Understand how to minimize the independence complications that might arise for members in public practice from: a) Borrowing money. b) Leasing (and leasing out) real estate. c) Entering into various business relationships, such as co-ownership.

I. Loans

A. If a covered member borrows from (or loans to) an attest client or any of its officers, directors, or 10% owners, there is likely an independence problem, especially if the client is not a lending institution.

B. If the attest client is a lending institution making a loan to covered members or their immediate family members, independence would not be impaired if it is (a) an immaterial unsecured loan, (b) a home mortgage, or (c) a secured loan, so long as **all** of these safeguards are met:

   1. Normal lending procedures, terms, and requirements were applied.

   2. The loan occurred before the lending institution become an attest client, or came from a lending institution for which independence was not required and later sold to an attest client.

   3. Loans are kept current, and terms are not altered by extending maturity date, lowering interest rate, and so on.

   4. The estimated fair value of the collateral equals or exceeds the outstanding balance; any deficit is not material to the covered member's net worth.

C. If a covered member keeps payments current and otherwise complies with loan or lease terms, these also do **not** impair independence:

   1. Auto loans and leases collateralized by the car

   2. Loans fully collateralized by cash surrender value of an insurance policy

   3. Loans fully collateralized by cash deposits at the same lending institutions (e.g., passbook loans)

   4. Aggregate outstanding balances from credit card and overdraft reserve accounts of $10,000 or less

II. Leases

A. Capital leases (leases to own) impair independence.

B. Operating lease arrangements do not impair independence if all of these safeguards are met:

   1. The lease meets the generally accepted accounting principles criteria for an operating lease.

   2. The terms and conditions are comparable with similar leases.

   3. All amounts are paid in accordance with the terms of the lease.

III. Business Relationships

A. **Cooperative Ventures**—Cooperating with an attest client to provide services to a third party or to develop a product is problematic. A cooperative venture does not exist where all these safeguards are present:

   1. Participation of the firm and client is governed by separate agreements that do not create obligations between them.

   2. Neither assumes responsibilities for the other's activities or results.

   3. Neither has authority to act as the other's agent.

B. Joint Closely Held Investments—Joint financial investments may create an independence problem also.

1. **Permissible:** The firm and an attest client could both own the stock of a widely held public company, like Microsoft.

2. **Impermissible:**

   a. The firm and a client both own material stakes in a small company.

   b. A covered member and an officer of an attest client jointly buy a sailboat.

Family Relationships

After studying this lesson, you should be able to:

1. Understand to what the label "immediate family members" applies.

2. Understand to what the label "close relatives" applies.

3. Understand which restrictions apply to each category.

I. Introduction

A. Two categories of family relationships create potential independence problems:

1. **Immediate family members:** Spouses, spousal equivalents, and dependents

2. **Close relatives**: Parents, siblings, and nondependent children.

II. Immediate Family Members

A. With substantial exceptions that are about to be spelled out, immediate family members of covered members must comply with the same independence rules as covered members themselves. They may not work for attest clients or own financial interests in them (unless the interests are both indirect and immaterial).

B. Irrespective of the exceptions below, immediate family members cumulatively may not own more than 5% of an attest client.

C. **Immediate Family Members Employed by Attest Client**—A covered member's immediate family members may work for an attest client, just not in a "key position" such as one in which an employee has:

1. Primary responsibility for significant accounting functions that support material components of the financial statement;

2. Primary responsibility for the preparation of the financial statement; or

3. The ability to exercise influence over the contents of the financial statement, including when the individual is a member of the board of directors or similar governing body, chief executive officer, president, chief financial officer, chief operating officer, general counsel, chief accountancy officer, controller, director of internal audit, director of financial reporting, treasurer, or any equivalent position.

D. **Immediate Family Member Participation in an Employee Benefit Plan**—Immediate family members may not only work for an attest client in a nonkey position, they may also participate in an employee benefit plan that is an attest client or is sponsored by an attest client, so long as all of the following safeguards are followed:

1. The plan is offered to all employees in comparable employment positions;

2. The immediate family member does not serve in a position of governance for the plan; *and*

3. The immediate family member does not have the ability to supervise or participate in the plan's investment decisions or in the selection of the investment options made available to plan participants.

E. **Immediate Family Member Participation in an Employee Benefit Plan with Financial Interests in an Attest Client**—An immediate family member might work for a company that is not an attest client but participate in its employee benefit plan and learn that the plan holds stock of an attest client. The general rule is that in this setting an immediate family member may hold a direct financial interest or material indirect financial interest in an attest client if all of the following safeguards are met:

1. The covered member is neither on the attest team nor in a position to influence. (So, the immediate family member could be a 10-hour person or other partner in the office but not a team member or in a position to influence in relationship to the attest client);

2. Such investment is an unavoidable consequence of such participation; the immediate family member had no other investment options available for selection and

3. If the plan creates an option that would allow the immediate family members to invest in a nonattest client, the immediate family members should select that option and dispose of the attest client shares as soon as practicable but within 30 days.

III. Close Relatives

A. Generally, close relatives of covered members must follow the same independence rules as the covered members themselves, but the restrictions are looser than for immediate family members and they are looser for close relatives of covered members who are not on the engagement team.

B. Independence is impaired if the close relative of an audit team member has **either** of the following:

1. A key position with the attest client, *or*

2. A financial interest in the attest client that:

   a. The team member knows or has reason to know was material to the close relative, *or*

   b. Enabled the close relative to exercise significant influence over the attest client.

C. Independence is impaired if the close relative of a person in a position to influence or other partner in the office has **either** of the following:

1. A key position with an attest client, *or*

2. A financial interest that:

   a. The person in a position to influence or other partner in office has reason to believe was material to the close relative, **and**

   b. Enabled the close relative to exercise significant influence over the attest client.

D. There are no specific restrictions on close relatives of 10-hour people (though the Conceptual Framework should always be kept in mind).

Employment Relationships

Current Employment

> **After studying this lesson, you should be able to:**
>
> 1. Apply the rules that, to preserve independence, prevent various members of an accounting firm from working for an audit client in a wide range of positions.
>
> 2. Understand the rules that govern a situation where an attest client's employee wishes to come to work for the audit firm.

I. Current Employment

A. The employment rules focus on partners and professional employees of attest firms. They may not, without impairing independence, serve in these roles for an attest client: director, officer, employee, promoter, underwriter, voting trustee, or trustee for any pension or profit-sharing trust of the client's, or in any equivalent management position.

B. Professors—Partners and professional employees may serve as adjunct faculty members at a college that is an attest client so long as the following safeguards are all accurate regarding the faculty member. He or she:

1. Does not hold a key position with the client

2. Is not on the attest engagement team

3. Is not in a position to influence

4. Is on a part-time and non-tenure basis

5. Does not participate in any employee benefit plan sponsored by the school, unless participation is required

6. Does not assume any management responsibilities or set policies

C. Honorary Director or Trustee of a Not-for-Profit Organization—Partners and professional employees may lend the prestige of their names to a not-for-profit that is an attest client so long as all of the following safeguards are in place:

1. The position is clearly honorary.

2. The partner or professional employee cannot vote and takes no management role in the organization.

3. All externally circulated materials identify the position as honorary.

D. Member of an Advisory Board—If criteria similar to those mentioned in the previous section are met, partners and professional employees may serve on an attest client's advisory board without impairing independence.

E. Member of Governmental Advisory Committee—Independence considerations do not prevent partners or professional employees from serving on a citizen's advisory committee studying possible changes in the form of a county government that is an attest client, or on an advisory committee appointed to study the financial status of the state in which the county is located.

F. Campaign Treasurer—Independence considerations preclude a firm from auditing a campaign organization whose campaign manager is a partner or professional employee of the firm. Similarly, if Joe is an elected head of a governmental unit or is a candidate running for that position, an audit firm would not be independent in auditing that governmental unit if Joe's campaign manager is a partner or professional employee of the firm. However, the firm would not necessarily lack independence to audit Joe's political party. The firm should apply the threats and safeguards framework to determine whether threats to independence could be lowered to an acceptable level.

G. Member of Federated Fund-Raising Organization—If a firm's partner or professional employee serves as director or officer of a federated fund-raising organization such as United Way, which not only gives funds to a particular local charity but also exercises control over that charity, then the firm may not audit that local charity. Even if United Way does not exercise control, there are sufficient independence concerns that the Conceptual Framework should be invoked.

H. Member of Organization that Receives Funds from Fund-Raising Organization—When a partner or professional employee is a director of an organization that receives funding from a foundation that exists solely to raise funds for that organization, the firm may not audit the foundation, unless the directorship is clearly honorary.

II. Former Employment or Association with an Attest Client

A. Independence concerns arise when people who are employed by attest clients or who were associated with them as officers, directors, promoters, underwriters, voting trustees, or trustees for a pension fund or profit-sharing fund of the clients, join the firm as **covered members.**

B. Independence is impaired if one of these people participates as a **team member** or someone in a **position to influence** when the attest engagement covers any period of time when the person was employed by or associated with the audit client.

C. However, if the people become merely other partners in the office or 10-hour people, then independence is not impaired so long as they **dissociate** themselves from the client prior to becoming a covered member. Dissociation includes **all** of the following five steps:

1. Ceasing to participate in all the client's health and welfare benefit plans, unless the client is legally required to allow the covered member to participate in the plan (e.g., COBRA), and the covered member pays 100% of his or her portion of the cost

2. Ceasing to participate in all other employee benefit plans by liquidating or transferring all vested benefits in the client's defined benefit plans, defined contribution plans, and similar arrangements at the earliest permissible

3. Disposing of any direct or material indirect financial interest in the client

4. Collecting or repaying any loans to or from the client other than those specifically permitted or grandfathered by the code

5. Assessing other relationships with the client to determine if they create threats to independence that would require the application of safeguards to reduce threats to an acceptable level

Subsequent Employment

After studying this lesson, you should be able to:

1. Know the rules that must be followed to preserve independence when certain covered members are considering going to work for an attest client.

2. Know the rules that must be followed to preserve independence when covered members do go to work for an attest client.

I. **Considering Subsequent Employment with an Attest Client**

   A. When an attest team member or person in a position to influence is considering employment with the attest client, independence is impaired unless the team member:

   1. Promptly reports such consideration or offer to an appropriate person in the firm, *and*

   2. Removes him- or herself from the engagement until the offer is rejected or the position is no longer sought.

   B. When a *covered member* learns that a team member or a person in a position to influence is considering employment with a client and has not taken the steps listed above, that member should alert the firm.

   1. The firm must consider what additional procedures may be necessary to provide *reasonable assurance* that the person acted properly.

   2. The policy does not explicitly cover other partners in office or 10-hour people.

II. **Subsequent Employment with an Attest Client**

   A. A firm's independence will be considered impaired when a partner or professional employee goes to work for an attest client in a *key position,* unless all of the following conditions are met:

   1. Amounts due the former employee for ownership interest in the firm and unfunded, vested retirement interests are not material to the firm, and the underlying formula used to calculate payments remains fixed.

   2. The former employee is not in a position to influence the accounting firm's operations or financial policies.

   3. The former employee does not participate or **appear** to participate in the firm's business and is not associated with the firm (even if unpaid). An *appearance of participation* results from such actions as:

      a. The former employee consults with the firm.

      b. The firm provides the former employee with an office and related amenities.

      c. The individual's name is included in the firm's office directory.

      d. The individual's name is included as a member of the firm in other membership lists of business, professional, or civic organizations, unless designated as retired.

   4. The ongoing attest engagement team considers modifying audit procedures to adjust for the risk created by the former employee's knowledge of the audit plan that he or she has now taken to the client. Also, it should consider whether remaining team members can appropriately stand up to a former employee if they have to deal with him or/ her.

   5. If the former employee joins the client in a **key position within one year of dissociating from the firm**, and has significant interaction with the attest engagement team, an appropriate professional in the firm should review the subsequent engagement to determine whether appropriate skepticism was maintained.

B. Sarbanes-Oxley (SOX) imposes stricter rules where public companies are involved. SOX imposes a one-year cooling-off period that requires the lead partner, the concurring partner, or any other member of the audit engagement team who provides more than 10 hours of audit, review, or attest services to observe a one-year cooling-off period before going to work for a client in a financial oversight position. The positions that cannot be assumed within the one-year period include (a) chief executive officer, chief financial officer, controller, chief accountancy officer, or any equivalent officers; (b) any financial oversight role; and (c) any position preparing financial statements. If a former audit firm employee violates these rules, independence is impaired. The one-year cooling-off period is that year preceding the beginning of the audit, so the cooling-off period actually can extend to nearly two years if the member has begun an audit cycle before leaving the firm.

Other Associations and Relationships

> **After studying this lesson, you should be able to:**
>
> **1.** Appreciate the intricacies of avoiding independence problems while in various relationships with attest clients, such as social clubs, trade associations, condominium associations, and credit unions.
>
> **2.** Know the rules that govern the giving of gifts and entertainment in an attest setting.

I. **Member of a Social Club**—If a covered member belongs to a social club, such as a country club, that is an attest client, there should be no independence problem if the membership is primarily a social matter.

II. **Member of a Trade Association**—Independence is impaired if a covered member belongs to a trade association that is an attest client. If a partner or professional employee is employed by or associated with a trade association in an important role (director, trustee, etc.), independence is again impaired.

III. **Member of a Common Interest Realty Association (CIRA)**—If a covered member buys an interest in a condominium, cooperative, or other common interest realty association, his or her firm may nonetheless audit the common interest realty association, but only if **all** of the following safeguards are met:

   A. The common interest realty association performs functions similar to local governments, such as public safety, road maintenance, and utilities;

   B. The covered member's annual assessment is not material to either the common interest realty association or the member;

   C. Liquidation of the common interest realty association or sale of common assets would not result in a distribution to the covered member; *and*

   D. The common interest realty association's creditors would not be permitted to recover out of the member's assets if the common interest realty association became insolvent.

IV. **Member of a Credit Union**—When a covered member is a member of a credit union and became eligible to join only because of the professional services he or she provided to the credit union, independence is impaired. However, if the member individually qualifies to join the credit union irrespective of professional services provided, then independence is not impaired.

V. **Gifts and Entertainment**

   A. **Gifts**—In dependence is impaired if the firm, a team member, or someone in a position to influence accepts a gift from an attest client, unless the value is clearly insignificant to the recipient.

   B. **Entertainment**—Entertainment may be accepted without impairing independence so long as it is reasonable in the circumstances. The circumstances to be considered include:

   1. Nature of the gift or entertainment

   2. Occasion giving rise to the gift or entertainment

   3. Cost or value of the gift or entertainment

   4. Nature, frequency, and value of other gifts and entertainment

   5. Whether the entertainment was associated with the active conduct of business

   6. Whether other attest clients also participated in the entertainment; *and*

   7. Client and firm employees who participated in the entertainment

VI. **Actual or Threatened Litigation**

   A. **Litigation Between Client and Member**—If the client (or its management) sues the audit firm (or vice versa), the key question is whether the firm and client are in threatened or actual positions of material adverse interests. A minor dispute or one not related to the engagement (such as a billing dispute) would not impair independence. However, the code gives these examples of impaired independence:

1. An **attest client's current** management sues or seriously threatens to sue firm alleging deficiencies in the audit work.

2. A **covered member** sues the client's current management alleging fraud or deceit.

B. **Litigation by Client Security Holders**—Client shareholders filing a suit claiming securities fraud or some other wrong by both the client and the audit firm presumptively does **not** automatically impair independence. But if there are cross-claims between the client and its managers on one hand and the attest firm of the other (or a serious risk of them), independence is impaired if there is a *significant risk* that a material settlement or judgment will result.

C. **Other Third-Party Litigation**—Litigation by non-shareholder third parties, such as lenders, who might also sue the auditor and/or the client is treated similarly.

D. Final resolution of litigation or other dispute eliminates the independence threat and reduces it to an acceptable level.

Nonaudit Services

Code Provisions

After studying this lesson, you should be able to:

1. Understand the differences between the code's approach and Sarbanes-Oxley's approach to the provision of nonaudit services to public company attest clients.

2. Understand and be able to apply the "big picture" code rules, such as the general requirements that always must be met for those who provide nonaudit services to attest clients.

I. Introduction

A. The code governs provision of nonaudit services to private company audit clients and indicates that communications about the following matters that would **not** normally be considered nonaudit services:

   1. The client's selection and application of accounting standards or policies and financial statement disclosure requirements;

   2. The appropriateness of the client's methods used in determining accounting and financial reporting;

   3. Adjusting journal entries that the member has prepared or proposed for client management consideration; *and*

   4. The form or content of the financial statement.

B. Covered members should monitor the total amount of their nonaudit services to ensure that their total involvement with the client does not become so extensive that it would constitute performing a separate service.

C. **Management Responsibilities**—Members must not assume any management responsibilities of attest clients. "Management responsibilities involve leading and directing an entity, including making significant decisions regarding the acquisition, deployment, and control of human, financial, physical, and intangible resources." Examples of such impermissible activities include:

   1. Setting policy or strategic direction for the attest client

   2. Directing or accepting responsibility for actions of the attest client's employees except to the extent permitted when using internal auditors to provide assistance for services performed under auditing or attestation standards

   3. Authorizing, executing, or consummating transactions or otherwise exercising authority on behalf of an attest client or having the authority to do so

   4. Preparing source documents, in electronic or other form, that evidence the occurrence of a transaction

   5. Having custody of an attest client's assets

   6. Deciding which recommendations of the member or other third parties to implement or prioritize

   7. Reporting to those charged with governance on behalf of management

   8. Serving as an attest client's stock transfer or escrow agent, registrar, general counsel or equivalent

   9. Accepting responsibility for the management of an attest client's project

10. Accepting responsibility for the preparation and fair presentation of the attest client's financial statements in accordance with the applicable financial reporting framework

11. Accepting responsibility for designing, implementing, or maintaining internal control

II. **General Requirements for Performing Nonaudit Services**—When covered members do provide nonaudit services for an attest client, **if other rules do not state otherwise**, independence would not be impaired if **all** of the following three safeguards are met.

A. In order to ensure that the ultimate management of the attest client stays with the client's management, the members must determine that the client and its management agree to:

1. Assume all management responsibilities;

2. Oversee the service, by designating an individual, preferably within senior management, who possesses the skill, knowledge, and/or experience to do the job. The member should assess the situation to ensure that the individual is up to the task;

3. Evaluate the adequacy and results of the services performed and

4. Accept responsibility for the results of the services.

B. The members must **not** assume management responsibilities (as outlined above) and additionally must satisfy themselves that the audit client and its management will:

1. Be able to meet the criteria listed in the previous paragraph

2. Make an informed judgment on the results of the member's nonaudit services

3. Accept responsibility for making the significant judgments and decisions that are the proper responsibility of management

C. Before performing nonaudit services, members must establish (and document in writing) their understanding with the attest client regarding:

1. Objectives of the engagement

2. Services to be performed

3. The attest client's acceptance of its responsibilities

4. The member's responsibilities

5. Any limitations on the engagement

D. If all of these general requirements are met, then independence is not impaired, unless other rules (that we are about to explore) so provide.

E. If the general requirements are met, then a member may:

1. Provide advice, research materials, and recommendations to assist management in performing its functions and making decisions

2. Attend board meetings as a nonvoting advisor

3. Interpret financial statements, forecasts, or other analyses

4. Provide management with advice regarding its potential plans strategies, or relationships

III. **Sarbanes-Oxley (SOX)**

A. SOX limits the nonattest (also known as consulting or advisory services) that attest firms may provide to attest clients that are **public companies**. SOX does not apply if the firms are not public companies, so the code governs if an accounting firm audits a private company.

B. SOX limitations on nonaudit services are based on three fundamental notions: (a) accounting firms should not audit their own work, (b) auditors should not advocate for their clients, and (c) accounting firms should not serve as their clients' managers.

C. SOX provides that an independent auditor cannot perform the following nonaudit services for a public company audit client:

1. Bookkeeping or other services related to the accounting records of financial statements

2. Financial information systems design and implementations

3. Appraisal or valuation services, fairness opinions, or contributions-in-kind reports

4. Actuarial services

5. Internal audit outsourcing services

6. Management functions or human resources

7. Broker or dealer, investment advisor, or investment banking services

8. Legal services and expert services unrelated to the audit

9. Any other service that the Public Company Accounting Oversight Board (PCAOB) determines is impermissible.

D. SOX does not prohibit attest firms from providing tax services to their attest clients, but PCAOB rules do provide that a public company's auditor's independence is impaired regarding a tax client if the firm:

1. Enters into a contingent fee arrangement with an audit client

2. Provides marketing, planning, or opinion services in favor of the tax treatment of a *confidential transaction,* or if the transaction is based on an *aggressive* interpretation of tax law

3. Provides tax services to members of management who serve in a financial reporting oversight role for a client (or to their immediate family)

E. SOX requires that rather than the audit client's management selecting the auditor, client **audit committees** should select, evaluate, and compensate the auditors. In addition, these audit committees, which are to be composed entirely of outside directors and therefore presumably independent of overt management influence, must **preapprove** any permitted nonaudit services (such as tax services) purchased by a company from its auditor.

F. Also, when a firm seeks the permission of an audit client's audit committee to provide tax services, it must: (a) describe the proposed services in writing to the committee, (b) discuss with the committee the potential effects on independence, and (c) document that discussion.

Specific Services

After studying this lesson, you should be able to:

1. Understand the types of nonaudit services that can be provided to a private company attest client.

2. Understand the types of nonaudit services that cannot be provided to a private company attest client.

Overview

Appraisal, Valuation, or Actuarial	Impaired	Not Impaired
Results would be material to the financial statement and services involve high degree of subjectivity*	x	
Services not requiring high degree of subjectivity†		x
Services performed for nonfinancial statement purposes‡		x

*Examples: valuing employee stock option plan, business combination, or appraisals of assets and liabilities.

†Examples: valuing a client's pension or postemployment benefit liabilities.

‡Examples: appraising or actuarial services for tax planning, estate and gift taxation, and divorce proceedings.

Benefit Plan Administration	Impaired	Not Impaired
Communicate summary plan data to plan trustee		x
Advise client management regarding impact of plan provisions		x
Process transactions initiated by plan participants		x
Prepare account valuations		x
Prepare and transmit participant statement to plan participants		x
Make policy decisions on client's behalf	x	
Interpret plan for participants without management's concurrence	x	
Make disbursements on plan's behalf	x	
Take custody of plan assets	x	
Serve as a plan fiduciary	x	

Bookkeeping, Payroll, and Other Disbursements	Impaired	Not Impaired
Record management-approved transactions in client's general ledger		x
Post client-coded transactions to client's general ledger		x
Prepare financial statements based on client's trial balance information		x
Post client-approved journal entry to client's trial balance		x
Propose standard, adjusting, or correcting journal entries		x
Generate unsigned checks using client's source documents		x
Process a client's payroll using client-provided records		x
Transmit client approved payroll or other disbursement information to a financial institution chosen by client		x
Prepare reconciliation for client's evaluation		x
Determine or make changes in accounting records without client approval	x	
Approve or authorize client transactions	x	
Prepare source documents	x	
Make changes to source documents without client approval	x	
Accept responsibility to authorize payment of client funds	x	
Accept responsibility to sign or cosign checks	x	
Maintain client's bank account, take custody of client funds, or make credit or banking decisions for client	x	
Approve vendor invoices for payments	x	

Business Risk Consulting	Impaired	Not Impaired
Assist management in its assessment of client's business risk control processes		x
Recommend a plan for improving control processes and assisting in implementation		x
Make or approve business risk decisions	x	
Present business risk consideration to board on management's behalf	x	

Corporate Finance Consulting	Impaired	Not Impaired
Assist in developing corporate strategies		x
Assist in identifying sources of capital meeting client's criteria		x
Introduce management to sources of capital meeting client's criteria		x
Assist management in analyzing effects of proposed transactions		x
Advise client in transaction negotiations		x
Assist in drafting offering documents		x
Participate in transaction negotiations in advisory capacity		x
Be named as financial advisory in client's offering documents		x
Commit the client to a transaction	x	
Consummate transaction on client's behalf	x	
Act as a promoter, underwriter, broker-dealer, or guarantor of client's securities	x	
Act as a distributor of client's offering documents	x	
Maintain custody of client's securities	x	

Executive or Employee Search	Impaired	Not Impaired
Recommend position description or candidate specifications		x
Solicit, screen, and recommend candidates based on client- approved criteria		x
Recommend qualified candidates based on client-approved criteria		x
Advise employer on employee hiring or benefits		x
Hire or terminate client employees	x	
Commit client to employee compensation or benefits	x	

Forensic Accounting Services	Impaired	Not Impaired
Expert witness for a client	x	
Expert for a large group where attest clients (a) < 20% of members, voting interest, and claims (b) are not *lead* plaintiffs, and (c) do not have sole decision-making power to select expert witness		x
Fact witness		x
Litigation consulting: providing advice to attest client (without serving as expert witness)		x
Litigation consulting: serving as trier of fact, special master, court-appointed expert, or arbitrator	x	
Litigation consulting: mediator		x

Information Systems	Impaired	Not Impaired
Install or integrate a client's financial information system if it is off-the-shelf (not designed by member)		x
Assist in setting up client's chart of accounts and financial statement format		x
Design, develop, install, or integrate client's information system that is unrelated to client's financial statements or accounting records		x
Provide training and instruction to client's employees on information and control system		x
Perform network maintenance		x
Design or develop a client's financial information system	x	
Make other than insignificant modifications to source code underlying a client's existing financial information system	x	
Supervise client personnel in the daily operation of financial information system	x	
Operate client's network	x	

Internal Audit	Impaired	Not Impaired
Assess whether performance complies with management policies		x
Identify opportunities for improvement		x
Recommend improvement for management consideration		x
Performing ongoing monitoring activities or control activities (e.g., reviewing customer credit info as part of sales process) that affects execution of transactions	x	
Performing separate evaluations of a significant control such that member is, in effect, performing routine operations built into client's business process	x	
Having management rely on member's work as primary basis for client's assertions on design of operating effectiveness of internal controls	x	
Determining which, if any, recommendations for improving internal control system should be implemented	x	
Reporting to board or audit committee on behalf of management regarding internal audit affairs	x	
Approving or being responsible for overall internal audit work including determining internal audit risk and scope, project priorities, and frequency of performance of audit procedures	x	
Being connected with client as employee or in any management position (e.g., being listed as an employee in client's directory)	x	

Investment—Advisory or Management	Impaired	Not Impaired
Recommend allocation of funds that client should invest in various asset classes		x
Perform bookkeeping and reporting of client's portfolio balance		x
Review management of client's portfolio by others to determine if managers are meeting client's investment objectives		x
Transmit client's investment selection to broker		x
Make investment decisions on client's behalf	x	
Execute transactions to buy or sell for client	x	
Take custody of client assets, such as a security purchased by client	x	

Tax Services	Impaired	Not Impaired
Assuming that CPA does not have custody or control over client's funds and that client employee reviews and approves tax return prior to transmission to taxing authority, and, if required for filing, signs tax return, then:		
• Preparing tax return		x
• Transmitting tax return to taxing authority		x
• Transmitting payment		x
Signing and filing tax return on behalf of client management if authorized by management and requirements are met	x	
Representing client in administrative proceedings before taxing authority		x
Representing client in court to resolve a tax dispute	x	

Members in Business

I. **Introduction**

A. **Members in business** are members who are "employed or engaged on a contractual or volunteer basis in an executive, staff, governance, advisory, or administrative capacity in such areas as industry, the public sector, education, the not-for-profit sector and regulatory or professional bodies." This would include staff accountants, internal auditors, and other accountants not engaged in public practice.

B. Members in business do not have to worry about independence rules. They have other responsibilities that generally mirror those of members in public practice, so it should not take long to master their part of the Code of Professional Conduct.

II. **Conceptual Framework**

A. The Conceptual Framework for members in business generally tracks that of members in public practice. Six of the seven threats identified for members in public practice also apply to members in business: (a) adverse interest threats, (b) advocacy threats, (c) familiarity threats, (d) self-interest threats, (e) self-review threats, and (f) undue influence threats. The examples given differ, naturally, because of the difference in work setting.

B. Examples of adverse interest threats include:

   1. A member in business's close relative is an investor in her employer's closest competitor.

   2. A member in business has sued her employer.

C. Examples of advocacy threats include:

   1. Obtaining favorable financing is dependent on the information that the member in business includes in a prospectus.

   2. The member in business gives or fails to give information that he knows will unduly influence the conclusions reached by a third party.

D. Examples of familiarity threats include:

   1. A member in business has a long relationship with a third party and therefore stops reviewing the quality of the third-party's work.

   2. A member in business hires a relative as a subordinate.

   3. A member in business regularly accepts gifts or entertainment from a firm that sells goods or services to the member's employer.

E. Self-interest threats include:

   1. A member in business's close relative owns stock in the employer.

   2. A member in business is eligible for a performance-related bonus, and its value will be directly affected by the member in business's decisions.

F. Self-review threats include:

   1. An internal auditor accepts work that she previously performed before she was promoted to her current position.

2. A member in business accepts work that she previously performed that will be the basis for providing another professional service—for example, Sally gives tax advice to her client and later, while doing attest work for the client, automatically accepts the validity of the tax advice.

G. Undue influence threats include members in business being pressured to

1. Become associated with misleading information

2. Deviate from company policy, *or*

3. Change a conclusion regarding a tax or accounting position.

H. When attempting to eliminate these threats or reduce them to an acceptable level, members in business cannot turn to safeguards generated by their accounting firm, of course, but can turn to those created by:

1. The profession, legislation, or regulation, *or*

2. Their employer.

III. Integrity and Objectivity

A. Offering or Accepting Gifts or Entertainment—Members in business should not accept any gifts or entertainment that would violate the law or the policies of other firms of their own employer. Gifts or entertainment not reasonable in the circumstances would create a violation of the integrity and objectivity rule.

B. Preparing and Reporting Information—Members in business must never:

1. Make or direct another to make a false entry

2. Fail to correct inaccurate financial statements or entries; *or*

3. Sign or permit another to sign a document containing materially false information.

C. Subordination of Judgment—The rules against subordination of judgment for members in business are essentially identical for those of members in public practice that are contained in Part 1 of the Code of Professional Conduct.

D. Obligation of a Member to His or Her Employer's External Accountant—Members in business are to "be candid and not knowingly misrepresent facts or knowingly fail to disclose material facts to their employers" external auditor.

E. Educational Services—When teaching at a university or performing other educational services, a member in business is viewed as performing professional services and therefore must act with integrity and objectivity.

IV. General Standards

A. Like members in public practice, members in business must:

1. Act with professional competence

2. Exercise due professional care

3. Adequately plan and supervise performance of professional services

4. Have sufficient relevant data to back up any conclusions or recommendations they make

B. Members in business are expected to:

1. Comply with applicable standards promulgated by bodies like the Securities and Exchange Commission and Internal Revenue Service

2. Not imply that financial statements they are preparing and submitting to third parties were prepared in accordance with independence rules when they were not

V. Accounting Principles

   A. Like members in public practice, members in business may not claim that financial statements are presented in accordance with generally accepted accounting principles when they are not.

VI. Discreditable Acts—Members in business are held to essentially the same standards as members in public practice when it comes to defining discreditable acts, which include:

   A. Discrimination and harassment in employment

   B. Solicitation or disclosure of CPA Exam questions and answers

   C. Failure to file a tax return or pay a tax liability

   D. Negligence in preparing financial statement or other records

   E. Failure to follow the rules for preparation of financial statements required by agencies like the Securities and Exchange Commission, Federal Communications Commission, and state commissioners

   F. Entering into prohibited indemnification agreements and limited liability provisions

   G. Disclosing confidential information without the employer's permission or the application of another recognized exception (such as validly issued subpoena, etc.)

   H. Promoting or marketing their firm by use of false, misleading, or deceptive ads

   I. Improper (misleading) use of the CPA credential

Other Members

After studying this lesson, you should be able to:

1. Recognize the two basic types of "other members"—retired and unemployed.

2. Understand that other members should not engage in discreditable acts.

I. **Definition**—*Other members* are, by definition, unemployed, retired, or otherwise not working in the profession, so most of the code that applies to members in public practice and members in business does not apply to them.

II. **Discreditable Acts**—Other members are, at a minimum, not to engage in discreditable acts, including:

   A. Discrimination and harassment in employment practices

   B. Solicitation or disclosure of CPA Examination questions and answers

   C. Failure to file a tax return or pay a tax liability

   D. Improper disclosure of confidential information obtained from former employment or previous volunteer work

   E. False, misleading, or deceptive acts in promoting or marketing services

   F. Improper (misleading) use of the CPA credential

Requirements of SEC and PCAOB

Securities and Exchange Commission (SEC)

> **After studying this lesson, you should be able to:**
>
> 1. Understand the ethical requirements of the SEC.
>
> 2. Recognize situations that present threats to compliance with the ethical requirements of the SEC.
>
> 3. Apply the ethical requirements and independence rules of the SEC to situations that could present threats to compliance during an audit of an issuer.

I. **Introduction**

   A. The SEC rules for independence are very similar to AICPA rules. Although there are some differences, the results are usually the same under both approaches. Any student who masters the AICPA Code of Professional Conduct and has knowledge of the SOX requirements and a modicum of common sense should be able to handle questions regarding the SEC rules. Nonetheless, this lesson outlines those rules in some detail.

   B. Rule 2-01 of the SEC's Regulation S-X provides specific rules regarding auditor independence in connection with public company audit clients. It also includes the Sarbanes-Oxley (SOX) independence requirements. Remember that if there are any differences between the AICPA approach and the rules of the SEC or PCAOB, the latter take precedence if the audit client is a public company.

      1. Many of SOX's provisions that are relevant here are covered in more detail in the BEC lesson on corporate governance, including requirements for retention of audit records, punishment for destroying audit documents prematurely, and so on.

   C. SEC independence rules are, overall, concerned with whether a relationship with or provision of a service to an audit client:

      1. Creates a conflict of interest for the auditor;

      2. Results in the accountant auditing his or her own work;

      3. Results in the accountant acting as an audit client's manager or employee; *or*

      4. Places the accountant in a position of being an advocate for the audit client.

II. **Key Definitions**

   A. **Financial Reporting Oversight Role (FROR)**—A role in which a person is in a position to or does exercise influence over the contents of the F/S or anyone who prepares them. Examples: director, CEO, president, CFO, COO, general counsel, CAO, controller, director of internal audit, director of financial reporting, treasurer, or any equivalent position.

   B. **Audit and Professional Engagement Period**—Includes the period covered by any F/S being audited or reviewed (the "audit period") and the period of the engagement (the "professional engagement period"). The professional engagement period begins at the earlier of when the accountant signs an initial engagement letter or begins the audit and ends when the audit client or the accountant notifies the SEC that the client is no longer the accountant's audit client.

   C. **Close Family Member (CFM)**—A person's spouse, spousal equivalent, parent, dependent, nondependent child, and sibling.

   D. **Covered Persons**—The following partners, principals, shareholders, and employees of an accounting firm:

      1. **Audit engagement team**, which includes "all partners, principals, shareholders and professional employees participating in an audit, review, or attestation engagement of an

audit client, including audit partners and all persons who consult with others on the audit engagement . . . regarding technical or industry-specific issues, transactions, or events" (comparable to AICPA "team");

2. **Chain of command**, which includes all persons who: (a) supervise or have direct management responsibility for the audit, including at all successively senior levels through the accounting firm's chief executive; (b) evaluate the performance or recommend the compensation of the audit engagement partner; *or* (c) provide quality control or other oversight of the audit (PTIs);

3. Any other partner, principal, shareholder, or managerial employee of the accounting firm who has provided 10 or more hours of non-audit services (NAS) to the audit client for the period beginning on the date such services are provided and ending on the date the accounting firm signs the report on the F/S for the fiscal year during which those services are provided, or who expects to provide 10 or more hours of NAS to the audit client on a recurring basis (10-hour persons); *and*

4. Any other partner, principal, or shareholder from an "office" of the accounting firm in which the lead audit engagement partner primarily practices in connection with the audit (OPIOs—other partners in the office).

E. **Immediate Family Member (IFM)**—A person's spouse, spousal equivalent, and dependents.

III. **Basic Requirements**—To be qualified to audit a public company, a CPA:

A. Must be registered and in good standing under the laws of his or her state; *and*

B. Must be and appear to be independent and capable of exercising objective and impartial judgment.

IV. **Financial Relationships**—Investments in audit clients can imperil independence.

A. **Direct Investments**—The accounting firm, any of its covered persons or any or their immediate family members (IFMs) may not have direct investments in an audit client, such as owning stocks, bonds, notes, options, and so on.

1. A "direct investment" includes one through an intermediary if:

   a. The firm, covered persons or IFMs, alone or together, either supervise or participate in the intermediary's investment decisions, *or*

   b. The intermediary is a nondiversified mutual fund that has invested 20% or more its money in an audit client.

B. **Five Percent Investments**—Independence is impaired if any partner, principal, shareholder, or professional employee of the accounting firm (and any of their IFMs or CFMs) owns >5% or more of the client's stock.

C. **Trustee of a Trust**—Independence is impaired if the accounting firm or any covered persons or IFMs serve as voting trustees of a trust or executors of an estate containing an audit client's securities, *unless* they have no authority to make investment decisions for the trust or estate.

D. **Material Indirect Interests**—As with the AICPA Code, accounting firms, covered persons, and their IFMs may not only not have direct financial interests in an audit client (whether material or immaterial), they may not have indirect interests that are *material*. It is permitted for these persons to own 5% or less of a *diversified* investment company, even if the company owns some shares of an audit client.

E. **Related Entities**—Independence is destroyed if the firm, covered persons, or IFMs:

1. Have any direct or material indirect investment in an entity that is not an audit client where:

   a. An audit client has an investment in that entity that is material to the audit client and has the ability to exercise significant control over that entity, *or*

   b. The entity has an investment in an audit client that is material to that entity and has the ability to exercise significant influence over that audit client.

2. Have any material investment in an entity over which an audit client is able to exercise significant influence; *or*

3. Have the ability to exercise significant influence over an entity that has the ability to exercise significant influence over an audit client.

V.   Other Financial Relationships—Independence is impaired if the firm, its covered persons, or their IMFs have:

A.   Loans/Debtor Creditor Relationships—Any loan to or from an audit client, its officers or directors, or its 10% owners, *except* for the following loans obtained from a *financial institution* under its normal lending procedures, terms, and requirements:

1. Automobile loans and leases collateralized by the automobile;

2. Loans fully collateralized by the cash surrender value of an insurance policy;

3. Loans fully collateralized by cash deposits at the same financial institution; *and*

4. A mortgage loan collateralized by the borrower's primary residence provided the loan was not obtained while the covered person was a covered person.

B.   Savings and Checking Accounts—Any savings, checking, or similar account at a bank, savings and loan, or similar institution that is an audit client if the account has a balance that exceeds the amount insurable by the FDIC, *except* that an accounting firm may have an uninsured balance provided that the likelihood of the institution experiencing financial difficulties is remote.

C.   Broker-Dealer Accounts—Brokerage or similar accounts maintained with a broker-dealer that is an audit client, if:

1. Any such account includes assets other than cash or securities; *or*

2. The value of assets in the accounts exceeds the amount protected by the Securities Investor Protection Corporation (SIPC), which is $500,000 for securities and $250,000 for cash.

D.   Credit Cards—Any aggregate outstanding credit card balance > $10,000 owed to a lender that is an audit client.

E.   Insurance Products—Any individual policy issued by an insurer that is an audit client, *unless*:

1. The policy was obtained when the covered person was *not* a covered person in the firm; *and*

2. The likelihood of the insurer becoming insolvent is remote.

VI.   Exceptions—Notwithstanding the provisions in the previous two sections, independence will not be impaired in these cases:

A.   Inheritance and Gifts—Any person who acquires an unsolicited financial interest (as through gift or inheritance) will not lose independence if he or she disposes of the interest as soon as practicable, but always less than 30 days after the person has knowledge of and the right to dispose of the interest.

B.   New Audit Engagement—A person has a financial interest that would normally impair independence *but* that person did not audit the client's F/S the previous year and disposes of the interest before either (a) signing an engagement letter, or (b) commencing any audit procedures.

C.   Employee Compensation and Benefit Plans—An IFM has an impermissible financial interest in an audit client that was an unavoidable consequence of participation in his or her employer's employee compensation or benefits program, provided that the financial interest (other than unexercised employee stock options) is disposed of as soon as practicable but always no later than 30 days after the person has the right to dispose of the financial interest. This exception applies to IFMs of OPIOs and 10-hour persons.

VII.   Audit Clients' Financial Relationships—CPAs are not independent in these cases:

A.   Investments by the Audit Client in the Accounting Firm—(a) An audit client has, or has agreed to acquire, any direct investment in the accounting firm, *or* (b) the audit client's officers or directors own >5% of the equity securities of the accounting firm.

B. **Underwriting**—Their firm engages an audit client to act as an underwriter, broker-dealer, market-maker, promoter, or analyst for securities issued by the accounting firm.

VIII. Employment Relationships—An accountant is not independent if he or she has an employment relationship with the audit client such as those listed next:

A. **Employment at Audit Client of Accountant**—A current partner, principal, shareholder, or professional employee of the accounting firm is employed by the audit client or is a member of the board of directors.

B. **Employment at Audit Client of Certain Relatives of Accountant**—A CFM of a covered person is in an accounting **role** or FROR at an audit client.

C. **Employment at Audit Client of Former Employee of Accounting Firm**

1. A former partner, principal shareholder, or professional employee at an accounting firm is in an accounting or FROR at an audit client, *unless* the individual:

    a. Does not influence the accounting firm's operations or financial policies;

    b. Has no capital balances in the accounting firm; *and*

    c. Has no financial arrangement with the accounting firm other than one providing for regular payment of a fixed dollar amount (which is not dependent on the revenue, profits, or earnings of the accounting firm):

        i. Pursuant to a fully funded retirement plan; *or*

        ii. in the case of a former professional employee who was not a partner, principal, or shareholder of the accounting firm and who has been dissociated from the accounting for more than five years that is immaterial to the former employee.

2. A former partner, principal, shareholder, or professional employee of an accounting firm is in an FROR at an audit client (except an investment company, where slightly different rules apply), *unless* the individual was not a member of the audit engagement team during the one-year period preceding the date of the initiation of the audit.

Example

ABC's Audit cycle runs May 15 to May 14. Sandy is on the audit team of PriceCooperHouse. She resigns on June 15, just one month into the audit cycle. She must wait until the end of that cycle and then allow a complete cycle to pass before she can go to work in an accounting or FROR capacity. Had she quit on May 14, 2017, she could have started at ABC on May 15, 2018. But since she resigned on June 15, 2017, she must wait until May 15, 2019.

If the individual worked for the audit firm but did not participate in the client's audit before going to work for the client in an FROR, this is not considered a problem.

Persons who provided 10 or fewer hours of attest services during the relevant period are not covered by the requirement.

Nor are persons who are employed by the issuer due to a merger or because of an emergency situation.

D. **Employment at Accounting Firm of Former Employee of Audit Client**—A former officer, director, or employee of an audit client becomes a partner, principal, shareholder, or professional employee of the accounting firm, *unless* the individual does not participate in, and is not in a position to influence, the audit of F/S covering any period he or she was employed by the audit client.

IX. Business Relationships

A. An accountant is not independent if at any time during the audit and professional engagement, the accounting firm or any covered person in the firm has any direct or material indirect business relationship with an audit client or with persons associated with the audit client in a decision-making capacity, such as an audit client's officers, directors, or substantial shareholders.

    B. **Exception**—An accounting firm or covered persons can provide professional services to an audit client or buy services from a client in the ordinary course of business without an impermissible business relationship arising.

X. **Non-Audit Services**—SOX provisions, as implemented by the SEC, indicate that independence is impaired if an auditor provides any of the following non-audit services (NAS) to a public company audit client, *unless* it is reasonable to conclude that the results of these services will not be subject to audit procedures during the audit of the client's F/S:

    A. Bookkeeping services, including

        1. Maintaining or preparing the client's accounting records

        2. Preparing the client's F/S that are filed with the SEC

        3. Preparing or originating source data underlying the F/S

    B. Financial information systems design and implementation, including:

        1. Directly or indirectly operating, or supervising the operation of, the audit client's information system or managing the audit client's local-area network

        2. Designing or implementing a hardware or software system that aggregates source data underlying the F/S or generates information that is significant to the client's F/S

    C. Appraisal or valuation services

    D. Actuarial services

    E. Internal audit outsourcing services

    F. Management functions

    G. Human resources, such as:

        1. Searching for prospective candidates for managerial positions

        2. Engaging in psychological testing, or other formal testing or evaluation programs

        3. Undertaking reference checks of prospective candidates for executive or director positions

        4. Acting as a negotiator on an audit client's behalf, such as determining compensation, fringe benefits, and so on

        5. Recommending that the client hire a specific candidate for a specific job (although it is okay to advise a client on a candidate's competence for financial accounting, administrative, or control positions)

    H. Broker-dealer, investment adviser, or investment banking services

    I. Legal services

    J. Expert services unrelated to the audit

XI. **Contingent Fees**—An accountant is not independent if it provides *any* service or product to a public company audit client for a contingent fee or commission.

XII. **Partner Rotation**—SOX mandates that:

    A. There are no requirements that public companies rotate audit *firms*.

    B. Lead and concurring audit partners must be rotated every five years (five on, five off).

    C. Other partners providing more than 10 hours of attest services must be rotated every seven years (seven on, two off).

    D. There are exemptions for firms with fewer than five public company audit clients and fewer than 10 audit partners.

> **Note**
> *Audit firms may provide these services to nonaudit clients that are public companies and to private companies (even if they are audit clients) so long as AICPA restrictions are followed. Other NAS, such as most tax services, may be performed for public company audit clients, but only if (a) preapproved by the client's audit committee and (b) disclosed in the client's periodic reports filed with the SEC.*

XIII. Audit Committee Administration of the Engagement—SOX shifts control of the audit process from the CEO and CFO to the audit committee, and an auditor is not independent unless these new rules are followed. Both the audit engagement itself and provision of permitted NAS are to be preapproved by the audit committee.

    A. Some NAS provided by the audit firm (those services providing 5% or less of total revenues from the audit client during the audit year) do not require preapproval by the audit committee. However, the audit committee must approve of these services before the current audit engagement has been completed.

XIV. Compensation—SOX provides that an accountant is not independent if any audit partner earns or receives compensation based on selling NAS to the audit client.

XV. Quality Controls—An accounting firm's independence will not be impaired solely because a covered person is not independent, *provided*:

    A. The covered person did not know of the circumstances giving rise to the lack of independence;

    B. The covered person's lack of independence was corrected as promptly as possible once it became known; *and*

    C. The accounting firm has a quality control system in place that provides reasonable assurance that independence rules will be complied with.

    D. For firms annually auditing more than 500 companies, their quality control system provides such reasonable assurance only if it has the following features:

        1. Written independence policies and procedures;

        2. An automated system tracking investments of partners and managerial employees that might impair independence;

        3. For all professionals, a system that provides timely information about entities from which the accountant is required to maintain independence;

        4. An annual or ongoing firm-wide training program on independence rules;

        5. An annual internal inspection and testing program to monitor adherence to independence rules;

        6. Notification to all firm employees of the name and title of the member of senior management responsible for compliance with independence rules; *and*

        7. A disciplinary mechanism to ensure compliance.

Public Company Accounting Oversight Board (PCAOB)

After studying this lesson, you should be able to:

1. Understand the ethical requirements of the PCAOB.

2. Recognize situations that present threats to compliance with the ethical requirements of the PCAOB.

3. Apply the ethical requirements and independence rules of the PCAOB to situations that could present threats to compliance during an audit of an issuer.

4. Be able to explain the role the PCAOB plays in governing the audit profession, including in registering, inspecting, and punishing firms that audit public companies.

I. Introduction

A. In 2002, Sarbanes-Oxley (SOX) replaced decades of self-regulation by public accounting firms when it created the PCAOB to govern public company audit firms under the supervision of the SEC.

1. The PCAOB, among other things:

a. Registers accounting firms that audit public companies

b. Establishes auditing, quality control, ethics, independence, and other standards

c. Inspects firms

d. Annual inspections are conducted for firms doing more than 100 audits per year.

e. Inspections occur once every three years for firms auditing fewer companies.

f. Investigates and punishes wrongdoing

B. SOX also enacted several provisions relating to auditor independence—including rules regarding which consulting services audit firms can offer to their public company audit clients, rules on audit partner rotation and cooling-off periods, and rules on auditor compensation. These rules are covered in the previous lesson on the SEC's ethics rules.

C. This lesson covers rules the PCAOB has issued on ethics and independence. An earlier lesson covered its other major responsibilities (registering public accounting firms, inspecting registered public accounting firms, issuing standards for attestation activities and quality control, enforcement).

D. All PCAOB rules must be approved by the SEC, so it is not a surprise that its ethics and independence rules are consistent with the SEC requirements explicated in a previous lesson.

E. Early on, in 2003, the PCAOB adopted the AICPA's Code of Professional Conduct provisions regarding independence as its own interim standards. Although that version of the Code has since been replaced by the current electronic version and the PCAOB has issued many of its own rules (discussed below), the substance of the rules remains the same so there remains much consistency between PCAOB rules and AICPA rules regarding independence. However, if the SEC and PCAOB issue any rules that are more restrictive than AICPA rules, they override those AICPA rules for public company audits.

II. PCAOB Independence and Ethics Rules

A. **Independence Required**—Rule 3520 provides that "a registered public accounting firm and its associated persons must be independent of the firm's audit client throughout the audit and professional engagement." No surprise there. CPAs must comply with not only PCAOB rules and SEC rules, but also "all other independence criteria applicable to the engagement."

B. Contingency Fees and Commissions—Rule 3521, consistent with AICPA rules, provides that if a firm or any affiliate provides "any service or product" to an audit client in exchange for a contingent fee or commission, independence is impaired. Elsewhere, the PCAOB defines contingent fee to include any arrangement in which the amount of a fee is dependent upon a specified finding or result being obtained. Consistent with AICPA rules, a fee is not considered contingent if it is fixed by courts or other public authorities and is not dependent on a particular finding or result.

C. Tax Consulting—Although the SEC and PCAOB considered prohibiting public company audit firms from providing any tax services to public company audit clients, they chose not to do so. However, Rule 3522 puts some limitations on those tax services by providing that firms are not independent if during their audit engagements they provide services related to marketing, planning or opining in favor of tax transactions that are:

1. **Confidential**—A "confidential transaction" is one that is offered to a taxpayer under conditions of confidentiality and for which the taxpayer has paid the advisor a fee; *or*

2. **Aggressive**—An "aggressive tax position transaction" is one initially recommended by the accounting firm and a "significant purpose" of which is tax avoidance, *unless* the proposed tax treatment is at least *more likely than not* to be allowable under applicable tax laws. Examples of such impermissible aggressive transactions are ones that are the same or similar to transactions the IRS has already determined to be tax avoidance transactions.

D. Tax Services for FRORs—Rule 3523 provides that public company accounting firms may also forfeit their independence by providing "any tax service" to a person in a "financial reporting oversight role" (FROR) at the audit client or to an immediate family member (IFM) (spouse, spousal equivalent, and dependents) of such a person.

1. FROR is defined as a role in which a person can or does exercise influence over the contents of financial statements or anyone who prepares them. Examples of FRORs include: directors, CEOs, presidents, CFOs, COOs, general counsel, CAOs, controllers, directors of internal audit, directors of financial reporting, treasurers, or other equivalent positions.

2. The rule contains three exceptions. Independence is not impaired if the person:

   a. Is in an FROR only because he or she is a member of the client's board of directors

   b. Is in an FROR only because of his or her relationship to an affiliate of the entity being audited where the affiliate's financial statements are not material to the consolidated financial statements of the audit client or are audited by a different audit firm.

   c. Was not in an FROR before a hiring, promotion or similar change in employment and the tax services are:

      i. Provided pursuant to an engagement in process before the change in employment; and

      ii. Completed on or before 180 days after the employment event

E. Approving Permissible Tax Consulting—SOX allows certain tax consulting services to be provided to public company audit clients so long as they are pre-approved by the client's audit committee. Rule 3524 sets out the procedure for seeking such approval, requiring that the accounting firm:

1. Describe in writing:

   a. The scope of the service, the fee structure for the engagement, and any other related agreement between the firm and the audit client.

   b. Any compensation arrangement or other agreement, such as a referral fee or fee-sharing arrangement between the firm and any person (other than the audit client) regarding the promoting, marketing, or recommending of a transaction covered by the service.

2. Discuss with the audit committee the potential effects of the services on the firm's independence.

3. Document the discussion.

F. **Approving Permissible NAS**—SOX prohibits audit firms from providing certain non-audit services (NAS) related to internal controls over financial reporting, but allows others if pre-approved by the public company client's audit committee. Regarding those that are allowed, Rule 3525 sets out the procedure for seeking such approval, providing, consistent with Rule 3524 regarding tax services, that the firm should:

1. Describe in writing to the audit committee the scope of the service;

2. Discuss with the audit committee the potential effects of the service on the firm's independence; and

3. Document the discussion.

G. **Accepting New Audit Clients**—Rule 3526 provides that before accepting a public company as a new audit client, a registered firm must:

1. Describe in writing to the audit committee all relationships between the firm and its affiliates on the one hand and the client and its FROR employees as of the date of the communication that "may reasonably be thought to bear on independence";

2. Discuss with the audit committee these relationships and their potential effect on independence; and

3. Document the discussion.

   a. Note: at least annually with respect to each public company audit client a firm should go through this three-step procedure regarding existing relationships and affirm to the audit committee in writing that it remains independent.

III. Other PCAOB Ethics Rules

A. Rule 3502 provides that public accountants have a responsibility to not—knowingly or recklessly, by action or omission—contribute to violations of SOX, of PCAOB rules, of federal securities laws, or of professional standards.

B. Rule 3700 establishes advisory groups to assist the PCAOB in establishing its own professional standards.

C. Relatedly, to increase transparency the PCAOB recently required firms to file a form for each issuer audit disclosing:

1. The name of the engagement partner;

2. The name, location, and extent of participation of each other accounting firm participating in the audit whose work constituted at least 5% of total audit hours; *and*

3. The number and aggregate extent of participation of all other accounting firms participating in the audit whose individual participation was less than 5% of total audit hours.

Requirements of GAO and DOL

Government Accountability Office (GAO)

After studying this lesson, you should be able to:

1. Recognize situations that present threats to compliance with the ethical requirements of the Government Accountability Office Government Auditing Standards.

I. **General Accountability Office's Government Auditing Standards—Ethical Principles**

   A. The GAO's guidelines apply to those who conduct audits of:

   1. Government entities (e.g., federal, state and local)

   2. Entities that receive government awards (e.g., colleges, trade schools, charities, local governments) in compliance with generally accepted government auditing standards (GAGAS)

   3. **Independence and ethical principles**—Those who audit pursuant to GAGAS are expected to audit:

      a. Independently; *and*

      b. In accordance with these key ethical principles:

         i. The public interest

         ii. Integrity

         iii. Objectivity

         iv. Proper use of government information, resources, and positions—these are to be used for official purposes and not for an auditor's personal gain

         v. **Professional behavior**—Includes compliance with all relevant legal, regulatory, and professional obligations, avoidance of conflicts of interest, sensitivity to appearance of impropriety, and putting forth an honest effort to meet technical and professional standards.

II. **Independence Introduction**

   A. **Independence** comprises:

   1. **Independence of mind**—Performing an audit without being affected by influences that compromise professional judgment enables an auditor to act with integrity, objectivity, and professional skepticism.

   2. **Independence in appearance**—No reasonable and informed third party should be given reason to conclude that the integrity, objectivity, and/or professional skepticism of the auditor are compromised.

   B. **Time period**—Independence must be maintained during:

   1. Any period of time falling within the period covered by the financial statements or subject matter of the audit, *and*

   2. The period of the professional engagement, which begins at the earlier of the signing of an initial engagement letter or some other agreement to perform an audit and ends with the formal or informal notification of the termination of the professional relationship or issuance of a report, whichever is later.

C. **Four Key Independence Considerations**

1. Conceptual framework for making independence determinations

2. Requirements for and guidance on independence for audit organizations (AOs) structurally located within the entities they audit

3. Requirements for and guidance on independence for performing nonaudit services (NAS)

4. Requirements for and guidance on necessary documentation of the auditor's independence

III. **Conceptual Framework**

A. Like the AICPA and many other bodies, the GAO has adopted a conceptual framework for making independence determinations for situations where no clear rule applies. If you have mastered the AICPA conceptual framework, you should have little difficulty with the GAO conceptual framework.

B. Like the AICPA framework, the GAO's conceptual framework involves three steps:

1. **Identifying threats** to independence

2. **Evaluating the significance** of the threats identified, both individually and in the aggregate

3. **Applying safeguards** as necessary to eliminate threats or reduce them to an acceptable level

C. If threats are identified and no available safeguards can eliminate them or reduce them to an acceptable level, **independence is considered to be impaired**.

D. **Threats**—The following are broad categories of threats to independence which should be identified and evaluated:

1. Self-interest threat—The threat that a financial or other interest will inappropriately influence an auditor's judgment or behavior

2. Self-review threat—The threat that an AO will evaluate its own NAS and not appropriately evaluate the results of previous judgments made or actions taken

3. Bias threat—The threat that an auditor will, as a result of political, ideological, social, or other convictions, take a position that is not objective

4. Familiarity threat—The threat that aspects of a relationship with management or personnel of the audited entity, such as a close or long relationship or involvement of an immediate or close family member will undermine objectivity

5. Undue influence threat—The threat that external influences or pressures will impact an auditor's independence and objectivity

6. Management participation threat—The threat to objectivity resulting from an auditor's performing management functions of the audited entity

7. *Structural threat*—The threat that an AO's placement within a government entity, in combination with the structure of the entity being audited, will impact the AO's ability to perform work and report results objectively

E. **Safeguards by the Auditor**—A nonexclusive list of safeguards the AO itself might apply to eliminate the threats to independence or at least reduce them to an acceptable level include:

1. Consulting an independent third party, such as a professional organization, a regulatory body, or another auditor

2. Involving another AO to perform or re-perform part of the audit

3. Having a professional staff member who was not a member of the audit team review the work performed

4. Removing an individual from an audit team

F. **Safeguards by the Audited Entity**—A nonexclusive list of safeguards that might arise from the audited entity itself include:

   1. A requirement that persons other than management ratify or approve the appointment of an AO to perform the audit (as SOX requires for public companies)

   2. Internal entity procedures ensuring objective choices in commissioning NAS

   3. An entity governance structure that provides appropriate oversight and communications regarding the audit organization's services (comparable to the independent audit committee required by SOX for public companies)

G. Threats to independence should be evaluated both individually and in the aggregate.

H. Threats to independence are not acceptable if they either:

   1. Could impact the auditor's ability to perform an audit without being affected by influences that compromise professional judgment; *or*

   2. Could expose the auditor or AO to circumstances that would cause a reasonable and informed third party to conclude that integrity, objectivity, or professional skepticism of the AO, or a member of the audit team, had been compromised.

I. **Mitigating Structural Threats**—Independence can be threatened when auditors in government entities report either to external auditor, to senior management within the audited entity, or to both.

   1. Constitutional or statutory safeguards may mitigate the effects of structural threats to independence. For external AOs, such safeguards may include governmental organizations under which the AO is:

   a. At a level of government other than the one of which the audited entity is a part (e.g., federal auditors may be auditing a state government program, or state auditors may be auditing a county government program)

   b. Placed within a different branch of government from that of the audited entity (e.g., legislative auditors audit an executive branch program)

   2. Structural threats may be mitigated if the head of an AO meets *any* of the following criteria in accordance with constitutional or statutory requirements:

   a. Directly elected by voters of the jurisdiction being audited;

   b. Elected or appointed by a legislative body, subject to removal by a legislative body, and reports the results of audits to and is accountable to a legislative body;

   c. Appointed by someone other than a legislative body, so long as the appointment is confirmed by a legislative body and removal from the position is subject to oversight or approval by a legislative body, and reports the results of audits to and is accountable to a legislative body; *or*

   d. Appointed by, accountable to, reports to, and can only be removed by a statutorily created governing body, the majority of whose members are independently elected or appointed and are outside the organization being audited.

   3. For AOs under a different structure than those just listed, *all* of the following safeguards should be in place:

   a. Statutory protections to prevent the audited entity from abolishing the AO;

   b. Statutory protection that if the head of the AO is removed, the head of the agency reports this to the legislative body;

   c. Statutory protection preventing the audited entity from interfering with the initiation, scope, timing, and completion of any audit;

   d. Statutory protection preventing the audited entity from interfering with audit reporting, findings, conclusions or the manner, means, or timing of the AO's reports;

    e. Statutory protection requiring the AO to report regularly to a legislative body or other independent governing body;

    f. Statutory protections giving the AO sole authority over the selection, retention, advancement, and dismissal of its staff; *and*

    g. Statutory access to records and documents related to the agency, program, or function being audited and access to officials or others as needed to conduct the audit.

J. **Internal Auditor Independence**

  1. Internal auditors working under the direction of the audited entity's management are considered independent for purposes of reporting internally if the head of the audit organization meets *all* of the following:

    a. Accountable to head of the government entity or to those charged with governance;

    b. Reports audit results both to the head of the government entity and to those charged with governance;

    c. Located organizationally outside the staff or line management function of the areas being audited;

    d. Has access to those charged with governance; *and*

    e. Is sufficiently removed from political pressure to conduct audits and report findings objectively without fear of political reprisal.

  2. If internal auditors audit external organizations, such as contractors, and no independence impairments exist, the auditor is considered an external party to the audited entities.

IV. Provision of Nonaudit Services to Audited Entities

A. Before providing NAS to an audited entity, the AO should determine that the audited entity has designated an individual with suitable skills, knowledge, or experience as well as a sufficient understanding to oversee the services provided by the auditor.

  1. If an AO were to assume management responsibilities for an audited entity, the management participation threat would be so great that no safeguards could reduce them to an acceptable level. Management responsibilities include leading and directing an entity, including making decisions regarding the acquisition, deployment, and control of human, financial, physical, and intangible resources. Examples of specific management actions that would impair independence include:

    a. Setting policies and strategic direction for the audited entity

    b. Directing and accepting responsibility for the actions of the audited entity's employees in the performance of their routine, recurring activities

    c. Having custody of an audited entity's assets

    d. Reporting to those charged with governance on behalf of management

    e. Deciding which of the auditor's or outside third party's recommendations to implement

    f. Accepting responsibility for the management of an audited entity's project

    g. Accepting responsibility for designing, implementing, or maintaining internal control

    h. Providing services that are intended to be used as management's primary basis for making decisions that are significant to the subject matter of the audit

    i. Developing an audited entity's performance measurement system when that system is material or significant to the subject matter of the audit

    j. Serving as a voting member of an audited entity's management committee or board of directors

B. Before performing NAS for audited entities, auditors should obtain assurances that audited entity management will do *all* the following:

   1. Assume all management responsibilities

   2. Oversee the NAS by designating a member within senior management who possessed suitable skill, knowledge, or experience

   3. Evaluate the adequacy and results of the NAS performed

   4. Accept responsibility for the results of the NAS

C. Auditors preparing to perform NAS should establish and document their understanding with the audited entity's management regarding:

   1. Objectives of the NAS

   2. Services to be performed

   3. Audited entity's acceptance of its responsibilities

   4. The auditor's responsibilities

   5. Any limitations of the NAS

D. **Routine Activities**—Giving routine advice and responding to questions as a direct part of the audit are not considered NAS and do not impair independence. Examples of such routine activities directly related to the audit include:

   1. Providing advice to the audited entity regarding an accounting matter relevant to the audit

   2. Researching and responding to the audited entity's technical questions on relevant tax laws as an ancillary part of providing tax services

   3. Providing advice on routine business matters

   4. Educating the audited entity on matters within the technical expertise of the auditors

   5. Providing information to the audited entity that is readily available to the auditors, such as best practices and benchmarking studies

E. Certain NAS requirements that directly support the audited entity's operations will necessarily impair independence. Among others, these include:

   1. Determining or changing journal entries, account codes or classifications for transactions, or other accounting records for the audited entity without obtaining management's approval

   2. Authorizing or approving the entity's transactions

   3. Preparing or making changes to source documents (e.g., purchase orders, payroll time records, general ledgers, customer orders, contracts) without management approval

F. Obviously, auditors may not accept responsibility for the preparation and fair presentation of F/S that the auditor will subsequently audit.

G. If the auditor has determined that the NAS requirements have been met and that any significant threats to independence have been eliminated or reduced to an acceptable level, then the following services, unless otherwise expressly prohibited, may be performed for an audited entity:

   1. Recording transactions approved by management

   2. Preparing F/S based on information in the trial balance

   3. Posting entries approved by management to the trial balance

   4. Preparing account reconciliations for management's evaluation

   5. Proposing standard, adjusting, or correcting journal entries or other changes affecting the F/S to the audited entity's management for its review and acceptance so long as the auditor is satisfied that management understands the nature and impact of the entries

H. Internal Audit Assistance—The following will always impair independence when provided to an audit client:

1. Setting internal audit policies or the strategic direction of internal audit activities

2. Performing procedures that form part of the internal control, such as reviewing and approving changes to employee data access privileges

3. Determining the scope of the internal audit function and resulting work

I. Internal Control Monitoring—To perform ongoing monitoring procedures on behalf of management that are built into the routine, recurring operating activities of an organization will always constitute a management participation threat that imperils independence.

J. Information Technology Systems Service—Examples of IT NAS that would impair independence when provided to an audit client include:

1. Designing or developing a financial or other IT system that will play a significant role in the management of an area of operations that is or will be the subject matter of an audit

2. Providing services that entail making other than insignificant modifications to the source code underlying such a system

3. Operating or supervising the operation of such a system

K. Valuation Services—Providing valuation services that have a material effect on the F/S will impair independence if the valuation involves a significant degree of subjectivity.

L. Miscellaneous NAS—Other NAS requirements that will always impair independence when provided to an audited entity include:

1. Non-tax-disbursement examples:

    a. Accepting responsibility to authorize payment of audited entity funds

    b. Accepting responsibility for signing or cosigning audited entity checks, even if only in an emergency

    c. Maintaining an audited entity's bank account or otherwise having custody of its funds or making credit or banking decisions for the audited entity

    d. Approving vendor invoices for payment

2. Benefit plan administration examples:

    a. Making policy decisions on behalf of an audited entity's management

    b. When dealing with plan participants, interpreting the plan document on behalf of management without first obtaining management's concurrence

    c. Making disbursements on behalf of the plan

    d. Having custody of a plan's assets

    e. Serving a plan as a fiduciary as defined by ERISA

3. **Investment**—Advisory or management examples:

    a. Making investment decisions on behalf of the audited entity's management

    b. Executing a transaction to buy or sell

    c. Having custody of an audited entity's assets, even taking temporary possession of securities purchased by an audited entity

    4. Corporate finance examples:

        a. Committing the audited entity to the terms of a transaction or consummating a transaction in its behalf

        b. Acting as a promoter, underwriter, broker-dealer, or guarantor of audited entity securities, or distributor of private placement memoranda or offering documents

        c. Maintaining custody of an audited entity's securities.

    5. Executive or employee personnel matters

        a. Committing the audited entity to employee compensation or benefit arrangements

        b. Hiring or terminating audited entity employees

    6. Business risk consulting examples:

        a. Making or approving business risk decisions

        b. Presenting business risk considerations to those charged with governance on behalf of management

V. **Documentation**—To establish independence, auditors should document:

    A. Threat to independence that requires the application of safeguards, along with the safeguards applied

    B. Safeguards required if an audit organization is structurally located within a government entity and is considered independent based on those safeguards

    C. Consideration of audited entity management's ability to effectively oversee an NAS to be provided by the auditor

    D. The auditor's understanding with an audited entity for which the auditor will perform an NAS

VI. **Professional Judgment**—This includes exercising reasonable care and professional skepticism. It represents the application of knowledge, skills, and experience.

    A. Professional judgment is used:

        1. In applying the conceptual framework to determine independence in a specific situation

        2. To assign competent staff to the audit

        3. To define the scope of the audit

        4. To determine risk in the audit

        5. To determine sufficient and appropriate audit evidence to support findings

        6. To report results

        7. To maintain appropriate quality control over the audit process

VII. **Competence**—The audit staff must possess professional competence adequate to address the audit objectives and perform the work in accordance with GAGAS.

    A. Competence derives from education and experience.

    B. Audit firms should have a process for recruiting, hiring, continuously developing, assigning, and evaluating staff in order to maintain a competent workforce.

    C. Competence provides the basis for sound professional judgments.

VIII. **Technical Knowledge**—The staff assigned to perform a GAGAS audit should collectively possess the necessary technical knowledge, skill, and experience.

IX. **Continuing Professional Education (CPE)**—Auditors performing GAGAS audits should undertake at least 24 hours of government auditing CPE every two years. Auditors performing more senior auditor responsibilities or more than 20% of their time charged to GAGAS audits must also have 56 hours of CPE every two years.

X. **Quality Control and Assurance**—Audit firms performing GAGAS audits must:

A. Establish and maintain a system of quality control designed to provide the organization with reasonable assurances that both the organization and its staff comply with professional standards and applicable legal and regulatory requirements.

B. Undergo an independent peer review at least every three years.

C. Adopt policies and procedures that address:

1. Leadership responsibilities for quality within the AO

2. Independence, legal, and ethical requirements

3. Initiation, acceptance, and continuation of audits

4. Human resources

5. Audit performance, documentation, and reporting

6. Monitoring of quality

Department of Labor (DOL)

After studying this lesson, you should be able to:

1. Understand the Department of Labor's independence rules for auditing employee benefit plans regulated by ERISA.

I. **Department of Labor**—Interpretive Bulletin Relating to Guidelines on Independence of Accountant Retained by Employee Benefit Plan.

    A. Employee Benefit Plans (plans) are broadly regulated by the Department of Labor's (DOL's) Employee Benefits Security Administration (EBSA) pursuant to the Employee Retirement Income Security Act (ERISA).

    B. Statutory law provides that an accountant retained by a plan to examine plan financial information and render an opinion on the financial statements and schedules required to be contained in a plan's annual report must be "independent."

    C. Unfortunately, despite having been strongly urged to simply adopt AICPA guidelines for independence, DOL's guidelines, contained in 29 C.F.R. 2509-75-9, date to the 1970s and are inconsistent with modern independence rules.

    D. The rules provide that an accountant will **not** be considered independent with respect to a plan, due to the following:

        1. **Financial ties**—Independence will be considered to be impaired if during the period of the engagement, at the date of the opinion, or during the period covered by the financial statements, "the accountant or his or her firm or a member thereof had, or was committed to acquire, any direct financial interest or any material indirect financial interest in such plan, or the plan sponsor . . ."

            a. Because this provision covers any member of an accountant's firm, its coverage is much broader than that of current AICPA guidelines.

            b. The term *member* means all partners or shareholder employees in the firm and all professional employees participating in the audit or located in an office of the firm participating in a significant portion of the audit.

        2. **Employment ties**—During the same period, the same entities may not be connected to a plan or plan sponsor as a:

            a. Promoter;

            b. Underwriter;

            c. Investment advisor;

            d. Voting trustee;

            e. Director;

            f. Officer; *or*

            g. Employee of the plan or plan sponsor.

        3. However, employees of a plan or plan sponsor who have left to join the accounting firm may nonetheless be deemed independent if:

            a. They have completely disassociated themselves from the plan or plan sponsor; *and*

            b. Do not participate in auditing financial statements of the plan covering any period of his or her employment by the plan or plan sponsor.

4. However, independence may be considered impaired if an accountant or a member of an accounting firm maintains financial records for the plan. An accounting firm should not audit its own work.

E. According to the rule, an engagement to provide professional services, including actuarial services, to the plan sponsor does not ruin an accountant's independence so long as the accountant does not violate the rules on financial ties and employment mentioned above.

F. However, the firm should take care not to engage in a prohibited transaction pursuant to 29 U.S.C. 1106(a)(1)(C), which prohibits certain transactions between a plan and a *party in interest* to minimize conflicts of interest and thereby prevent fiduciaries from lining their own pockets with the plan's funds.

Assessing Risk and Developing a Planned Response

Financial Statement Audits

Accounting vs. Auditing

After studying this lesson, you should be able to:

1. Explain the respective responsibilities of management and the auditor in financial reporting.

2. Outline the role of and distinction between GAAP and GAAS.

I. **Financial Accounting**—The accounting focuses primarily on the preparation and distribution of the general-purpose, historical financial statements (balance sheet, income statement, statement of cash flows, and statement of retained earnings), which are representations of management.

    A. These financial statements are distributed to interested parties outside of the reporting entity itself, such as actual or potential shareholders and creditors, major customers and suppliers, employees, regulators, and others for their decision-making (resource allocation) needs.

    B. Users' specific decision-making circumstances will involve different issues and they may have different information priorities and concerns, but most will want to evaluate whether management has performed well.

    C. Since management's performance will be evaluated, at least in part, by financial statements prepared by management itself, users need to know whether the financial statements are reliable when evaluating the performance of management.

II. **Auditing**—The auditor's primary role is to provide an impartial (independent) report on the reliability of management's financial statements.

> **Purpose of an audit**—"The purpose of an audit is to provide financial statement users with an opinion by the auditor on whether the financial statements are presented fairly, in all material respects, in accordance with the applicable financial reporting framework. An auditor's opinion enhances the degree of confidence that the intended users can place in the financial statements."
>
> From the AICPA's Preface to *Codifications of Statements on Auditing Standards, Principles Underlying an Audit Conducted in Accordance with Generally Accepted Auditing Standards.*.

III. **The Role of Standards**—Think of "standards" as the criteria by which quality will be evaluated. The preparation of the financial statements and the performance of the audit are subject to very different standards.

    A. Standards applicable to evaluating the presentation of the financial statements:

> **Applicable financial reporting framework**—"The financial reporting framework adopted by management and, where appropriate, those charged with governance in the preparation of the financial statements that is acceptable in view of the nature of the entity and the objective of the financial statements, or that is required by law or regulation."
>
> **Financial reporting framework**—"A set of criteria used to determine measurement, recognition, presentation, and disclosure of all material items appearing in the financial statements; for example: U.S. generally accepted accounting principles (GAAP), International Financial Reporting Standards (IFRSs), issued by the International Accounting Standards Board (IASB), or a special purpose framework."

        1. The financial reporting framework adopted by an entity for its financial statement presentation in the U.S. may be based on IFRSs (issued by the IASB) or U.S. GAAP.

2. **Accounting Standards Setters Associated with U.S. GAAP**—The nature of the reporting entity determines which particular accounting standards must be followed under the label of U.S. GAAP.

   a. Federal governmental entities follow pronouncements of the Federal Accounting Standards Advisory Board (FASAB).

   b. State and local governmental entities follow pronouncements of the Governmental Accounting Standards Board (GASB).

   c. Other entities (such as corporations) follow pronouncements of the Financial Accounting Standards Board (FASB).

B. **Standards Applicable to Evaluating the Auditor's Performance**

1. **Outside the U.S.**—"International Standards on Auditing" (ISAs) are issued by the International Auditing and Assurance Standards Board, an audit-related standard-setting body within the International Federation of Accountants, known as IFAC.

2. **Within the U.S.**—The nature of the reporting entity determines which auditing standards are applicable to an audit of the entity's financial statements.

   a. **Governmental entities**—When required by law, regulation, or agreement, Generally Accepted Government Auditing Standards (GAGAS), issued by the U.S. Government Accountability Office (GAO) are applicable.

   b. **Public companies (companies registered with the Securities and Exchange Commission, also referred to as "issuers," that is, issuers of securities to the public)**— The auditing standards of the Public Company Accounting Oversight Board (PCAOB) are Applicable.

   c. **Private companies (referred to as "nonissuers") and other entities**—The auditing standards of the AICPA's Auditing Standards Board are applicable; these pronouncements collectively are referred to by the AICPA as generally accepted auditing standards (GAAS).

ICPA's "clarity and convergence" project—The AICPA reissued substantially all of their existing Statements on Auditing Standards (SASs) in a clarified format intended to make the SASs easier to understand. In addition, the AICPA substantially converged their auditing standards to be consistent with the requirements of IFAC's International Standards on Auditing. Although some differences in those respective requirements remain (and will be covered elsewhere in CPAexcel®), those standards are now very, very similar. The recent AICPA pronouncements are referred to as "Clarified Standards."

The PCAOB adopted the then-existing AICPA auditing standards in April 2003 as "interim standards, on an initial, transitional basis." Since that time, the PCAOB has been issuing its own Auditing Standards. Much of the existing PCAOB auditing standards remain those of the AICPA existing as of April 16, 2003.

GAAS and Principles

After studying this lesson, you should be able to:

1. Identify the seven principles underlying an audit conducted in accordance with GAAS under the AICPA's "Clarified" auditing standards

2. Identify the 10 Generally Accepted Auditing Standards (GAAS) associated with the AICPA's past auditing standards, which still remain as part of the PCAOB auditing standards.

I. **Generally Accepted Auditing Standards (GAAS)**—Historically, the AICPA identified 10 standards comprising GAAS that used to serve as a framework for U.S. auditing standards. The AICPA replaced these 10 standards with seven principles in connection with its Clarified Auditing Standards. The AICPA no longer uses the term *GAAS* to refer to these 10 standards representing criteria to measure the quality of the auditor's performance. Instead the AICPA now uses the term GAAS to refer to the body of authoritative professional standards issued in the form of Statements on Auditing Standards.

II. **Clarity and Convergence Project**—In connection with its *clarity and convergence project* the AICPA has replaced its Statements on Auditing Standards to be similar to the International Standards on Auditing (ISAs) issued by the International Federation of Accountants (specifically IFAC's International Auditing & Assurance Standards Board—IAASB). As part of that effort, the AICPA has also replaced its use of 10 criteria formerly known as "Generally Accepted Auditing Standards" with seven *principles* to provide a framework for understanding and explaining an audit.

   A. The seven principles are not requirements and have no authoritative status. However, they are intended to be helpful as a framework for audit standard setting.

   B. The seven principles reflect most of the considerations that had been addressed in the previous 10 generally accepted auditing standards (the former reporting standards seem to have changed the most relative to these principles).

   C. The seven principles are organized around four primary themes—(1) purpose/premise; (2) responsibilities; (3) performance; and (4) reporting (as a memory aid, remember: PR-PR).

III. **Purpose of an Audit and Premise Upon Which an Audit Is Conducted**

   A. The purpose of an audit is to provide financial statement users with an opinion by the auditor on whether the financial statements are presented fairly, in all material respects, in accordance with the applicable financial reporting framework. An auditor's opinion enhances the degree of confidence that intended users can place in the financial statements.

   B. An audit in accordance with generally accepted auditing standards is conducted on the premise that management and, where appropriate, those charged with governance, have responsibility for

      1. The preparation and fair presentation of the financial statements in accordance with the applicable financial reporting framework; this includes the design, implementation, and maintenance of internal control relevant to the preparation and fair presentation of financial statements that are free from material misstatement, whether due to fraud or error

      2. Providing the auditor with all information, such as records, documentation, and other matters that are relevant to the preparation and fair presentation of the financial statements; any additional information that the auditor may request from management and, where appropriate, those charged with governance; and unrestricted access to those within the entity from whom the auditor determines it necessary to obtain audit evidence

C. Responsibilities—Note that the term *responsibilities principle* takes the place of what previously had been called *general standards* describing characteristics the auditor brings to the engagement.

   1. Auditors are responsible for having appropriate competence and capabilities to perform the audit; complying with relevant ethical requirements; and maintaining professional skepticism and exercising professional judgment, throughout the planning and performance of the audit.

D. Performance—Note that the term *performance principle* takes the place of what previously had been called *fieldwork standards* governing the auditor's evidence-gathering activities.

   1. To express an opinion, the auditor obtains reasonable assurance about whether the financial statements as a whole are free from material misstatement, whether due to fraud or error.

   2. To obtain reasonable assurance, which is a high, but not absolute, level of assurance, the auditor

   a. Plans the work and properly supervises any assistants

   b. Determines and applies appropriate materiality level or levels throughout the audit

   c. Identifies and assesses risks of material misstatement, whether due to fraud or error, based on an understanding of the entity and its environment, including the entity's internal control

   d. Obtains sufficient appropriate audit evidence about whether material misstatements exist, through designing and implementing appropriate responses to the assessed risks

   3. The auditor is unable to obtain absolute assurance that the financial statements are free from material misstatement because of inherent limitations, which arise from

   a. The nature of financial reporting

   b. The nature of audit procedures

   c. The need for the audit to be conducted within a reasonable period of time and so as to achieve a balance between benefit and cost

E. Reporting

   1. Based on an evaluation of the audit evidence obtained, the auditor expresses, in the form of a written report, an opinion in accordance with the auditor's findings, or states that an opinion cannot be expressed. The opinion states whether the financial statements are presented fairly, in all material respects, in accordance with the applicable financial reporting framework.

Professional Standards

After studying this lesson, you should be able to:

1. Understand the role of guidance associated with Statements on Auditing Standards including interpretive publications and other auditing publications.

2. Identify the two types of professional requirements (unconditional requirements and presumptively mandatory requirements) and the wording associated with each.

I. **The AICPA's Use of the Term GAAS and Guidance Associated with It**

    A. **Statements on Auditing Standards (SASs)**—The SASs constitute GAAS and must be followed by auditors when AICPA auditing standards are applicable. (Specifically, the Rule of Conduct, *Compliance With Standards,* of the AICPA Code of Professional Conduct requires that auditors adhere to the standards promulgated by the Auditing Standards Board.) Under the clarified auditing standards, any reference to GAAS now specifically means this authoritative body of professional standards (SASs) issued by the Auditing Standards Board.

        1. The auditor is expected to have sufficient knowledge of the SASs to identify those applicable to the audit.

        2. The auditor should be prepared to justify any departures from the SASs.

        3. Materiality and audit risk also underlie the application of the SASs, particularly those related to performing the audit (evidence gathering) and reporting.

    B. **Interpretive Publications**—Consist of the appendices to the SASs, auditing interpretations of the SASs, auditing guidance included in AICPA Audit and Accounting Guides, and AICPA auditing Statements of Position.

        1. Interpretive publications are **not** considered to be auditing standards, however.

        2. These are issued under the authority of the Auditing Standards Board after all ASB members have had an opportunity to comment on the interpretive publication.

        3. Auditors should be aware of (and consider) interpretive publications applicable to their audits. When auditors do not apply such auditing guidance, they should be prepared to explain how they complied with the SAS provisions related to such interpretive publications.

    C. **Other Auditing Publications**—Include articles in the *Journal of Accountancy* and the AICPA's *CPA Letter* (and other professional publications), continuing professional education programs, textbooks, etc.

        1. Other auditing publications have no authoritative status—they may be useful to the auditor in understanding and applying the SASs, however.

        2. To assess the appropriateness of the other auditing publications—consider the degree to which the publication is recognized as helpful in applying the SASs and the degree to which the author is recognized as an authority on auditing matters. (Other auditing publications reviewed by the AICPA Audit and Attest Standards staff are presumed to be appropriate.)

II. **Categories of Professional Requirements**—The various AICPA standards (i.e., Statements on Auditing Standards, Statements on Standards for Attestation Engagements, Statements on Standards for Accounting and Review Services, and Statements on Quality Control Standards) distinguish between **two types of professional requirements:**

A. Unconditional requirements—Must comply with the requirement without exception (indicated by "must" in applicable standards);

B. Presumptively mandatory requirements—In rare circumstances, the practitioner may depart from such a *requirement*, but must document the justification for the departure and how the alternate procedures performed were adequate to meet the objective of the requirement (indicated by "should" in applicable standards).

Note
Explanatory material is descriptive guidance within the body of the standards that does not impose a requirement (indicated by may, might, or could in applicable standards).

Quality Control Standards (SQCS)

After studying this lesson, you should be able to:

1. Describe the relationship of GAAS to the AICPA's Statements on Quality Control Standards (SQCS).

2. List the six elements that comprise a firm's quality control system.

I. **Relationship of GAAS to the SQCS**—An individual audit engagement is governed by GAAS, whereas a CPA firm's collective portfolio of accounting and auditing services (sometimes called the A&A practice, which involves entities' financial statements and, thereby, involves the public interest) is governed by the AICPA's SQCS. SQCS are issued by the AICPA's Auditing Standards Board (in particular, the section of the SQCS dealing with "A Firm's System of Quality Control" is QC10). The relevant AICPA guidance applicable to an individual audit engagement is provided by AU 220, *Quality Control for an Engagement Conducted in Accordance with [GAAS]*.

II. **Focus of the System of Quality Control**—A CPA firm is required to have a "system of quality control" for its accounting and auditing services (covering audit, attestation, compilation, and review services; note that the SQCS are not applicable to tax or consulting services) to provide reasonable assurance that engagements are performed in accordance with professional standards and applicable regulatory and legal requirements, and that the issuance of reports are appropriate in the circumstances.

A. **Nature and Scope**—The policies and procedures will vary with the circumstances (e.g., firm size and number of offices, complexity of services offered, and the level of experience of the professional staff).

B. **Inherent Limitations**—Similar to any internal control system, a quality control system provides "reasonable" (a high, but not absolute) assurance, reflecting implicit cost-benefit trade-offs.

III. **Six Elements of a Quality Control System**—These are interrelated (e.g., monitoring and the quality of personnel involved affect the other elements).

A. **Leadership Responsibilities for Quality**—Policies and procedures should promote an internal culture that emphasizes a commitment to quality (sometimes called the "tone at the top"). For an individual audit engagement, the engagement partner should take responsibility for overall audit quality, although performance of certain procedures may, of course, be delegated to other members of the engagement team.

B. **Relevant Ethical Requirements**—Policies and procedures should address the independence of personnel as necessary (should obtain written confirmation of compliance with independence requirements from all appropriate personnel at least annually).

C. **Acceptance and Continuance of Client-Relationships and Engagements**—Policies and procedures should carefully assess the risks associated with each engagement (including issues related to management integrity) and the firm should only undertake engagements that can be completed with professional competence.

D. **Human Resources**—Policies and procedures should address important personnel issues (including initial hiring, assignments to engagements, professional development and continuing professional education, and promotion decisions).

> **Note**
> *The purpose of AU 220, Quality Control for an Engagement Conducted in Accordance with [GAAS], is to assist the auditor in implementing the firm's quality control procedures specifically at the engagement level. This pronouncement states that the auditor's objective is to implement quality control procedures at the engagement level that provide reasonable assurance that (a) the audit complies with professional standards and applicable legal and regulatory requirements and (b) the auditor issues an appropriate report.*

> **Note**
> *If the engagement team identifies a threat to independence that safeguards may not eliminate or reduce to an acceptable level, the engagement partner is required to report the matter to the relevant person(s) in the firm to determine the appropriate action (to either eliminate the threat or withdraw from the engagement when withdrawal is allowed under applicable law or regulation).*

E. **Engagement Performance**—Policies and procedures should focus on compliance with all applicable firm and professional standards and applicable regulatory requirements, and encourage personnel to consult as necessary with professional (or other) literature or other human resources within or outside of the firm for appropriate guidance.

F. **Monitoring**—Policies and procedures should provide an ongoing assessment of the adequacy of the design and the operating effectiveness of the system of quality control. Controls that are effective at one point in time, may deteriorate over time owing to neglect or changed circumstances. It is important that the controls are properly monitored so that timely adjustments can be made as necessary to keep the quality control policies and procedures working effectively over time.

IV. **Differences of Opinion**—The firm should establish policies and procedures for dealing with and resolving differences of opinion within the engagement team, with those consulted, and between the engagement partner and the engagement quality control reviewer (including that the conclusions reached are documented and implemented and that the report is not released until the matter is resolved).

V. **Documentation of the Operation of Quality Control Policies and Procedures**—The firm should establish policies and procedures requiring appropriate documentation of the operation of each element of the system of quality control.

VI. **Definitions**

A. **Engagement Partner**—The person in the firm who is responsible for the audit engagement and its performance and for the auditor's report.

B. **Engagement Quality Control Review**—A process designed to provide an objective evaluation, before the report is released, of the significant judgments the engagement team made and the conclusions it reached in formulating the auditor's report. (The engagement quality control review process is only for those audit engagements, if any, for which the firm has determined that an engagement quality control review is required, in accordance with its policies and procedures.)

C. **Engagement Quality Control Reviewer**—This is the person in the firm, a suitably qualified external person, or a team made up of such individuals, none of whom is part of the engagement team, with sufficient and appropriate experience and authority to objectively evaluate the significant judgments that the engagement team made and the conclusions it reached in formulating the auditor's report.

VII. **The Main Difference Between the Clarified SAS and the Corresponding International Standard on Auditing**—The SAS requires that the quality control review must be completed before the engagement partner releases the auditor's report, whereas the ISA requires that the quality control review be completed before the engagement partner dates the auditor's report.

Overview of Audit Process

After studying this lesson, you should be able to:

1. Identify the primary dimensions of the audit process: a) engagement planning; b) internal control considerations; c) substantive audit procedures; and d) reporting.

I. Engagement Planning

A. Decide whether to accept (or continue) the engagement—Recall the quality control standards regarding client acceptance/continuation issues.

B. Perform risk assessment procedures to address the risks of material misstatement, whether due to error or fraud.

C. Evaluate requirements for staffing and supervision.

D. Prepare the required written audit plan (sometimes called the *audit program*) that specifies the nature, timing, and extent of auditing procedures for every audit area (which is usually prepared after control risk has been assessed, so that detection risk can be appropriately set in each audit area).

II. Internal Control Considerations

A. Obtain an understanding of internal control for planning purposes as required, emphasizing the assessment of the risk of material misstatement in individual audit areas and document the understanding of internal control.

B. If contemplating *reliance* on certain identified internal control strengths as a basis for reducing substantive testing, the auditor must then perform appropriate *tests of control* to determine that those specific controls are operating effectively, that is, working as intended.

III. Substantive Audit Procedures (Evidence-Gathering Procedures Whose Purpose is to Detect Material Misstatements, if There Are Any)—Note that the word *substantive* is derived from *substantiate*, which means *to verify*. These are evidence-gathering procedures designed to verify the financial statement elements and to detect any material misstatements.

A. **Analytical Procedures**—Those evidence-gathering procedures that suggest *reasonableness* (or *unreasonableness*) based upon a comparison to appropriate expectations or benchmarks, such as prior year's financial statements, comparability to industry data (including ratios) or other interrelationships involving financial and/or nonfinancial data.

B. **Tests of Details**—Those evidence-gathering procedures consisting of either of two types:

1. **Tests of ending balances**—Where the final balance is assessed by testing the composition of the year-end balance (e.g., testing a sample of individual customers' account balances that make up the general ledger accounts receivable control account balance).

2. **Tests of transactions**—Where the final balance is assessed by examining those debits and credits that caused the balance to change from last year's audited balance to the current year's balance.

IV. Reporting—Conclusions are expressed in writing using standardized language to avoid miscommunication.

Overview of Auditor's Report

After studying this lesson, you should be able to:

1. Describe the structure and content of the so-called standard unqualified audit report under the AICPA's Clarified Standards.

I. Prior to the issuance of the Clarified Standards, the so-called standard unqualified audit report under AICPA Professional Standards consisted of three paragraphs (comprised of a total of nine sentences). The change in the audit reporting language is one of the major differences caused by the Clarified Standards.

   A. **Introductory Paragraph**—Three sentences:

   1. Identify the entity's financial statements.

   2. Identify management's responsibilities.

   3. Identify the auditor's responsibilities.

   B. **Scope Paragraph**—Five sentences:

   1. Audit is conducted in accordance with GAAS.

   2. Audit provides reasonable assurance.

   3. Audit examines evidence on a test basis.

   4. Audit includes assessing accounting principles used and significant estimates made.

   5. Audit provides a reasonable basis for the opinion.

   C. **Opinion Paragraph**—One long sentence:

   1. Express an opinion that the financial statements are fairly stated in conformity with GAAP (or other applicable accounting framework).

A sample unqualified audit report under the "old" (now superseded) standards is provided below, so that the differences relative to the sample unqualified audit report under the "new" Clarified Standards will be more clearly recognized.

Standard Unqualified Auditor's Report—Under the "Old" AICPA Professional Standards

Independent Auditor's Report

We have audited the balance sheets of ABC Company at December 31, 20X2 and 20X1, and the related statements of income, retained earnings, and cash flows for the years then ended. These financial statements are the responsibility of the Company's management. Our responsibility is to express an opinion on these financial statements based on our audits.

We conducted our audits in accordance with auditing standards generally accepted in the United States of America. Those standards require that we plan and perform the audit to obtain reasonable assurance about whether the financial statements are free of material misstatement. An audit includes examining, on a test basis, evidence supporting the amounts and disclosures in the financial statements. An audit also includes assessing the accounting principles used and significant estimates made by management, as well as evaluating the overall financial statement presentation. We believe that our audits provide a reasonable basis for our opinion.

In our opinion, the financial statements referred to above present fairly, in all material respects, the financial position of ABC Company at December 31, 20X2 and 20X1, and the results of their operations and their cash flows for the years then ended, in conformity with accounting principles generally accepted in the United States of America.

/s/ CPA firm (signed by audit engagement partner)

Date (The auditor's report should not be dated earlier than the date on which the auditor has obtained sufficient appropriate audit evidence to support the opinion.)

II. **Auditor's Report**—Under the AICPA's Clarified Standards, the auditor's report has been reformatted and expanded to reflect four main sections:

A. The first section has no label, but it identifies the nature of the engagement and the entity's financial statements involved (consists of one sentence).

B. The second section is labeled **Management's Responsibility for the Financial Statements**—(1 sentence) it states that management is responsible for the fair presentation of the financial statements and the implementation of internal control.

C. The third section is labeled **Auditor's Responsibility**, which consists of three separate paragraphs.

   1. The first consists of three sentences:

      a. Responsibility to express an opinion

      b. Conducted the audit in accordance with (GAAS)

      c. Plan and perform the audit to provide reasonable assurance.

   2. The second consists of five sentences:

      a. Perform procedures to obtain audit evidence about the amounts and disclosures.

      b. The procedures depend on the auditor's judgment, including assessment of risks of material misstatement, whether due to fraud or error.

      c. In making those risk assessments, the auditor considers internal control.

      d. The auditor expresses no such opinion (*on internal control, when not engaged to report on internal control in an "integrated audit"*).

      e. An audit includes evaluating the appropriateness of accounting policies used and the reasonableness of significant accounting estimates.

   3. The third consists of one sentence—expressing the auditor's belief that the audit evidence is sufficient and appropriate to provide a basis for the opinion.

D. The fourth section is labeled **Opinion**—(one sentence) it expresses the auditor's opinion (in the same wording as that used in the previous AICPA standards).

In the Clarified Standards, the AICPA has replaced the term *unqualified* with *unmodified*. Two versions of the sample unmodified auditor's report are provided below. The first presents the typical unmodified audit report in paragraph form; and the second presents it on a sentence-by-sentence basis for ease of review.

Sample Unmodified Auditor's Report Under AICPA Clarified Standards

<u>Independent Auditor's Report</u>

[Appropriate Addressee]

We have audited the accompanying consolidated financial statements of ABC Company and its subsidiaries, which comprise the consolidated balance sheets as of December 31, 20X1 and 20X0, and the related consolidated statements of income, changes in stockholders' equity and cash flows for the years then ended, and the related notes to the financial statements.

Management's Responsibility for the Financial Statements

Management is responsible for the preparation and fair presentation of these consolidated financial statements in accordance with accounting principles generally accepted in the United States of America; this includes the design, implementation, and maintenance of internal control relevant to the preparation and fair presentation of consolidated financial statements that are free from material misstatement, whether due to fraud or error.

Auditor's Responsibility

Our responsibility is to express an opinion on these consolidated financial statements based on our audits. We conducted our audits in accordance with auditing standards generally accepted in the United States of America. Those standards require that we plan and perform the audit to obtain reasonable assurance about whether the consolidated financial statements are free from material misstatement.

An audit involves performing procedures to obtain audit evidence about the amounts and disclosures in the consolidated financial statements. The procedures selected depend on the auditor's judgment, including the assessment of the risks of material misstatement of the consolidated financial statements, whether owing to fraud or error. In making those risk assessments, the auditor considers internal control relevant to the entity's preparation and fair presentation of the consolidated financial statements in order to design audit procedures that are appropriate in the circumstances, but not for the purpose of expressing an opinion on the effectiveness of the entity's internal control. Accordingly, we express no such opinion. An audit also includes evaluating the appropriateness of accounting policies used and the reasonableness of significant accounting estimates made by management, as well as evaluating the overall presentation of the consolidated financial statements.

We believe that the audit evidence we have obtained is sufficient and appropriate to provide a basis for our audit opinion.

Opinion

In our opinion, the consolidated financial statements referred to above present fairly, in all material respects, the financial position of ABC Company and its subsidiaries as of December 31, 20X1 and 20X0, and the results of their operations and their cash flows for the years then ended in accordance with accounting principles generally accepted in the United States of America.

[Auditor's signature—Firm name, signed by audit engagement partner]

[**Auditor's city and state**—This is a new requirement under the Clarified Standards]

[Date of the auditor's report—When the auditor has obtained sufficient appropriate audit evidence as a reasonable basis for the opinion]

Sample Unmodified Auditor's Report Under AICPA Clarified Standards (Sentence by Sentence):

Independent Auditor's Report

[Introductory Paragraph]

1. We have audited the accompanying consolidated financial statements of ABC Company and its subsidiaries, which comprise the consolidated balance sheets as of December 31, 20X1 and 20X0, and the related consolidated statements of income, changes in stockholders' equity and cash flows for the years then ended, and the related notes to the financial statements.

Management's Responsibility for the Financial Statements

1. Management is responsible for the preparation and fair presentation of these consolidated financial statements in accordance with accounting principles generally accepted in the United States of America; this includes the design, implementation, and maintenance of internal control relevant to the preparation and fair presentation of consolidated financial statements that are free from material misstatement, whether owing to fraud or error.

Auditor's Responsibility

[First of three paragraphs]

1. Our responsibility is to express an opinion on these consolidated financial statements based on our audits.

2. We conducted our audits in accordance with auditing standards generally accepted in the United States of America.

3. Those standards require that we plan and perform the audit to obtain reasonable assurance about whether the consolidated financial statements are free from material misstatement.

[Second of three paragraphs]

1. An audit involves performing procedures to obtain audit evidence about the amounts and disclosures in the consolidated financial statements.

2. The procedures selected depend on the auditor's judgment, including the assessment of the risks of material misstatement of the consolidated financial statements, whether owing to fraud or error.

3. In making those risk assessments, the auditor considers internal control relevant to the entity's preparation and fair presentation of the consolidated financial statements in order to design audit procedures that are appropriate in the circumstances, but not for the purpose of expressing an opinion on the effectiveness of the entity's internal control.

4. Accordingly, we express no such opinion.

5. An audit also includes evaluating the appropriateness of accounting policies used and the reasonableness of significant accounting estimates made by management, as well as evaluating the overall presentation of the consolidated financial statements.

[Third of three paragraphs]

1. We believe that the audit evidence we have obtained is sufficient and appropriate to provide a basis for our audit opinion.

Opinion

1. In our opinion, the consolidated financial statements referred to above present fairly, in all material respects, the financial position of ABC Company and its subsidiaries as of December 31, 20X1 and 20X0, and the results of their operations and their cash flows for the years then ended in accordance with accounting principles generally accepted in the United States of America.

Different Types of Engagements

After studying this lesson, you should be able to:

1. Recognize which AICPA Professional Standards are applicable to engagements to review and/or compile financial statements of a private company and which standards are applicable to other attestation engagements; and

2. Recognize that "engagement letters" are required for any audit engagement, and review or compile an entity's financial statements under AICPA Professional Standards.

I. **AICPA's Statements on Standards for Accounting and Review Services (SSARSs)**—These are applicable when the CPA is associated with the financial statements of a private company, but that association is something less than a full-scope *audit engagement*.

    A. **Compilation**—This occurs when the CPA is engaged simply to assemble into financial statement format the financial records of a private company, without expressing any degree of assurance on the reliability of those financial statements.

    B. **Review**—This occurs when the CPA is engaged to provide a lower level of assurance (relative to that of an audit) on financial statements of a private company by performing limited procedures, including reading the financial statements, performing analytical procedures, and making appropriate inquiries of client personnel.

II. **AICPA's Statements on Standards for Attestation Engagements (SSAEs)**—These are applicable when the CPA provides assurance about written representations or subject matter other than historical financial statements (e.g., management may make representations about its superior product performance that may be made more reliable by the CPA's independent verification and report).

III. **Responsibilities Vary for Different Types of Engagements**

    A. **Understanding with the Client**—When associated with financial statement subject matter, AICPA Professional Standards require the CPA to establish an understanding with the entity involved as to the services to be rendered and the parties' respective responsibilities. The CPA must document that understanding in a written engagement letter between the CPA and the client entity. This should not be surprising, since the "public interest" is associated with such financial statement subject matter.

> **Note**
> A written engagement letter must be obtained for engagements to audit, review, or compile an entity's financial statements under AICPA Professional Standards.

    B. **Levels of Assurance**—The level of assurance varies with the type of service involved and should be clearly addressed in the engagement letter between the CPA and the client entity.

        1. **Audit**—An audit conveys a high level of assurance about the reliability of the financial statements, and is expressed as positive assurance in the form of an opinion (recall that the SASs apply to audits of "nonissuers").

        2. **Review**—A review conveys a lower (i.e., "moderate") level of assurance about financial statements (for a private company under the AICPA's SSARSs).

        3. **Compilation**—A compilation conveys no assurance about the reliability of the financial statements (for a private company under the AICPA's SSARSs).

> **Note**
> The SSARSs and SSAEs will be explored in detail at an appropriate point later in the course materials. They are merely introduced here so that candidates will be reminded early on that the AICPA Professional Standards encompass a variety of types of standards governing different services associated with the CPA profession.

IV. **Other Attest Engagements**—The CPA may convey either a high or moderate level of assurance about nonfinancial statement representations under the SSAEs. (The subject matter of the engagement involves something other than historical financial statements, and, hence, more flexibility exists to negotiate with the entity about the level of assurance to be conveyed and/or the procedures to be used as a basis for conclusions.)

PCAOB Responsibilities

The Sarbanes-Oxley Act of 2002 (SOA) was enacted by Congress in response to a series of highly visible financial reporting frauds and audit failures that undermined investor confidence in the U.S. capital markets. Said to be the most significant revision of securities laws since the 1930s, SOA ended self-regulation of the accounting profession and created the Public Company Accounting Oversight Board (PCAOB), a private-sector not-for-profit corporation, to provide a new regulatory mechanism over auditors of public companies, among other things.

After studying this lesson, you should be able to:

1. Know the five primary responsibilities of the Public Company Accounting Oversight Board that were established by the Sarbanes-Oxley Act of 2002.

2. Understand the primary sections ("Titles") of the Sarbanes-Oxley Act of 2002 that directly affect auditors of public companies ("issuers").

I. **The Sarbanes-Oxley Act of 2002 and the PCAOB**

   A. **Public Company Accounting Oversight Board (PCAOB)**—Five primary responsibilities:

   1. **Registration of public accounting firms**—U.S. and non-U.S. accounting firms that prepare audit reports of any U.S. public company (*issuer* of securities) must register with the PCAOB. (This includes non-U.S. accounting firms that play a substantial role in the preparation of such audit reports.)

   2. **Inspections of registered public accounting firms**—PCAOB is directed to conduct a continuous program of inspections that assess compliance with SOA, PCAOB rules, SEC rules, and applicable professional standards. (A written report is required for each such inspection.)

      a. **Firms that provide audit reports for at least 100 issuers**—PCAOB must inspect annually.

      b. **Firms that provide audit reports for fewer than 100 issuers**—PCAOB must inspect every three years (triennially).

   3. **Standard setting**—PCAOB is directed to establish auditing and related attestation, quality control, ethics and independence standards and rules to be used by registered public accounting firms in the preparation of audit reports for issuers. (The Office of the Chief Auditor and the Standing Advisory Group (SAG) assist PCAOB in establishing such auditing and professional practice standards.)

   4. **Enforcement**—PCAOB has broad authority to investigate registered public accounting firms and persons associated with such firms.

      a. PCAOB rules require cooperation by registered public accounting firms and associated persons—must produce documents and provide testimony as directed. (PCAOB may also seek information from others, including clients of registered firms.)

      b. PCAOB sanctions may range from revocation of a firm's registration or barring a person from participating in audits of public companies to lesser sanctions such as monetary penalties or imposition of remedial measures, including additional training or new quality control procedures.

   5. **Funding**—PCAOB's budget is funded by (1) registration and annual fees from public accounting firms and (2) an annual *accounting support fee* assessed on issuers (based on their relative monthly market capitalization).

II. **Overview of the Sarbanes-Oxley Act of 2002**

   A. **Purpose of the Legislation**—To address a series of perceived corporate misconduct and alleged audit failures (including Enron, Tyco, and WorldCom, among others) and to strengthen investor confidence in the integrity of the U.S. capital markets.

B. The Sarbanes-Oxley Act of 2002 consists of 11 *Titles* (the first four of which are directly applicable to auditors).

C. **Title I**—Established the PCAOB, gave standard-setting authority to the PCAOB (regarding auditing, quality control, and independence standards), and created its role in overseeing the accounting firms required to register with the PCAOB.

D. **Title II**—Established independence requirements for external auditors, which addressed perceived conflicts of interest (limiting non-audit services, establishing a five-year rotation for the audit partner and review partner, and restricting members of the audit firm from taking key management positions (including CEO, CFO, controller, or chief accounting officer) during the one-year period preceding the audit engagement).

    1. Services that the auditor is prohibited from providing: (1) bookkeeping or other services related to the accounting records; (2) financial information systems design and implementation; (3) appraisal or valuation services; (4) actuarial services; (5) internal audit outsourcing services; (6) management functions or human resources; (7) broker or dealer, investment advisor, or investment banking services; (8) legal services and expert services unrelated to the audit; and (9) any other service that the PCAOB determines is impermissible.

    2. The issuer's audit committee is required to approve any non-audit services (including tax services) that are not specifically prohibited.

E. **Title III**—Established requirements related to *corporate responsibility* to make executives take responsibility for the accuracy of financial reporting (including a requirement for certification by the entity's *principal officers*) and to make it illegal for management to improperly influence the conduct of an audit.

F. **Title IV**—Addressed a variety of *enhanced financial disclosures,* the most well-known of which deals with required internal control reporting (Section 404), among other matters.

PCAOB on Engagement Quality Review

> **After studying this lesson, you should be able to:**
>
> **1.** Understand the auditor's responsibilities for an "engagement quality review" (and for concurring approval of issuance) under PCAOB Auditing Standards.
>
> **2.** Know the primary differences between the requirements of PCAOB Auditing Standards and the AICPA's Statements on Quality Control Standards (SQCS).

I. Engagement Quality Review

II. Introduction and Overview

    A. Applicability of Standard—Requires an engagement quality review (and concurring approval of issuance) for engagements conducted under PCAOB standards (1) for an audit; (2) for a review of interim financial information; and (3) for an attestation engagement regarding compliance reports of brokers and dealers (or a review engagement regarding exemption reports of brokers and dealers).

    B. Objective of the Engagement Quality Reviewer—To perform an evaluation of the significant judgments made by the engagement team and the related conclusions reached and in preparing any engagement report(s).

    C. Qualifications of an Engagement Quality Reviewer—(1) Must be an *associated person* of a registered public accounting firm; and (2) must have competence, independence, integrity, and objectivity:

> **Note**
> "An outside reviewer who is not already associated with a registered public accounting firm would become associated with the firm issuing the report if he or she ... (1) receives compensation from the firm issuing the report for performing the review or (2) performs the review as agent for the firm issuing the report."

        1. Associated person of a registered public accounting firm— Should be able to withstand any pressure from the engagement partner or others and may be someone from outside the firm; if the reviewer is from within the firm, he/she should be a partner or have an equivalent position. (There is no such requirement for a reviewer from outside the firm.)

        2. Competence—Must be qualified to serve as the engagement partner on the engagement under review.

        3. Objectivity—The engagement quality reviewer (and any assisting personnel) should not make engagement team decisions or assume any responsibilities of the engagement team.

        4. "Cooling-off" restriction—The person serving as engagement partner during either of the two audits preceding the audit subject to engagement quality review is not permitted to serve as engagement quality reviewer (unless the registered firm qualifies for a specific exemption to this requirement).

III. Engagement Quality Review for an Audit or a Review under PCAOB Standards

    A. Engagement Quality Review Process—To evaluate the significant judgments and conclusions of the engagement team, the engagement quality reviewer should (1) hold discussions with the engagement partner and other members of the engagement team; and (2) review documentation.

    B. Evaluation of Engagement Documentation—The engagement quality reviewer should evaluate whether the documentation that was reviewed (1) indicates that the engagement team responded appropriately to significant risks; and (2) supports the conclusions reached by the engagement team.

C. Concurring Approval of Issuance

1. The engagement quality reviewer cannot express such approval if there is any significant engagement deficiency [when (a) the engagement team failed to obtain sufficient appropriate evidence; (b) the engagement team reached an inappropriate overall conclusion; (c) the engagement report is not appropriate; or (d) the firm is not independent of its client].

2. The firm cannot give permission to the client to use the engagement report until the engagement quality reviewer provides concurring approval of issuance.

IV. Documentation of an Engagement Quality Review

A. Documentation should contain sufficient information to permit an experienced auditor, having no prior association with the engagement, to understand the procedures performed and conclusions reached by the engagement quality reviewer.

B. Documentation of an engagement quality review should be included in the engagement documentation (and be subject to other PCAOB requirements regarding retention of and changes to audit documentation).

V. PCAOB Standards Have Several Differences Relative to AICPA's Statements on Quality Control Standards (SQCS)

A. **Engagement Quality Review**—SQCS do not require an engagement quality review for any type of engagement, whereas the PCAOB establishes such a requirement.

B. **Cooling-off Restriction**—SQCS do not impose a "cooling-off" restriction or a requirement that the reviewer must be an associated person of a registered public accounting firm.

C. **Concurring Approval of Issuance**—SQCS require any engagement quality review performed be completed before the engagement report is released without requiring a concurring approval of issuance.

D. **Documentation Retention and Changes**—SQCS do not specifically require that engagement quality review documentation must be retained with other engagement documentation and be subject to specific policies regarding retention and changes.

Planning Activities

Pre-Engagement Planning Issues

After studying this lesson, you should be able to:

1. Understand the auditor's requirement under the applicable Statements on Quality Control Standards as they are used to specifically consider the "acceptance and continuance of clients and engagements."

2. Understand the auditor's responsibilities in agreeing upon the terms of the audit engagement with management.

3. Understand the auditor's responsibilities to communicate with the predecessor auditor when an entity changes auditors.

I. **Statements on Quality Control Standards**—Recall the AICPA's Statements on Quality Control Standards (SQCS) that are applicable to a CPA's financial statement related services.

   A. One of the six elements of a quality control system is *acceptance and continuance of clients and engagements*. Auditors should avoid clients whose management lacks integrity or clients who are viewed as too risky owing to industry considerations or entity-specific issues.

   B. The auditor should also evaluate the compliance with applicable ethics requirements, especially regarding independence issues and competencies to properly perform the engagement, before proceeding with other significant audit-related activities.

Question
What if the successor believes that the financial statements covered by the predecessor's report require revision?

Answer:
Try to arrange a meeting with the three parties (i.e., the successor, predecessor, and client management). If the client refuses to meet to discuss issues reflecting on the appropriateness of the previously issued financial statements, the successor should consider the risks of being the entity's auditor.

Question
What if the auditor is unable to observe the beginning inventory?

Answer:
If unable to verify the beginning inventory, the auditor may be unable to reach a conclusion about the cost of goods sold and, hence, the net income. As a result, the auditor may not be able to express an opinion on the fairness of the income statement, statement of cash flows, or statement of retained earnings. However, the auditor could still express an opinion on the balance sheet itself.

II. **Terms of Engagement**—The relevant AICPA guidance is provided by AU 210, *Terms of Engagement*. This pronouncement addresses the auditor's responsibilities in agreeing upon the terms of the audit engagement with management (and those charged with governance, when appropriate).

   A. **Auditor's Objective under AU 210**—The auditor's objective is to accept an audit engagement involving a new or existing audit client only when the basis for the audit has been agreed upon by (1) establishing when the *preconditions for an audit* are present; and (2) confirming that a common understanding of the terms of the engagement exists between the auditor and management (and those charged with governance, as applicable).

> **Definition**
> *Preconditions for an Audit:* The use by management of an acceptable financial reporting framework in the preparation of the financial statements and the agreement of management to the premise on which an audit is conducted.

1. Management should acknowledge its responsibility for (a) the fair presentation of the financial statements; (b) the design and implementation of effective internal control over financial reporting; and (c) providing the auditor with all information relevant to the financial statements and any additional information requested by the auditor, and providing access to all entity personnel relevant to the audit of the financial statements. (The auditor should determine whether the financial reporting framework is appropriate and obtain an agreement that management acknowledges and understands its responsibilities.)

2. If the preconditions are not present, the auditor should not accept the engagement; instead, the auditor should discuss the matter with management.

3. If management imposes a limitation on the scope of the audit that the auditor believes would result in a disclaimer of opinion (called a *limited engagement*), the auditor normally should not accept the engagement. If such an entity is required by law or regulation to have an audit, the auditor is then allowed to accept the limited engagement, so as long as a disclaimer of opinion is acceptable under the applicable law or regulation.

4. **Agreement on audit engagement terms**—The agreement of the terms of the engagement should be documented in an audit engagement letter and address the following:

   a. The objective and scope of the audit;

   b. The auditor's responsibilities;

   c. Management's responsibilities;

   d. A statement about the inherent limitations of an audit;

   e. A statement identifying the applicable financial reporting framework;

   f. Reference to the expected content of any reports to be issued; and

   g. Other matters as warranted in the auditor's judgment.

B. **Initial audits**—*Initial audit* refers to when the prior year's financial statements have been audited by a different auditor (referred to as the *predecessor auditor*).

1. Before accepting the engagement, the auditor should request that management authorize the predecessor auditor to respond to the auditor's inquiries relevant to the decision whether to accept the engagement.

2. The predecessor is expected to respond fully and to indicate when the response is limited. The auditor should evaluate the predecessor's response in deciding whether to accept the engagement. If management does not authorize the predecessor to respond (or otherwise limits the predecessor's response), the auditor should consider that fact in deciding whether to accept the engagement.

3. The auditor's communication with the predecessor auditor may be written or verbal. Typical matters expected to be addressed include the following:

   a. Information that might bear on the integrity of management

   b. Any disagreements with management about accounting or auditing issues

   c. Communications involving those charged with governance with respect to fraud and/or noncompliance with applicable laws or regulations

   d. Communications involving management and those charged with governance regarding significant deficiencies in internal control

   e. The predecessor's understanding about the reasons for the entity's change in auditors

Question
What if the auditor believes that the financial statements covered by the predecessor's report require revision?

Answer:
Try to arrange a three-way meeting involving the auditor, predecessor, and entity management. If management refuses to meet to discuss issues related to the appropriateness of previously issued financial statements, the auditor should consider those matters in deciding whether to accept the engagement.

C. **Recurring Audit Engagements**—If the auditor concludes that the terms of the preceding engagement are still applicable to the current engagement, the auditor should remind management of the terms of the engagement (and document that reminder).

1. The auditor may remind management of the terms of the engagement in writing or verbally. When the communication is oral, it is desirable to document the significant matters discussed (including with whom and when).

2. It may be appropriate to revise the terms of the previous engagement. This is the case, for example, when there is a change in senior management or a significant change in ownership; when there is a change in the financial reporting framework adopted; when there is a change in legal or regulatory requirements; when there is any indication that management misunderstands the nature of the audit; or when there are special terms to the engagement.

D. **Acceptance of a Change in the Terms of the Audit Engagement**

1. If the auditor is asked to change the audit engagement to an engagement resulting in a lower level of assurance (prior to completing the audit engagement), the auditor should determine whether reasonable justification for doing so exists; if not, the auditor should decline the request.

2. Suppose that the auditor concludes no reasonable justification for such a change exists, but management will not permit the auditor to continue the original audit engagement. The auditor should: (a) withdraw from the audit engagement when possible; (b) communicate the circumstances to those charged with governance; and (c) determine whether there is any legal or other obligation to report the matter to any other parties.

3. **Reasonable basis for a change**—Reasonable justification would exist when there is a change in circumstances affecting management's requirements, or if there was a misunderstanding about the nature of the service originally requested. The resulting report should not refer to any audit procedures performed prior to changing the engagement to a review or other service.

III. **Sample Engagement Letter**

CPA Firm's Letterhead

(Date)

  Ms. Nancy Pritchett*

  ABC Company**

  1803 King Avenue

  Columbus, OH 43212

Dear Ms. Pritchett:

This letter confirms our understanding of the services we will provide to ABC Company for the fiscal year ended December 31, 20XX. Moreover, this letter constitutes the entire agreement between us

---

regarding the services covered by this letter, and it supersedes any prior proposals, correspondence, and understandings, whether written or oral.

Services and Related Report

We will audit the balance sheet of ABC Company as of December 21, 20XX, and the related statements of income, retained earnings, and cash flows for the year then ended, for the purpose of expressing an opinion on them. Upon completion of our audit, we will provide you with our audit report on those financial statements.

Our Responsibilities and Limitations

Our responsibility is to express an opinion on the financial statements based on our audit, and is limited to the period covered by our audit. If circumstances preclude us from issuing an unqualified opinion, we will discuss the reasons with you in advance. If, for any reason, we are unable to complete the audit or are unable to form an opinion, we may decline to express an opinion or decline to issue a report for the engagement.

We are responsible for conducting the audit in accordance with generally accepted auditing standards. Those standards require that we obtain reasonable, but not absolute, assurance about whether the financial statements are free of errors or fraud that would have a material effect on the financial statements, as well as other illegal acts having a direct and material effect on the financial statements. Accordingly, a material misstatement may remain undetected. An audit is not designed to detect errors, fraud, or the effects of illegal acts that might be immaterial to the financial statements. We will inform you of all matters of fraud that come to our attention. We will also inform you of any illegal acts that come to our attention, unless they are clearly inconsequential.

We will obtain an understanding of internal control over financial reporting sufficient to properly plan the audit and to determine the nature, timing, and extent of audit procedures to be performed. The audit will not be designed to provide assurance on internal control over financial reporting or to detect significant deficiencies in internal control. However, we will report to you any significant deficiencies in internal control that we identify.

An audit includes examining, on a test basis, evidence supporting the amounts and disclosures in the financial statements. Judgment is required in determining the areas and number of transactions selected for our testing. An audit also includes assessing the accounting principles used and significant estimates made by management, as well as evaluating the overall financial statement presentation. Our procedures will include appropriate tests of documentary evidence supporting the transactions recorded in the accounts, tests of the physical existence of inventory, and direct confirmation of accounts receivable and certain other assets and liabilities by correspondence with selected customers, banks, legal counsel, and creditors. At the conclusion of our audit, we will request certain written representations from senior management about the financial statements and related matters.

Management's Responsibilities

The financial statements are the responsibility of the Company's management. That responsibility includes properly recording transactions in the accounting records and establishing and maintaining internal control sufficient to permit the preparation of financial statements in conformity with generally accepted accounting principles.

The Company's management is responsible for adjusting the financial statements to correct any material misstatements and for affirming to us in the representation letter that the effects of any uncorrected misstatements aggregated by us during the engagement and pertaining to the latest period presented are immaterial, both individually and in the aggregate, to the financial statements taken as a whole. Management is also responsible for ensuring that the Company complies with all applicable laws and regulations.

The Company's management is also responsible for making available to us, on a timely basis, all of the Company's original accounting records and related information, documentation, and company personnel to whom we may direct our inquiries. That includes providing access to us to the minutes of all meetings of stockholders, the board of directors, and committees of the board of directors for which such minutes are taken.

<u>Timing, Fees, and Other Matters</u>

Assistance to be supplied by the Company's personnel, including the preparation of certain specific schedules and analyses of accounts, is described in a separate attachment. Timely completion of this work is necessary for us to complete our audit on a timely basis.

The results of our audit tests, the responses to our inquiries, and the written representation furnished by management, comprise the evidence that we will reply upon in forming our opinion on the financial statements. The resulting audit documentation for this engagement is the property of (*name of the CPA firm*) and access will be limited to authorized persons to protect the confidentiality of company-specific information.

As part of our engagement for the year ending December 31, 20XX, we will review the federal and state income tax returns for ABC Company. We will be available during the year to consult with you on the tax effects of any proposed transactions or anticipated changes in your business activities.

Our fees will be billed as work progresses and are based on the amount of time required plus out-of-pocket expenses incurred by our audit team. Individual hourly rates vary according to the degree of responsibility involved and the experience and skill required. We will notify you on a timely basis of any circumstances we encounter that might affect our initial estimate of total fees, which we anticipate will range from $xx,xxx to $xx,xxx, excluding the aforementioned out-of-pocket expenses. Invoices are payable upon presentation.

If this letter accurately reflects your understanding, please sign where indicated in the space provided below and return it to us. We appreciate the opportunity to serve you and look forward to a mutually enjoyable association.

Sincerely yours,

(Name of the CPA Firm)

_____

Engagement Partner's Signature

<u>Accepted and agreed to:</u>

_____

(ABC Company Representative's Signature)

(Title)

(Date)

*The engagement letter should be addressed to whoever engaged the CPA firm (which might be the entity's CEO, board of directors, or someone else). The client representative responsible for the engagement who signs the engagement letter should be given a copy of the signed engagement letter and the CPA firm should retain the original letter for engagement documentation purposes.

**Assume that ABC Company is a "nonissuer" (i.e., a private company) such that PCAOB auditing standards do not apply. Hence, there is no mention here of PCAOB auditing standards or the audit of internal control that is applicable to SEC registrants under the Sarbanes-Oxley Act of 2002.

Planning and Supervision

Recall the AICPA's specific Performance Principle dealing with "planning, materiality, risk assessment, and evidence," which states: "To obtain reasonable assurance, which is a high, but not absolute, level ofassurance, the auditor: plans the work and properly supervises any assistants."

I. AICPA Guidance—The relevant AICPA guidance is provided by AU 300, *Planning An Audit*. This pronouncement states that the auditor's objective is to plan the audit so that it will be performed in an effective manner.

    A. Involvement of Key Engagement Team Members—The engagement partner and other key members of the audit team should be involved in planning activities.

        1. The nature and extent of planning varies with the size and complexity of the entity, the audit team's experience with the entity, and changes in circumstances occurring during the engagement. Likewise, the extent of supervision and review can vary depending upon the size and complexity of the entity, the nature of the audit area involved, the assessed risks of material misstatement, and the competence of the audit personnel involved.

        2. Planning is an ongoing iterative process, not a one-time activity. Planning encompasses risk assessment procedures, understanding the applicable legal and regulatory framework, the determination of materiality, the involvement of specialists, and so forth.

        3. The engagement partner may delegate portions of planning and supervision to other personnel, but a discussion about the risk of material misstatement (including fraud risks) among key members of the audit team, including the engagement partner, is required.

    B. Preliminary Engagement Activities—The auditor should address the following matters at the beginning of the engagement:

        1. Perform appropriate procedures to address quality control issues related to the continuance of the client relationship and the specific audit engagement (including consideration of issues regarding management integrity).

        2. Evaluate compliance with relevant ethical requirements related to quality control considerations (particularly regarding independence issues).

        3. Establish an understanding of the terms of the engagement.

    C. Planning Activities

        1. The auditor should establish an *overall audit strategy* dealing with the scope and timing of the audit work, which affects the development of the required *audit plan*. (An audit plan is more detailed than the overall strategy and deals with the nature, timing, and extent of audit procedures to be performed.) In establishing the overall audit strategy, the auditor should:

            a. Identify relevant characteristics of the engagement affecting its scope.

            b. Identify the reporting objectives of the engagement and required communications.

            c. Consider the factors that are significant in utilizing the audit team.

            d. Consider the results of preliminary engagement activities.

            e. Determine the nature, timing, and extent of necessary resources for the engagement.

    f. The overall strategy affects the auditor's decisions regarding the allocation of audit resources to specific audit areas and how those resources are managed and supervised.

    g. Communication with those charged with governance—The auditor is required to communicate with those charged with governance about an overview of the planned scope and timing of the engagement. The auditor may discuss planning issues with management, but should be careful to avoid divulging details that might reduce the effectiveness of the audit by making the auditor's procedures and scope too predictable.

  2. The auditor should also develop an *audit plan*. (In practice, the term *audit program* is often used in place of what the AICPA calls the *audit plan*.) The audit plan encompasses (a) the nature and extent of planned risk assessment procedures; (b) the nature, timing, and extent of planned *further audit procedures* at the relevant assertion level; and (c) other planned audit procedures necessary to comply with GAAS. Note: Because planning is an iterative process, the auditor should make appropriate changes to the overall strategy and to the audit plan as necessary during the course of the audit if unexpected circumstances are encountered.

D. Specialized Skills—The auditor should determine whether there is a need for specialized skills on the engagement. In the past, the AICPA used the term specialist to describe what they now call "a professional possessing specialized skills."

  1. A professional having specialized skills may be someone within or outside of the audit firm. Examples include valuation experts, appraisers, actuaries, tax specialists, IT professionals, etcetera.

  2. The auditor should be sufficiently knowledgeable about the matters involved to communicate the objectives of the work, to evaluate whether the planned procedures will meet the auditor's needs, and to evaluate the results of the procedures performed.

E. Documentation—The auditor should address the following matters in the audit documentation: (1) the overall audit strategy; (2) the audit plan; and (3) any significant changes made to the audit strategy or the audit plan during the audit engagement, along with the reasons for any such changes.

II. PCAOB Standards—The relevant PCAOB guidance is provided by their auditing standards on *Audit Planning*. The auditor's planning-related responsibilities are virtually the same under the PCAOB standards as they are under the AICPA standards.

Materiality

After studying this lesson, you should be able to:

1. Understand the concept of materiality, which is essential in evaluating the "fairness" of the financial statements within some range of acceptability.

2. Understand the role of both quantitative and qualitative considerations that might influence the auditor's judgments about materiality.

3. Recognize the meaning of the term "performance materiality."

I. **AICPA Guidance**—The relevant AICPA guidance is provided by AU 320, *Materiality in Planning and Performing An Audit*. This pronouncement states that the auditor's objective is to apply the concept of materiality appropriately in planning and performing the audit.

II. **Materiality**—The concept of materiality can be described as "an understanding of what is important" in financial reporting based on the auditor's perception of the users' needs.

   A. A definition of *materiality* from the FASB's Conceptual Framework project (specifically, Statement on Financial Accounting Concepts No. 2) follows:

> "The magnitude of an omission or misstatement of accounting information that, in the light of surrounding circumstances, makes it probable that the judgment of a reasonable person relying on the information would have been changed or influenced by the omission or misstatement." (Note that this definition emphasizes that materiality judgments involve both quantitative and qualitative considerations.)

   B. The determination of materiality is a matter of professional judgment, and involves both **quantitative** (the relative magnitude of the items in question) and **qualitative** (the surrounding circumstances) considerations.

   C. The auditor considers the concept of materiality throughout the audit process, including (a) in planning and performing the audit; (b) in evaluating the effect of uncorrected misstatements on the entity's financial statements; and (c) in forming the auditor's opinion.

   1. **In planning the audit**—The auditor should determine the materiality for the financial statements as a whole in connection with establishing the overall audit strategy. The auditor should determine **performance materiality** in connection with assessing the risks of material misstatement and determining the nature, timing, and extent of further audit procedures at the relevant assertion level.

Note
Previous AICPA auditing standards distinguished between planning-stage materiality and evaluation-stage materiality. Current standards no longer make that distinction, but, instead, introduce the term performance materiality, which seems similar to what was meant by the term planning-stage materiality in the past.

Definitions
Performance Materiality: The amount(s) set by the auditor at less than materiality for the financial statements as a whole to reduce to an appropriately low level the probability that the aggregate of uncorrected and undetected misstatements exceeds materiality for the financial statements as a whole; if applicable, it is also the amount(s) set by the auditor at less than the materiality level(s) for particular classes of transactions, account balances, or disclosures.

Tolerable Misstatement: The application of performance materiality to a particular sampling procedure.

   2. **Revision during the audit**—The auditor should revise materiality for the financial statements as a whole and, if applicable, the materiality level(s) for specific classes of transactions or

account balances when the auditor becomes aware of information affecting the auditor's initial judgments. The auditor should also determine whether "performance materiality" should be revised and whether the nature, timing, and extent of further audit procedures are appropriate.

D. **Documentation**—The auditor should document the following matters:

1. Materiality for the financial statements as a whole

2. Materiality level(s) for particular classes of transactions, account balances, or disclosures, as applicable

3. Performance materiality

4. Any revision of those considerations during the audit engagement

E. **Considerations that May Affect the Auditor's Materiality Judgment**

1. **Quantitative guidelines**—In practice, auditors frequently apply a variety of "benchmarks" as a starting point in determining the appropriate materiality levels. A few examples of frequently used general guidelines follow (these are not specifically identified in the AICPA auditing standards, however):

   a. 5% to 10% of net income or earnings before taxes

   b. 0.50% to 2% of the larger of net sales or total assets

   c. 5% of owners' equity for private companies

2. **Qualitative matters**—The surrounding circumstances and perceived risks might affect the auditor's judgment of what is material to the users. There are too many such factors to list here, but two examples follow:

   a. **Public versus private companies**—A lower materiality threshold may apply to public companies owing to more exposure to litigation and because the owners of private companies may be closer to the day-to-day operations and, therefore, have different information needs.

   b. **Unstable versus stable industry**—A lower materiality threshold may apply to a company in an unstable industry, which is by nature more susceptible to business failure.

3. **Tolerable misstatement** (which, in practice, is sometimes referred to as "tolerable error")—This term refers to the maximum error in a population that the auditor is willing to accept. This should be established in such a way that tolerable misstatement, combined for the entire audit plan, does not exceed materiality for the financial statements taken as a whole.

III. **PCAOB Standards**—The relevant PCAOB guidance is provided by *Consideration of Materiality in Planning and Performing an Audit*. The auditor's responsibilities regarding materiality under the PCAOB standards are very similar to those under AICPA standards, although the PCAOB standard does not use the term "performance materiality."

Audit Risk

After studying this lesson, you should be able to:

1. Understand the concept (and definition) of *audit risk* that underlies a risk-based audit approach relevant to planning, fieldwork, and audit reporting.

2. Understand the components of the "audit risk model" that are applicable to individual audit areas or major classes of transactions to be audited.

I. **Audit Risk**

A. **Definition of Audit Risk**—"The risk that the auditor expresses an inappropriate audit opinion when the financial statements are materially misstated. Audit risk is a function of the risks of material misstatement and detection risk." (Source—AU 200, *Overall Objectives of the Independent Auditor and the Conduct of an Audit in Accordance with [GAAS]*.) Note that the concept of audit risk is really a probability and that audit risk and materiality are interrelated by the definition of audit risk.

B. The presence of audit risk is indicated in the auditor's report by reference to *reasonable assurance,* meaning that audit risk cannot be reduced to a zero probability (which would imply "absolute assurance") owing to the inherent limitations of an audit. *Reasonable assurance* is defined as follows: "In the context of an audit of financial statements, a high, but not absolute, level of assurance." Note that *reasonable assurance* means a "high level of assurance" and a "low level of audit risk."

II. **Basic Auditor Responsibility**—The auditor should properly plan and perform the audit to obtain reasonable assurance that material misstatements, whether caused by errors or fraud, are detected.

III. **Considerations at the Financial Statement Level**—The one overriding audit planning objective is to limit audit risk to an appropriately low level (as determined by the auditor's judgment), which involves the following:

A. Determining the extent and nature of the auditor's risk assessment procedures

B. Identifying and assessing the risk of material misstatement

C. Determining the nature, timing, and extent of further audit procedures

D. Evaluating whether the financial statements taken as a whole are presented fairly in conformity with GAAP

IV. **Risk of Material Misstatement**—The *risk of material misstatement* (RMM) is defined as: "The risk that the financial statements are materially misstated prior to the audit." RMM exists at two levels: (1) the overall financial statement level; and (2) the assertion level for classes of transactions, account balances, and disclosures.

A. **RMM at the Overall Financial Statement Level**—This refers to risks that are "pervasive" to the financial statements and that potentially affect many assertions.

B. **RMM at the Assertion Level**—The auditor assesses RMM at the assertion level for the purpose of determining the nature, timing, and extent of further audit procedures to obtain sufficient appropriate audit evidence. RMM at the assertion level consists of two components: (1) inherent risk; and (2) control risk (see below).

C. At the assertion level, audit risk consists of three component risks: (1) inherent risk (IR); (2) control risk (CR); and (3) detection risk (DR). RMM consists of inherent risk and control risk.

$$AR = IR \times CR \times DR$$

> **Definitions**
>
> *Inherent Risk (IR):* The probability that a material misstatement would occur in the particular audit area in the absence of any internal control policies and procedures.
>
> *Control Risk (CR):* The probability that a material misstatement that occurred in the first place would not be detected and corrected by internal controls that are applicable.
>
> *Detection Risk (DR):* The probability that a material misstatement that was not prevented or detected and corrected by internal control was not detected by the auditor's substantive audit procedures (i.e., an undetected material misstatement exists in a relevant assertion).

V. Variations on the above Audit Risk Model

    A. $AR = RMM \times DR$, where:

        1. "Risk of material misstatement" (RMM)—the auditor's combined assessment of inherent risk and control risk (if IR and CR are not separately assessed).

> Note that $RMM = IR \times CR$

    B. $AR = RMM \times TD \times AP$, where:

        1. DR can be broken into two components involving the likelihood that the auditor's two basic categories of substantive procedures fail to detect a material misstatement that exists (1) "tests of details risk" (TD) and (2) "substantive analytical procedures risk (AP)."

> Note that $DR = TD \times AP$

    C. $AR = IR \times CR \times TD \times AP$

VI. Quantification of the Risk Components

    A. The component risks do not necessarily have to be quantified; for example, they could be assessed qualitatively as high, medium, or low.

    B. Each component is considered from left to right in order: audit risk is set, then inherent risk is assessed, then control risk is assessed, and finally the implications for the appropriate level of detection risk are considered.

    C. "Detection risk" is the only component risk that is specifically the auditor's responsibility— "inherent risk" arises because of the particular audit area under investigation and "control risk" reflects management's responsibility to design and implement internal controls. Note that the auditor must "assess" inherent risk and control risk, but the auditor actually makes the decisions that, in effect, result in some level of detection risk, which should take into consideration the auditor's assessment of the risk of material misstatement.

        1. If IR and CR are seen by the auditor as too high, the auditor must compensate by decreasing DR.

        2. If IR and CR are perceived as low, the auditor may consider accepting a higher DR.

    D. Increasing or decreasing DR is accomplished by adjusting the nature, timing, and/or extent of the auditor's substantive audit procedures. These might be viewed as the auditor's three strategic variables that, in effect, "set" DR based on the auditor's professional judgment about the following:

        1. **Nature**—What specific audit procedures to perform (perhaps shifting the relative emphasis placed on the "soft evidence" analytical procedures versus the "hard evidence" tests of details)?

2. **Timing**—When will the procedures be performed? At an "interim" date (prior to year-end) or at "final" (after year-end when the books have been closed) and the auditor is actually auditing the numbers that the entity intends to report in its financial statements)?

3. **Extent**—Are large samples required for the auditor's test work or can somewhat smaller sample sizes be justified? How extensively should substantive procedures be performed?

Analytical Procedures

Definition

Analytical Procedures: Evaluations of financial information through analysis of plausible relationships among both **financial and nonfinancial data.** (This includes any necessary follow-up investigation of fluctuations, significant differences, or inconsistent relationships.)

I. **AICPA Guidance**—The relevant AICPA guidance is provided by AU 520, *Analytical Procedures*. This pronouncement states that the auditor's objectives are to: (1) obtain relevant and reliable audit evidence when using substantive analytical procedures; and (2) design and perform analytical procedures near the end of the audit that assist the auditor when forming an overall conclusion about whether the financial statements are consistent with the auditor's understanding of the entity.

> **Note**
> *AU 520 replaces a previous AICPA auditing standard (then designated "AU 329"). The AICPA's nonauthoritative Summary of Changes, addressing the Clarified Standards, pointed out, "The clarified SAS does not change or expand the requirements of extant AU section 329 in any significant respect."*

   A. **Substantive Analytical Procedures**—When performing analytical procedures for substantive purposes, the auditor should: (1) determine the suitability of the particular analytical procedures for given assertions; (2) evaluate the reliability of the data from which the auditor developed the expectation; (3) develop an expectation of recorded amounts (or ratios) and evaluate whether the expectation is sufficiently precise; and (4) compare the recorded amounts (or ratios) with the auditor's expectations and determine whether any difference is acceptable without further investigation.

   1. Substantive procedures may consist of substantive analytical procedures, tests of details, or some combination of both. The auditor makes judgments about the effectiveness and efficiency of such procedures to limit the assessed risk of material misstatement to an acceptably low level.

   2. **Nature of assertion**—The effectiveness and efficiency of analytical procedures used for substantive purposes depends on four important considerations: (1) the nature of the assertion involved; (2) the plausibility and predictability of the relationship; (3) the availability and reliability of the data used as a basis for developing the expectation; and (4) the precision of the expectation. Analytical procedures may be particularly effective in testing for omissions (regarding the "completeness" assertion) of transactions that would be hard to detect with procedures that focus on recorded amounts. In other words, tests of details may not be effective when underlying source documents do not exist for transactions that went totally unrecorded, so analytical procedures may represent the best chance of detecting such omissions.

   3. **Plausibility and predictability of relationship**—Developing a meaningful "expectation" to compare to the entity's recorded amount is critically important to the skillful use of analytical procedures.

      a. Relationships in a stable environment are usually more predictable than those in a dynamic environment.

b. Relationships involving income statement accounts tend to be more predictable than those involving balance sheet accounts (since the income statement deals with a period of time rather than a single moment in time).

c. Relationships involving transactions subject to management discretion tend to be less predictable.

4. **Availability and reliability of data**—Reliability increases when the data used are reliable, which is enhanced when the data are (a) obtained from independent external sources; (b) are subject to audit testing (either currently or in the past); or (c) are developed under conditions of effective internal control.

5. **Precision of expectation**—The likelihood of detecting a misstatement decreases as the level of aggregation of the data increases. In other words, relationships of interest to the auditor may be obscured by the noise in the data at high levels of aggregation. For example, analyzing sales by month broken down by product line is more likely to be helpful to the auditor than simply comparing the current year's sales in total to the prior year's sales.

B. **Analytical Procedures when Forming Overall Conclusions**—The auditor should perform analytical procedures near the end of the audit that assist the auditor in forming an overall conclusion as to whether the financial statements are consistent with the auditor's understanding of the entity. These procedures may be similar to those used as "risk assessment procedures," and include reading the financial statements and considering any unusual or unexpected relationships that were not previously identified. As a result, the auditor may revise the assessment of the risks of material misstatement and modify the planned further audit procedures.

C. **Investigating Results of Analytical Procedures**—The auditor should investigate any identified significant differences by (1) inquiring of management (and corroborating management's responses with appropriate audit evidence, as necessary); and (2) performing other necessary audit procedures.

D. **Documentation**—The auditor should include the following matters in the audit documentation:

1. The auditor's expectation and the factors considered in developing it;

2. The results of the comparison of the recorded amounts (or ratios) with the expectations; *and*

3. Any additional auditing procedures performed to investigate significant differences identified by that comparison.

In summary, analytical procedures serve three audit purposes (two of which are required):

1. For risk assessment (required!)

2. For substantive purposes (widely used voluntarily, but not technically required)

3. As a final review (required!)

Detecting Fraud

After studying this lesson, you should be able to:

1. Understand (and be able to state) the auditor's fundamental responsibility to detect and communicate matters related to fraud in a financial statement audit.

2. Identify and distinguish between the two types of "fraud" that might be relevant to a financial statement audit, as discussed in the AICPA Professional Standards.

3. Identify the three categories of "risk factors" that the auditor is required to consider when assessing the risk of material misstatement due to fraud, based on AICPA Professional Standards.

I. **AICPA Guidance**—The relevant AICPA guidance is provided by AU 240, *Consideration of Fraud in a Financial Statement Audit*. This pronouncement states that the auditor's objectives are to: (1) identify and assess the risks of material misstatement due to fraud; (2) obtain sufficient appropriate audit evidence regarding the assessed risks of material misstatement due to fraud, through designing and implementing appropriate responses; and (3) respond appropriately to fraud or suspected fraud identified during the audit.

Definitions

Fraud: An intentional act by one or more individuals among management, those charged with governance, employees, or third parties, involving the use of deception that results in a misstatement in the financial statements.

Fraud Risk Factors: Events or conditions that indicate (a) an incentive or pressure to perpetrate fraud; (b) provide an opportunity to commit fraud; or (c) indicate attitudes or rationalizations to justify a fraudulent action.

A. There are two different types of misstatements that are relevant to the auditor's consideration of fraud:

1. **Fraudulent financial reporting**—This type of fraud involves misstatements that are intended to deceive financial statement users (e.g., the intent is to inflate the entity's stock price). Fraudulent financial reporting often involves management override of controls, recording fictitious journal entries, concealing facts, and altering underlying records to achieve the deception. This scenario is typically associated with a conspiracy involving multiple members of senior management to deceive the auditors, as well as financial statement users.

2. **Misappropriation of assets**—This type of fraud involves theft of assets causing the financial statements to be misstated owing to false entries intended to conceal the theft. Misappropriation of assets often involves embezzlement of receipts, stealing physical assets or intellectual property, and diverting the entity's assets for personal use. This scenario is typically associated with an individual bad actor operating individually to perpetrate and conceal the theft.

> **Note**
> AICPA Professional Standards focus on the auditor's responsibility for providing reasonable assurance of detecting material misstatements, whether due to error or fraud. The distinction depends upon whether the misstatement is intentional (which is the essence of fraud) or not. Intent may be difficult to determine, for example, when addressing accounting estimates, which are subjective by nature.

II. **The Auditor's Basic Responsibility Relates to Planning**

A. In general, the auditor is required to design (plan) the audit to provide "reasonable assurance" of detecting misstatements that are material to the financial statements. In particular, the auditor should specifically assess the risk of material misstatement due to fraud (in addition to error), and design the audit procedures to be responsive to that risk assessment. That risk assessment should be performed at both the financial statement level and the assertion level.

B. Specifically, key audit team members must have a "brainstorming" discussion to consider how and where the financial statements might be susceptible to material misstatement owing to fraud and to emphasize the importance of maintaining professional skepticism. That discussion involving key members of the engagement team should consider such matters as the following:

1. Known internal and external fraud risk factors relevant to the entity

2. The risk of management override of controls

3. Indications of "earnings management"

4. The importance of maintaining professional skepticism throughout the engagement

5. How the auditor might respond to the risk of material fraud

---

Question
Does failure to detect a material misstatement imply a substandard audit?

Answer:
No! An auditor may be unable to detect a material misstatement owing to forgery, collusion, or upper management involvement, etc.

III. Inquiry and Analytical Procedures—To obtain information needed to identify the risks of material fraud the auditor emphasizes "inquiry" and "analytical procedures." (The auditor's important inquiries should be documented in the Management Representations Letter at the end of fieldwork!)

A. Inquiry—The auditor should question management personnel about their knowledge of fraud, suspected fraud, or allegations of fraud; inquire about specific controls that management has implemented to mitigate fraud risks; and inquire about management's communications with those charged with governance about fraud-related issues. The auditor may also choose to question others (e.g., audit committee, internal auditors, operating personnel, in-house legal counsel, etc.) about fraud-related issues.

B. Analytical Procedures—The auditor should perform analytical procedures involving revenue accounts, in particular. In general, the auditor should consider whether any unexpected results associated with analytical procedures might have been intentional.

C. There is a presumption that improper revenue recognition is a fraud risk. The auditor should ordinarily presume that there is a risk of material misstatement owing to fraud related to revenue recognition, and perform appropriate audit procedures (such as analytical procedures).

IV. Fraud Risk Factors—The auditing standards identify three characteristics generally associated with fraud: (1) incentive/pressure; (2) opportunity; and (3) attitude/rationalization. These three categories of risk factors are sometimes referred to as the *fraud triangle*.

A. Fraudulent Financial Reporting—Example risk factors the auditor should consider:

1. Incentive/pressure—Reasons that management might be motivated to commit fraudulent financial reporting.

a. Financial stability/profitability—When the entity is threatened by deteriorating economic conditions, for example: operating losses threaten bankruptcy; there are recurring negative cash flows from operations; there is vulnerability to rapid changes due to technology or other factors; there are increasing business failures in the industry; or the entity reports unusual profitability relative to others in the industry.

b. Excessive pressure to meet the expectations of outsiders—Senior management may face significant pressure to meet external expectations, for example: there are overly optimistic press releases; the entity is only barely able to meet the stock exchange's listing requirements; the entity is having difficulty meeting debt covenants; or the entity must obtain additional outside financing to retool production to be competitive.

2. **Opportunities**—Circumstances that might give management a way to commit fraudulent financial reporting.

   a. **Nature of the industry or the entity's operations**—For example: significant related-party transactions not in the ordinary course of business; ability to dominate suppliers or customers in a certain industry sector; unnecessarily complex transactions close to year-end raise "substance over form" issues; significant bank accounts or business operations in "tax-haven" jurisdictions with no clear business justification; major financial statement elements that involve significant estimates by management that are difficult to corroborate.

   b. **Ineffective monitoring of management**—For example, domination of management by a single person or small group without compensating controls or; ineffective oversight by those charged with governance.

   c. **Complex or unstable organizational structure**—For example, organization consists of unusual legal entities; high turnover of senior management, counsel, or board members.

   d. **Internal controls are deficient**—For example, inadequate monitoring of controls; high turnover rates in accounting, internal auditing, and information technology staff; ineffective accounting and information systems (There are significant deficiencies that rise to the level of material weaknesses.)

3. **Attitudes/rationalizations**—Attitudes, behaviors, or justifications of management that might be associated with fraudulent financial reporting:

   a. Lack of commitment to establishing and enforcing ethical standards

   b. Previous violations of securities laws (or other regulations)

   c. Excessive focus by management on the entity's stock price

   d. Management's failure to correct reportable conditions

   e. Pattern of justifying inappropriate accounting as immaterial

   f. Management has a strained relationship with the predecessor or current auditor

B. **Misappropriation of Assets**—Example risk factors the auditor should consider:

1. **Incentive/pressure**—An employee or member of management might be motivated to commit the misappropriation for a variety of reasons, such as the following: employees who have access to cash (or other assets susceptible to theft), may have personal financial problems, or they may have adverse relationships with the entity under audit, (perhaps in response to anticipated future layoffs or recent decreases to their benefits or compensation levels).

2. **Opportunities**—Circumstances that might give someone a way to commit the misappropriation include the following:

   a. **When assets are inherently vulnerable to theft**—For example, there are large amounts of liquid assets on hand, or inventory items are small, but valuable.

   b. **Inadequate internal control over assets**—For example, there is inadequate segregation separation of duties, inadequate documentation or reconciliation for assets, or inadequate management understanding related to information technology.

3. **Attitudes/rationalizations**—The individual perpetrating the misappropriation might possess attitudes or justifications that might be associated with that rationalize the improper behaviors and avoid any feelings of remorse for this misconduct. Generally, the auditor cannot normally observe these attitudes, but should consider the implications of such matters when they are discovered. The following might be of interest to the auditor:

   a. The employee's behavior indicates dissatisfaction with the entity under audit.

    b. There are changes in the employee's behavior or lifestyle that are suspicious.

    c. The employee exhibits a disregard for internal control related to assets by overriding existing controls or failing to correct known deficiencies.

C. Consideration of the Effects of the Risk Factors

    1. The auditor should use judgment in considering the individual or collective effects of the risk factors and recognize that the effects of these risk factors vary widely.

    2. Specific controls may mitigate the associated risks, and specific control deficiencies may add to the risks.

D. Conditions may be discovered during fieldwork that cause the assessment of these risks in the planning stage to be modified. Factors that might cause the auditor's concerns to increase include the following examples:

    1. There are discrepancies in the accounting records including inaccuracies or unsupported balances.

    2. There is conflicting or missing evidence including missing documents or the absence of original documents that should be available (perhaps only photocopies are available).

    3. There is a problematic relationship between the auditor and the entity including restricted access of the auditor to records or personnel and undue time pressures imposed by management.

E. Responses to Risk Assessment—In response to this risk assessment related to fraud, the auditor may conclude that the planned procedures should be modified or that control risk should be reconsidered. The auditor might make some "overall responses" (at the financial statement level, such as assigning more experienced staff to the engagement) and make other responses "at the assertion level" (by designing audit procedures for which the nature, timing, and extent of those procedures are responsive to the assessed risks of fraud).

    1. Overall responses—The auditor may decide to assign more experienced personnel or information technology specialists to the engagement. The auditor should incorporate a degree of "unpredictability" in audit testing, whether at the financial statement level or the assertion level (e.g., visiting some locations for inventory counts on an unannounced basis) or selecting some items for testing that are below materiality levels.

    2. Responses at the assertion level—The auditor may decide to increase the emphasis on audit procedures that provide a stronger basis for conclusions or to confirm the terms of sales transactions, in addition to receivable balances; the auditor may move important audit testing to year-end, instead of performing those tests at an interim date; and/or the auditor may increase sample sizes for audit testing.

    3. Addressing management override of controls—The auditor should obtain an understanding of the entity's controls over journal entries and inquire about unusual activity. Selected journal entries at the end of the period should be examined. The auditor should also review accounting estimates for bias, and might perform a "retrospective review" of significant accounting estimates in the prior year. The auditor should specifically evaluate any significant unusual transactions outside the entity's normal course of business.

F. Management Override—Auditors should plan procedures specifically to address management override of internal control. Management override means that upper management may not be affected by controls that are imposed on subordinates throughout the organization. (Therefore, management may be able to sidestep those controls without leaving an audit trail for discovery.)

    1. Examine adjusting journal entries—The auditor should be especially attentive to nonstandard journal entries (involving unusual accounts or amounts and those involving complex issues or significant uncertainty). Likewise, the auditor should also be especially attentive to journal entries near the end of the reporting period (both for the fiscal year and any applicable interim reporting periods, such as quarterly reports).

2. **Evaluate accounting estimates for bias**—The auditor should consider performing a "retrospective review," which means evaluating prior years' estimates for reasonableness in light of facts occurring after those estimates were made. In other words, did later events support or refute the appropriateness of management's estimates in prior periods? That may affect the auditor's perception of the reliability of management's estimates in the current period.

3. **Evaluate the business rationale for any unusual transactions**—The auditor should look for appropriate authorization of any unusual transactions by those charged with governance.

Fraud: Evaluation and Communication

After studying this lesson, you should be able to:

1. Understand the auditor's responsibility to evaluate fraud issues in light of the overall results of the audit procedures performed.

2. Identify the specific fraud issues that the auditor should document.

3. Understand the auditor's responsibility to communicate the identified fraud issues to management, those charged with governance, or others.

I. **Evaluation of Audit Test Results**—Near the end of the audit, the auditor should evaluate whether the results of the auditing procedures affect the auditor's initial assessment of material fraud risk. (The analytical procedures related to revenue should be performed through the end of the period.)

    A. When evaluating identified misstatements of the financial statements, the auditor should consider whether such misstatements might be indicative of fraud. For example, the auditor might consider the organizational level involved. If a misstatement may be the result of fraud involving management, the auditor should reevaluate the assessment of material fraud risk and the auditor's response to the assessed risks.

    B. If the misstatement is (or may be) the result of fraud and the effect could be material to the financial statements (or if the auditor has been unable to evaluate the materiality involved):

        1. Attempt to obtain additional evidence to determine the facts as to the cause and whether the financial statements are misstated. Discuss the issues and any further investigation required with an appropriate level of management (at least one level above those believed to be involved) and with those charged with governance (especially if senior management appears to be involved).

        2. If the auditor encounters circumstances related to fraud that call into question whether it is appropriate to continue the audit, the auditor should determine the applicable professional and legal responsibilities, and consider whether it is appropriate to withdraw from the engagement. If the auditor withdraws, then the matter should be discussed with management and those charged with governance. (Circumstances that may call into question the auditor's ability to continue the audit include the following: (a) the entity does not take appropriate action regarding fraud; (b) audit evidence suggests that there is a significant risk of pervasive fraud; and (c) the auditor has significant concerns about the competence or integrity of management or those charged with governance.)

II. **Required Documentation**—The auditor should document the following matters related to the consideration of fraud in the financial statement audit:

    A. The discussion among engagement personnel about fraud in planning the audit, including how and when the discussion occurred, the team members who participated, and the subject matter discussed;

    B. The procedures performed to obtain information necessary to assess the risks of material fraud;

    C. Specific risks of material fraud that were identified at the financial statement level and at the assertion level, including a description of how the auditor responded to those identified risks (including the linkage of audit procedures to the risk assessment);

    D. Reasons supporting the auditor's conclusion if revenue recognition was not identified as a fraud risk contrary to the presumption that revenue recognition is a fraud risk;

    E. The results of procedures performed to further address the risk of management override of controls;

F. Other conditions and analytical relationships that caused the auditor to perform additional auditing procedures; *and*

G. The nature of any communication about fraud made to management, those charged with governance, regulators, and others.

III. Required Communications When Fraud Is Detected or Suspected—The auditor's communication of fraud issues with management (or those charged with governance) may be written or oral, but should be timely. As indicated above, such communication should be documented in the audit documentation.

A. If the fraud is not material to the financial statements and senior management is not involved in the fraud, the appropriate level of management (which is usually considered to be at least one level above where the fraud is believed to have occurred) should be notified. Determining the appropriate level of management for such communication is a matter of judgment, and includes consideration of the likelihood of collusion within management.

B. If the fraud is material to the financial statements or if senior management is involved in the fraud, those charged with governance should be notified.

C. **Other Matters Related to Fraud**—The auditor may choose to discuss a variety of other matters with those charged with governance, including the following:

1. Concerns about the adequacy of management's assessment of the entity's controls to prevent and detect fraud

2. Failure by management to respond appropriately to identified fraud or to address identified significant deficiencies in internal control

3. Concerns about the entity's control environment, including the competence or integrity of management

4. Concerns about management's efforts to "manage earnings"

5. Concerns about the authorization of transactions that do not appear to be within the normal course of the entity's business

D. The auditor should consider whether any identified fraud risk factors may constitute a "significant deficiency" (or material weakness) regarding internal control that should be reported to senior management and those charged with governance.

E. **Whistleblowing**—Informing others (outside) the entity such as regulatory and enforcement authorities, is ordinarily prohibited by the auditor's confidentiality requirements, although the duty of confidentiality may be overridden by law or regulation (or the requirements of audits for governmental entities). Accordingly, it would be appropriate for the auditor to seek legal guidance when facing such circumstances. The auditing (and ethical) standards historically have identified four basic exceptions to the auditor's confidentiality requirements:

1. The auditor must respond truthfully to a valid legal subpoena.

2. The auditor must comply with applicable legal and regulatory requirements (including complying with the SEC's 8-K requirements about important matters, such as the entity's decision to change auditors).

3. A predecessor auditor must respond appropriately to the successor auditor's inquiries when the former client has given permission for the predecessor auditor to respond to the auditor's questions.

4. The auditor must report fraud to the applicable funding agency under the requirements of government auditing standards.

Detecting Illegal Acts

After studying this lesson, you should be able to:

1. State the auditor's fundamental responsibility to detect and communicate illegal acts in a financial statement audit.

I. **AICPA Guidance**—The relevant AICPA guidance is provided by AU 250, *Consideration of Laws and Regulations in an Audit of Financial Statements*. This pronouncement states that the auditor's objectives are to: (1) obtain sufficient appropriate audit evidence regarding material amounts and disclosures about laws and regulations generally recognized to have a direct effect on the financial statements; (2) perform specified audit procedures that may identify instances of noncompliance with other laws and regulations that may have a material effect on the financial statements; and (3) respond appropriately to noncompliance (or suspected noncompliance) with laws and regulations identified during the audit.

> **Definition**
> *Legal and Regulatory Framework:* Those laws and regulations to which an entity is subject; noncompliance may result in fines, litigation, or other consequences that may have a material effect on the financial statements.

    A. **Fundamental Auditor Responsibility**—The essence of the auditor's responsibility is to obtain reasonable assurance that the financial statements are free from material misstatement, whether caused by fraud or error, considering the applicable legal and regulatory framework.

        1. **Inherent limitations**—The auditor cannot be expected to detect all noncompliance with all laws and regulations, since that is a legal determination and because many laws focus on an entity's operations instead of on the financial statements. (Note that the personal misconduct of management, those charged with governance, or others is outside the meaning of the term *noncompliance*.)

        2. The SAS distinguishes between two categories of considerations:

            a. Laws and regulations **having a direct effect** on the amounts and/or disclosures in the financial statements—The auditor should obtain sufficient appropriate audit evidence regarding material amounts and disclosures.

            b. Other laws and regulations **not having a direct effect** on the financial statements—The auditor should perform specified audit procedures that may identify noncompliance that may have a material effect on the financial statements. The specified audit procedures include inquiry of management and those charged with governance about compliance issues, inspection of any correspondence with regulatory authorities, reading minutes, and so forth.

    B. **Auditor's Consideration of Compliance with Laws and Regulations**—In obtaining an understanding of the entity and its environment, the auditor should obtain an understanding of

        1. The entity's applicable legal and regulatory framework; *and*

        2. How the entity is complying with that framework.

    C. **Audit Procedures when Noncompliance is Identified or Suspected**

        1. **If information suggests possible noncompliance**—The auditor should obtain an understanding of the circumstances of the act involved and gather further information to evaluate the financial statement effect. The auditor should also evaluate the implications of noncompliance to other aspects of the audit engagement, including risk assessment and the reliability of written representations.

2. **If the auditor suspects noncompliance**—The auditor should discuss the matter with management (at least one level above those suspected to be involved) and with those charged with governance, as appropriate.

3. **If unable to obtain sufficient information as to compliance**—The auditor should evaluate the effect of the lack of sufficient appropriate audit evidence on the auditor's report (and consider the need for obtaining legal advice).

D. **Reporting of Identified or Suspected Noncompliance**

1. **Reporting noncompliance to those charged with governance**—The auditor should communicate with those charged with governance any noncompliance with laws and regulations (unless it is clearly inconsequential). When management or those charged with governance is involved, the auditor should communicate to the next higher level of authority. If no higher level of authority within the entity exists, the auditor should consider obtaining legal advice.

2. **Reporting noncompliance in the auditor's report**—If a material effect on the financial statements has not been appropriately reported, the auditor should modify the opinion (expressing either a qualified or adverse opinion). If the auditor has been prevented from obtaining sufficient appropriate audit evidence to evaluate the financial statement impact of the matter, the auditor should modify the opinion (expressing either a qualified opinion or disclaimer of opinion) for a scope limitation.

3. **Reporting noncompliance to regulatory/enforcement authorities**—The auditor should determine whether there is a responsibility to report the matter to parties outside the entity, which may take priority over confidentiality responsibilities. The auditor should consider obtaining legal advice about this issue.

4. **Withdrawal**—If the entity refuses to accept a modified opinion and if withdrawal is possible under applicable law or regulation, the auditor may withdraw from the engagement and inform those charged with governance of the reasons in writing. Likewise, if the entity does not take the appropriate corrective action regarding noncompliance issues, the auditor may withdraw if such action is permitted by applicable law or regulation.

E. **Documentation**—The auditor should document the identified or suspected noncompliance and the results of the discussion with management, those charged with governance, and others, as applicable. Such documentation might include:

1. Copies of records or documents

2. Minutes of the discussion with management, those charged with governance, and others

Using the Work of a "Specialist"

After studying this lesson, you should be able to:

1. Understand the distinction between the terms *auditor's specialist* and *management's specialist* as used by the AICPA.

2. Identify the considerations that would be relevant to an auditor's selection of a particular specialist.

3. Know when it would be appropriate for the auditor to reference the involvement of the auditor's specialist in the auditor's report.

I. **AICPA Guidance**—The relevant AICPA guidance is provided by AU 620, *Using the Work of an Auditor's Specialist*. This pronouncement states that the auditor's objectives are to determine: (1) whether to use the work of an auditor's specialist; and (2) whether the work of the auditor's specialist is adequate for the auditor's purposes.

Definitions

Auditor's Specialist: An individual or organization possessing expertise in a field other than accounting or auditing, whose work in that field is used by the auditor to assist the auditor in obtaining sufficient appropriate audit evidence.

Management's Specialist: An individual or organization possessing expertise in a field other than accounting or auditing, whose work in that field is used by the entity to assist the entity in preparing the financial statements.

A. Note that the auditor is still responsible for the expressed opinion, so the auditor's responsibility is not reduced by using the work of an auditor's specialist.

B. Examples of a "field of expertise other than accounting or auditing" include the following: the valuation of complex financial instruments; actuarial calculations of liabilities for employee benefits; the valuation of environmental liabilities and cleanup costs; estimation of oil and other mineral reserves; and the interpretation of contracts, laws, and regulations; and so forth.

II. **Basic Requirements of the Auditor with Respect to Using an Auditor's Specialist**—Some considerations may differ for an *internal* auditor's specialist (who is affiliated with the auditor's firm or a firm that is part of an affiliated network) or an *external* auditor's specialist (who is not affiliated with the auditor's firm).

A. **Determining the Need**—The auditor should determine whether an auditor's specialist is needed to obtain sufficient appropriate audit evidence, taking into consideration the following:

   1. The nature of the matter involved;

   2. The risks of material misstatement involved;

   3. The significance of the matter to the audit;

   4. The auditor's experience with any previous work of the auditor's specialist; *and*

   5. Whether the auditor's specialist is subject to the audit firm's quality controls (which would apply to an internal specialist, but not to an external one).

B. **Competence, Capabilities, and Objectivity of the Specialist**—The auditor should evaluate the competence, capabilities, and objectivity of the auditor's specialist for the auditor's purposes.

1. The auditor should consider information about the competence, capabilities, and objectivity of an auditor's specialist, which might be obtained from the following:

   a. Personal experience with the specialist's previous work

   b. Discussions with the specialist or with other auditors familiar with the specialist

   c. Knowledge of the specialist's credentials or professional/industry affiliations, including whether the work is subject to any particular technical performance standards or industry requirements

   d. Any journal articles or books written by the specialist

2. For an external auditor's specialist, the auditor should inquire about any relationships that might threaten the specialist's objectivity. The auditor should consider any threats to the specialist's objectivity, along with any safeguards that might reduce such threats to an acceptable level.

C. **Obtaining an Understanding of the Field of Expertise**—The auditor should obtain a sufficient understanding of the field of expertise of the auditor's specialist so that the auditor can

1. Determine the nature, scope, and objectives of the work; *and*

2. Evaluate the adequacy of that work for the auditor's purposes. This understanding may be obtained from having experience with other entities requiring that same field of expertise, through specific education in that field, or through discussion with the auditor's specialist.

D. **Agreement with the Auditor's Specialist**—The auditor and the auditor's specialist should agree (in writing when appropriate) about the following:

1. The nature, scope, and objectives of the work involved;

2. Their respective roles and responsibilities;

3. The nature, timing, and extent of communications between the auditor and the auditor's specialist, including any reports to be delivered; *and*

4. The requirements for the auditor's specialist to adhere to confidentiality considerations applicable to an audit engagement. The agreement between the auditor and the external specialist is usually in the form of an engagement letter.

E. **Evaluating the Adequacy of the Work**

1. The auditor should evaluate the adequacy of the work performed by the auditor's specialist, including the following matters:

   a. The relevance and reasonableness of the conclusions;

   b. The relevance and reasonableness of any underlying assumptions and the methods used; *and*

   c. The relevance, completeness, and accuracy of any source data used by the auditor's specialist.

2. The auditor may perform specific procedures to evaluate such work, including:

   a. Making inquiries of the specialist;

   b. Reviewing the specialist's working papers; *and*

   c. Performing certain corroborative procedures, such as performing analytical procedures, examining published data, or confirming some matters with third parties, among other possibilities.

F. **If the Work is not Adequate**—The auditor and the auditor's specialist should agree on any further work to be performed, or the auditor should perform additional audit procedures that are appropriate to the circumstances (which could include engaging another auditor's specialist). If the auditor is unable to resolve the matter, it could constitute a scope limitation that would result in a modified opinion.

G. Reference to the Auditor's Specialist in the Auditor's Report

1. If the auditor's report contains an *unmodified* opinion, the auditor should not refer to the work of an auditor's specialist.

2. If the auditor's report contains a *modified* opinion and the auditor believes that it would help readers understand the reason for the modification, the auditor may reference the work of an external auditor's specialist. Normally, such a reference would first require the permission of the auditor's specialist. The auditor should also point out, in the auditor's report, that such a reference does not reduce the auditor's responsibility for the expressed opinion.

Required Communications with Those Charged with Governance

After studying this lesson, you should be able to:

1. State the specific matters that the auditor is required to communicate "with those charged with governance" (and be able to define that term).

2. Understand the impact that ineffective two-way communication with those charged with governance may have on the audit engagement.

I. **AICPA Guidance**—The relevant AICPA guidance is provided by AU 260, *The Auditor's Communication with Those Charged with Governance*. This pronouncement states that the auditor's objectives are to: (1) communicate clearly the auditor's responsibilities related to the audit and an overview of the planned scope and timing of the audit and (2) obtain from those charged with governance information relevant to the audit.

> **Definitions**
>
> *Those Charged with Governance:* The person(s) or organization(s) with responsibility for overseeing the strategic direction of the entity and the obligations related to the accountability of the entity (encompasses the term "board of directors" or "audit committee" used elsewhere in the auditing standards).
>
> *Management:* The person(s) with executive responsibility for the conduct of the entity's operations.

A. **Basic Auditor Responsibility**—The auditor should communicate those matters that are significant and relevant to the responsibilities of those charged with governance in overseeing the financial reporting process.

> **Note**
> The auditor is not required to perform any specific procedures to identify such matters to communicate with those charged with governance.

B. **Benefits**—Effective two-way communication with those charged with governance is important to having a constructive relationship, obtaining information relevant to the audit, and assisting those charged with governance in their role of overseeing financial reporting.

II. **Communication with Management**—The auditor may choose to discuss some matters with management before communicating them with those charged with governance, unless that is inappropriate. For example, the auditor would not normally discuss issues involving management's competence or integrity. Likewise, the auditor may choose to discuss some matters with the internal auditor(s) before communicating the matters with those charged with governance.

III. **Matters Required to Be Communicated with Those Charged with Governance**—(Note that the auditor may choose to communicate additional matters.)

A. **The Auditor's Responsibilities under GAAS**—The auditor should communicate the auditor's responsibility for expressing an opinion on the fairness of the financial statements, and point out that management is responsible for presenting the financial statements in conformity with the applicable financial reporting framework. These responsibilities could be communicated by an engagement letter.

B. **The Planned Scope and Timing of the Audit**—The auditor should communicate an overview of the planned scope and timing of the audit engagement.

C. **Significant Findings from the Audit**—The auditor should communicate:

1. The auditor's views about the qualitative aspects of the entity's significant accounting policies including the quality (not just the acceptability) of significant accounting practices, estimates, and disclosures;

2. Significant difficulties encountered during the audit including significant delays caused by management, unreasonable time pressure, unavailability of expected information, etc.;

3. Disagreements with management over accounting and auditing matters whether or not those disagreements were satisfactorily resolved; *and*

4. Any other matters that the auditor believes would be important to those charged with governance in their oversight of financial reporting.

5. **Uncorrected misstatements**—The auditor should request that uncorrected misstatements be corrected and communicate any uncorrected misstatements accumulated by the auditor, including the financial statement effect.

6. **Other matters**—The auditor should communicate the following matters:

    a. Material misstatements communicated to management that were corrected;

    b. Any significant findings or issues discussed with management;

    c. Any known instances where management consulted with other accountants about accounting or auditing matters; *and*

    d. The written representations that the auditor requested from management.

IV. **The Communication Process**—Clear communication by the auditor facilitates effective two-way communication with those charged with governance. Generally, the communication may be oral or in writing (effective communication may include formal presentations, written reports, or informal discussions, as determined by the auditor's judgment).

A. The auditor should communicate the significant findings from the audit in writing when oral communication is inadequate in the auditor's judgment.

B. When a significant matter is discussed with an individual member or subset of those charged with governance (such as the chair of the audit committee or others), the auditor should evaluate whether the matter should be summarized in a subsequent communication to all those charged with governance.

C. **Timing of Communications**—The auditor should communicate on a timely basis so that those charged with governance can take appropriate action. However, that timing may vary depending upon the circumstances.

D. **Adequacy of the Communication Process**—The auditor should evaluate whether the two-way communication has been adequate for purposes of the audit.

1. An inadequate two-way communication may suggest an unsatisfactory control environment, which the auditor should consider.

2. If the two-way communication is inadequate, the auditor should consider whether a scope limitation may exist and consider the possible effect on the assessment of the risks of material misstatement. This might warrant modification of the opinion, or even withdrawal.

V. **Documentation of the Communication**—The auditor should document matters communicated orally, and (when communicated in writing, the auditor should keep a copy of that communication).

VI. **Other Statements on Auditing Standards**—Other statements require that certain specific matters should be communicated to those charged with governance regarding:

A. **Illegal Acts**—The auditor should communicate any illegal acts that come to the auditor's attention.

B. **Going-Concern Issues**—When substantial doubt about the entity's ability to continue as a going concern remains after considering management's strategy, the auditor should communicate (1) the nature of the conditions identified; (2) the possible effect on the financial statements and disclosures; and (3) the effects on the auditor's report:

C. **Fraud**—The auditor should:

1. Inquire of the audit committee about the risks of fraud and the audit committee's knowledge of any fraud or suspected fraud;

2. Communicate any fraud discovered involving senior management and any fraud that causes a material misstatement (whether or not management is involved); *and*

3. Obtain an understanding with those charged with governance regarding communications about misappropriations committed by lower-level employees.

D. **Communicating Internal Control Matters Identified in an Audit**—The auditor should communicate to management and those charged with governance any identified significant deficiencies in internal control (including material weaknesses).

PCAOB on Communications with Audit Committees

> **After studying this lesson, you should be able to:**
>
> 1. Recognize the matters about which the auditor is obligated to communicate with the company's audit committee under PCAOB auditing standards.
>
> 2. Know the meaning of the terms "critical accounting estimate" and "critical accounting policies and practices" as used by the PCAOB.
>
> 3. Know the PCAOB's requirements regarding the form and timing of the auditor's communications with a company's audit committee.

I. Communications With Audit Committees

II. Introduction

The PCAOB encourages effective *two-way communication* between the auditor and the audit committee. Specifically, it requires the auditor to communicate with a company's audit committee regarding the conduct of an audit and to obtain information from the audit committee relevant to the audit. It also requires the auditor to establish an understanding of the terms of the engagement with the audit committee and to obtain an engagement letter. Communications are required only to the extent that the matters are relevant to the integrated audit, so there may be fewer matters to communicate when auditing a smaller, less complex company.

Definitions

Audit Committee: A committee (or equivalent body) established by and among the board of directors of a company for the purpose of overseeing the accounting and financial reporting processes of the company and audits of the financial statements of the company; if no such committee exists with respect to the company, the entire board of directors of the company.

Critical Cccounting Estimate: An accounting estimate where (a) the nature of the estimate is material due to the levels of subjectivity and judgment necessary to account for highly uncertain matters or the susceptibility of such matters to change and (b) the impact of the estimate on financial condition or operating performance is material.

Critical Accounting Policies and Practices: A company's accounting policies and practices that are both most important to the portrayal of the company's financial condition and results, and require management's most difficult, subjective, or complex judgments, often as a result of the need to make estimates about the effects of matters that are inherently uncertain.

III. Objectives

The auditor's objectives are to: (1) communicate to the audit committee the auditor's responsibilities regarding the audit and establish an understanding of the terms of the audit engagement with the audit committee; (2) obtain information from the audit committee relevant to the audit; (3) communicate to the audit committee information about the strategy and timing of the audit; and (4) provide the audit committee with timely observations about the audit that are significant.

IV. Appointment and Retention

A. **Significant Issues Discussed with Management in Connection with the Auditor's Appointment or Retention**—The auditor should discuss with the audit committee any significant issues that the auditor discussed with management in connection with the auditor's appointment/retention.

B. **Establishing an Understanding of the Terms of the Audit.**

1. The auditor should establish an understanding of the terms of the engagement with the audit committee, including the following matters: (a) the objective of the audit; (b) the auditor's responsibilities; and (c) management's responsibilities.

2. The auditor should provide an engagement letter to the audit committee annually.

V. Obtaining Information and Communicating the Audit Strategy

    A. Obtaining Information Relevant to the Audit—The auditor should inquire of the audit committee about matters relevant to the audit, including their knowledge of (possible) violations of laws or regulations.

    B. Overall Audit Strategy, Timing of the Audit, and Significant Risks—The auditor should communicate an overview of the audit strategy (including timing of the audit) and discuss any significant risks identified during the auditor's risk assessment. The auditor should communicate the need for specialized skills or knowledge and plans to use the work of the entity's internal auditors or others (including other CPA firms) in the integrated audit.

VI. Results of the Audit

    A. Accounting Policies and Practices, Estimates, and Significant Unusual Transactions—The auditor should communicate the following matters: (1) *significant* accounting policies and practices; (2) *critical accounting policies and practices* (and the reasons they are considered critical); (3) *critical accounting estimates* (including a description of management's processes, significant assumptions, and significant changes to those processes or assumptions); and (4) significant unusual transactions (matters that are outside the normal course of business). If management communicates any of those matters, the auditor is not required to communicate them again at the same level of detail.

    B. Auditor's Evaluation of the Quality of Financial Reporting—The auditor should communicate the following matters:

        1. Qualitative aspects of significant accounting policies and practices (including any indications of management bias);

        2. Assessment of critical accounting policies and practices;

        3. Conclusions regarding critical accounting estimates;

        4. Significant unusual transactions (and their business rationale);

        5. The conformity of the financial statement presentation with applicable financial reporting framework;

        6. Any new accounting pronouncements affecting financial reporting; *and*

        7. Alternative accounting treatments discussed with management.

    C. Other Information in Documents Containing Audited Financial Statements—The auditor should communicate the auditor's responsibilities for *other information* presented in documents containing the audited financial statements.

    D. Difficult or Contentious Matters—The auditor should communicate any difficult or contentious matters for which the auditor consulted outside the engagement team.

    E. Management Consultation with Other Accountants—The auditor should communicate views about any known instances where management consulted with other accountants about significant accounting or auditing matters.

    F. Going-Concern Issues—The auditor should communicate about the following going-concern matters: (1) The conditions or events causing the auditor to have *substantial doubt about the company's ability to continue for a going concern for a reasonable period of time*; (2) the basis for the auditor's conclusion, if the auditor concludes that such substantial doubt is alleviated by management's plans; and (3) if the auditor concludes that substantial doubt remains after considering management's plans, the effect on the financial statements and the auditor's report.

    G. Uncorrected and Corrected Misstatements

        1. Uncorrected misstatements—The auditor should provide the audit committee with a schedule of uncorrected misstatements that the auditor presented to management, and discuss with the audit committee the basis for the determination that the uncorrected misstatements were immaterial.

2. **Corrected misstatements**—The auditor should communicate those corrected misstatements (other than those that are clearly *trivial*) that were detected by the auditor, and discuss the implications of those matters relative to internal control over financial reporting.

H. **Material Written Communications**—The auditor should communicate other *material written communications* between the auditor and management.

I. **Departure from the Auditor's Standard Report**—When the auditor expects to modify the opinion or include explanatory language to the audit report (or an explanatory paragraph), the auditor should communicate the reasons for that.

J. **Disagreements with Management**—The auditor should communicate any disagreements with management over significant matters, whether or not satisfactorily resolved.

K. **Difficulties Encountered in Performing the Audit**—The auditor should communicate any significant difficulties encountered, such as: (1) significant delays or the unavailability of personnel; (2) unreasonable time pressures to complete the audit; (3) unreasonable management restrictions; and (4) unexpected difficulties in obtaining sufficient appropriate audit evidence.

L. **Other Matters**—The auditor should communicate any other matters arising out of the audit that are significant to overseeing the company's financial reporting.

VII. **Form and Documentation of Communications**—The auditor's communications may be oral or in writing, unless otherwise specified.

VIII. **Timing**—The auditor should communicate all of these required matters to the audit committee on a timely basis and prior to the issuance of the auditor's report.

Internal Control—Concepts and Standards

Obtaining an Understanding of Internal Control

> **After studying this lesson, you should be able to:**
>
> 1. Understand the auditor's responsibility to obtain an understanding of an entity's internal control (in connection with the second Standard of Fieldwork under GAAS, which is now associated with one of the AICPA's "Performance" Principles underlying an audit under GAAS)
>
> 2. Explain three different ways that an auditor might document the understanding of internal control.

I. **Review Phase**—The auditor should obtain an initial understanding of internal controls and document that understanding.

    A. The auditor obtains an **understanding of internal control** and the flow of documents related to the entity's transactions primarily through:

        1. Inquiry of appropriate personnel

        2. Observation of client activities

        3. Review of documentation—The auditor reviews relevant documentation, including the client's accounting manuals, prior-year's audit documentation (working papers), etc.

    B. The auditor's internal control analysis tends to focus on the entity's major transaction cycles.

    C. **Transaction Cycle**—Defined to be a group of essentially homogeneous transactions, that is, transactions of the same type.

    D. **Implication**—A specific transaction cycle is the highest level of aggregation about which meaningful generalizations of control risk can be made, since control risk is constant within that transaction cycle. Each transaction within a specific transaction cycle is captured, processed, and recorded subject to the same set of internal control policies and procedures.

    E. **Examples of Typical Transaction Cycles**—Typical examples, include the following:

        1. Revenue/receipts

        2. Expenditures/disbursements

        3. Payroll

        4. Financing/investing activities

        5. Inventory, especially if inventory is manufactured, rather than purchased

    F. **Document the Auditor's Understanding**—The auditor should document that understanding of internal control. The extensiveness of the review and documentation varies with the circumstances (e.g., the emphasis on understanding internal controls increases if reliance on internal control is planned):

        1. **Flow charts of transaction cycles**—A graphical depiction of the client's accounting systems for major categories of transactions with emphasis on the origination, processing, and distribution of important underlying accounting documents.

            a. **Advantages**—A fairly systematic approach that is unlikely to overlook important considerations; tailored to client-specific circumstances; fairly easy for others to review and understand; and fairly easy to update from year to year.

    b.   **Disadvantages**—Can be rather tedious and time consuming to prepare initially although available commercial software today may eliminate much of that difficulty; the auditor might fail to recognize relevant internal control deficiencies by getting too absorbed in the details of documenting the client's system.

Assessing Risk and Developing a Planned Response

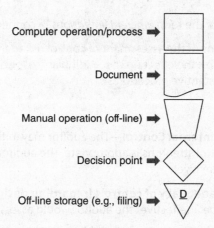

Computer operation/process ➡

Document ➡

Manual operation (off-line) ➡

Decision point ➡

Off-line storage (e.g., filing) ➡

2. **Internal control questionnaires (ICQs)**—Questionnaires consisting of a listing of questions about client's control procedures and activities; a "no" answer is usually designed to indicate a control weakness.

    a.   **Advantages**—Generic questionnaires can be prepared in advance for clients in various industry categories with every conceivable question, so that no important question related to controls is likely to be omitted; deficiencies are easily identified by a client's "no" response to any question.

    b.   **Disadvantages**—Generic questionnaires are not tailored to client-specific circumstances and irrelevant questions are annoying to client personnel; the client personnel responding to the checklist of questions may conceal deficiencies by inaccurate answers without the auditor's knowledge.

3. **Narrative write-ups**—A written memo describing the important control-related activities in the transaction cycles under consideration.

    a.   **Advantages**—Memos can be tailored to a client's unique circumstances, can be as detailed or general as desired, and are relatively easy to prepare (and easy for reviewers to read it).

    b.   **Disadvantages**—It is relatively easy to overlook relevant internal control issues (strengths or weaknesses) because the analysis is fairly unstructured.

G. **Perform a Walkthrough**—The auditor may select a few transactions to trace them through the client's accounting system. The purpose is merely to get some feedback as to whether the auditor has accurately understood (and documented) the way the client entity is processing transactions. The walkthrough is not considered evidence or a form of documentation and should not be confused with tests of control.

Evaluating Internal Control

After studying this lesson, you should be able to:

1. Understand the purpose of performing "tests of control" and the circumstances that warrant performing such tests.

2. Understand the meaning of the term *inherent limitations* in connection with internal control.

3. Understand the implications of the assessment of control risk to the level of detection risk that may be appropriate (and, thereby, the effect on the "audit plan"—specifically on the nature, timing, and extent of the auditor's substantive procedures).

I. **Preliminary Evaluation of Internal Control**—The auditor may initially consider whether reliance on certain specific internal control strengths is appropriate. The auditor may consider assessing control risk at less than the maximum level.

   A. Consider the apparent **adequacy of controls (regarding design effectiveness)**—If internal control is perceived to be "ineffective," the auditor would assess control risk at the maximum level.

      1. Consider the possible types of errors or problems that could occur.

      2. Consider the kinds of procedures that would prevent and/or detect such errors or problems.

      3. Determine whether such controls are in place.

      4. Evaluate the implications of any identified weaknesses.

   B. Consider **cost-benefit trade-offs**—Reliance on internal controls "buys" a reduction of substantive audit work to some degree, but it "costs" additional effort to perform tests of control (and this may or may not be cost beneficial, even if the design of internal control is perceived to be effective).

   C. The auditor should document the basis for conclusions about internal control either way, whether internal control is perceived to be effective or ineffective.

II. **Perform Tests of Controls**—If reliance is planned (regarding operating effectiveness)—*Reliance* means the same thing as *to assess control risk at less than the maximum level* for purposes of accepting a somewhat higher level of detection risk.

   A. Perform tests of controls—but only for those specific control policies and procedures (strengths that justify accepting a somewhat higher level of detection risk) on which reliance is planned.

   B. The purpose of performing tests of control is to verify that the controls that looked good on paper (design effectiveness) were actually working as intended throughout the period (**operating effectiveness**).

   C. Circumstances that warrant performing tests of control (associated with a reliance strategy): (1) when the auditor's risk assessment includes an expectation regarding the operating effectiveness of controls; or (2) when the performance of substantive procedures alone do not limit audit risk to an acceptably low level.

   D. **When Performing Tests of Controls**—Select a sample of transactions and verify that the control procedures of interest were, in fact, performed on the transactions in the sample which usually requires that the control procedure be documented as it is performed. Undocumented controls may be tested by the auditor's observation of the entity's performance of such controls.

III. **Reevaluate Planned Reliance Based on the Results of These Tests of Controls**—Determine whether the results of the tests of controls are consistent with the planned reliance on internal controls. (What looked good on paper may not be working satisfactorily in reality.)

IV. Develop a Detailed Audit Plan—(Also referred to as an *audit program*) The auditor should prepare a written audit plan that specifies the nature, timing, and extent of further audit procedures to be performed, and the auditor should document the conclusions about control risk in planning the audit:

    A. A wholly substantive audit approach means *no reliance* on internal control (which means the same thing as *assessing control risk at the maximum level*). In other words, the auditor plans to meet the audit risk objectives by performing only substantive audit procedures without any expectation about the operating effectiveness of internal control. Tests of control would not be performed.

    B. Auditors may base their audit conclusions on both tests of controls and substantive audit procedures, although the auditor must always perform substantive procedures to some extent (i.e., the auditor cannot rely entirely on the operating effectiveness of internal control as a sole basis for conclusions), related to detection risk in the audit risk model.

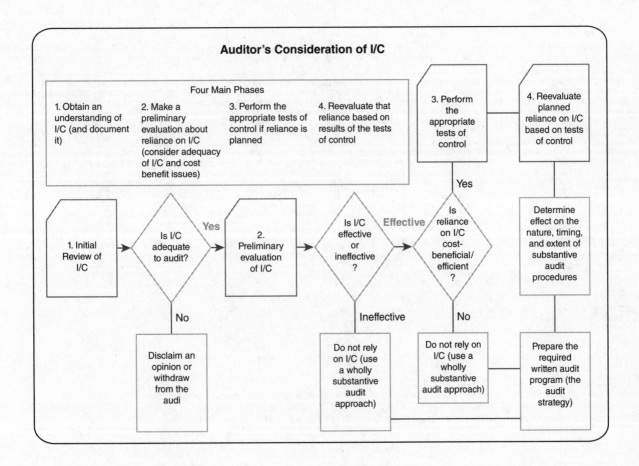

V. Inherent Limitations—The design and implementation of internal control is a management function (not the auditor's responsibility!) and management must evaluate the applicable costs and benefits in the design and implementation of their internal control policies and procedures.

    A. The costs of internal controls should not outweigh the benefits attributable to those controls. As a result, controls provide reasonable (not absolute) assurance.

    B. Mistakes may occur as a result of employees' misunderstandings, misjudgments, carelessness, fatigue, etc.

C. Segregation of duties may break down due to collusion (a conspiracy among employees or management to circumvent internal controls) or management's "override" of controls—override refers to management imposing controls downward on subordinates without intending to be affected by those controls themselves.

Question

Why must auditors consider an entity's internal control in planning the audit engagement?

Answer:

In order to plan an effective and efficient audit, auditors must assess control risk as a basis for setting the appropriate level of detection risk related to their substantive auditing procedures (specifically, to determine the nature, timing, and extent of those substantive procedures).

Assessing Control Risk Under AICPA Standards

> **After studying this lesson, you should be able to:**
>
> 1. Understand the auditor's responsibility to perform risk assessment procedures.
>
> 2. Understand the entity and its environment, including internal control (with emphasis on the five interrelated components of internal control), in accordance with AICPA Professional Standards.

I. Responsibilities under AICPA Professional Standards

    A. The relevant AICPA guidance is provided by AU 315, *Understanding the Entity and Its Environment and Assessing the Risks of Material Misstatement*. This pronouncement states that the auditor's objective is to "identify and assess the risks of material misstatement, whether due to fraud or error, at the financial statement and relevant assertion levels through understanding the entity and its environment, including its internal control, thereby providing a basis for designing and implementing responses to the assessed risks of material misstatement."

> This SAS provides guidance regarding the second Standard of Fieldwork of GAAS: "The auditor must obtain a sufficient understanding of the entity and its environment, including its internal control, to assess the risk of material misstatement of the financial statements whether due to fraud or error, and to design the nature, timing, and extent of further audit procedures."
>
> That requirement is now embedded in one of the Performance Principles. "To obtain reasonable assurance, which is a high, but not absolute, level of assurance, the auditor . . . identifies and assesses risks of material misstatement, whether due to fraud or error, based on an understanding of the entity and its environment, including the entity's internal control."

    B. The AU section focuses on the auditor's requirements related to

        1. Risk assessment procedures

        2. Understanding the entity and its environment, including its internal control

        3. Assessing the risks of material misstatement

        4. Documentation

II. Risk Assessment Procedures—The auditor should perform risk assessment procedures to obtain an understanding of the entity and its environment, including its internal control (the nature, timing, and extent of the risk assessment procedures vary with the engagement's circumstances, such as the entity's size and complexity and the auditor's experience with it).

    A. Inquiries of Management and Others—The auditor should obtain information from inquiries made of management and others, including internal auditors, production and marketing personnel, those charged with governance, and outsiders (such as external legal counsel or valuation experts used by the entity).

    B. Observation and Inspection—The auditor's risk assessment procedures should include observation of entity operations, inspection of documents (e.g., internal control manuals), reading reports prepared by management and those charged with governance (e.g., minutes of meetings), and visits to the entity's facilities.

    C. Analytical Procedures—The auditor's analytical procedures performed in planning may assist the auditor in understanding the entity and its environment and identify specific risks relevant to the audit.

D. Review Information—The auditor should review information about the entity and its environment obtained in prior periods. The auditor should consider whether changes may have affected the relevance of that information (perhaps by making inquiries or performing a walkthrough of transactions through the entity's systems).

E. Discussion among Audit Team Members—The audit team should discuss the susceptibility of the entity's financial statements to material misstatements.

1. **Key members should be involved in the discussion**—But professional judgment is required to determine who should be included in that discussion. (For a multilocation audit, there may be multiple discussions for key members at each major location.)

2. **Objective of this discussion**—The purpose of the discussion is for members of the audit team to understand the potential for material misstatements of the financial statements (due to error or fraud) in specific areas assigned to them and how their work may affect other parts of the audit.

3. **The discussion should include critical issues**—Such matters include the areas of significant audit risk, the potential for management override of controls; important controls; materiality at the financial statement level and the relevant assertion level; etc.

III. Understanding the Entity and Its Environment—Including its internal control.

A. The auditor's understanding of the entity and its environment consists of understanding the following: (1) industry, regulatory, and other external factors; (2) nature of the entity; (3) objectives and strategies and related business risks that may cause material misstatement of the financial statements; (4) measurement and review of the entity's financial performance; and (5) internal control.

1. **Industry, regulatory, and other external factors**—There may be specific risks of material misstatement due to the nature of the business, the degree of regulation, or other economic, technical, and competitive issues.

2. **Nature of the entity**—This refers to the entity's operations, ownership, governance, financing, etc. (Understanding these considerations may help the auditor understand the classes of transactions, account balances, and disclosures that are relevant to the financial statements.)

3. **Objectives and strategies**—The auditor should obtain an understanding of the entity's objectives and strategies, including any related business risks that may cause material misstatement of the financial statements. Strategies are operational approaches by which management intends to achieve its objectives. Business risks result from circumstances that could adversely affect the entity's ability to achieve its objectives. (Note that the auditor does not have a responsibility to identify all business risks.)

4. **Measurement and review of the entity's financial performance**—The auditor should obtain an understanding of the entity's performance measures (and their review) and indicate aspects of the entity's performance that management considers important, which may help the auditor to understand whether such pressures increase the risks of material misstatement.

5. **Obtain a sufficient understanding of internal control**—The auditor should perform risk assessment procedures to evaluate the design of controls relevant to the audit to identify types of potential misstatements. Note that inquiry alone is not sufficient to evaluate the design and implementation of a control. Consider factors that affect the risks of material misstatement; and design the tests of controls, if applicable, and the substantive procedures that are appropriate in the circumstances.

> **Note**
> *The auditor must perform substantive tests to some degree for all significant audit areas—cannot assess control risk so low that substantive testing is omitted entirely!*

B. The Auditor's Consideration of Internal Control—Internal control may also be referred to as *internal control structure*. The auditor should obtain a sufficient understanding of internal control to evaluate the design of controls relevant to the audit.

Definition

Internal Control: A process—effected by those charged with governance, management, and other personnel—that is designed to provide reasonable assurance about the achievement of the entity's objectives with regard to reliability of financial reporting, effectiveness and efficiency of operations, and compliance with applicable laws and regulations.

C. **The Auditor's Primary Consideration**—The auditor should consider whether (and how) a specific control prevents, or detects and corrects, material misstatements in relevant assertions related to classes of transactions, account balances, or disclosures.

D. Internal control consists of five interrelated components:

1. **Control environment**—The policies and procedures that determine the overall control consciousness of the entity, sometimes called "the tone at the top."

The auditor should evaluate the following elements that comprise the entity's control environment:

Communication and enforcement of integrity and ethical values

Commitment to competence

Participation of those charged with governance (including their interaction with internal and external auditors)

Management's philosophy and operating style

The entity's organizational structure

The entity's assignment of authority and responsibility (including internal reporting relationships)

Human resource policies and practices

2. **Risk assessment**—The policies and procedures involving the identification, prioritization, and analysis of relevant risks as a basis for managing those risks.

The auditor's responsibilities include:

Inquiring about business risks that management has identified relevant to financial reporting and considering their implications to the financial statements

Considering how management identified (and decided how to manage) business risks relevant to financial reporting

Considering the implications to the risk assessment process when the auditor identifies business risks that management failed to identify

3. **Information and communication systems**—The policies and procedures related to the identification, capture, and exchange of information in a form and time frame that enable people to carry out their responsibilities.

The auditor's responsibilities include obtaining the following:

Sufficient knowledge to understand the classes of transactions that are significant to the financial statements and the procedures and relevant documents related to financial reporting

An understanding of how incorrect processing of transactions is resolved

An understanding of the automated (IT) and manual procedures used to prepare the financial statements and how misstatements may occur

An understanding of how transactions originate with the entity's business processes

Sufficient knowledge to understand how the entity communicates financial reporting roles and responsibilities

4. **Control activities**—The policies and procedures that help ensure that management directives are carried out, especially those related to

   a. Authorization,

   b. Segregation of duties,

   c. Performance reviews,

   d. Information processing, *and*

   e. Physical controls.

> The auditor's responsibilities include:
>
> Obtaining an understanding of how IT affects control activities relevant to planning the audit (especially with respect to application controls and general controls); and
>
> Considering whether the entity has established effective controls related to IT (especially with respect to maintaining the integrity of information and the security of data).

5. **Monitoring**—The policies and procedures involving the ongoing assessment of the quality of internal control effectiveness over time.

> The auditor should obtain an understanding of the sources of the information related to the entity's monitoring activities and the basis upon which management considers the information to be reliable.

E. **Inherent Limitations of Internal Control**—Internal control provides reasonable, not absolute, assurance about achieving the entity's objectives. Internal control may be ineffective owing to human failures (mistakes and misunderstandings) and controls may be circumvented by collusion or management override of controls. The cost of an internal control procedure should not exceed the benefit expected to be derived from it.

Performing Procedures in Response to Assessed Risks

After studying this lesson, you should be able to:

1. Assess the risk of material misstatement.

2. Document various internal control matters.

3. Link audit responses to the risks of material misstatement at the financial-statement level and the relevant-assertion level, in accordance with AICPA Professional Standards.

I. **Responsibilities under AICPA Professional Standards**

   A. The primary relevant AICPA guidance is provided by AU 315, *Understanding the Entity and Its Environment and Assessing the Risks of Material Misstatement*. This pronouncement states that the auditor's objective is to "identify and assess the risks of material misstatement, whether due to fraud or error, at the financial statement and relevant assertion levels through understanding the entity and its environment, including its internal control, thereby providing a basis for designing and implementing responses to the assessed risks of material misstatement."

   B. Additional relevant guidance is provided by AU 330, *Performing Audit Procedures in Response to Assessed Risks and Evaluating the Audit Evidence Obtained*. The auditor's objective is "to obtain sufficient appropriate audit evidence regarding the assessed risks of material misstatement through designing and implementing appropriate responses to those risks."

II. **Assessing the Risk of Material Misstatement**

   A. **Auditor's Responsibility**—The auditor should identify and assess the risks of material misstatement

      1. At the financial statement level; *and*

      2. At the relevant assertion level related to classes of transactions, account balances, and disclosures.

   B. **Internal Control Considerations**—A weak control environment (such as management's lack of competence) may have pervasive financial statement effects and require an overall response by the auditor. The auditor's understanding of internal control may also raise questions about the auditability of the entity's financial statements (e.g., sufficient appropriate evidence may not be available).

   C. **Significant Risks**—These are risks that the auditor believes require special audit consideration. The auditor should consider the nature of the risks identified (e.g., whether the risk may relate to fraud, significant economic developments, the complexity of transactions, related-party transactions, subjective measurement, or nonroutine transactions that are unusual for the entity).

   D. **Risks for which Substantive Procedures Alone do not Provide Sufficient Appropriate Audit Evidence**—The auditor should evaluate the design and implementation of controls over such risks, since it is not possible to reduce detection risk to an acceptably low level with substantive procedures by themselves: for example, when IT is a significant part of the entity's information system and transactions are initiated, authorized, recorded, processed, and reported electronically without an audit trail.

   E. **Revision of Risk Assessment**—Risk assessment is an iterative process and the assessment of risks may change as additional evidence is obtained. (For example, when performing tests of controls, evidence may be obtained that controls are ineffective, or when performing substantive procedures, misstatements may be detected that suggest that controls are ineffective.)

III. Documentation—The form of the documentation requires professional judgment and varies with the circumstances, including the complexity of the entity and the extent to which IT is used. The documentation may include narrative descriptions, questionnaires, flowcharts, and checklists.

    A. The auditor should document the following matters:

        1. The discussion with members of the audit team about the potential for misstatements due to error or fraud including how and when that discussion occurred, the subject matter discussed, the team members involved, and significant decisions reached about the planned responses to those risks;

        2. Major elements of the understanding of each of the five components of internal control to assess the risk of material misstatement, the sources of information used for that understanding, and the risk assessment procedures performed;

        3. The assessment of the risks of material misstatement (both at the financial statement level and at the relevant assertion level) and the basis for that assessment; *and*

        4. The risks identified and the related controls the auditor evaluated.

    B. Another standard (AU 330) focuses on the auditor's requirements related to:

        1. Overall responses to the risks of material misstatement at the financial statement level;

        2. Responses to the risks of material misstatement at the relevant assertion level (in determining the nature, timing, and extent of further audit procedures, including tests of the operating effectiveness of controls and substantive procedures);

        3. Evaluating the sufficiency and appropriateness of the audit evidence obtained; *and*

        4. Documentation.

IV. Overall Responses to the Risks of Material Misstatement at the Financial Statement Level

    A. As the risk of material misstatement increases, the auditor may assign more experienced staff to the engagement; provide closer supervision; use specialists; use more unpredictable audit procedures; and/or make appropriate changes in the nature, timing, or extent of further audit procedures.

    B. The assessment of the risk of material misstatement may influence the auditor's strategy in using a *substantive approach* or a *combined approach* that uses both tests of controls (regarding the operating effectiveness of controls) and substantive procedures.

V. Responses to the Risks of Material Misstatement at the Relevant Assertion Level—The assessment of the risk of material misstatement may affect the auditor's decisions regarding the nature, timing, and extent of further audit procedures, including the tests of the operating effectiveness of controls and the substantive procedures.

    A. Substantive procedures must be performed to some degree for all relevant assertions related to each material class of transactions, account balance, or disclosure (i.e., the auditor cannot rely totally on the effectiveness of the entity's internal controls).

    B. Nature—This refers to the purpose of further audit procedures (tests of controls or substantive procedures) and their type (inspection, observation, inquiry, confirmation, recalculation, reperformance, or analytical procedures).

    C. Timing—This refers to when the further audit procedures are performed (at year-end or before year-end, called "interim"); performing substantive procedures at year-end is usually more effective with a higher risk of material misstatement.

    D. Extent—This refers to the quantity of an audit procedure to be performed (such as sample size) based on the auditor's judgment; computer-assisted audit techniques (CAATs) may be used to extensively test electronic transactions/files.

    E. Tests of Controls—To determine the operating effectiveness of controls

        1. The auditor should perform tests of controls when the auditor's risk assessment includes an expectation of the operating effectiveness of controls. (Note that this is frequently referred to as "relying" on internal control as a partial basis for the auditor's conclusions, or "assessing control risk at less than the maximum level.")

2. The auditor should also perform tests of control when substantive procedures alone do not provide sufficient appropriate evidence at the relevant assertion level. For example, when the entity uses IT extensively and no audit trail exists.

3. **Nature of tests of controls**—Tests of control might include making inquiries of entity personnel; inspection of documents, reports, or files, indicating performance of the control; observation of the application of the control; and auditor reperformance of the control. Note that inquiry alone is not sufficient to test controls. When controls are not documented, the auditor may be able to obtain evidence about their operating effectiveness by observation or the use of CAATs.

4. **Timing of tests of controls**—When obtaining evidence about the effectiveness of controls for an interim period, the auditor should determine what evidence is required for the remaining period. If planning to rely on controls that have changed since last tested, the auditor should test those controls currently. If planning to rely on controls that have not changed since last tested, the auditor should test the operating effectiveness of those controls at least every third year (i.e., no more than two years should pass before retesting such controls).

> **Note**
> *When the auditor identifies a significant risk of material misstatement, but plans to rely on the effectiveness of controls that mitigate that risk, the auditor should test those controls in the current period.*

5. **Extent of tests of controls**—When a control is applied on a transaction basis (e.g., matching approved purchase orders to suppliers' invoices) and if the control operates frequently, the auditor should use audit sampling techniques to test operating effectiveness; when a control is applied on a periodic basis (e.g., monthly reconciliation of the accounts receivable subsidiary ledger to the general ledger), the auditor should perform procedures appropriate for testing smaller populations.

F. **Substantive Procedures**—The issues related to the auditor's search for material misstatements will be discussed later in connection with lessons on audit evidence.

VI. Evaluating the Sufficiency and Appropriateness of the Audit Evidence Obtained

A. An audit is an iterative process, so the planned audit procedures may need to be modified; for example, identified misstatements from substantive procedures may alter the auditor's judgment about the effectiveness of controls.

B. Consider all relevant audit evidence—The auditor should consider all relevant audit evidence, whether it appears to corroborate or contradict the relevant assertions.

VII. Documentation—The auditor should document the following:

A. The overall responses to address the assessed risk of misstatement at the financial statement level;

B. The nature, timing, and extent of the further audit procedures;

C. The linkage of those procedures with the assessed risks at the relevant assertion level;

D. The results of the audit procedures; *and*

E. The conclusions reached in the current audit about the operating effectiveness of controls tested in a prior audit.

Internal Control—Required Communications

After studying this lesson, you should be able to:

1. Know the meaning of the terms *significant deficiency* and *material weakness*.

2. Understand the auditor's responsibility to communicate identified internal control deficiencies to management and those charged with governance, in accordance with AICPA Professional Standards.

I. Required Communications Related to Internal Control Deficiencies (Weaknesses)

Definitions

Control Deficiency: When the design or operation of a control does not allow management or employees, in the normal course of performing their assigned functions, to prevent or detect misstatements on a timely basis.

Deficiency in Design: When a control necessary to meet the control objective is missing, or when the control objective is not always met, even if the control operates as designed.

Deficiency in Operation: When a properly designed control does not operate as designed, or when the person performing the control does not have the authority or competence to effectively perform the control.

Significant Deficiency: A deficiency (or combination of deficiencies) in internal control that is less severe than a material weakness, yet important enough to merit attention by those charged with governance.

Material Weakness: A deficiency (or combination of deficiencies) in internal control such that there is a reasonable possibility that a material misstatement of the entity's financial statements will not be prevented or detected and corrected on a timely basis.

A. **Evaluating Control Deficiencies**—The auditor must determine whether identified deficiencies are significant deficiencies or material weaknesses.

1. The auditor should consider both the likelihood and potential magnitude of misstatement in making that evaluation—multiple control deficiencies affecting the same financial statement item increases the likelihood of misstatement.

2. The auditor may wish to consider the possible mitigating effects of compensating controls that can reduce the severity of the effects of a deficiency.

3. Risk factors that affect whether there is a reasonable possibility that a deficiency will result in a misstatement include the following:

   a. The nature of the accounts, classes of transactions, disclosures, and assertions involved;

   b. The susceptibility of the related asset or liability to loss or fraud;

   c. The subjectivity, complexity, or extent of judgment involved;

   d. The interaction or relationship of the control with other controls;

   e. The interaction among the deficiencies; *and*

   f. The possible future consequences of the deficiency.

4. Specific indicators of material weaknesses include the following:

   a. Identification of any fraud involving senior management (whether or not material);

    b. Restatement of previously issued financial statements to correct a material misstatement due to error or fraud;

    c. Identification of a material misstatement in the financial statements by the auditor that would not have been identified by the entity's internal control; *and*

    d. Ineffective oversight of the entity's financial reporting and internal control by those charged with governance.

II. Communicating Identified Control Deficiencies—The auditor must communicate the significant deficiencies and material weaknesses identified in the audit.

  A. Form of Communication—Identified significant deficiencies and material weaknesses must be communicated in writing to management and those charged with governance. Certain matters may not be communicated to management when communication would be inappropriate (e.g., matters that raise questions about management integrity or competence). Lesser matters (not significant deficiencies) may be communicated to the appropriate level of operational management with the authority to take remedial action. Such lesser matters may be communicated either orally or in writing.

  B. Timing—The required communication is best made by the "report release date" and should be made no later than 60 days following the report release date. The "report release date" is the date that the auditor grants the entity permission to use the auditor's report in connection with the audited financial statements.

  C. Early Communication is Permitted—The auditor may choose to verbally communicate certain significant deficiencies and material weaknesses during the audit (e.g., to permit timely correction). However, all identified significant deficiencies and material weaknesses must still be communicated in writing no later than 60 days following the report release date, including those matters communicated orally during the audit.

  D. Other Matters—The auditor may choose to communicate other matters believed to be beneficial to the entity (including deficiencies that are not "significant deficiencies") either in writing or verbally. If communicated verbally, the auditor must document such communication.

  E. The written communication about significant deficiencies and material weaknesses should:

    1. State that the purpose of the audit was to express an opinion on the financial statements, not to express an opinion on the effectiveness of internal control

    2. State that the auditor is not expressing an opinion on the effectiveness of internal control

    3. State that the auditor's consideration of internal control was not designed to identify all significant deficiencies or material weaknesses.

    4. Include the definition of the terms *material weakness* and *significant deficiency*, as applicable.

    5. Identify the matters that are considered to be material weaknesses and significant deficiencies, as applicable.

    6. State that the communication is intended solely for the use of management, those charged with governance, and others within the organization (it should not be used by anyone other than those specified parties)—if such a communication is required to be given to a governmental authority, that specific reference may be added.

> **Note**
> *The auditor may include additional statements regarding the general inherent limitations of internal control, including the possibility of management override, but such comments are not required.*

Sample Written Communication about Internal Control Deficiencies

In planning and performing our audit of the financial statements of ABC Company (the "Company") as of and for the year ended December 31, 20XX, in accordance with auditing standards generally accepted in the United States of America, we considered the Company's internal control over financial reporting (internal control) as a basis for designing our auditing procedures for the purpose of expressing our opinion on the financial statements, but not for the purpose of expressing an opinion on the effectiveness of the Company's internal control. Accordingly, we do not express an opinion on the effectiveness of the Company's internal control.

Our consideration of internal control was for the limited purpose described in the preceding paragraph and was not designed to identify all deficiencies in internal control that might be significant deficiencies or material weaknesses and therefore, there can be no assurance that all deficiencies, significant deficiencies, or material weaknesses have been identified. However, as discussed below, we identified certain deficiencies in internal control that we consider to be material weaknesses (and other deficiencies that we consider to be significant deficiencies—*add this phrase only if applicable*).

A deficiency in internal control exists when the design or operation of a control does not allow management or employees, in the normal course of performing their assigned functions, to prevent, or detect and correct misstatements on a timely basis. A material weakness is a deficiency, or a combination of deficiencies, in internal control, such that there is a reasonable possibility that a material misstatement of the entity's financial statements will not be prevented, or detected and corrected on a timely basis. (We consider the following deficiencies in the Company's internal control to be material weaknesses:)

(*Describe the material weaknesses that were identified.*)

(A significant deficiency is a deficiency, or a combination of deficiencies, in internal control that is less severe than a material weakness, yet important enough to merit attention by those charged with governance. We consider the following deficiencies to be significant deficiencies in internal control:)

(*Describe the significant deficiencies that were identified.*)

This communication is intended solely for the information and use of management, (*identify the body or individuals charged with governance*), others within the organization, and (*identify any specified governmental authorities*) and is not intended to be and should not be used by anyone other than these specified parties.

F. The auditor should not issue a written communication stating that no significant deficiencies were identified—However, the auditor is permitted to add a comment that no material weaknesses were identified, perhaps as requested to submit to a governmental authority.

G. Management may issue a written response to the auditor's communication to indicate corrective action taken or planned or stating management's belief that the costs of correction exceed the benefits—If such a written response is included with the auditor's communication, the auditor should add a paragraph to disclaim an opinion on management's written response.

Using the Work of an Internal Audit Function

After studying this lesson, you should be able to:

1. Understand the independent auditor's responsibilities to evaluate the internal auditors' competence and objectivity when considering the role of an entity's internal audit function for purposes of assessing control risk and/or providing assistance with substantive procedures.

I. **AICPA Guidance**—The relevant AICPA guidance is provided by AU 610 (SAS No. 128), *Using the Work of Internal Auditors,* which has been clarified to be consistent with International Standards on Auditing.

> **Note**
> The requirements of this standard do not apply if (1) the activities of the internal audit function are not relevant to the audit, or (2) the external auditor does not expect to use the work of the internal audit function in obtaining audit evidence. There is no requirement that external auditors use the work of an internal audit function.
>
> The AICPA defines an **internal audit function** as "a function of an entity that performs assurance and consulting activities designed to evaluate and improve the effectiveness of the entity's governance, risk management, and internal control processes."

II. **Two Ways to Use the Work of an Internal Audit Function**—The external auditor may use the internal audit function to (1) obtain audit evidence that modifies the nature, timing, or extent of audit procedures to be performed by the external auditor; and/or (2) provide direct assistance to the external auditor under the external auditor's direction, supervision, and review.

   A. Using the internal audit function **to obtain audit evidence** means, in effect, substituting the internal auditors' work (related to tests of controls and/or substantive procedures) in place of work that would otherwise be performed by the external auditor.

   1. There are three necessary conditions before the external auditor may use the internal audit function to obtain audit evidence

      a. **Objectivity**—The internal audit function's organizational status (dealing with the level to whom the function reports, such as those charged with governance, rather than middle management) and relevant policies and procedures must support the objectivity of the internal auditors.

      b. **Competence**—The internal auditors must be competent (related to their education, experience, certification, etc.) to perform reliable work.

      c. **Systematic and disciplined approach**—The internal audit function must apply a "systematic and disciplined approach, including quality control." The external auditor should not rely on "internal audit–like" work that is conducted in an informal, unstructured, or ad hoc way. However, the degree of formality and structure may vary with the nature, size, and complexity of the entity involved.

   2. **Significant judgments**—The external auditor should make all significant audit judgments.

   3. The external auditor should perform more of the work directly when (a) the degree of judgment involved increases, (b) the assessed risk of material misstatement increases, (c) the organizational status and objectivity of the internal auditors decreases, or (d) the competence of the internal auditors decreases.

   4. Procedures to be performed by the external auditor when using the work of the internal audit function to obtain audit evidence include the following:

    a. The external auditor should read the internal audit function's reports related to the work the external auditor plans to use;

    b. The external auditor should perform procedures to determine whether the internal audit function's work was adequately planned, performed, reviewed, and documented, and whether the conclusions reached were appropriate; *and*

    c. The external auditor should reperform some of the internal audit function's work that the external auditor plans to use.

  5. **Communication with those charged with governance**—The external auditor should communicate plans to use the work of the internal audit function to obtain audit evidence.

B. Using the internal audit function **to provide direct assistance** means using internal auditors to perform audit procedures subject to the external auditor's direction, supervision, and review.

  1. There are two necessary conditions before the external auditor may use the internal audit function to obtain audit evidence.

> **Note**
> *A systematic and disciplined approach is not a requirement for using the internal audit function to provide direct assistance, since the internal auditors' work is subject to the direction, supervision, and review of the external auditor.*

    a. **Objectivity**—The internal audit function's organizational status and relevant policies and procedures must support the objectivity of the internal auditors.

    b. **Competence**—The internal auditors must be competent to perform reliable work.

  2. **Determining the nature and extent of the internal auditors' direct assistance**—The external auditor should consider the internal audit function's objectivity and competence, the assessed risk of material misstatement, and the amount of judgment involved.

  3. Procedures to be performed by the external auditor when using the internal audit function to provide direct assistance

    a. The external auditor should obtain written acknowledgment from management or those charged with governance (either as part of the engagement letter or as a separate document) that the internal auditors will be allowed to follow the external auditor's directives without interference.

    b. The external auditor should appropriately direct, supervise, and review the work performed by the internal auditors.

    c. The external auditor should test some of the work performed by the internal auditors.

  4. Communication with those charged with governance—The external auditor should communicate how the auditor plans to use the internal auditors to provide direct assistance.

III. Documentation Requirements

A. When using the internal audit function to obtain audit evidence, the external auditor should document the following:

  1. The evaluation of the internal audit function's organizational status and objectivity of the internal auditors, the function's competence, and the application of a systematic and disciplined approach;

  2. The nature and extent of the work used and the basis for that decision; *and*

  3. The external auditor's procedures performed to evaluate the work of the internal audit function.

B. When using the internal audit function to provide direct assistance—the external auditor should document the following:

1. The evaluation of the internal audit function's organizational status and objectivity of the internal auditors and the function's competence;

2. The basis for the external auditor's decision about the nature and extent of the work performed by the internal auditors; and

3. Identification of the working papers prepared by the internal auditors, and the nature and extent of the external auditor's review and testing of the internal auditors' work.

Note
There is no division of responsibility regarding the work of the internal auditors. The external auditor's report should not refer to the internal auditors' work in the audit report! The external auditor remains fully responsible for all the conclusions expressed.

Performing Further Procedures and Obtaining Evidence

Internal Control: Transaction Cycles

Specific Transaction Cycles

After studying this lesson, you should be able to:

1. Understand what is meant by the term *transaction cycle* and why auditors tend to focus on transaction cycles when assessing control risk.

2. Identify several examples of transaction cycles that an auditor might consider.

I. **Transaction Cycle**—A transaction cycle is a group of essentially homogeneous transactions, that is, transactions of a particular type. The bulk of a company's economic activities can be grouped into a relative few categories called transaction cycles.

II. **Implication**—Within a given category of transactions, control risk is essentially constant, since all transactions within that category are processed subject to the same configuration of internal control policies and procedures. A transaction cycle is, therefore, the highest level of aggregation for which control risk may be viewed as a constant.

III. **Transaction Cycles Covered in This Lesson**

   A. Revenue/receipts

   B. Expenditures/disbursements

   C. Payroll

   D. Inventory, especially manufactured inventory (since purchased inventory would be similar to expenditures/disbursements as presented here)

   E. Fixed assets

   F. Investing/financing

Exam Hint
As a tool to analyze the audit considerations of internal control policies and procedures in each transaction cycle, remember that internal controls (specifically, "control activities") should "SCARE"! Note that this is intended to be a helpful memory aid simply to recall some basic points of emphasis that are useful to auditors in looking at the relative strength or weakness of controls in a particular transaction cycle. In this context, "SCARE" represents:

Segregation of duties,

Controls (as in physical controls),

Authorization,

Reviews (as in performance reviews), *and*

EDP/IT (information processing).

IV. **The Framework "SCARE"**—This acronym is easy to remember and it is helpful in identifying relevant internal control considerations that are associated with "control activities" in the AICPA Professional Standards:

   A. **Segregation of Duties**—This is also referred to as separation of duties and involves separating incompatible functions to the extent possible. The same employee should not normally (1) authorize transactions (execution function), (2) have access to the related assets (custody function), and (3) perform accounting activities (record keeping function) in the ordinary course of duties. In essence, these three

> **Note**
> *The applicable SAS describes control activities in terms of five specific considerations: (1) authorization; (2) segregation of duties; (3) physical controls; (4) information processing; and (5) performance reviews.*

activities are like points on a triangle and each point of the triangle should ideally be vested in different employees, subject to cost-benefit considerations.

B. Controls (Physical Controls)—Access to assets (and to important accounting documents and computer systems) should be limited to authorized personnel. In addition, assets should be periodically counted, as appropriate, and compared to the corresponding accounting records for agreement. This is important in safeguarding assets and in establishing accountability for assets.

C. Authorization—Transactions should be executed in accordance with management's authorization.

D. Reviews (Performance Reviews)—Actual performance should be compared to appropriate budgets and forecasts. Internal data should be compared to external sources of information as appropriate. Analyses of relationships should be performed and investigative and corrective action should be taken as needed.

E. EDP/IT (Information Processing)—Information technology (IT) controls consist of two basic categories:

> **Note**
> EDP *as used here is an outdated reference to* electronic data processing *that has been replaced by the more contemporary term* IT *for information technology.*

1. General controls, which are policies and procedures that have widespread effect on many specific applications

2. Application controls, which refer specifically to the processing of particular computer applications

Revenue/Receipts—Sales

> **After studying this lesson, you should be able to:**
>
> **1.** Identify the primary accounting documents and internal control objectives associated with an entity's revenue-receipts cycle (with emphasis on sales recognition).
>
> **2.** Understand the primary control activities normally associated with an entity's revenue-receipts cycle (with emphasis on sales recognition).

I.   Flow Chart of Typical Internal Controls for Sales

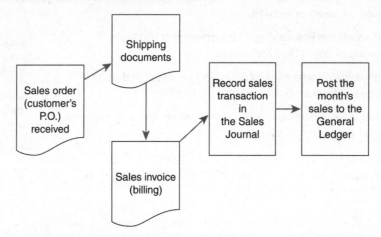

II. Internal Control Objectives—The objectives of internal controls in this area are to provide reasonable assurance that:

   A. Goods and services are provided in accordance with management's authorization (and based on approved orders).

   B. Terms of sale (including prices and any discounts) are in accordance with management's authorization.

   C. Credit terms and limits are properly established (as authorized).

   D. Deliveries of goods and services result in accurate and timely billings.

   E. Any sales-related discounts and adjustments (including returns) are in accordance with management's authorization.

III. Audit Considerations (Framed by "SCARE")—The entity's control activities should address the following matters:

   A. Segregation of duties—Separate the execution (authorization), record-keeping (accounting), and custody (access) functions.

   1. Credit to customers should be granted by an independent department (separate from sales staff which may be paid on commission and which may have an incentive to view everyone as creditworthy).

   2. An independent employee should review the statements to customers.

   3. Returns should be accounted for by an independent clerk in the shipping/receiving area.

   B. Controls (Physical Controls)

   1. Computer passwords should be used to limit unauthorized access to the accounting systems.

   2. Any inventory involved should be secured with access limited to authorized personnel.

C. Authorization—The entity's transactions should be executed as authorized by management.

1. Management should review the terms of sales transactions and indicate that approval on the sales invoice (billing).

2. Management should usually establish general approvals of transactions within specified limits and specifically approve transactions outside of those prescribed limits.

3. Management should approve the entity's adjusting journal entries.

D. Reviews (Performance Reviews)

1. The entity's recorded sales should be compared to appropriate budgets and forecasts.

2. Related accounting documents should be compared on a timely basis—for example, sales invoices and shipping documents should be compared to verify that the sales transactions were recorded in the proper period, which is referred to as proper cutoff.

E. EDP/IT (Information Processing)—The auditor should agree the financial statement amount(s) to the applicable general ledger account(s).

1. Important accounting documents (e.g., shipping documents and sales invoices) should be prenumbered and the numerical sequence should be accounted for.

2. An aged trial balance for accounts receivable should be agreed (or reconciled) to the general ledger control account; the aging provides important information about the quality of the receivables and the need for follow-up audit procedures.

Revenue/Receipts—Cash

After studying this lesson, you should be able to:

1. Identify the primary accounting documents and internal control objectives associated with an entity's revenue-receipts cycle (with emphasis on cash collection).

2. Understand the primary control activities normally associated with an entity's revenue-receipts cycle (with emphasis on cash collection).

I. **Flow Chart of Typical Processing of Cash Receipts**

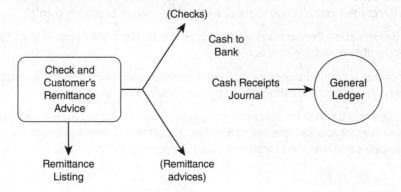

II. **Internal Control Objectives**—The objectives of internal controls in this area are to provide reasonable assurance that:

A. Access to cash receipts records and accounts receivable records is limited to authorized personnel.

B. Detailed cash and account balance records are reconciled with control accounts and bank statements at least monthly.

C. All cash receipts are correctly recorded in the period received.

III. **Audit Considerations (Framed by "SCARE")**—The entity's control activities should address the following matters:

A. **Segregation of Duties**

1. A listing of cash receipts (sometimes referred to as a *remittance listing* or *log of cash receipts*) is prepared upon opening the mail in the mail room; checks are restrictively endorsed immediately ("for deposit only . . . ")

2. Cash-related activities, which are handled by separate personnel as appropriate are as follows:

    a. Opening the mail—handling the checks received, and verifying the accuracy of the payment indicated on the enclosed "remittance advice" (the stub returned with the customer's payment on account)

    b. Making the deposit—deposits should be made daily

    c. Applying payments received to the appropriate customers' accounts receivable

    d. Preparing the bank reconciliation on a timely basis

B. **Controls (Physical Controls)**

1. Employees with access to cash receipts should be "bonded," which is a type of insurance for which the employer pays an insurance premium and which involves background checks on the applicable employees.

2. Receipts should be deposited daily, not accumulated in someone's desk drawer for an occasional deposit.

3. Access to cash receipts (including access to documents) should be limited to those authorized—that includes the appropriate use of passwords.

4. The company might use a *lockbox* whereby payments from customers are directly received by the bank, thereby avoiding the company's mail room.

C. Authorization—The entity's transactions should be executed as authorized by management.

1. Adjusting journal entries should be approved by management.

2. Bank reconciliations should be appropriately reviewed with the reviewer's approval indicated.

D. Reviews (Performance Reviews)

1. The initial cash receipts listing from the mail room should be compared to the total according to the cash receipts journal, and traced to that day's bank deposit to show that what was received was, in fact, deposited.

2. The cash accounts should be reconciled with the bank statements on a timely basis by someone not involved in handling cash receipts or updating the accounting records.

E. EDP/IT (Information Processing)

1. In general, there should be adequate documentation supporting transactions and account balances (important documents should be prenumbered and the numerical sequence properly accounted for).

2. For cash transactions received *on site,* there should be adequate *point of sale* cash registers and use of prenumbered receipts.

Expenditures/Disbursements

After studying this lesson, you should be able to:

1. Identify the primary accounting documents and internal control objectives associated with an entity's expenditure/disbursements cycle.

2. Understand the primary control activities normally associated with an entity's expenditure/disbursements cycle.

I. Flow Chart of Typical Processing for Expenditures/Disbursements

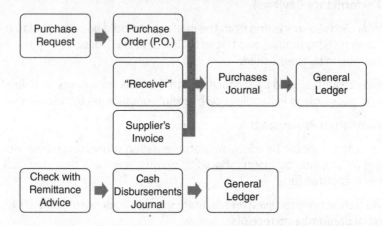

II. Objectives of Internal Controls over Purchases and Accounts Payable—The objectives are to provide reasonable assurance that:

A. Goods and services are obtained in accordance with management's authorization and based on approved orders—considering quantity, quality, vendors, etc. This is usually handled by a separate "Purchasing Department" to centralize these activities.

B. The terms of acquisitions (including prices and quantities) are in accordance with management's authorization.

C. All goods and services received are accurately accounted for on a timely basis.

D. Adjustments to vendor accounts are made according to management's authorization.

E. Only authorized goods and services are accepted and paid for (and payments are timely to take advantage of any cash discounts available for prompt payment).

F. Amounts payable for goods and services received are accurately recorded and properly classified.

G. Access to purchasing, receiving, and accounts payable records is limited to authorized personnel.

III. Objectives of Internal Controls over Cash Disbursements—The objectives are to provide reasonable assurance that:

A. Disbursements are for authorized expenditures as approved by management.

B. Disbursements are recorded at the proper amounts and with the appropriate classifications.

C. Periodic comparisons are made between the supporting detailed accounting records (including bank reconciliations) and the general ledger control accounts.

D. Any adjusting journal entries for cash accounts are in accordance with management's authorization.

E. Access to cash and disbursement records is limited to authorized personnel.

IV. **Audit Considerations (Framed by "SCARE")**—The entity's control activities should address the following matters related to the expenditures/disbursement transactions cycle:

A. **Segregation of Duties**

1. A separate purchasing department handles the purchasing activities (after a duly approved request for goods or services has been received from the department making the request).

2. The purchasing personnel (execution function) are independent of those in receiving (custody function) and in accounting (record-keeping function), including the accounts payable personnel. The accounts payable personnel should also be independent of those involved in processing the related cash disbursements.

3. Bank reconciliations are prepared by someone not having other involvement in handling cash receipts, cash disbursements, or record keeping.

B. **Controls (Physical Controls)**

1. There should be appropriate physical control over unused checks to limit access to authorized personnel.

2. Employees with the ability to initiate cash disbursements should be "bonded."

3. Access to cash disbursements or to related documents should be limited to authorized personnel.

C. **Authorization**—The entity's transactions should be executed as authorized by management.

1. All adjusting journal entries should be approved by management.

2. Only authorized personnel should be able to order goods and services on the company's behalf.

3. The department requesting the purchase of goods or services should indicate their acceptance of the goods or services received and approval, before payment is made.

D. **Reviews (Performance Reviews)**

1. An appropriate employee should compare the suppliers' monthly statements with recorded payables.

2. An appropriate employee should compare the purchase order, "receiver," and vendor's invoice for agreement to establish that the invoice is for goods and services received and as authorized. (The invoice should be approved before payment is made and available cash discounts for prompt payment should be taken.)

E. **EDP/IT (Information Processing)**

1. Detailed records should be maintained to support the general ledger payable account.

2. Prenumbered purchase orders should be used (and the numerical sequence accounted for).

3. Prenumbered checks should be used (and the numerical sequence accounted for).

4. The supporting documents (including vendors' invoices) should be canceled as "paid" immediately upon payment to prevent double payments.

5. Two signatures should be required on checks. (Any signature plates should be kept in a secure place to prevent unauthorized use.)

F. Note the difference between a "vouchers payable" system and an "accounts payable" system:

1. An **accounts payable** system keeps track of payables by the name of the vendor. (Hence, payables are identified by the total amount owed to the various individual suppliers.)

2. A **vouchers payable** system keeps track of individual transactions without summarizing amounts owed in total to individual vendors. (There can be numerous vouchers payable to an individual vendor, but the payables are identified by voucher number, not by vendor name. An entity that uses a vouchers payable system can confirm individual transactions, but cannot confirm the total amount owed to a given vendor, which has implications to the vendor's auditor and how confirmation requests should be designed.)

Payroll Cycle

After studying this lesson, you should be able to:

1. Identify the primary accounting documents and internal control objectives associated with an entity's payroll cycle.

2. Understand the primary control activities normally associated with an entity's payroll cycle.

I. **Flow Chart of Typical Internal Controls for Payroll**

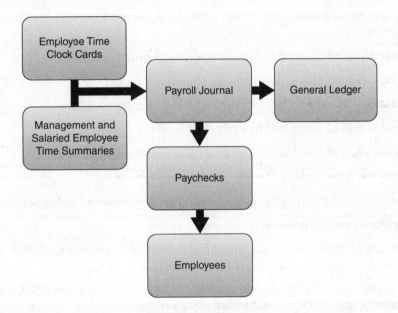

II. **Objectives of Internal Controls over Payroll**—The objectives are to provide reasonable assurance that:

A. Payroll withholdings and deductions are based on appropriate supporting authorizations.

B. Compensation is made only to valid employees at authorized rates and for services actually rendered.

C. Gross pay, withholdings, deductions, and net pay are correctly computed.

D. Payroll costs and liabilities are appropriately classified and summarized in the proper periods.

E. Appropriate comparisons are made of personnel, payroll, and work records at reasonable intervals.

F. Net pay and related withholdings are remitted to the appropriate employees and agencies.

G. Access to sensitive personnel files and payroll records is limited to authorized personnel.

III. **Audit Considerations (Framed by "SCARE")**—The entity's control activities should address the following matters:

A. **Segregation of Duties**

1. The following activities should be performed by different personnel when circumstances permit:

a. Establishing and maintaining employee files in the personnel department

b. Timekeeping

    c. Payroll preparation and updating the accounting records

    d. Check distribution

    e. Reconciling the payroll bank account with the general ledger account

  2. The treasurer should typically sign the payroll checks.

  3. An appropriate departmental supervisor should distribute the payroll checks to employees in that department.

  4. Unclaimed checks should be controlled. That is, they should be returned to treasury, secured, and eventually destroyed, if not claimed within an appropriate time.

B. Controls (Physical Controls)

  1. Access to personnel files (containing sensitive information) should be limited to authorized personnel.

  2. Access to payroll checks should be limited to authorized personnel.

  3. Personnel with access to payroll checks should be bonded.

C. Authorization—The entity's transactions should be executed as authorized by management.

  1. Payroll should be authorized by a responsible official.

  2. Payroll computations should be verified by an independent person.

  3. Overtime payments should be approved by management.

  4. Payroll for management should also be appropriately reviewed and approved.

D. Reviews (Performance Reviews)

  1. A company should maintain current and accurate payroll information (which should be periodically matched with information in the personnel files).

  2. The payroll checks written should be reconciled to the payroll register, serving as the supporting accounting record for each payroll period.

  3. Other appropriate reconciliations should be made on a timely basis: for example, in a manufacturing environment, someone should reconcile the job cost time sheets to time clock cards. (For strict internal control purposes, a company should use time clocks where possible.)

E. EDP/IT (Information Processing)

  1. Payroll checks should be prenumbered (and the numerical sequence accounted for).

  2. A company should maintain a separate checking account specifically for payroll transactions to establish more accountability and control over these important transactions.

Miscellaneous Cycles

After studying this lesson, you should be able to:

1. Identify the internal-control objectives associated with miscellaneous transaction cycles (manufactured inventory, fixed assets, and investing/financing).

2. Understand the primary control activities normally associated with miscellaneous transaction cycles.

I. **Production/Manufacturing Inventory**

    A. **The Major Objectives of Internal Controls**—In this area, the primary objectives are to provide reasonable assurance that:

        1. The resources obtained and used in production (including raw materials, work-in-process, and finished goods) are accurately recorded on a timely basis.

        2. Transfers of finished products to customers or others are accurately recorded.

        3. Related expenditures are appropriately classified.

        4. Access to all categories of inventory (and inventory-related documents) is limited to authorized personnel.

        5. Comparisons of actual inventory on hand are made to recorded amounts at least annually.

    B. **Audit Considerations (Framed by "SCARE")**—The entity's control activities should address the following matters:

        1. **Segregation of duties**

            a. To the extent possible, the company should separate the authorization of inventory-related transactions, the custody of (or access to) inventory, and the accounting record keeping activities.

            b. Sales returns (inventory) should be immediately counted by the receiving clerk and a *receiver* (i.e., a receiving document) prepared to verify the quantity and condition of the goods received.

        2. **Controls (physical controls)**

            a. Access to the inventory should be limited to authorized personnel (the inventory should be physically secured with access restricted to personnel having authorized keys or passcodes).

            b. Access to the important accounting documents, including applicable shipping documents, should be limited to authorized personnel.

        3. **Authorization**—The entity's transactions should be executed as authorized by management.

            a. The acquisition and distribution of inventory should be consistent with management's authorization.

            b. Management should establish general approvals of transactions within specified limits, and specifically approve transactions above those limits.

            c. Any adjusting journal entries (including sales returns and allowances, or adjustments to inventory, such as write-downs) should be approved by management.

        4. **Reviews (performance reviews)**

            a. Actual inventory should be compared periodically to recorded inventory (and any unusual differences should be investigated).

b. In a manufacturing context, appropriate reconciliations should be made of underlying accounting records (including applicable job order cost sheets or process cost worksheets) to the applicable inventory-related general ledger accounts.

5. EDP/IT (information processing)

a. The company should use prenumbered purchase orders for raw materials and components of production, along with prenumbered receivers, the receiving document. (The numerical sequence of these documents should be properly accounted for.)

b. The company should consider using a perpetual inventory system for items with high cost per unit.

c. The company should maintain adequate support for related general ledger control accounts.

II. Fixed Assets Cycle—The major objectives of internal controls in this area are to provide reasonable assurance that:

A. Transactions involving property, plant, and equipment are accurately recorded and classified; and are in accordance with management's authorization.

B. Estimates used in the determination of depreciation, depletion, and amortization of the assets' cost basis are reasonable and consistent over time; any changes should be properly approved.

C. Fixed assets are reasonably secure from loss with appropriate property insurance in force.

D. Supporting detailed records are maintained and periodically compared to the assets on hand.

E. Any adjusting journal entries related to fixed assets are approved by the management.

III. Investing/Financing Cycle—The major objectives of internal controls in this area are to provide reasonable assurance that:

A. Transactions involving investments and financing are accurately recorded and classified on a timely basis; and as authorized by management.

1. Investing—As used here, this refers to decisions related to the composition of the company's portfolio of investment assets, both current and noncurrent.

2. Financing—This refers to decisions related to the structure of the company's noncurrent liabilities and stockholders' equity sections of the balance sheet.

B. Investment assets should be reasonably secure from loss with procedures established to monitor the associated risks. Access should be limited to authorized personnel with appropriate segregation of duties.

C. Supporting detailed records should be maintained and compared periodically to actual investment-related assets of the company.

D. Any adjusting journal entries related to investment-related assets, liabilities, or stockholders' equity are approved by management.

Audit Evidence: Concepts and Standards

Overview of Substantive Procedures

After studying this lesson, you should be able to:

1. Know the two categories of "substantive" audit procedures (and the two categories of "tests of details").

2. Know the meaning of the term *analytical procedures*, the three general purposes served by analytical procedures, and the four considerations that determine the efficiency and effectiveness of analytical procedures that are used for substantive purposes.

3. Familiarize yourself with the fundamental ratios that are most often associated with the auditor's substantive analytical procedures.

I. **The Audit Risk Model**—Recall the *audit risk model* that applies to the assertion level for classes of transactions, account balances, and disclosures (note that this audit risk model does not apply at the overall financial statement level): **AR = IR × CR × DR**; where detection risk is the only component within the auditor's direct influence and which is essentially set by specifying the nature, timing, and extent of the auditor's substantive audit procedures.

A. **Nature**—The auditor has to decide what specific substantive procedures to perform. This includes determining how much emphasis should be placed on *tests of det ails* (which tend to be labor intensive and expensive, but which provide a relatively stronger basis for conclusions for most financial statement assertions) versus substantive *analytical procedures* (which tend to be less labor intensive and less expensive, but which provide a relatively weaker basis for conclusions for most financial statement assertions).

B. **Timing**—The auditor has to decide whether to perform the important substantive procedures, at an "interim" date (meaning any date prior to year-end and before the books are closed) or at "final" (at year-end and after the books are closed).

C. **Extent**—The auditor has to decide how large the samples sizes should be. Since the audit work is performed on a test basis, should the sample sizes be relatively large or can smaller sample sizes be justified?

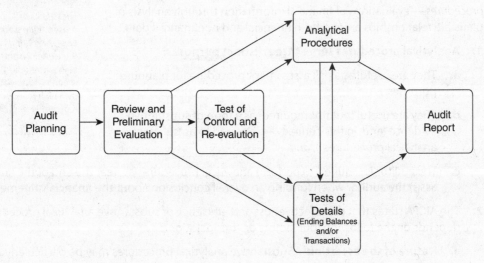

D. AU 330, *Performing Audit Procedures in Response to Assessed Risks and Evaluating the Audit Evidence Obtained,* states:

"In some cases, the auditor may find it impossible to design effective substantive procedures that, by themselves, provide sufficient appropriate audit evidence at the relevant assertion level. This may occur when an entity conducts its business using IT and no documentation of transactions is produced or maintained, other than through the IT system."

In such cases, the auditor would be required to perform tests of the relevant controls, in addition to the planned substantive procedures.

Question
Under these circumstances, what would be the consequences if the required tests of controls indicate that internal control is ineffective and cannot be relied on?

Answer:
If the auditor's substantive procedures by themselves are insufficient and if internal control is ineffective, the auditor would not have obtained sufficient appropriate evidence to afford a reasonable basis for the opinion. In other words, these circumstances would constitute a scope limitation!

II. **Substantive Audit Procedures**—These are audit procedures that are directly related to the financial statement elements and disclosures. Recall that the word substantive is derived from substantiate, which means "to verify that substantive procedures are those audit procedures designed to verify the entity's financial statement elements and disclosures" or, in other words, "to search for material misstatements if there are any."

   A. **Tests of Details**—These are the relatively precise (but usually rather expensive, labor-intensive) procedures (that suggest whether the client's recorded amounts are right or not).

Definition
Tests of Ending Balances: Verifying the client's recorded amounts by directly testing the composition making up the ending account balance.

Tests of Transactions: Verifying the client's recorded amounts by testing those relative few debits and credits (the transactions) that caused the account balance to change from last year's audited balance to this year's recorded balance.

   B. **Analytical Procedures**—Recall the AICPA definition of *analytical procedures*—"evaluations of financial information through analysis of plausible relationships among both financial and nonfinancial data."

Note
These tests of reasonableness involve analyzing trends and interrelationships—the key is developing a meaningful expectation by which to judge the reasonableness of the client's recorded amount.

   1. **Analytical procedures serve three distinct purposes:**

      a. They are useful as a risk assessment procedure for planning purposes;

      b. They are useful (but not required) as a form of substantive evidence (and, in this context, are referred to as "substantive analytical procedures"); *and*

      c. The auditor is required to perform analytical procedures as near the end of the audit to assist the auditor when forming an overall conclusion about the financial statements.

   2. The AICPA states that the effectiveness and efficiency of substantive analytical procedures depends on the following four factors or considerations:

      a. **Nature of the assertion**—Substantive analytical procedures may be particularly effective in testing for omissions of transactions that would be hard to detect with procedures that focus on recorded amounts. In other words, the skillful use of analytical procedures may be more effective than tests of details in addressing the completeness assertion, since there may be no supporting documents to examine for transactions that were not recorded in the first place!

    b. **Plausibility and predictability of the relationship**—Developing a meaningful expectation to compare to the client's recorded balance is critical to the skillful use of analytical procedures, so the predictability of the relationship is very important.

        i. Relationships in a stable environment are usually more predictable than those in a dynamic environment.

        ii. Relationships involving income statement accounts tend to be more predictable than those involving balance sheet accounts (since the income statement deals with a period of time rather than a single moment in time).

        iii. Relationships involving transactions subject to management discretion tend to be less predictable.

    c. **Availability and reliability of data used**—The reliability of the expectation increases when the data used is (1) obtained from independent outside sources; (2) when it is subject to audit testing (either currently or in the past); or (3) is developed under conditions of effective internal control.

    d. **Precision of the expectation**—The likelihood of detecting a misstatement decreases as the level of aggregation of the data increases. (That is, procedures would be less effective for "high altitude" global comparisons than for more focused, specific comparisons. In other words, relationships of interest to the auditor might be obscured by the noise in the data at a high level of aggregation, whereas those relationships might be more identifiable at a lower level of aggregation. For example, the auditor could focus on sales by month broken down by product line instead of simply comparing current annual sales currently to the prior year.)

3. **Selected ratios**—Such ratios may be tested in Auditing and Attestation as *analytical procedures* or in Financial Accounting and Reporting as *financial statement analysis*.

Definition

Liquidity Ratios (also known as solvency ratios): Measures of an entity's short-term ability to meet its obligations.

---

    a. *Working Capital* = Current assets – Current liabilities. This is a definition, not a ratio.

    b. *Current ratio* = Current assets/Current liabilities

    c. *Quick ratio (acid-test ratio)* = (Cash + Marketable securities + A/R)/Current liabilities

    d. *Current cash to debt ratio* = Net cash from operations/Average current liabilities

---

Definition

Activity Ratios (also known as turnover or efficiency ratios): Measures of an entity's effectiveness putting its assets to use.

---

    e. *Asset turnover* = Net sales/Average total assets

    f. *Receivable turnover* = Net (credit) sales/Average trade receivable (net)

    g. *Number of days sales in receivables* = 365 days/Receivable turnover

    h. *Inventory turnover* = Cost of goods sold/Average inventory

    i. *Number of days sales in inventory* = 365 days/Inventory turnover

---

Definition

Profitability Ratios: Measures of an entity's operating success (failure) for a period of time.

j. *Profit margin on sales* = Net income/Net sales

k. *Gross profit percentage* = (Sales – Cost of goods sold)/Sales

l. *Rate of return on assets* = Net income/Average total assets

m. *Rate of return on common stockholders' equity* = (Net income – Dividends attributable to preferred stockholders)/Average common stockholders' equity

n. *Earnings per share* = (Net income – Preferred dividends)/Average number of common shares outstanding

o. *Price earnings ratio (P-E ratio)* = Market price of stock/earnings per share

---

Definition

Coverage Ratios (also known as leverage ratios): Measures of the entity's ability to meet its obligations over time (i.e., measures of long-term risk to creditors and the extent to which the entity has borrowed up to its available capacity).

---

p. *Debt to total assets ratio* = Total liabilities/Total assets

q. *Debt to equity ratio* = Total liabilities/Total stockholders' equity

r. *Times interest earned* = Income before interest expense and income taxes/Interest expense

s. *Cash to debt coverage ratio* = Net cash from operations/Average total liabilities

The Nature of Evidence

After studying this lesson, you should be able to:

1. Understand the meaning of the terms sufficient and appropriate.

2. Know what constitutes *audit evidence.*

3. Identify the financial statement assertions specified in AICPA Professional Standards (separately by category of assertion: account balances at period end; transactions and events during the period; and presentation and disclosure), which can be used as broad audit objectives for which evidence must be obtained.

I. **Responsibilities under AICPA Professional Standards**—The relevant AICPA guidance is provided by AU 500, *Audit Evidence.* This pronouncement states that the auditor's objective is to "obtain sufficient appropriate audit evidence to be able to draw reasonable conclusions on which to base the auditor's opinion."

> One of the "Performance Principles" addresses the importance of obtaining sufficient appropriate audit evidence: "To obtain reasonable assurance, which is a high but not absolute level of assurance, the auditor

A. obtains sufficient appropriate audit evidence about whether material misstatements exist, through designing and implementing appropriate responses to the assessed risks."

II. **Audit Evidence**

> **Definitions**
>
> *Audit Evidence:* Information used by the auditor in arriving at the conclusions on which the auditor's opinion is based. Audit evidence includes both information contained in the accounting records underlying the financial statements and other information.
>
> *Accounting Records:* The records of initial accounting entries and supporting records, such as checks and records of electronic fund transfers, invoices, contracts, the general and subsidiary ledgers, journal entries and other adjustments to the financial statements that are not reflected in journal entries, and records, such as work sheets and spreadsheets, supporting cost allocations, computations, reconciliations and disclosures.
>
> *Other Information Constituting Audit Evidence:* Includes minutes of meetings, confirmations, industry analysts' reports, internal control manuals, and any other information obtained by inquiry, observation, and inspection.

III. **Sufficient Appropriate Audit Evidence**—"Sufficient" refers to the quantity of evidence, whereas "appropriate" refers to the quality of evidence in terms of its relevance and reliability.

A. The quantity of evidence required (related to "sufficient") is directly related to the risk of misstatement (the greater the risk, the more evidence is needed) and inversely related to the quality of evidence (the higher the quality, the less evidence is needed).

> **Note**
> *The auditor should obtain audit evidence by testing the accounting records, by analysis, review, and reconciling related information; however, the accounting records by themselves do not provide sufficient appropriate audit evidence.*

B. "Reliability" is affected by the source and nature of evidence and depends upon individual circumstances—however, the SAS offers the following guidelines:

   1. Evidence obtained directly by the auditor is more reliable than evidence obtained indirectly or by inference (e.g., observation of the application of a control is more reliable than inquiry of entity personnel about the application of a control).

   2. Evidence is more reliable when obtained from independent (knowledgeable) sources outside the entity;

   3. Evidence generated internally is more reliable when the related controls are effective;

   4. Evidence is more reliable when it exists in documentary form (whether paper or electronic); and

   5. Evidence provided by original documents is more reliable than evidence based on photocopies/facsimiles (faxes).

C. The auditor should consider the reliability of information used, but the auditor is not normally responsible for authenticating the entity's documents. The auditor should obtain evidence about the accuracy and completeness of information used to perform further audit procedures (either in connection with the actual audit procedure or by testing controls related to the information).

D. More assurance is obtained from consistent audit evidence obtained from different sources or of a different nature ("corroborating" information) than from evidence considered individually. When evidence from different sources is inconsistent, the auditor should determine what audit procedures are needed to resolve the inconsistency.

E. Professional judgment is required for "reasonable assurance," and the auditor does not examine all available evidence. The auditor may appropriately consider the cost of information relative to its usefulness, although cost alone is not a valid basis for omitting an audit procedure. Audit evidence is usually "persuasive" (or suggestive) and is rarely "conclusive" (or compelling). The auditor should not be satisfied with evidence that is less than persuasive.

IV. Using "Assertions" to Obtain Audit Evidence—In stating that the financial statements are consistent with GAAP, management makes several "assertions" (which are implicit or explicit statements of fact).

A. Historically, the auditing standards discussed five traditional financial statement assertions:

   1. Existence/occurrence;

   2. Completeness;

   3. Rights and obligations;

   4. Valuation and allocation; *and*

   5. Presentation and disclosure.

B. AICPA Professional Standards now classify assertions in three separate categories for the auditor's consideration, related to:

   1. Account balances;

   2. Presentation and disclosure; and

   3. Classes of transactions and events.

C. There are four assertions specific to "account balances at period end"

   1. **Existence**—That the assets, liabilities, and equity interests exist.

   2. **Completeness**—That all assets, liabilities, and equity interests that should have been recorded have been recorded. There are no omissions.

   3. **Rights and obligations**—That the entity holds or controls the rights to its assets, and the liabilities are the obligations of the entity. Any restrictions on the rights to the assets or obligations for the liabilities must be disclosed.

4. **Valuation and allocation**—That assets, liabilities, and equity interests are included in the financial statements at appropriate amounts (relative to the requirements of GAAP) and any resulting valuation or allocation adjustments are appropriately recorded.

D. **There are four assertions about "presentation and disclosure."**

1. **Occurrence and rights and obligations**—That the disclosed events and transactions have occurred and pertain to the entity.

2. **Completeness**—That all disclosures that should have been included have been included. There are no omissions of required disclosures.

3. **Classification and understandability**—That financial information is appropriately presented, described, and clearly expressed.

4. **Accuracy and valuation**—That financial and other information are disclosed fairly and at appropriate amounts.

E. **There are five assertions about "classes of transactions and events during the period."**

1. **Accuracy**—That amounts and other data have been recorded appropriately.

2. **Occurrence**—That transactions and events that have been recorded have occurred. In other words, they are properly recorded and valid.

3. **Completeness**—That all transactions and events that should have been recorded have been recorded. There are no omissions.

4. **Cutoff**—That transactions and events have been recorded in the correct accounting period. Note that there are only two ways to record a transaction in the wrong period. One is by recorded a transaction prematurely, which violates the "occurrence" assertion; and the other is to record a transaction belatedly, which violates the "completeness" assertion.

Note
"Cutoff" is actually redundant in this context, since establishing "occurrence" (that the recorded transactions are properly recorded) and "completeness" (that there are no omissions of transactions that should have been recorded) together establish that the transactions, in fact, have been recorded in the correct accounting period ("cutoff"). However, "cutoff" is an important issue that auditors must address, so this redundancy emphasizes an important auditing concept.

5. **Classification**—That transactions and events have been recorded in the proper accounts.

	Categories of Assertions		
	Account Balances at End of Period	Presentation and Disclosure	Transactions and Events During the Period
Existence/Occurrence	Applicable	Applicable	Applicable
Completeness	Applicable	Applicable	Applicable
Rights and Obligations	Applicable	N/A separately (included with Occurrence)	N/A
Accuracy and Valuation; or Valuation and Allocation	Applicable	Applicable	Applicable
Classification; or Classification and Understandability	N/A	Applicable	Applicable
Cutoff	N/A — implicit	N/A	Applicable

F. This SAS points out that the auditor may use the assertions as presented above or express them differently as long as the relevant issues have been addressed. For example, the auditor may combine the assertions about transactions and events with those about account balances; and the auditor may decline to identify a separate assertion about "cutoff" if occurrence and completeness have been established.

G. The auditor should use "relevant assertions" (those that have a meaningful bearing on whether the account is fairly stated) to assess the risk of material misstatement. The auditor should evaluate the nature of the assertion, the volume of transactions or data involved, and the complexity of the systems (including IT) by which the entity processes and controls the information related to the assertion.

Assertions and Types of Audit Procedures

> **After studying this lesson, you should be able to:**
>
> 1. Understand the auditor's responsibility to plan and perform substantive procedures in order to be responsive to the assessed risks of material misstatement, according to AICPA Professional Standards.
>
> 2. Know the three categories of audit procedures.

I. **Audit Procedures for Obtaining Evidence**—The auditor's basis for conclusion is comprised of three categories of procedures:

    A. Risk assessment procedures

    B. Tests of controls

    C. Substantive procedures

Definitions

Risk Assessment Procedures: The audit procedures performed to obtain an understanding of the entity and its environment, including the entity's internal control, to identify and assess the risks of material misstatement, whether due to fraud or error, at the financial statement and relevant assertion levels.

Tests of Control: An audit procedure designed to evaluate the operating effectiveness of controls in preventing, or detecting and correcting, material misstatements at the assertion level. (Note that the auditor must perform tests of controls when the risk assessment includes an expectation of the operating effectiveness of controls or when the substantive procedures alone do not provide sufficient appropriate audit evidence.)

Substantive Procedures: An audit procedure designed to detect material misstatements at the assertion level. Substantive procedures comprise (a) tests of details (classes of transactions, account balances, and disclosures) and (b) substantive analytical procedures.

II. **Menu of Specific Substantive Audit Procedures**—The auditor may use computer-assisted audit techniques (CAATs) to assist the auditor when information is in electronic form:

    A. Inspection of Records/Documents—Examining records or documents, whether internal or external, whether paper or electronic, or other media;

    B. Inspection of Tangible Assets—Physical examination of the assets;

    C. Observation—Looking at a process or procedure being performed by others;

    D. Inquiry—Seeking information of knowledgeable persons inside or outside the entity and evaluating their responses. Note that inquiry alone does not provide sufficient appropriate audit evidence either for substantive purposes or for tests of controls.

    E. Confirmation—Obtaining a representation directly from a knowledgeable third party;

    F. Recalculation—Checking the mathematical accuracy of documents;

    G. Reperformance—The auditor's execution of procedures or controls originally performed as part of the entity's internal controls;

    H. Analytical Procedures—Includes "scanning" to review accounting data to identify unusual items to be tested further. CAATs may be especially useful in identifying significant or unusual items.

> **Note**
> *Analytical procedures are defined as "evaluations of financial information through analysis of plausible relationships among both financial and nonfinancial data."*

III. The Auditor Should Plan and Perform Substantive Procedures—The auditor should design the substantive procedures to be responsive to the assessed risks of material misstatements. The purpose of substantive procedures is to detect material misstatements at the relevant assertion level.

A. The auditor should perform some substantive procedures for all relevant assertions related to each material class of transactions, account balance, and disclosure (regardless of the assessed risk of material misstatement), since there are inherent limitations to internal control and the assessment of risk is judgmental.

B. The auditor's substantive procedures should include the following related to the financial reporting process:

1. Agree the financial statement information to the underlying accounting records.

2. Examine material journal entries and other adjustments made during the preparation of the financial statements.

C. Nature of Substantive Procedures—These should be responsive to the planned level of detection risk; they consist of:

1. Tests of details

2. Substantive analytical procedures (should consider testing the controls over the preparation of information used in connection with analytical procedures)

D. Timing of Substantive Procedures—May be performed at an interim date (before year-end) or at final (at or after year-end)

1. Performing substantive procedures at an interim date increases detection risk. The auditor should perform additional substantive procedures (or substantive procedures combined with tests of control) to mitigate the increased risk and provide a reasonable basis for extending the audit conclusions from the interim date to year-end.

2. It is not necessary to rely on internal controls (i.e., test the operating effectiveness of controls) to extend the audit conclusions from the interim date to year-end. However, the auditor should consider whether only performing additional substantive procedures is sufficient.

3. When planning to perform substantive analytical procedures for the period following the interim date, the auditor should consider whether the period-end balances are reasonably predictable as to amount, relative significance, and composition.

E. Extent of Substantive Procedures—Determine the implications to sample sizes (considering the planned level of detection risk, materiality, tolerable misstatement, expected misstatement, and the nature of the population).

F. Evaluating the Sufficiency and Appropriateness of the Audit Evidence Obtained

1. **Consider all relevant audit evidence**—The auditor should consider whether the audit evidence appears to corroborate or to contradict the relevant assertions in the financial statements.

2. The sufficiency and appropriateness of audit evidence as a basis for the auditor's conclusions are matters of professional judgment. The auditor's judgment may be influenced by factors such as the following:

   a. The significance of the potential misstatement and the likelihood that it may have a material effect

   b. The understanding of the entity and its environment, including internal control

   c. The effectiveness of management's responses and controls to address the risks

   d. The results of the audit procedures performed (including whether the procedures identified instances of fraud or error)

   e. The persuasiveness of the audit evidence obtained

    f.   The source and reliability of available information

    g.   The experience gained in previous audits with such misstatements

3. **Documentation**—As covered in the course materials on internal controls, the auditor should document the following matters:

    a.   The overall responses to address the assessed risk of misstatement at the financial statement level

    b.   The nature, timing, and extent of the further audit procedures

    c.   The linkage of those procedures with the assessed risks at the relevant assertion level;

    d.   The results of the audit procedures

    e.   The conclusions reached in the current audit about the operating effectiveness of controls tested in a prior audit

PCAOB Risk Assessment Audit Standards

After studying this lesson, you should be able to:

1. Recognize the set of pronouncements that comprise the PCAOB's "risk assessment" project.

2. Understand the auditor's fundamental responsibilities associated with the various risk assessment Auditing Standards issued by the PCAOB.

3. Know the primary differences between the risk-assessment-related standards of the PCAOB and those of the AICPA.

I. PCAOB Risk Assessment Standards

The PCAOB issued a suite of eight Auditing Standards comprising its "risk assessment" project in 2010. In general, these PCAOB risk assessment standards are remarkably similar to the risk assessment standards previously issued (and now clarified) by the AICPA (Statements on Auditing Standards) and by the International Federation of Accountants (International Standards on Auditing), although a few (mostly minor) differences are identified below.

A. PCAOB Auditing Standard No. 8, *Audit Risk* [AS 1101]

B. PCAOB Auditing Standard No. 9, *Audit Planning* [AS 2101]

C. PCAOB Auditing Standard No. 10, *Supervision of the Audit Engagement* [AS 1201]

D. PCAOB Auditing Standard No. 11, *Consideration of Materiality in Planning and Performing an Audit* [AS 2105]

E. PCAOB Auditing Standard No. 12, *Identifying and Assessing Risks of Material Misstatement* [AS 2110]

F. PCAOB Auditing Standard No. 13, *The Auditor's Responses to the Risks of Material Misstatement* [AS 2301]

G. PCAOB Auditing Standard No. 14, *Evaluating Audit Results* [AS 2810]

H. PCAOB Auditing Standard No. 15, *Audit Evidence* [AS 1105]

II. PCAOB vs. AICPA—Structural Differences

These PCAOB Auditing Standards are applicable to integrated audits of an issuer's financial statements and the internal controls over financial reporting. In contrast, the AICPA's Statements on Auditing Standards focus solely on audits of nonissuers' financial statements.

III. Summaries—Summaries of the essence of these PCAOB risk assessment standards.

A. PCAOB on Audit Risk

1. **Auditor's objective**—To conduct the audit of financial statements in a manner that reduces audit risk to an appropriately low level.

2. **"Reasonable assurance" means reducing audit risk to an appropriately low level**—The auditor must plan and perform the audit to obtain reasonable assurance about whether the financial statements are free of material misstatements due to error or fraud.

3. The auditor should assess the risks of material misstatement at two levels: (1) at the financial statement level (where the risk of material misstatement is pervasive and potentially involves many assertions); and (2) at the assertion level (where the risk of material misstatement involves inherent risk and control risk).

B. PCAOB on Audit Planning

1. **Auditor's objective**—To plan the audit so that the audit is conducted effectively.

2. "Planning the audit includes establishing the overall audit strategy for the engagement and developing an audit plan, which includes, in particular, planned risk assessment procedures and planned responses to the risks of material misstatement. Planning is not a discrete phase of an audit but, rather, a continual and iterative process that might begin shortly after (or in connection with) the completion of the previous audit and continues until the completion of the current audit."

   a. **Overall strategy**—Involves rather high-level audit resource allocation issues involving the scope, timing, and direction of the audit (guides the development of the more specific audit plan).

   b. **Audit plan**—Deals with the planned nature, timing, and extent of the risk assessment procedures, the tests of controls, the substantive procedures, and any other procedures required to comply with PCAOB standards.

3. **Engagement partner responsibilities**—"The engagement partner is responsible for the engagement and its performance. Accordingly, the engagement partner is responsible for planning the audit and may seek assistance from appropriate engagement team members in fulfilling this responsibility."

C. **PCAOB on Supervision of the Audit Engagement**

1. **Auditor's objective**—To supervise the audit engagement so that the work is performed as directed and supports the conclusions reached.

2. The extent of supervision required varies with the engagement's circumstances, including the size and complexity of the company, the nature of the work assigned to engagement personnel, the capabilities of each engagement team member, and the risks of material misstatement. (The extent of supervision should be commensurate with those risks.)

3. **Engagement partner responsibilities**—"The engagement partner is responsible for the engagement and its performance. Accordingly, the engagement partner is responsible for proper supervision of the work of engagement team members and for compliance with PCAOB standards, including standards regarding using the work of specialists, other auditors, internal auditors, and others who are involved in testing controls."

D. **PCAOB on Consideration of Materiality in Planning and Performing an Audit**

1. **Auditor's objective**—To apply the concept of materiality appropriately in planning and performing audit procedures.

2. The auditor should plan and perform the audit to detect misstatement that, individually or in the aggregate, would result in material misstatement of the financial statements.

3. The auditor should use the same materiality considerations for planning the audit of internal control over financial reporting as for the audit of the financial statements.

4. The materiality level for the financial statements should be expressed as a specified amount to determine the nature, timing, and extent of audit procedures.

5. The auditor should determine tolerable misstatement for purposes of assessing risks of material misstatement at the account or disclosure levels.

E. **PCAOB on "Identifying and Assessing Risks of Material Misstatement"**

1. **Auditor's objective**—To identify and appropriately assess the risks of material misstatement, thereby providing a basis for designing and implementing responses to the risks of material misstatement.

2. The auditor should perform risk assessment procedures sufficient to provide a reasonable basis for identifying and assessing the risks of material misstatement and designing further audit procedures.

3. These risk assessment procedures should include (a) obtaining an understanding of the company and its environment; (b) obtaining an understanding of internal control over

financial reporting; (c) considering information from the client acceptance/retention evaluation, planning activities, prior audits, and other engagements for the company; (d) performing analytical procedures; and (e) inquiring of the audit committee, management, and others within the company about the risks of material misstatement.

4. The auditor should begin by identifying and assessing the risks of material misstatement at the financial statement level and then work down to the significant accounts and disclosures and their relevant assertions.

F. **PCAOB on "The Auditor's Responses to the Risks of Material Misstatement"**

1. **Auditor's objective**—To address the risks of material misstatement through appropriate overall audit responses and audit procedures.

2. **Overall responses**—The auditor should consider (a) making appropriate assignments of responsibilities based on capabilities of team members; (b) providing appropriate supervision; (c) incorporating a degree of unpredictability in planned procedures; (d) evaluating the company's selection and application of significant accounting principles (especially in subjective areas); and (e) determining whether it is necessary to make pervasive changes to the nature, timing, and extent of audit procedures.

3. **Responses involving the nature, timing, and extent of audit procedures**—The auditor should address the assessed risks of material misstatement for each relevant assertion of each significant account and disclosure.

   a. There are two categories of audit procedures performed in response to the assessed risks of material misstatement: (1) tests of controls; and (2) substantive procedures.

   b. The auditor should perform substantive procedures that are responsive to any identified significant risks (including fraud risks).

   c. In responding to fraud risks, the auditor should address the risk of management override of controls by examining journal entries, reviewing accounting estimates for biases, and evaluating the business rationale for significant unusual transactions.

G. **PCAOB on "Evaluating Audit Results"**

1. **Auditor's objective**—To evaluate the results of the audit to determine whether the audit evidence obtained is sufficient and appropriate to support the opinion.

2. The auditor must reach a conclusion as to whether sufficient appropriate audit evidence has been obtained to support the opinion.

3. The auditor should consider all relevant audit evidence (whether it corroborates or contradicts the financial statements) and evaluate the following:

   a. The results of analytical procedures performed as the overall review

   b. Misstatements (other than "trivial" ones) accumulated during the audit (with emphasis on uncorrected misstatements)

   c. The qualitative aspects of the company's accounting practices, including potential for management bias

   d. Conditions identified related to fraud risk

   e. The presentation of the financial statements (including disclosures) relative to the applicable financial reporting framework

   f. The sufficiency and appropriateness of the evidence obtained

H. **PCAOB on "Audit Evidence"**

1. **Auditor's objective**—To plan and perform the audit to obtain appropriate audit evidence that is sufficient to support the opinion.

2. **Sufficient appropriate audit evidence**

    a. Sufficiency relates to the *quantity* of evidence required—The amount of evidence needed increases as the risk of material misstatement increases; the amount of evidence needed decreases as the quality of the underlying evidence increases.

    b. Appropriateness relates to the *quality* of evidence, which involves (1) relevance and (2) reliability.

3. Financial statement assertions are factual representations that are implicitly or explicitly made by management—The PCAOB identified the five traditional financial statement assertions previously presented in a now-superseded Statement on Auditing Standards:

    a. **Existence**—That the assets or liabilities exist at a given date or that the recorded transactions have occurred during a given period

    b. **Completeness**—That there are no omissions of transaction or accounts that should have been recorded

    c. **Rights and obligations**—That the company has the rights to the assets and the obligations for the liabilities at a given date

    d. **Valuation or allocation**—That the financial statement elements are presented at appropriate amounts relative to the applicable accounting framework

    e. **Presentation and disclosure**—That the elements of the financial statements are properly classified, described, and disclosed relative to the applicable accounting framework

---

Note

The PCAOB's discussion about these five traditional financial statement assertions is a relatively major difference compared to the AICPA's Statement on Auditing Standards dealing with audit evidence. The SAS presents the discussion of assertions in three categories: (1) account balances at the period end (four assertions); (2) transactions and events during the period (five assertions); and presentation and disclosure (four assertions).

The Auditing Standards Board replaced an earlier SAS that had focused on the five traditional financial statement assertions in order to make U.S. auditing standards more consistent with International Standards on Auditing.

The PCAOB commented on the alternative treatments of assertions: "The auditor may base his or her work on financial statement assertions that differ from those in this standard if the assertions are sufficient for the auditor to identify the potential misstatements…"

IV. **Summary of Differences**—Summary of fundamental differences between the PCAOB risk assessment standards and the AICPA Auditing Standards Board risk assessment standards.

   A. The PCAOB risk assessment standards apply to integrated audits of issuers (encompassing both the company's financial statements and internal control over financial reporting), whereas the AICPA risk assessment standard apply solely to audits of non-issuers' financial statements.

   B. The PCAOB standards tended to provide a bit more specific guidance in certain areas (such as the engagement partner's responsibilities) that were originally addressed in somewhat more general terms in the AICPA standards; however, the AICPA's clarified auditing standards are now very similar to PCAOB auditing standards in these areas.

   C. A more significant difference involves the treatment of "assertions" in their respective standards dealing with the topic of audit evidence—the PCAOB focuses on the five traditional financial statement assertions (as presented in an earlier SAS that has since been superseded in an attempt to align U.S. auditing standards more closely with international standards); the resulting current AICPA standard classifies 13 assertions into three categories: (1) account balances at the period end (for which there are four assertions); (2) transactions and events for the period (for which there are five assertions); and (3) presentation and disclosure (for which there are four assertions).

Evaluation of Misstatements Identified During the Audit

I. **Responsibilities under AICPA Professional Standards**—The relevant AICPA guidance is provided by AU 450, *Evaluation of Misstatements Identified During the Audit*. This pronouncement states that the auditor's objectives are to evaluate the effect of (1) identified misstatements on the audit; and (2) uncorrected misstatements, if any, on the financial statements.

Definitions

Misstatement: A difference between the amount, classification, presentation, or disclosure of a reported financial statement item and the amount, classification, presentation, or disclosure that is required for the item to be in accordance with the applicable reporting framework. (Misstatements also involve matters deemed necessary for the financial statements to be presented fairly, in all material respects.)

Uncorrected Misstatements: Misstatements that the auditor has accumulated during the audit and that have not been corrected.

II. **Expectations Regarding Identified Misstatements and Uncorrected Misstatements**

A. **Accumulation of Identified Misstatements**—The auditor should accumulate all misstatements identified during the audit (except for those that are *clearly trivial*, which means *inconsequential*). The auditor may wish to distinguish among the following three types of misstatements:

1. **Factual misstatements**—Misstatements for which there is no doubt.

2. **Judgmental misstatements**—Differences due to the judgments of management that the auditor considers unreasonable or to the selection of accounting policies that the auditor views as inappropriate.

3. **Projected misstatements**—The auditor's best estimate of misstatements in populations as suggested by audit sampling.

B. **Consideration of Identified Misstatements as the Audit Progresses**—The auditor should determine whether the overall audit strategy and audit plan need to be revised as a result of the identified misstatements. That would be necessary if the aggregate of accumulated misstatements (and other misstatements that may exist) approaches what is considered to be material.

C. **Communication and the Correction of Misstatements**—The auditor should communicate all misstatements accumulated during the audit on a timely basis with the *appropriate level* of management and request they correct the misstatements. The appropriate level is the one that has the authority to evaluate the misstatements and take necessary action.

1. **If management has examined a class of transactions or account balance at the auditor's request (e.g., as a result of an audit sample that indicates a misstatement) and has made**

a correction—The auditor should perform additional procedures to determine whether any misstatements remain.

2. **If management refuses to correct some (or all) of the misstatements**—The auditor should obtain an understanding of management's reasons and take that into consideration when evaluating whether the financial statements are materially misstated.

D. **Evaluating the Effect of Uncorrected Misstatements**

1. **Reassess materiality**—The auditor should reassess materiality to verify that it is appropriate in view of the entity's actual financial results.

2. **Determine whether uncorrected misstatements are material**—The auditor should consider (a) the size and nature of the misstatements; and (b) the effect of uncorrected misstatements related to prior periods.

3. Other (undetected) misstatements may exist when a misstatement results from a break down in internal control, or when inappropriate assumptions or valuation methods have been widely used. The auditor should consider whether the detected and undetected misstatements might exceed materiality.

4. Circumstances affecting the evaluation of materiality include the following: (a) compliance and regulatory requirements; (b) debt covenants; (c) the effect on future periods' financial statements; (d) the effects on changes in earnings (such as changing income to a loss or vice versa) or other trends; (e) the impact on ratios; (f) the effects on segment information; (g) an effect that increases management compensation; (h) the omission of information important to users' understanding; and (i) the misclassification between operating/non-operating items or recurring/non-recurring items.

E. **Documentation of misstatements**—The auditor should document the following three matters in the audit documentation: (1) the amount below which misstatements would be viewed as *clearly trivial*; (2) all misstatements accumulated during the audit and whether they have been corrected; and (3) the auditor's conclusion (and the basis for that conclusion) about whether the uncorrected misstatements are material, individually or in the aggregate.

Audit Documentation

After studying this lesson, you should be able to:

1. Understand the auditor's responsibilities to prepare and obtain documentation, in accordance with AICPA Professional Standards.

2. Know the major differences between AICPA Professional Standards and PCAOB Auditing Standards with respect to documentation "completion" requirements and "retention" requirements.

3. Know the distinction between the auditor's "permanent file" and the current year's audit documentation.

I. **Responsibilities under AICPA Professional Standards**—The relevant AICPA guidance is provided by AU 230, *Audit Documentation*. This pronouncement states that the auditor's objective is "to prepare documentation that provides:

A. A sufficient and appropriate record of the basis for the auditor's report; *and*

B. Evidence that the audit was planned and performed in accordance with (GAAS) and applicable legal and regulatory requirements."

> **Definition**
> *Audit Documentation*: This is the record of audit procedures performed, relevant audit evidence obtained, and conclusions reached (terms such as *working papers* or *work papers* are also sometimes used).

II. **Purposes of Audit Documentation**

A. Provides the principal support for the auditor's report (regarding the procedures performed and the conclusions reached).

B. Documents the auditor's compliance with GAAS and any applicable legal and regulatory requirements;

1. That the work was adequately planned and supervised;

2. That an understanding of the entity and its environment, including internal control, was obtained and evaluated as necessary to assess the risks of material misstatement and to design the audit to be responsive to those risks; *and*

3. That the procedures applied and the evidence obtained provide a reasonable basis for the opinion expressed.

C. The audit documentation assists in controlling the audit work—that is, breaking the overall audit project into manageable tasks that can be delegated to the various members of the audit team (while documenting the work performed and the conclusions reached, and identifying the work yet to be completed).

III. **Ownership and Custody Issues**

A. **Ownership**—Audit documentation is the auditor's property (the auditor should safeguard it and establish a formal retention policy).

B. **Confidentiality**—The audit documentation is subject to the restrictions imposed by AICPA ethics rules on confidentiality. (The auditor should prevent unauthorized access to the audit documentation, since it contains entity-specific confidential information.)

C. Auditors should apply appropriate controls over the audit documentation to protect the integrity of the information at all stages of the audit, to prevent unauthorized changes, and to limit access to authorized personnel.

IV. AICPA Requirements

    A. Audit documentation should permit an experienced auditor without prior connection to the audit to understand the following:

        1. The nature, timing, and extent of procedures performed;

        2. The results of those procedures;

        3. The conclusions reached on significant matters; *and*

        4. Whether the accounting records agree or reconcile with the audited financial statements.

    B. Audit documentation should include abstracts or copies of significant contracts or agreements examined—if needed by an experienced auditor to understand the basis for conclusions.

    C. Audit documentation should identify the specific items tested by the auditor (or the *identifying characteristics* of items tested in connection with the substantive procedures and any tests of control so that the items tested can be determined as necessary).

    D. The auditor should also document audit findings or issues that are *significant* (including actionstaken to address them and the basis for conclusions reached), and should also document discussions of significant findings or issues with management (including issues discussed, and when and with whom). Such findings and issues include:

        1. Significant matters regarding the selection, application, and consistency of accounting principles

        2. Circumstances causing difficulty in applying necessary audit procedures

        3. Results of audit procedures indicating a possible material misstatement

        4. Findings that could result in modification of the audit report

        5. Audit adjustments (whether or not recorded by management) that could have a material effect individually or when aggregated

    E. If information is identified that contradicts or is inconsistent with the auditor's final conclusions—the auditor should document how the auditor addressed the contradiction or inconsistency in forming the conclusions.

    F. Identification of preparer and reviewer—the auditor should document who performed the audit work and who reviewed the specific audit documentation.

    G. Should document the *report release date*—That is defined as the date the auditor grants the entitypermission to use the auditor's report on the audited financial statements.

V. Revisions—Any revisions to audit documentation after the date of the auditor's report should comply with the following requirements:

    A. Documentation Completion Date—The auditor should complete the assembly of the final audit file no later than 60 days after the report release date. The PCAOB specifies a limit of 45 days for audits of public companies.

    B. Before the Documentation Completion Date—The auditor may add information received after the report date or delete unnecessary documentation up to the documentation completion date.

    C. After the Documentation Completion Date—The auditor must not delete any audit documentation before the end of the retention period; the auditor may add to the documentation, but must document any materials added, by whom, when, reasons for the change, and the effect, if any, on the auditor's conclusions.

    D. Retention Requirements—The AICPA requires that the audit documentation be retained for at least five years from the report release date. (The PCAOB requires retention for at least seven years for audits of public companies.)

VI. Additional Documentation—Other Statements on Auditing Standards require additional specific documentation, including, for example, the following:

  A. Aggregated Misstatements—The auditor must document:

  1. The nature and effect of misstatements that the auditor aggregates

  2. The auditor's conclusions as to whether the aggregated misstatements are material to the financial statements

  B. Analytical Procedures—The auditor must document:

  1. The expectation and factors (sources) considered in developing it, when not otherwise apparent

  2. The results of the comparison of that expectation to the recorded amounts (or to ratios based on recorded amounts)

  3. Any additional procedures performed (and the results of those procedures) to investigate unexpected differences from that comparison

  C. Going-Concern Issues—The auditor must document:

  1. The conditions giving rise to the going concern issue

  2. The elements of management's plan considered important to overcoming the situation

  3. Evidence obtained to evaluate the significant elements of management's plans

  4. The auditor's conclusion as to whether *substantial doubt* remains

  5. The auditor's conclusion as to whether an explanatory paragraph should be added to the auditor's report

VII. Quantity of Content—The quantity, type, and content of the audit documentation depends on the auditor's professional judgment and may include consideration of the following matters:

  A. The risk of material misstatement in the area involved

  B. The amount of judgment involved in performing the work and interpreting the results (including the nature of the audit procedures involved)

  C. The nature and extent of any exceptions identified

  D. The significance of the evidence to the assertion involved

  E. The need to document a conclusion not readily determinable from the documentation of the work performed

VIII. Types of Files Related to Audit Working Papers

  A. Permanent File—Involves matters having ongoing audit significance and may include:

  1. Description of the client's industry, a brief history of client, and a description of the client's facilities

  2. Abstracts or copies of important legal documents and important long-term contracts—documents such as the company's articles of incorporation and bylaws and contracts such as debt agreements, leases, and labor contracts (including pension plans and profit- sharing agreements)

  3. Documentation of the auditor's understanding of internal control for the major transaction cycles

  4. **Historical financial information**—Such as ratio analysis of the client's operations or other data having ongoing usefulness

  B. Current Year's Audit Files—The current year's audit files include the auditor's documentation of important administrative matters (such as the audit team's time budget) along with the supporting working papers related to the financial statement items.

1. Audit plan (sometimes called the audit program).

2. Memoranda (documenting planning activities, consideration of fraud, assessment of internal control, etc.).

3. Abstracts or copies of relevant client documents (including minutes of board of directors' meetings or meetings of those charged with governance).

4. Letters (confirmations, attorney letters, management representation letter, engagement letter, etc.).

5. Analyses and schedules (either prepared by client personnel or by the audit team).

C. **Bulk File**—Where documentation that is too voluminous can be stored (e.g., magnetic tapes, extensive computer printouts, etc.).

D. **Correspondence File**—Where letters and e-mail messages to and from clients are organized so that the audit team can conveniently review communications related to each client organization.

E. **Report File**—Where prior years' audit reports and management letters are organized (by client) so that the audit team can conveniently review formal reports previously issued for each client.

PCAOB on Audit Documentation

After studying this lesson, you should be able to:

1. Know the documentation requirements under PCAOB Auditing Standards.

2. Know the primary differences between PCAOB documentation requirements for issuers relative to AICPA documentation requirements for nonissuers (regarding documentation retention and the documentation completion date).

I. Audit Documentation

Definition

Audit Documentation: The written record of the basis for the auditor's conclusions that provides the support for the auditor's representations. Also serves as a **basis for the review** of the quality of the audit work—the documentation should be prepared in sufficient detail to permit an experienced auditor without prior connection to the engagement to understand the procedures performed and the conclusions reached (and to determine who performed the work and on what date).

II. Basic Documentation Requirement
—(1) Demonstrate that the engagement complied with PCAOB standards; (2) support the basis for the auditor's conclusions regarding every relevant financial statement assertion; and (3) demonstrate that the underlying accounting records agree to or reconcile with the financial statement elements.

III. Documentation of Specific Matters

A. Document audit procedures involving inspection of documents (including walkthroughs, tests of controls, and substantive tests of details)—Identify the specific items tested (or the source and specific selection criteria); include abstracts or copies of significant contracts or agreements examined.

B. For matters documented in a **central repository** or in a particular office of the public accounting firm (including issues such as auditor independence, staff training, client acceptance/retention, etc.)—The audit documentation should appropriately reference the central repository.

C. Must document all **significant findings or issues** (also document the actions taken to address them and the basis for the conclusions reached)—Including the application of accounting principles, circumstances causing modification of planned audit procedures, matters that could result in modification of the auditor's report, material misstatements, significant deficiencies or material weaknesses in internal control over financial reporting, difficulties in applying audit procedures, and disagreements among members of the engagement team about final conclusions on significant matters, among other things.

D. All significant findings or issues must be identified in an **engagement completion document** insufficient detail so that a reviewer can obtain a thorough understanding of the matters.

IV. Retention of and Subsequent Changes to Audit Documentation

A. Must retain audit documentation for **seven years** from the **report release date**—The report release date is when the auditor grants permission to use the auditor's report in connection with the issuance of the company's financial statements. (Recall that the AICPA requires a retention period of five years for audits of *nonissuers*.)

B. A complete and final set of audit documentation should be assembled no later than **45 days** after the report release date—That is called the **documentation completion date.** (Recall that the AICPA allows auditors of nonissuers to have a maximum of 60 days for this purpose.)

C. After the documentation completion date—No documentation can be deleted, but documentation can be added (must indicate the date the information was added, the name of the person preparing the additional documentation, and the reason for adding it).

D. The office of the firm issuing the auditor's report is responsible for ensuring that all documentation complies with PCAOB requirements—Documentation of other auditors associated with the engagement (in other offices of the firm or in different firms) must be retained or accessible to the office issuing the report.

Confirmation

I. **Responsibilities under AICPA Professional Standards**—The relevant AICPA guidance is provided by AU 505, *External Confirmations*. This pronouncement states that the auditor's objective is "to design and perform external confirmations to obtain relevant and reliable audit evidence."

> **Definition**
>
> *External Confirmation*: Audit evidence obtained as a direct written response to the auditor from a third party ("the confirming party"), either in paper form or by electronic or other medium (e.g., through the auditor's direct access to information held by a third party).
>
> *Positive Confirmation Request*: A request that the confirming party respond directly to the auditor by providing the requested information or indicating whether the confirming party agrees or disagrees with the information in the request.
>
> *Negative Confirmation Request*: A request that the confirming party respond directly to the auditor only if the confirming party disagrees with the information provided in the request.

II. **Tailor Objectives/Assertions**—The auditor should tailor the confirmations to the specific audit objectives/assertions. Confirmations are most useful in addressing the existence/occurrence assertion. There are two basic types of confirmation requests:

A. **Positive Confirmation Request**—Where a response is requested whether or not the other party agrees with the client's recorded amount. A nonresponse is viewed as a "loose end" that must be addressed.

1. When individual accounts are large

2. Requires second (or possibly third) requests as a follow-up procedure for nonresponses

3. If no response is obtained, the auditor must perform *alternative procedures*.

B. **Negative Confirmation Request**—Where a response is only requested in the event of **disagreement**. A nonresponse is viewed as evidence of agreement by the recipient:

1. Could easily misinterpret a nonresponse as suggesting agreement when, instead, the other party did not even open the envelope!

2. Therefore, negative confirmations usually require a larger sample size than would positive confirmations.

3. The auditor may justify using negative confirmations when:

a. The population consists of a large number of small, rather homogeneous items;

b. The assessed risk of material misstatement is low, and the relevant controls are operating effectively; *and*

c. Recipients are expected to pay attention to the request, and a low rate of exceptions is expected.

C. **Alternative Procedures**—Alternative (sometimes called "alternate") audit procedures are usually required when no response is received for a positive confirmation request:

1. **Receivables**—The auditor would first look to see whether cash was received subsequent to the date of the confirmation request. Second best, the auditor would examine the documents underlying the apparent validity of the recorded transaction.

2. **Payables**—The auditor would usually verify subsequent cash disbursements as evidence of payment of the account.

III. **Control of Requests and Responses**—The auditor should "maintain control over the confirmation requests and responses." If the response is by fax, the auditor should consider a direct call to the respondent; and if the response is verbal, encourage a written reply.

IV. **Responding to Risks of Material Misstatement**—AU 330, *Performing Audit Procedures in Response to Assessed Risks and Evaluating the Audit Evidence Obta ined,* states, "The auditor should use external confirmation procedures for accounts receivable, except when one or more of the following is applicable:

A. The overall account balance is immaterial.

B. External confirmation procedures for accounts receivable would be ineffective.

C. The auditor's assessed level of risk of material misstatement at the relevant assertion level is low, and the other planned substantive procedures address the assessed risk. In many situations, the use of external confirmation procedures for accounts receivable and the performance of other substantive procedures are necessary to reduce the assessed risk of material misstatement to an acceptably low level."

AU 330 also states, "If the auditor has determined that an assessed risk of material misstatement at the relevant assertion level is a significant risk, the auditor should perform substantive procedures that are specifically responsive to that risk."

Example
If the auditor identified that management is under pressure to meet earnings expectations, there may be a risk that management is inflating sales by improperly recognizing revenue related to sales agreements with terms that preclude revenue recognition or by invoicing sales before shipment. In these circumstances, the auditor may, for example, design external written confirmation requests not only to confirm outstanding amounts, but also to confirm the details of the sales agreements, including date, any rights of return, and delivery terms. In addition, the auditor may find it effective to supplement such external written confirmations with inquiries of nonfinancial personnel in the entity regarding any changes in sales agreements and delivery terms.

Accounting Estimates

After studying this lesson, you should be able to:

1. Understand the auditor's responsibilities to apply a risk-based audit approach to evaluate the reasonableness of accounting estimates in accordance with AICPA Professional Standards.

2. Know the definition of "estimation uncertainty" and how that concept may result in a "significant risk."

3. Know the auditor's responsibilities when an accounting estimate results in a "significant risk."

I. **Responsibilities under AICPA Professional Standards**—The relevant AICPA guidance is provided by AU 540, *Auditing Accounting Estimates, Including Fair Value Accounting Estimates and Related Disclosures*. This pronouncement states that the auditor's objective is to obtain sufficient appropriate audit evidence about whether the accounting estimates (including fair value accounting estimates) are reasonable and whether the related disclosures are adequate in view of the applicable financial reporting framework.

> **Definition**
>
> *Accounting Estimate*: An approximation of a monetary amount in the absence of a precise means of measurement.
>
> *Auditor's Point Estimate (or Auditor's Range)*: The amount (or range of amounts) derived from audit evidence for use in evaluating the recorded or disclosed amount(s).
>
> *Estimation Uncertainty*: The susceptibility of an accounting estimate and related disclosures to an inherent lack of precision in its measurement.
>
> *Management's Point Estimate*: The amount selected by management for recognition or disclosure as an accounting estimate.
>
> *Outcome of an Accounting Estimate*: The actual monetary amount that results from resolution of the underlying matter addressed by the accounting estimate.

II. **The Risk-Based Audit Approach**

   A. **Basis for Risk Assessment**—The auditor should obtain an understanding of the following:

      1. The requirements of the applicable financial reporting framework

      2. How management makes the accounting estimates and the data used, including how management has assessed the effect of estimation uncertainty

   B. **Identifying and Assessing Risks of Material Misstatement**—The auditor should evaluate the degree of estimation uncertainty involved, and determine whether any of those accounting estimates result in significant risks. (Recall that significant risks require the auditor to obtain an understanding of whether relevant controls mitigate such risks.)

   C. **Responding to the Assessed Risks of Material Misstatement**

      1. The auditor should determine whether management has complied with the requirements of the applicable financial reporting framework, and whether the methods used to make the estimate are appropriate and consistently applied.

      2. In responding to the assessed risks, the auditor should do one (or more) of the following:

         a. Determine whether events occurring up to the date of the auditor's report provide evidence about the accounting estimate;

         b. Test how management made the estimate, along with the data used;

      c. Test the operating effectiveness of applicable controls, along with performing appropriate substantive procedures; *and/or*

      d. Develop a point estimate (or range) to evaluate management's point estimate.

   3. The auditor should consider the need for specialized skills or knowledge.

D. Further Substantive Procedures to Respond to Significant Risks—The auditor should evaluate the following:

   1. How management addressed estimation uncertainty in making the accounting estimate;

   2. Whether management's significant assumptions are reasonable; *and*

   3. When relevant, whether management has the intent and ability to carry out specific actions.

E. Evaluating the Reasonableness of the Accounting Estimates—The auditor should evaluate whether the accounting estimates are reasonable (or are misstated) relative to the applicable financial reporting framework. The auditor is not responsible for predicting future conditions, transactions, or events, however.

F. Disclosures—The auditor should obtain sufficient appropriate audit evidence as to whether the disclosures meet the requirements of the applicable financial reporting framework. For accounting estimates resulting in significant risks, the auditor should evaluate the adequacy of the disclosure of estimation uncertainty.

G. Indicators of Possible Management Bias—The auditor should consider whether the accounting estimates might indicate possible management bias.

H. Documentation—The auditor should include documentation regarding (1) the basis for the auditor's conclusions about the reasonableness of accounting estimates resulting in significant risks and their disclosure; and (2) any indications of possible management bias. The auditor usually obtains written representations as to whether management believes assumptions used in making accounting estimates are reasonable.

III. Additional Guidance Regarding Estimation Uncertainty

A. Nature of Estimation Uncertainty—The nature of estimation uncertainty varies with the nature of the accounting estimate, the extent to which there is an accepted method (or model) to be used, and the subjectivity of any assumptions or the degree of judgment involved. The risks of material misstatement increase when there is high estimation uncertainty.

B. Understanding Management's Assessment—In obtaining an understanding of whether and how management has assessed estimation uncertainty, the auditor might consider whether management has performed a *sensitivity analysis* and monitors outcomes of prior accounting estimates.

C. When the Estimation Uncertainty is High—The auditor may consider a combination of responses to the assessed risks, including reviewing outcomes, testing how management made its estimate, testing applicable controls, and developing a point estimate (or range) to evaluate management's point estimate.

D. Narrowing a Range—The auditor's range should encompass all reasonable outcomes, not all possible outcomes. A high estimation uncertainty (significant risk) may be indicated if it is not possible to narrow the range to less than or equal to performance materiality.

E. Reporting—When there is significant uncertainty, the auditor may add an emphasis-of-matter paragraph to the auditor's report.

Fair Value Estimates

After studying this lesson, you should be able to:

1. Understand the auditor's responsibilities to apply a risk-based audit approach to evaluate the reasonableness of fair value accounting estimates in accordance with AICPA Professional Standards.

2. Recognize the role of "observable inputs" and "unobservable inputs" in evaluating estimation uncertainty for fair value accounting estimates.

I. **Responsibilities under AICPA Professional Standards**—The relevant AICPA guidance is provided by AU 540, *Auditing Accounting Estimates, Including Fair Value Accounting Estimates and Related Disclosures*. This pronouncement states that the auditor's objective is to obtain sufficient appropriate audit evidence about whether the accounting estimates (including fair value accounting estimates) are reasonable and whether the related disclosures are adequate in view of the applicable financial reporting framework.

> **Note**
> *The prior discussion related to auditing accounting estimates is also applicable to the discussion here related to auditing fair value accounting estimates, which is based on the same Statement on Auditing Standards. The focus here is on audit considerations that are specific to fair value measurements and disclosures.*

II. **The Risk-Based Audit Approach**

    A. **Basis for Risk Assessment**—The auditor should obtain an understanding of the applicable financial reporting requirements, and how management makes the fair value accounting estimate (and data used), including how management assessed the effect of estimation uncertainty.

    B. **Identifying and Assessing Risks of Material Misstatement**—The auditor should evaluate the degree of estimation uncertainty involved and determine whether any of those fair value accounting estimates result in significant risks.

    C. **Responding to the Assessed Risks of Material Misstatement**—The auditor should determine whether management complied with the applicable financial reporting requirements, and whether the methods used to make the fair value accounting estimate are appropriate and are consistently applied. The auditor should consider the need for specialized skills or knowledge.

    D. **Further Substantive Procedures to Respond to Significant Risks**—The auditor should evaluate how management addressed estimation uncertainty; whether management's significant assumptions are reasonable; and, when relevant, whether management has the intent and ability to carry out specific actions.

    E. **Evaluating the Reasonableness of the Estimates**—The auditor should evaluate whether the fair value accounting estimates are reasonable relative to the requirements of the applicable financial reporting framework.

    F. **Disclosures**—The auditor should obtain sufficient appropriate audit evidence as to whether the disclosures meet the requirements of the applicable financial reporting framework. The auditor should also evaluate the adequacy of disclosure of the estimation uncertainty for any identified significant risks.

    G. **Indicators of Possible Management Bias**—The auditor should consider whether the fair value accounting estimates might indicate possible management bias.

    H. **Documentation**—The auditor should document the following:

        1. The basis for the auditor's conclusions about the reasonableness of fair value accounting estimates resulting in significant risks and their disclosure, *and*

        2. Any indications of possible management bias.

III. Additional Guidance Regarding Estimation Uncertainty Particularly for Fair Value Accounting Estimates

    A. Nature of Estimation Uncertainty—High estimation uncertainty results in an increased risk of material misstatement when, for example:

        1. Fair value accounting estimates for derivative instruments are not publicly traded.

        2. Fair value accounting estimates are based on a highly specialized entity-developed model or when the assumptions (inputs) cannot be observed in the marketplace.

> "… the existence of published price quotations ordinarily is the best audit evidence of fair value."

    B. Examples of Fair Value Accounting Estimates—Complex financial instruments (not traded in an open market); share-based payments; property held for disposal; certain assets or liabilities acquired in a business combination, including intangibles; and nonmonetary exchange of assets.

    C. For fair value accounting estimates, assumptions (inputs) affect estimation uncertainty and vary as follows:

        1. Observable inputs—Assumptions that market participants would use in pricing an asset or liability based on market data from sources independent of the reporting entity or

        2. Unobservable inputs—An entity's own judgments about what assumptions market participants would use. Estimation uncertainty increases when the fair value estimates are based on unobservable inputs.

    D. Testing how Management Makes the Estimate—The auditor may decide to test how management made their estimate (and the data used) when the accounting estimate is a fair value accounting estimate using observable and unobservable inputs.

    E. Evaluating the Method of Measurement—Determining whether the method or model used by management is appropriate requires professional judgment.

    F. Evaluating the Use of Models for Fair Value Accounting Estimates—Matters the auditor may consider in testing the model include the following:

        1. Whether the model is validated for suitability prior to usage

        2. Whether appropriate controls exist over changes

        3. Whether the model is periodically tested for validity (when inputs are subjective)

        4. Whether adjustments are made to the model's outputs

        5. Whether the model is adequately documented, including key parameters and limitations

    G. Considering Specialized Skills or Knowledge—In considering the need for specialized skills or knowledge, the auditor may consider whether any complex calculations or models are involved in making fair value accounting estimates when no observable market exists.

    H. Indicators of Possible Management Bias—An example of an indicator of possible management bias would be the use of an entity's own assumptions for fair value accounting estimates that are inconsistent with observable market conditions.

    I. Communication with Those Charged with Governance—Another SAS requires the auditor to communicate the auditor's views about the qualitative aspects of the entity's significant accounting practices, including accounting estimates. The auditor should determine that they are informed about the process used by management in developing sensitive accounting estimates, as well as the auditor's basis for conclusions about those matters.

Lawyer's Letters

After studying this lesson, you should be able to:

1. Understand procedures the auditor would perform related to legal liability issues.

2. Understand the agreement between the AICPA and American Bar Association regarding matters that can be communicated to the auditor in the "lawyer's letter" in response to a "letter of inquiry" (with emphasis on "asserted" and "unasserted claims").

3. Be familiar with the language used in a typical "letter of inquiry to legal counsel."

I. **Responsibilities under AICPA Professional Standards**—The relevant AICPA guidance is provided by AU 501, *Audit Evidence—Specific Considerations for Selected Items*. This pronouncement states that the auditor's objective is "to obtain sufficient appropriate audit evidence regarding the completeness of litigation, claims, and assessments involving the entity" (among other matters specifically addressed by the SAS).

II. **Audit Procedures Related to Legal Contingencies**

A. Management is the primary source of information about these legal contingencies. The auditor should make appropriate inquiries of management.

B. The auditor should read the minutes of all meetings of those charged with governance where significant issues, including matters related to legal liability, affecting the financial statements likely would be discussed.

C. To corroborate management's responses to the auditor's inquiries about the identity of lawyers who have rendered significant legal services to the client (and to whom a letter of inquiry should be sent)—the auditor should examine the charges to the related expense account and then examine (vouch to) the appropriate underlying invoices.

D. The auditor should draft a *letter of inquiry* for management to send to those lawyers who have rendered litigation-related services to the entity. The lawyer's response to the letter of inquiry is simply called the *lawyer's letter* (or *attorney's letter*). The primary purpose of the lawyer's letter is to corroborate management's responses to the auditor's inquiries about legal-related contingencies. When the entity's in-house counsel has responsibility for such litigation-related matters, the auditor should send a similar letter of inquiry to the in-house counsel and obtain a written response.

E. One or more lawyer's letters are expected to be included in the audit documentation. However, the SAS allows for the possibility that the entity may not have any relevant "litigation, claims, or assessments" having financial reporting significance. In that case, the auditor would include a specific statement of fact in the management representations letter stating that the entity had no legal counsel to address current or potential litigation issues.

III. **Inquiries of the Client's Lawyer(s)**—The letter of inquiry normally includes the entity's listing of various legal matters that the lawyer is handling (classified separately as Asserted Claims and Unasserted Claims) to facilitate the lawyer's response.

IV. **Asserted Claims**—With respect to asserted claims and active litigation "asserted" means that someone has already filed a claim or has at least announced the intention to make such a claim, which is synonymous with the AICPA's term "pending or threatened litigation." According to the American Bar Association, the lawyer should inform the auditor directly about any omissions of asserted claims in the lawyer's letter responding to the letter of inquiry.

V. **Unasserted Claims**—With respect to unasserted claims and potential litigation, "unasserted" means that the entity has exposure to litigation, but no one has yet announced an intention to sue.

A. The lawyer cannot (according to the American Bar Association's *Statement of Policy Regarding Lawyers' Responses to Auditors' Requests for Information*) inform the auditor directly about any omission of unasserted claims as identified in the letter of inquiry.

B. However, lawyers must tell their client about any such omissions and request that client management then inform the auditors.

C. Note that this issue (whether the entity's lawyer has informed management of any omission of an unasserted claim that management should discuss with their auditors) is specifically addressed in the management representations letter.

D. An unasserted claim must be disclosed according to GAAP if the following two conditions exist:

    1. It is probable that a claim will be asserted, *and*

    2. It is at least reasonably possible that a material unfavorable outcome will occur.

VI. Scope Limitation—A limitation in the lawyer's response is a scope limitation sufficient to preclude an unqualified opinion (a nonresponse would likely result in a disclaimer of opinion owing to a major scope limitation).

VII. Sample Letter of Inquiry to Legal Counsel

Illustrative Letter of Inquiry to Legal Counsel

(Prepared on Client's Letterhead)

(*Date*[1])

(*Name of Lawyer*)

(*Address of Lawyer*)

Dear _____:

In connection with an audit of our financial statements at (*balance-sheet date*) and for the (*period*) then ended, management of the Company has prepared, and furnished to our auditors (*state name and address of auditors*), a description and evaluation of certain contingencies, including those set forth below involving matters with respect to which you have been engaged and to which you have devoted substantive attention on behalf of the Company in the form of legal consultation or representation. These contingencies are regarded by management of the Company as material for this purpose.[2] Your response should include matters that existed at (*balance-sheet date*) and during the period from that date to the date of your response.

Pending or Threatened Litigation (excluding unasserted claims)

(Ordinarily, the information would include the following: (1) the nature of the litigation; (2) the progress of the case to date; (3) how management is responding or intends to respond to the litigation (e.g., to contest the case vigorously or to seek an out-of-court settlement); and (4) an evaluation of the likelihood of an unfavorable outcome and an estimate, if one can be made, of the amount or range of potential loss.)

Please furnish to our auditors such explanation, if any, that you consider necessary to supplement the foregoing information, including an explanation of those matters as to which your views may differ from those stated and an identification of the omission of any pending or threatened litigation, claims, and assessments or a statement that the list of such matters is complete.

Unasserted Claims and Assessments (considered by management to be probable of assertion, and that, if asserted, would have at least a reasonable possibility of an unfavorable outcome)

(Ordinarily, the information would include the following: (1) the nature of the litigation; (2) how management intends to respond if the claim is asserted; and (3) an evaluation of the likelihood of an unfavorable outcome and an estimate, if one can be made, of the amount or range of potential loss.)

Please furnish to our auditors such explanation, if any, that you consider necessary to supplement the foregoing information, including an explanation of those matters as to which your views may differ from those stated.

We understand that whenever, in the course of performing legal services for us with respect to a matter recognized to involve an unasserted possible claim or assessment that may call for financial statement disclosure, if you have formed a professional conclusion that we should disclose or consider disclosure concerning such possible claim or assessment, as a matter of professional responsibility to us, you will so advise us and will consult with us concerning the question of such disclosure and the applicable requirements of Statement of Financial Accounting Standards No. 5. Please specifically confirm to our auditors that our understanding is correct.

Please specifically identify the nature of and reasons for any limitation on your response.

(The auditor may request the client to inquire about additional matters, for example, unpaid or unbilled charges or specified information on certain contractually assumed obligations of the company, such as guarantees of indebtedness of others.)

Very truly yours,

(*Authorized Signature for Client*)[3]

---

[1]The sending of this letter should be timed so that the lawyer's response is dated as close as practicable to the date of the auditor's report. However, the auditor and client should consider early mailing of a draft inquiry as a convenience for the lawyer in preparing a timely response to the formal letter of inquiry.

[2]Management may indicate a specific materiality limit if an understanding has been reached with the auditor.

[3]If a client has not needed to retain legal counsel, the auditors may express an unmodified opinion on the financial statements even though they have not obtained a letter from legal counsel of the Company. In these circumstances, the auditors should obtain written representation from the Company that legal counsel has not been retained for matters concerning business operations that may involve current or prospective litigation.

Management Representations Letters

I. **Responsibilities under AICPA Professional Standards**—The relevant AICPA guidance is provided by AU 580, *Written Representations*. This pronouncement states that the auditor's objectives are

   A. "To obtain written representations from management that they believe they have fulfilled their responsibility for the preparation and fair presentation of the financial statements and for the completeness of information provided to the auditor;

   B. Support other audit evidence relevant to the financial statements by means of written representations determined necessary by the auditor; *and*

   C. Respond appropriately to written representations provided by management … or if management … (does) not provide the written representations requested by the auditor."

II. **Document Verbal Responses to Auditor's Inquiries**

   A. An auditor is required to obtain written representations from management to corroborate management's verbal responses to important inquiries by the auditor.

   B. This letter from management is addressed directly to the auditors.

   C. The letter should be signed by those members of management with overall responsibility for financial and operating matters—ordinarily the chief executive officer (CEO) and the chief financial officer (CFO).

   1. Their unwillingness to sign the management representations letter would be a scope limitation probably resulting in a disclaimer of opinion or withdrawal from the engagement.

   2. If any such representations are contradicted by other evidence—the auditor should investigate the circumstances and evaluate the implications to reliance on other management representations.

   D. The representations letter should cover all periods encompassed by the auditor's report. If current management was not present for all periods covered, tailor the representations to the circumstances.

   E. Date of the management representations letter—the representations letter should be dated the same as the date of the auditor's report.

III. **The Specific Content of the Representations Depend on the Circumstances**—Usually include the following provisions as applicable.

   A. **Regarding the Financial Statements:**

   1. That management is responsible for the fairness of the financial statements

   2. That management is responsible for internal control over financial reporting

   3. That management is responsible for internal control to prevent and detect fraud

   4. That significant assumptions used for any accounting estimates are reasonable

   5. That related party transactions have been properly accounted for and disclosed

   6. That subsequent events have been properly accounted for and disclosed

7. That any uncorrected misstatements are immaterial

8. That the effects of litigation and claims have been properly accounted for and disclosed

B. Regarding the Information Provided:

1. That all relevant financial records and unrestricted access to personnel were made available to the auditor

2. That all transactions have been recorded

3. That management has made available the results of their assessment of fraud risks

4. That regarding fraud, there is no fraud involving management or employees having significant internal control responsibilities, or others where the financial statement effect could be material

5. That management has no knowledge of suspected fraud communicated by employees, former employees, or others

6. That management has disclosed all instances of noncompliance with laws and regulations relevant to financial reporting

7. That there are no (undisclosed) litigations, claims, and assessments relevant to the financial statements

8. That management has disclosed all known related party relationships and transactions

C. Sample Management Representations Letter

Illustrative Management Representation Letter

(Prepared on the Entity's Letterhead)

(To Auditor)

(Date)

This representation letter is provided in connection with your audit of the financial statements of ABC Company, which comprise the balance sheet as of December 31, 20XX, and the related statements of income, changes in stockholders' equity, and cash flows for the year then ended, and the related notes to the financial statements, for the purpose of expressing an opinion on whether the financial statements are presented fairly, in all material respects, in accordance with accounting principles generally accepted in the United States (U.S. GAAP).

Certain representations in this letter are described as being limited to matters that are material. Items are considered material, regardless of size, if they involve an omission or misstatement of accounting information that, in the light of surrounding circumstances, makes it probable that the judgment of a reasonable person relying on the information would be changed or influenced by the omission or misstatement.

Except where otherwise stated below, immaterial matters less than $[insert amount] collectively are not considered to be exceptions that require disclosure for the purpose of the following representations. This amount is not necessarily indicative of amounts that would require adjustment to or disclosure in the financial statements.

We confirm that (*to the best of our knowledge and belief, having made such inquiries as we considered necessary for the purpose of appropriately informing ourselves*) [*as of (date of auditor's report)*,]:

Financial Statements

– We have fulfilled our responsibilities, as set out in the terms of the audit engagement dated (insert date), for the preparation and fair presentation of the financial statements in accordance with U.S. GAAP.

– We acknowledge our responsibility for the design, implementation, and maintenance of internal control relevant to the preparation and fair presentation of financial statements that are free from material misstatement, whether due to fraud or error.

- We acknowledge our responsibility for the design, implementation, and maintenance of internal control to prevent and detect fraud.

- Significant assumptions used by us in making accounting estimates, including those measured at fair value, are reasonable.

- Related party relationships and transactions have been appropriately accounted for and disclosed in accordance with the requirements of U.S. GAAP.

- All events subsequent to the date of the financial statements and for which U.S. GAAP requires adjustment or disclosure have been adjusted or disclosed.

- The effects of uncorrected misstatements are immaterial, both individually and in the aggregate, to the financial statements as a whole. A list of the uncorrected misstatements is attached to the representation letter.

- The effects of all known actual or possible litigation and claims have been accounted for and disclosed in accordance with U.S. GAAP.

(*Any other matters that the auditor may consider appropriate*.)

Information Provided

- We have provided you with:

  - Access to all information, of which we are aware that is relevant to the preparation and fair presentation of the financial statements such as records, documentation, and other matters;

  - Additional information that you have requested from us for the purpose of the audit; and

  - Unrestricted access to persons within the entity from whom you determined it necessary to obtain audit evidence.

- All transactions have been recorded in the accounting records and are reflected in the financial statements.

- We have disclosed to you the results of our assessment of the risk that the financial statements may be materially misstated as a result of fraud.

- We have (*no knowledge of any*) (*disclosed to you all information that we are aware of regarding*) fraud or suspected fraud that affects the entity and involves:

  - Management;

  - Employees who have significant roles in internal control; or

  - Others when the fraud could have a material effect on the financial statements

- We have (*no knowledge of any*) (*disclosed to you all information that we are aware of regarding*) allegations of fraud, or suspected fraud, affecting the entity's financial statements communicated by employees, former employees, analysts, regulators or others.

- We have disclosed to you all known instances of noncompliance or suspected noncompliance with laws and regulations whose effects should be considered when preparing financial statements.

- We (*have disclosed to you all known actual or possible*) (*are not aware of any pending or threatened*) litigation, claims, and assessments whose effects should be considered when preparing the financial statements [and we have not consulted legal counsel concerning litigation, claims, or assessments].

- We have disclosed to you the identity of the entity's related parties and all the related party relationships and transactions of which we are aware.

(*Any other matters that the auditor may consider necessary*.)

(*Name and Signature of Chief Executive Officer with Title*)

(*Name and Signature of Chief Financial Officer with Title*)

Related-Party Issues

After studying this lesson, you should be able to:

1. Know the definition of the term *related parties*.

2. Understand the auditor's responsibility to address related-party issues, in accordance with AICPA Professional Standards.

I. **Responsibilities under AICPA Professional Standards**—The relevant AICPA guidance is provided by the clarified SAS, AU 580, *Related Parties*. This pronouncement states that the auditor's objectives are:

   A. To obtain an understanding of related-party relationships and transactions to address fraud risk factors and evaluate whether the financial statements achieve fair presentation and

   B. To obtain sufficient appropriate audit evidence about whether related-party relationships and transactions are properly accounted for and adequately disclosed in the financial statements.

II. **Definitions**

   A. FASB definition of *related parties*: The essence of this definition is that one party has the ability to influence the conduct of the other party.

   "Affiliates of the enterprise; entities for which investments are accounted for by the equity method by the enterprise; trusts for the benefit of employees, such as pension and profit-sharing trusts that are managed by or under the trusteeship of management; principal owners of the enterprise; its management; members of the immediate families of principal owners of the enterprise and its management; and other parties with which the enterprise may deal if one party controls or can significantly influence the management or operating policies of the other to an extent that one of the transacting parties might be prevented from fully pursuing its own separate interests."

   B. AICPA definition of *arm's-length transaction*:

   "A transaction conducted on such terms and conditions between a willing buyer and a willing seller who are unrelated and are acting independently of each other and pursuing their own best interests. "

III. **The Historical Cost Principle**—The historical cost principle in accounting is based on the notion of an exchange price negotiated in an arms-length transaction, which results in an accurate measure of the value exchanged. However, related parties could potentially set the transaction price at whatever value they wish, without regard to the "real" economic value. Auditors are generally not in a position to provide reliable, independent appraisals of transaction prices between related parties. As a result, auditors are particularly concerned with the adequacy of disclosure about transactions between related parties.

IV. **The Auditor's Responsibilities Under the SAS**

   A. **Risk Assessment**—The auditor should assess the risk of material misstatement that could result from the entity's related-party relationships and transactions. The auditor should view any significant related-party transactions outside the entity's normal course of business as significant risks.

   1. The auditor should inquire of management about

   a. The identity of the entity's related parties

   b. The nature of the relationships involved

   c. Whether the entity engaged in any transactions with those related parties during the period, and, if so, the purpose of the transactions

2. The auditor should also inquire about (and perform other risk assessment procedures) to obtain an understanding of the applicable controls established to (a) identify and account for such related-party relationships and transactions; (b) authorize and approve significant transactions with related parties, as well as those that are outside the normal course of business. (The risk of management override of controls is higher when management has significant influence with parties with whom the entity does business.)

    a. Examples of arrangements that may indicate undisclosed related-party relationships

        i. Participation in partnerships with other parties

        ii. Agreements with other parties having conditions outside the normal course of business

        iii. Guarantees involving other parties

    b. Examples of transactions outside the normal course of business

        i. Complex equity transactions (restructurings or acquisitions)

        ii. Transactions with offshore entities

        iii. Sales transactions with unusually large discounts

        iv. Transactions with circular arrangements (such as repurchase agreements)

    c. The auditor should stay alert for any indications of related-party relationships or transactions that management has failed to disclose to the auditor. The auditor should be attentive to such matters when

        a. Reviewing bank confirmations and other records or documents

        b. Reading the minutes of meetings of those charged with governance

    d. Relevant information about the related parties should be shared with the members of the engagement team.

3. **Response to Risk Assessment**—The auditor should obtain sufficient appropriate audit evidence about the assessed risks of material misstatement due to related-party relationships and transactions.

    1. **When there is a significant risk about related-party transactions**—The auditor may perform substantive procedures such as the following:

        a. Confirm specific terms of the transactions with the related parties

        b. Inspect evidence in the possession of the entity or the related party

        c. Confirm (or discuss) information with intermediaries, such as banks or others

        d. Review audited financial statements, income tax returns, or reports issued by regulatory agencies to assess the financial condition of the other party

    2. Procedures to obtain an understanding of the business relationships involving a related party (and to determine the need for further substantive procedures) include the following:

        a. Inquiries of management and those charged with governance

        b. Inquiries of the related parties

        c. Inspection of contracts with the related party

        d. Review of employee whistleblowing reports, if available

        e. Background research, perhaps using the Internet

4. **Evaluation**—The auditor should evaluate whether the identified related-party relationships and transactions have been appropriately accounted for and properly disclosed and whether the financial statements achieve *fair presentation* regarding those related-party relationships

and transactions. The substance of the transactions is normally more important than their legal form.

    1.   If the auditor identifies related-party transactions not previously disclosed by management—The auditor should:

        a. Communicate relevant information to members of the engagement team

        b. Ask management to identify all transactions with the newly identified related party

        c. Inquire about why the entity's controls did not identify the related-party relationship

        d. Perform appropriate substantive audit procedures

        e. Reconsider the risk that there may be other undisclosed related-party relationships

        f. Evaluate whether management's failure to disclose the matter might have been intentional

    2.   If the auditor identifies significant related-party transactions outside the entity's normal course of business—The auditor should determine whether those transactions have been appropriately authorized. The auditor should also inspect any underlying agreements to evaluate whether the terms are consistent with management's explanations or whether the business rationale might suggest fraud.

  5. **Communication**—The auditor should communicate with those charged with governance any significant matters involving the entity's related parties.

  6. **Documentation**—The auditor should include in the audit documentation the names of the identified related parties and the nature of the related-party relationships and transactions.

B. **Procedures to Identify the Existence of Related Parties**

  A. Inquire of management as to the existence of any related-party relationships.

  B. Review prior year's audit documentation for continuing engagements.

  C. Might inquire of the predecessor auditors for a first-year engagement (if applicable).

  D. Review any applicable SEC filings (for public companies) that list related parties.

  E. Review stockholder listings of closely held companies to identify major stockholders.

C. **Procedures to Identify Transactions with the Related Parties**

  A. Inquire of management about any such transactions. Review any conflict-of-interest statements furnished to the company by management.

  B. Review minutes of board of directors' meetings for mention of significant activities with related parties.

  C. Review the accounting records for any large, unusual, or nonrecurring transactions, especially near the end of the reporting period.

  D. Examine underlying documents for unusual or large transactions (such as investment transactions) and transactions that have terms or conditions that are inconsistent with prevailing market conditions (such as loans with abnormal interest rates or without stated maturity dates):

      1. Guarantees of loans (either payable or receivable) might be identified on confirmations of such loans

      2. Transactions with major customers, suppliers, borrowers, or lenders might indicate undisclosed relationships

      3. Invoices from law firms might indicate work performed for related parties or related-party transactions

PCAOB on Related Parties

After studying this lesson, you should be able to:

1. Understand how to identify and assess the risks of material misstatement involving related party relationships and transactions under PCAOB auditing standards.

2. Understand how to respond to the assessed risks of material misstatement involving related party relationships and transactions and to evaluate their financial statement effects under PCAOB auditing standards.

3. Know the auditor's responsibilities for communicating with an entity's audit committee about related party relationships and transactions under PCAOB auditing standards.

I. **Related Parties**

II. **Introduction and Overview**

    A. Until 2014, the PCAOB guidance with respect to related-party issues was a now-superseded AICPA Statement on Auditing Standards adopted by the PCAOB on a temporary basis in 2003. The PCAOB updated its guidance on related-party relationships and transactions by incorporating the PCAOB's risk assessment standards issued in 2010.

    B. **Objective**—The auditor's objective is "to obtain sufficient appropriate audit evidence to determine whether related parties and relationships and transactions with related parties have been properly identified, accounted for, and disclosed in the financial statements."

    C. **Risk Assessment**—The auditor should identify and assess the risks of material misstatement at the financial statement and assertion levels, including the risks of material misstatement associated with related parties and transactions with related parties.

    D. **Response to Risk Assessment**—The auditor should design and implement audit responses addressing the assessed risks of material misstatement, including the risks of material misstatement associated with related parties and transactions with related parties.

> **Note**
> *If management makes an assertion that transactions with related parties were conducted on terms equivalent to those prevailing in arm's-length transactions, the auditor should determine whether evidence obtained supports or refutes such assertions. Such an assertion may result in a qualified or adverse opinion, since it may be impossible for management to determine what the terms would have been had the parties not been related.*

III. **Perform Risk Assessment Procedures**—The auditor should perform procedures to obtain an understanding of the nature of the relationships between the company and its related parties, including the terms and business purposes of transactions with related parties.

    A. The auditor should obtain an understanding of the company's process for

        1. Identifying related parties and transactions with related parties;

        2. Authorizing and approving transactions with related parties; *and*

        3. Accounting for and disclosing relationships and transactions with related parties in the financial statements.

    B. The auditor should make appropriate inquiries of management, others who may be knowledgeable about related-party issues, and the audit committee (or chair).

        1. Inquire of management about the following:

            a. The names of the company's related parties, the nature of the relationships, and any changes from the prior period;

            b. Background information about the related parties, including location, industry, size, etc.;

    c. The transactions involving related parties during the period, including the terms and business purposes of those transactions; *and*

    d. Any related-party transactions that were not authorized according to the company's established policies (including any exceptions that were granted and the reasons).

  2. Inquire of others who may have knowledge of the matters identified above. These may include internal auditors, in-house legal counsel, the chief compliance/ethics officer, and the human resources director.

  3. Inquire of the audit committee (or its chair) about the audit committee's understanding of the company's relationships, significant related-party transactions, and whether any member of the audit committee has any concerns about related-party issues.

C. Communication—The auditor should communicate relevant information about related-party issues to engagement team members (and, when using the work of other auditors, the auditor should communicate relevant information about related-party issues to those other auditors).

IV. Response to Risk Assessment—The auditor should respond appropriately to the assessed risks of material misstatement associated with related parties and transactions with related parties.

A. For any related-party transactions that are required to be disclosed or that are determined to be a significant risk, the auditor should do the following:

  1. Read the underlying documents for consistency with explanations from inquiries and other audit evidence about the business purpose;

  2. Determine whether the transaction has been authorized and approved in accordance with the company's established policies and whether any exceptions to the company's established policies were granted;

  3. Evaluate the financial capability of the related parties with respect to significant responsibilities (relevant information might include the audited financial statements of the related parties, reports of regulatory agencies, financial publications, and income tax returns if available); *and*

  4. Perform other procedures as necessary regarding the assessed risks of material misstatement.

B. Intercompany Accounts—The auditor should address the risks of material misstatement regarding the company's intercompany accounts.

V. Evaluation of Financial Statement Treatment—The auditor should evaluate whether the company has properly identified its related parties and transactions with related parties.

A. The auditor should read the minutes of board meetings and evaluate any significant unusual transactions, including transactions with executives.

B. If the auditor believes that previously undisclosed related-party relationships or transactions may exist, the auditor should perform procedures (beyond inquiry of management) to determine whether those relationships or transactions do exist.

C. If the auditor determines that previously undisclosed related-party relationships or transactions exist, the auditor should do the following:

  1. Inquire of management about the possible existence of other transactions with the related party previously undisclosed;

  2. Evaluate why the matter was previously undisclosed to the auditor;

  3. Communicate relevant information to other members of the audit team;

  4. Consider the need to perform additional procedures to identify other relationships or transactions previously undisclosed;

  5. Perform the procedures identified above for transactions with related parties required to be disclosed or determined to be a significant risk; *and*

6. Reconsider the auditor's risk assessment: (1) Evaluate the implications to the auditor's assessment of internal control; (2) reassess the risk of material misstatement and perform additional procedures as necessary; and (3) evaluate the implications for the audit if the auditor believes the undisclosed matter indicates that fraud or an illegal act may be involved.

D. Communications with the Audit Committee

A. In general, the auditor should communicate the auditor's evaluation of the company's identification and financial reporting of related-party relationships and transactions.

B. The auditor should also communicate other significant matters associated with related-party relationships and transactions, such as the following:

1. Related-party relationships or transactions with parties that were previously undisclosed to the auditor

2. Significant related-party transactions that have not been authorized in accordance with the company's established policies or for which exceptions to the company's established policies were made

3. Related-party transactions identified by the auditor that appear to lack an appropriate business purpose

4. Management's assertion included in the financial statements that the terms of a related-party transaction were equivalent to that of an arm's-length transaction (and the evidence obtained by the auditor that is consistent or inconsistent with that assertion)

E. Indicators of Related Parties and Transactions Undisclosed to the Auditor

The PCAOB provides examples of information (and sources of information) that may indicate to the auditor that related parties or related-party transactions previously undisclosed to the auditor might exist.

A. Examples of **information** that may indicate that related parties or transactions with related parties previously undisclosed to the auditor might exist

1. Purchasing or selling at significantly different than market prices

2. Sales transactions that have unusual terms (e.g., "bill and hold" transactions) or engaging in transactions that lack economic substance

3. Borrowing or lending at significantly different than normal terms

4. Advancing funds that are used to pay for an otherwise uncollectible receivable

5. Guarantees outside the normal course of business

B. Examples of **sources of information** that may indicate that related parties or transactions with related parties previously undisclosed to the auditor might exist:

1. Filings with the SEC and other regulatory agencies

2. Confirmation responses and lawyer letters

3. Internal reports (e.g., reports prepared by the entity's internal auditors and records from the company's whistleblower program)

4. Shareholder registers identifying major shareholders

5. Contracts and other agreements with management or others involving significant unusual transactions

Subsequent Events and Related Issues

After studying this lesson, you should be able to:

1. Know what is meant by the term *subsequent events*, and distinguish between those that require adjustments to the financial statement and those that require disclosure without adjustment.

2. Understand the auditing procedures associated with identifying subsequent events issues.

3. Recognize the effect that subsequent events issues may have on dating the auditor's report.

4. Understand the auditor's responsibilities when subsequently discovered facts become known to the auditor before (and after) the report release date.

5. Understand the predecessor auditor's responsibility when considering the reissuance of the auditor's report on prior period financial statements.

I. **Responsibilities under AICPA Professional Standards**—The relevant AICPA guidance is provided by AU 560, *Subsequent Events and Subsequently Discovered Facts*. This pronouncement states that the auditor's objectives are

   A. To obtain sufficient appropriate audit evidence about whether subsequent events are properly reflected in the financial statements;

   B. To respond appropriately to subsequently discovered facts; and

   C. For a predecessor auditor who is requested to reissue a previously issued report, to perform specified procedures to determine whether the previously issued report is still appropriate.

> **Definitions**
>
> *Subsequent Events:* Events occurring between the date of the financial statements and the date of the auditor's report.
>
> *Subsequently Discovered Facts:* Facts that become known to the auditor after the date of the auditor's report that, had they been known to the auditor at that date, may have caused the auditor to revise the auditor's report.

II. **Subsequent Events Requiring Adjustment**—Where such an event provides new or better information about circumstances in existence as of the balance sheet date.

 Example
A lawsuit that could only be estimated at the balance sheet date was settled for a fixed amount prior to the issuance of the audit report; with the benefit of this new information, there is no need to estimate the financial statement consequences, since the actual consequence is now known and can be used to adjust the income statement and balance sheet.

III. **Subsequent Events Requiring Disclosure Only**—Where disclosure of a material event or transaction is necessary so that the financial statements will not be misleading, even though the subsequent events issue is unrelated to circumstances existing at the balance sheet date.

 Example
After the balance sheet date, a tornado wiped out the company's facilities and the company had no casualty insurance; disclosure would be required to prevent financial statement readers from being misled about the entity's circumstances, but adjustment would not be required since the financial statement presentation was appropriate at year-end.

IV. Audit Procedures Regarding Subsequent Events

    A. Inquire of Management—Include an appropriate reference to such subsequent events in the management representations letter. The auditor should also obtain an understanding of management's procedures to identify subsequent events, as appropriate.

    B. Review the minutes of meetings of those charged with governance. (Include all meetings up to the date of the audit report.)

    C. The lawyer's letter may be relevant to this issue (regarding legal contingencies).

    D. Scan journals and ledgers subsequent to year-end (through fieldwork) for any unusual items.

V. Subsequently Discovered Facts Known Before the Report Release Date—Subsequently discovered facts that became known to the auditor before the report release date

    A. The auditor should discuss the matter with management (and possibly those charged with governance) and determine whether the financial statements require revision. If so, the auditor should inquire as to how management will address the matter.

    B. If Management Revises the Financial Statements—The auditor should perform appropriate audit procedures on the revision.

    C. If Management Does Not Revise the Financial Statements—If the auditor believes that revision is necessary, the auditor should appropriately modify the opinion.

VI. Subsequently Discovered Facts Known After the Report Release Date

    A. The auditor should discuss the matter with management (and possibly those charged with governance) and determine whether the financial statements require revision. If so, the auditor should inquire as to how management will address the matter.

    B. If Management Revises the Financial Statements—The auditor should

        1. Perform appropriate audit procedures on the revision;

        2. Assess whether management's actions are timely and appropriate to ensure that users are informed; *and*

        3. If the opinion on the revised financial statements differs from that previously expressed; add an emphasis-of-matter or other matter paragraph (that identifies the date of the previous report, the opinion previously expressed, and the reason for the different opinion now expressed).

    C. If Management Does Not Revise the Financial Statements—If the auditor believes that revision is necessary, the auditor should determine whether those financial statements have already been made available to third parties.

        1. If the financial statements have not been made available to third parties, the auditor should notify management and those charged with governance that the financial statements should not be made available to third parties before making necessary revisions and a new audit report has been provided.

        2. If the financial statements have been made available, the auditor should determine whether management has taken timely and appropriate steps to ensure that users have been informed not to rely on those financial statements.

        3. If management does not take the necessary steps to inform the users, the auditor should notify management and those charged with governance that the auditor will try to prevent users' reliance on the auditor's report.

VII. If a Predecessor Auditor Reissues the Auditor's Report

    A. The predecessor should perform the following procedures to determine whether the previously issued auditor's report is still appropriate:

        1. Read the financial statements of the subsequent period (and compare those financial statements with the ones previously audited and reported on to identify any significant changes);

2. Inquire of and request written representations from management about any issues, including subsequent events, that might affect the previous representations from management; *and*

3. Obtain a representation letter from the successor auditor about any known matters affecting the financial statements audited by the predecessor.

B. If a Subsequently Discovered Fact Becomes Known to the Predecessor

1. The predecessor auditor should discuss the matter with management (and possibly those charged with governance) and determine whether the financial statements require revision. If so, the auditor should inquire as to how management will address the matter.

2. If management revises the financial statements and the predecessor auditor plans to issue a new auditor's report—the predecessor should:

    a. Perform the procedures necessary to evaluate the revision (and date the audit report appropriately or dual-date the report for the revision);

    b. Assess steps taken by management to ensure that users do not rely on the erroneous financial statements; *and*

    c. If the opinion on the revised financial statements differs from that previously expressed, add an emphasis-of-matter or other matter paragraph (that identifies the date of the previous report, the opinion previously expressed, and the reason for the different opinion now expressed).

VIII. Dating the Auditor's Report—Applicable to subsequent events, as well as to subsequently discovered facts involving the auditor or the predecessor auditor.

A. Dating the Auditor's Report—The auditor's report should not be dated earlier than the date on which the auditor has obtained "sufficient appropriate audit evidence to support the opinion."

1. Earlier auditing standards used to emphasize the *completion of fieldwork* as the relevant date for the audit report.

2. Current standards emphasize that the audit report should not be dated before the completion of fieldwork, and may be dated later than that. For example, management must take responsibility for the financial statement presentation, including footnotes; and the auditor must review and evaluate the audit documentation before having *sufficient appropriate evidence* both of which may follow the so-called completion of fieldwork.

B. Subsequent Events—Dating the auditor's report when a subsequent event occurs after the completion of fieldwork but prior to the issuance of the auditor's report

1. If the financial statements are adjusted without any accompanying disclosure, the report should be dated whenever the auditor has obtained *sufficient appropriate audit evidence* (which may be the completion of fieldwork or later). In this case, there is no need to consider *dual dating*.

2. If the financial statements are (a) adjusted along with additional footnote disclosure; or (b) disclosure is added without adjustment—the audit report may be either "dual dated" (using one date for the overall audit report and a later date to address a specific subsequent event) or the entire audit report may be dated as of the later date (which makes the auditor responsible, in general, for all subsequent events up to that later date).

Example
Dual-Dating the Audit Report
"February 16, 20X1, except for Note XY, as to which the date is March 1, 20X1"

C. Subsequently Discovered Facts—If management revised the financial statements

1. **Before the report release date**—The auditor should either date the auditor's report as of a later date (and extend the audit procedures to the new date and obtain an updated management representations letter as of the new date) or dual-date the auditor's report for the revision.

2. **After the report release date (also applicable to a predecessor auditor)**—The auditor should date the audit report appropriately or dual-date the report for the revision.

Going-Concern Issues

After studying this lesson, you should be able to:

1. Know the indicators that would cause the auditor to have "substantial doubt about an entity's ability to continue as a going concern" (and the audit procedures that would likely detect such issues).

2. Understand the additional evidence-gathering responsibilities (and documentation requirements) the auditor has when substantial doubt about the entity's ability to continue occurs.

3. Understand the audit reporting implications of going-concern issues.

I. **Responsibilities under AICPA Professional Standards**—The relevant AICPA guidance is provided by AU 570, *The Auditor's Consideration of an Entity's Ability to Continue as a Going Concern*. This pronouncement states that the auditor's objectives are to:

   A. Evaluate and conclude whether there is substantial doubt about the entity's ability to continue as a going concern for a reasonable period of time.

   B. Assess the possible financial statement effects, including the adequacy of disclosure about the entity's ability to continue as a going concern for a reasonable period of time.

   C. Determine the implications for the auditor's report.

> **Definition**
> *Reasonable Period of Time*: A period of time not to exceed one year beyond the date of the financial statements being audited.

II. **Audit Procedures to Identify Whether There Is *Substantial Doubt***—The auditor's usual audit procedures would ordinarily be sufficient to identify circumstances related to a going-concern issue. In other words, the auditor normally does not need to design audit procedures to specifically search for going concern issues. Such procedures would include:

   A. Analytical procedures

   B. Review for subsequent events

   C. Review compliance with terms of loan agreements. (Noncompliance with debt covenants usually results in that debt becoming immediately due and payable!)

   D. Read the minutes of meetings of those charged with governance for any discussion of significant issues

   E. Inquire of the entity's attorney(s) about lawsuits by requesting a "lawyer's letter"

III. **Indicators of Substantial Doubt**

   A. **Negative Trends**—Recurring losses, negative cash flows, or working capital deficiencies.

   B. **Other Indicators**—Defaults on debt, violations of debt covenants, disposals of major assets, or restructuring of debt.

   C. **Internal Matters**—Labor problems, dependence on single projects or customers, or harmful long-term commitments.

   D. **External Matters**—Lawsuits, catastrophic losses, harmful legislation, a downturn in the economy causing many companies in an adversely affected industry to fail, or a loss of major customers or suppliers.

IV. Additional Evidence-Gathering Responsibilities—When the auditor has *substantial doubt about the entity's ability to continue as a going concern*, the auditor's reporting responsibilities extend to one year after the balance sheet date.

Note
The auditor cannot be expected to predict the future, however!

A. Inquire about management's strategy to overcome the financial difficulties for example, to dispose of assets, to borrow or restructure existing debt, to delay expenditures, or to issue additional stock. These are *mitigating factors* that might be expected to generate meaningful cash inflows or reduce the entity's cash outflows. The auditor should assess whether management's plans would likely mitigate the adverse effects of the entity's circumstances.

B. Plan and perform audit procedures to evaluate the feasibility of those elements of management's plans deemed most important. For example, the auditor should evaluate the feasibility of management's plans to obtain additional financing or to dispose of certain assets.

C. Written Representations—The auditor should obtain written representations from management about two matters:

1. Management's plans designed to mitigate the adverse effects of such conditions and the likelihood that those plans can be executed; *and*

2. Management's belief that the financial statements disclose all relevant matters about the going-concern issue of which management is aware.

V. Reporting Responsibilities—When the auditor continues to have substantial doubt about the entity's ability to continue as a going concern, despite management's plans to mitigate the adverse effects of such conditions:

A. Evaluate the adequacy of disclosure relative to the requirements of the applicable financial reporting framework. (If the auditor believes that this "substantial doubt" has been mitigated as a result of the perceived effectiveness of management's plans, the auditor should also consider the adequacy of the disclosure of those matters that initially caused the auditor to have substantial doubt, along with the appropriate disclosure of the mitigating factors.)

B. The auditor should add an *emphasis-of-matter* (after the opinion paragraph) to draw the reader's attention to the going-concern uncertainties if the management's disclosure of these uncertainties is adequate and the auditor intends to issue an unmodified opinion. However, if the disclosures are inadequate, then the auditor should appropriately modify the opinion.

C. The auditor could possibly disclaim an opinion if sufficient appropriate evidence cannot be obtained to evaluate the adequacy of the entity's financial statement treatment of these uncertainties in relation to GAAP (as a scope limitation). If disclaiming an opinion, the auditor should not include the emphasis-of-matter paragraph.

D. The SAS points out that the auditor should not use *conditional language* in expressing a conclusion regarding the existence of substantial doubt about the entity's ability to continue as a going concern. As an example of inappropriate conditional language that is prohibited, the SAS offered the following: "The Company has been unable to renegotiate its expiring credit agreements. Unless the Company is able to obtain financial support, there is substantial doubt about its ability to continue as a going concern."

Sample emphasis-of-matter paragraph (presented after the opinion paragraph):

The accompanying financial statements have been prepared assuming that the Company will continue as a going concern. As discussed in Note X to the financial statements, the Company has suffered recurring losses from operations and has a net capital deficiency that raises substantial doubt about its ability to continue as a going concern. Management's plans in regard to these matters are also described in Note X. The financial statements do not include any adjustments that might result from the outcome of this uncertainty. Our opinion is not modified with respect to this matter.

VI. Documentation Requirements—The auditor should document the following matters related to going-concern issues:

A. The conditions that caused the auditor to believe that there is substantial doubt about the entity's ability to continue as a going concern

B. The elements of management's plans considered particularly important

C. The procedures the auditor performed to evaluate those significant elements of management's plans, and the evidence obtained

D. The auditor's conclusion as to whether substantial doubt about the entity's ability to continue as a going concern for a reasonable period of time remains or is alleviated by management's strategy

E. The consideration and effect of that conclusion on the auditor's report

VII. Required Communication with Those Charged with Governance—When substantial doubt about the entity's ability to continue as a going concern remains, the auditor should communicate:

A. The nature of the conditions identified

B. The possible effect on the financial statements and disclosures

C. The effects on the auditor's report

Audit Evidence: Specific Audit Areas

Introduction to Auditing Individual Areas

> **After studying this lesson, you should be able to:**
>
> 1. Identify the four assertions for account balances, at the end of the period, as broad audit objectives applicable to balance-sheet line items for which the auditor must gather evidence as a basis for evaluation.
>
> 2. Identify certain audit procedures that are generally applicable to each of these assertions and other audit procedures that are generally applicable to every individual audit area.

I. **Audit Procedures Generally Applicable to the Four Assertions for Account Balances**—Note that these assertions represent broad audit objectives for which the auditor must gather evidence to determine whether the financial statement elements are fairly presented in accordance with the applicable accounting framework (e.g., GAAP).

    A. **Existence**—Related to the validity of recorded items.

        1. **Confirmation**—(Especially when concerned about overstatements.) For example, cash, accounts receivable, inventory held by others, and investments held by others.

        2. **Observation**—Especially for inventory or investment securities held by the entity.

        3. **Agree (vouch) to underlying documents**—Agree items from the accounting records to the supporting source documents to evaluate the appropriateness of recorded items: for example, as an alternate procedure for accounts receivable; to verify additions to property, plant, and equipment accounts; and for various liabilities, such as notes payable.

    B. **Completeness**—Related to omissions of amounts that should have been recorded.

        1. **Cutoff tests**—Trace from supporting source documents back to the accounting records looking for omissions. For example, trace from shipping documents to cost of goods sold or to the sales journal, or perform a "search for unrecorded liabilities."

        2. **Analytical procedures**—These are applicable to every audit area, but be specific: calculate a particular ratio or compare something specific to another specific thing!

    C. **Rights and Obligations**—Related to any restrictions to the entity's rights to their assets or to the obligations for their liabilities.

        1. **Inquire of applicable client personnel**—Inquire about compensating balances with banks, the use of specific assets as collateral for debts, review debt agreements for collateral, etc.; the management representation letter should document these inquiries regarding important matters.

        2. **Examine authorization of transactions**—to ascertain whether any unusual conditions apply.

    D. **Valuation and Allocation**—Related to the appropriateness of dollar measurements.

        1. **Recalculate account balances**—(Verify the client's calculations), for example, for depreciation expense and prepaid insurance.

        2. **Trace to subsequent cash receipts or disbursements**—Includes tracing to cash receipts or cash disbursements journal and to the applicable bank statement.

        3. **Analytical procedures**—review the aged trial balance for accounts receivable to evaluate the apparent reasonableness of the allowance for uncollectibles. (In connection with such analytical procedures, the auditor may also inspect underlying sales invoices or shipping documents to test the accuracy of the entity's data underlying the analytical procedures.)

4. **Examine published price quotations for fair value measurements, when applicable**—Verify mathematical accuracy. Verify that the supporting ledgers or other accounting records agree to the reported balance per the general ledger before performing other audit procedures on those supporting accounting records for purposes of reaching a conclusion about the fairness of the general ledger account balance involved. *Foot* and *cross-foot* the underlying records to verify that they, in fact, add up.

II. **Audit Procedures Generally Applicable to Every Individual Audit Area**

A. **Consider the Implications of Internal Control**—Remember the acronym **"SCARE"** [for "segregation of duties, controls (as in physical controls), authorization, reviews (as in performance reviews), and EDP (for information processing)]" discussed in the "Internal Control Concepts and Standards" section) to identify control activities of interest to the auditor relevant to planning the **nature, timing, and extent of substantive procedures** that underlie detection risk, based on the assessed level of control risk.

B. **Substantive Procedures usually Performed in Every Individual Audit Area**

1. Agree the financial statement elements (or the trial balance from which the financial statement elements are derived) to the underlying accounting records (i.e., to the general ledger).

2. Scan the entity's journals and ledgers for any unusual items.

3. Make appropriate inquiries of management and other personnel (and document those important inquiries and management's responses in the management representations letter).

4. Perform specific analytical procedures—consider historical trends and events within the industry.

Cash

After studying this lesson, you should be able to:

1. Verify the appropriateness of each of the items on an entity's bank reconciliation, supporting the entity's reported cash balance.

2. Be familiar with the content of the standard bank confirmation form.

3. Understand what is meant by the term *kiting* and how the auditor might address this issue.

I. Review the Client's Bank Reconciliation for Each Cash Account

A. Request a **cutoff bank statement** approximately 10 days after year-end, to test the reconciling items on the year-end bank reconciliation. (This request must come from management to the entity's financial institution to provide information directly to the entity's auditors.)

1. **Deposits in-transit**—Verify that items listed as deposits in transit on the bank reconciliation have been processed as deposits on the cutoff bank statement (testing for existence/occurrence regarding the validity of those reconciling items); these should appear in chronological order on the cutoff bank statement.

2. **Outstanding checks**—Look for checks processed with the cutoff bank statement and having a date prior to year-end; trace those items to the client's list of outstanding checks for completeness. (Note that checks outstanding at year-end will not necessarily clear the bank in order or within the period encompassed by the cutoff bank statement.)

B. **Confirm** directly with the bank the balance according to the bank statement (usually confirm two separate bank-related matters: (1) cash balances with emphasis on the existence assertion; and (2) liabilities to the bank with emphasis on the completeness assertion)—Note that such evidence obtained from independent sources outside the client organization is viewed as very reliable evidence.

Sample Bank Reconciliation As of 12/31/X1:

Balance per bank @ 12/31/X1	$X[1]
Add: Deposits in transit	X[2]
Less: Outstanding checks	(X)[3]
Adjusted balance as of 12/31/X1	$X
Balance per books @ 12/31/X1	X[4]
Add: Credits directly by bank (e.g., interest)	X[5]
Less: Charges by bank (service charges, etc.)	(X)[5]
Adjusted balance as of 12/31/X1	$X

Legend:

[1] Confirmed as of 12/31/X1... (A-3).

[2] Agreed to bank cutoff statement (A-4).

[3] Reviewed canceled checks (dated December or earlier and processed in January) returned with bank cutoff statement (A-4); no omissions from the outstanding check listing were noted.

[4] Agreed to General Ledger as of 12/31/X1.

[5] Agreed to client's December bank statement.

Standard Form to Confirm Account
Balance Information with Financial Institutions

_____
Customer Name

Financial
Institution's
Name and
Address

[   ]

[   ]

We have provided to our accountants the following information as of the close of business on_____, 20___, regarding our deposit and loan balances. Please confirm the accuracy of the information, noting any exceptions to the information provided. If the balances have been left blank, please complete this from by furnishing the balance in the appropriate space below.* Although we do not request nor expect you to conduct a comprehensive, detailed search of your records, if during the process of comleting this confirmation additional information about other deposit and loan accounts we may have with you comes to your attention, please include such information below. Please use the enclosed envelope to return the form directly to our accountants.

1. At the close of business on the date listed above, our records indicated the following deposit balance(s):

Account Name	Account No.	Interest Rate	Balance

2. We were directly liable to the financial institution for loans at the close of business on the date listed above as follows:

Account No./Description	Balance	Due Date	Interest Rate	Date through which interest is paid	Description of Collateral

_____
Customer's Authorized Signature

_____
Date

The information presented above by the customer is in agreement with our records. Although we have not conducted a comprehensive, detailed search of our records, no other deposit or loan accounts have come to our attention except as noted below.

_____
Financial Institution Authorized Signature / Title

_____
Date

Exceptions and/or comments

Please return this form directly to our accountants: [   ]

*Ordinarily, balances are intentionally left blank if they
are not available at the time the form is prepared.

[   ] D 451 5951

Approved 1990 by American Bankers Association, American Institute of Certified Public Accountants, and Bank Administration Institute.
Additional forms available from: AICPA - Order Department, P.O. Box 1003, NY, NY 10108-1003

II. Multiple Checking Accounts with Transfers Among Them

A. Prepare a schedule of interbank (or intercompany) transfers to verify that both sides of the transfer are properly accounted for (i.e., verify that the cash receipts journal and the cash disbursements journal both reflect the transfer in the same proper period) and to detect any **kiting.**

B. Kiting is an overstatement of the true cash balance at year-end caused by recording the receipt, while failing to record the disbursement, associated with a transfer between cash accounts. (Note that recording the disbursement, while failing to record the receipt part of a transfer between cash accounts would result in a misstatement—however, it would be an understatement of the cash balance and, therefore, would be inconsistent with kiting, which results specifically in an overstatement.)

III. **If Fraud (Misappropriation) Is Suspected**—The auditor may prepare a **proof of cash**. This compares the beginning balance per the bank plus deposits minus checks clearing the bank versus the beginning balance per the books plus receipts minus disbursements according to the books.

IV. **Petty Cash**—May count cash on hand at the client's request. (If the auditor chooses to perform any specific audit procedures for an immaterial account, such as petty cash, analytical procedures are usually sufficient, such as simply comparing the current year's general ledger balance to the prior year's general ledger balance.)

V. **Inquire of Management**—About any **restrictions on cash balances**. If there is a minimum balance requirement for cash, then that restriction should be disclosed.

> **Note**
> *The* management representations letter *usually addresses any compensating balances (minimum balance requirements) that constitute a restriction on spendable cash. (The usual management representations comment that addresses all general restrictions on the entity's rights to its assets is: "The company has satisfactory title to all owned assets, and there are no liens or encumbrances on such assets nor has any asset been pledged as collateral.")*

Accounts Receivable

After studying this lesson, you should be able to:

1. Recognize that the four assertions for account balances at the end of the period represent a framework for preparing an audit plan to evaluate the fairness of accounts receivable.

2. Know how to identify the appropriate substantive audit procedures to address each of those assertions when auditing accounts receivable.

I. **Recall the four assertions** that Professional Standards identify for account balances at the end of the period: (1) existence; (2) completeness; (3) rights and obligations; and (4) valuation and allocation.

   A. **Related to the Existence/Occurrence Assertion**—Confirm selected individual customers' accounts.

   B. Verify that the subsidiary A/R ledger agrees or reconciles with the A/R general ledger balance:

   1. Recall that the *accounting records* constitute one category of evidence. The second category is *other information* according to SAS No. 106 and is covered in the review module on Audit Evidence.

   2. It is important to establish the logical connection between the detailed accounting records being used for the audit procedure (in this case, the subsidiary ledger of individual customer accounts) and that which is the object of the auditor's intended conclusions (specifically, the general ledger balance for A/R).

   C. **Confirm all accounts** that are determined to be individually material and confirm selected other accounts on a test basis.

   1. **Positive confirmations**—Request a response whether the individual customer agrees or disagrees with the stated balance. A nonresponse indicates a situation that should be followed up by the auditor.

   2. **Negative confirmations**—Request a response only if the individual customer disagrees with the stated balance.

      a. A nonresponse is taken as evidence supporting the client's representation.

      b. The risk is that the recipient of the request might have thrown it away without even verifying the balance owed.

      c. Accordingly, negative confirmations are usually used only for rather small balances under conditions of effective internal control (i.e., low control risk).

   D. **Investigate All Exceptions (Disagreements) Received**—Determine whether the client's records are accurate and, if not, whether the financial statements are materially misstated.

   E. If no response is received to a positive confirmation request, the auditor should send a second confirmation request, and perform **alternate procedures** if still no response is received.

   1. **Subsequent cash receipts (the preferred alternate procedure)**—Trace collections on the account subsequent to the date of the confirmation to the cash receipts journal and to the bank statement (suggests the balance was valid if it was subsequently collected).

   2. **Vouch to (inspect) the underlying documents (the last resort if the account has not been collected)**—Examine the documents (customer's purchase order, client's sales invoice, and shipping documents) supporting the validity (*occurrence*) of the transactions comprising the account balance.

II. **Related to the Valuation Assertion**—Evaluate the reasonableness of management's estimates of *allowance for uncollectibles* and the *allowance for sales returns*.

A. Note that confirmations may contribute, in part, to the auditor's conclusions about the **fairness of the dollar valuation**; however, that contribution relates to establishing the reasonableness of the gross A/R and additional procedures are required to assess the net realizable value of the A/R.

B. **Review the Client's Aged Trial Balance of Accounts Receivable**

    1. Inquire about any large, delinquent items.

    2. Estimate the percentage of uncollectible accounts within each category of age (based on prior year's working papers tempered by current economic conditions).

C. Review **receivers (documents used by the entity's receiving department to capture deliveries) after year-end** for sales returns; consider prior years' returns in view of current economic conditions.

D. Review **adjusting journal entries** (e.g. write-offs) for appropriate authorization.

III. Related to the Completeness Assertion

A. Perform a **cutoff test** of sales. Examine the shipping documents for the last few shipments before year-end and the first few shipments after year-end; compare these shipping documents with the related sales invoices to assess whether the sales were recorded in the appropriate period.

B. Compare these shipping documents around the end of the period with the related sales invoices (related to the sales journal) to assess whether the sales were recorded in the appropriate period.

C. Proper cutoff involves two assertions (existence/occurrence and completeness). Usually the auditor performs certain specific audit procedures directed at testing the validity of recorded transactions (i.e., existence/occurrence) but completeness is primarily addressed by these cutoff procedures (along with applicable analytical procedures).

IV. Related to the Rights and Obligations Assertion—Inquire of management:

A. About receivables pledged as collateral for debts (and review loan agreements to identify such collateral)

B. About shipments on consignment that are not actual sales

C. About any receivables due from employees or management that should be classified separately from ordinary trade receivables

D. Document such inquiries (and management's response) in the management representations letter.

> **Note**
> *Lapping is an attempt to cover up a theft of receipts, where a clerk might try to apply a later receipt to the prior customer's account (and so on) until the scam ends by writing off someone's account as uncollectible. Lapping is a type of fraud (specifically, misappropriation of assets) that is associated with an improper segregation of duties whereby someone with access to the customer's payment also has the authority to make entries in the accounting records to cover up the theft.*

Inventory

After studying this lesson, you should be able to:

1. Recognize that the four assertions for account balances at the end of the period represent a framework for preparing an audit plan to evaluate the fairness of inventory.

2. Identify appropriate substantive audit procedures to address each of those assertions when auditing inventory.

Recall the four assertions that that Professional Standards identify for account balances at the end of the period: (1) existence; (2) completeness; (3) rights and obligations; and (4) valuation and allocation.

I. **Relevant AICPA Guidance**—The relevant AICPA guidance is provided by AU 501, *Audit Evidence— Specific Considerations for Selected Items*. Part of this standard focuses specifically on inventory, which is summarized here. The standard states that the auditor's objective is to obtain sufficient appropriate audit evidence about the **existence and condition** of inventory.

II. **Related to the Existence Assertion**—The auditor participates in the client's physical count of inventory (the observation of inventory):

    A. **Note**—The **client counts** the entire inventory and the **auditor observes** the client's taking of the inventory (while taking independent *test counts*). The auditor participates in this process for two primary reasons, referred to as *dual purpose* tests.

        1. **Internal control objectives**—The auditor should study the client's written procedures and instructions given to the employees or others counting the inventory to assess the adequacy of the design of these procedures in achieving an accurate physical count; the auditor's focus here is assessing control risk related to inventory reporting.

        2. **Substantive audit objectives**—The auditor should take a sample of inventory items and verify the physical existence of quantities reflected in the client's detailed records supporting the ending inventory; the auditor's focus here is assessing the fairness of the reported inventory.

Recall that the *direction* of the test is critical to the inference associated with an audit procedure:

To test existence for inventory—The auditor should select items from the client's (final) inventory listing, which is essentially the subsidiary ledger for the adjusted general ledger balance. The auditor should agree those selected items to the underlying inventory count tags (and the auditor's own count sheets) that serve as source documents.

To test completeness for inventory—The direction of the test is just the opposite. The auditor should select items from the underlying inventory count tags (including the auditor's own count sheets) and agree those to the client's inventory listing to establish that there were no omissions from the client's inventory listing.

    B. **Related to Audit Procedures**—Emphasizing quantities:

        1. **Auditor's attendance at physical inventory counting**—Involves (a) inspecting the inventory to ascertain its existence and evaluate its condition (and performing test counts); (b) observing compliance with management's instructions and the performance of procedures for recording and controlling the results of the physical count; and (c) obtaining audit evidence about the reliability of management's count procedures

        2. Review the client's written inventory-taking procedures to determine that the physical count will be complete and accurate (regarding dates, locations, personnel involved, and

instructions about accounting for the prenumbered inventory tags, cutoff procedures, and error resolution procedures)

3. Assessing the accuracy of the client's reported inventory **quantities**. The auditor should perform test counts for a sample of the prenumbered inventory tags, trace these counts into the client's count sheets (to verify the accuracy of the client's counts on a test basis) and to the client's final inventory listing that supports the general ledger balance. Note that the entity's final inventory listing (reflecting both quantities and dollar amounts) serves as the "subsidiary ledger" for inventory and represents the dollar amount for inventory to which the general ledger account will be adjusted.

4. Focus on the client's prenumbered inventory tags. Determine that all tags have been properly accounted for (i.e., all tags are used, unused and returned, or have been voided and returned to a responsible official).

5. The auditor should be alert for and inquire about obsolete or damaged items (e.g., dusty or damaged cartons) related to the valuation assertion; the auditor should also be alert for empty containers or hollow spaces.

C. If the physical count of inventory occurs on a date other than the date of the financial statements, the auditor should perform audit procedures to determine whether changes in inventory between those dates are properly recorded.

D. If the auditor is unable to attend physical inventory counting due to unforeseen circumstances, the auditor should make some physical counts on an alternative date and perform audit procedures on intervening transactions.

E. If attendance at physical inventory counting is impracticable, the auditor should perform alternative audit procedures to obtain sufficient appropriate audit evidence regarding the existence and condition of inventory. If that is not possible, then the auditor should appropriately modify the auditor's opinion.

F. If there is a material amount of inventory stored in a **public warehouse**, the auditor can confirm such inventory with the custodian (or could consider physical observation).

III. **Related to the Valuation Assertion**

A. **Price Tests**—Regarding the **unit costs** (not selling prices!) attributed to inventory items:

1. Affected by the client's inventory methods (perpetual versus periodic inventory system) and cost flow assumptions (LIFO, FIFO, average)

2. For merchandising (nonmanufacturing) inventory—Examine the appropriate underlying invoices

3. For manufactured inventory—Review the supporting job order cost records (or the process cost worksheets) and test to underlying documents.

B. **Test Extensions**—Recalculate the product of quantity times cost/unit for selected items:

1. Add up these extensions to verify that the items tested are reflected in the total of the detailed inventory listing supporting the client's general ledger balance. This can be described as "verifying the mathematical accuracy" to establish the connection between the general ledger balance and the supporting detailed listing;

2. Scan the detailed inventory listing for any unusual items;

3. Review the client's reconciliation (or the adjusting journal entry) of the general ledger balance to the detailed inventory listing.

C. **Lower of Cost or Market Considerations**—Inquire of management as to the existence of any damaged, obsolete, or excess inventory items that might require a write-down from historical cost to net realizable value; be attentive to these issues when participating in the observation of inventory.

IV. Related to the Completeness Assertion—Procedures that might identify material omissions of inventory:

    A. Test **inventory cutoff** (recall "FOB-shipping point" versus "FOB-destination" as a technical issue determining when title to goods is transferred):

        1. **Related to increases in inventory**—Review "receivers" (receiving documents used by the entity's receiving department to capture deliveries) for a few days before and after year-end (part of "purchases" cutoff test);

        2. **Related to decreases to inventory**—Review shipping documents for a few days before and after year-end (related to "sales" and, hence, "cost of goods sold" cutoff test).

    B. **Analytical Procedures (Perhaps by Location or by Product-Line)**—Compare the current year to the prior year and inquire about any significant differences in:

        1. Gross profit rates

        2. Inventory turnover (primarily applicable to the valuation assertion regarding slow-moving inventory)

        3. Shrinkage rates

        4. Total inventory

V. Related to the Rights and Obligations Assertion

    A. Inquire of management about any inventory that might be held on consignment or pledged as collateral for borrowings (and review loan agreements to identify such collateral).

    B. Document such inquiries (and management's response) in the management representations letter.

VI. Other Issues Related to Auditing Inventory

    A. **Use of Specialists**—An auditor may need to engage an outside expert if the determination of **quantities** and/or **quality** is too complex (e.g., electronics, precious jewels).

    B. If an auditor is unable to verify the **beginning** inventory for a first-year audit, but is able to verify the **ending** inventory:

        1. The auditor may render an opinion on the balance sheet and disclaim an opinion on the income statement, statement of retained earnings, and the statement of cash flows (due to the inability to verify cost of goods sold and, hence, net income).

        2. It may be possible to establish the reasonableness of a new client's beginning inventory from alternate procedures—through the use of analytical procedures or by reviewing a predecessor auditor's working papers.

Investments in Securities and Derivative Instruments

After studying this lesson, you should be able to:

1. Understand the auditor's responsibilities, under AICPA Professional Standards, when auditing investments (including derivative instruments and hedging activities).

2. Recognize that the four assertions for account balances at the end of the period represent a framework for preparing an audit plan to evaluate the fairness of investments.

3. Identify appropriate substantive audit procedures to address each of those assertions when auditing investments.

I. **Relevant AICPA Guidance**—The relevant AICPA guidance is provided by AU 501, *Audit Evidence—Specific Considerations for Selected Items*. Part of this standard focuses specifically on investments in securities and derivative instruments, which is summarized here. The standard states that the auditor's objective is to obtain sufficient appropriate audit evidence about the **valuation** of investments in securities and derivative instruments.

II. **Auditing Investments in Securities**—Including derivatives, measured at fair value

> **Note**
> *The Statements on Auditing Standards that preceded the clarified standards tended to address GAAP issues specifically, whereas the clarified standards are intended to be neutral with respect to the applicable financial reporting framework. Accordingly, the clarified standard no longer addresses FASB-specific issues related to investments and derivatives. The AICPA has indicated that more technical guidance about auditing derivatives will be provided in an AICPA Audit Guide on this topic.*

  A. The auditor should determine whether the applicable financial reporting framework specifies the method to be used to determine fair value (and evaluate whether the stated fair value is consistent with that method).

  B. Quoted market prices (obtained from financial publications, national exchanges, or NASDAQ) usually provide sufficient evidence of fair value.

  C. If estimates of fair value are obtained from third-party sources (such as broker-dealers)—the auditor should obtain an understanding of their methods used.

  D. If management uses a valuation model—the auditor should obtain sufficient appropriate audit evidence about the fair value based on that model. It might be good to use more than one pricing source to see if there is any consensus when the valuation is subjective or sensitive to changes in the underlying assumptions.

  E. **Impairment Losses**—the auditor should evaluate management's conclusion about the need to recognize an impairment loss, and obtain sufficient appropriate audit evidence supporting any impairment recorded. Determining whether a decline in fair value is other than temporary requires professional judgment, including consideration of the following:

    1. Whether the fair value is significantly below the carrying value (and the period of time for which that has been the case)

    2. Whether the financial condition of the issuer has deteriorated

    3. Whether the security has been downgraded by a rating agency

    4. Whether dividends have been reduced or eliminated or scheduled interest payments have not been made

    5. Whether the entity recorded losses from the security after the period-end

    6. **Unrealized appreciation or depreciation due to the ineffectiveness of a hedge**—The auditor should obtain an understanding of the methods used to determine whether the hedge is effective, including the portion that is ineffective.

III. Investments in Securities When Valuations Are Based on Cost—The usual auditing procedures may include inspection of documentation of the purchase price, confirmation with outside parties, and testing the amortization of any discount or premium.

IV. Investments in Securities When Valuations Are Based on the Investee's Financial Results—(Another SAS addresses investments accounted for using the equity method.)

A. **Reading the Audited Financial Statements of the Investee May Provide Sufficient Appropriate Audit Evidence**—If unable to obtain sufficient appropriate audit evidence, the auditor should determine the effect on the auditor's report.

B. **May Need to Obtain Additional Audit Evidence**—When there are significant differences in fiscal year-ends or in accounting principles used, the auditor may make inquiries of investor management about the investee. The auditor may need to obtain evidence about any related party transactions between the investor and investee to evaluate the adequacy of disclosure about related-party issues. If there is a lack of comparability, owing to different fiscal year-ends, the auditor may need to add an emphasis-of-matter paragraph to the auditor's report.

V. Summary of Procedures with Emphasis on Four Balance-Sheet-Related Assertions—Summary of procedures used in auditing traditional investment securities (i.e., stocks and bonds) with emphasis on the four balance-sheet-related assertions.

A. **Related to the Existence Assertion**—The auditor mainly uses inspection and confirmation.

1. Physically inspect any securities in the possession of the client entity.

2. Confirm any stocks and bonds held by an independent custodian.

B. **Related to the Completeness Assertion**—The auditor primarily uses analytical procedures to address the risk of omissions.

1. Evaluate investment income or loss accounts:

a. Verify revenue through confirmation when investments are held by an independent custodian.

b. May trace cash receipts to a bank statement

c. May recalculate the interest income on debt instruments or dividends received on stock investments

2. Compare dividends, interest, or other investment income (loss) to prior year's working papers for reasonableness; dividends can be verified by consulting dividend record books produced by commercial investment advisory services.

3. Review the minutes of the meetings of those charged with governance for approval of any large transactions.

C. **Related to the Valuation Assertion**—The appropriate audit procedures will vary with the nature of the securities involved.

1. For bonds:

a. Verify the interest earned by calculations (based on the face value, interest yield, and period held).

b. Review the amortization of any premium or discount.

c. Inquire about management's intention to hold the security to maturity (and document that inquiry in the management representations letter).

2. For investments (in stocks or bonds) that are marked to market as required by the applicable accounting standards:

a. Compare the carrying value at the beginning of the period to the prior year's working papers; agree to underlying documents, examine canceled checks for any current year additions to investments and trace the proceeds of any sales to a bank statement.

    b. Verify the year-end fair value (trace to an independent outside source, such as the *Wall Street Journal* or other appropriate quotation)—evaluate the adequacy of disclosure as required by the applicable accounting standards.

    c. Inquire of management about any impairments that may be other than temporary.

3. For investments in stock accounted for by the equity method:

    a. Compare the carrying value at the beginning of the period to the prior year's audit working papers; agree (vouch) transactions to underlying documents and examine canceled checks for any current year's additions to investments.

    b. Examine the investee's current year's audited financial statements to verify the investor's percentage share of income (loss) and any dividend distributions.

    c. Inquire of management about any impairments relative to the investment's carrying value.

D. Related to the Rights and Obligations Assertion—The auditor primarily uses inquiry and review.

1. Inquire about management's intent and ability affecting investment classifications (and document the inquiry in the management representations letter)—recall the following basic GAAP considerations:

    a. Trading securities

        i. Balance sheet—Reported at fair value (in current assets)

        ii. Income statement—Unrealized holding gains/losses should be reported on the income statement (include interest and dividends, too)

    b. Available-for-sale securities

        i. Balance sheet—Should be reported at fair value (either current or noncurrent assets, as appropriate); use unrealized holding gains and losses as a separate component of stockholders' equity.

        ii. Income statement—The unrealized holding gains/losses should be reported in other comprehensive income, not included in net income!

    c. Held-to-maturity (debt) securities

        i. Balance sheet—Should be reported at the amortized cost basis (either as current or noncurrent assets, as appropriate).

        ii. Income statement—No recognition of fluctuations in market value should be recorded! Should report interest as revenue.

2. Inquire of management about any restrictions applicable to investments (including any securities pledged as collateral for debt).

3. Review cash receipts and cash disbursements subsequent to year-end for any material transactions affecting investments, perhaps requiring disclosure.

Fixed Assets

Since the composition of the fixed assets' balances is usually substantially carried over from one period to the next, the auditor usually emphasizes substantive tests of transactions (that is, the continuing auditor usually verifies the ending balance by examining the debits and credits that caused the balance to change from the prior year).

After studying this lesson, you should be able to:

1. Recognize that the four assertions for account balances at the end of the period represent a framework for preparing an audit plan to evaluate the fairness of fixed assets.

2. Identify the appropriate substantive audit procedures to address each of those assertions when auditing fixed assets.

Recall the four assertions that Professional Standards identify for account balances at the end of the period: (1) existence; (2) completeness; (3) rights and obligations; and (4) valuation and allocation.

I.   Related to the Existence Assertion

   A.   Consider the adequacy of the accounting records. Verify that the client's detailed fixed asset listing supports the related general ledger account balance.

   B.   **For Additions**—Vouch to (inspect) the underlying documents (examine the purchase order, vendor's invoice, and the entity's canceled check if payment has been made); look for approval in the minutes of meetings of those charged with governance if the addition is a "major" one.

   C.   **For Disposals**—Trace any proceeds received to the cash receipts journal and bank statement; review for appropriate approval.

Note
Instead of performing tests of ending balances, the continuing auditor will normally verify the appropriateness of the year-end balance of fixed assets by performing substantive tests of transactions. In other words, if there are relatively few transactions that have caused the fixed asset balance to change from last year to this year, the auditor will, in effect, back into the ending balance by taking the beginning balance (audited last year), add any additions, and subtract any disposals. Since there are likely only a few additions and/or disposals, it is more efficient to examine those few transactions, rather than verify a sample of the individual items that comprise the year-end fixed asset balance.

II.   Related to the Valuation Assertion

   A.   Review the calculations for depreciation expense—compare the useful lives and methods used to prior years for consistency, and recalculate on a test basis.

   B.   Consider whether there have been any *impairments* of long-lived assets requiring a write-down from the historical cost-based carrying value—make appropriate inquiries of management (and document such inquiries and management's response in the management representations letter).

III.   Related to the Completeness Assertion

   A.   Review the client's *repairs and maintenance expense* account and examine underlying documents for material items to determine whether any of those recorded expenses should instead be capitalized.

   B.   Review any lease agreements to determine if lease capitalization might be required.

IV.   Related to the Rights and Obligations Assertion

   A.   Inquire of management about any fixed assets pledged as security for borrowings (and review loan agreements to identify such collateral).

   B.   Document such inquiries (and management's response) in the management representations letter.

Current Liabilities

After studying this lesson, you should be able to:

1. Recognize that the four assertions for account balances at the end of the period represent a framework for preparing an audit plan to evaluate the fairness of current liabilities.

2. Know how to identify appropriate substantive audit procedures to address each of those assertions when auditing current liabilities.

I. **Accounts Payable (or Vouchers Payable)**—Primarily use substantive tests of ending balances.

   A. Recall the difference between **accounts payable and vouchers payable** systems described in the review materials related to Internal Control—Transaction Cycles:

      1. **Accounts payable**—In an accounts payable system, the payables are tracked by the name of the vendor. The total payable to another party, which constitutes a receivable to them, is susceptible to confirmation if desired.

      2. **Vouchers payable**—In a vouchers payable system, the payables are tracked by individual transaction without summarizing the amounts owed by vendor name. The total payable to another party is not susceptible to confirmation, only individual transactions could be confirmed.

   B. Recall the four assertions that AICPA Professional Standards identify for account balances at the end of the period: (1) existence; (2) completeness; (3) rights and obligations; and (4) valuation and allocation.

   C. **Related to the Completeness Assertion** (for liabilities, the auditor's primary concern involves completeness not existence!)—Perform a **search for unrecorded liabilities.** This is done toward the end of fieldwork to provide the best chance of detecting any significant unrecorded liabilities.

      1. Review cash disbursements **subsequent to year-end** and, for all disbursements over some specified dollar amount (>$X), examine the related vendors' invoices and the entity's related receiving documents to identify transactions that should have been reported as liabilities as of year-end; compare those apparent liabilities to the details comprising the recorded payables to identify apparent liabilities that are unrecorded.

      2. Examine any unpaid invoices on hand at the date of the "search" along with the entity's related receiving documents to identify any transactions that should have been reported as a liability as of year-end.

      3. Inquire of management about their knowledge of any unrecorded liabilities and whether all invoices have been made available to the auditor. Document such inquiries and management's response in the management representations letter.

   D. **Related to the Existence and Valuation Assertions**

      1. Verify the mathematical accuracy of payables by comparing the general ledger balance to the supporting detailed listing of payables.

      2. Vouch selected items to the underlying vendor's invoices.

      3. Could confirm selected payables, but usually do not—Confirmation primarily establishes the validity (existence) of the recorded items, but there is a relatively low risk that the company would overstate its true liabilities; the far bigger risk is that material liabilities may have been omitted (i.e., completeness).

      4. Usually valuation is not a significant audit issue, since there is a presumption that the client will pay 100% of what is owed; the auditor should look to see that the client takes advantage of any available cash discounts for prompt payment.

E. Related to the **rights and obligations assertion**—Inspect the specific terms of the payables and inquire about any related party transactions. Separately classify notes payable for borrowings from accounts payable for ordinary operating activities.

II. **Other Current Liabilities**—The auditor uses analytical procedures extensively to evaluate other miscellaneous payables:

A. **Wages and Salaries Payable**—The auditor can compute the estimated accrual, in view of the number of days to be accrued relative to a whole pay period.

B. **Dividends Payable**—The auditor can compute, in view of the declared dividends/share (per the minutes of meetings of those charged with governance) times the number of shares outstanding.

C. **Interest Payable (and the Related Interest Expense)**—The auditor can compute an estimate of accrued interest for the time period involved, based on the interest rate (and payment dates) specified in the underlying debt agreements.

Long-Term Liabilities

After studying this lesson, you should be able to:

1. Recognize that the four assertions for account balances at the end of the period represent a framework for preparing an audit plan to evaluate the fairness of long-term liabilities.

2. Identify appropriate substantive audit procedures to address each of those assertions when auditing long-term liabilities.

Recall the four assertions that Professional Standards identify for account balances at the end of the period: (1) existence; (2) completeness; (3) rights and obligations; and (4) valuation and allocation.

I. **Related to the Completeness Assertion**—Use substantive tests of transactions (to address decreases in debt):

   A. Verify due dates for payments in the loan agreements.

   B. Trace cash disbursements from the accounting records to the bank statement.

   C. Examine canceled notes if paid in full.

   D. Could confirm year-end balances, but confirmations are most applicable to establishing the validity of recorded items (i.e., existence).

II. **Related to the Existence/Occurrence Assertion**—Use substantive tests of transactions (to address increases in debt):

   A. Obtain copies of new loan agreements for the auditor's review and documentation.

   B. Verify authorization of new debt in minutes of meetings of those charged with governance.

   C. Trace receipts from the accounting records to the bank statement.

III. **Related to the Valuation Assertion**—There are few measurement issues associated with most liabilities, but long-term liabilities should be based on present values:

   A. Trace related cash receipts and disbursements from the accounting records to the bank statements.

   B. Examine the underlying loan contracts related to the stated dollar amounts.

   C. Recalculate the amortization of any premium or discount using the effective interest method.

   D. Apply analytical procedures to the related expense accounts (e.g., interest)—Note that the balance sheet item and the related income statement item are usually addressed on the same audit documentation (working paper).

IV. **Related to the Rights and Obligations Assertion**—The auditor should make appropriate inquiries of management and review the loan documents:

   A. **Debt Covenants**—Important restrictions should be disclosed. (Note that violations of such covenants can cause the entire balance to become immediately payable.)

   B. **Collateral**—Any assets pledged as security for the debt should be disclosed.

   C. The current portion of long-term debt should be reclassified to current liabilities—Read the loan documents to identify the principal to be paid within the next year; examine the cash payments for the current-year installment paid if the debt is scheduled to be paid in equal installments.

Stockholders' Equity

After studying this lesson, you should be able to:

1. Recognize that the four assertions for account balances at the end of the period represent a framework for preparing an audit plan to evaluate the fairness of stockholders' equity.

2. Identify appropriate substantive audit procedures to address each of those assertions when auditing stockholders' equity.

Recall the four assertions that Professional Standards identify for account balances at the end of the period: (1) existence; (2) completeness; (3) rights and obligations; and (4) valuation and allocation.

I. **Related to the Existence Assertion**—Confirm the outstanding shares of stock if there is an external registrar. (Verify that the stock was issued in accordance with the company's articles of incorporation and with the approval of those charged with governance.)

II. **Related to the Completeness Assertion**

   A. Review the minutes of meetings of those charged with governance to identify authorized transactions.

   B. Account for all certificate numbers to establish that no unauthorized shares were issued.

III. **Related to the Rights and Obligations Assertion**

   A. Review the minutes of board meetings to verify that any stock and dividend transactions were duly authorized by those charged with governance.

   B. Review contracts with employee stock option plans to verify compliance with such agreements.

   C. Inquire of management about any restrictions that might exist on the availability of retained earnings for purposes of dividend distribution—the financial statements should disclose any restrictions on retained earnings available for dividend distribution.

IV. **Related to the Valuation Assertion**

   A. Review cash receipts and disbursements (and minutes of meetings of those charged with governance) for increases or decreases in stock accounts.

   B. Compare the subsidiary ledger to the general ledger stock accounts. (Examine stock certificates or read the applicable minutes of meetings of those charged with governance to verify the par or stated value per share.)

Payroll

When the auditor chooses to examine the payroll function handled in-house by the company (as opposed to an outside payroll service), recall the internal control considerations associated with the payroll transaction cycle covered in the lesson "Specific Transaction Cycles."

After studying this lesson, you should be able to:

1. Recognize that the five assertions for transactions and events during the period represent a framework for preparing an audit plan to evaluate the fairness of income statement items, such as payroll expense.

2. Identify appropriate substantive audit procedures to address payroll expense.

Recall the five assertions that Professional Standards identify for "classes of transactions and events for the period under audit": (1) accuracy; (2) occurrence; (3) completeness; (4) cutoff; and (5) classification.

I. Related to the Accuracy and Occurrence Assertions

A. Examine personnel records on a test basis, to determine that the levels of compensation and support for all deductions exist for all employees. (Officers' compensation should be documented in the minutes of meetings of those charged with governance.)

B. Trace selected transactions from the payroll register to the general ledger and to the payroll bank account.

C. Recalculate selected entries on the payroll register.

II. Related to the Completeness Assertion

A. Review time reports and time cards to verify support for production records.

B. Apply analytical procedures (and recalculation) to verify that the payroll-related accruals at year-end are reasonable.

III. Related to the Cutoff Assertion—Cutoff is effectively addressed when occurrence and completeness have been addressed; in other words, when the auditor has established that recorded transactions are properly recorded and that there are no omissions of transactions that should have been recorded, the auditor has established that the transactions have been recorded in the correct accounting period.

AICPA professional standards also state, "… there may not be a separate assertion related to cutoff of transactions and events when the occurrence and completeness assertions include appropriate consideration of recording transactions in the correct accounting period."

IV. Related to the Classification Assertion

A. The comments related to accuracy and occurrence apply to recording the transactions in the proper accounts, as well.

B. Review outside reports related to pension, other post-retirement benefits (e.g., insurance), and profit-sharing plans.

C. Verify payroll deductions and taxes, trace cash disbursements for withholdings to appropriate agencies.

D. Note that ordinarily, income statement elements (including revenue and expense items) are primarily audited by analytical procedures. Typically, tests of details will be performed only when the analytical procedures suggest that a risk of material misstatement exists and that a more detailed investigation is warranted. Payroll-related expenses would normally be subject to such analytical procedures, too. The discussion above is presented to provide insights about how such transactions could be tested in detail if the auditor deemed that appropriate.

Audit Sampling

Introduction to Sampling

> **After studying this lesson, you should be able to:**
>
> 1. Understand the distinction between statistical and nonstatistical audit sampling.
>
> 2. Understand the distinction between sampling risk and nonsampling risk.
>
> 3. Understand the distinction between false rejection (a Type 1 Error) and false acceptance (a Type 2 Error) comprising sampling risk that are applicable to control and substantive procedures tests.

> **Definition**
>
> *Sampling:* "The selection and evaluation of less than 100% of the population of audit relevance such that the auditor expects the items selected to be representative of the population …"

I. **Responsibilities under AICPA Professional Standards**—The relevant AICPA guidance is provided by AU 530, *Audit Sampling*. This pronouncement states that the auditor's objective is to provide a reasonable basis for the auditor to draw conclusions about the population from which the sample is selected.

II. **There Are Two General Approaches to Sampling**—May depend on the auditor's perceptions of cost/benefit trade-offs.

    A. **Nonstatistical Sampling**—Also called judgmental sampling

    B. **Statistical**—The benefits relate to objectivity:

        1. Relates to the **sufficiency** of the evidence—The determination of the sample size in a statistical sampling application establishes how much evidence is required.

        2. The results may seem more defensible to others (such as the courts).

        3. A common misconception is that statistical sampling eliminates the need for judgment. Actually, numerous judgments must be made; however, these judgments are made more explicit.

        4. Sampling applications occur in either of two contexts:

> **Definitions**
>
> *Attributes Sampling:* Sampling for purposes of deciding whether internal controls are working as designed (tests of controls).
>
> *Variables Sampling:* Sampling for purposes of deciding whether account balances (such as inventory or receivables) are fairly stated (substantive tests of details).

III. **Uncertainty and Audit Sampling—Risk Considerations** (Recall the definition of *audit risk*)—The probability that the auditor fails to modify the opinion on financial statements containing a material misstatement. Auditors may use the following model to evaluate the risk components explicitly:

> $AR = RMM * AP * TD$, where
>
> AR = audit risk;
>
> RMM = risk of material misstatement, consisting of the combined assessments of inherent risk and control risk;
>
> AP = risk that analytical procedures performed for substantive purposes will not detect a material misstatement that occurred; and
>
> TD = risk that tests of details will fail to detect a material misstatement that was not otherwise detected.

IV. Whether Nonstatistical Sampling or Statistical Sampling Is Used—The auditor is fundamentally seeking a sample that is truly representative of the population, so that the auditor gets an accurate signal about the population's characteristics in a highly efficient way.

V. Sampling Risk—Is the risk that the sample may not be truly representative of the population; in other words, the chance of an erroneous conclusion that the auditor takes by examining a subset of the population, rather than the entire population.

    A. Type 1 Errors (False Rejection)

        1. Tests of controls => the risk of **underreliance** on internal controls (also known as risk of assessing control risk too high).

        2. Substantive testing => the risk of incorrect rejection.

        3. Type 1 errors relate to efficiency—the auditor will probably achieve the appropriate conclusions, although not in the most efficient manner (perhaps taking more than one sample, maybe at the urging of the client who has faith in the effectiveness of the internal control or the fairness of the financial statement element).

    B. Type 2 Errors (False Acceptance)

        1. Tests of controls => the risk of **overreliance** on internal controls (also known as the risk of assessing control risk too low).

        2. Substantive testing => the risk of incorrect acceptance.

        3. Type 2 errors relate to effectiveness—now the auditor may have failed to meet the overall objective, which is to limit audit risk to an acceptably low level. (The client will have no incentive to argue about this conclusion, so the auditors will not have any reason to take a second look.)

> **Note**
> *If there were no variation within a population (i.e., if all items were homogeneous), the auditor would only need a sample of one item to assess the whole population! The variability of the population causes the sample size to increase and is responsible for the sampling risk.*

VI. Nonsampling Risk—Refers to any other mistakes by the auditor (i.e., other than sampling risk), not a direct consequence of using a sampling approach:

    A. Inappropriate auditing procedures.

    B. Failure to correctly identify "errors" or amounts sampled, misinterpreting the results, etc.

Attributes Sampling

After studying this lesson, you should be able to:

1. Understand the meaning of the term "attributes sampling."

2. Know the eight steps that comprise an attributes-sampling application.

3. Know how to determine the sample size for an attributes sampling application using AICPA tables.

I. **Attributes Sampling**—Statistical sampling for the purpose of identifying the percentage frequency of a characteristic in a population of interest to the auditor; this term is usually used to refer to audit sampling to ascertain the operating effectiveness of internal control (where, for each transaction in the sample, the control procedure of interest was either performed or not performed—there are only two outcomes, similar to '"hit or miss" or "heads or tails")

II. **Eight Steps Comprise an Attributes Sampling**

   A. **Identify the Sampling Objective**—That is, the purpose of the test.

   B. **Define What Constitutes an Occurrence**—Sometimes called a deviation or error when a control procedure of interest was not properly performed.

   C. **Identify the Relevant Population**

   1. Specify the relevant time period.

   2. Specify the sampling unit—what it is that the auditor is selecting (e.g., sales transactions).

   D. **Determine the Sampling Method**—How the specific items (or transactions) are to be selected for the sample.

   1. **Statistical sampling approaches**

      a. **Random number**—Each transaction has the same probability of being selected (the best approach).

      b. **Systematic**—For example, selecting every 100th item

   2. **Judgmental sampling approaches**—not appropriate for attributes sampling!

      a. **Block**—A group of contiguous items (e.g., the sales transactions for the entire month of June)

      b. **Haphazard**—Arbitrary selection, with no conscious biases. Subconscious biases may exist without the auditor's awareness, however.

   E. **Determine the Sample Size**—Based on AICPA tables.

Factor (holding all others constant)	Relationship
Expected error rate (related to the variation in population)	Direct
Tolerable (deviation) rate (related to precision)	Inverse
Risk of overreliance	Inverse
Risk of underreliance (implicit)	Inverse
Population size (implicit)	Direct

   F. **Select the Sample**—Identify the occurrences associated with all the items in the sample.

   G. **Evaluate the Sample Results**—This means make a decision as to whether the auditor can rely on the effectiveness of the internal control procedure under consideration.

   1. Calculate the **observed deviation rate** = (# errors)/n.

2. Determine the point estimate, the best single indicator of the percentage of times that the control procedure was performed as designed in the population (ignoring, for the moment, the uncertainty surrounding whether the sample is truly representative of the population).

3. Calculate a confidence interval for the **achieved upper precision limit** (in view of the actual errors observed). There are AICPA tables to determine the achieved upper precision limit. *(The topic determination of confidence intervals is not likely to be tested on the CPA Exam!)*

4. Compare the achieved upper precision limit to the stated **tolerable rate**; the auditor can only rely on the internal control procedure if the error rate, based on the upper bound of the confidence interval (the achieved upper precision limit from the tables) is less than or equal to the stated tolerable rate.

5. Consider the **qualitative characteristics** of the internal control deviations for any implication to the rest of the audit.

6. Make the appropriate decision—Should the auditor rely on the specific control procedure (i.e., **assess control risk at less than the maximum**) or not?

   Note
   This table has been adapted from material copyrighted by the American Institute of Certified Public Accountants, Inc.

   H. **Document the Auditor's Sampling Procedures**

III. **Attributes Sampling Example**

Statistical Sample Sizes for Tests of Controls

5% Risk of Overreliance						
Expected Population	**Tolerable Rate**					
Deviation Rate	**2%**	**3%**	**4%**	**5%**	**6%**	**7%**
.25	236	157	117	93	78	66
.50	*	157	117	93	78	66
.75	*	208	117	93	78	66
1.00	*	*	156	**93**	78	66
1.25	*	*	156	124	78	66
1.50	*	*	192	124	103	66
1.75	*	*	227	153	103	88
2.00	*	*	*	181	127	88
* Sample size is too large to be cost-effective for most audit applications.						

IV. **Attributes Sampling—Numerical Example**

   A. Suppose that an auditor specified the following parameters for a statistical sampling application related to internal controls in the revenue/receipts transaction cycle:

   Acceptable risk of overreliance on Internal control (a Type II error)   **5%**

   (The auditor is willing to rely on the control procedure if the statistical test indicates that the control is working as prescribed at least 95% of the time.)

   Estimated population deviation rate   **1%**

   Tolerable deviation rate   **5%**

   B. **Requirement**—Identify the required sample size using the AICPA tables for attributes sampling.

   C. **Solution**—The 5% **risk of overreliance** (Type II Error) determines the applicable page of the AICPA tables; the 5% **tolerable rate** determines the applicable column of the AICPA table; and the 1% **estimated population deviation rate** determines the applicable row of the AICPA table.

   1. The resulting sample size is **93**.

Variables Sampling

After studying this lesson, you should be able to:

1. Understand the meaning of the term "variables sampling" and the various specific approaches (difference estimation, ratio estimation, mean-per-unit estimation, and probability-proportionate-to-size sampling).

2. Know the eight steps that comprise a variables-sampling application.

3. Know the factors that affect the sample size for a variables-sampling application.

4. Understand the role of "stratification" in audit sampling.

I.   **Relies Heavily on the Classic Normal Distribution**—(With the bell-shaped curve.)

   A.   This distribution is determined by two parameters:

   1.   The **mean**, related to central tendency; and

   2.   **Variance** (or its square root, standard deviation), related to dispersion or variability.

> **Note**
> If 68% of the area is under the bell-shaped curve, it is within one standard deviation of the mean; if 95.5% of the area is under the bell-shaped curve, is within two standard deviations of the mean.

II.   **Basic Steps**—The **eight basic steps in a variables sampling plan** are practically the same as in the attributes sampling case:

   A.   **Identify the Sampling Objective**—The purpose of "variables sampling" is to determine the inferred audit value of a population of interest (e.g., for accounts receivable or inventory).

> **Note**
> Auditors should examine all the items that are individually material (i.e., we are not sampling these).

   B.   **Identify the Relevant Population:**

   1.   Specify what constitutes the sampling unit.

   2.   Be careful to assure that conclusions are properly extended to the appropriate population (i.e., completeness of the population).

   C.   **Select the Specific Sampling Technique**—The choices are difference estimation, ratio estimation, mean-per-unit estimation, or probability-proportionate-to-size sampling.

   D.   **Calculate the Sample Size**—Since tables do not exist for this in variables sampling. Recall the **five factors and relationships** to sample size identified for attributes sampling applications—these factors are still applicable to variables sampling.

Factor (holding all others constant)	Relationship
Estimated population standard deviation (related to the variation in population)	Direct
Allowance for sampling risk (also called "tolerable misstatement") [related to precision]	Inverse
Risk of incorrect acceptance (Type II)	Inverse
Population size (explicitly considered for variables sampling)	Direct
Risk of incorrect rejection (Type I error, only implicitly considered)	Inverse

The **basic formula**, based on classical statistics:

$n = (S * \text{Z-coefficient} * N / A)^2$

where:

n represents the sample size to be determined.

S represents the estimated population standard deviation (related to the variability of the population).

Z-coefficient represents a measure of reliability for some level of specified "confidence" (typically about 2).

N represents the size of the population (number of accounts or items of inventory, etc.).

A represents the specified allowance for sampling risk, related to the statistical concept of "precision."

Note

It is very unlikely that the AICPA will require calculations of sample size! However, they frequently test these concepts. In particular, they might ask questions related to the factors that influence the sample size and whether that influence is directly or inversely related. The formula identified above is a useful way to keep these relationships straight.

E. **Determine the Method of Selection**—Random (the preferred approach) or systematic.

F. **Conduct the Sample**

G. **Evaluate the Sample** and project to population:

1. Calculate a point estimate (the implied audit value) for the population based on the sample's audited values.

2. Construct a confidence interval to determine whether to accept or reject the client's recorded balance as consistent with the audit evidence.

Note

The AICPA has rarely tested calculations in this area. On a few occasions, they have required calculations of a "point estimate" for a population; however, calculations of the confidence interval surrounding a point estimate are beyond the scope of the CPA Exam!

H. Document the Auditor's Sampling Procedures and Judgments.

Definition

Stratification: The auditor may reduce the overall variability within a population by classifying similar items into sub-populations (within each group, the variability may be much smaller); the resulting aggregate sample size may be smaller as a result of reducing the combined effects of variability.

III. Variables Sampling—Specific Sampling Techniques—Note that the CPA Exam has rarely emphasized calculations related to statistical sampling; however, the exam has historically tested the concepts related to sampling.

- **A. Difference Estimation**—This approach involves identifying the dollar differences between the sample's audit values and applicable book values.

  1. **Sample size**—As previously described. Note that we usually need at least 30 differences between audit and book values in our sample when using "difference estimation."

  2. Estimate the population's implied audit value.

- **B.** Calculate the average difference between the audit value (av) and book value (bv) for items in the sample:

$$d = (av - bv)/n$$

- **C.** Extend that average difference to the population by multiplying it by the number of items in the population:

$$D = d * N$$

- **D.** Calculate the implied population audit value (the "point estimate") by adding the calculated difference for the population to the population's book value:

$$AV = BV + D, \text{ where D can be either positive or negative}$$

  1. Construct a confidence (precision) interval around the population's audit value to compare to the client's recorded balance—This is beyond the scope of the CPA Examination.

- **E. Ratio Estimation**—This approach involves identifying the ratio of the audit values and book values for the sampled items.

  1. Note that this approach is useful when the dollar amount of the differences between the audit and the book values is expected to be proportional to the book values.

  2. Sample size—as previously described.

  3. Estimate the population's implied audit value:

- **F.** Calculate the ratio for the sample, where the ratio has the sample's audit value in the numerator and the sample's book value in the denominator:

$$R = av/bv$$

G. Estimate the population's audit value (a point estimate) by multiplying the population's book value by that "ratio:"

$$AV = R * BV$$

    1. Construct a confidence (precision) interval around the population's audit value to compare to the client's recorded balance—this is beyond the scope of the CPA Examination.

H. Mean-per-Unit Estimation (MPU)

    1. Useful when difference or ratio estimation cannot be used—for example, for inventory when perpetual records do not exist (i.e., there is no "book" value for each individual sample item).

    2. Sample size—as previously described.

    3. Estimate the population's implied audit value.

        a. Calculate the average audit value for items in the sample:

$$MPU = av/n$$

        b. Multiply that average (MPU) times the number of items in the population:

$$AV = MPU * N$$

    4. Construct a confidence (precision) interval around the population's audit value to compare to the client's recorded balance—this is beyond the scope of CPA Exam!

I. Probability-Proportional-to-Size (PPS) Sampling—An introduction:

    1. The *sampling unit* is an individual dollar (when a given dollar is selected for the sample, it attaches to the related account or item which is then examined in its entirety); note that individually material items are automatically selected.

    2. PPS is useful if there are relatively few differences between audit and book values; otherwise, the sample size can become very large and the PPS application then becomes inefficient.

    3. The main advantage is efficiency—it can achieve the maximum possible stratification (which then minimizes the effects of variability on sample size).

    4. The main disadvantage is that PPS does not work very well in auditing negative balances (understatements) or zero (unrecorded) balances. Applies best to audit concerns involving overstatements (e.g., accounts receivable or inventory when few misstatements are expected).

PPS sampling will be addressed in more depth in the next lesson.

Probability-Proportional-to-Size (PPS) Sampling

After studying this lesson, you should be able to:

1. Understand the relevant sampling unit for probability-proportionate-to-size sampling.

2. Determine the sample size and the sampling interval for a probability-proportionate-to-size sampling application.

3. Determine the projected misstatement for a probability-proportionate-to-size sampling application.

I. **PPS "Sampling Unit"**—PPS sampling defines the "sampling unit" to be an individual dollar associated with the financial statement element involved. (Variations of this approach are referred to as dollar-unit sampling or monetary-unit sampling.) For example, suppose accounts receivable consists of 7500 customer accounts having a total balance of $3,000,000. The population is viewed as consisting of 3,000,000 individual items (dollars) rather than 7500 accounts. However, when an individual dollar is selected as part of the sample, it attaches to the related account or logical record, which is then examined in its entirety. Accordingly, the probability that an individual account will be selected is "proportional" to that individual account's balance relative to the total for all accounts.

II. **Primary Advantage of PPS Sampling**—The main advantage of PPS sampling is efficiency. If there are few differences between audit and book values, PPS sampling may result in smaller sample sizes than the other sampling methods. If there are many differences, however, PPS sample sizes can become too large to be practical.

III. **Primary Disadvantage of PPS Sampling**—The main disadvantage of PPS sampling is that it does not work very well in auditing negative balances (understatements) or zero (unrecorded) balances. It applies best to audit circumstances involving concerns about overstatements, such as for accounts receivable or inventory; and, then, only when few misstatements are expected.

IV. **Basic Steps in a PPS Sampling Application**

A. **Determine the Sample Size**—based on three considerations:

1. The "reliability factor" (from an AICPA table based on the risk of incorrect acceptance and the number of overstatements permitted—see the table below);

2. The population book value; *and*

3. The tolerable misstatement (net of any expected misstatements).

$$n = \frac{\text{Reliability factor (from tables)} \times \text{Book value}}{\text{Tolerable misstatement, net of expected misstatements}}$$

Alternatively, **n = Book value/Sampling interval**, where:

Sampling interval = Tolerable misstatement (net of expected misstatements)/Reliability factor

RELIABILITY FACTORS

Number of Overstatements	Risk of Incorrect Acceptance				
	1%	5%	10%	15%	20%
0	4.61	3.00	2.31	1.90	1.61
1	6.64	4.75	3.89	3.38	3.00
2	8.41	6.30	5.33	4.72	4.28
3	10.05	7.76	6.69	6.02	5.52
4	11.61	9.16	8.00	7.27	6.73
5	13.11	10.52	9.28	8.50	7.91

B. **Select the Sample**—PPS samples are usually selected using "systematic selection" with a random starting point and a specified "sample interval."

$$\text{Sample interval} = \frac{\text{Population book value}}{\text{Sample size}}$$

C. **Evaluate the Recorded Book Value**—To "evaluate" the entity's recorded balance relative to the implied audit value for the population, the auditor should calculate the "upper limit on misstatement," which corresponds to the upper limit of a confidence interval. Such computations are beyond the scope of CPA Exam, but a few concepts (especially "projected misstatement") may be worth remembering.

Upper limit on misstatement

= [Basic precision + Projected misstatement + Incremental allowance]

where:

Basic precision:

Basic precision = Reliability factor × Sample interval
(for 0 misstatements)

Projected misstatement:

For accounts having a book value greater than or equal to the sample interval, the actual misstatement should be used to determine the "projected misstatement."

For accounts having book values less than the sample interval, the auditor would have to apply the "tainting percentage" to the sample interval from which that account was selected. Suppose that the sample interval is $2,000 and that an account having a book value of $250 has an audit value of $200. The "tainting" is $50/$250 = .20; and, since the account's book value is less than the sample interval, the projected misstatement for this account would be .20 × $2,000 = $400.

When there are no misstatements in the sample, the projected misstatement is zero.

Incremental allowance:

The incremental allowance is zero if there are no misstatements of accounts having book values less than the sample interval. The concept is only relevant when there are misstatements of accounts having book values less than the sample interval, but the calculation itself is a technical issue that is beyond the scope of the CPA Exam.

Example Problems

Difference Estimation Problem

I. **Calculating a Point Estimate**—Using statistical sampling to assist in verifying the year-end accounts payable balance, an auditor has accumulated the following data (based on a 1984 AICPA Exam question):

	No. of Accounts	Book Balance	Audit Value
Population	4100	$5,000,000	??
Sample	200	$250,000	$300,000

II. **Required**—Using **difference estimation**, calculate the implied value for the year-end accounts payable balance.

Difference Estimation Solution

I. **Calculating a Point Estimate**—Using statistical sampling to assist in verifying the year-end accounts payable balance, an auditor has accumulated the following data (based on a 1984 AICPA Exam question):

	No. of Accounts	Book Balance	Audit Value
Population	4100	$5,000,000	??
Sample	200	$250,000	$300,000

II. **Required**—Using **difference estimation**, calculate the implied value for the year-end accounts payable balance.

  A. First, calculate the average difference for items in the sample:

  d = (av – bv)/n => ($300,000 – $250,000)/200 = $250

  B. Second, extend that average difference to the population by multiplying it by the number of items in the population:

  D = d * N => $250 * 4,100 = $1,025,000

  C. Third, estimate the population's audit value by adding that difference to the population's book value:

  AV = BV + D => $5,000,000 + $1,025,000 = **$6,025,000**

Exam Tip
Even though ratio estimation and difference estimation calculate different point estimates, that does not mean that the auditor would reach different conclusions about the fairness of the client's book balance. The calculation of the applicable confidence intervals would also differ accordingly. However, the calculation of confidence intervals is currently beyond the scope of the CPA Exam.

Ratio Estimation Problem

I. **Calculating a Point Estimate**—Using statistical sampling to assist in verifying the year-end accounts payable balance, an auditor has accumulated the following data (based on a 1984 CPA Exam question):

	No. of Accounts	Book Balance	Audit Value
Population	4100	$5,000,000	??
Sample	200	$250,000	$300,000

II. **Required**—Using **ratio estimation**, calculate the implied value for the year-end accounts payable balance.

Ratio Estimation Solution

I. **Calculating a Point Estimate**—Using statistical sampling to assist in verifying the year-end accounts payable balance, an auditor has accumulated the following data (based on a 1984 CPA Exam question):

	No. of Accounts	Book Balance	Audit Value
Population	4100	$5,000,000	??
Sample	200	$250,000	$300,000

II. **Required**—Using **ratio estimation**, calculate the implied value for the year-end accounts payable balance.

Ratio = av/bv => $300,000/$250,000 = 1.2

A. Estimated population Audit Value = ratio * population Book Value

=> 1.2 * $5,000,000 = **$6,000,000**

MPU Estimation Problem

I. **Calculating a Point Estimate**—Using statistical sampling to assist in verifying the year-end accounts payable balance, an auditor has accumulated the following data (based on a 1984 CPA Exam question):

	No. of Accounts	Book Balance	Audit Value
Population	4100	$5,000,000	??
Sample	200	$250,000	$300,000

II. **Required**—Using **mean-per-unit estimation**, calculate the implied value for the year-end accounts payable balance.

MPU Estimation Solution

I. Calculating a Point Estimate—Using statistical sampling to assist in verifying the year-end accounts payable balance, an auditor has accumulated the following data (based on a 1984 CPA Exam question):

	No. of Accounts	Book Balance	Audit Value
Population	4100	$5,000,000	??
Sample	200	$250,000	$300,000

II. Required—Using **mean-per-unit estimation**, calculate the implied value for the year-end accounts payable balance.

A. First, calculate the mean per unit (i.e., the average audit value for items in the sample):

MPU = av/n => $300,000/200 = $1,500 per unit

B. Second, calculate the implied audit value for the population by multiplying that MPU times the number of items in the population:

av = MPU * N => $1500 * 4,100 = **$6,150,000**

Exam Tip
Even though MPU estimation calculates a different point estimate than ratio estimation or difference estimation, it does not mean that the auditor would reach different conclusions about the fairness of the client's book balance. The calculation of the applicable confidence intervals would also differ accordingly. However, the calculation of confidence intervals is currently beyond the scope of the CPA Exam.

PPS Sampling Problem

A Numerical Problem—Sample Size for PPS Sampling

I.   Hill has decided to use probability-proportional-to-size (PPS) sampling, sometimes called dollar-unit sampling, in the audit of a client's accounts receivable balances. Hill plans to use the following PPS sampling table:

Reliability Factors for Errors of Overstatement

Number of Overstatements	Risk of Incorrect Acceptance				
	1%	5%	10%	15%	20%
0	4.61	3.00	2.31	1.90	1.61
1	6.64	4.75	3.89	3.38	3.00
2	8.41	6.30	5.33	4.72	4.28
3	10.05	7.76	6.69	6.02	5.52
4	11.61	9.16	8.00	7.27	6.73

Additional Information

Tolerable misstatement (net of effect of expected misstatement)	$ 24,000
Risk of incorrect acceptance	20%
Number of misstatements allowed	1
Recorded amount of accounts receivable	$240,000
Number of accounts	360

II. **Required**—What sample size should Hill use?

PPS Sampling Solution

A Numerical Problem—Sample Size for PPS Sampling

I.   Hill has decided to use probability-proportional-to-size (PPS) sampling, sometimes called dollar-unit sampling, in the audit of a client's accounts receivable balances. Hill plans to use the following PPS sampling table:

Reliability Factors for Errors of Overstatement

Number of Overstatements	Risk of Incorrect Acceptance				
	1%	5%	10%	15%	20%
0	4.61	3.00	2.31	1.90	1.61
1	6.64	4.75	3.89	3.38	3.00
2	8.41	6.30	5.33	4.72	4.28
3	10.05	7.76	6.69	6.02	5.52
4	11.61	9.16	8.00	7.27	6.73

Additional Information

Tolerable misstatement (net of effect of expected misstatement)	$ 24,000
Risk of incorrect acceptance	20%
Number of misstatements allowed	1
Recorded amount of accounts receivable	$240,000
Number of accounts	360

II.   **Required**—What sample size should Hill use?

   A.   n = reliability factor from tables * Book value/tolerable error

   B.   => (3.0 * $240,000)/$24,000 = **30**

IT (Computer) Auditing

IT Controls—General Controls

After studying this lesson, you should be able to:

1. Understand the meaning of the term "general controls" relevant to an IT (computerized) environment.

2. Know the five categories of such general controls.

I. **The Study and Evaluation of Internal Control**—This is somewhat different in a computerized environment:

   A. **The basic control objectives are the same, however!**

   B. Particular considerations in an Electronic Data Processing (EDP) (often referred to as an Information Technology [IT]) environment:

      1. A **disadvantage** is that the **segregation of duties** may be undermined—If someone gets unauthorized access to the computer system, it may be difficult to separate incompatible activities.

      2. Another **disadvantage** is that the usual **audit trail may be lacking**. There may be no "paper trail" auditors are accustomed to following.

      3. An **advantage** is that **computer processing is uniform**—Computers don't have "good" days and "bad" days; if a particular transaction is processed correctly one time, an identical transaction will be processed correctly, too.

   C. The **specific evidence gathering procedures** may differ.

II. **General Controls**—Controls that have pervasive effects on all the specific applications; there are five categories of general controls:

   A. **Organization and Operation**

      1. **Segregation of duties**—Especially within the EDP department; also between the EDP and various user departments

      2. Focus on the **primary areas of responsibility**—As much as possible, try to separate the following activities within the EDP department:

         a. **Systems analyst**—Responsible for designing the system

         b. **Programmer**—Responsible for writing the code that makes up the programs

         c. **Operator**—Responsible for running the system

         d. **Librarian**—Responsible for keeping track of the programs and files and verifying that access is limited to authorized personnel

         e. **Security**—Responsible for protecting the programs and data files and implementing procedures to safeguard the system

   B. **Systems Development and Documentation**—Regarding the appropriate authorization and documentation of new systems; any changes should be appropriately documented.

C. **Hardware and Systems Software**

 1. **Built-in controls**

    a. **Parity check**—Especially related to transmissions of information between system hardware components. A *bit* added to each character so that the loss of any portion of the data might be detected.

    b. **Echo check**—Especially related to transmissions of information over the phone lines. A signal that what was sent was, in fact, received.

    c. **Diagnostic routines**—That check internal operations of hardware components (usually when booting up the system).

    d. **Boundary protection**—For running multiple jobs concurrently.

 2. **Operating system**—Controls and instructions built into the software that runs the hardware.

D. **Access**—The access to data, software, and the hardware should be limited to authorized personnel.

E. **Data and Procedures**—Including physical safeguards that can protect the data files:

 1. **File labels**—Internal and external labels that might prevent using a file for an unintended or inappropriate use

 2. **File protection rings**—A processing control related to magnetic tapes that prevents critical data from being overwritten (similar to a "read only" switch on a floppy disk)

 3. **File protection plans**—Duplicates or prior generations. "Grandfather" and "father" versions that can be used to recreate a current file by updating earlier files with current transaction data

IT Controls—Application Controls

After studying this lesson, you should be able to:

1. Understand the meaning of the term application controls, relevant to an IT (computerized) environment.

2. Know the 3 categories of application controls (input, processing, and output) and specific examples of controls associated with each.

I. **Application Controls**—Related to the specific computer processing applications; now the emphasis is placed on the specific input, processing, and output activities.

   A. **Input**

      1. **Objectives**—That the input of data is accurate and as authorized.

      2. **Examples**

         a. **Preprinted forms**—So that employees will know exactly where to look for particular items of information.

         b. **Keypunch**—Verification/duplication.

         c. **Control totals**—Where useful comparisons are made to verify that all of the data were input properly.

            i. **Batch totals**—Totals that actually mean something (e.g., the day's cash withdrawals at an ATM location).

            ii. **Hash totals**—Totals that have no meaningful interpretation per se, even though a total can be arithmetically determined (e.g., adding up employees' social security numbers to verify that no employees were dropped from a payroll application).

            iii. **Record count**—Keeping track of the number of records processed to determine that the appropriate number was accounted for.

         d. **Logic checks**—Refers to certain computer edit routines that might signal when erroneous data have been input.

            i. **Limit tests**—Are the data all within some predetermined range? For example, a payroll program may specify an upper limit for how many hours can be legitimately worked.

            ii. **Validity checks**—Are the data recognized as legitimate possibilities (e.g., gender codes can only be "M" or "F")?

            iii. **Missing data checks**—Are there any omissions from any fields in which data should have been present?

            iv. **Check digits**—A check digit is an arithmetic manipulation of a numerical field that captures the information content of that field and then gets "tacked" onto the end of that numeric field.

         e. **Error resolution procedures**—Whenever the control procedures flag a data input problem, there should be procedures to pull out the item, fix the problem, and then put the item back in line for data entry.

   B. **Processing**

      1. **Objectives**—That the processing of data is accurate and as authorized

2. **Examples**

   a. **Control totals**—Same as for the corresponding section under Input above

   b. **Checkpoint/restart**—For particularly long processing runs, there should be built-in checkpoint/restart procedures so that, if the program crashes, it does not have to be restarted from the very beginning.

   c. **Limit on processing time**—A predetermined limit for computer processing time might be specified; if that time is exceeded, the program can assume an error has occurred and shut down the processing run.

   d. **Internal (e.g., headers) and external labels**—Should be used on all files to reduce the likelihood of mistakes caused by using the wrong files.

   e. **Error resolution procedures (the same idea as for Input)**—Whenever the control procedures flag a data-processing problem, there should be procedures to pull out the item, fix the problem, and then put the item back in line for the necessary data processing.

C. **Output**

   1. **Objectives**—That the output of data (and the distribution of any related reports) is accurate and as authorized.

   2. **Examples**

      a. **Control totals (the same idea as for Input and Processing)**

      b. **Output limits**—A predetermined page (or time) limit might be specified; if those limits are exceeded, the program can assume an error has occurred and stop the output activity.

      c. **Error resolution procedures (the same idea as for Input and Processing)**—Whenever the control procedures flag a data output problem, there should be procedures to pull out the item, fix the problem, and then put the item back in line for proper output.

IT Evidence-Gathering Procedures

The auditor's evidence gathering procedures may be affected by a computerized environment—"auditing through the computer" (as opposed to "auditing around the computer").

After studying this lesson, you should be able to:

1. Understand the costs and benefits associated with developing generalized audit software versus customizing software to a specific entity's circumstances.

2. Understand specific procedures that the auditor may perform in an IT environment to test relevant controls.

I. **Audit Software (Focus is on Substantive Test Work)**—Especially to access the client's files, but may also be used to help achieve the audit objectives:

    A. **Generalized Software**—Canned audit programs to access and test client's files; initially expensive to develop, but can be efficient if used on numerous engagements

    B. **Customized Software**—Programs specifically written to access the files of a particular client; may be cheaper in the short run, but more expensive in the long run if such costs are incurred for many clients

    C. **Data Mining Software**—Commercially available software (such as ACL or Idea) can be easily used to access client's electronic data and perform a broad range of substantive audit tasks (such as performing analytical procedures and sampling for confirmation work)

II. **Procedures Related to Tests of Controls**—When those IT-related controls are internal and unobservable:

    A. **Test Data**—Introducing "dummy" transactions under the auditor's control:

        1. Include some known errors to test the client's internal controls by checking whether the client's system catches those known errors.

        2. The auditor need not include every possible type of error; include only those kinds of errors that are of interest to the auditor.

        3. But be careful not to contaminate the client's database.

    B. **Integrated Test Facility (ITF)**—Create a fictitious division or department within the client and process the "dummy" data along with the client's "live" data; again, be careful not to contaminate the client's actual files.

    C. **Parallel Simulation**—Processing the client's actual data on the auditor's software and then comparing auditor's output to client's output for agreement.

    D. **Tagging Specific Client Transactions and Tracing Them Through the Client's System**—Such tagging is analogous to an electronic tag attached to an animal in the wilderness so that researchers can follow the animal's movement.

> **Note**
> Test data, ITF, *and* parallel simulation *test how well the client's systems work (after the fact), especially in detecting errors.*

    E. **Embedded Audit Modules** (and audit hooks)—Systems that don't have a permanent audit trail require that any auditing occurs while processing take place.

        1. **Embedded audit modules**—Routines that are built into the application program to perform an ongoing audit function.

2. **Audit hooks**—An exit point that is built into the application program where an audit module can be added subsequently.

Note
Tagging, embedding audit modules, and audit hooks test the working of the system while processing takes place.

Note
Inquiry, observation, and inspection can be used to gather evidence about external, observable EDP-related controls that are not otherwise documented.

Other IT Considerations

After studying this lesson, you should be able to:

1. Understand a variety of other terms and concepts associated with processing and networking in an IT environment.

I. **Hardware versus Software**

    A. **Hardware**—The central processing unit (CPU) and all the other related equipment.

    B. **Software**—The systems programs and all the applications programs:

        1. **Operating system**—The set of instructions that runs the CPU and the related peripheral equipment.

        2. **Compiler**—Translates the source program into object program:

            a. **Source program**—Written in a specific programming language (e.g., FORTRAN, COBOL).

            b. **Object program**—The instructions in machine readable form.

II. **Modes of Operation**—Related to when the transactions are processed:

    A. **Batch Processing**—When transactions are collected for periodic processing (e.g., daily updates for an ATM machine).

    B. **Online, Real-Time Processing:**

        1. **Online**—Means that the user is in direct communication with the computer's central processing unit (CPU).

        2. **Real-time**—Means that the data files are immediately updated.

III. **Service Organizations**—Independent computer centers may be engaged to process a client's transactional data; using such a service organization is a form of "outsourcing" and represents an alternative to having a company's own IT department.

IV. **Distributed Systems**—Involves a single database, which is literally distributed across multiple computers connected by a communication link. In other words, a network of remote computers connected to the main system (i.e. a *host* server) whereby each location can then have input/output, processing, and printing capabilities.

V. **Database Systems**—A set of interconnected files that eliminates the redundancy associated with maintaining separate files for different subsets of the organization; a key concern is limiting the users' access to the appropriate parts of the database as authorized.

VI. **Hierarchical vs. Relational Database Structures**

    A. **Hierarchical**—Data elements at one level encompass the data elements immediately below (constructed like a company's organizational chart). These structures are largely outdated.

    B. **Relational**—An integrated database having the structure of a spreadsheet (where each row consists of fields related to a particular customer or item and each column consists of a specific information field that is applicable to each customer or item).

VII. **Networks**—Basic definitions

    A. **Local Area Network (LAN)**—A network of hardware and software interconnected throughout a building or campus (usually limited to a few miles in scope).

    B. **Wide Area Network (WAN)**—A larger version of a LAN that might span a whole city or country.

C. **Value-Added Network (VAN)**—A network that facilitates EDI transactions (see the section on e-commerce below) between the buying and selling companies in such transactions, but the VAN is maintained by an independent company.

D. **Internet**—A worldwide network of privately controlled computers.

E. **Intranet**—A local area network that uses internet technology to facilitate communications throughout a particular organization (perhaps using a *firewall* to insulate the organization's system from unauthorized, outside entry).

F. **Extranet**—Same as intranet, except that important external constituents (e.g., major customers or suppliers) are also connected.

VIII. **Electronic Commerce**

A. **Electronic Funds Transfer (EFT)**—Involves the transfer of monies between financial accounts (usually associated with financial institutions).

B. **Electronic Data Interchange (EDI)**—Involves an electronic transaction between companies (one is selling, the other is buying).

   1. The usual hardcopy documents (e.g., purchase orders, sales invoices) don't exist!

   2. The goal is greater efficiency and less paperwork—should result in lower receivable/payable balances.

   3. **Point-to-Point (Point of Sale) Transactions**—Involve direct computer-to-computer communication between the parties.

   4. **Value-Added Network**—As indicated above, an independent company may develop the electronic infrastructure to facilitate these electronic business activities (along with support services).

IX. **Using the Internet**—Security and information reliability remain major concerns, although no direct investment is specifically required to engage in e-commerce transactions. Note that the AICPA developed *WebTrust* as an assurance service to address such concerns for a consumer/buyer.

Forming Conclusions and Reporting

Audit Reports

Introduction to Audit Reports

After studying this lesson, you should be able to:

1. State the Reporting Principle under the clarified standards (and how that compares to the now-superseded Reporting Standards of GAAS).

2. Know the structure and content of the **unmodified** auditor's report (and how that compares to what was previously known as the standard **unqualified** audit report.

3. Recognize the various alternative audit reports in addition to the unmodified auditor's report introduced here.

I. **Relevant AICPA Guidance**—The relevant AICPA guidance is provided by AU 700, *Forming an Opinion and Reporting on Financial Statements*. The standard states that the auditor's objectives are to form an opinion on the financial statements based on an evaluation of the audit evidence obtained, and express clearly that opinion through a written report.

II. **Principles**—Recall that the seven principles identified as a framework for audit standard setting in the Clarified Standards include one principle specifically dealing with reporting:

> "Based on an evaluation of the audit evidence obtained, the auditor expresses, in the form of a written report, an opinion in accordance with the auditor's findings, or states that an opinion cannot be expressed. The opinion states whether the financial statements are presented fairly, in all material respects, in accordance with the applicable financial reporting framework."

III. **Standard Unqualified Audit Report**—Prior to the Clarified Standards, the AICPA auditing standards referred to the Standard **Unqualified** Audit Report—Such an audit report consisted of three paragraphs known as the introductory, scope, and opinion paragraphs, as shown below.

Standard Unqualified Auditor's Report

Independent Auditor's Report

We have audited the balance sheets of ABC Company at December 31, 20X2 and 20X1, and the related statements of income, retained earnings, and cash flows for the years then ended. These financial statements are the responsibility of the Company's management. Our responsibility is to express an opinion on these financial statements based on our audits.

We conducted our audits in accordance with auditing standards generally accepted in the United States of America. Those standards require that we plan and perform the audit to obtain reasonable assurance about whether the financial statements are free of material misstatement. An audit includes examining, on a test basis, evidence supporting the amounts and disclosures in the financial statements. An audit also includes assessing the accounting principles used and significant estimates made by management, as well as evaluating the overall financial statement presentation. We believe that our audits provide a reasonable basis for our opinion.

In our opinion, the financial statements referred to above present fairly, in all material respects, the financial position of ABC Company at December 31, 20X2 and 20X1, and the results of their operations and their cash flows for the years then ended, in conformity with accounting principles generally accepted in the United States of America.

/s/ CPA firm (signed by audit engagement partner)

Date (The auditor's report should not be dated earlier than the date on which the auditor has obtained sufficient appropriate audit evidence to support the opinion.)

> In the Clarified Standards, the AICPA has replaced the previous term *unqualified* with *unmodified*.

IV. **Clarified Standards**—Under the AICPA's Clarified Standards, the auditor's unmodified report has been reformatted and expanded to reflect four main sections:

A. The first section ordinarily has no label, and merely identifies the nature of the engagement and the entity's financial statements involved (consisting of one sentence). However, if the auditor's report includes a section after the opinion paragraph labeled **Report on Other Legal and Regulatory Requirements**, then the introductory paragraph should be labeled **Report on the Financial Statements**. (Samples of both versions of audit reports are provided below.)

B. The second section is labeled **Management's Responsibility for the Financial Statements** (one sentence)—States that management is responsible for the fair presentation of the financial statements and the design and implementation of internal control.

C. The third section is labeled **Auditor's Responsibility**, which consists of three separate paragraphs.

    1. **The first consists of three sentences**—(1) responsibility to express an opinion; (2) conducted the audit in accordance with (GAAS); and (3) plan and perform the audit to provide reasonable assurance.

    2. **The second consists of five sentences**—(1) perform procedures to obtain audit evidence about the amounts and disclosures; (2) the procedures depend on the auditor's judgment, including assessment of risks of material misstatement, whether due to fraud or error; (3) in making those risk assessments, the auditor considers internal control; (4) auditor expresses no such opinion (on internal control, when not engaged to report on internal control in an integrated audit); and (5) an audit includes evaluating the appropriateness of accounting policies used and the reasonableness of significant accounting estimates.

    3. **The third consists of one sentence**—Expressing the auditor's belief that the audit evidence is sufficient and appropriate to provide a basis for the opinion.

D. The fourth section is labeled **Opinion** (one sentence)—Expresses the auditor's opinion (in the same wording as that used in the previous AICPA standards).

E. **Signature Block**—The AICPA now requires identification of the CPA's city/state, in addition to the signature and date.

V. **Alternative Audit Reports**—These various auditor's reports will be discussed in detail in subsequent lessons.

A. Auditor's report includes an emphasis-of-matter paragraph.

B. Auditor's report includes an other-matter paragraph.

C. **Auditor Expresses a Qualified Opinion**—The auditor expresses one or more reservations about (1) the financial statement presentation (owing to a material departure from the requirements of the applicable financial reporting framework); or (2) the audit engagement (owing to a scope limitation about a material matter for which the auditor was unable to obtain sufficient appropriate audit evidence).

D. **Auditor Expresses an Adverse Opinion**—The auditor states that the financial statements are not fairly stated (as a result of a departure from the requirements of the applicable financial reporting framework that is material and pervasive).

E. **Auditor Expresses a Disclaimer of Opinion**—A report in which the auditor expresses no conclusion about the fairness of the entity's financial statements (due to a scope limitation that is material and pervasive).

VI. **Comparative Financial Statements**—The continuing auditor should report appropriately on the financial statements of each period presented that the auditor has audited. The type of opinion need not be the same for each period. (Sample reports will be provided in connection with specific lessons on the various modified audit reports.)

   A. **Prior Period Financial Statements Audited by a Predecessor Auditor Whose Report is not Reissued**—The auditor should add an other-matter paragraph stating: (1) that the financial statements of the prior period were audited by a predecessor auditor; (2) the type of opinion given (and the reason for any modification); (3) the nature of any emphasis-of-matter paragraph or other-matter paragraph; and (4) the date of the predecessor's report.

   B. **Predecessor's Audit Report on Prior Period Financial Statements is Reissued**—The predecessor should obtain a representation letter from the (successor) auditor regarding matters that might affect the predecessor's prior period audit report, but the predecessor should not refer to the successor auditor in the predecessor's reissued audit report.

   C. **Prior Period Financial Statements not Audited**

   1. If those financial statements were compiled or reviewed (and the report on the prior period financial statements is not reissued)—the auditor should include an other-matter paragraph that identifies: (1) the nature of the service performed in the prior period; (2) a description of any modifications noted; (3) a statement that the service does not provide a basis for an opinion; and (4) the date of the report.

   2. If the prior period financial statements were not audited, reviewed, or compiled—the auditor's report should include an other-matter paragraph pointing out that fact.

VII. **Reporting for Audits Conducted in Accordance with PCAOB Standards and GAAS when the Audit is not Within the PCAOB's Jurisdiction**

   A. When conducting an audit in accordance with PCAOB standards and the audit is not within the PCAOB's jurisdiction—the auditor must also conduct the audit in accordance with GAAS.

   B. The audit report should follow the PCAOB's format, amended to state that the audit was also conducted in accordance with GAAS.

   C. Examples of when an audit might be conducted in accordance with PCAOB standards (although not within the PCAOB's jurisdiction)—audits for clearing agencies and futures commission merchants registered with the U.S. Commodities Futures Trading Commission (CFTC) or audits required by contract to adhere to PCAOB standards

VIII. **Sample Auditor's Reports Presented Below**

   A. Unmodified auditor's report on the current-year (and prior-year) comparative financial statements with no reference to legal and regulatory requirements, so the introductory paragraph is not separately labeled.

   B. Unmodified auditor's report is presented on a sentence-by-sentence basis to facilitate the review of the contents of such an auditor's report.

   C. Unmodified auditor's report on the current-year (and prior-year) comparative financial statements now including a reference to legal and regulatory requirements, so the introductory paragraph is labeled **Report on the Financial Statements.**

   D. Auditor's report when the audit uses PCAOB Standards, although the audit is not within the PCAOB's jurisdiction.

**Sample Unmodified Auditor's Report Under AICPA Clarified Standards
(Without Reference to Legal and Regulatory Requirements):**

Independent Auditor's Report

(Appropriate Addressee)

We have audited the accompanying consolidated financial statements of ABC Company and its subsidiaries, which comprise the consolidated balance sheets as of December 31, 20X1 and 20X0, and the related consolidated statements of income, changes in stockholders' equity and cash flows for the years then ended, and the related notes to the financial statements.

Management's Responsibility for the Financial Statements

Management is responsible for the preparation and fair presentation of these consolidated financial statements in accordance with accounting principles generally accepted in the United States of America; this includes the design, implementation, and maintenance of internal control relevant to the preparation and fair presentation of consolidated financial statements that are free from material misstatement, whether due to fraud or error.

Auditor's Responsibility

Our responsibility is to express an opinion on these consolidated financial statements based on our audits. We conducted our audits in accordance with auditing standards generally accepted in the United States of America. Those standards require that we plan and perform the audit to obtain reasonable assurance about whether the consolidated financial statements are free from material misstatement.

An audit involves performing procedures to obtain audit evidence about the amounts and disclosures in the consolidated financial statements. The procedures selected depend on the auditor's judgment, including the assessment of the risks of material misstatement of the consolidated financial statements, whether due to fraud or error. In making those risk assessments, the auditor considers internal control relevant to the entity's preparation and fair presentation of the consolidated financial statements in order to design audit procedures that are appropriate in the circumstances, but not for the purpose of expressing an opinion on the effectiveness of the entity's internal control. Accordingly, we express no such opinion. An audit also includes evaluating the appropriateness of accounting policies used and the reasonableness of significant accounting estimates made by management, as well as evaluating the overall presentation of the consolidated financial statements.

We believe that the audit evidence we have obtained is sufficient and appropriate to provide a basis for our audit opinion.

Opinion

In our opinion, the consolidated financial statements referred to above present fairly, in all material respects, the financial position of ABC Company and its subsidiaries as of December 31, 20X1 and 20X0, and the results of their operations and their cash flows for the years then ended in accordance with accounting principles generally accepted in the United States of America.

(Auditor's signature—Firm name, signed by audit engagement partner)

(**Auditor's city and state**—This is a new requirement under the Clarified Standards)

(Date of the auditor's report—When the auditor has obtained sufficient appropriate audit evidence as a reasonable basis for the opinion.)

Unmodified Auditor's Report Under AICPA Clarified Standards (Presented Sentence by Sentence):

Independent Auditor's Report

(Introductory Paragraph)

1. We have audited the accompanying consolidated financial statements of ABC Company and its subsidiaries, which comprise the consolidated balance sheets as of December 31, 20X1 and 20X0, and the related consolidated statements of income, changes in stockholders' equity and cash flows for the years then ended, and the related notes to the financial statements.

Management's Responsibility for the Financial Statements

1. Management is responsible for the preparation and fair presentation of these consolidated financial statements in accordance with accounting principles generally accepted in the United States of America; this includes the design, implementation, and maintenance of internal control relevant to the preparation and fair presentation of consolidated financial statements that are free from material misstatement, whether due to fraud or error.

Auditor's Responsibility

(First of three paragraphs)

1. Our responsibility is to express an opinion on these consolidated financial statements based on our audits.

2. We conducted our audits in accordance with auditing standards generally accepted in the United States of America.

3. Those standards require that we plan and perform the audit to obtain reasonable assurance about whether the consolidated financial statements are free from material misstatement.

(Second of three paragraphs)

4. An audit involves performing procedures to obtain audit evidence about the amounts and disclosures in the consolidated financial statements.

5. The procedures selected depend on the auditor's judgment, including the assessment of the risks of material misstatement of the consolidated financial statements, whether due to fraud or error.

6. In making those risk assessments, the auditor considers internal control relevant to the entity's preparation and fair presentation of the consolidated financial statements in order to design audit procedures that are appropriate in the circumstances, but not for the purpose of expressing an opinion on the effectiveness of the entity's internal control.

7. Accordingly, we express no such opinion.

8. An audit also includes evaluating the appropriateness of accounting policies used and the reasonableness of significant accounting estimates made by management, as well as evaluating the overall presentation of the consolidated financial statements.

(Third of three paragraphs)

9. We believe that the audit evidence we have obtained is sufficient and appropriate to provide a basis for our audit opinion.

Opinion

1. In our opinion, the consolidated financial statements referred to above present fairly, in all material respects, the financial position of ABC Company and its subsidiaries as of December 31, 20X1 and 20X0, and the results of their operations and their cash flows for the years then ended in accordance with accounting principles generally accepted in the United States of America.

**Sample Unmodified Auditor's Report Under AICPA Clarified Standards
(Including Reference to Legal and Regulatory Requirements):**

Independent Auditor's Report

(Appropriate Addressee)

Report on the Financial Statements[1]

We have audited the accompanying consolidated financial statements of ABC Company and its subsidiaries, which comprise the consolidated balance sheets as of December 31, 20X1 and 20X0, and the related consolidated statements of income, changes in stockholders' equity and cash flows for the years then ended, and the related notes to the financial statements.

Management's Responsibility for the Financial Statements

Management is responsible for the preparation and fair presentation of these consolidated financial statements in accordance with accounting principles generally accepted in the United States of America; this includes the design, implementation, and maintenance of internal control relevant to the preparation and fair presentation of consolidated financial statements that are free from material misstatement, whether due to fraud or error.

Auditor's Responsibility

Our responsibility is to express an opinion on these consolidated financial statements based on our audits. We conducted our audits in accordance with auditing standards generally accepted in the United States of America. Those standards require that we plan and perform the audit to obtain reasonable assurance about whether the consolidated financial statements are free from material misstatement.

An audit involves performing procedures to obtain audit evidence about the amounts and disclosures in the consolidated financial statements. The procedures selected depend on the auditor's judgment, including the assessment of the risks of material misstatement of the consolidated financial statements, whether due to fraud or error. In making those risk assessments, the auditor considers internal control relevant to the entity's preparation and fair presentation of the consolidated financial statements in order to design audit procedures that are appropriate in the circumstances, but not for the purpose of expressing an opinion on the effectiveness of the entity's internal control.[2] Accordingly, we express no such opinion. An audit also includes evaluating the appropriateness of accounting policies used and the reasonableness of significant accounting estimates made by management, as well as evaluating the overall presentation of the consolidated financial statements.

We believe that the audit evidence we have obtained is sufficient and appropriate to provide a basis for our audit opinion.

Opinion

In our opinion, the consolidated financial statements referred to above present fairly, in all material respects, the financial position of ABC Company and its subsidiaries as of December 31, 20X1 and 20X0, and the results of their operations and their cash flows for the years then ended in accordance with accounting principles generally accepted in the United States of America.

Report on Other Legal and Regulatory Requirements

(The form and content of this section of the auditor's report will vary depending on the nature of the auditor's other reporting responsibilities.)

(Auditor's signature)

(Auditor's city and state)

(Date of the auditor's report)

[1] The subtitle **Report on the Financial Statements** is unnecessary in circumstances when the second subtitle, **Report on Other Legal and Regulatory Requirements,** is not applicable.

[2] When the auditor has responsibility for expressing an opinion on the effectiveness of internal control in conjunction with the audit of the entity's financial statements, the sentence would be stated as follows: "In making those risk assessments, the auditor considers internal control relevant to the entity's preparation and fair presentation of the consolidated financial statements in order to design audit procedures that are appropriate in the circumstances." In addition, the next sentence, "Accordingly, we express no such opinion," would be omitted.

Sample Audit Report When the Audit Uses PCAOB Standards, Although the Audit Is Not Within the PCAOB's Jurisdiction:

Report of Independent Registered Public Accounting Firm

We have audited the accompanying consolidated balance sheets of ABC Company and subsidiaries as of December 31, 20X2 and 20X1, and the related consolidated statements of operations, changes in stockholders' equity, and cash flows for the years then ended. These consolidated financial statements are the responsibility of the Company's management. Our responsibility is to express an opinion on these consolidated financial statements based on our audits.

We conducted our audits in accordance with the auditing standards of the Public Company Accounting Oversight Board (United States) and in accordance with auditing standards generally accepted in the United States of America. Those standards require that we plan and perform the audit to obtain reasonable assurance about whether the consolidated financial statements are free of material misstatement. An audit includes examining, on a test basis, evidence supporting the amounts and disclosures in the consolidated financial statements. An audit also includes assessing the accounting principles used and significant estimates made by management, as well as evaluating the overall financial statement presentation. We believe that our audits provide a reasonable basis for our opinion.

In our opinion, the consolidated financial statements referred to above present fairly, in all material respects, the consolidated financial position of ABC Company and subsidiaries as of December 31, 20X2 and 20X1, and the results of their operations and their cash flows for the years then ended, in conformity with accounting principles generally accepted in the United States of America.

(Signature)

(City and State or Country)

(Date)

This sample report is based on the following circumstances:

1. The audit of an entity's consolidated financial statements is not within the jurisdiction of the PCAOB;

2. The audit is conducted in accordance with PCAOB auditing standards and also auditing standards generally accepted in the United States;

3. The auditor has not been engaged to audit internal control over financial reporting; *and*

4. The financial statements are prepared in accordance with U.S. GAAP.

PCAOB on Audit Reports

After studying this lesson, you should be able to:

1. Know the audit report (and review report) requirements applicable to issuers under PCAOB Auditing Standards.

I. References in Auditors' Reports to the Standards of the (PCAOB)

II. Standards Adopted

PCAOB adopted the AICPA's auditing standards in existence on April 16, 2003, as "interim standards, on an initial, transitional basis."

III. Required Changes

Made the following required changes to the auditor's report, relative to the 2003 AICPA guidelines. The AICPA later changed its reporting model in its clarified auditing standards.

A. Title of the Report—Replaced "Independent Auditor's Report" with **"Report of Independent Registered Public Accounting Firm."**

B. Scope Paragraph—Replaced reference to "auditing standards generally accepted in the United States of America" with **"the standards of the Public Company Accounting Oversight Board (United States)."**

C. Opinion Paragraph—Replaced reference to "accounting principles generally accepted in the United States of America" with **"U.S. generally accepted accounting principles."**

D. Signature—Required firms to **add their city and state** (or country, as applicable) along with their signature and date of their audit report.

IV. Examples of Reporting Language Specified by PCAOB

Sample Audit Report Using the PCAOB's Template: Report No. 1

Report of Independent Registered Public Accounting Firm

We have audited the accompanying balance sheets of ABC Company at December 31, 20X3 and 20X2, and the related statements of operations, stockholders' equity, and cash flows for each of the three years in the period ended December 31, 20X3. These financial statements are the responsibility of the Company's management. Our responsibility is to express an opinion on these financial statements based on our audits.

We conducted our audits in accordance with the standards of the Public Company Accounting Oversight Board (United States). Those standards require that we plan and perform the audit to obtain reasonable assurance about whether the financial statements are free of material misstatement. An audit includes examining, on a test basis, evidence supporting the amounts and disclosures in the financial statements. An audit also includes assessing the accounting principles used and significant estimates made by management, as well as evaluating the overall financial statement presentation. We believe that our audits provide a reasonable basis for our opinion.

In our opinion, the financial statements referred to above present fairly, in all material respects, the financial position of ABC Company at December 31, 20X3 and 20X2, and the results of its operations and its cash flows for each of the three years in the period ended December 31, 20X3, in conformity with U.S. generally accepted accounting principles.

(Signature)

(City and State or Country)

(Date)

Sample Review Report Using the PCAOB's Template: Report No. 2

<u>Report of Independent Registered Public Accounting Firm</u>

We have reviewed the accompanying (*describe the interim financial information or statements reviewed*) of ABC Company as of September 30, 20X3 and 20X2, and for the three-month and nine-month periods then ended. This interim financial information (statements) is (are) the responsibility of the company's management.

We conducted our review in accordance with the standards of the Public Company Accounting Oversight Board (United States). A review of interim financial information consists principally of applying analytical procedures and making inquiries of persons responsible for financial and accounting matters. It is substantially less in scope than an audit conducted in accordance with the standards of the Public Company Accounting Oversight Board, the objective of which is the expression of an opinion regarding the financial statements taken as a whole. Accordingly, we do not express such an opinion.

Based on our review, we are not aware of any material modifications that should be made to the accompanying interim financial information (statements) for it (them) to be in conformity with U.S. generally accepted accounting principles.

(Signature)

(City and State or Country)

(Date)

Note: Effective in 2017, the PCAOB requires each registered public accounting firm to file with the PCAOB its "Form AP, Auditor Reporting of Certain Audit Participants," for every audit of an issuer. This Form AP requires disclosure of the following:

1. The engagement partner's name;

2. The name, location, and extent of participation of any other accounting firm whose participation in the audit accounts for 5% or more of the total audit hours; *and*

3. The number and extent in total of all other accounting firms whose participation in the audit accounts for less than 5% of the total audit hours.

These Form APs will be accessible on the PCAOB's website.

Audits of Group Financial Statements

After studying this lesson, you should be able to:

1. Know how a reference to a component auditor affects the auditor's report.

2. Understand the difference between a component and a group, and distinguish between the group's auditor and a component auditor.

I. **Relevant AICPA Guidance**—The relevant AICPA guidance is provided by AU 600, *Special Considerations—Audits of Group Financial Statements (Including the Work of Component Auditors)*. The standard states that the auditor's objectives are to determine whether to act as the auditor of the group financial statements, and, if so, (1) to determine whether to make reference to the audit of the component auditor; (2) to communicate clearly with component auditors; and (3) to obtain sufficient appropriate audit evidence regarding the financial information of the components and the consolidation process to express an opinion on the group financial statements.

II. **Selected Definitions**

> **Definitions**
>
> *Component*: An entity for which group or component management prepares financial information that is required by the applicable financial reporting framework to be included in the group financial statements.
>
> *Component Auditor*: An auditor who performs work on the financial information of a component that will be used as audit evidence for the group audit. (**A component auditor may be part of the group engagement partner's firm, a network-affiliated firm, or another unrelated firm.**)
>
> *Group*: All the components whose financial information is included in the group financial statements. A group always has more than one component.
>
> *Group Financial Statements*: Financial statements that include the financial information of more than one component. This term also refers to combined financial statements aggregating the financial information prepared by components that are under common control.
>
> *Group-Wide Controls*: Controls designed, implemented, and maintained by group management over group financial reporting.
>
> *Significant Component*: A component identified by the group engagement team that (a) is of individual financial significance to the group; or (b) due to its specific nature, is likely to include significant risks of material misstatement of the group financial statements.

III. **Responsibilities of the Group Engagement Partner and the Group Engagement Team**

    A. **Group Engagement Partner**—The group engagement partner is responsible for (1) the supervision and performance of the group audit engagement in compliance with professional standards and applicable regulatory requirements; and (2) determining whether the auditor's report is appropriate in the circumstances.

    B. **Acceptance and Continuance**—The group engagement team should obtain an understanding of the group, its components, and their environments sufficient to identify the significant components.

        1. The group engagement partner should evaluate whether sufficient appropriate audit evidence will be obtained, including the use of the component auditors' work, to act as the auditor of the group financial statements.

        2. If sufficient appropriate audit evidence would not be obtained, the auditor should not accept a new engagement or should withdraw from a continuing engagement. (If withdrawal is not permitted, the auditor should disclaim an opinion.)

C. Assess the Risks of Material Misstatement of the Group Financial Statements—The auditor should obtain an understanding of the group, its components, and their environments (including group-wide controls) and obtain an understanding of the consolidation process and the instructions issued by group management to components.

D. Obtain an Understanding of the Component Auditor(s)

1. Recall that the term component auditor applies to auditors of other offices of the group engagement partner's firm (for an engagement involving multiple offices of the same firm), to a network-affiliated firm, or to another unrelated firm (that is not subject to the quality controls of the group engagement partner's firm).

2. The group engagement team should obtain an understanding of (a) the component auditor's independence and professional competence; (b) the extent to which the group engagement team will be involved in the work of the component auditor; (c) whether the group engagement team will be able to obtain information affecting the consolidation process from the component auditor.

E. The group engagement team should determine materiality (1) for the group financial statements as a whole, (2) for the components to be audited by the group engagement team or by component auditors, and (3) the threshold for determining clearly trivial to the group financial statements.

F. Responding to Assessed Risks—If work to be performed on the consolidation process or the financial information of the components is based on an expectation that group-wide controls are operating effectively, the group engagement team (or the component auditor) should test the operating effectiveness of those controls.

G. Consolidation Process—The group engagement team should perform further audit procedures on the consolidation process to respond to the assessed risks of material misstatement associated with the consolidation process, including evaluating whether all components have been included and whether there are any indicators of possible management bias or fraud.

H. Communications with a Component Auditor—The group engagement team should communicate its requirements of the component on a timely basis, and request that the component auditor communicate matters relevant to the group engagement team's conclusions.

I. Involvement in the Work of the Component Auditors—For a significant component for which the auditor of the group financial statements is assuming responsibility for the component auditor's work, the auditor should (a) discuss with the component auditor the significance of the component to the group and the susceptibility of the component to material misstatement; and (b) review the component auditor's documentation of identified significant risks of material misstatement to the group financial statements.

J. Documentation—The group engagement team's audit documentation should include the following:

1. An analysis of components indicating those that are significant (and the type of work performed);

2. Written communications between the group engagement team and the component auditors about the group engagement team's requirements;

3. Those components for which reference to the component auditors' reports were made in the auditor's report; *and*

4. The financial statements of the component and the report of the component auditor for components referenced in the auditor's report on the group financial statements.

K. Determining Whether to Reference a Component Auditor in the Auditor's Report

1. Reference to the component auditor should not be made unless: (a) the component's financial statements are prepared using the same financial reporting framework used by the group; (b) the component auditor has performed an audit on the component's financial statements in

accordance with GAAS (or PCAOB standards, if applicable); and **(c) the component auditor has issued an audit report on the component's financial statements that is not restricted as to use.**

2. If the group engagement partner decides to assume responsibility for the component auditor's work—No reference should be made to the component auditor in the auditor's report.

3. If the group engagement partner decides to name the component auditor in the auditor's report—The component auditor's permission should be obtained and the component auditor's report should be presented along with the auditor's report on the group financial statements.

L. Effect of Reference to a Component Auditor on the Auditor's Report

1. No effect on the introductory paragraph or management's responsibility section.

2. Auditor's responsibility section—The first paragraph should be modified to identify the component audited by other auditors and the magnitude of the financial statements involved.

3. The opinion paragraph should refer to "In our opinion, **based on our audit and the report of the other auditors, …**"

M. Sample Report that Refers to a Component Auditor

Independent Auditor's Report

(Appropriate Addressee)

Report on the Consolidated Financial Statements

We have audited the accompanying consolidated financial statements of ABC Company and its subsidiaries, which comprise the consolidated balance sheets as of December 31, 20X1 and 20X0, and the related consolidated statements of income, changes in stockholders' equity and cash flows for the years then ended, and the related notes to the financial statements.

Management's Responsibility for the Financial Statements

Management is responsible for the preparation and fair presentation of these consolidated financial statements in accordance with accounting principles generally accepted in the United States of America; this includes the design, implementation and maintenance of internal control relevant to the preparation and fair presentation of consolidated financial statements that are free from material misstatement, whether due to fraud or error.

Auditor's Responsibility

Our responsibility is to express an opinion on these consolidated financial statements based on our audit. **We did not audit the financial statements of B Company, a wholly-owned subsidiary, whose statements reflect total assets and revenues constituting 20% and 22%, respectively, of the related consolidated totals. Those statements were audited by other auditors, whose report has been furnished to us, and our opinion, insofar as it relates to the amounts included for B Company, is based solely on the report of the other auditors.** We conducted our audits in accordance with auditing standards generally accepted in the United States of America. Those standards require that we plan and perform the audit to obtain reasonable assurance about whether the consolidated financial statements are free from material misstatement.

An audit involves performing procedures to obtain audit evidence about the amounts and disclosures in the consolidated financial statements. The procedures selected depend on the auditor's judgment, including the assessment of the risks of material misstatement of the consolidated financial statements, whether due to fraud or error. In making those risk assessments, the auditor considers internal control relevant to the entity's preparation and fair presentation of the consolidated financial statements in order to design audit procedures that are appropriate in the circumstances, but not for the purpose of expressing an opinion on the effectiveness of the entity's internal control. Accordingly, we express no such opinion. An audit also includes evaluating the appropriateness of accounting policies used and the reasonableness of significant accounting estimates made by management, as well as evaluating the overall presentation of the consolidated financial statements.

We believe that the audit evidence we have obtained is sufficient and appropriate to provide a basis for our audit opinion.

Opinion

In our opinion, **based on our audit and the report of the other auditors**, the consolidated financial statements referred to above presents fairly, in all material respects, the financial position of ABC Company and its subsidiaries as of December 31, 20X1 and 20X2, in accordance with accounting principles generally accepted in the United States of America.

(Auditor's Signature)

(Auditor's City and State)

(Date of the Auditor's Report)

Emphasis-of-Matter Paragraphs and Other-Matter Paragraphs

After studying this lesson, you should be able to:

1. Know the definition of (and distinction between) emphasis-of-matter and other matter paragraphs in the auditor's report.

2. Know the three matters for which an emphasis-of-matter paragraph is required.

3. Know how an emphasis-of-matter and/or other-matter paragraph would be presented in the auditor's report.

I. **Responsibilities under AICPA Professional Standards**—The relevant AICPA guidance is provided by AU 706: *Emphasis-of-Matter Paragraphs and Other-Matter Paragraphs in the Independent Auditor's Report*. This pronouncement states that the auditor's objective is to draw the users' attention, as necessary, to (1) a matter, already appropriately presented/disclosed in the financial statements, that is important to the users' understanding of the financial statements (emphasis-of-matter paragraph); or (2) any other matter that is relevant to the users' understanding of the audit, the auditor's responsibilities, or the auditor's report (other-matter paragraph).

Definitions

Emphasis-of-Matter Paragraph: A paragraph that refers to a matter appropriately presented or disclosed in the financial statements that, in the auditor's judgment, is of such importance that it is fundamental to users' understanding of the financial statements.

Other-Matter Paragraph: A paragraph that refers to a matter other than those presented or disclosed in the financial statements that, in the auditor's judgment, is relevant to users' understanding of the audit, the auditor's responsibilities, or the auditor's report.

II. **Emphasis-of-Matter Paragraph**

A. Matters for which an emphasis-of-matter paragraph is **required**:

1. When the auditor has substantial doubt about the entity's ability to continue as a going concern

2. When there is an inconsistency in accounting principles used

3. When the financial statements are prepared in accordance with special purpose frameworks. (This topic will be discussed in another lesson.)

B. Circumstances for which an auditor may consider it necessary to add an emphasis-of-matter paragraph: (1) an uncertainty as to the outcome of unusually important litigation or regulator action; (2) a major casualty having a significant effect; (3) significant transactions with related parties; or (4) unusually important subsequent events.

C. Presentation of the emphasis-of-matter paragraph:

1. Presented immediately after the opinion paragraph

2. Should have an appropriate heading, such as "Emphasis of Matter"

3. Should reference the specific matter being emphasized and identify where relevant disclosures can be found in the financial statements

4. State that the auditor's opinion is not modified with respect to the matter emphasized.

D. Example of such a paragraph for a going-concern issue:

Emphasis-of-Matter (presented after the opinion paragraph):

The accompanying financial statements have been prepared assuming that the Company will continue as a going concern. As discussed in Note X to the financial statements, the Company has suffered recurring losses from operations and has a net capital deficiency that raise substantial doubt about its ability to continue as a going concern. Management's plans in regard to these matters are also described in Note X. The financial statements do not include any adjustments that might result from the outcome of this uncertainty. Our opinion is not modified with respect to this matter.

III. Other-Matter Paragraph

A. Circumstances for which an Auditor May Consider it Necessary to Add an Other-Matter Paragraph:

1. **Relevant to users' understanding of the audit**—In rare situations, the auditor may add an other-matter paragraph to explain why it was not possible for the auditor to withdraw from an engagement in which a scope limitation that was pervasive resulted in a disclaimer of opinion.

2. **Relevant to users' understanding of the auditor's responsibilities or the auditor's report**—For example, when the opinion expressed on the prior year's financial statements is different than the opinion previously expressed (as a result of management's correction of a material departure from the applicable financial reporting framework).

B. Presentation of the Other-Matter Paragraph

1. When the other-matter paragraph is intended to draw users' attention to a matter relevant to their understanding of the audit of the financial statements—The other-matter paragraph should be presented immediately after the opinion paragraph and after any emphasis-of-matter paragraph(s).

   a. When the other-matter paragraph is intended to draw users' attention to a matter relating to other reporting responsibilities addressed in the auditor's report—The paragraph may be included in the section of the report labeled "Report on Other Legal and Regulatory Requirements."

   b. When relevant to all the auditor's responsibilities or users' understanding of the auditor's report—The other-matter paragraph may also be included as a separate section following the "Report on the Financial Statements" and the "Report on Other Legal and Regulatory Requirements."

2. Should have an appropriate heading, such as "Other Matter."

C. Example of such a paragraph when the opinion expressed on the prior year's financial statements is different than the opinion previously expressed:

Other Matter (presented after the opinion and emphasis-of-matter paragraphs):

In our report dated March 1, 20X1, we expressed an opinion that the 20X0 financial statements did not fairly present the financial position, results of operations, and cash flows of ABC Company in accordance with accounting principles generally accepted in the United States of America because of two departures from such principles: (1) ABC Company carried its property, plant, and equipment at appraisal values, and provided for depreciation on the basis of such values, and (2) ABC Company did not provide for deferred income taxes with respect to differences between income for financial reporting purposes and taxable income. As described in Note X, the Company has changed its method of accounting for these items and restated its 20X0 financial statements to conform with accounting principles generally accepted in the United States of America. Accordingly, our present opinion on the restated 20X0 financial statements, as presented herein, is different from that expressed in our previous report.

IV. Communication with Those Charged with Governance—The auditor should communicate with those charged with governance about the proposed wording of any expected emphasis-of-matter or other-matter paragraph(s).

Note

The Statements on Auditing Standards that preceded the clarified auditing standards used the term *explanatory paragraph* in a variety of contexts, including emphasis of a matter and explaining the basis for an opinion that was other than unqualified. Sometimes the explanatory paragraph preceded the opinion, sometimes it followed the opinion, and in some circumstances the auditor had a choice to place the explanatory paragraph either before or after the opinion paragraph. Under the clarified auditing standards, the term explanatory paragraph is no longer used.

Qualified for Scope Limitation

After studying this lesson, you should be able to:

1. Understand when and how to express a qualified audit opinion for a scope limitation affecting the auditor's basis for conclusions.

I. **Relevant AICPA Guidance**—The relevant AICPA guidance is provided by AU 705, *Modifications to the Opinion in the Independent Auditor's Report*. The standard states that the auditor's objective is to express clearly an appropriately modified opinion when (1) the auditor concludes that the financial statements as a whole are misstated; or (2) **the auditor is unable to obtain sufficient appropriate audit evidence to conclude that the financial statements as a whole are free from material misstatement.** This lesson focuses on the second matter, which is known as a scope limitation.

> **Definitions**
> *Modified opinion*: A qualified opinion, an adverse opinion, or a disclaimer of opinion.
>
> *Pervasive*: (a) Effects that are not confined to specific elements, accounts or items of the financial statements; (b) effects that, if so confined, represent or could represent a substantial proportion of the financial statements; or (c) regarding disclosures, are fundamental to users' understanding of the financial statements.

II. **Opinion Scope Limitation Involves Judgment**

   A. **Qualified Opinion**—The auditor should express a qualified opinion when the auditor is unable to obtain sufficient appropriate audit evidence, and the auditor concludes that the possible effect on the financial statements, if any, could be **material, but not pervasive**. (This lesson focuses on the qualified opinion in connection with a scope limitation.)

   B. **Disclaimer of Opinion**—The auditor should express a disclaimer of opinion when the auditor is unable to obtain sufficient appropriate audit evidence, and the auditor concludes that the possible effect on the financial statements, if any, could be **material and pervasive**. (A separate lesson focuses on the disclaimer of opinion.)

III. **Circumstances Resulting in a Scope Limitation**

   A. **Circumstances beyond the Control of the Entity**—For example, the entity's accounting records have been destroyed.

   B. **Circumstances Related to the Nature or Timing of the Auditor's Work**—For example, the auditor determines that substantive procedures alone are not sufficient and the entity's controls are ineffective; the auditor is unable to obtain audited financial statements of an investee (accounted for using the equity method); or the timing of the auditor's appointment does not permit the auditor to observe the physical counting of inventories.

   C. **Limitations Imposed by Management**—For example, management prevents the auditor from requesting external confirmation of certain account balances. The auditor should request that management remove any such limitation.

   1. If management refuses—The auditor should communicate the matter to those charged with governance and determine whether it is possible to perform alternative procedures to obtain sufficient appropriate audit evidence.

   2. If unable to obtain sufficient appropriate audit evidence (and if the effects could be both material and pervasive)—The auditor should withdraw from the audit (when practicable) or issue a disclaimer of opinion.

IV. Effect of a Qualification for a Scope Limitation on the Auditor's Report

    A. No effect on the introductory paragraph or management's responsibility section.

    B. Auditor's responsibility section—Modify the last sentence to state, "We believe that the audit evidence we have obtained is sufficient and appropriate to provide a basis for our qualified audit opinion."

    C. Add a "Basis for Qualified Opinion" paragraph (with such a label) before the opinion paragraph.

    D. Qualify the opinion using appropriate language such as: "In our opinion, **except for the possible effects of the matter described in the Basis for Qualified Opinion paragraph**, the financial statements referred to above present fairly . . ." and label the opinion paragraph "Qualified Opinion."

V. Sample Audit Report Qualified for a Scope Limitation

Independent Auditor's Report

(Appropriate Addressee)

We have audited the accompanying financial statements of ABC Company, which comprise the balance sheet as of December 31, 20X1, and the related statements of income, changes in stockholders' equity and cash flows for the year then ended, and the related notes to the financial statements.

Management's Responsibility for the Financial Statements

Management is responsible for the preparation and fair presentation of these financial statements in accordance with accounting principles generally accepted in the United States of America; this includes the design, implementation, and maintenance of internal control relevant to the preparation and fair presentation of financial statements that are free from material misstatement, whether due to fraud or error.

Auditor's Responsibility

Our responsibility is to express an opinion on these financial statements based on our audit. We conducted our audit in accordance with auditing standards generally accepted in the United States of America. Those standards require that we plan and perform the audit to obtain reasonable assurance about whether the financial statements are free from material misstatement.

An audit involves performing procedures to obtain audit evidence about the amounts and disclosures in the consolidated financial statements. The procedures selected depend on the auditor's judgment, including the assessment of the risks of material misstatement of the consolidated financial statements, whether due to fraud or error. In making those risk assessments, the auditor considers internal control relevant to the entity's preparation and fair presentation of the consolidated financial statements in order to design audit procedures that are appropriate in the circumstances, but not for the purpose of expressing an opinion on the effectiveness of the entity's internal control. Accordingly, we express no such opinion. An audit also includes evaluating the appropriateness of accounting policies used and the reasonableness of significant accounting estimates made by management, as well as evaluating the overall presentation of the financial statements.

We believe that the audit evidence we have obtained is sufficient and appropriate to provide a basis for our qualified audit opinion.

Basis for Qualified Opinion

ABC Company's investment in XYZ Company, a foreign affiliate acquired during the year and accounted for under the equity method, is carried at $xxx on the balance sheet at December 31, 20X1, and ABC Company's share of XYZ Company's net income of $xxx is included in ABC Company's net income for the year then ended. We were unable to obtain sufficient appropriate audit evidence about the carrying amount of ABC Company's investment in XYZ Company as of December 31, 20X1 and ABC Company's share of XYZ Company's net income for the year then ended because we were denied access to the financial information, management, and the auditors of XYZ Company. Consequently, we were unable to determine whether any adjustments to these amounts were necessary.

Qualified Opinion

In our opinion, except for the possible effects of the matter described in the Basis for Qualified Opinion paragraph, the financial statements referred to above present fairly, in all material respects, the financial position of ABC Company as of December 31, 20X1, and the results of its operations and its cash flows for the year then ended in accordance with accounting principles generally accepted in the United States of America.

(Auditor's signature)

(Auditor's city and state)

(Date of the auditor's report)

Qualified for Misstatement

After studying this lesson, you should be able to:

1. Understand when and how to express a qualified audit opinion for a misstatement (including inadequate disclosure) affecting the fair presentation of an entity's financial statements.

I. **Relevant AICPA Guidance**—The relevant AICPA guidance is provided by AU 705, *Modifications to the Opinion in the Independent Auditor's Report*. The standard states that the auditor's objective is to express clearly an appropriately modified opinion when (1) the auditor concludes that the financial statements as a whole are misstated; or (2) the auditor is unable to obtain sufficient appropriate audit evidence to conclude that the financial statements as a whole are free from material misstatement. (This lesson focuses on the first matter, since the scope limitation is discussed in a separate lesson.)

> **Definitions**
> *Modified Opinion*: A qualified opinion, an adverse opinion, or a disclaimer of opinion.
>
> *Pervasive*: (a) Effects that are not confined to specific elements, accounts, or items of the financial statements; (b) effects that, if so confined, represent or could represent a substantial proportion of the financial statements; or (c) regarding disclosures, are fundamental to users' understanding of the financial statements.

II. **Opinion Choice for a Misstatement (Including Inadequate Disclosure) Involves Judgment**

  A. **Qualified Opinion**—The auditor should express a qualified opinion when the auditor concludes that misstatements are **material, but not pervasive** to the financial statements.

  B. **Adverse Opinion**—The auditor should express an adverse opinion when the auditor concludes that misstatements are **material, and pervasive** to the financial statements. (A separate lesson focuses on the adverse opinion.)

III. **Effect of a Qualification for a Misstatement on the Auditor's Report**

  A. No effect on the introductory paragraph or management's responsibility section

  B. Auditor's **Responsibility Section**—Modify the last sentence to state, "We believe that the audit evidence we have obtained is sufficient and appropriate to provide a basis for our qualified audit opinion."

  C. Add a "Basis for Qualified Opinion" paragraph (with such a label) before the opinion paragraph. The auditor should include a description and quantification of the financial effects of the misstatement (when practicable); likewise, the auditor should include the omitted information (when practicable).

  D. Qualify the opinion using appropriate language such as: "In our opinion, **except for the effects of the matter described in the Basis for Qualified Opinion paragraph**, the financial statements referred to above present fairly . . ." and label the opinion paragraph "Qualified Opinion."

IV. **Sample Audit Report Qualified for a Misstatement**

Independent Auditor's Report

(Appropriate Addressee)

We have audited the accompanying financial statements of ABC Company, which comprise the balance sheet as of December 31, 20X1, and the related statements of income, changes in stockholders' equity and cash flows for the year then ended, and the related notes to the financial statements.

Management's Responsibility for the Financial Statements

Management is responsible for the preparation and fair presentation of these financial statements in accordance with accounting principles generally accepted in the United States of America; this includes the design, implementation, and maintenance of internal control relevant to the preparation and fair presentation of financial statements that are free from material misstatement, whether due to fraud or error.

Auditor's Responsibility

Our responsibility is to express an opinion on these financial statements based on our audit. We conducted our audit in accordance with auditing standards generally accepted in the United States of America. Those standards require that we plan and perform the audit to obtain reasonable assurance about whether the financial statements are free from material misstatement.

An audit involves performing procedures to obtain audit evidence about the amounts and disclosures in the consolidated financial statements. The procedures selected depend on the auditor's judgment, including the assessment of the risks of material misstatement of the consolidated financial statements, whether due to fraud or error. In making those risk assessments, the auditor considers internal control relevant to the entity's preparation and fair presentation of the consolidated financial statements in order to design audit procedures that are appropriate in the circumstances, but not for the purpose of expressing an opinion on the effectiveness of the entity's internal control. Accordingly, we express no such opinion. An audit also includes evaluating the appropriateness of accounting policies used and the reasonableness of significant accounting estimates made by management, as well as evaluating the overall presentation of the financial statements.

We believe that the audit evidence we have obtained is sufficient and appropriate to provide a basis for our qualified audit opinion.

Basis for Qualified Opinion

The Company has stated inventories at cost in the accompanying balance sheets. Accounting principles generally accepted in the United States of America require inventories to be stated at the lower of cost or market. If the Company stated inventories at the lower of cost or market, a write down of $xxx and $xxx would have been required as of December 31, 20X1 and 20X0, respectively. Accordingly, cost of sales would have been increased by $xxx and $xxx, and net income, income taxes, and stockholders' equity would have been reduced by $xxx, $xxx, and $xxx, and $xxx, $xxx, and $xxx, as of and for the years then ended in accordance with accounting principles generally accepted in the United States of America.

Qualified Opinion

In our opinion, except for the effects of the matter described in the Basis for Qualified Opinion paragraph, the financial statements referred to above present fairly, in all material respects, the financial position of ABC Company as of December 31, 20X1 and 20X0, and the results of its operations and its cash flows for the years then ended in accordance with accounting principles generally accepted in the United States of America.

(Auditor's signature)

(Auditor's city and state)

(Date of the auditor's report)

Adverse Opinion

After studying this lesson, you should be able to:

1. Understand how to express an adverse audit opinion when a material and pervasive misstatement causes an entity's financial statement presentation to be misleading.

I. Relevant AICPA Guidance—The relevant AICPA guidance is provided by AU 705, *Modifications to the Opinion in the Independent Auditor's Report*. The standard states that the auditor's objective is to express clearly an appropriately modified opinion when (1) **the auditor concludes that the financial statements as a whole are misstated**; or (2) the auditor is unable to obtain sufficient appropriate audit evidence to conclude that the financial statements as a whole are free from material misstatement. (This lesson focuses on the first matter, since the scope limitation is discussed elsewhere.)

Definitions

Modified Opinion: A qualified opinion, an adverse opinion, or a disclaimer of opinion.

Pervasive: (a) Effects that are not confined to specific elements, accounts, or items of the financial statements; (b) effects that, if so confined, represent or could represent a substantial proportion of the financial statements; or (c) regarding disclosures, are fundamental to users' understanding of the financial statements.

II. Opinion Choice for a Misstatement (Including Inadequate Disclosure) Involves Judgment

A. Qualified Opinion—The auditor should express a qualified opinion when the auditor concludes that misstatements are *material, but not pervasive* to the financial statements. (A separate lesson focuses on the qualified opinion.)

B. Adverse Opinion—The auditor should express an adverse opinion when the auditor concludes that misstatements are *material, and pervasive* to the financial statements.

III. Effect of an Adverse Opinion on the Auditor's Report

A. No effect on the introductory paragraph or management's responsibility section.

B. Auditor's responsibility section—modify the last sentence to state, "We believe that the audit evidence we have obtained is sufficient and appropriate to provide a basis for our adverse audit opinion."

C. Add a "Basis for Adverse Opinion" paragraph (with such a label) before the opinion paragraph. The auditor should include a description and quantification of the financial effects of the misstatement (when practicable); likewise, the auditor should include the omitted information (when practicable).

D. Express the adverse opinion using appropriate language such as: "In our opinion, **because of the significance of the matter discussed in the Basis for Adverse Opinion paragraph, the financial statements referred to above do not present fairly** . . ." and label the opinion paragraph "Adverse Opinion."

IV. Sample Audit Report with an Adverse Opinion for Misstatement

Independent Auditor's Report

(Appropriate Addressee)

We have audited the accompanying consolidated financial statements of ABC Company and its subsidiaries, which comprise the consolidated balance sheets as of December 31, 20X1, and the related consolidated statements of income, changes in stockholder' equity and cash flows for the year then ended, and the related notes to the financial statements.

Management's Responsibility for the Financial Statements

Management is responsible for the preparation and fair presentation of these consolidated financial statements in accordance with accounting principles generally accepted in the United States of America; this includes the design, implementation, and maintenance of internal control relevant to the preparation and fair presentation of consolidated financial statements that are free from material misstatement, whether due to fraud or error.

Auditor's Responsibility

Our responsibility is to express an opinion on these consolidated financial statements based on our audit. We conducted our audit in accordance with auditing standards generally accepted in the United States of America. Those standards require that we plan and perform the audit to obtain reasonable assurance about whether the financial statements are free from material misstatement.

An audit involves performing procedures to obtain audit evidence about the amounts and disclosures in the consolidated financial statements. The procedures selected depend on the auditor's judgment, including the assessment of the risks of material misstatement of the consolidated financial statements, whether due to fraud or error. In making those risk assessments, the auditor considers internal control relevant to the entity's preparation and fair presentation of the consolidated financial statements in order to design audit procedures that are appropriate in the circumstances, but not for the purpose of expressing an opinion on the effectiveness of the entity's internal control. Accordingly, we express no such opinion. An audit also includes evaluating the appropriateness of accounting policies used and the reasonableness of significant accounting estimates made by management, as well as evaluating the overall presentation of the consolidated financial statements.

We believe that the audit evidence we have obtained is sufficient and appropriate to provide a basis for our adverse audit opinion.

Basis for Adverse Opinion

As described in Note X, the Company has not consolidated the financial statements of subsidiary XYZ Company that it acquired during 20X1 because it has not yet been able to ascertain the fair values of certain of the subsidiary's material assets and liabilities at the acquisition date. This investment is therefore accounted for on a cost basis by the Company. Under accounting principles generally accepted in the United States of America, the subsidiary should have been consolidated because it is controlled by the Company. Had XYZ Company been consolidated, many elements in the accompanying consolidated financial statements would have been materially affected. The effects on the consolidated financial statements of the failure to consolidate have not been determined.

Adverse Opinion

In our opinion, because of the significance of the matter discussed in the Basis for Adverse Opinion paragraph, the consolidated financial statements referred to above do not present fairly the financial position of ABC Company and its subsidiaries as of December 31, 20X1, or the results of their operations or their cash flows for the years then ended.

(Auditor's signature)

(Auditor's city and state)

(Date of the auditor's report)

Disclaimer of Opinion

After studying this lesson, you should be able to:

1. Understand how to express a disclaimer of opinion for a scope limitation when the possible effects are viewed as *material and pervasive*.

I. **Relevant AICPA Guidance**—The relevant AICPA guidance is provided by AU 705, *Modifications to the Opinion in the Independent Auditor's Report.* The standard states that the auditor's objective is to express clearly an appropriately modified opinion when (1) the auditor concludes that the financial statements as a whole are misstated; or (2) the auditor is unable to obtain sufficient appropriate audit evidence to conclude that the financial statements as a whole are free from material misstatement. This lesson focuses on the second matter, which is known as a *scope limitation*.

> **Definitions**
> *Modified Opinion*: A qualified opinion, an adverse opinion, or a disclaimer of opinion.
>
> *Pervasive*: (a) Effects that are not confined to specific elements, accounts, or items of the financial statements; (b) effects that, if so confined, represent or could represent a substantial proportion of the financial statements; or (c) regarding disclosures, are fundamental to users' understanding of the financial statements.

II. **Opinion Choice for a Scope Limitation Involves Judgment**

   A. **Qualified Opinion**—The auditor should express a qualified opinion when the auditor is unable to obtain sufficient appropriate audit evidence, and the auditor concludes that the possible effect on the financial statements, if any, could be *material, but not pervasive*. (Another lesson focuses on the qualification for a scope limitation.)

   B. **Disclaimer of Opinion**—The auditor should express a disclaimer of opinion when the auditor is unable to obtain sufficient appropriate audit evidence, and the auditor concludes that the possible effect on the financial statements, if any, could be *material and pervasive*.

III. **Circumstances Resulting in a Scope Limitation**

   A. **Circumstances beyond the Control of the Entity**—For example, the entity's accounting records have been destroyed.

   B. **Circumstances Related to the Nature or Timing of the Auditor's Work**—For example, the auditor determines that substantive procedures alone are not sufficient and the entity's controls are ineffective; the auditor is unable to obtain audited financial statements of an investee (accounted for using the equity method); or the timing of the auditor's appointment does not permit the auditor to observe the physical counting of inventories.

   C. **Limitations Imposed by Management**—For example, management prevents the auditor from requesting external confirmation of certain account balances. The auditor should request that management remove any such limitation.

      1. If management refuses—The auditor should communicate the matter to those charged with governance and determine whether it is possible to perform alternative procedures to obtain sufficient appropriate audit evidence.

      2. If unable to obtain sufficient appropriate audit evidence (and if the effects could be both material and pervasive)—The auditor should withdraw from the audit (when practicable) or issue a disclaimer of opinion.

IV. **Effect of a Disclaimer of Opinion on the Auditor's Report**

   A. Minor effect on the introductory paragraph ("We were engaged to audit ...") and no effect on the management's responsibility section.

B. Auditor's responsibility section—Revise this section to consist of the following two sentences: "Our responsibility is to express an opinion on these financial statements based on conducting the audit in accordance with auditing standards generally accepted in the United States of America. **Because of the matter described in the Basis for Disclaimer of Opinion paragraph, however, we were not able to obtain sufficient appropriate audit evidence to provide a basis for an audit opinion.**"

C. Add a "Basis for Disclaimer of Opinion" paragraph (with such a label) before the opinion paragraph.

D. Disclaim an opinion using appropriate language such as: **"Because of the significance of the matter described in the Basis for Disclaimer of Opinion paragraph, we have not been able to obtain sufficient appropriate audit evidence to provide a basis for an audit opinion. Accordingly, we do not express an opinion on these financial statements."**

Add an appropriate title preceding the paragraph, such as "Disclaimer of Opinion."

V. Sample Audit Report with a Disclaimer of Opinion for a Scope Limitation

---

Independent Auditor's Report

(Appropriate Addressee)

We were engaged to audit the accompanying financial statements of ABC Company, which comprise the balance sheet as of December 31, 20X1, and the related statements of income, changes in stockholders' equity and cash flows for the year then ended, and the related notes to the financial statements.

Management's Responsibility for the Financial Statements

Management is responsible for the preparation and fair presentation of these financial statements in accordance with accounting principles generally accepted in the United States of America; this includes the design, implementation, and maintenance of internal control relevant to the preparation and fair presentation of financial statements that are free from material misstatement, whether due to fraud or error.

Auditor's Responsibility

Our responsibility is to express an opinion on these financial statements based on conducting the audit in accordance with auditing standards generally accepted in the United States of America. **Because of the matter described in the Basis for Disclaimer of Opinion paragraph, however, we were not able to obtain sufficient appropriate audit evidence to provide a basis for an audit opinion.**

Basis for Disclaimer of Opinion

The company's investment in XYZ Company, a joint venture, is carried at $xxx on the Company's balance sheet, which represents over 90% of the Company's net assets as of December 31, 20X1. We were not allowed access to the management and the auditors of XYZ Company. As a result, we were unable to determine whether any adjustments were necessary relating to the Company's proportional share of XYZ Company's assets that it controls jointly, its proportional share of XYZ Company's liabilities for which it is jointly responsible, its proportional share of XYZ Company's income and expenses for the year, and the elements making up the statements of changes in stockholders' equity and cash flows.

Disclaimer of Opinion

Because of the significance of the matter described in the Basis for Disclaimer of Opinion paragraph, we have not been able to obtain sufficient appropriate audit evidence to provide

---

a basis for an audit opinion. Accordingly, we do not express an opinion on these financial statements.

(Auditor's signature)

(Auditor's city and state)

(Date of the auditor's report)

Consistency of Financial Statements

After studying this lesson, you should be able to:

1. Identify how the auditor's report should address a material inconsistency in the financial statements caused by a change in accounting principle or a correction of previously issued financial statements.

I. **Relevant AICPA Guidance**—The relevant AICPA guidance is provided by AU 708, *Consistency of Financial Statements*. The standard states that the auditor's objectives are to (1) evaluate the consistency of the financial statements for the periods presented; and (2) communicate appropriately in the auditor's report when comparability has been materially affected (a) by a change in accounting principle or (b) by adjustments to correct a material misstatement in previously issued financial statements.

II. **Evaluating Consistency**

A. The auditor should evaluate whether the comparability between periods has been affected by either a material change in accounting principle or a material restatement of financial statements.

B. **When the Auditor's Opinion Covers Two (or More) Periods**—The auditor should evaluate the consistency between such periods, as well as the consistency of the earliest period covered by the auditor's opinion with the prior period.

C. **Change in Accounting Principle**

D. The auditor should evaluate a change in accounting principles about four matters:

1. Whether the adopted principle is in accordance with the applicable financial reporting framework;

2. Whether the method of accounting for the effect of the change is in accordance with the applicable financial reporting framework;

3. Whether the disclosures about the change are adequate; *and*

4. Whether the entity has justified that the alternative adopted is **preferable**. (The issuance of an accounting pronouncement that requires or expresses a preference for an accounting principle is considered sufficient justification for a change in principle.)

E. **When Those Four Criteria are Met (and the Change has a Material Effect on the Financial Statements)**—The auditor should include an *emphasis-of-matter* paragraph in the auditor's report to describe the change and reference the footnote disclosure applicable to the change. The auditor should state that the auditor's opinion is not modified regarding the matter.

1. Include the emphasis-of-matter paragraph in subsequent periods until the new principle is applied in all periods presented.

2. If the change is accounted for by retrospective application to the financial statements, the emphasis-of-matter paragraph is only needed in the period of the change.

F. **When Those Four Criteria Have not all Been Met (and the Change has a Material Effect on the Financial Statements)**—The auditor should evaluate whether the change results in a material misstatement and consider whether the auditor's report should be modified.

G. **When a Change in the Reporting Entity Results in Financial Statements that are Essentially Those of a Different Reporting Entity**—The auditor should include an emphasis-of-matter paragraph in the auditor's report describing the change in the entity and referencing the entity's disclosure. However, that is unnecessary when the change in entity results from a transaction or event, such as the purchase or disposition of a subsidiary.

H. Correction of a Material Misstatement in Previously Issued Financial Statements

1. **When the financial statements are restated to correct a prior material misstatement**—The auditor should include an emphasis-of-matter paragraph in the auditor's report. (That paragraph need not be included in subsequent periods.) The auditor should state that the auditor's opinion is not modified regarding the matter.

2. **If the financial statement disclosures relating to the restatement are not adequate**—The auditor should evaluate the inadequacy of disclosure and consider whether the auditor's report should be modified.

3. A change from an accounting principle that is not in accordance with the applicable financial reporting framework to one that is in accordance is a correction of a misstatement.

III. Effect on the Auditor's Report

A. The auditor need not refer to consistency, unless there is an inconsistency due to a material change in accounting principle or restatement.

B. Sample emphasis-of-matter paragraph for a voluntary change in principle:

Emphasis-of-Matter

As discussed in Note X to the financial statements, the entity has elected to change its method of accounting for (*describe accounting method change*) in (*insert year(s) of financial statements that reflect the accounting method change*). Our opinion is not modified with respect to this matter.

C. Sample emphasis-of-matter paragraph for a restatement:

Emphasis-of-Matter

As discussed in Note X to the financial statements, the 20X2 financial statements have been restated to correct a misstatement. Our opinion is not modified with respect to this matter.

PCAOB on Evaluating Consistency of Financial Statements

After studying this lesson, you should be able to:

1. Understand the auditor's responsibilities under PCAOB Auditing Standards to identify "consistency" issues involving either a change in accounting principle or a restatement to correct previously issued financial statements.

I. Evaluating Consistency of Financial Statements

II. Purpose of These PCAOB Auditing Standards

To establish requirements and provide direction for the auditor's evaluation of the consistency of financial statements and the effect of that evaluation on the auditor's report.

A. Identifies two types of issues related to consistency that might affect the auditor's report: (1) a change in accounting principle; and (2) an adjustment to correct a misstatement in previously issued financial statements (i.e., *restatements*).

B. When Reporting on Two or More Periods—The auditor should evaluate the consistency between those periods and with the prior period, if that prior period is presented along with the financial statements reported on.

III. Changes in Accounting Principle

Involving a change from one generally accepted accounting principle to another, including the situation where the accounting principle formerly used is no longer generally accepted.

A. GAAP is specified by FASB guidance entitled *Accounting Changes and Error Corrections*. The PCAOB auditing standards point out that, when a company uses retrospective application to account for a change in accounting principle, the financial statements generally will be viewed as consistent. (However, the previous years' financial statements will appear different from those that the auditor previously reported on.)

B. When There is a Change in Accounting Principle—The auditor should evaluate whether **(1) the newly adopted principle is GAAP; (2) the method of accounting for the effect of the change conforms to GAAP; (3) the disclosures related to the change are adequate; and (4) the company has justified that the alternative accounting principle is preferable.**

   1. **When the four criteria have been met**—The auditor should add an explanatory paragraph to the auditor's report to identify the inconsistency.

   2. **When the four criteria have not been met**—The auditor should treat the matter as a GAAP departure and modify the audit report appropriately.

   3. **When an investor uses the "equity method" and the investee has a change in accounting principle that is material to the investor's financial statements**—The auditor should add an explanatory paragraph to emphasize the matter.

C. When There is a Change in Accounting Estimate Effected by a Change in Accounting Principle—The auditor should evaluate and report on the matter like other changes in accounting principle.

D. When There is a Change in the Reporting Entity Resulting from a Transaction or Event, Such as the Purchase or Disposition of a Subsidiary—It does not require recognition in the auditor's report. (However, if there is a change in the reporting entity that does not result from such a transaction or event, then an explanatory paragraph would be required.)

IV. Correction of a Material Misstatement in Previously Issued Financial Statements

A. The correction of a material misstatement in previously issued financial statements should be recognized in the auditor's report by the addition of an explanatory paragraph.

B. Restatements of previously issued financial statements require related disclosures to be made—The auditor should evaluate the adequacy of the company's disclosures.

V. Change in Classification

A. Changes in classification in previously issued financial statements normally do not require recognition in the auditor's report (unless the change represents a change in accounting principle or the correction of a material misstatement).

B. Accordingly, the auditor should evaluate a material change in financial statement classification (and the related disclosure) to determine whether such a change is also a change in accounting principle or a correction of a material misstatement.

> The auditing requirements under PCAOB auditing standards are substantially the same as those of the AICPA's Clarified Auditing Standards (specifically, AU 708, "Consistency of Financial Statements." The now-superseded SAS No. 1 (specifically, AU 420, *Consistency of Application of [GAAP]*) previously stated that "error correction not involving principle" (e.g., mathematical mistakes, oversight, or misuse of facts) did not have to be identified in the auditor's report. However, the guidance in the Clarified Auditing Standard now treats restatements as an inconsistency that warrants mention in the auditor's report, similar to PCAOB requirements.

Opening Balances—Initial Audits

After studying this lesson, you should be able to:

1. Describe the auditor's responsibility for verifying *opening balances* (and consistency) in an initial audit engagement.

2. Know that the auditor cannot refer to the predecessor as providing a partial basis for the auditor's report.

3. Know how the inability to verify beginning inventory would impact the auditor's report when the effect is material and pervasive.

I. Relevant AICPA Guidance—The relevant AICPA guidance is provided by AU 510, *Opening Balances—Initial Audit Engagements, Including Reaudit Engagements.* The standard states that the auditor's objective is to obtain sufficient audit evidence about whether (a) opening balances contain misstatements that materially affect the current period's financial statements; and (b) appropriate accounting policies reflected in the opening balances have been consistently applied in the current period (or changes are appropriately accounted for and adequately presented and disclosed).

II. Selected Definitions

Definitions

Initial Audit Engagement: An engagement in which (a) the financial statements for the prior period were not audited; or (b) the financial statements for the prior period were audited by a predecessor auditor.

Opening Balances: Those account balances that exist at the beginning of the period. (also include matters requiring disclosure that existed at the beginning of the period, such as contingencies and commitments).

Predecessor Auditor: The auditor from a different audit firm who has reported on the most recent audited financial statements (or was engaged to perform, but did not complete, an audit of the financial statements).

Reaudit: An initial audit engagement to audit financial statements that have been previously audited by a predecessor auditor.

III. Audit Procedures

A. The auditor should read the most recent financial statements and any predecessor's audit report for information relevant to opening balances.

B. The auditor should request management to authorize the predecessor to respond fully to inquiries by the auditor and to allow the auditor to review the predecessor auditor's audit documentation.

1. The predecessor may request a *consent and acknowledgment letter* from the entity to document the authorization regarding the communication with the auditor. Such a letter is not required, but the SAS provides an example.

2. The predecessor may also request a *successor auditor acknowledgment letter* to document the auditor's agreement regarding the use of the predecessor auditor's audit documentation before permitting access to it. Such a letter is not required, but the SAS provides an example.

3. The extent to which the predecessor permits access to the audit documentation is a matter of professional judgment.

4. The auditor's use of the predecessor's information is influenced by the auditor's assessment of the predecessor's competence and independence.

C. **Evaluate the Entity's Opening Balances**

   1. Obtain sufficient appropriate audit evidence as to whether opening balances contain misstatements affecting the current period financial statements by (a) determining whether the prior closing balances have been properly brought forward; (b) determining whether the opening balances reflect the application of appropriate accounting policies; and (c) evaluating whether current period audit procedures provide evidence relevant to the opening balances (such as reviewing the predecessor's audit documentation).

   2. If the opening balances contain material misstatements affecting the current period, the auditor should determine the effect on the current period's financial statements and communicate the misstatements to the appropriate level of management and those charged with governance.

D. **Evaluate the Consistency of Accounting Policies**—The auditor should obtain sufficient appropriate audit evidence as to whether the accounting policies reflected in the opening balances have been consistently applied in the current period (and whether any changes have been properly reported).

E. Discovery of possible material misstatements in financial statements reported on by a predecessor auditor.

   1. The auditor should request management to inform the predecessor of the situation and arrange a three-way meeting to resolve the matter.

   2. If management does not cooperate (or if the auditor is not satisfied with the resolution of the matter), the auditor should evaluate the implications to the current engagement and whether to withdraw. The auditor may also wish to consult with legal counsel for guidance.

IV. **Audit Reporting Considerations**

A. **Reference to Predecessor**—The auditor should not refer to the predecessor's work or report as a partial basis for the auditor's opinion.

B. **Opening Balances**

   1. If unable to obtain sufficient appropriate audit evidence regarding the opening balances, the auditor should either express a qualified opinion or disclaim an opinion, as appropriate.

   2. If there is a material misstatement in the opening balances, the auditor should either express a qualified or adverse opinion, as appropriate.

C. **Consistency of Accounting Policies**—The auditor should either express a qualified or adverse opinion (as appropriate) if the current period's accounting policies are not consistently applied in relation to the opening balances (or if any material changes are not properly reported).

V. **Sample Report**—A sample report follows with a disclaimer of opinion on results of operations and cash flows and an unmodified opinion on financial position (owing to the inability to verify opening inventory such that the effect is deemed to be material and pervasive).

A. Modify introductory sentence—"… and were engaged to audit …"

B. Do not change to Management's Responsibility section.

C. Modify Auditor's Responsibility section—Modify the first two paragraphs and comment on the "basis for unmodified opinion on financial position" at the end.

D. Add a "Basis for Disclaimer" paragraph on results of operations and cash flows.

E. Disclaim an opinion on results of operations and cash flows.

F. Provide an opinion only on financial position.

G. Sample report with a disclaimer of opinion on results of operations and cash flows and an unmodified opinion on financial position (owing to the inability to verify opening inventory)

Independent Auditor's Report

(Appropriate Addressee)

We have audited the accompanying balance sheet of ABC Company, as of December 31, 20X1, and were engaged to audit the related statements of income, changes in stockholders' equity and cash flows for the year then ended, and the related notes to the financial statements.

Management's Responsibility for the Financial Statements

Management is responsible for the preparation and fair presentation of these financial statements in accordance with accounting principles generally accepted in the United States of America; this includes the design, implementation, and maintenance of internal control relevant to the preparation and fair presentation of financial statements that are free from material misstatement, whether due to fraud or error.

Auditor's Responsibility

Our responsibility is to express an opinion on these financial statements based on conducting the audit in accordance with auditing standards generally accepted in the United States of America. Because of the matters described in the Basis for Disclaimer of Opinion paragraph, however, we were not able to obtain sufficient appropriate audit evidence to provide a basis for an audit opinion on the income statement and the cash flow statement.

We conducted our audit of the balance sheet in accordance with auditing standards generally accepted in the United States of America. Those standards require that we plan and perform the audit to obtain reasonable assurance about whether the balance sheet is free of material misstatement.

An audit involves performing procedures to obtain audit evidence about the amounts and disclosures in the consolidated financial statements. The procedures selected depend on the auditor's judgment, including the assessment of the risks of material misstatement of the consolidated financial statements, whether due to fraud or error. In making those risk assessments, the auditor considers internal control relevant to the entity's preparation and fair presentation of the consolidated financial statements in order to design audit procedures that are appropriate in the circumstances, but not for the purpose of expressing an opinion on the effectiveness of the entity's internal control. Accordingly, we express no such opinion. An audit also includes evaluating the appropriateness of accounting policies used and the reasonableness of significant accounting estimates made by management, as well as evaluating the overall presentation of the financial statements.

We believe that the audit evidence we have obtained is sufficient and appropriate to provide a basis for our unmodified opinion on the financial position.

Basis for Disclaimer of Opinion on the Results of Operations and Cash Flows

We were not appointed as auditors of the company until after December 31, 20X0, and thus did not observe the counting of the physical inventories at the beginning of the year. We were unable to satisfy ourselves by alternative means concerning inventory quantities held at December 31, 20X0. Since opening inventories enter into the determination of the net income and cash flows, we were unable to determine whether adjustments might have been necessary relating to the profit for the year reported in the income statement and the net cash flows from operating activities reported in the cash flow statement.

Disclaimer of Opinion on the Results of Operations and Cash Flows

Because of the significance of the matter described in the Basis for Disclaimer of Opinion paragraph, we have not been able to obtain sufficient appropriate audit evidence to provide a basis for an audit opinion on the income statement and the cash flow statement. Accordingly, we do not express an opinion on the results of operations and cash flows for the year ended December 31, 20X1.

Opinion on the Financial Position

In our opinion, the balance sheet presents fairly, in all material respects, the financial position of ABC Company, as of December 31, 20X1, in accordance with accounting principles generally accepted in the United States of America.

(Auditor's signature)

(Auditor's city and state)

(Date of the auditor's report)

Other Information Along with Financial Statements

After studying this lesson, you should be able to:

1. Identify the auditor's responsibility for *other information* included in a document containing the audited financial statements.

I. **Relevant AICPA Guidance**—The relevant AICPA guidance is provided by AU 720, *Other Information in Documents Containing Audited Financial Statements*. The standard states that the auditor's objective is to respond appropriately when the auditor becomes aware that documents containing audited financial statements and the auditor's report include other information that could undermine the credibility of those financial statements and the auditor's report.

> **Definitions**
>
> *Other Information*: Information other than the financial statements and the auditor's report that is included in a document containing audited financial statements and the auditor's report (can be financial and nonfinancial information, but excludes *required supplementary information*).
>
> *Inconsistency*: Other information that conflicts with information contained in the audited financial statements (may raise doubt about the auditor's conclusions and the basis for the auditor's opinion).
>
> *Misstatement of Fact*: Other information that is unrelated to matters appearing in the audited financial statements that is incorrectly presented (may undermine the credibility of the document containing the audited financial statements).

II. **Auditor Responsibilities**

   A. When the audited financial statements and auditor's report is included in a document containing *other information*, the auditor should read the other information to identify any material inconsistencies with the financial statements.

   1. **Examples of other information**—Financial summaries or highlights, management reports on operations, employment data, financial ratios, selected quarterly data, employment data, names of officers/directors, etc.

   2. Other information does not include press releases, cover letters accompanying documents containing the audited financial statements, information in analyst briefings, or information posted to the entity's Web site.

   B. **Material Inconsistencies Identified Prior to the Report Release Date**

   1. Request that management make appropriate revision.

   2. **If management refuses**—Inform those charged with governance and (a) include an *other-matter* paragraph to the auditor's report, (b) withhold the auditor's report, or (c) withdraw from the engagement (when permitted).

   C. **Material Inconsistencies Identified After the Report Release Date**

   1. **If management agrees to make the revision**—The auditor may review steps taken by management to ensure that users of the financial statements and other information are informed of the need for revision.

   2. **If management refuses**—Inform those charged with governance and take appropriate action (such as seeking advice from the auditor's legal counsel).

   D. **Material Misstatements of Fact**—The auditor should discuss the matter with management and, if there is a material misstatement of fact, the auditor should request management to consult with a qualified third party (such as the entity's legal counsel). If management refuses to correct a material misstatement of fact, the auditor should communicate the matter to those charged with governance.

III. Reporting Issues—Disclaiming an Opinion on the Other Information

Note
The auditor is not required to reference the other information in the auditor's report, but may choose to include a disclaimer of opinion on it to avoid any confusion.

Other Matter

Our audit was conducted for the purpose of forming an opinion on the basic financial statements as a whole. The (*identify the other information*) is presented for purposes of additional analysis and is not a required part of the basic financial statements. Such information has not been subjected to the auditing procedures applied in the audit of the basic financial statements, and accordingly, we do not express an opinion or provide any assurance on it.

Supplementary Information Related to Financial Statements

> **After studying this lesson, you should be able to:**
>
> 1. Identify the auditor's responsibilities when engaged to report on *supplementary information in relation to the audited financial statements*.
>
> 2. Prepare an appropriate other-matter paragraph when expressing an opinion on the supplementary information in relation to the audited financial statements in a combined report on the audited financial statements.

I. **Relevant AICPA Guidance**—The relevant AICPA guidance is provided by AU 725, *Supplementary Information in Relation to the Financial Statements as a Whole.* The standard states that the auditor's objective is to evaluate the presentation of the supplementary information and report on whether it is fairly stated, in all material respects, in relation to the financial statements as a whole.

II. **Fairly Stated**—When engaged to determine whether supplementary information is fairly stated in relation to the financial statements.

   A. The auditor should determine whether:

   1. The supplementary information was derived from (or directly related to) the underlying records used to prepare the financial statements.

   2. The supplementary information relates to the same period as the financial statements.

   3. The auditor served as the auditor of the financial statements.

   4. Either an unmodified or qualified opinion was expressed on the financial statements (must not have issued an adverse opinion or disclaimer of opinion).

   5. The supplementary information will either accompany the entity's audited financial statements or the audited financial statements will be made *readily available* by the entity. (Note: *Readily available* means without further action by the entity. Being available upon the user's request is not considered *readily available*).

   B. The auditor should obtain management's agreement that management has responsibility for:

   1. Preparing the supplementary information in accordance with applicable criteria

   2. Providing the auditor with written representations

   3. Including the auditor's report on the supplementary information in any document containing the supplementary information that references the auditor's association with it

   4. Presenting the supplementary information with the audited financial statements (or making the audited financial statements *readily available* to the intended users of the supplementary information)

   C. The auditor should perform the following procedures:

   1. Inquire of management about the purpose of the supplementary information and the criteria used to prepare it.

   2. Obtain an understanding about the methods used and whether those methods have changed (and if changed, the reasons for any changes).

   3. Compare and reconcile the supplementary information to the financial statements or to the underlying records used for the financial statements.

   4. Inquire of management about any significant assumptions used.

5. Evaluate the appropriateness and completeness of the supplementary information in relationship to the audited financial statements.

6. Obtain appropriate written representations from management.

III. Reporting on Supplementary Information in Relation to Audited Financial Statements

A. **Form of Report**—The auditor may issue a separate report on the supplementary information (in addition to the report on the audited financial statements) or combine the report on the supplementary information with the report on the financial statements. (If the latter, then add an other-matter paragraph regarding the supplementary information.)

B. If the auditor expressed an adverse opinion or a disclaimer of opinion on the financial statements, the auditor is prohibited from reporting on the supplementary information.

C. If the supplementary information is materially misstated in relation to the financial statements, the auditor should discuss the matter with management and propose appropriate revision. If management does not revise the supplementary information, the auditor should either appropriately modify the opinion on the supplementary information or withhold the separate report on it.

D. Sample other-matter paragraph when the auditor expresses an unmodified opinion on the financial statements and on the supplementary information in a combined report:

Other Matter

Our audit was conducted for the purpose of forming an opinion on the financial statements as a whole. The (*identify accompanying supplementary information*) is presented for purposes of additional analysis and is not a required part of the financial statements. Such information is the responsibility of management and was derived from and relates directly to the underlying accounting and other records used to prepare the financial statements. The information has been subjected to the auditing procedures applied in the audit of the financial statements and certain additional procedures, including comparing and reconciling such information directly to the underlying accounting and other records used to prepare the financial statements or to the financial statements themselves, and other additional procedures in accordance with auditing standards generally accepted in the United States of America. In our opinion, the information is fairly stated in all material respects in relation to the financial statements as a whole.

Required Supplementary Information

After studying this lesson, you should be able to:

1. Identify the auditor's responsibilities when required *supplementary information* is associated with audited financial statements.

2. Prepare an appropriate emphasis-of-matter or other-matter paragraph when commenting on required supplementary information (or its omission) in connection with audited financial statements.

I. **Relevant AICPA Guidance**—The relevant AICPA guidance is provided by AU 730, *Required Supplementary Information*. The standard states that the auditor's objectives are to (1) describe in the auditor's report whether required supplementary information is presented, and (2) communicate when the supplementary information has not been presented in accordance with the established guidelines (or when material modification is necessary).

Definitions

Required supplementary information: Information that a designated accounting standard setter requires to accompany an entity's basic financial statements (the information is not part of the basic financial statements, but authoritative guidelines for measurement and presentation have been established).

Designated accounting standard setter: A body designated by the AICPA council to establish GAAP pursuant to the Rule of Conduct on *Compliance Standards*.

II. **Procedures to Be Performed by the Auditor**

   A. Inquire of management about the methods used to prepare the information, including (1) whether it is measured and presented in accordance with prescribed guidelines; (2) whether the methods of measurement or presentation have been changed relative to prior period; and (3) whether any significant assumptions affect the measurement or presentation of it.

   B. Compare the information for consistency with (1) management's responses to the auditor's inquiries; (2) the basic financial statements; and (3) other knowledge obtained during the audit of the basic financial statements.

III. **Reporting Implications**

   A. The auditor should include an other-matter paragraph in the auditor's report commenting appropriately on the required supplementary information. The supplementary information cannot affect the auditor's opinion on the financial statements, since it is outside of those financial statements.

   B. The specific language to be used depends upon the particular circumstances.

   1. Whether the required supplementary information is included and the auditor has applied the procedures described above (no material departures);

   2. Whether the required supplementary information is omitted;

   3. Whether some required supplementary information is missing and some is presented in accordance with prescribed guidelines;

   4. Whether the auditor has identified any material departures from prescribed guidelines;

   5. Whether the auditor is unable to complete required procedures; or

   6. Whether the auditor has unresolved doubts as to whether the required supplementary information is presented in accordance with prescribed guidelines.

Example language when the required supplementary information is included and the auditor has performed the applicable procedures without identifying any material departures:

[*Identify the applicable financial reporting framework (e.g., accounting principles generally accepted in the United States of America)*] require that the (*identify the required supplementary information*) on page XX be presented to supplement the basic financial statements. Such information, although not a part of the basic financial statements is required by (*identify designated accounting standard setter*) who considers it to be an essential part of financial reporting for placing the basic financial statements in an appropriate operational, economic, or historical context. We have applied certain limited procedures to the required supplementary information in accordance with auditing standards generally accepted in the United States of America, which consisted of inquiries of management about the methods of preparing the information and comparing the information for consistency with management's responses to our inquiries, the basic financial statements, and other knowledge we obtained during our audit of the basic financial statements. We do not express an opinion or provide any assurance on the information because the limited procedures do not provide us with sufficient evidence to express an opinion or provide any assurance.

PCAOB on Auditing Supplemental Information

After studying this lesson, you should be able to:

1. Know the meaning of the term "supplemental information" as used by the PCAOB.

2. Know the auditor's responsibility for performing audit procedures on supplemental information under PCAOB auditing standards.

3. Know the auditor's responsibilities for reporting on supplemental information under PCAOB auditing standards.

I. **Auditing Supplemental Information Accompanying Audited Financial Statements**

II. **Introduction and Overview**

   A. The PCAOB issued this guidance primarily because of recent changes in the regulatory environment. For example, the 2010 Dodd-Frank Act gave the PCAOB oversight responsibility for audits of brokers and dealers registered with the SEC. These brokers and dealers are required to file certain schedules of information with the SEC. The previous PCAOB standards on supplemental information (adopted from the AICPA standards in 2003) addressed supplemental information only in *auditor-submitted documents* and did not specify audit procedures to be applied to supplemental information that is filed with a regulatory authority, such as the SEC. The current PCAOB standards apply to supplemental information, whether it is required by regulatory authorities or provided voluntarily, when audited in connection with financial statements audited under PCAOB auditing standards.

   B. **Objective**—The auditor's objective is "to obtain sufficient appropriate audit evidence to express an opinion on whether the supplemental information is fairly stated, in all material respects, in relation to the financial statements as a whole."

Definition

Supplemental Information: "Refers to the following information when it accompanies audited financial statements:

a. Supporting schedules that brokers and dealers are required to file pursuant to Rule 17a-5 under the Securities Exchange Act of 1934;

b. Supplemental information (i) required to be presented pursuant to the rules and regulations of a regulatory authority and (ii) covered by an independent public accountant's report on that information in relation to financial statements that are audited in accordance with PCAOB standards; or

c. Information that is (i) ancillary to the audited financial statements, (ii) derived from the company's accounting books and records, and (iii) covered by an independent public accountant's report on that information in relation to the financial statements that are audited in accordance with PCAOB standards."

   C. **Overview of the Performance and Reporting Requirements**

   1. The auditor is required to perform audit procedures specifically to test the supplemental information.

   2. The auditor is required to evaluate (a) whether the supplemental information is fairly presented in relation to the audited financial statements; and (b) whether the supplemental information complies with the relevant regulatory requirements (or other criteria, if applicable).

   3. The auditor is required to coordinate audit work on the supplemental information with audit work on the related financial statements.

4. The auditor is required to clearly report the auditor's responsibilities and conclusions when reporting on supplemental information.

III. Performing Audit Procedures on the Supplemental Information

A. The nature, timing, and extent of the procedures to be applied to the supplemental information may vary with the circumstances, including the following: (1) the risk of material misstatement; (2) the applicable materiality levels relevant to the information; (3) the audit evidence obtained with respect to the financial statements; and (4) the type of opinion expressed on the financial statements.

B. In performing procedures on the supplemental information, the auditor should:

1. Obtain an understanding of the purpose of the information and the criteria used by management for its presentation;

2. Obtain an understanding of the methods used to prepare the information, evaluate the appropriateness of those methods, and determine whether those methods are consistent with those used in the prior period;

3. Inquire of management about any significant assumptions underlying the presentation of the information;

4. Determine that the information reconciles to the financial statements or other applicable records;

5. Perform procedures to test the completeness and accuracy of the information (if not already tested in connection with the audit of the financial statements);

6. Evaluate whether the information complies with relevant regulatory requirements (or other applicable criteria); *and*

7. Obtain appropriate management representations: (a) that management acknowledges responsibility for the fair presentation of the information; (b) that management believes the information is fairly stated; (c) that the methods used have not changed from the prior period (if changed, state that the reasons for the changes are appropriate); (d) that the information complies with regulatory requirements or other applicable criteria; and (e) that management believes any underlying assumptions are appropriate.

IV. Evaluation of Audit Results

A. **Overall Evaluation**—The auditor should evaluate whether the information is fairly stated in relation to the financial statements, including whether the information is presented in conformity with regulatory requirements or other applicable criteria.

B. **Accumulated Misstatements**—The auditor should communicate accumulated misstatements to management to give management a chance to make corrections.

C. **Uncorrected Misstatements**—The auditor should evaluate whether uncorrected misstatements are material (based on relevant quantitative and qualitative factors).

V. Reporting on Supplemental Information

A. **Combined or Separate Reports Permitted**—Unless prohibited by regulatory requirements, the auditor may either issue a separate report on the supplemental information and the financial statements or issue a combined report on both.

B. **Effects of Modifications to the Report on Financial Statements**—The auditor should evaluate whether any modification of the report on the financial statements is relevant to the opinion to be expressed on the supplemental information.

1. **Qualified opinion on the financial statements**—The auditor should express a qualified opinion on the supplemental information if the basis for the qualification also applies to the supplemental information.

2. **Adverse opinion (or disclaimer) on the financial statements**—The auditor should likewise express an adverse opinion (or disclaimer) on the supplemental information.

PCAOB's Sample (Separate) Report on Supplemental Information:

The (identify supplemental information) has been subjected to audit procedures performed in conjunction with the audit of (Company's) financial statements. The (supplemental information) is the responsibility of the Company's management. Our audit procedures included determining whether the (supplemental information) reconciles to the financial statements or the underlying accounting and other records, as applicable, and performing procedures to test the completeness and accuracy of the information presented in the (supplemental information). In forming our opinion on the (supplemental information), we evaluated whether the (supplemental information), including its form and content, is presented in conformity with (specify the relevant regulatory requirement or other criteria, if any). In our opinion, the (identify supplemental information) is fairly stated, in all material respects, in relation to the financial statements as a whole.

Alert to Restrict Report

After studying this lesson, you should be able to:

1. Identify the circumstances for which the auditor should include an *alert* to restrict the use of the auditor's written communication.

2. Identify the appropriate wording associated with an alert to restrict the use of the auditor's written communication.

I. **Relevant AICPA Guidance**—The relevant AICPA guidance is provided by AU 905, *Alert That Restricts the Use of the Auditor's Written Communication*. The standard states that the auditor's objective is to restrict the use of the auditor's written communication by including an alert when the potential exists for that communication to be misunderstood if taken out of the context of its intended use.

II. **Using an Alert to Restrict the Use of the Auditor's Report**

    A. Such an alert should be included as a separate paragraph of the report when:

        1. The subject matter is based on criteria that are only suitable for (or available to) a limited number of users; *or*

        2. The matters are presented in a *by-product report* that is not the primary objective of the engagement.

        3. **Including an Alert**—The auditor is not prohibited from including such an alert in any other auditor's report or written communication.

        4. **Purpose of the Alert**—The purpose of the alert is to restrict the use of the auditor's written communication because of the potential for misunderstanding if taken out of the context for which the written communication is intended.

        5. **Content of the Alert**—The auditor should state that the written communication is intended solely for the use of the specified parties (and either identify or refer to those parties).

        6. **Adding Other Specified Parties**—The auditor should obtain acknowledgment in writing from such other parties as to their understanding of the nature of the engagement, the criteria used, and the auditor's written communication. They can be added after the release of the auditor's written communication (by amending the written communication to add them, but without changing the original date of the auditor's written communication).

        7. **Distribution of the Auditor's Written Communication**—The auditor is not responsible for enforcing the distribution of the auditor's written communication after its release. The purpose of the alert is to appropriately communicate such restricted distribution.

III. **Sample Reporting Language for an Alert to Restrict the Use of the Auditor's Report**

    A. A typical alert consists of one sentence at the end of the auditor's report:

> This (report, letter, presentation, or communication) is intended solely for the information and use of (list or refer to the specified parties) and is not intended to be and should not be used by anyone other than these specified parties.

B. Alert for engagements performed in accordance with Government Auditing Standards:

The purpose of this (*report, letter, presentation, or communication*) is solely to (*describe the purpose of the auditor's written communication, such as to describe the scope of our testing of internal control over financial reporting and compliance, and the results of that testing, and not to provide an opinion on the effectiveness of the entity's internal control over financial reporting or on compliance*). This (*report, letter, presentation, or communication*) is an integral part of an audit performed in accordance with Government Auditing Standards in considering (*describe the results that are being assessed, such as the entity's internal control over financial reporting and compliance*). Accordingly, this (*report, letter, presentation, or communication*) is not suitable for any other purpose.

Financial Statements Using Another Country's Framework

After studying this lesson, you should be able to:

1. Identify the auditor's responsibilities when engaged to report on financial statements prepared in accordance with a financial reporting framework generally accepted in another country.

2. Identify the reporting language that would be appropriate when issuing an audit report on financial statements prepared in accordance with a financial reporting framework generally accepted in another country.

I. **Relevant AICPA Guidance**—The relevant AICPA guidance is provided by AU 910, *Financial Statements Prepared in Accordance With a Financial Reporting Framework Generally Accepted in Another Country*. The standard states that the auditor's objective, when engaged to report on financial statements prepared in accordance with a financial reporting framework generally accepted in another country, is to address appropriately the special considerations that are relevant to: (1) the acceptance of the engagement; (2) the planning and performance of the engagement; and (3) the formation of an opinion and reporting on the financial statements.

II. **Acceptance of the Engagement**

    A. **Considerations**—The auditor should obtain an understanding of (1) the purpose for which the financial statements are prepared; (2) the intended users of the financial statements; and (3) steps taken by management to determine that the framework is acceptable in the circumstances.

    B. **Users**—The auditor should consider whether the intended users are likely to be familiar with the applicable financial reporting framework.

III. **Performance of the Engagement**

    A. **Use Solely Outside the U.S.**—When auditing financial statements intended for use solely outside the U.S., the auditor should comply with GAAS, except for requirements related to the form and content of the auditor's report. The auditor should obtain an understanding of the entity's selection and application of accounting policies.

    B. **Consultation with Others**—The auditor may wish to consult with others having expertise in applying that country's reporting framework.

IV. **Reporting**

    A. **For Use Only Outside the U.S.**—The auditor should report either using (1) a U.S. form of report (including a statement that refers to the note to the financial statements that describes the basis of presentation, including the country involved); or (2) the report form and content of the other country (identify the other country in the report).

    B. **For Use Both Outside and Inside the U.S.**—If the financial statements are also intended for use in the U.S., the auditor should report using the U.S. form of report, including an emphasis-of-matter paragraph that (1) identifies the financial reporting framework used; (2) refers to the note to the financial statements describing that framework; and (3) indicates that such a framework differs from U.S. GAAP.

    C. **Summary of the Differences in the Audit Reporting Language Relative to U.S. Form.**

        1. The first sentence would be changed as follows: … financial statements, which, as described in note X to the financial statements, have been prepared on the basis of (*specify the financial reporting framework generally accepted*) in (*name of the country*)."

        2. The sentence describing management's responsibilities would be changed as follows: "Management is responsible for the preparation and fair presentation of these financial statements in accordance with (*specify the financial reporting framework generally accepted*) in (*name of country*);"

3. The second sentence in the section on the auditor's responsibility would be changed as follows: "We conducted our audit in accordance with auditing standards generally accepted in the United States of America (and [*in name of country*])."

4. The opinion would be changed as follows: "In our opinion, the financial statements referred to above present fairly, in all material respects, ... in accordance with (*specify the financial reporting framework generally accepted*) in (*name of country*)."

V. **Sample Report—U.S. form of Independent Auditor's Report to report on financial statements prepared in accordance with a financial reporting framework generally accepted in another country that are intended for use only outside the United States:**

Independent Auditor's Report

(Appropriate Addressee)

We have audited the accompanying financial statements of ABC Company, which comprise the balance sheet as of December 31, 20X1, and the related statements of income, changes in stockholders' equity, and cash flows for the year then ended, and the related notes to the financial statements, which, as described in note X to the financial statements, have been prepared on the basis of (*specify the financial reporting framework generally accepted*) in (*name of country*).

Management's Responsibility for the Financial Statements

Management is responsible for the preparation and fair presentation of these financial statements in accordance with (*specify the financial reporting framework generally accepted*) in (*name of country*); this includes the design, implementation, and maintenance of internal control relevant to the preparation and fair presentation of financial statements that are free from material misstatement, whether due to fraud or error.

Auditor's Responsibility

Our responsibility is to express an opinion on these financial statements based on our audit. We conducted our audit in accordance with auditing standards generally accepted in the United States of America (and [*in name of country*]). Those standards require that we plan and perform the audit to obtain reasonable assurance about whether the financial statements are free from material misstatement.

An audit involves performing procedures to obtain audit evidence about the amounts and disclosures in the financial statements. The procedures selected depend on the auditor's judgment, including the assessment of the risks of material misstatement of the financial statements, whether due to fraud or error. In making those risk assessments, the auditor considers internal control relevant to the entity's preparation and fair presentation of the financial statements in order to design audit procedures that are appropriate in the circumstances, but not for the purpose of expressing an opinion on the effectiveness of the entity's internal control. Accordingly, we express no such opinion. An audit also includes evaluating the appropriateness of accounting policies used and the reasonableness of significant accounting estimates made by management, as well as evaluating the overall presentation of the financial statements.

We believe that the audit evidence we have obtained is sufficient and appropriate to provide a basis for our audit opinion.

Opinion

In our opinion, the financial statements referred to above present fairly, in all material respects, the financial position of ABC Company as of December 31, 20X1, and the results of its operations and its cash flows for the year then ended in accordance with (*specify the financial reporting framework generally accepted*) in (*name of country*).

(Auditor's signature)

(Auditor's city and state)

(Date of the auditor's report)

Reporting on Summary Financial Statements

After studying this lesson, you should be able to:

1. Identify the auditor's responsibilities when engaged to report on an entity's *summary financial statements*.

2. Identify the reporting language that would be appropriate when issuing an audit report on summary financial statements.

I. **Relevant AICPA Guidance**—The relevant AICPA guidance is provided by AU 810, *Engagements to Report on Summary Financial Statements*. The standard states that the auditor's objectives are (1) to determine whether it is appropriate to accept the engagement to report on summary financial states; and (2) if engaged, to perform the necessary procedures, to form an opinion on whether the summary financial statements are consistent with the audited financial statements from which they have been derived, and to clearly express that opinion (and the basis for it) through a written report.

> **Definitions**
>
> *Applied Criteria*: The criteria applied by management in the preparation of the summary financial statements.
>
> *Summary Financial Statements*: Historical financial information that is derived from financial statements but that contains less detail than the financial statements, while still providing a structured representation consistent with that provided by the financial statements.

II. **Engagement Acceptance**

A. The auditor must have been engaged to audit the financial statements as a whole in order to accept an engagement to report on summary financial statements.

B. Before accepting an engagement to report on summary financial statements— The auditor should (1) determine whether the applied criteria are acceptable; and (2) obtain a written agreement from management acknowledging their responsibilities and accepting the expected form and content of the auditor's report.

III. **Procedures to Be Performed by the Auditor**

A. Evaluate whether the summary financial statements adequately disclose their summarized nature and identify the audited financial statements.

B. When unaccompanied by the audited financial statements, evaluate whether the audited financial statements are **readily available** to users.

C. Evaluate whether the summary financial statements adequately disclose the applied criteria.

D. Compare the summary financial statements with the related audited financial statements.

E. Evaluate whether the summary financial statements are prepared in accordance with the applied criteria.

F. Evaluate whether the summary financial statements contain necessary information at an appropriate level of aggregation so they are not misleading.

> **Note**
> *Audited financial statements are viewed as readily available if users can obtain them without any further action by the entity. Management's statement that they are available upon request, would **not** be considered readily available*

G. Obtain a written representations letter that addresses the following matters:

1. Management has prepared the summary financial statements in accordance with the applied criteria (and that the applied criteria are acceptable).

2. Management has made the audited financial statements readily available to the intended users.

3. If the date of the report on the summary financial information is later than the date of the report on the audited financial statements, include a statement as to whether management believes any of its previous representations need to be modified and whether any subsequent events require adjustment to or disclosure in the audited financial statements.

4. The representation letter should be dated the same as the auditor's report.

IV. Form of the Auditor's Opinion

A. Only an Unmodified or Adverse Opinion is Permitted—The summary financial statements are either consistent or not consistent with the audited financial statements; accordingly, a qualified opinion is not permitted.

    1. Unmodified opinion—When issuing an unmodified opinion on the summary financial statements, the opinion should state that they are consistent, in all material respects, with the audited financial statements from which they have been derived, in accordance with the applied criteria.

    2. Adverse opinion—When issuing an adverse opinion on the summary financial statements, the opinion should state that the financial statements are not consistent, in all material respects, with the audited financial statements in accordance with the applied criteria.

B. Adverse Opinion or Disclaimer of Opinion—When the auditor's report on the audited financial statements contains an adverse opinion or a disclaimer of opinion, the auditor should either withdraw from the engagement to report on the summary financial statements (when withdrawal is possible) or disclaim an opinion on the summary financial statements.

V. Auditor's Report on Summary Financial Statements—Include the following elements:

A. A title that includes the word *independent*

B. Addressee

C. Introductory paragraph that (1) identifies the summary financials; (2) identifies the audited financial statements from which the summary financials were derived; (3) refers to the auditor's report on the financial statements and the date; and (4) states that the summary financials do not include all the disclosures required for complete financial statements

D. Description of management's responsibility

E. Statement about the auditor's responsibility

F. A paragraph that clearly describes an opinion

G. The auditor's signature, city and state, and date of the report

VI. Sample Audit Report on Summary Financial Statements

Independent Auditor's Report on Summary Financial Statements

(Appropriate Addressee)

The accompanying summary financial statements, which comprise the summary balance sheet as of December 31, 20X1, the summary income statement, summary statement of changes in stockholders' equity and summary cash flow statement for the year then ended, and the related notes, are derived from the audited financial statements of ABC Company as of and for the year ended December 31, 20X1. We expressed an unmodified audit opinion on those audited financial statements in our report dated February 15, 20X2. The audited financial statements, and the summary financial statements derived therefrom, do not reflect the effects of events, if any, that occurred subsequent to the date of our report on the audited financial statements.

The summary financial statements do not contain all the disclosures required by (*describe financial reporting framework applied in the preparation of the financial statements of ABC Company*). Reading the summary financial statements, therefore, is not a substitute for reading the audited financial statements of ABC Company.

Management's Responsibility for the Summary Financial Statements

Management is responsible for the preparation of the summary financial statements on the basis described in Note X.

Auditor's Responsibility

Our responsibility is to express an opinion about whether the summary financial statements are consistent, in all material respects, with the audited financial statements based on our procedures, which were conducted in accordance with auditing standards generally accepted in the United States of America. The procedures consisted principally of comparing the summary financial statements with the related information in the audited financial statements from which the summary financial statements have been derived, and evaluating whether the summary financial statements are prepared in accordance with the basis described in Note X. We did not perform any audit procedures regarding the audited financial statements after the date of our report on those financial statements.

Opinion

In our opinion, the summary financial statements of ABC Company as of and for the year ended December 31, 20X1 referred to above are consistent, in all material respects, with the audited financial statements from which they have been derived, on the basis described in Note X.

(Auditor's signature)

(Auditor's city and state)

(Date of the auditor's report)

Interim Financial Information

After studying this lesson, you should be able to:

1. Identify the auditor's responsibilities when engaged to report on an entity's *interim financial information*.

2. Identify the reporting language that would be appropriate when issuing a review report on an audit entity's interim financial information.

I. **Relevant AICPA Guidance**—The relevant AICPA guidance is provided by AU 930, *Interim Financial Information*. The standard states that the auditor's objective is to obtain a basis for reporting whether the auditor is aware of any material modifications that should be made to the interim financial information for it to be in accordance with the applicable financial reporting framework through performing limited procedures.

> **Definition**
> *Interim Financial Information*: Financial information prepared and presented in accordance with an applicable financial reporting framework that comprises either a complete or condensed set of financial statements covering a period(s) less than one full year or covering a 12-month period ending on a date other than the entity's fiscal year end.

II. **Engagement Acceptance**

    A. Before accepting an engagement to review the interim financial information, the auditor should (1) determine whether the financial reporting framework to be applied is acceptable; and (2) obtain the agreement of management regarding the engagement terms.

    B. **Agreement on Engagement Terms**—The auditor should agree upon the terms of the engagement with management (or those charged with governance) and record those terms in an engagement letter that includes: (1) the objectives and scope of the engagement; (2) the responsibilities of management; (3) the responsibilities of the auditor; (4) the limitations of a review engagement; and (5) identification of the applicable financial reporting framework.

III. **Engagement Performance**

    A. Obtain an understanding of the entity and its environment, including internal control related to the preparation of annual and interim financial information. This should be sufficient to (1) identify the types of potential misstatements (and likelihood of occurrence) and (2) select the inquiries and analytical procedures for the auditor's basis for conclusions.

    B. Analytical procedures, inquiries, and other review procedures.

        1. **Analytical procedures**—The auditor should apply analytical procedures to the interim information to identify unusual items that may indicate a material misstatement, including the following:

            a. Comparing the interim financial information with comparable information for the immediately preceding period and with the corresponding period(s) in the previous year;

            b. Comparing recorded amounts or ratios developed from recorded amounts to expectations; and

            c. Comparing disaggregated revenue data.

        2. **Inquiries and other review procedures**—The auditor should make the following inquiries and perform the following other procedures in a review of interim financial information.

            a. Read the available minutes of meetings of stockholders, directors, and appropriate committees;

      b. Obtain reports from any component auditors related to reviews of significant components or inquire of those auditors if reports have not been issued;

      c. Inquire of management about the matters normally associated with a management representations letter;

      d. Obtain evidence that the interim financial information agrees to (or reconciles with) the accounting records;

      e. Read the interim financial information; *and*

      f. Read other information in documents containing the interim financial information to see if any of it is materially inconsistent.

   3. Inquiry concerning litigation, claims, and assessments—The auditor should inquire of legal counsel if information about litigation, claims, and assessments does not appear to be presented in accordance with the applicable financial reporting framework.

   4. Going-concern issues—If information indicates that there may be substantial doubt about an entity's ability to continue as a going concern, the auditor should inquire of management about plans for dealing with adverse effects and consider the adequacy of disclosure about such matters.

   5. The auditor should consider the reasonableness and consistency of management's responses, but the auditor is not required to corroborate management's responses with other evidence.

C. Evaluating the Results of Interim Review Procedures—The auditor should evaluate, individually and in the aggregate, misstatements to determine whether material modification should be made to the interim financial information.

D. Written Representations from Management—The auditor should obtain written representations from management for all interim financial information presented as of the date of the auditor's review report. If management does not provide the written representation requested, the auditor should withdraw from the engagement to review the interim financial information.

IV. Reporting on a Review of Interim Financial Information

  A. Form of the Review Report—The report should be in writing and include the following:

   1. Title

   2. Addressee

   3. An introductory paragraph

   4. A section on "Management's Responsibility for the Financial Statements"

   5. A section on "Auditor's Responsibility"

   6. A concluding section that expresses conclusions (negative assurance)

   7. The signature, city and state, and date of the review report

  B. Each page of the interim financial information should be clearly marked *unaudited*.

  C. If Comparative Information is Presented that has Not Been Reviewed—The report should indicate that the auditor assumes no responsibility for it.

  D. Modification of the Auditor's Review Report—When the interim financial information has not been prepared in accordance with the applicable financial reporting framework in all material respects, the auditor should consider whether modification of the review report is sufficient to address the matter.

   1. If modification is sufficient—The auditor should modify the review report by describing the nature of the departure, and stating the effects on the interim financial information (or providing the appropriate information when disclosure is inadequate), if practicable.

   2. If modification is not sufficient—The auditor should withdraw from the review engagement.

E. Interim Financial Information Accompanying Audited Financial Statements—The auditor should include an *other-matter paragraph* in the report on audited financial statements when the following conditions exist:

1. The interim financial information that has been reviewed is included in a document containing the audited financial statements.

2. The interim information accompanying the audited financial statements does not appear to be presented in accordance with the applicable financial reporting framework.

3. The auditor's separate review report, which refers to the departure, is not presented with the interim financial information.

V. Sample Review Report of the Entity's Auditor

Independent Auditor's Review Report

(Appropriate Addressee)

Report on the Financial Statements

We have reviewed the accompanying (*describe the interim financial information or statements reviewed*) of ABC Company and subsidiaries as of September 30, 20X1, and for the three-month and nonemonth periods then ended.

Management's Responsibility

The Company's management is responsible for the preparation and fair presentation of the interim financial information in accordance with (*identify the applicable financial reporting framework; for example, accounting principles generally accepted in the United States of America*); this responsibility includes the design, implementation, and maintenance of internal control sufficient to provide a reasonable basis for the preparation and fair presentation of interim financial information in accordance with the applicable financial reporting framework.

Auditor's Responsibility

Our responsibility is to conduct our review in accordance with auditing standards generally accepted in the United States of America applicable to reviews of interim financial information. A review of interim financial information consists principally of applying analytical procedures and making inquiries of persons responsible for financial and accounting matters. It is substantially less in scope than an audit conducted in accordance with auditing standards generally accepted in the United States of America, the objective of which is the expression of an opinion regarding the financial information. Accordingly, we do not express such an opinion.

Conclusion

Based on our review, we are not aware of any material modifications that should be made to the accompanying interim financial information for it to be in accordance with (*identify the applicable financial reporting framework; for example, accounting principles generally accepted in the United States of America*).

(Auditor's signature)

(Auditor's city and state)

(Date of the auditor's report)

VI. Filings with the SEC Under Federal Securities Statutes

A. **Relevant AICPA Guidance**—The relevant AICPA guidance is provided by AU 925, *Filings with the U.S. SEC Under the Securities Act of 1933*. The standard states that the auditor's objective is to perform specified procedures at or shortly before the effective date of the registration statement to sustain the burden of proof that the auditor has performed a reasonable investigation [under Section 11(b)(3)(B)].

Definitions

Auditor's Consent: A statement signed and dated by the auditor giving consent to use the auditor's report in a registration statement.

Awareness Letter: A letter signed and dated by the auditor to acknowledge the auditor's awareness that the review report on interim financial information is being used in a registration statement (also known as an *acknowledgment letter*).

Effective Date of the Registration: The date on which the registration statement becomes effective for purposes of evaluating the auditor's liability under Section 11 of the Securities Act of 1933.

B. **Responsibilities under Federal Securities Statutes**—The Securities Act of 1933 promotes fair disclosure and prohibits fraud in initial public offerings of securities.

1. **Management's** responsibilities are the same as with the financial statements used for other purposes—that is, the financial statements are the representations of management.

2. The **independent accountant's** responsibilities are similar to other types of reporting—Section 11 of the 1933 Act prohibits false or misleading statements (or material omissions) in registration statements.

   a. Section 11 defense—After a reasonable investigation, the independent accountant had reasonable grounds to believe that the financial statements were fairly stated (but the CPA has the burden of proof).

   b. Statutory responsibility is determined in light of the circumstances on the effective date of the registration statement.

   c. The CPA should read the relevant parts of any prospectus filed under the 1933 Act to verify that the independent accountant's name is not being used inappropriately. (Note that a *prospectus* is an informational document required to be filed with the SEC in connection with a registration statement to offer securities for sale; the prospectus cannot be used to finalize sales of such securities until the registration statement is declared effective by the SEC.)

   d. When the registration statement references the interim financial information reviewed by the accountant—the prospectus should clearly indicate that the review report is not part of the registration statement within the meaning of the 1933 Act. The auditor's review report is only required if the registration statement indicates that the unaudited interim information has been reviewed. (If unaudited financial statements are presented along with audited financial statements in a filing with the SEC, the unaudited financial statements should be labeled "unaudited" and should not be referenced in the auditor's report.)

C. **Subsequent Events Procedures in Connection with Filings under the Securities Act of 1933**

1. Extend the procedures regarding subsequent events from the audit report date up to (or as near as practicable) to the effective date of the registration statement.

2. Following fieldwork, the auditor may usually rely on inquiries of appropriate client personnel—obtain written representations from management regarding those financial and accounting matters.

3. An auditor who has reported on the financial statements from prior periods, but not the most recent audited financial statements included in the registration statement, is responsible for events subsequent to the date of the prior-period's audited financial statements. The auditor should:

   a. Read the applicable portions of the prospectus and registration statement.

   b. Obtain a letter of representations from the successor auditor as to whether the successor's audit identified any matters that might have a material effect on the prior period's financial statements.

Sample Reports

Unmodified Opinion (Reference to Legal Requirements)

Independent Auditor's Report

(Appropriate Addressee)

Report on the Financial Statements[1]

We have audited the accompanying consolidated financial statements of ABC Company and its subsidiaries, which comprise the consolidated balance sheets as of December 31, 20X1 and 20X0, and the related consolidated statements of income, changes in stockholders' equity and cash flows for the years then ended, and the related notes to the financial statements.

Management's Responsibility for the Financial Statements

Management is responsible for the preparation and fair presentation of these consolidated financial statements in accordance with accounting principles generally accepted in the United States of America; this includes the design, implementation, and maintenance of internal control relevant to the preparation and fair presentation of consolidated financial statements that are free from material misstatement, whether due to fraud or error.

Auditor's Responsibility

Our responsibility is to express an opinion on these consolidated financial statements based on our audits. We conducted our audits in accordance with auditing standards generally accepted in the United States of America. Those standards require that we plan and perform the audit to obtain reasonable assurance about whether the consolidated financial statements are free from material misstatement.

An audit involves performing procedures to obtain audit evidence about the amounts and disclosures in the consolidated financial statements. The procedures selected depend on the auditor's judgment, including the assessment of the risks of material misstatement of the consolidated financial statements, whether due to fraud or error. In making those risk assessments, the auditor considers internal control relevant to the entity's preparation and fair presentation of the consolidated financial statements in order to design audit procedures that are appropriate in the circumstances, but not for the purpose of expressing an opinion on the effectiveness of the entity's internal control.[2] Accordingly, we express no such opinion. An audit also includes evaluating the appropriateness of accounting policies used and the reasonableness of significant accounting estimates made by management, as well as evaluating the overall presentation of the consolidated financial statements.

We believe that the audit evidence we have obtained is sufficient and appropriate to provide a basis for our audit opinion.

Opinion

In our opinion, the consolidated financial statements referred to above present fairly, in all material respects, the financial position of ABC Company and its subsidiaries as of December 31, 20X1 and 20X0, and the results of their operations and their cash flows for the years then ended in accordance with accounting principles generally accepted in the United States of America.

Report on Other Legal and Regulatory Requirements

(Auditor's signature)

(Auditor's city and state)

(Date of the auditor's report)

[1] The subtitle "Report on the Financial Statements" is unnecessary in circumstances when the second subtitle, "Report on Other Legal and Regulatory Requirements," is not applicable.

[2] When the auditor has responsibility for expressing an opinion on the effectiveness of internal control in conjunction with the audit of the entity's financial statements, the sentence would be stated as follows: "In making those risk assessments, the auditor considers internal control relevant to the entity's preparation and fair presentation of the consolidated financial statements in order to design audit procedures that are appropriate in the circumstances." In addition, the next sentence, "Accordingly, we express no such opinion," would be omitted.

Unmodified Opinion (No Reference to Legal Requirements)

Independent Auditor's Report

(Appropriate Addressee)

We have audited the accompanying consolidated financial statements of ABC Company and its subsidiaries, which comprise the consolidated balance sheets as of December 31, 20X1 and 20X0, and the related consolidated statements of income, changes in stockholders' equity and cash flows for the years then ended, and the related notes to the financial statements.

Management's Responsibility for the Financial Statements

Management is responsible for the preparation and fair presentation of these consolidated financial statements in accordance with accounting principles generally accepted in the United States of America; this includes the design, implementation, and maintenance of internal control relevant to the preparation and fair presentation of consolidated financial statements that are free from material misstatement, whether due to fraud or error.

Auditor's Responsibility

Our responsibility is to express an opinion on these consolidated financial statements based on our audits. We conducted our audits in accordance with auditing standards generally accepted in the United States of America. Those standards require that we plan and perform the audit to obtain reasonable assurance about whether the consolidated financial statements are free from material misstatement.

An audit involves performing procedures to obtain audit evidence about the amounts and disclosures in the consolidated financial statements. The procedures selected depend on the auditor's judgment, including the assessment of the risks of material misstatement of the consolidated financial statements, whether due to fraud or error. In making those risk assessments, the auditor considers internal control relevant to the entity's preparation and fair presentation of the consolidated financial statements in order to design audit procedures that are appropriate in the circumstances, but not for the purpose of expressing an opinion on the effectiveness of the entity's internal control.[1] Accordingly, we express no such opinion. An audit also includes evaluating the appropriateness of accounting policies used and the reasonableness of significant accounting estimates made by management, as well as evaluating the overall presentation of the consolidated financial statements.

We believe that the audit evidence we have obtained is sufficient and appropriate to provide a basis for our audit opinion.

Opinion

In our opinion, the consolidated financial statements referred to above present fairly, in all material respects, the financial position of ABC Company and its subsidiaries as of December 31, 20X1 and 20X0, and the results of their operations and their cash flows for the years then ended in accordance with accounting principles generally accepted in the United States of America.

(Auditor's signature)

(Auditor's city and state)

(Date of the auditor's report)

[1] When the auditor has responsibility for expressing an opinion on the effectiveness of internal control in conjunction with the audit of the entity's financial statements, the sentence would be stated as follows: "In making those risk assessments, the auditor considers internal control relevant to the entity's preparation and fair presentation of the consolidated financial statements in order to design audit procedures that are appropriate in the circumstances." In addition, the next sentence, "Accordingly, we express no such opinion," would be omitted.

Unmodified Opinion (Sentence by Sentence)

Independent Auditor's Report

(Appropriate Addressee)

(Introductory Paragraph)

We have audited the accompanying consolidated financial statements of ABC Company and its subsidiaries, which comprise the consolidated balance sheets as of December 31, 20X1 and 20X0, and the related consolidated statements of income, changes in stockholders' equity and cash flows for the years then ended, and the related notes to the financial statements.

Management's Responsibility for the Financial Statements

Management is responsible for the preparation and fair presentation of these consolidated financial statements in accordance with accounting principles generally accepted in the United States of America; this includes the design, implementation, and maintenance of internal control relevant to the preparation and fair presentation of consolidated financial statements that are free from material misstatement, whether due to fraud or error.

Auditor's Responsibility

(First of three paragraphs)

1. Our responsibility is to express an opinion on these consolidated financial statements based on our audits.

2. We conducted our audits in accordance with auditing standards generally accepted in the United States of America.

3. Those standards require that we plan and perform the audit to obtain reasonable assurance about whether the consolidated financial statements are free from material misstatement.

(Second of three paragraphs)

4. An audit involves performing procedures to obtain audit evidence about the amounts and disclosures in the consolidated financial statements.

5. The procedures selected depend on the auditor's judgment, including the assessment of the risks of material misstatement of the consolidated financial statements, whether due to fraud or error.

6. In making those risk assessments, the auditor considers internal control relevant to the entity's preparation and fair presentation of the consolidated financial statements in order to design audit procedures that are appropriate in the circumstances, but not for the purpose of expressing an opinion on the effectiveness of the entity's internal control.

7. Accordingly, we express no such opinion.

8. An audit also includes evaluating the appropriateness of accounting policies used and the reasonableness of significant accounting estimates made by management, as well as evaluating the overall presentation of the consolidated financial statements. (Third of three paragraphs)

9. We believe that the audit evidence we have obtained is sufficient and appropriate to provide a basis for our audit opinion.

Opinion

In our opinion, the consolidated financial statements referred to above present fairly, in all material respects, the financial position of ABC Company and its subsidiaries as of December 31, 20X1 and

20X0, and the results of their operations and their cash flows for the years then ended in accordance with accounting principles generally accepted in the United States of America.

(Auditor's signature)

(Auditor's city and state)

(Date of the auditor's report)

Independent Auditor's Report

(Appropriate Addressee)

We have audited the accompanying financial statements of ABC Company, which comprise the balance sheet as of December 31, 20X2 and 20X1, and the related statements of income, changes in stockholders' equity and cash flows for the years then ended, and the related notes to the financial statements.

Management's Responsibility for the Financial Statements

Management is responsible for the preparation and fair presentation of these financial statements in accordance with accounting principles generally accepted in the United States of America; this includes the design, implementation, and maintenance of internal control relevant to the preparation and fair presentation of financial statements that are free from material misstatement, whether due to fraud or error.

Auditor's Responsibility

Our responsibility is to express an opinion on these financial statements based on our audits. Except as explained in the Basis for Disclaimer of Opinion paragraph, we conducted our audits in accordance with auditing standards generally accepted in the United States of America. Those standards require that we plan and perform the audit to obtain reasonable assurance about whether the financial statements are free from material misstatement.

An audit involves performing procedures to obtain audit evidence about the amounts and disclosures in the consolidated financial statements. The procedures selected depend on the auditor's judgment, including the assessment of the risks of material misstatement of the consolidated financial statements, whether due to fraud or error. In making those risk assessments, the auditor considers internal control relevant to the entity's preparation and fair presentation of the consolidated financial statements in order to design audit procedures that are appropriate in the circumstances, but not for the purpose of expressing an opinion on the effectiveness of the entity's internal control. Accordingly, we express no such opinion. An audit also includes evaluating the appropriateness of accounting policies used and the reasonableness of significant accounting estimates made by management, as well as evaluating the overall presentation of the financial statements.

We believe that the audit evidence we have obtained is sufficient and appropriate to provide a basis for our audit opinions on the balance sheets as of December 31, 20X2 and 20X1, and the statements of income, changes in stockholders' equity and cash flows for the year ended December 31, 20X2.

Basis for Disclaimer of Opinion on 20X1 Operations and Cash Flows

We did not observe the taking of the physical inventory as of December 31, 20X0, since that date was prior to our appointment as auditors for the Company, and we were unable to satisfy ourselves regarding inventory quantities by means of other auditing procedures. Inventory amounts as of December 31, 20X0 enter into the determination of net income and cash flows for the year ended December 31, 20X1.

Disclaimer of Opinion on 20X1 Operations and Cash Flows

Because of the significance of the matter described in the Basis for Disclaimer of Opinion paragraph, we have not been able to obtain sufficient appropriate audit evidence to provide a basis for an audit opinion on the results of operations and cash flows for the year ended December 31, 20X1.

Accordingly, we do not express an opinion on the results of operations and cash flows for the year ended December 31, 20X1.

Opinion

In our opinion, the balance sheets of ABC Company as of December 31, 20X2 and 20X1, and the statements of income, changes in stockholders' equity and cash flows for the year ended December 31, 20X2, present fairly, in all material respects, the financial position of ABC Company as of December 31, 20X2 and 20X1, and the results of its operations and its cash flows for the year ended December 31, 20X2 in accordance with accounting principles generally accepted in the United States of America.

(Auditor's signature)

(Auditor's city and state)

(Date of the auditor's report)

Independent Auditor's Report

(Appropriate Addressee)

We have audited the accompanying financial statements of ABC Company, which comprise the balance sheet as of December 31, 20X1 and 20X0, and the related statements of income, changes in stockholders' equity and cash flows for the years then ended, and the related notes to the financial statements.

Management's Responsibility for the Financial Statements

Management is responsible for the preparation and fair presentation of these financial statements in accordance with accounting principles generally accepted in the United States of America; this includes the design, implementation, and maintenance of internal control relevant to the preparation and fair presentation of financial statements that are free from material misstatement, whether due to fraud or error.

Auditor's Responsibility

Our responsibility is to express an opinion on these financial statements based on our audits. We conducted our audits in accordance with auditing standards generally accepted in the United States of America. Those standards require that we plan and perform the audit to obtain reasonable assurance about whether the financial statements are free from material misstatement.

An audit involves performing procedures to obtain audit evidence about the amounts and disclosures in the consolidated financial statements. The procedures selected depend on the auditor's judgment, including the assessment of the risks of material misstatement of the consolidated financial statements, whether due to fraud or error. In making those risk assessments, the auditor considers internal control relevant to the entity's preparation and fair presentation of the consolidated financial statements in order to design audit procedures that are appropriate in the circumstances, but not for the purpose of expressing an opinion on the effectiveness of the entity's internal control. Accordingly, we express no such opinion. An audit also includes evaluating the appropriateness of accounting policies used and the reasonableness of significant accounting estimates made by management, as well as evaluating the overall presentation of the financial statements.

We believe that the audit evidence we have obtained is sufficient and appropriate to provide a basis for our qualified audit opinion.

Basis for Qualified Opinion

The Company has excluded, from property and debt in the accompanying 20X1 balance sheet, certain lease obligations that were entered into in 20X1 which, in our opinion, should be capitalized in accordance with accounting principles generally accepted in the United States of America. If these lease obligations were capitalized property would be increased by $xxx, long-term debt by $xxx, and retained earnings by $xxx as of December 31, 20X1, and net income and earnings per share would be increased (decreased) by $xxx and $xxx, respectively, for the year then ended.

Qualified Opinion

In our opinion, except for the effects on the 20X1 financial statements of not capitalizing certain lease obligations as described in the Basis for Qualified Opinion paragraph, the financial statements referred to above present fairly, in all material respects, the financial position of ABC Company as of

December 31, 20X1 and 20X0, and the results of its operations and its cash flows for the years then ended in accordance with accounting principles generally accepted in the United States of America.

(Auditor's signature)

(Auditor's city and state)

(Date of the auditor's report)

Qualified for Scope

Independent Auditor's Report

(Appropriate Addressee)

We have audited the accompanying financial statements of ABC Company, which comprise the balance sheet as of December 31, 20X1, and the related statements of income, changes in stockholders' equity and cash flows for the year then ended, and the related notes to the financial statements.

Management's Responsibility for the Financial Statements

Management is responsible for the preparation and fair presentation of these financial statements in accordance with accounting principles generally accepted in the United States of America; this includes the design, implementation, and maintenance of internal control relevant to the preparation and fair presentation of financial statements that are free from material misstatement, whether due to fraud or error.

Auditor's Responsibility

Our responsibility is to express an opinion on these financial statements based on our audit. We conducted our audit in accordance with auditing standards generally accepted in the United States of America. Those standards require that we plan and perform the audit to obtain reasonable assurance about whether the financial statements are free from material misstatement.

An audit involves performing procedures to obtain audit evidence about the amounts and disclosures in the consolidated financial statements. The procedures selected depend on the auditor's judgment, including the assessment of the risks of material misstatement of the consolidated financial statements, whether due to fraud or error. In making those risk assessments, the auditor considers internal control relevant to the entity's preparation and fair presentation of the consolidated financial statements in order to design audit procedures that are appropriate in the circumstances, but not for the purpose of expressing an opinion on the effectiveness of the entity's internal control. Accordingly, we express no such opinion. An audit also includes evaluating the appropriateness of accounting policies used and the reasonableness of significant accounting estimates made by management, as well as evaluating the overall presentation of the financial statements.

We believe that the audit evidence we have obtained is sufficient and appropriate to provide a basis for our qualified audit opinion.

Basis for Qualified Opinion

ABC Company's investment in XYZ Company, a foreign affiliate acquired during the year and accounted for under the equity method, is carried at $xxx on the balance sheet at December 31, 20X1, and ABC Company's share of XYZ Company's net income of $xxx is included in ABC Company's net income for the year then ended. We were unable to obtain sufficient appropriate audit evidence about the carrying amount of ABC Company's investment in XYZ Company as of December 31, 20X1 and ABC Company's share of XYZ Company's net income for the year then ended because we were denied access to the financial information, management, and the auditors of XYZ Company. Consequently, we were unable to determine whether any adjustments to these amounts were necessary.

Qualified Opinion

In our opinion, except for the possible effects of the matter described in the Basis for Qualified Opinion paragraph, the financial statements referred to above present fairly, in all material respects, the financial position of ABC Company as of December 31, 20X1, and the results of its operations and its cash flows for the year then ended in accordance with accounting principles generally accepted in the United States of America.

(Auditor's signature)

(Auditor's city and state)

(Date of the auditor's report)

Qualified for Material Misstatement

(Appropriate Addressee)

Report on the Financial Statements[i]

We have audited the accompanying financial statements of ABC Company, which comprise the balance sheet as of December 31, 20X1 and 20X0, and the related statements of income, changes in stockholders' equity and cash flows for the years then ended, and the related notes to the financial statements.

Management's Responsibility for the Financial Statements

Management is responsible for the preparation and fair presentation of these financial statements in accordance with accounting principles generally accepted in the United States of America; this includes the design, implementation, and maintenance of internal control relevant to the preparation and fair presentation of financial statements that are free from material misstatement, whether due to fraud or error.

Auditor's Responsibility

Our responsibility is to express an opinion on these financial statements based on our audits. We conducted our audits in accordance with auditing standards generally accepted in the United States of America. Those standards require that we plan and perform the audit to obtain reasonable assurance about whether the financial statements are free from material misstatement.

An audit involves performing procedures to obtain audit evidence about the amounts and disclosures in the consolidated financial statements. The procedures selected depend on the auditor's judgment, including the assessment of the risks of material misstatement of the consolidated financial statements, whether due to fraud or error. In making those risk assessments, the auditor considers internal control relevant to the entity's preparation and fair presentation of the consolidated financial statements in order to design audit procedures that are appropriate in the circumstances, but not for the purpose of expressing an opinion on the effectiveness of the entity's internal control. Accordingly, we express no such opinion. An audit also includes evaluating the appropriateness of accounting policies used and the reasonableness of significant accounting estimates made by management, as well as evaluating the overall presentation of the financial statements.

We believe that the audit evidence we have obtained is sufficient and appropriate to provide a basis for our qualified audit opinion.

Basis for Qualified Opinion

The Company has stated inventories at cost in the accompanying balance sheets. Accounting principles generally accepted in the United States of America require inventories to be stated at the lower of cost or market. If the Company stated inventories at the lower of cost or market, a write down of $xxx and $xxx would have been required as of December 31, 20X1 and 20X0, respectively. Accordingly, cost of sales would have been increased by $xxx and $xxx, and net income, income taxes, and stockholders' equity would have been reduced by $xxx, $xxx, and $xxx, and $xxx, $xxx, and $xxx, as of and for the years then ended in accordance with accounting principles generally accepted in the United States of America.

Qualified Opinion

In our opinion, except for the effects of the matter described in the Basis for Qualified Opinion paragraph, the financial statements referred to above present fairly, in all material respects, the financial position of ABC Company as of December 31, 20X1 and 20X0, and the results of its operations and its cash flows for the years then ended in accordance with accounting principles generally accepted in the United States of America.

Report on Other Legal and Regulatory Requirements

(Form and content of this section of the auditor's report will vary depending on the nature of the auditor's other reporting responsibilities.)

(Auditor's signature)

(Auditor's city and state)

(Date of the auditor's report)

[i] The subtitle "Report on the Financial Statements" is unnecessary in circumstances when the second subtitle, "Report on Other Legal and Regulatory Requirements," is not applicable.

Qualified for Inadequate Disclosure

Independent Auditor's Report

(Appropriate Addressee)

We have audited the accompanying financial statements of ABC Company, which comprise the balance sheet as of December 31, 20X1 and 20X0, and the related statements of income, changes in stockholders' equity and cash flows for the years then ended, and the related notes to the financial statements.

Management's Responsibility for the Financial Statements

Management is responsible for the preparation and fair presentation of these financial statements in accordance with accounting principles generally accepted in the United States of America; this includes the design, implementation, and maintenance of internal control relevant to the preparation and fair presentation of financial statements that are free from material misstatement, whether due to fraud or error.

Auditor's Responsibility

Our responsibility is to express an opinion on these financial statements based on our audits. We conducted our audits in accordance with auditing standards generally accepted in the United States of America. Those standards require that we plan and perform the audit to obtain reasonable assurance about whether the financial statements are free from material misstatement.

An audit involves performing procedures to obtain audit evidence about the amounts and disclosures in the consolidated financial statements. The procedures selected depend on the auditor's judgment, including the assessment of the risks of material misstatement of the consolidated financial statements, whether due to fraud or error. In making those risk assessments, the auditor considers internal control relevant to the entity's preparation and fair presentation of the consolidated financial statements in order to design audit procedures that are appropriate in the circumstances, but not for the purpose of expressing an opinion on the effectiveness of the entity's internal control. Accordingly, we express no such opinion. An audit also includes evaluating the appropriateness of accounting policies used and the reasonableness of significant accounting estimates made by management, as well as evaluating the overall presentation of the financial statements.

We believe that the audit evidence we have obtained is sufficient and appropriate to provide a basis for our qualified audit opinion.

Basis for Qualified Opinion

The company's financial statements do not disclose (*describe the nature of the omitted information that is not practicable to present in the auditor's report*). In our opinion, disclosure of this information is required by accounting principles generally accepted in the United States of America.

Qualified Opinion

In our opinion, except for the omission of the information described in the Basis for Qualified Opinion paragraph, the financial statements referred to above present fairly, in all material respects, the financial position of ABC Company as of December 31, 20X1 and 20X0, and the results of its operations and its cash flows for the years then ended in accordance with accounting principles generally accepted in the United States of America.

(Auditor's signature)

(Auditor's city and state)

(Date of the auditor's report)

Adverse Opinion

Independent Auditor's Report

(Appropriate Addressee)

We have audited the accompanying consolidated financial statements of ABC Company and its subsidiaries, which comprise the consolidated balance sheets as of December 31, 20X1, and the related consolidated statements of income, changes in stockholders' equity and cash flows for the year then ended, and the related notes to the financial statements.

Management's Responsibility for the Financial Statements

Management is responsible for the preparation and fair presentation of these consolidated financial statements in accordance with accounting principles generally accepted in the United States of America; this includes the design, implementation, and maintenance of internal control relevant to the preparation and fair presentation of consolidated financial statements that are free from material misstatement, whether due to fraud or error.

Auditor's Responsibility

Our responsibility is to express an opinion on these consolidated financial statements based on our audit. We conducted our audit in accordance with auditing standards generally accepted in the United States of America. Those standards require that we plan and perform the audit to obtain reasonable assurance about whether the financial statements are free from material misstatement.

An audit involves performing procedures to obtain audit evidence about the amounts and disclosures in the consolidated financial statements. The procedures selected depend on the auditor's judgment, including the assessment of the risks of material misstatement of the consolidated financial statements, whether due to fraud or error. In making those risk assessments, the auditor considers internal control relevant to the entity's preparation and fair presentation of the consolidated financial statements in order to design audit procedures that are appropriate in the circumstances, but not for the purpose of expressing an opinion on the effectiveness of the entity's internal control. Accordingly, we express no such opinion. An audit also includes evaluating the appropriateness of accounting policies used and the reasonableness of significant accounting estimates made by management, as well as evaluating the overall presentation of the consolidated financial statements.

We believe that the audit evidence we have obtained is sufficient and appropriate to provide a basis for our adverse audit opinion.

Basis for Adverse Opinion

As described in Note X, the Company has not consolidated the financial statements of subsidiary XYZ Company that it acquired during 20X1 because it has not yet been able to ascertain the fair values of certain of the subsidiary's material assets and liabilities at the acquisition date. This investment is therefore accounted for on a cost basis by the Company. Under accounting principles generally accepted in the United States of America, the subsidiary should have been consolidated because it is controlled by the Company. Had XYZ Company been consolidated, many elements in the accompanying consolidated financial statements would have been materially affected. The effects on the consolidated financial statements of the failure to consolidate have not been determined.

Adverse Opinion

In our opinion, because of the significance of the matter discussed in the Basis for Adverse Opinion paragraph, the consolidated financial statements referred to above do not present fairly the financial position of ABC Company and its subsidiaries as of December 31, 20X1, or the results of their operations or their cash flows for the years then ended.

(Auditor's signature)

(Auditor's city and state)

(Date of the auditor's report)

Disclaimer of Opinion for Scope

Independent Auditor's Report

(Appropriate Addressee)

Report on the Financial Statements[i]

We were engaged to audit the accompanying financial statements of ABC Company, which comprise the balance sheet as of December 31, 20X1, and the related statements of income, changes in stockholders' equity and cash flows for the year then ended, and the related notes to the financial statements.

Management's Responsibility for the Financial Statements

Management is responsible for the preparation and fair presentation of these financial statements in accordance with accounting principles generally accepted in the United States of America; this includes the design, implementation, and maintenance of internal control relevant to the preparation and fair presentation of financial statements that are free from material misstatement, whether due to fraud or error.

Auditor's Responsibility

Our responsibility is to express an opinion on these financial statements based on conducting the audit in accordance with auditing standards generally accepted in the United States of America. Because of the matter described in the Basis for Disclaimer of Opinion paragraph, however, we were not able to obtain sufficient appropriate audit evidence to provide a basis for an audit opinion.

Basis for Disclaimer of Opinion

The company's investment in XYZ Company, a joint venture, is carried at $xxx on the Company's balance sheet, which represents over 90% of the Company's net assets as of December 31, 20X1. We were not allowed access to the management and the auditors of XYZ Company. As a result, we were unable to determine whether any adjustments were necessary relating to the Company's proportional share of XYZ Company's assets that it controls jointly, its proportional share of XYZ Company's liabilities for which it is jointly responsible, its proportional share of XYZ Company's income and expenses for the year, and the elements making up the statements of changes in stockholders' equity and cash flows.

Disclaimer of Opinion

Because of the significance of the matter described in the Basis for Disclaimer of Opinion paragraph, we have not been able to obtain sufficient appropriate audit evidence to provide a basis for an audit opinion. Accordingly, we do not express an opinion on these financial statements.

Report on Other Legal and Regulatory Requirements

(Form and content of this section of the auditor's report will vary depending on the nature of the auditor's other reporting responsibilities.)

(Auditor's signature)

(Auditor's city and state)

(Date of the auditor's report)

[i] The subtitle "Report on the Financial Statements" is unnecessary in circumstances when the second subtitle, "Report on Other Legal and Regulatory Requirements," is not applicable.

Unmodified on B/S, Disclaimer on I/S and Cash Flows

Sample report with a disclaimer of opinion on results of operations and cash flows and an unmodified opinion on financial position (due to inability to verify opening inventory):

Independent Auditor's Report

(Appropriate Addressee)

We have audited the accompanying balance sheet of ABC Company, as of December 31, 20X1, and were engaged to audit the related statements of income, changes in stockholders' equity, and cash flows for the year then ended, and the related notes to the financial statements.

Management's Responsibility for the Financial Statements

Management is responsible for the preparation and fair presentation of these financial statements in accordance with accounting principles generally accepted in the United States of America; this includes the design, implementation, and maintenance of internal control relevant to the preparation and fair presentation of financial statements that are free from material misstatement, whether due to fraud or error.

Auditor's Responsibility

Our responsibility is to express an opinion on these financial statements based on conducting the audit in accordance with auditing standards generally accepted in the United States of America. Because of the matters described in the Basis for Disclaimer of Opinion paragraph, however, we were not able to obtain sufficient appropriate audit evidence to provide a basis for an audit opinion on the income statement and the cash flow statement.

We conducted our audit of the balance sheet in accordance with auditing standards generally accepted in the United States of America. Those standards require that we plan and perform the audit to obtain reasonable assurance about whether the balance sheet is free of material misstatement.

An audit involves performing procedures to obtain audit evidence about the amounts and disclosures in the consolidated financial statements. The procedures selected depend on the auditor's judgment, including the assessment of the risks of material misstatement of the consolidated financial statements, whether due to fraud or error. In making those risk assessments, the auditor considers internal control relevant to the entity's preparation and fair presentation of the consolidated financial statements in order to design audit procedures that are appropriate in the circumstances, but not for the purpose of expressing an opinion on the effectiveness of the entity's internal control. Accordingly, we express no such opinion. An audit also includes evaluating the appropriateness of accounting policies used and the reasonableness of significant accounting estimates made by management, as well as evaluating the overall presentation of the financial statements.

We believe that the audit evidence we have obtained is sufficient and appropriate to provide a basis for our unmodified opinion on the financial position.

Basis for Disclaimer of Opinion on the Results of Operations and Cash Flows

We were not appointed as auditors of the company until after December 31, 20X0, and thus did not observe the counting of the physical inventories at the beginning of the year. We were unable to satisfy ourselves by alternative means concerning inventory quantities held at December 31, 20X0. Since opening inventories enter into the determination of the net income and cash flows, we were unable to determine whether adjustments might have been necessary relating to the profit for the year reported in the income statement and the net cash flows from operating activities reported in the cash flow statement.

Disclaimer of Opinion on the Results of Operations and Cash Flows

Because of the significance of the matter described in the Basis for Disclaimer of Opinion paragraph, we have not been able to obtain sufficient appropriate audit evidence to provide a basis for an audit opinion on the income statement and the cash flow statement. Accordingly, we do not express an opinion on the results of operations and cash flows for the year ended December 31, 20X1.

Opinion on the Financial Position

In our opinion, the balance sheet presents fairly, in all material respects, the financial position of ABC Company, as of December 31, 20X1, in accordance with accounting principles generally accepted in the United States of America.

(Auditor's signature)

(Auditor's city and state)

(Date of the auditor's report)

Emphasis-of-Matter Paragraph

Independent Auditor's Report

(Appropriate Addressee)

Report on the Financial Statements

We have audited the accompanying financial statements of ABC Company, which comprise the balance sheet as of December 31, 20X1, and the related statements of income, changes in stockholders' equity and cash flows for the year then ended, and the related notes to the financial statements.

Management's Responsibility for the Financial Statements

Management is responsible for the preparation and fair presentation of these financial statements in accordance with accounting principles generally accepted in the United States of America; this includes the design, implementation, and maintenance of internal control relevant to the preparation and fair presentation of financial statements that are free from material misstatement, whether due to fraud or error.

Auditor's Responsibility

Our responsibility is to express an opinion on these financial statements based on our audit. We conducted our audit in accordance with auditing standards generally accepted in the United States of America. Those standards require that we plan and perform the audit to obtain reasonable assurance about whether the financial statements are free from material misstatement.

An audit involves performing procedures to obtain audit evidence about the amounts and disclosures in the financial statements. The procedures selected depend on the auditor's judgment, including the assessment of the risks of material misstatement of the financial statements, whether due to fraud or error. In making those risk assessments, the auditor considers internal control relevant to the entity's preparation and fair presentation of the financial statements in order to design audit procedures that are appropriate in the circumstances, but not for the purpose of expressing an opinion on the effectiveness of the entity's internal control.[1] Accordingly, we express no such opinion. An audit also includes evaluating the appropriateness of accounting policies used and the reasonableness of significant accounting estimates made by management, as well as evaluating the overall presentation of the financial statements.

We believe that the audit evidence we have obtained is sufficient and appropriate to provide a basis for our audit opinion.

Opinion

In our opinion, the financial statements referred to above present fairly, in all material respects, the financial position of ABC Company as of December 31, 20X1, and the results of its operations and its cash flows for the year then ended in accordance with accounting principles generally accepted in the United States of America.

Emphasis of Matter

As discussed in Note X to the financial statements, the Company is a defendant in a lawsuit (*briefly describe the nature of the litigation consistent with the Company's description in the note to the financial statements*). Our opinion is not modified with respect to this matter.

Report on Other Legal and Regulatory Requirements

(Form and content of this section of the auditor's report will vary depending on the nature of the auditor's other reporting responsibilities.)

(Auditor's signature)

(Auditor's city and state)

(Date of the auditor's report)

[1] When the auditor has responsibility for expressing an opinion on the effectiveness of internal control in conjunction with the audit of the entity's financial statements, the sentence would be stated as follows: "In making those risk assessments, the auditor considers internal control relevant to the entity's preparation and fair presentation of the consolidated financial statements in order to design audit procedures that are appropriate in the circumstances." In addition, the next sentence, "Accordingly, we express no such opinion," would be omitted.

Other-Matter Paragraph

Independent Auditor's Report

(Appropriate Addressee)

Report on the Financial Statements

We have audited the accompanying financial statements of ABC Company, which comprise the balance sheet as of December 31, 20X1 and 20X0, and the related statements of income, changes in stockholders' equity and cash flows for the years then ended, and the related notes to the financial statements.

Management's Responsibility for the Financial Statements

Management is responsible for the preparation and fair presentation of these financial statements in accordance with accounting principles generally accepted in the United States of America; this includes the design, implementation, and maintenance of internal control relevant to the preparation and fair presentation of financial statements that are free from material misstatement, whether due to fraud or error.

Auditor's Responsibility

Our responsibility is to express an opinion on these financial statements based on our audits. We conducted our audits in accordance with auditing standards generally accepted in the United States of America. Those standards require that we plan and perform the audit to obtain reasonable assurance about whether the financial statements are free from material misstatement.

An audit involves performing procedures to obtain audit evidence about the amounts and disclosures in the financial statements. The procedures selected depend on the auditor's judgment, including the assessment of the risks of material misstatement of the financial statements, whether due to fraud or error. In making those risk assessments, the auditor considers internal control relevant to the entity's preparation and fair presentation of the financial statements in order to design audit procedures that are appropriate in the circumstances, but not for the purpose of expressing an opinion on the effectiveness of the entity's internal control. Accordingly, we express no such opinion. An audit also includes evaluating the appropriateness of accounting policies used and the reasonableness of significant accounting estimates made by management, as well as evaluating the overall presentation of the financial statements.

We believe that the audit evidence we have obtained is sufficient and appropriate to provide a basis for our audit opinion.

Opinion

In our opinion, the financial statements referred to above present fairly, in all material respects, the financial position of ABC Company as of December 31, 20X1 and 20X0, and the results of its operations and its cash flows for the years then ended in accordance with accounting principles generally accepted in the United States of America.

Other Matter

In our report dated March 1, 20X1, we expressed an opinion that the 20X0 financial statements did not fairly present the financial position, results of operations, and cash flows of ABC Company in accordance with accounting principles generally accepted in the United States of America because of two departures from such principles: (1) ABC Company carried its property, plant, and equipment at appraisal values, and provided for depreciation on the basis of such values, and (2) ABC Company did not provide for deferred income taxes with respect to differences between income for financial reporting purposes and taxable income. As described in Note X, the Company has changed its method of accounting for these items and restated its 20X0 financial statements to conform with accounting principles generally accepted in the United States of America. Accordingly, our present opinion on the restated 20X0 financial statements, as presented herein, is different from that expressed in our previous report.

Report on Other Legal and Regulatory Requirements

(Form and content of this section of the auditor's report will vary depending on the nature of the auditor's other reporting responsibilities.)

(Auditor's signature)

(Auditor's city and state)

(Date of the auditor's report)

Reference to Component Auditor

Independent Auditor's Report

(Appropriate Addressee)

Report on the Consolidated Financial Statements

We have audited the accompanying consolidated financial statements of ABC Company and its subsidiaries, which comprise the consolidated balance sheets as of December 31, 20X1 and 20X0, and the related consolidated statements of income, changes in stockholders' equity and cash flows for the years then ended, and the related notes to the financial statements.

Management's Responsibility for the Financial Statements

Management is responsible for the preparation and fair presentation of these consolidated financial statements in accordance with accounting principles generally accepted in the United States of America; this includes the design, implementation and maintenance of internal control relevant to the preparation and fair presentation of consolidated financial statements that are free from material misstatement, whether due to fraud or error.

Auditor's Responsibility

Our responsibility is to express an opinion on these consolidated financial statements based on our audit. We did not audit the financial statements of B Company, a wholly-owned subsidiary, whose statements reflect total assets and revenues constituting 20% and 22%, respectively, of the related consolidated totals. Those statements were audited by other auditors, whose report has been furnished to us, and our opinion, insofar as it relates to the amounts included for B Company, is based solely on the report of the other auditors. We conducted our audits in accordance with auditing standards generally accepted in the United States of America. Those standards require that we plan and perform the audit to obtain reasonable assurance about whether the consolidated financial statements are free from material misstatement.

An audit involves performing procedures to obtain audit evidence about the amounts and disclosures in the consolidated financial statements. The procedures selected depend on the auditor's judgment, including the assessment of the risks of material misstatement of the consolidated financial statements, whether due to fraud or error. In making those risk assessments, the auditor considers internal control relevant to the entity's preparation and fair presentation of the consolidated financial statements in order to design audit procedures that are appropriate in the circumstances, but not for the purpose of expressing an opinion on the effectiveness of the entity's internal control. Accordingly, we express no such opinion. An audit also includes evaluating the appropriateness of accounting policies used and the reasonableness of significant accounting estimates made by management, as well as evaluating the overall presentation of the consolidated financial statements.

We believe that the audit evidence we have obtained is sufficient and appropriate to provide a basis for our audit opinion.

Opinion

In our opinion, based on our audit and the report of the other auditors, the consolidated financial statements referred to above presents fairly, in all material respects, the financial position of ABC Company and its subsidiaries as of December 31, 20X1 and 20X2, in accordance with accounting principles generally accepted in the United States of America.

(Auditor's signature)

(Auditor's city and state)

(Date of the auditor's report)

Single Financial Statement

Specific Element (Special Purpose Framework)

Independent Auditor's Report

(Appropriate Addressee)

We have audited the accompanying schedule of royalties applicable to engine production of the Q Division of ABC Company for the year ended December 31, 20X1, and the related notes (the schedule).

Management's Responsibility for the Financial Statements

Management is responsible for the preparation and fair presentation of the schedule in accordance with the financial reporting provisions of Section Z of the license agreement between ABC Company and XYZ Corporation dated January 1, 20X1 (the contract). Management is also responsible for the design, implementation, and maintenance of internal control relevant to the preparation and fair presentation of financial statements that are free from material misstatement, whether due to fraud or error.

Auditor's Responsibility

Our responsibility is to express an opinion on the schedule based on our audit. We conducted our audit in accordance with auditing standards generally accepted in the United States of America. Those standards require that we plan and perform the audit to obtain reasonable assurance about whether the schedule is free from material misstatement.

An audit involves performing procedures to obtain audit evidence about the amounts and disclosures in the schedule. The procedures selected depend on the auditor's judgment, including the assessment of the risks of material misstatement of the schedule, whether due to fraud or error. In making those risk assessments, the auditor considers internal control relevant to the entity's preparation and fair presentation of the schedule in order to design audit procedures that are appropriate in the circumstances, but not for the purpose of expressing an opinion on the effectiveness of the entity's internal control. Accordingly, we express no such opinion. An audit also includes evaluating the appropriateness of accounting policies used and the reasonableness of significant accounting estimates made by management, as well as evaluating the overall presentation of the schedule.

We believe that the audit evidence we have obtained is sufficient and appropriate to provide a basis for our audit opinion.

Opinion

In our opinion, the schedule referred to above presents fairly, in all material respects, the royalties applicable to engine production of the Q Division of ABC Company for the year ended December 31, 20X1, in accordance with the financial reporting provisions of Section Z of the contract.

Basis of Accounting

We draw attention to Note X of the schedule, which describes the basis of accounting. The schedule was prepared by ABC Company on the basis of the financial reporting provisions of Section Z of the contract, which is a basis of accounting other than accounting principles generally accepted in the United States of America, to comply with the financial reporting of the contract referred to above. Our opinion is not modified with respect to this matter.

Restriction on Use

Our report is intended solely for the information and use of ABC Company and XYZ Corporation and is not intended to be and should not be used by anyone other than these specified parties.

(Auditor's signature)

(Auditor's city and state)

(Date of the auditor's report)

Incomplete Presentation

Independent Auditor's Report

(Appropriate Addressee)

We have audited the accompanying Historical Summaries of Gross Income and Direct Operating Expenses of ABC Apartments for each of the three years in the period ended December 31, 20X1, and the related notes (the historical summaries).

Management's Responsibility for the Financial Statements

Management is responsible for the preparation and fair presentation of these historical summaries in accordance with accounting principles generally accepted in the United States of America; this includes the design, implementation, and maintenance of internal control relevant to the preparation and fair presentation of the financial statement that is free from material misstatement, whether due to fraud or error.

Auditor's Responsibility

Our responsibility is to express an opinion on the historical summaries based on our audit. We conducted our audit in accordance with auditing standards generally accepted in the United States of America. Those standards require that we plan and perform the audit to obtain reasonable assurance about whether the historical summaries are free from material misstatement.

An audit involves performing procedures to obtain audit evidence about the amounts and disclosures in the historical summaries. The procedures selected depend on the auditor's judgment, including the assessment of the risks of material misstatement of the historical summaries, whether due to fraud or error. In making those risk assessments, the auditor considers internal control relevant to the entity's preparation and fair presentation of the historical summaries in order to design audit procedures that are appropriate in the circumstances, but not for the purpose of expressing an opinion on the effectiveness of the entity's internal control. Accordingly, we express no such opinion. An audit also includes evaluating the appropriateness of accounting policies used and the reasonableness of significant accounting estimates made by management, as well as evaluating the overall presentation of the historical summaries.

We believe that the audit evidence we have obtained is sufficient and appropriate to provide a basis for our audit opinion.

Opinion

In our opinion, the historical summaries referred to above present fairly, in all material respects, the gross income and direct operating expenses described in Note X of ABC Apartments for each of the three years in the period ended December 31, 20X1, in accordance with accounting principles generally accepted in the United States of America.

Emphasis of Matter

We draw attention to Note X to the historical summaries, which describes that the accompanying historical summaries were prepared for the purpose of complying with the rules and regulations of Regulator DEF (for inclusion in the filing of Form Z of ABC Company) and are not intended to be a complete presentation of the company's revenues and expenses. Our opinion is not modified with respect to this matter.

(Auditor's signature)

(Auditor's city and state)

(Date of the auditor's report)

Application of Accounting Principles (Second Opinion)

Written Report to the Requesting Party about the Application of Accounting Principles (Sometimes called a *Second Opinion*):

Introduction

We have been engaged to report on the appropriate application of the requirements of accounting principles generally accepted in the United States of America to the specific transaction described below. This report is being issued to ABC Company for assistance in evaluating accounting policies for the described specific transaction. Our engagement has been conducted in accordance with the Statement on Auditing Standards Reports on Application of Requirements of an Applicable Financial Reporting Framework.

Description of Transactions

The facts, circumstances, and assumptions relevant to the specific transaction as provided to us by the management of ABC Company are as follows:

(*Include text discussing the facts, circumstances, and assumptions relevant to the specific transaction.*)

Appropriate Accounting Principles

(*Include text discussing accounting principles generally accepted in the United States of America and how they apply to the described transaction.*)

Concluding Comments

The ultimate responsibility for the decision on the appropriate application of the requirements of accounting principles generally accepted in the United States of America for an actual transaction rests with the preparers of financial statements, who should consult with their continuing accountant. Our conclusion on the appropriate application of the requirements of accounting principles generally accepted in the United States of America for the described specific transaction is based solely on the facts provided to us as previously described; should these facts and circumstances differ, our conclusion may change.

Restricted Use

This report is intended solely for the information and use of those charged with governance and management of ABC Company and is not intended to be and should not be used by anyone other than these specified parties.

Report on Summary Financial Statements

Independent Auditor's Report

(Appropriate Addressee)

The accompanying summary financial statements, which comprise the summary balance sheet as of December 31, 20X1, the summary income statement, summary statement of changes in stockholders' equity and summary cash flow statement for the year then ended, and the related notes, are derived from the audited financial statements of ABC Company as of and for the year ended December 31, 20X1. We expressed an unmodified audit opinion on those audited financial statements in our report dated February 15, 20X2. The audited financial statements, and the summary financial statements derived therefrom, do not reflect the effects of events, if any, that occurred subsequent to the date of our report on the audited financial statements.

The summary financial statements do not contain all the disclosures required by (*describe financial reporting framework applied in the preparation of the financial statements of ABC Company*). Reading the summary financial statements, therefore, is not a substitute for reading the audited financial statements of ABC Company.

Management's Responsibility for the Summary Financial Statements

Management is responsible for the preparation of the summary financial statements on the basis described in Note X.

Auditor's Responsibility

Our responsibility is to express an opinion about whether the summary financial statements are consistent, in all material respects, with the audited financial statements based on our procedures, which were conducted in accordance with auditing standards generally accepted in the United States of America. The procedures consisted principally of comparing the summary financial statements with the related information in the audited financial statements from which the summary financial statements have been derived, and evaluating whether the summary financial statements are prepared in accordance with the basis described in Note X. We did not perform any audit procedures regarding the audited financial statements after the date of our report on those financial statements.

Opinion

In our opinion, the summary financial statements of ABC Company as of and for the year ended December 31, 20X1 referred to above are consistent, in all material respects, with the audited financial statements from which they have been derived, on the basis described in Note X.

(Auditor's signature)

(Auditor's city and state)

(Date of the auditor's report)

Review Report on Interim Financial Statements

Independent Auditor's Report

(Appropriate Addressee)

Report on the Financial Statements

We have reviewed the accompanying (*describe the interim financial information or statements reviewed*) of ABC Company and subsidiaries as of September 30, 20X1, and for the three-month and nine-month periods then ended.

Management's Responsibility

The Company's management is responsible for the preparation and fair presentation of the interim financial information in accordance with (*identify the applicable financial reporting framework; for example, accounting principles generally accepted in the United States of America*); this responsibility includes the design, implementation, and maintenance of internal control sufficient to provide a reasonable basis for the preparation and fair presentation of interim financial information in accordance with the applicable financial reporting framework.

Auditor's Responsibility

Our responsibility is to conduct our review in accordance with auditing standards generally accepted in the United States of America applicable to reviews of interim financial information. A review of interim financial information consists principally of applying analytical procedures and making inquiries of persons responsible for financial and accounting matters. It is substantially less in scope than an audit conducted in accordance with auditing standards generally accepted in the United States of America, the objective of which is the expression of an opinion regarding the financial information. Accordingly, we do not express such an opinion.

Conclusion

Based on our review, we are not aware of any material modifications that should be made to the accompanying interim financial information for it to be in accordance with (*identify the applicable financial reporting framework; for example, accounting principles generally accepted in the United States of America*).

(Auditor's signature)

(Auditor's city and state)

(Date of the auditor's report)

Other Reports

Reports on Application of Requirements of Framework

After studying this lesson, you should be able to:

1. Identify the reporting accountant's responsibilities when engaged to provide a second opinion on the requirements of the applicable financial reporting framework.

2. Identify the reporting language that would be appropriate when issuing a written report on the requirements of the applicable financial reporting framework.

I. **Relevant AICPA Guidance**—The relevant AICPA guidance is provided by AU 915, *Reports on Application of Requirements of an Applicable Financial Reporting Framework*. The standard states that the auditor's objective, when engaged to issue a written report or provide oral advice on the application of the requirements of an applicable financial reporting framework to a specific transaction or on the type of report that may be issued on a specific entity's financial statements, is to appropriately address: (1) the acceptance of the engagement; (2) the planning and performance of the engagement; and (3) reporting on the specific transaction or type of report.

Definitions

Hypothetical Transaction: A transaction or financial reporting issue that does not involve facts or circumstances of a specific entity.

Reporting Accountant: An accountant, other than a continuing accountant, who prepares a written report or provides oral advice on the application of the requirements of an applicable financial reporting framework to a specific transaction or on the type of report that may be issued on a specific entity's financial statements. (A reporting accountant who is also engaged to provide accounting advice to a specific entity on a recurring basis is commonly referred to as an *advisory accountant*.)

Specific Transaction: A completed or proposed transaction or group of related transactions or a financial reporting issue involving facts and circumstances of a specific entity.

II. **Engagement Acceptance**

A. The reporting accountant should consider the following: (1) the circumstances under which the written report or oral advice is requested; (2) the purpose of the request; and (3) the intended use of the written report or oral advice.

B. The reporting accountant should not accept any engagement involving a *hypothetical transaction*.

C. If it is appropriate to accept an engagement under this SAS, the reporting accountant should establish an understanding with the requesting party that: (1) management is responsible for the proper accounting treatment and should consult with the continuing accountant; (2) management acknowledges that the reporting accountant may need to consult with the continuing accountant and, if requested, that management will authorize the continuing accountant to respond to the reporting accountant's inquiries; and (3) management will notify those charged with governance and the continuing accountant about the engagement.

III. **Engagement Planning and Performance**

A. The reporting accountant should:

1. Obtain an understanding of the specific transaction(s) or the conditions relevant to the type of report that may be issued;

2. Review the requirements of the applicable financial reporting framework;

3. Consult with other professionals or others, if appropriate;

4. Consider existing relevant precedents or analogies;

5. Request permission from management to consult with the continuing accountant and request that management authorize the continuing accountant to respond fully to the reporting accountant's inquiries; *and*

6. Consult with the continuing accountant regarding the facts.

B. **Consulting with the Continuing Accountant**—The reporting accountant (who is engaged to issue a written report or provide oral advice on the application of the requirements of an applicable financial reporting framework to a specific transaction) should consult with the continuing accountant **unless**:

1. The reporting accountant is engaged to provide recurring accounting and reporting advice and (a) **does not believe that a second opinion is being requested**; (b) has full access to management; and (c) believes that the relevant information has been obtained.

2. The reporting accountant deems it unnecessary to consult with the continuing accountant, the reporting accountant should **document** the justification for not consulting.

C. **Continuing Accountant's Responses**—The continuing accountant's responsibilities for responding to inquiries of the reporting accountant are the same as those of a predecessor auditor responding to an auditor's inquiries. The continuing accountant may indicate whether the method of accounting recommended by the continuing accountant is disputed by management and convey the continuing accountant's conclusion on the application of the requirements of an applicable financial reporting framework.

IV. **Written Report**

A. The report should be addressed to the requesting party and include the following:

1. A description of the engagement and reference to this SAS;

2. Identification of the specific entity, a description of any specific transaction(s), and a statement about the source of information;

3. A statement describing the application of the requirements of an applicable financial reporting framework (and country involved);

4. A statement that management is responsible for the proper accounting treatment and they should consult with their continuing accountants;

5. A statement that any differences in the facts or circumstances may change the report; *and*

6. A restriction that the report is intended solely for the specified parties. (The restricted distribution of the report does not prevent distribution of the report to the continuing accountant.)

B. The requirements associated with the written report may be useful when providing oral advice, too.

V. **Sample Written Report to the Requesting Party**

Introduction

We have been engaged to report on the appropriate application of the requirements of accounting principles generally accepted in the United States of America to the specific transaction described below. This report is being issued to ABC Company for assistance in evaluating accounting policies for the described specific transaction. Our engagement has been conducted in accordance with Statement on Auditing Standards Reports on Application of Requirements of an Applicable Financial Reporting Framework.

Description of Transactions

The facts, circumstances, and assumptions relevant to the specific transaction as provided to us by the management of ABC Company are as follows:

(*Include text discussing the facts, circumstances, and assumptions relevant to the specific transaction.*)

Appropriate Accounting Principles

(*Include text discussing accounting principles generally accepted in the United States of America and how they apply to the described transaction.*)

Concluding Comments

The ultimate responsibility for the decision on the appropriate application of the requirements of accounting principles generally accepted in the United States of America for an actual transaction rests with the preparers of financial statements, who should consult with their continuing accountant. Our conclusion on the appropriate application of the requirements of accounting principles generally accepted in the United States of America for the described specific transaction is based solely on the facts provided to us as previously described; should these facts and circumstances differ, our conclusion may change.

Restricted Use

This report is intended solely for the information and use of those charged with governance and management of ABC Company and is not intended to be and should not be used by anyone other than these specified parties.

F/S with Special Purpose Frameworks

After studying this lesson, you should be able to:

1. Identify the four specific bases of accounting associated with the term *special purpose framework*.

2. Identify the reporting language that would be appropriate when issuing an audit report on financial statements prepared using a special purpose framework, and the differences in such reporting language depending upon the particular basis of accounting involved.

I. **Relevant AICPA Guidance**—The relevant AICPA guidance is provided by AU 800, *Special Considerations—Audits of Financial Statements Prepared in Accordance With Special Purpose Frameworks*. The standard states that the auditor's objectives are to (1) the acceptance of the engagement; (2) the planning and performance of that engagement; and (3) forming an opinion and reporting on the financial statements.

> **Definition**
> *Special Purpose Framework*: A financial reporting framework other than GAAP that is one of the following bases of accounting: (1) cash basis, (2) tax basis, (3) regulatory basis, or (4) contractual basis, or (5) other basis (that "uses a definite set of logical, reasonable criteria that is applied to all material items appearing in financial statements").

II. **Engagement Acceptance**

   A. **Acceptability of the Financial Reporting Framework**—The auditor should obtain an understanding of (a) the purpose for which the financial statements are prepared; (b) the intended users; and (c) the steps taken by management to determine that the applicable financial reporting framework is acceptable in the circumstances.

   B. **Preconditions for an Audit**—The auditor should obtain the agreement of management that it understands its responsibility to include all informative disclosures that are appropriate for the special purpose framework used, including (a) a description of the special purpose framework; (b) informative disclosures similar to those required by GAAP; (c) a description of any significant interpretations of the contract on which the special purpose financial statements are based, when applicable; and (d) additional disclosures beyond those specifically required that may be necessary to achieve fair presentation.

III. **Engagement Planning and Performance**

   A. **When the Engagement is Based on an Underlying Contract**—The auditor should obtain an understanding of any *significant interpretations* of the contract that management made.

   B. An interpretation is significant when adoption of another reasonable interpretation would have produced a material difference.

IV. **Forming an Opinion and Reporting Considerations**

   A. **Description of the Applicable Financial Reporting Framework**—The auditor should consider whether the financial statements are appropriately titled (should not use financial statement names that imply GAAP), include a summary of significant accounting policies, and adequately describe how the special purpose framework differs from GAAP. These differences do not have to be quantified, however.

   B. **Fair Presentation**—The auditor should determine whether informative disclosures are included similar to those required by GAAP, and whether additional disclosures are needed to achieve fair presentation.

C. Auditor's Report—The report should describe the *purpose for which the financial statements are prepared* (**if regulatory basis or contractual basis**) or reference a note containing that information about the special purpose framework used.

D. Alerting Readers in an Emphasis-of-Matter Paragraph—The auditor's report on special purpose financial statements should include an *emphasis-of-matter* ("Basis of Accounting") paragraph that (1) indicates that the financial statements are prepared in accordance with the applicable special purpose framework; (2) refers to the note that describes that framework; and (3) states that the special purpose framework is a basis of accounting other than GAAP. (The only exception to such an alert involves *regulatory basis financial statements intended for general use* for which no such alert is needed.)

E. Restricting the Use of the Auditor's Report to the Intended Users—The auditor's report should also include an *other-matter* paragraph that restricts the use of the auditor's report to those within the entity, the parties to the contract/agreement, or the regulatory agencies to whom the entity is subject **when the financial statements are prepared in accordance with either** (1) a contractual basis of accounting; or (2) a regulatory basis of accounting. (The only exception to such a restriction involves *regulatory basis financial statements intended for general use* for which no such restriction is needed. And no such restriction applies to cash basis or tax basis.)

F. Regulatory Basis Financial Statements Intended for General Use—If the financial statements are prepared in accordance with a regulatory basis of accounting and are intended for general use, the auditor should not include the *emphasis-of-matter* or *other-matter* paragraphs. Instead, the auditor should express (1) an opinion as to whether the financial statements are prepared in accordance with GAAP (which they are not); and (2) an opinion in a separate paragraph as to whether the financial statements are prepared in accordance with the special purpose framework.

G. Auditors Report Prescribed by Law or Regulation—If the prescribed specific layout, form, or wording of the auditor's report is not acceptable (or would cause the auditor to make an inappropriate statement), the auditor should either reword the prescribed form or attach separately an appropriately worded audit report.

Question
Which special purpose frameworks require a *description of purpose for which such financial statements are prepared*?

Answer:
Only regulatory basis (whether intended for general use or not) and contractual basis. (Cash basis and tax basis do not!)

Question
Which special purpose frameworks require an emphasis-of-*matter* paragraph alerting readers to the special purpose framework?

Answer:
Cash basis, tax basis, regulatory basis (if restricted), and contractual basis do. (Only regulatory basis intended for general use does not require such an alert!)

Question
Which special purpose frameworks require an *other-matter* paragraph to restrict the distribution of the auditor's report to specified users?

Answer:
Only regulatory basis (if restricted) and contractual basis do. (Cash basis, tax basis, and regulatory basis intended for general use do not require such a restriction!)

V. Sample Audit Report for Financial Statements Prepared on a Cash Basis

Independent Auditor's Report

(Appropriate Addressee)

We have audited the accompanying financial statements of ABC Partnership, which comprise the statement of assets and liabilities arising from cash transactions as of December 31, 20X1, and the related statement of revenue collected and expenses paid for the year then ended, and the related notes to the financial statements.

Management's Responsibility for the Financial Statements

Management is responsible for the preparation and fair presentation of these financial statements in accordance with the cash basis of accounting described in Note X; this includes determining that the cash basis of accounting is an acceptable basis for the presentation of the financial statements in the circumstances. Management is also responsible for the design, implementation, and maintenance of internal control relevant to the preparation and fair presentation of financial statements that are free from material misstatement, whether due to fraud or error.

Auditor's Responsibility

Our responsibility is to express an opinion on these financial statements based on our audit. We conducted our audit in accordance with auditing standards generally accepted in the United States of America. Those standards require that we plan and perform the audit to obtain reasonable assurance about whether the financial statements are free from material misstatement.

An audit involves performing procedures to obtain audit evidence about the amounts and disclosures in the financial statements. The procedures selected depend on the auditor's judgment, including the assessment of the risks of material misstatement of the financial statements, whether due to fraud or error. In making those risk assessments, the auditor considers internal control relevant to the partnership's preparation and fair presentation of the financial statements in order to design audit procedures that are appropriate in the circumstances, but not for the purpose of expressing an opinion on the effectiveness of the partnership's internal control. Accordingly, we express no such opinion. An audit also includes evaluating the appropriateness of accounting policies used and the reasonableness of significant accounting estimates made by management, as well as evaluating the overall presentation of the financial statements.

We believe that the audit evidence we have obtained is sufficient and appropriate to provide a basis for our audit opinion.

Opinion

In our opinion, the financial statements referred to above present fairly, in all material respects, the assets and liabilities arising from cash transactions of ABC Partnership as of December 31, 20X1, and its revenue collected and expenses paid during the year then ended in accordance with the cash basis of accounting described in Note X.

Basis of Accounting

We draw attention to Note X of the financial statements, which describes the basis of accounting. The financial statements are prepared on the cash basis of accounting, which is a basis of accounting other than accounting principles generally accepted in the United States of America. Our opinion is not modified with respect to this matter.

(Auditor's signature)

(Auditor's city and state)

(Date of the auditor's report)

Audits of Single F/S and Specific Elements, Accounts, or Items

After studying this lesson, you should be able to:

1. Identify the auditor's responsibilities when engaged to report on a single financial statement or specific element of a financial statement.

2. Identify the reporting language that would be appropriate when issuing an audit report on a single financial statement or specific element of a financial statement.

I. **Relevant AICPA Guidance**—The relevant AICPA guidance is provided by AU 805, *Special Considerations—Audits of Single Financial Statements and Specific Elements, Accounts, or Items of a Financial Statement*. The standard states that the auditor's objective is to appropriately address the special considerations that are relevant to (1) the acceptance of the engagement; (2) the planning and performance of the engagement; and (3) reporting on the single financial statement or the specific element.

II. **Engagement Acceptance**

   A. **Application of GAAS**—If not engaged to audit the complete set of financial statements, the auditor should determine whether the audit of a single financial statement or a specific element of those financial statements in accordance with GAAS is practicable.

   B. **Acceptability of the Financial Reporting Framework**—The auditor should obtain an understanding of (a) the purpose for which the single financial statement or specific element of a financial statement is prepared; (b) the intended users; and (c) the steps taken by management to determine that the application of the financial reporting framework is acceptable and that disclosure is adequate.

III. **Engagement Planning and Performance**

   A. **If the Specific Element is Based on Stockholders' Equity**—The auditor should obtain sufficient appropriate evidence to enable the auditor to express an opinion about financial position. (This effectively means that the auditor should have audited the whole balance sheet in order to report on an element based on stockholders' equity.)

   B. **If the Specific Element is Based upon the Entity's Net Income or the Equivalent**—The auditor should obtain sufficient appropriate evidence to enable the auditor to express an opinion about both financial position and results of operations. (This effectively means that the auditor should have audited the complete set of financial statements in order to report on an element based on net income.)

   C. **Considerations when Planning and Performing the Audit**—Written representations from management about the complete set of financial statements would be replaced by representations about the single financial statement or the specific element in accordance with the applicable financial reporting framework.

IV. **Forming an Opinion and Reporting Considerations**

   A. Reporting on the entity's complete set of financial statements and a single financial statement or a specific element of those financial statements:

   1. If the auditor is engaged to audit a single financial statement or a specific element of a financial statement in connection with an audit of the complete set of financial statements— The auditor should (1) issue a separate report and express a separate opinion for each engagement, and (2) indicate in the report on a specific element of a financial statement the date of the auditor's report on the complete set of financial statements and the nature of that opinion under an appropriate heading.

2. An audited single financial statement or an audited specific element of a financial statement may normally be published along with the entity's audited complete set of financial statements if the single financial statement or specific element is sufficiently differentiated from the complete set of financial statements.

3. If the presentation does not sufficiently differentiate the single financial statement or specific element from the audited financial statements—The auditor should ask management to address the situation; and the auditor should not release the auditor's report until satisfied with the resolution.

B. Modified opinion, emphasis-of-matter paragraph, or other-matter paragraph in the auditor's report on the entity's financial statements:

1. If the modified opinion on the set of financial statements is relevant to the audit of the specific element (i.e., the modification is material and pervasive with respect to the specific element)—The auditor should (a) express an adverse opinion on the specific element when the modification applicable to the set of financial statements is a result of a material misstatement in the financial statements; or (b) disclaim an opinion on the specific element when the modification applicable to the set of financial statements is a result of a scope limitation. (Note: Otherwise that would be equivalent to expressing a *piecemeal opinion*, which is prohibited.)

2. If the modified opinion on the set of financial statements is relevant to the audit of the specific element and the auditor still considers it appropriate to express an unmodified opinion on that specific element—The auditor should only do that if (a) that opinion is expressed in a report that does not accompany the report containing the adverse opinion or disclaimer of opinion, and (b) the specific element does not constitute a major portion of the entity's complete set of financial statements or the specific element is not based on stockholders' equity or net income or equivalent.

3. A single statement constitutes a major portion of a complete set of financial statements, so the auditor should not express an unmodified opinion on the single financial statements when an adverse opinion or disclaimer of opinion is expressed on the complete set of financials.

4. If the report on the complete set of financial statements includes an emphasis-of-matter or other-matter paragraph relevant to the single financial statement or the specific element— The auditor should include a similar emphasis-of-matter or other-matter paragraph in the report on the single financial statement or specific element.

C. Reporting on an incomplete presentation (that is otherwise in accordance with GAAP)—The auditor should include an emphasis-of-matter paragraph in the auditor's report that (1) states the purpose for which the presentation is prepared and refers to a note in the financial statements that describes the basis of presentation; and (2) indicates that the presentation is not intended to be a complete presentation.

V. Sample Report on a Single Financial Statement (Based on a General Purpose Framework)

Independent Auditor's Report

(Appropriate Addressee)

We have audited the accompanying balance sheet of ABC Company as of December 31, 20X1, and the related notes (the financial statement).

Management's Responsibility for the Financial Statements

Management is responsible for the preparation and fair presentation of the financial statement in accordance with accounting principles generally accepted in the United States of America; this includes the design, implementation, and maintenance of internal control relevant to the preparation and fair presentation of the financial statement that is free from material misstatement, whether due to fraud or error.

Auditor's Responsibility

Our responsibility is to express an opinion on the financial statement based on our audit. We conducted our audit in accordance with auditing standards generally accepted in the United States of America. Those standards require that we plan and perform the audit to obtain reasonable assurance about whether the financial statement is free from material misstatement.

An audit involves performing procedures to obtain audit evidence about the amounts and disclosures in the financial statement. The procedures selected depend on the auditor's judgment, including the assessment of the risks of material misstatement of the financial statement, whether due to fraud or error. In making those risk assessments, the auditor considers internal control relevant to the entity's preparation and fair presentation of the financial statement in order to design audit procedures that are appropriate in the circumstances, but not for the purpose of expressing an opinion on the effectiveness of the entity's internal control. Accordingly, we express no such opinion. An audit also includes evaluating the appropriateness of accounting policies used and the reasonableness of significant accounting estimates made by management, as well as evaluating the overall presentation of the financial statement.

We believe that the audit evidence we have obtained is sufficient and appropriate to provide a basis for our audit opinion.

Opinion

In our opinion, the financial statement referred to above presents fairly, in all material respects, the financial position of ABC Company as of December 31, 20X1, in accordance with accounting principles generally accepted in the United States of America.

(Auditor's signature)

(Auditor's city and state)

(Date of the auditor's report)

Reporting on Compliance with Requirements in an F/S Audit

After studying this lesson, you should be able to:

1. Identify the auditor's responsibilities when engaged to report on an entity's compliance with contractual or regulatory requirements in connection with an audit of the entity's financial statements.

2. Identify the reporting language that would be appropriate when issuing a report on compliance with contractual or regulatory requirements either in a separate report on compliance or a combined report on the audited financial statement and on compliance issues.

I. **Relevant AICPA Guidance**—The relevant AICPA guidance is provided by AU 806, *Reporting on Compliance with Aspects of Contractual Agreements or Regulatory Requirements in Connection with Audited Financial Statements*. The standard states that the auditor's objective, when requested to report on an entity's compliance with aspects of contractual agreements or regulatory requirements in connection with the audit of financial statements, is to report appropriately on such matters.

II. **Reports on Compliance with Aspects of Contractual Agreements or Regulatory Requirements**

A. The auditor should include a statement that nothing came to the auditor's attention to cause the auditor to believe that the entity failed to comply with the specified aspects of the contractual agreements or regulatory requirements only if: (1) the auditor did not identify any such noncompliance; (2) the auditor expressed an unmodified or qualified opinion on the financial statements involved; and (3) the covenants or regulatory requirements related to accounting matters that have been subjected to procedures applied in the audit.

B. When instances of noncompliance have been identified—the auditor's report on compliance should describe that noncompliance. Note: If the entity has obtained a waiver for such noncompliance, the auditor may include a statement that a waiver has been obtained; but, all instances of noncompliance must be described in the report, including those for which a waiver has been obtained.

C. When the auditor has issued an adverse opinion or disclaimed an opinion—the auditor should issue a report on compliance only when instances of noncompliance were identified.

D. The report on compliance should be in writing and should be presented either as a separate report or may be combined with the auditor's report on the financial statements.

E. Include a paragraph conveying an *appropriate alert* that restricts the distribution of the report on compliance issues to the specified users.

III. **A Separate Report on Compliance with Aspects of Contractual Agreements When No Instances of Noncompliance Are Identified**

Independent Auditor's Report

(Appropriate Addressee)

We have audited, in accordance with auditing standards generally accepted in the United States of America, the financial statements of XYZ Company, which comprise the balance sheet as of December 31, 20X2, and the related statements of income, changes in stockholders' equity, and cash flows for the year then ended, and the related notes to the financial statements, and have issued our report thereon dated February 16, 20X3.

In connection with our audit, nothing came to our attention that caused us to believe that XYZ Company failed to comply with the terms, covenants, provisions, or conditions of sections XX to YY, inclusive, of the Indenture dated July 21, 20X0, with ABC Bank, insofar as they relate to accounting matters. However, our audit was not directed primarily toward obtaining knowledge of such noncompliance. Accordingly, had we performed additional procedures, other matters may have come to our attention regarding the Company's noncompliance with the above-referenced terms, covenants, provisions, or conditions of the Indenture, insofar as they relate to accounting matters.

This report is intended solely for the information and use of the board of directors and management of XYZ Company and ABC Bank and is not intended to be and should not be used by anyone other than these specified parties.

(Auditor's signature)

(Auditor's city and state)

(Date of the auditor's report)

IV. A Separate Report on Compliance with Aspects of Contractual Agreements When Instances of Noncompliance Are Identified

---

Independent Auditor's Report

(Appropriate Addressee)

We have audited, in accordance with auditing standards generally accepted in the United States of America, the financial statements of XYZ Company, which comprise the balance sheet as of December 31, 20X2, and the related statements of income, changes in stockholders' equity, and cash flows for the year then ended, and the related notes to the financial statements, and have issued our report thereon dated March 5, 20X3.

In connection with our audit, we noted that XYZ Company failed to comply with the Working Capital provision of section XX of the Loan Agreement dated March 1, 20X2, with ABC Bank. Our audit was not directed primarily toward obtaining knowledge as to whether XYZ Company failed to comply with the terms, covenants, provisions, or conditions of sections XX to YY, inclusive, of the Loan Agreement, insofar as they relate to accounting matters. Accordingly, had we performed additional procedures, other matters may have come to our attention regarding noncompliance with the above-referenced terms, covenants, provisions, or conditions of the Loan Agreement, insofar as they relate to accounting matters.

This report is intended solely for the information and use of the board of directors and management of XYZ Company and ABC Bank and is not intended to be and should not be used by anyone other than these specified parties.

(Auditor's signature)

(Auditor's city and state)

(Date of the auditor's report)

V. A Combined Report on Audited Financial Statements and Compliance with Aspects of Contractual Agreements When No Instances of Noncompliance Are Identified

---

Independent Auditor's Report

(Appropriate Addressee)

We have audited the accompanying financial statements of ABC Company, which comprise the balance sheet as of December 31, 20X1, and the related statements of income, changes in stockholders' equity, and cash flows for the year then ended, and the related notes to the financial statements.

Management's Responsibility for the Financial Statements

Management is responsible for the preparation and fair presentation of these financial statements in accordance with accounting principles generally accepted in the United States of America; this includes the design, implementation, and maintenance of internal control relevant to the preparation and fair presentation of financial statements that are free from material misstatement, whether due to fraud or error.

Auditor's Responsibility

Our responsibility is to express an opinion on these financial statements based on our audit. We conducted our audit in accordance with auditing standards generally accepted in the United States of America. Those standards require that we plan and perform the audit to obtain reasonable assurance about whether the financial statements are free from material misstatement.

An audit involves performing procedures to obtain audit evidence about the amounts and disclosures in the financial statements. The procedures selected depend on the auditor's judgment, including the assessment of the risks of material misstatement of the financial statements, whether due to fraud or error. In making those risk assessments, the auditor considers internal control relevant to the entity's preparation and fair presentation of the financial statements in order to design audit procedures that are appropriate in the circumstances, but not for the purpose of expressing an opinion on the effectiveness of the entity's internal control. Accordingly, we express no such opinion. An audit also includes evaluating the appropriateness of accounting policies used and the reasonableness of significant accounting estimates made by management, as well as evaluating the overall presentation of the financial statements.

We believe that the audit evidence we have obtained is sufficient and appropriate to provide a basis for our audit opinion.

Opinion

In our opinion, the financial statements referred to above present fairly, in all material respects, the financial position of ABC Company as of December 31, 20X1, and the results of its operations and its cash flows for the year then ended in accordance with accounting principles generally accepted in the United States of America.

Other Matter

In connection with our audit, nothing came to our attention that caused us to believe that ABC Company failed to comply with the terms, covenants, provisions, or conditions of sections XX to YY, inclusive, of the Indenture dated July 21, 20X0 with XYZ Bank, insofar as they relate to accounting matters. However, our audit was not directed primarily toward obtaining knowledge of such noncompliance. Accordingly, had we performed additional procedures, other matters may have come to our attention regarding the Company's noncompliance with the above-referenced terms, covenants, provisions, or conditions of the Indenture, insofar as they relate to accounting matters.

Restricted Use Relating to the Other Matter

The communication related to compliance with the aforementioned Indenture described in the Other Matter paragraph is intended solely for the information and use of the boards of directors and management of ABC Company and XYZ Bank and is not intended to be and should not be used by anyone other than these specified parties.

(Auditor's signature)

(Auditor's city and state)

(Date of the auditor's report)

Service Organizations—User Auditors

After studying this lesson, you should be able to:

1. Identify the user auditor's responsibilities when auditing a *user entity* that has outsourced some degree of transaction processing to a *service organization*.

2. Understand the implications that a service auditor's report may have to the user auditor's report on the user entity's financial statement.

I. Relevant AICPA Guidance—The relevant AICPA guidance is provided by AU 402, *Audit Considerations Relating to an Entity Using a Service Organization*. The standard states that the user auditor's objectives, when the user entity uses the services of a service organization, are to: (1) obtain an understanding of the nature and significance of the services provided and their effect on the user entity's internal control relevant to the audit sufficient to assess the risks of material misstatement, and (2) design and perform audit procedures that are responsive to those risks.

Definitions

Complementary User Entity Controls: Controls that management of the service organization assumes, in the design of its service, will be implemented by user entities, and which, if necessary to achieve the control objectives stated in management's description of the service organization's system, are identified as such in that description.

Service Auditor: A practitioner who reports on controls at a service organization

Service Organization: A service organization used by another service organization to perform some of the services provided to user entities that are relevant to those user entities' internal control over financial reporting. (This SAS also applies to subservice organizations.)

Type 1 Report: Report on management's description of a service organization's system and the **suitability of the design** of controls.

Type 2 Report: Report on management's description of a service organization's system and the **suitability of the design and operating effectiveness of controls**.

User Auditor: An auditor who audits and reports on the financial statements of a user entity.

User Entity: An entity that uses a service organization and whose financial statements are being audited.

II. User Auditor Responsibilities

A. Obtain an understanding of the services provided by a service organization, including internal controls.

1. The services of a service organization are relevant to the audit of a user entity when those services (and the controls over those services) affect the user entity's information system related to financial reporting and safeguarding assets.

2. The user auditor should evaluate the design and implementation of relevant controls at the user entity related to the service organization's services.

3. The user auditor should determine whether a sufficient understanding of the nature and significance of the service organization's services and their effect on the user entity's internal control relevant to the audit have been obtained to assess the risks of material misstatement.

4. If the user auditor is unable to obtain a sufficient understanding from the user entity—the user auditor should obtain that understanding by:

    a. Obtaining and reading the service auditor's Type 1 or Type 2 report;

    b. Contacting the service organization (through the user entity) to obtain specific information, or visiting the service organization and performing necessary procedures about relevant controls; *or*

    c. Using another auditor to perform procedures to provide the necessary information about controls at the service organization.

5. Using a Type 1 or Type 2 report to support the user auditor's understanding.

    a. The user auditor should be satisfied about (1) the service auditor's professional competence and independence and (2) the standards that the service auditor followed in issuing the report.

    b. The user auditor should (1) evaluate whether the report provides sufficient appropriate evidence for understanding the user entity's relevant internal controls and (2) determine whether any *complementary user entity controls* identified by the service organization are relevant in assessing the risks of material misstatement.

B. Responding to the Assessed Risks of Material Misstatement

1. **Evidence at the user entity**—The user auditor should determine whether sufficient appropriate audit evidence is available at the user entity; and, if not, perform further audit procedures at the service organization.

2. **Tests of controls**—When the user auditor's risk assessment includes an expectation that controls at the service organization are operating effectively, the user auditor should obtain evidence about such operating effectiveness by either obtaining a Type 2 report or performing appropriate tests of controls at the service organization (or using another auditor to perform those tests of controls).

3. **A user entity may outsource some or all of its finance function to a service organization**—In that case, a significant portion of the audit evidence resides at the service organization. Necessary substantive procedures may be performed at the service organization by the user auditor or by the service auditor on the user auditor's behalf. The user auditor is still responsible for obtaining sufficient appropriate audit evidence.

C. Inquiry about Fraud, Noncompliance, and Uncorrected Misstatements—The user auditor should inquire of the user entity's management as to whether they are aware of any fraud, noncompliance with laws and regulations, or uncorrected misstatements at the service organization affecting the financial statements of the user entity.

III. Reporting Issues to the User Auditor

A. Modified Opinion

1. **Scope limitation**—If the user auditor is unable to obtain sufficient appropriate audit evidence about the services provided by the service organization relevant to the user entity's financial statements, the user auditor should modify the opinion for a scope limitation.

2. **Reference to service auditor**—The user auditor may refer to the service auditor in the user auditor's report containing a modified opinion if that reference would be relevant to understanding the user auditor's modification. The user auditor should indicate that such reference does not change the user auditor's responsibility for that opinion.

B. Unmodified Opinion—The user auditor should not refer to the service auditor in the user auditor's report containing an unmodified opinion. The user auditor is responsible for the opinion expressed, and *no division of responsibility* is permitted.

Service Organizations—Service Auditors

After studying this lesson, you should be able to:

1. Understand the service auditor's requirements under AICPA Attestation Standards when engaged to report on internal control over financial reporting at a service organization.

2. Identify the nature of the two different types of reports on internal control that a service auditor may be engaged to issue.

I. Relevant AICPA Guidance

The relevant AICPA guidance applicable to the service auditor is provided by AT-C 320, *Reporting on an Examination of Controls at a Service Organization*.

II. Distinction Between the Service Auditor and the User Auditor

Definitions

Service Auditor: Practitioner who reports on controls at a service organization.

User Auditor: An auditor who audits and reports on the financial statements of a user entity. (In other words, the auditor of an entity that has outsourced the processing of its transactions to the service organization for whom such processing may be more efficient; the user auditor must consider relevant internal controls of the service organization in auditing the financial statements of such a user entity.)

III. Applicability

A. **The Attestation Standards Apply to Internal Control Reporting by the Service Auditor**— The service auditor may be engaged to issue either of two types of reports on internal control applicable to a service organization.

   1. **On the adequacy of the design of internal control** (Called a "Type 1 engagement" by AICPA Professional Standards)—Whether the control policies and procedures are suitably designed and placed in operation.

   2. **On the operating effectiveness of internal control (based on tests of controls)** (called a "Type 2 engagement" by AICPA Professional Standards)—Whether the policies and procedures are suitably designed and working effectively to provide reasonable assurance of achieving the stated control objectives.

B. **Examples of Such Services**—Bank trust departments, mortgage banks that service mortgages for others, IT centers (e.g., processing checks for financial institutions or handling the details of subscriptions for magazine publishers).

C. Management of the service organization is required to provide the service auditor with a written assertion (1) about the fairness of the presentation of the description of the system and (2) about the suitability of the design; and, in a *Type 2 engagement*, management is also required to provide a written assertion (3) about the operating effectiveness of the controls. Those assertions should either accompany the service auditor's report or be included in the service organization's description of the system of internal control.

IV. Responsibilities of Service Auditors (Governed by SSAEs)—Must be independent of service organization, but not necessarily independent of all **user** entities.

A. **Procedures**

   1. **Inquiry**—of service organization management and other personnel.

   2. **Inspection**—of documentation (flowcharts, narrative memoranda, or questionnaires).

   3. **Observation**—of internal control activities.

4. Obtainment of management's written representations as deemed appropriate.

5. Performance of test of control—If reporting on the operating effectiveness of internal control, the service auditor must perform appropriate **tests of controls**.

B. **Reporting on the Adequacy of the Design of Internal Control** (i.e., reporting on the internal control policies and procedures placed in operation, which are also known as a "Type 1" engagement)—the service auditor's report ordinarily consists of the following sections:

1. **Scope**—Identify the nature of the engagement and the **specific date** involved.

2. Service organization's responsibilities

3. **Service auditor's responsibilities**—Reference the attestation standards established by the AICPA and describe an examination; also, **disclaim an opinion on operating effectiveness**

4. Inherent limitations of internal control

5. **Opinion**—(1) that the description fairly presents the system that was designed and implemented as of the specific date; and (2) that the controls related to the stated control objectives were suitably designed to provide reasonable assurance that the control objectives would be achieved if the controls operated effectively as of the specific date.

6. **Restricted use**—Distribution should be restricted to the service organization, user entities, and the user entities' independent auditors.

C. **Reporting on the operating effectiveness of internal control** (i.e., reporting on the policies and procedures placed in operation **and** on their operating effectiveness, which are also known as a "Type 2" engagement)—the service auditor's report ordinarily consists of the following sections:

1. **Scope**—Identify the nature of the engagement and the period involved.

2. Service organization's responsibilities

3. **Service auditor's responsibilities**—Reference the attestation standards established by the AICPA and describe an examination.

4. Inherent limitations of internal control

5. **Opinion**—(1) that the description fairly presents the system that was designed and implemented throughout the period; (2) that the controls related to the stated control objectives were suitably designed to provide reasonable assurance that the control objectives would be achieved if the controls operated effectively throughout the period; and (3) that the controls tested operated effectively throughout the period.

6. **Description of tests of controls**—Reference the pages of the service auditor's report identifying the specific controls tested and the nature, timing, and results of those tests.

> **Note**
> *Management specifies the control objectives to be tested—Should cover a reporting period of **at least six months**.*

7. **Restricted use**—Distribution should be restricted to the service organization, user entities, and the user entities' independent auditors.

V. **Service Organization Control Reports**—The AICPA has developed a "menu" of assurance-related service opportunities for CPAs under the heading of **Service Organization Control Reports** (or **SOC** Reports):

A variety of resources, including an "SOC Toolkit" is available on the AICPA's website at: http://www.aicpa.org/interestareas/frc/assuranceadvisoryservices/pages/soctoolkit_firms.aspx

SOC 1 Report:
"To give the auditor of a user entity's financial statements information about controls at a service organization that may be relevant to a user entity's internal control over financial reporting. A Type 2 SOC 1 report includes a detailed description of tests of controls performed by the CPA and results of the tests." [Such a report must be restricted to specified users.]

Note
The service auditor's report under AT-C 320 is an SOC 1 report.

SOC 2 Report:

"To give management of a service organization, user entities and others a report about controls at a service organization relevant to the security, availability or processing integrity of the service organization's system, or the confidentiality and privacy of the data processed by that system. A Type 2 SOC 2 report includes a detailed description of tests of controls performed by the CPA and results of the tests." [Such a report must be restricted to specified users.]

SOC 3 Report:

"To give users and interested parties a report about controls at the service organization related to security, availability, processing integrity, confidentiality or privacy. SOC 3 reports are a short-form report (i.e., no description of tests of controls and results) and may be used in a service organization's marketing efforts." [This is the only SOC report that is appropriate for "general use"; the others must be restricted to specified users.]

Comfort Letters

After studying this lesson, you should be able to:

1. Understand the purpose of *comfort letters* provided by accountants to underwriters and other financial intermediaries in connection with an entity's stock issuance.

2. Understand the basic structure of comfort letters and the nature of the assurance specifically provided by the entity's accountants/auditors.

I. **Relevant AICPA Guidance**—The relevant AICPA guidance is provided by AU 920: *Letters for Underwriters and Certain Other Requesting Parties*. The standard states that the auditor's objectives, when engaged to issue a letter to a requesting party in connection with a nonissuer entity's financial statements included in a securities offering, are to appropriately address: (1) the acceptance of the engagement and the scope of services, and (2) issue a letter with the appropriate form and content.

II. **Purpose**—Section 11 of the Securities Act of 1933 (the Act) provides for liability to underwriters and certain others (such as a broker-dealer or a financial intermediary) when there is a material omission or misstatement to a registration statement.

   A. A *comfort letter* from the entity's auditor may help underwriters or others having a statutory due diligence defense under Section 11 of the Act to establish a *reasonable investigation* (i.e., *due diligence*).

   B. Comfort letters are not required and are not filed with the SEC.

   C. The scope is specified in the underwriting agreement (between the entity and the underwriters or others); a copy of the agreement should be given to the auditor. The auditor should obtain from the requesting party either (1) a written opinion from legal counsel that the requesting party has a statutory due diligence defense under Section 11 of the 1933 Act, or (2) an appropriate representation letter that meets certain technical requirements. (Without that, the auditor should not provide negative assurance on the financial statements or on any of the requested matters.)

   D. The auditor should meet with the underwriters (or other requesting parties) to establish their specific needs and give them a *draft* of the expected comfort letter in advance to avoid misunderstandings.

   E. The auditor should avoid implying that the procedures performed were sufficient for the underwriter's (or other parties') purposes, since that is a legal determination.

III. **A Typical Comfort Letter**—Usually consists of the following:

   A. An introductory paragraph that identifies the particular registration statement and the audited financial statements and schedules with which the auditor is associated

   B. A statement as to the auditor's independences

   C. **Positive Expression of Opinion**—Whether the **audited** financial statements and schedules **comply as to form** with the accounting requirements of the Act and the SEC (if a review under GAAS has been performed); if a review of the interim information has not been performed, the auditor is limited to reporting the procedures performed along with the findings

   D. **Negative Assurance**—Whether the **unaudited** condensed interim financial information complies as to form with the requirements of the Act and the SEC

   E. **Negative Assurance**—Whether any material modifications should be made to the unaudited condensed consolidated financial statements

   F. **Negative Assurance**—Whether there has been any change during a specified period in capital stock, increase in long-term debt, or any decrease in other specified financial statement items

   G. A concluding paragraph that limits the distribution of the comfort letter to specified parties for the purposes stated

IV. Other Reporting Considerations

A. **Dating of the Letter**—A comfort letter is usually dated on or shortly before the effective date of the registration; the letter should state that the procedures identified in the letter did not cover the period after the cut-off date (to which the procedures apply) to the date of the letter.

B. **Addressee**—A comfort letter should be addressed only to the entity, named underwriters, broker-dealer, or the financial intermediary related to the securities.

C. Comment on the previously audited financial statements referred to in the registration statement.

1. Give **positive assurance** (opinion) as to whether the audited financial statements comply with the **form** and content required by the SEC.

2. Use the following language: "In our opinion (include the phrase 'except as disclosed in the registration statement,' if applicable) the consolidated financial statements and financial statement schedules audited by us and included in the registration statement comply as to form in all material respects with the applicable accounting requirements of the 1933 Act and the related rules and regulations adopted by the SEC."

D. Commenting on the **unaudited financial statements, condensed interim financial information**, or **capsule financial information**—The auditor should obtain an understanding of internal control over financial reporting.

1. **Unaudited financial statements and schedules and unaudited condensed interim financial information**—The auditor may express negative assurance that interim information complies as to form with SEC requirements, if the auditor has performed a review of the interim financial information. (If a review of the interim financial information has not been performed, the auditor is limited to reporting the procedures performed and the findings.)

2. **Capsule financial information**—This term refers to unaudited summarized interim information in narrative or tabular form. The auditor is permitted to express negative assurance on capsule financial information if (a) the auditor has appropriate knowledge of the entity's financial reporting practices; and (b) the auditor conducted an audit of the annual financial statements involved (or conducted a review of the interim financial information involved). Otherwise, the auditor is limited to reporting the procedures performed along with the findings.

E. Commenting on financial **forecasts; subsequent changes**; or **tables, statistics, and other financial information**.

1. **Forecasts**—The comfort letter should not provide negative assurance on the results of any procedures performed with respect to financial forecasts.

2. **Subsequent changes**—Comments usually relate to any changes in capital stock, increase in long-term debt, or decreases in other specified financial statement items (subsequent to the latest financial statements included in the registration statement).

3. The comfort letter may express negative assurance regarding "subsequent changes" within 135 days of the most recent period for which an audit or review was performed. The procedures usually are limited to reading the minutes and making inquiries of management (and obtaining the appropriate written representations). (After 135 days from the most recent period for which the auditor has performed an audit or review, the auditor is limited to reporting the procedures performed along with the findings.)

4. **Tables, statistics, and other financial information**—For the auditor to comment on tables, statistics, and other financial information in the comfort letter, there are several requirements: (a) the auditor must have conducted an audit of the entity's financial statements for a period including (or immediately preceding) the unaudited period (or have completed an audit for a later period); (b) the auditor must have obtained an understanding of the entity's internal control over financial reporting; (c) the information must be expressed in dollars (or percentages based on dollars); and (d) the information must be derived from the accounting records subject to the entity's internal control over financial reporting. The auditor's comments should clearly identify the specific information involved, and report the procedures performed and the findings.

F. A comfort letter should state that the auditor make no representation involving legal interpretations.

Typical Comfort Letter for a 1933 Act Offering

June 28, 20X6

[Addressee]

Dear Ladies and Gentlemen:

We have audited the consolidated financial statements of the Nonissuer Company, Inc. (the company) and subsidiaries, which comprise the consolidated balance sheets as of December 31, 20X5 and 20X4, and the related consolidated statements of income, changes in stockholders' equity, and cash flows for each of the years in the three-year period ended December 31, 20X5, and the related notes to the consolidated financial statements, all included in The Issuer Company's (the registrant) registration statement (no. 33-00000) on Form S-1 filed by the registrant under the Securities Act of 1933 (the Act); our report with respect thereto is also included in that registration statement. The registration statement, as amended on June 28, 20X6, is herein referred to as the registration statement.

In connection with the registration statement—

1. We are independent certified public accountants with respect to the company within the meaning of the 1933 Act and the applicable rules and regulations thereunder adopted by the SEC.

2. In our opinion [include the phrase "except as disclosed in the registration statement" if applicable], the consolidated financial statements audited by us and included in the registration statement comply as to form in all material respects with the applicable accounting requirements of the Act and the related rules and regulations adopted by the SEC.

3. We have not audited any financial statements of the company as of any date or for any period subsequent to December 31, 20X5; although, we have conducted an audit for the year ended December 31, 20X5, the purpose (and, therefore, the scope) of the audit was to enable us to express our opinion on the consolidated financial statements as of December 31, 20X5, and for the year then ended, but not on the financial statements for any interim period within that year. Therefore, we are unable to and do not express any opinion on the unaudited condensed consolidated balance sheet as of March 31, 20X6, and the unaudited condensed consolidated statements of income, stockholders' equity, and cash flows for the three-month periods ended March 31, 20X6 and 20X5, included in the registration statement, or on the financial position, results of operations, or cash flows as of any date or for any period subsequent to December 31, 20X5.

4. For purposes of this letter we have read the 20X6 minutes of meetings of the stockholders, the board of directors, and [include other appropriate committees, if any] of the company and its subsidiaries as set forth in the minute books at June 23, 20X6, officials of the company having advised us that the minutes of all such meetings through that date were set forth therein and having discussed with us the unapproved minutes of meetings held on [dates]; we have carried out other procedures to June 23, 20X6, as follows (our work did not extend to the period from June 24, 20X6 to June 28, 20X6, inclusive):

a. With respect to the three-month periods ended March 31, 20X6 and 20X5, we have—

i. Performed the procedures specified for a review in accordance with auditing standards generally accepted in the United States of America applicable to reviews of interim financial information, on the unaudited condensed consolidated balance sheet as of March 31, 20X6, and the unaudited condensed consolidated statements of income, stockholders' equity, and cash flows for the three-month periods ended March 31, 20X6 and 20X5, included in the registration statement.

ii. Inquired of certain officials of the company who have responsibility for financial and accounting matters whether the unaudited condensed consolidated financial statements referred to in a(i) comply as to form in all material respects with the applicable accounting requirements of the Act and the related rules and regulations adopted by the SEC.

b. With respect to the period from April 1, 20X6 to May 31, 20X6, we have—

i. Read the unaudited consolidated financial information of the company and subsidiaries for April and May of both 20X5 and 20X6 furnished to us by the company, officials of the company having advised us that no financial statements as of any date or for any period subsequent to May 31, 20X6, were available. (If applicable: The financial information for April and May of both 20X5 and 20X6 is incomplete in that it omits the statements of cash flows and other disclosures.)

ii. Inquired of certain officials of the company who have responsibility for financial and accounting matters whether the unaudited consolidated financial information referred to in b(i) is stated on a basis substantially consistent with that of the audited consolidated financial statements included in the registration statement.

The foregoing procedures do not constitute an audit conducted in accordance with generally accepted auditing standards. Also, they would not necessarily reveal matters of significance with respect to the comments in the following paragraph. Accordingly, we make no representations regarding the sufficiency of the foregoing procedures for your purposes.

5. Nothing came to our attention as a result of the foregoing procedures, however, that caused us to believe that—

a.

i. Any material modifications should be made to the unaudited condensed consolidated financial statements described in 4a(i), included in the registration statement, for them to be in conformity with generally accepted accounting principles.

ii. The unaudited condensed consolidated financial statements described in 4a(i) do not comply as to form in all material respects with the applicable accounting requirements of the Act and the related rules and regulations adopted by the SEC.

b.

i. At May 31, 20X6, there was any change in the capital stock, increase in long-term debt, or decrease in consolidated net current assets or stockholders' equity of the consolidated companies as compared with amounts shown in the March 31, 200X6 unaudited condensed consolidated balance sheet included in the registration statement, or

ii. for the period from April 1, 20X6 to May 31, 20X6, there were any decreases, as compared to the corresponding period in the preceding year, in consolidated net sales or in income from continuing operations or of net income, except in all instances for changes, increases, or decreases that the registration statement discloses have occurred or may occur.

6. As mentioned in 4b, company officials have advised us that no consolidated financial statements as of any date or for any period subsequent to May 31, 20X6, are available; accordingly, the procedures carried out by us with respect to changes in financial statements items after May 31, 20X6, have, of necessity, been even more limited than those with respect to the periods referred to in 4. We have inquired of certain officials of the company who have responsibility for financial and accounting matters whether (a) at June 23, 20X6, there was any change in the capital stock, increase in long-term debt, or any decreases in consolidated net current assets or stockholders' equity of the consolidated companies as compared with amounts shown in the March 31, 20X6, unaudited condensed consolidated balance sheet included in the registration statement, or (b) for the period from April 1, 20X6 to June 23, 20X6, there were any decreases as compared with the corresponding period in the preceding year, in consolidated net sales or in income from continuing operations or of net income.

On the basis of these inquiries and our reading of the minutes as described in 4, nothing came to our attention that caused us to believe that there was any such change, increase, or decrease, except in all instances for changes, increases, or decreases that the registration statement discloses have occurred or may occur.

7. This letter is solely for the information of the addressees and to assist the underwriters in conducting and documenting their investigation of the affairs of the company in connection with the offering of the securities covered by the registration statement, and it is not to be used, circulated, quoted, or otherwise referred to within or without the underwriting group for any other purpose, including but not limited to the registration, purchase, or sale of securities, nor is it to be filed with or referred to in whole or in part in the registration statement or any other document, except that reference may be made to it in the underwriting agreement or in any list of closing documents pertaining to the offering of the securities covered by the registration statement.

Government Auditing Standards

After studying this lesson, you should be able to:

1. Understand the distinction between "GAAS" and "GAGAS" (issued by the U.S. Government Accountability Office) and the additional responsibilities resulting from the Government Auditing Standards.

2. Understand the circumstances in which the Single Audit Act is applicable.

I. **Government Auditing Standards**—Government Auditing Standards (also known as Generally Accepted Government Auditing Standards or GAGAS) are issued by the U.S. Government Accountability Office (in GAO's Yellow Book) under the authority of the Comptroller General of the United States.

A. GAGAS must be followed when required by applicable law, regulation, or agreement. These standards may apply to a variety of different governmental engagements, including financial audits, performance audits, and attestation engagements.

> **Note**
> *These additional standards are presented at the end of this lesson as excerpted from GAO's 2011 Yellow Book.*

B. GAGAS go beyond the 10 criteria formerly known as GAAS, and include additional general, fieldwork, and reporting standards.

C. Summary of the primary reporting differences associated with GAGAS (relative to engagements under GAAS):

1. **Additional reporting requirements regarding internal control**—Government Auditing Standards require a written report on internal control in every financial audit under GAGAS. This includes commentary about the auditor's understanding of internal control for planning purposes and the assessment of control risk, as well as the scope of the auditor's testing of internal control. When the auditor communicates *significant deficiencies*, the auditor should also obtain a response from officials of the entity and include a copy of management's written response (or a summary of management's oral response) in the auditor's report.

2. **Additional reporting requirements regarding compliance with applicable laws and regulations**—Government Auditing Standards require a written report on compliance with applicable laws and regulations. This report should distinguish between (a) *general requirements* that apply to all federal financial programs; and (b) *specific requirements* that apply to a particular program by a specific statutory (legislative) requirement.

    a. The auditor should design the audit to provide reasonable assurance of detecting instances of noncompliance that have a "material and direct effect" on the entity's financial statements. (Similarly, the auditor should design the audit to provide reasonable assurance of detecting fraud that is material to the entity's financial statements.)

    b. Management is responsible for identifying laws and regulations that have a direct and material effect on the entity's financial statements, and it is common for auditors to obtain written representations from management that all such laws and regulations have been appropriately identified.

    c. The auditor's report on compliance should comment on the scope of the auditor's testing of the entity's compliance with applicable laws and regulations.

    d. The auditor's report on compliance should also include (1) any known instances of fraud that are viewed as more than inconsequential; (2) any known instances of illegal acts that are viewed as more than inconsequential; (3) other identified violations of contracts or grants that are material; and (4) any known instances of "abuse" that are material.

    e. Auditors may have a duty to report instances of fraud, illegal acts, or abuse to authorities outside the entity (such as a federal inspector general, etc.) when (1) management fails to meet its legal requirements to report such matters; or (2) when management fails to appropriately respond to identified instances of fraud, illegal acts, or abuse.

3. **Additional reporting requirements regarding illegal acts**—Government Auditing Standards also require the auditor to report any known instances of illegal acts that could result in **criminal prosecution**.

II. **Single Audit Act of 1984, as Amended**—The Single Audit Act is applicable to state and local governmental entities that have expenditures of federal assistance (grants) now aggregating at least $750,000 in a given year. It imposes certain requirements on such entities and their auditors that go beyond GAAS and even GAGAS.

   A. Management's responsibilities under the Single Audit Act include the following:

   1. Prepare the financial statements along with a schedule of expenditures of federal assistance.

   2. Prepare a *corrective action plan* to respond to any current-year audit findings.

   3. Submit certain necessary forms, including the audit report to the designated Federal Audit Clearinghouse on a timely basis.

   B. The auditor's responsibilities under the Single Audit Act include the following:

   1. The audit should be conducted in accordance with GAGAS.

   2. The auditor should identify each *major program* to be audited based on appropriate risk assessment considerations (and materiality should be determined separately for each major program).

   3. The auditor should evaluate whether the financial statements and schedule of expenditures of federal assistance are fairly presented using appropriate criteria.

   4. The auditor should obtain an appropriate understanding of internal control over the federal assistance programs and perform testing of internal control over designated major programs.

   5. The auditor should evaluate the entity's compliance with applicable laws, regulations, or other requirements having a direct and material effect on designated major programs.

   6. The auditor should report any identified audit findings, including material instances of noncompliance with applicable laws, regulations, or other requirements involving designated major programs; identified instances of fraud; and significant deficiencies in internal controls over designated major programs.

   C. **Summary Comments Regarding the Single Audit Act**

   1. **Efficiency**—A single coordinated audit of the aggregate federal financial assistance provided to a state or local governmental entity (with emphasis on the entity's major programs) is intended to result in greater efficiency compared to the alternative, which would be having multiple audits of the entity conducted on a grant-by-grant basis.

   2. **Added requirements**—A single coordinated audit of the aggregate federal financial assistance involves more than just a financial statement audit. Additional testing of internal control is required for major programs, and additional testing is also required for major programs regarding the entity's compliance with applicable laws, regulations, or other requirements applicable to major programs.

   3. **Multiple reports**—The auditor should issue reports on (a) the fairness of the entity's financial statements (and schedule of expenditures of federal assistance); (b) internal control over financial reporting (with emphasis on major programs); and (c) compliance with applicable laws, regulations, and other requirements. If audit findings were identified, the auditor should also prepare a *Schedule of Findings and Questioned Costs*.

III. GAGAS—Excerpted from GAO's Yellow Book (2011 Edition)

General Standards

1. **Independence**—"In all matters relating to the audit work, the audit organization and the individual auditor, whether government or public, must be independent."

2. **Professional Judgment**—"Auditors must use professional judgment in planning and performing audits and in reporting the results."

3. **Competence**—"The staff assigned to perform the audit must collectively possess adequate professional competence needed to address the audit objectives and perform the work in accordance with GAGAS."

4. **Quality Control and Assurance**—"Each audit organization performing audits in accordance with GAGAS must:

   a. "Establish and maintain a system of quality control that is designed to provide the audit organization with reasonable assurance that the organization and its personnel comply with professional standards and applicable legal and regulatory requirements, and

   b. "Have an external peer review performed by reviewers independent of the audit organization being reviewed at least once every three years."

Additional GAGAS Requirements for Performing Financial Audits:

1. **Auditor Communication**—"In addition to the AICPA requirements for auditor communication, when performing a GAGAS financial audit, auditors should communicate pertinent information that in the auditors' professional judgment needs to be communicated to individuals contracting for or requesting the audit, and to cognizant legislative committees when auditors perform the audit pursuant to a law or regulation, or they conduct the work for the legislative committee that has oversight of the audited entity. This requirement does not apply if the law or regulation requiring an audit of the financial statements does not specifically identify the entities to be audited, such as audits required by the Single Audit Act Amendments of 1996."

2. **Previous Audits and Attestation Engagements**—"When performing a GAGAS audit, auditors should evaluate whether the audited entity has taken appropriate corrective action to address findings and recommendations from previous engagements that could have a material effect on the financial statements or other financial data significant to the audit objectives. When planning the audit, auditors should ask management of the audited entity to identify previous audits, attestation engagements, and other studies that directly relate to the objectives of the audit, including whether related recommendations have been implemented. Auditors should use this information in assessing risk and determining the nature, timing, and extent of current audit work, including determining the extent to which testing the implementation of the corrective actions is applicable to the current audit objectives."

3. **Fraud, Noncompliance with Provisions of Laws, Regulations, Contracts, and Grant Agreements, and Abuse**—"In addition to the AICPA requirements concerning fraud and noncompliance with provisions of laws and regulations, when performing a GAGAS financial audit, auditors should extend the AICPA requirements pertaining to the auditors' responsibilities for laws and regulations to also apply to consideration of compliance with provisions of contracts or grant agreements."

4. **Developing Elements of a Finding**—"In a financial audit, findings may involve deficiencies in internal control; noncompliance with provisions of laws, regulations, contracts, or grant agreements; fraud; or abuse. As part of a GAGAS audit, when auditors identify findings, auditors should plan and perform procedures to develop the elements of the findings that are relevant and necessary to achieve the audit objectives."

5. **Audit Documentation**—"In addition to the AICPA requirements for audit documentation, auditors should comply with the following additional requirements when performing a GAGAS financial audit."

a. "Document supervisory review, before the report release date, of the evidence that supports the findings, conclusions, and recommendations contained in the auditors' report."

b. "Document any departures from the GAGAS requirements and the impact on the audit and on the auditors' conclusions when the audit is not in compliance with applicable GAGAS requirements due to law, regulation, scope limitations, restrictions on access to records, or other issues impacting the audit."

Additional GAGAS Requirements for Reporting on Financial Audits:

1. **Reporting auditors' compliance with GAGAS**—"When auditors comply with all applicable GAGAS requirements for financial audits, they should include a statement in the auditors' report that they performed the audit in accordance with GAGAS. Because GAGAS incorporates by reference the AICPA SASs, GAGAS does not require auditors to cite compliance with the AICPA standards when citing compliance with GAGAS."

2. **Reporting on internal control and compliance with provisions of laws, regulations, contracts, and grant agreements**—"When providing an opinion or a disclaimer on financial statements, auditors should also report on internal control over financial reporting and on compliance with provisions of laws, regulations, contracts, or grant agreements that have a material effect on the financial statements. Auditors report on internal control and compliance, regardless of whether or not they identify internal control deficiencies or instances of noncompliance.

   "Auditors should include either in the same or in separate report(s) a description of the scope of the auditors' testing of internal control over financial reporting and of compliance with provisions of laws, regulations, contracts, or grant agreements."

3. **Communicating deficiencies in internal control, fraud, noncompliance with provisions of laws, regulations, contracts, and grant agreements, and abuse**—"When performing GAGAS financial audits, auditors should communicate in the report on internal control over financial reporting and compliance, based upon the work performed, (1) significant deficiencies and material weaknesses in internal control; (2) instances of fraud and noncompliance with provisions of laws or regulations that have a material effect on the audit and any other instances that warrant the attention of those charged with governance; (3) noncompliance with provisions of contracts or grant agreements that has a material effect on the audit; and (4) abuse that has a material effect on the audit."

4. **Reporting views of responsible officials**—"When performing a GAGAS financial audit, if the auditors' report discloses deficiencies in internal control, fraud, noncompliance with provisions of laws, regulations, contracts, or grant agreements, or abuse, auditors should obtain and report the views of responsible officials of the audited entity concerning the findings, conclusions, and recommendations, as well as any planned corrective actions."

5. **Reporting confidential or sensitive information**—"When performing a GAGAS financial audit, if certain pertinent information is prohibited from public disclosure or is excluded from a report due to the confidential or sensitive nature of the information, auditors should disclose in the report that certain information has been omitted and the reason or other circumstances that make the omission necessary."

6. **Distributing reports**—"Distribution of reports completed in accordance with GAGAS depends on the relationship of the auditors to the audited organization and the nature of the information contained in the report. Auditors should document any limitation on report distribution."

Compliance Audits

SAS No. 117, *Compliance Audits,* was originally issued in clarified format. It has been reclassified as AU 935 to be compatible with International Standards on Auditing.

I. **Relevant AICPA Guidance**—The relevant AICPA guidance is provided by AU 935, *Compliance Audits.* The standard states that the auditor's objectives are to (1) obtain sufficient appropriate audit evidence to form an opinion and report whether the entity complied in all material respects with applicable compliance requirements (at the level specified in the governmental audit requirement), and (2) identify audit and reporting requirements specified in the governmental audit requirements that are supplementary to GAAS and Government Auditing Standards and perform procedures to address those requirements.

II. **Applicability**—When an auditor is engaged to perform a compliance audit in accordance with (1) generally accepted auditing standards (GAAS), (2) Government Auditing Standards (also called Generally Accepted Government Auditing Standards (GAGAS) from GAO's Yellow Book issued under the authority of the Comptroller General of the United States), and (3) a governmental audit requirement requiring an expression of opinion on compliance with applicable compliance requirements.

A. This SAS applies to the compliance audit, but not to the financial statement audit part of such an engagement—example engagements for which this SAS applies includes an audit under OMB Circular A-133, *Audits of States, Local Governments, and Non-Profit Organizations,* also includes a department-specific requirement such as "U.S. Department of Housing and Urban Development Audit Requirements Related to Entities Such as Public Housing Agencies, Nonprofit and For-Profit Housing Projects, and Certain Lenders."

B. **Definition of** *governmental audit requirement*—A governmental requirement established by law, regulation, rule, or provision of contracts or grant agreements requiring that an entity undergo an audit of its compliance with applicable compliance requirements related to one or more government programs.

III. **Compliance Auditing—Requirements and Guidance**

A. **This SAS Incorporated the AICPA's Risk Assessment Standards**

1. The auditor should perform risk assessment procedures to obtain an understanding of the applicable compliance requirements and internal controls over compliance—the nature and extent of the risk assessment procedures may vary with the circumstances (such as the complexity of the compliance requirements and the depth of the auditor's knowledge of internal control over compliance).

2. The auditor should assess the risks of material noncompliance (whether due to fraud or error) for each applicable compliance requirement and consider whether any of those are *pervasive* to compliance.

3. The auditor should perform further audit procedures in response to the assessed risks, such as develop an overall response to any risks that are pervasive to the entity's compliance; perform appropriate tests of details; and perform tests of controls when there is an expectation of operating effectiveness or when required to do so. (Note that an example of a *pervasive* risk of noncompliance would be financial difficulty that increases the risk that grant funds will be used for unauthorized purposes.)

B. Supplementary Audit Requirements—The auditor should identify *supplementary audit requirements* (beyond GAAS and GAGAS) specified in the governmental audit requirement.

1. Some governmental audit requirements specifically identify the applicable compliance requirements, whereas others provide a framework for the auditor to determine the applicable compliance requirements.

2. OMB Circular A-133, *Audits of States, Local Governments and Non-Profit Organizations*, provides a framework (Compliance Supplement) to determine the compliance requirements.

C. Written Representations—The auditor should obtain written representations from management tailored to the entity and the governmental audit requirement.

D. Subsequent Events—The auditor should perform procedures up to the date of the auditor's report to identify subsequent events related to the entity's compliance (e.g., reports from grantors regarding noncompliance or information about noncompliance obtained through other professional engagements for the entity); an example of a subsequent event warranting disclosure is the discovery of noncompliance causing the grantor to stop the funding.

E. Evaluating the Evidence and Forming an Opinion—Most governmental audit requirements specify that the auditor's opinion on compliance is at the *program* level (and materiality is usually determined based on the program taken as a whole).

1. The auditor should consider *likely questioned costs* (not just *known questioned costs*) and other noncompliance that may not result in questioned costs.

2. The auditor may include a variety of factors in assessing the risk of noncompliance, including: (a) the complexity of the compliance requirements; (b) how long the entity has been subject to those compliance requirements; (c) the degree of judgment involved in compliance; and (d) the entity's compliance in prior years.

F. Reporting—The auditor may issue (1) a separate report on compliance only; (2) a combined report on compliance and on internal control over compliance; or (3) a separate report on internal control over compliance.

Combined Report on Compliance with Applicable Requirements and Internal Control Over Compliance

Independent Auditor's Report

(Addressee)

Compliance

We have audited (entity's name) compliance with the (identify the applicable compliance requirements or reference the document that describes the applicable compliance requirements) applicable to (entity's) (identify the government program(s) audited or refer to a separate schedule that identifies the program(s)) for the year ended June 30, 20X1. Compliance with the requirements referred to above is the responsibility of (entity's) management. Our responsibility is to express an opinion on (entity's) compliance based on our audit.

We conducted our audit of compliance in accordance with auditing standards generally accepted in the United States of America; the standards applicable to financial audits contained in Government Auditing Standards issued by the Comptroller General of the United States; and (name of the governmental audit requirement or program-specific audit guide). Those standards and (name of the governmental audit requirement or program-specific audit guide) require that we plan and perform the audit to obtain reasonable assurance about whether noncompliance with the compliance requirements referred to above that could have a material effect on (identify the government program(s) audited or refer to a separate schedule that identifies the program(s)). An audit includes examining, on a test basis, evidence about (entity's) compliance with those requirements and performing such other procedures as we considered necessary in the circumstances. We believe that our audit provides a reasonable basis for our opinion. Our audit does not provide a legal determination of (entity's) compliance with those requirements.

In our opinion, (entity's name) complied, in all material respects, with the compliance requirements referred to above that are applicable to (identify the government program(s) audited) for the year ended June 30, 20X1.

Internal Control Over Compliance

Management of (entity's name) is responsible for establishing and maintaining effective internal control over compliance with the compliance requirements referred to above. In planning and performing our audit, we considered (entity's) internal control over compliance to determine the auditing procedures for the purpose of expressing our opinion on compliance, but not for the purpose of expressing an opinion on the effectiveness of internal control over compliance. Accordingly, we do not express an opinion on the effectiveness of (entity's) internal control over compliance.

A deficiency in internal control over compliance exists when the design or operation of a control does not allow management or employees, in the normal course of performing their assigned functions, to prevent, or detect and correct, noncompliance on a timely basis. A material weakness in internal control over compliance is a deficiency, or combination of deficiencies in internal control over compliance, such that there is a reasonable possibility that material noncompliance with a compliance requirement will not be prevented, or detected and corrected, on a timely basis.

This report is intended solely for the information and use of management, (identify the body or individuals charged with governance), others within the entity, (identify the legislative or regulatory body), and (identify the grantor agency(ies)) and is not intended to be and should not be used by anyone other than these specified parties.

(Signature)

(Auditor's city and state)

(Date)

G. **Documentation**—The auditor should document the risk assessment procedures performed, responses to the assessed risks of material noncompliance, the basis for materiality levels, and compliance with applicable *supplementary audit requirements*.

H. **Communication**—The auditor should communicate the following matters with those charged with governance: the auditor's responsibilities under GAAS, GAGAS, and the governmental audit requirements; an overview of the planned scope and timing of the compliance audit; and any significant findings.

I. **Reissuance of the Compliance Report**—When reissuing a compliance report, the auditor should add an explanatory paragraph describing why the report is being reissued and noting any changes from the previously issued report; if additional audit procedures are performed, the auditor's report date should be updated.

The Clarified SSARSs and General Principles

After studying this lesson, you should be able to:

1. Know the key words that distinguish "unconditional requirements," "presumptively mandatory requirements," and "application and other explanatory material," respectively.

2. Understand the accountant's responsibilities with respect to applicable "interpretive publications" and "other preparation, compilation, and review publications."

3. Know the preconditions that affect whether the accountant may properly accept an engagement to be performed under the clarified SSARSs.

Statements on Standards for Accounting and Review Services (SSARS) are issued by the AICPA's Accounting and Review Services Committee (ARSC) and are applicable to certain financial statement-related services that a CPA may provide to nonissuers. In October 2014, the ARSC replaced substantially all of the then-existing SSARSs with "clarified" SSARSs, similar to what the Auditing Standards Board previously did with the Statements on Auditing Standards. The purpose of this project was to make the clarified SSARSs easier to read and understand and, therefore, to improve the application of these standards in practice.

Accordingly, the ARSC adopted clarity drafting conventions, such as the following: (1) specified objectives for each of the clarified sections of the AR-C (i.e., the clarified SSARS sections); (2) included a section on definitions, as applicable, in each AR-C; (3) separated the professional "requirements" from the "application and other explanatory material" parts of each AR-C; and (4) adopted formatting techniques (e.g., using bullet lists) to improve the flow and readability of each AR-C.

The clarified SSARSs were issued as SSARS No. 21, *Statements on Standards for Accounting and Review Services: Clarification and Recodification*. It was comprised of four primary sections:

- Section 60, *General Principles for Engagements Performed in Accordance With [SSARS]*
- Section 70, *Preparation of Financial Statements*
- Section 80, *Compilation Engagements*
- Section 90, *Review of Financial Statements*

Historically, the SSARSs involved two types of engagements: reviews and compilations. The clarified SSARSs have added a third type of engagement: engagements to prepare financial statements for a client without issuing an accompanying report.

SSARS No. 22 provides guidance on "Compilation of Pro Form Financial Information" in clarified format (designated AR-C Section 120).

Compliance with the SSARSs is enforceable under the AICPA Code of Professional Conduct, specifically, the *Compliance With Standards* rule.

Supplemental (more detailed) outlines are provided elsewhere in Wiley CPAexcel® for each of the four AR-C sections identified above.

I. **Requirements**—The "General Principles" retained the two categories of requirements for SSARSs: "unconditional" and "presumptively mandatory."

    A. **Unconditional Requirements**—Indicated by the word "must." The accountant is required to comply with such a requirement without exception whenever the requirement is relevant.

    B. **Presumptively Mandatory Requirements**—Indicated by the word "should." The accountant is expected to comply with such a requirement, except in rare circumstances.

        1. Noncompliance is allowed if a required procedure would be ineffective in achieving the intent of the requirement for a specific engagement.

        2. When not complying with such a requirement, the accountant should perform alternative procedures to achieve the intent of the presumptively mandatory requirement.

        3. When departing from a presumptively mandatory requirement, the accountant must document the justification for such departure and how the alternative procedure(s) met the intent of that requirement.

    C. **"Application and Other Explanatory Material"** (including appendices of SSARSs) —These are not "requirements" and are presented separately within the SSARSs. Indicated by the words "may," "might," or "could," they may explain what a requirement means or provide examples of appropriate procedures.

II. **The Role of "Interpretive" and "Other" Publications**

    A. **Interpretive Publications**—The accountant should consider the guidance of applicable interpretive publications in performing the engagement. These are recommendations on the application of SSARSs in particular circumstances as issued by ARSC after ARSC members have had the opportunity to comment on the proposed interpretations.

Definition
Interpretive Publications: "Interpretations of SSARSs; exhibits to SSARSs; the AICPA Guide, *Preparation, Compilation, and Review Engagements,* guidance on preparation, compilations, and review engagements included in AICPA Audit and Accounting Guides; and AICPA Statements of Position, to the extent that those statements are applicable to such engagements."

    B. **Other Preparation, Compilation, and Review Publications**—The accountant should evaluate the relevance and appropriateness of such guidance to the engagement.

Definition
Other Preparation, Compilation, and Review Publications: "Publications other than interpretive publications."

---

        1. These other publications may be useful in understanding the SSARSs, but they have no authoritative status, and the accountant is not required to be aware of all such other publications.

        2. Other publications issued by the AICPA that have been approved by the AICPA's Audit and Attest Standards team are presumed to be appropriate. Those that have not been reviewed by the AICPA's Audit and Attest Standards team may be considered by the accountant, but their influence may be affected by the publication's stature and whether the author is a known expert.

III. Preconditions—Circumstances affecting acceptance and continuance of engagements in accordance with the SSARSs

    A. The accountant should not accept an engagement to be performed in accordance with the SSARSs if any of the following circumstances exist:

        1. There is reason to believe that relevant ethical requirements (e.g., independence requirements) will not be satisfied;

        2. Information that is needed to perform the engagement is unlikely to be either available or reliable; *or*

        3. There is reason to doubt management's integrity.

    B. Prior to accepting an engagement to be performed in accordance with the SSARSs, the accountant should perform the following actions:

        1. Determine that the ethical requirements regarding competence will be satisfied;

        2. Determine whether the financial reporting framework adopted by management is acceptable; *and*

        3. Obtain an agreement that management acknowledges and understands its responsibilities for the following:

            a. The selection of the financial reporting framework;

            b. The design, implementation, and maintenance of internal control relevant to the financial statements;

            c. The prevention and detection of fraud;

            d. Compliance with applicable laws and regulations;

            e. The accuracy and completeness of the records, documents, and explanations, including significant judgments made by management for the financial statements; *and*

            f. Providing the accountant with access to all relevant information related to the fair presentation of the financial statements, additional information requested by the accountant, and unrestricted access to personnel.

SSARSs—Preparation of Financial Statements

After studying this lesson, you should be able to

1. Distinguish between preparation engagements for which AR-C 70, *Preparation of Financial Statements*, is applicable and other engagements for which AR-C 70 is not applicable.

2. Understand the accountant's obligation to obtain written agreement of the terms of the preparation engagement.

3. Know the requirements associated with a preparation engagement, including the accountant's documentation requirements.

Note

In the past, the SSARSs dealt with only two types of engagements: reviews and compilations. The clarified SSARSs have added a third type of engagement: engagements to prepare financial statements, whether historical or prospective, for a client without issuing an accompanying report, which is the focus of AR-C 70, *Preparation of Financial Statements*. When engaged to prepare financial statements, the accountant is also required to comply with the requirements of AR-C 60 (*General Principles*), including meeting the "preconditions" for accepting the engagement. The accountant is not required to be independent for a preparation engagement.

I. **Obtain an Agreement on the Terms of the Engagement**

   A. The accountant and management (or those charged with governance, as applicable) should agree on the terms of the engagement, which should be documented in writing (typically in an engagement letter). The following should be documented:

      1. The engagement's objective;

      2. Management's responsibilities;

      3. The accountant's responsibilities;

      4. That each page of the financial statements will include a statement that no assurance is provided (if such a statement is not included on each page, then the accountant will issue a disclaimer to make that point clear);

      5. The limitations of the engagement;

      6. Identification of the applicable financial reporting framework; *and*

      7. Whether the financial statements are to contain known departures from the applicable financial reporting framework (including misstatements or omission of some or all of the required footnote disclosures).

   B. The agreement should be signed by the accountant (or firm) and management (or those charged with governance). If signed by those charged with governance, the accountant should still obtain management's agreement and understanding of its responsibilities (associated with "preconditions" for accepting the engagement).

II. **Prepare the Financial Statements**

   A. Each page of the financial statements should include a statement that "no assurance is provided" (or other words to that effect). The accountant's name (or firm) need not be identified. If that statement cannot be added to each page, the accountant should either (1) issue a disclaimer as to any assurance, (2) perform a compilation engagement in accordance with AR-C 80, or (3) withdraw.

   B. The accountant is required to obtain an appropriate understanding of the financial reporting framework to be used and the significant accounting policies applicable to the financial statements.

   C. If the financial statements use a special-purpose framework, the accountant should include a description of the financial reporting framework on the face of the financial statements or in a footnote.

D. When assisting management with significant judgments, the accountant should discuss those judgments with management so that management understands those judgments and can take responsibility for them.

E. When records, documents, or other information used in preparing the financial statements are viewed as incomplete or inaccurate, the accountant should request additional or corrected information.

F. When financial statements contain known departures from the applicable financial reporting framework (including omission of some or all required disclosures), the accountant should discuss the matter with management and disclose those departures in the financial statements. If the omission appears intended to mislead users of the financial statements, the accountant should not prepare the financial statements.

G. Preparing Prospective Financial Information

   1. Significant assumptions—The accountant should not prepare prospective financial information that omits disclosure of the summary of significant assumptions.

   2. Financial projections—The accountant should not prepare a financial projection that (a) fails to identify the hypothetical assumptions or that (b) omits a description of the limitations of the usefulness of the projection.

III. Documenting a Preparation Engagement

A. The accountant should document the preparation engagement in enough detail to clearly show the work performed and should include (1) the engagement letter (or other written documentation) and (2) a copy of the financial statements prepared.

B. Noncompliance with a "Presumptively Mandatory Requirement"—In rare circumstances, the accountant may depart from a relevant presumptively mandatory requirement; however, the accountant must document the reason(s) for the departure and how alternative procedures satisfied the intent of that presumptively mandatory requirement.

IV. Applicability of AR-C 70

A. In addition to preparing traditional financial statements, this section also applies to preparation of the following:

   1. Specified elements, accounts, or financial statement items;

   2. Supplementary information and required supplementary information;

   3. Pro forma financial information; *and*

   4. Prospective financial information (forecasts or projections).

B. An appendix identified the following examples to which AR-C 70 applies:

   1. Preparing financial statements prior to audit or review by another accountant;

   2. Preparing financial statements to be presented *alongside* the tax return;

   3. Preparing personal financial statements for presentation *alongside* a financial plan;

   4. Preparing single financial statements (e.g., just a balance sheet) with substantially all disclosures omitted; *and*

   5. Preparing financial statements using general ledger information outside of an accounting software system.

C. AR-C 70 identified certain engagements to which AR-C 70 does not apply:

   1. Engagements to perform audit, review, or compilation services;

   2. Preparing financial statements for submission to taxing authorities;

   3. Preparing financial statements as part of personal financial planning; *or*

   4. Preparing financial statements in connection with litigation services or business valuation services.

SSARSs—Compilation Engagements

After studying this lesson, you should be able to:

1. Know what is meant by the term "compilation."

2. Understand the accountant's responsibilities when performing a compilation engagement.

3. Know the structure and content of the accountant's report for a compilation engagement.

> **Note**
> A "compilation" engagement involves assisting management in presenting the financial statements (or other historical, pro forma, or prospective financial information) along with the accountant's accompanying report, which provides no assurance about those financial statements (or other financial information). The accountant is also required to comply with the requirements of AR-C 60, *General Principles*, including meeting the "preconditions" for accepting the compilation engagement. The accountant is not required to be independent for a compilation engagement, since no assurance is provided. Guidance is provided in the Clarified SSARSs, specifically by AR-C 80, *Compilation Engagements*.

I. **Obtain an Agreement on the Terms of the Engagement**

   A. The accountant and management (or those charged with governance, as applicable) should agree on the terms of the engagement, which should be documented in writing (typically in an engagement letter, but a contract would also be acceptable). The following should be documented:

      1. The engagement's objective;

      2. Management's responsibilities;

      3. The accountant's responsibilities;

      4. The limitations of the engagement (see the note below);

      5. Identification of the applicable financial reporting framework; *and*

      6. The expected form and content of the compilation report (and a statement that, depending on circumstances, the actual report issued may differ from the expected report in form and content).

> **Note**
> An exhibit to AR-C 80 provides a sample engagement letter for a compilation engagement, which includes the following example of a limitation of the engagement (regarding the accountant's liability):
>
> "You agree to hold us harmless and to release, indemnify, and defend us from any liability or costs, including attorney's fees, resulting from management's knowing misrepresentations to us."

   B. The agreement should be signed by the accountant (or firm) and management (or those charged with governance). If signed by those charged with governance, the accountant should still obtain management's agreement and understanding of its responsibilities (associated with the "preconditions" for accepting an engagement).

II. **Performance Responsibilities for a Compilation Engagement**

   A. **Understanding the Applicable Reporting Framework**—The accountant should obtain an appropriate understanding of the financial reporting framework and the significant accounting policies applicable to the entity's financial statements.

   B. **Read the Financials**—The accountant should read the financial statements to evaluate whether they are free of obvious material misstatements.

C. Incomplete/Unsatisfactory Records—If the accountant believes that the records or other information is incomplete or inaccurate, the accountant should request further or corrected information.

D. Revisions Required—If the accountant discovers a need for revision to the financial statements, the accountant should propose appropriate revisions to management.

E. Withdrawal—If management has failed to provide records or information as requested or if management does not make appropriate adjustments as proposed by the accountant, the accountant should withdraw (and inform management of the reasons for withdrawing).

III. Reporting Responsibilities for a Compilation Engagement

  A. The accountant's compilation report normally consists of the following:

    1. A statement that management (owners) of the identified entity is (are) responsible for the financial statements and that identifies the financial statements (and date/period) involved;

    2. A statement that the compilation was performed in accordance with SSARSs promulgated by the AICPA's Accounting and Review Services Committee;

    3. A statement that the accountant did not audit or review the financial statements, etc., and the accountant does not provide any assurance on them;

    4. A statement that disclaims an opinion or any form of assurance; *and*

    5. The signature of the accountant (or the accountant's firm), along with the city and state of the office, and the date of the report. (Presenting the report on the accountant's letterhead is an acceptable way to identify the accountant's city and state.)

Note

The accountant may request that management add a reference to each page of the financial statements, such as "See Accountant's Compilation Report" (or something similar), but that is not required.

Sample Compilation Report (Under Clarified SSARSs)

Accountant's Compilation Report

Management is responsible for the accompanying financial statements of XYZ Company, which comprise the balance sheets as of December 31, 20X1 and 20X2, the related statements of income, changes in stockholders' equity, and cash flows for the years then ended, and the related notes to the financial statements in accordance with accounting principles generally accepted in the United States of America. I (We) have performed compilation engagements in accordance with Statements on Standards for Accounting and Review Services promulgated by the Accounting and Review Services Committee of the AICPA. I (We) did not audit or review the financial statements nor was (were) I (we) required to perform any procedures to verify the accuracy or completeness of the information provided by management. Accordingly, I (we) do not express an opinion, a conclusion, or provide any form of assurance on these financial statements.

[Signature of accounting firm or accountant, as appropriate]

[Accountant's city and state]

[Date of the accountant's report]

B. In summary, the compilation report normally consists of four sentences:

1. Management is responsible for the accompanying financial statements of XYZ Company, which comprise the balance sheets as of December 31, 20X1 and 20X2, the related statements of income, changes in stockholders' equity, and cash flows for the years then ended, and the related notes to the financial statements in accordance with accounting principles generally accepted in the United States of America.

2. I (We) have performed compilation engagements in accordance with Statements on Standards for Accounting and Review Services promulgated by the Accounting and Review Services Committee of the AICPA.

3. I (We) did not audit or review the financial statements nor was (were) I (we) required to perform any procedures to verify the accuracy or completeness of the information provided by management.

4. Accordingly, I (we) do not express an opinion, a conclusion, or provide any form of assurance on these financial statements.

C. Compilation Report when Financial Statements Use a Special-Purpose Framework

1. When using a special-purpose framework, the report should include a separate paragraph stating that the financial statements are prepared in accordance with the particular special-purpose framework and that refers to the note to the financial statement describing the framework.

2. When the financial statements are prepared using a regulatory basis or a contractual basis of accounting, the report should identify the purpose for which the financial statements were prepared (or refer to a note that provides that information).

3. Unless the financial statements omit substantially all disclosures, the accountant should modify the report when the financial statements omit (a) a description of the special-purpose framework; (b) a summary of significant accounting policies; (c) a description of how the special-purpose framework differs from GAAP (although the differences need not be quantified); or (d) appropriate informative disclosures.

D. Reporting when the Accountant Is Not Independent

1. The last paragraph of the report should state that the accountant was not independent [either a single sentence without indicating the reason or with additional commentary indicating the reason(s) for the impairment].

2. If stating any reason(s) for the impairment, the accountant should identify all applicable reasons for the lack of independence.

E. Reporting when Substantially All Disclosures Are Omitted

1. If the omission of disclosures appears to be intended to mislead financial statement readers, the accountant should not issue a compilation report.

2. When the financial statements omit substantially all disclosures, the compilation report should include a paragraph pointing out that fact, including a statement that the financial statements are not designed for those who are uninformed about such matters. (The accountant should not issue a report on "comparative" financial statements of one year that omit substantially all disclosures along with financial statements of another year that include applicable disclosures. Such financial statements would not be viewed as comparable.)

3. If most disclosures are presented but selected disclosures are omitted, the report should identify the nature of the departure and any known effects.

F. Reporting Known Departures from the Applicable Financial Reporting Framework

1. Material departures that are not disclosed in the notes should be reported in a modified compilation report in a separate paragraph. (If the accountant believes that modification of the report is not an adequate way to communicate the deficiencies, the accountant should withdraw.)

2. The effects of the departure should be disclosed if known. The accountant is not required to determine the effects, however, and can state in the report that management has not made such a determination.

3. The accountant should not add a statement to the report stating that the "financial statements are not in conformity with [the applicable financial reporting framework]," which is equivalent to expressing a conclusion.

IV. Documentation Requirements for a Compilation Engagement—The documentation should provide a clear understanding of the accountant's work and, at a minimum, include the following:

A. The engagement letter (or other appropriate written documentation);

B. A copy of the financial statements; *and*

C. A copy of the compilation report.

SSARSs—Review Engagements

After studying this lesson, you should be able to:

1. Know what is meant by the term review of a nonissuer.

2. Understand the accountant's responsibilities for performing a review engagement in accordance with the SSARSs.

3. Know the structure and content of the accountant's report for a review engagement in accordance with the SSARSs.

Note

A "review" engagement involves obtaining "limited assurance" (primarily by analytical procedures and inquiry of management) as to whether material modifications should be made to an entity's financial statements to be presented in accordance with the applicable financial reporting framework. The accountant is also required to comply with the requirements of AR-C 60, *General Principles,* including meeting the "preconditions" for accepting the review engagement. The accountant is required to be independent for a review engagement, since "negative assurance" is provided. Guidance is provided in the Clarified SSARSs, specifically by AR-C 90, *Review Engagements*.

I. **Obtain an Agreement on the Terms of the Engagement**

   A. The accountant and management (or those charged with governance, as applicable) should agree on the terms of the engagement, which should be documented in writing (typically in an engagement letter). The following should be documented:

   1. The engagement's objective;

   2. Management's responsibilities;

   3. The accountant's responsibilities;

   4. The limitations of the engagement;

   5. Identification of the applicable financial reporting framework; *and*

   6. The expected form and content of the review report (and a statement that, depending on circumstances, the actual report issued may differ from the expected report in form and content).

   B. The agreement should be signed by the accountant (or firm) and management (or those charged with governance). If signed by those charged with governance, the accountant should still obtain management's agreement and understanding of its responsibilities (associated with the "preconditions" for accepting an engagement).

   C. **Understanding of the Industry and Knowledge of the Entity**—The accountant should obtain an understanding of the entity's industry, its business (including its organization and operations) and the accounting principles and practices used (including the nature of its financial statement elements).

II. **Designing and Performing Review Procedures**—The accountant should design and perform analytical procedures and make inquiries (and perform any other procedures as needed) to obtain "limited assurance" as a basis for the review report.

   A. **Risk Assessment**—The accountant should focus the review procedures in the areas believed to be at higher risk of material misstatements. However, the accountant does not obtain an understanding of internal control for purposes of assessing control risk.

   B. **Analytical Procedures**—The accountant should use analytical procedures as a basis for inquiry about relationships that appear unusual and should investigate significant differences relative to expectations by inquiring of management and performing other review procedures as needed.

C. **Inquiries of Management**—The accountant should inquire about (but is not required to corroborate) the following:

1. Whether the financial statements are fairly and consistently presented

2. Whether unusual situations impact the financial statements

3. Whether there are significant transactions, especially at period-end

4. The status of any uncorrected misstatements;

5. Any matters called into question by the review procedures

6. The effect of any subsequent events

7. Management's knowledge of fraud or suspected fraud involving management, employees with significant internal control responsibilities, or others where the effect could be material

8. Any allegations of fraud or suspected fraud by employees, former employees, or others

9. Any instances of noncompliance with laws and regulations that could be material to the financial statements

10. Significant adjusting journal entries relevant to the financial statements

11. Any communications from regulatory authorities

12. Related-party relationships and transactions with related parties

13. Litigation, claims, and assessments that should be considered

14. Whether management's significant assumptions affecting accounting estimates are reasonable

15. Any actions at meetings of stockholders, directors, or others that should be considered in the financial statements

16. Any other matters considered relevant by the accountant

D. **Reading the Financial Statements**—The accountant should read the financial statements for any indications of departures from the applicable framework.

E. **Reconciling to Underlying Records**—The accountant should verify that the financial statements agree to (or reconcile to) the accounting records.

F. **Incomplete/Unsatisfactory Records**—If the accountant believes that the records or other information is incomplete or inaccurate, the accountant should request further or corrected information.

G. **Written Representations**—The accountant should obtain written representations from the appropriate members of management (usually the chief executive officer and chief financial officer); the representations letter should have the same date as the review report. (If management does not provide the required representations, the accountant should withdraw.)

III. **Reporting Responsibilities for a Review Engagement**

A. The accountant's review report normally consists of the following:

1. A title, such as "Independent Accountant's Review Report"

2. An appropriate addressee

3. An introductory paragraph (without a label) that identifies the financial statements that were reviewed (and dates/periods involved), that states that a review consists primarily of analytical procedures and inquiries, and that states that a review is substantially less in scope than an audit (with a disclaimer of opinion)

4. A section entitled "Management's Responsibility for the Financial Statements" that identifies management's responsibilities for the financial statements and internal control

5. A section entitled "Accountant's Responsibility" that references the SSARSs promulgated by the ARSC of the AICPA and refers to "limited assurance" as a basis for reporting

6. A section entitled "Accountant's Conclusion" that provides negative assurance on the financial statements *and*

7. The signature of the accountant or the accountant's firm, the city and state where the accountant practices, and the date of the report.

Sample (Clarified) Review Report on Comparative Financial Statements

Independent Accountant's Review Report

[Appropriate Addressee]

I (We) have reviewed the accompanying financial statements of XYZ Company, which comprise the balance sheets as of December 31, 20X2 and 20X1, and the related statements of income, changes in stockholders' equity, and cash flows for the years then ended, and the related notes to the financial statements. A review includes primarily applying analytical procedures to management's (owners') financial data and making inquiries of company management (owners). A review is substantially less in scope than an audit, the objective of which is the expression of an opinion regarding the financial statements as a whole. Accordingly, I (we) do not express such an opinion.

Management's Responsibility for the Financial Statements

Management (Owners) is (are) responsible for the preparation and fair presentation of these financial statements in accordance with accounting principles generally accepted in the United States of America; this includes the design, implementation, and maintenance of internal control relevant to the preparation and fair presentation of financial statements that are free from material misstatement whether due to fraud or error.

Accountant's Responsibility

My (Our) responsibility is to conduct the review engagements in accordance with Statements on Standards for Accounting and Review Services promulgated by the Accounting and Review Services Committee of the AICPA. Those standards require me (us) to perform procedures to obtain limited assurance as a basis for reporting whether I am (we are) aware of any material modifications that should be made to the financial statements for them to be in accordance with accounting principles generally accepted in the United States of America. I (We) believe that the results of my (our) procedures provide a reasonable basis for our conclusion.

Accountant's Conclusion

Based on my (our) reviews, I am (we are) not aware of any material modifications that should be made to the accompanying financial statements in order for them to be in accordance with accounting principles generally accepted in the United States of America.

[Signature of accounting firm or accountant, as appropriate]

[Accountant's city and state]

[Date of the accountant's report]

B. Review report when financial statements use a special-purpose framework.

1. When using a special-purpose framework, the report should include an "emphasis-of-matter" paragraph stating that the financial statements are prepared in accordance with the special purpose framework and referencing the note to the financial statement describing the framework.

2. When the financial statements are prepared using a regulatory basis or a contractual basis of accounting, the report should identify the purpose for which the financial statements were prepared (or refer to a note that provides that information) and restrict the distribution of the report.

3. The accountant should modify the report when the financial statements omit (a) a description of the special-purpose framework, (b) a summary of significant accounting policies, (c) a description of how the special-purpose framework differs from GAAP (although the differences need not be quantified), or (d) appropriate informative disclosures.

C. Reporting Known Departures from the Applicable Financial Reporting Framework

1. If the accountant believes that modification of the report is not an adequate way to communicate the deficiencies, the accountant should withdraw.

2. When modifying the review report, the departure should be identified in a separate paragraph, labeled "Known Departures from the [*identify the applicable financial reporting framework*]." The effects on the financial statements should be included, if known. (The accountant is not required to make that determination if management has not, but the report should state that such determination has not been made by management.)

3. The "Accountant's Conclusion" paragraph would be modified (for example) as follows: "Based on my (our) review, except for the issue noted in the Known Departure from Accounting Principles Generally Accepted in the United States of America paragraph, I am (we are) not aware of any material modifications that should be made. . . ." (The "Known Departure" paragraph would follow the "Accountant's Conclusion" paragraph.)

4. The review report should avoid stating that the financial statements are not in accordance with the applicable framework, since that is effectively expressing an adverse opinion, which is inappropriate for a review.

D. Review Documentation

1. In general, the documentation should permit an experienced accountant with no prior connection to the engagement to understand the following:

    a. The nature, timing, and extent of review procedures performed in compliance with the SSARSs

    b. The evidence obtained from the procedures performed *and*

    c. Significant findings, conclusions reached, and significant professional judgments involved

2. Specifically, the documentation should include the following

    a. The engagement letter (or other written documentation)

    b. Communications about fraud or noncompliance with laws

    c. Communications about emphasis-of-matter or other-matter paragraph(s) in the accountant's review report

    d. Communications with other accountants associated with component financial statements

    e. The representation letter obtained from management *and*

    f. A copy of the financial statements and the review report

SSARSs—Other Topics

After studying this lesson, you should be able to:

1. Know how the accountant's report (for a compilation and for a review engagement) is affected when "required supplementary information" is relevant to the entity's financial statements.

2. Understand the accountant's responsibilities under SSARSs when "subsequently discovered facts" are identified before the report release date, as well as after the report release date.

3. Understand the accountant's responsibilities under SSARSs when engaged to compile "pro forma" financial information.

4. Know how the accountant's report (for a compilation and for a review engagement) is affected when the entity's financial statements are accompanied by "supplemental information."

5. Know the distinction between a "forecast" and a "projection" and the different types of professional services that are permitted for such prospective financial information.

SSARS No. 22 provides guidance on *Compilation of Pro Forma Financial Information* in clarified format (designated AR-C section 120). That topic will be addressed here.

In addition, certain other technical topics applicable to preparation engagements, compilations, and reviews in accordance with the SSARSs will also be addressed below.

I. Compilation of Pro Forma Financial Information

Note

The purpose of "pro forma" financial information is to show the significant effects on historical financial information that might have resulted had an actual or proposed transaction occurred at an earlier date. The Statements on Standards for Attestation Engagements provide guidance to practitioners when performing an "examination" or "review" engagement involving pro forma information. Compilation of pro forma financial information is addressed in the SSARSs.

    A. A Requirement to Perform a Compilation of Pro Forma Financial Information—The accountant must have compiled, reviewed, or audited the historical financial statements on which the pro forma information is based.

    B. Engagement Letter—The accountant and the entity (management) should establish an understanding in writing as to the nature and limitations of the services to be performed and the nature of the report to be issued.

        1. That understanding should specifically state that the engagement cannot be relied on to disclose errors, fraud, or illegal acts.

        2. That understanding also should state that the accountant will inform the appropriate level of management of any material errors and of any information coming to the accountant's attention that fraud or illegal acts may have occurred (excluding matters that are "clearly inconsequential").

    C. Performance Requirements—The accountant should read the compiled pro forma financial information (including the summary of significant assumptions) and consider whether that information appears to be free of obvious material errors.

    D. Reporting Requirements

        1. The pro forma financial information should be clearly labeled in a manner that distinguishes it from historical financial statements.

        2. Each page of the compiled pro forma financial information should include a reference such as "See Accountant's Compilation Report."

        3. The accountant is not required to be independent since no assurance is provided. If the accountant is not independent, the compilation report should indicate that fact.

4. The accountant may "assist" with the preparation of pro forma financial information without issuing a compilation report (when the accountant has not been engaged to "compile" such information).

5. The compilation report should not describe any other procedures performed by the accountant either prior to or during the compilation engagement.

II. Supplemental Information

Note
When the financial statements are accompanied by "supplemental information" associated with either a compilation or review engagement, the accountant should indicate the responsibility taken, if any, for such supplemental information either (1) in an other-matter paragraph in the compilation or review report or (2) in a separate report on that supplemental information.

A. When the Accountant Has Reviewed the Supplementary Information along with the Financial Statements—The report should state that (1) the supplementary information is presented for additional analysis and is not required as part of the financial statements; (2) the supplementary information is the responsibility of management; (3) the supplementary information was subjected to the review procedures applied to the review of the financial statements (and indicate whether the accountant is aware of any material modifications that should be made to it); and (4) the accountant has not audited the supplementary information and does not express an opinion on it.

B. When the Accountant Has Not Reviewed the Supplementary Information along with the Financial Statements—The report should state that (1) the supplementary information is presented for additional analysis and is not required as part of the financial statements; (2) the supplementary information is the responsibility of management; and (3) the accountant has not audited or reviewed the supplementary information, and does not express an opinion, a conclusion, or any assurance on it.

III. Required Supplementary Information

Note
When "required supplementary information" is relevant to financial statements associated with either a compilation or review engagement, the accountant's compilation or review report should include an "other-matter" paragraph that comments on the applicable circumstances:

A. That the required supplementary information is included and the accountant performed a compilation or review engagement on it;

B. That the required supplementary information is included and the accountant did not perform a compilation, review, or audit on it;

C. That the required supplementary information is omitted;

D. That some required supplementary information is included and some is omitted

E. That the accountant identified departures from the prescribed guidelines (established by the designated accounting standard-setting body); *or*

F. That the accountant has doubts as to whether the information is presented in accordance with the prescribed guidelines.

IV. Preparation or Compilation of Prospective Financial Information

> **Definitions**
>
> *Prospective financial information*: "Any financial information about the future. The information may be presented as complete financial statements or limited to one or more elements, items, or accounts."
>
> *Financial forecast*: "Prospective financial statements that present, to the best of the responsible party's knowledge and belief, an entity's expected financial position, results of operations, and cash flows. A financial forecast is based on the responsible party's assumptions reflecting conditions it expects to exist and the course of action it expects to take."
>
> *Financial projection*: Prospective financial statements that present, to the best of the responsible party's knowledge and belief, given one or more hypothetical assumptions, an entity's expected financial position, results of operations, and cash flows. A financial projection is sometimes prepared to present one or more hypothetical courses of action for evaluation, as in response to a question that begins for instance, "What would happen if …?"

A. Under the Clarified SSARSs

1. The accountant may perform either a preparation engagement or a compilation of prospective financial information (a review of such prospective financial information is not permitted).

2. When engaged to prepare prospective financial information or issue a compilation report on prospective financial information:

   a. **Significant assumptions**—The accountant should not prepare (or issue a compilation report on) prospective financial information that omits disclosure of the summary of significant assumptions; the entity's financial statements should also include a summary of significant accounting policies.

   b. **Financial projections**—The accountant should not prepare or issue a compilation report on a financial projection that (a) fails to identify the hypothetical assumptions or that (b) omits a description of the limitations of the usefulness of the projection; any report on a projection should be restricted to specified users, consisting of third parties in direct negotiation with the responsible party (which allows them to ask questions about the presentation).

3. When issuing a compilation report on prospective financial information—The report should include statements that (a) the forecasted/projected results may not be achieved; and (b) the accountant assumes no responsibility to update the report for matters occurring after the date of the report. (Any report on a "projection" must have restricted distribution; only a report on a "forecast" is permitted to have general distribution.)

B. Under the Clarified Statements on Standards for Attestation Engagements (SSAEs) —
The accountant may be engaged to perform an "examination" or an "agreed-upon procedures engagement" on prospective financial information (again, a review of prospective financial information is not permitted under the SSAEs). Examinations and agreed-upon procedures engagements under the SSAEs are addressed in other lessons of Wiley CPAexcel®.

1. **Examination engagements**—An examination results in a positive expression of opinion (similar to an audit report) focusing on the preparation of the prospective information and management's underlying assumptions; an examination report on a forecast is allowed to be issued for general distribution (but any report on a projection should have restricted distribution).

2. **Agreed-upon procedures engagements**—Any agreed-upon procedures report must be restricted to the specified users who take responsibility for the sufficiency of the procedures for their purposes; assurance is provided in the form of "procedures" and "findings".

V. Review Engagements—Other Miscellaneous Topics

A. Subsequent Events and Subsequently Discovered Facts

1. **Subsequent events**—The accountant should request that management consider the appropriateness of the financial statement treatment when subsequent events are identified.

2. **Subsequently discovered facts *before* the report release date:**

   a. The accountant should discuss the matter with management (and those charged with governance, as applicable) and determine how management intends to deal with the matter when the financial statements require revision.

   b. If management revises the financial statements, the accountant should perform review procedures on the revision and either change the date on the review report or "dual-date" the report.

   c. If management does not revise the financial statements, the accountant should modify the review report appropriately.

3. **Subsequently discovered facts *after* the report release date:**

   a. The accountant should discuss the matter with management (and those charged with governance, as applicable) and determine how management intends to deal with the matter when the financial statements require revision.

   b. If management revises the financial statements, the accountant should perform review procedures on the revision, and either change the date on the review report or "dual-date" the report. The accountant also should determine whether third parties possess those released financial statements and evaluate whether management is taking appropriate steps to inform them that the financial statements should not be used.

   c. If management is not taking the appropriate steps, including revision, the accountant should notify management and take action to prevent the use of the accountant's review report. The accountant may wish to seek legal guidance in that event.

B. Comparative Financial Statements

1. The report should refer to each applicable period for which financial statements are presented. (The type of engagement need not be the same for each period presented. For example, one period might be a compilation and another period might be a review; or one period might be a review and another period might be an audit.)

2. A continuing accountant should update the report on any prior periods' financial statements that are presented along with the current period.

3. **Reporting when the prior period was audited**—If the audit report on the prior period's financial statements is not presented, the review report should include an "other-matter" paragraph to indicate that the prior period's financials were audited; to identify the date of that audit report and the type of opinion expressed (and the reasons for any modifications); and to state that no audit procedures were performed after the date of the audit report.

4. **When changing reference to a previously reported departure**—The review report should include an "other-matter" paragraph to explain the removal of the previously reported departure.

C. Changing the Engagement from an Audit to a Review

1. The accountant should decide whether such a change is appropriate and consider (1) the reason(s) expressed for the change and (2) the incremental effort and cost to complete the audit.

2. A change in circumstances or a misunderstanding about the nature of an audit or review engagement usually would be considered a satisfactory reason for requesting a change in the engagement.

3. If an accountant was engaged to perform an audit but management refused to allow correspondence with the entity's attorney, the accountant normally would be prohibited from changing the engagement to review the entity's financial statements.

Sample Reports

F/S Prepared on Cash Basis

Independent Auditor's Report

(Appropriate Addressee)

We have audited the accompanying financial statements of ABC Partnership, which comprise the statement of assets and liabilities arising from cash transactions as of December 31, 20X1, and the related statement of revenue collected and expenses paid for the year then ended, and the related notes to the financial statements.

Management's Responsibility for the Financial Statements

Management is responsible for the preparation and fair presentation of these financial statements in accordance with the cash basis of accounting described in Note X; this includes determining that the cash basis of accounting is an acceptable basis for the presentation of the financial statements in the circumstances. Management is also responsible for the design, implementation, and maintenance of internal control relevant to the preparation and fair presentation of financial statements that are free from material misstatement, whether due to fraud or error.

Auditor's Responsibility

Our responsibility is to express an opinion on these financial statements based on our audit. We conducted our audit in accordance with auditing standards generally accepted in the United States of America. Those standards require that we plan and perform the audit to obtain reasonable assurance about whether the financial statements are free from material misstatement.

An audit involves performing procedures to obtain audit evidence about the amounts and disclosures in the financial statements. The procedures selected depend on the auditor's judgment, including the assessment of the risks of material misstatement of the financial statements, whether due to fraud or error. In making those risk assessments, the auditor considers internal control relevant to the partnership's preparation and fair presentation of the financial statements in order to design audit procedures that are appropriate in the circumstances, but not for the purpose of expressing an opinion on the effectiveness of the partnership's internal control. Accordingly, we express no such opinion. An audit also includes evaluating the appropriateness of accounting policies used and the reasonableness of significant accounting estimates made by management, as well as evaluating the overall presentation of the financial statements.

We believe that the audit evidence we have obtained is sufficient and appropriate to provide a basis for our audit opinion.

Opinion

In our opinion, the financial statements referred to above present fairly, in all material respects, the assets and liabilities arising from cash transactions of ABC Partnership as of December 31, 20X1, and its revenue collected and expenses paid during the year then ended in accordance with the cash basis of accounting described in Note X.

Basis of Accounting

We draw attention to Note X of the financial statements, which describes the basis of accounting. The financial statements are prepared on the cash basis of accounting, which is a basis of accounting other than accounting principles generally accepted in the United States of America. Our opinion is not modified with respect to this matter.

(Auditor's signature)

(Auditor's city and state)

(Date of the auditor's report)

F/S Prepared on Regulatory Basis (for General Use)

Independent Auditor's Report

(Appropriate Addressee)

We have audited the accompanying financial statements of XYZ City, Any State, which comprise cash and unencumbered cash for each fund as of December 31, 20X1, and the related statements of cash receipts and disbursements and disbursements budgeted and actual for the year then ended, and the related notes to the financial statements.

Management's Responsibility for the Financial Statements

Management is responsible for the preparation and fair presentation of these financial statements in accordance with the financial reporting provisions of Section Y of Regulation Z of Any State. Management is also responsible for the design, implementation, and maintenance of internal control relevant to the preparation and fair presentation of financial statements that are free from material misstatement, whether due to fraud or error.

Auditor's Responsibility

Our responsibility is to express an opinion on these financial statements based on our audit. We conducted our audit in accordance with auditing standards generally accepted in the United States of America. Those standards require that we plan and perform the audit to obtain reasonable assurance about whether the financial statements are free from material misstatement.

An audit involves performing procedures to obtain audit evidence about the amounts and disclosures in the financial statements. The procedures selected depend on the auditor's judgment, including the assessment of the risks of material misstatement of the financial statements, whether due to fraud or error. In making those risk assessments, the auditor considers internal control relevant to the partnership's preparation and fair presentation of the financial statements in order to design audit procedures that are appropriate in the circumstances, but not for the purpose of expressing an opinion on the effectiveness of the partnership's internal control. Accordingly, we express no such opinion. An audit also includes evaluating the appropriateness of accounting policies used and the reasonableness of significant accounting estimates made by management, as well as evaluating the overall presentation of the financial statements.

We believe that the audit evidence we have obtained is sufficient and appropriate to provide a basis for our audit opinions.

Basis for Adverse Opinion on U.S. Generally Accepted Accounting Principles

As described in Note X of the financial statements, the financial statements are prepared by XYZ City on the basis of the financial reporting provisions of Section Y of Regulation Z of Any State, which is a basis of accounting other than accounting principles generally accepted in the United States of America, to meet the requirements of Any State.

The effects on the financial statements of the variances between the regulatory basis of accounting described in Note X and accounting principles generally accepted in the United States of America, although not reasonably determinable, are presumed to be material.

Adverse Opinion on U.S. Generally Accepted Accounting Principles

In our opinion, because of the significance of the matter discussed in the "Basis for Adverse Opinion on U.S. Generally Accepted Accounting Principles" paragraph, the financial statements referred to above do not present fairly, in accordance with accounting principles generally accepted in the United States of America, the financial position of each fund of XYZ City as of December 31, 20X1, or changes in financial position or cash flows thereof for the year then ended.

Opinion on Regulatory Basis of Accounting

In our opinion, the financial statements referred to above present fairly, in all material respects, the cash and unencumbered cash of each fund of XYZ City as of December

31, 20X1, and their respective cash receipts and disbursements, and budgetary results for the year then ended in accordance with the financial reporting provisions of Section Y of Regulation Z of Any State described in Note X.

(Auditor's signature)

(Auditor's city and state)

(Date of the auditor's report)

Profit Participation

Independent Auditor's Report

We have audited, in accordance with generally accepted auditing standards, the financial statements of XYZ Company for the year ended December 31, 20X1, and have issued our report thereon, dated March 10, 20X2. We have also audited XYZ Company's schedule of Reed Smith's profit participation for the year ended December 31, 20x1. This schedule is the responsibility of the Company's management. Our responsibility is to express an opinion on this schedule based on our audit.

We conducted our audit of the schedule in accordance with auditing standards generally accepted in the United States of America. Those standards require that we plan and perform the audit to obtain reasonable assurance about whether the schedule of profit participation is free of material misstatement. An audit includes examining, on a test basis, evidence supporting the amounts and disclosures in the schedule. An audit also includes assessing the accounting principles used and significant estimates made by management, as well as evaluating the overall schedule presentation. We believe that our audit provides a reasonable basis for our opinion.

We have been informed that the documents that govern the determination of Reed Smith's profit participation are (a) the employment agreement between Reed Smith and XYZ Company dated February 1, 20X0, (b) the production and distribution agreement between XYZ Company and Television Network Incorporated dated March 1, 20X0, and (c) the studio facilities agreement between XYZ Company for the year ended December 31, 20X1, in accordance with the provisions of the agreements referred to above.

In our opinion, the schedule of profit participation referred to above presents fairly, in all material respects, Reed Smith's participation in the profits of XYZ Company for the year ended December 31, 20X1, in accordance with the provisions of the agreements referred to above.

This report is intended solely for the information and use of the board of directors and management of XYZ Company and Reed Smith and should not be used for any other purpose.

Note

Notice that, since the object of this report is "profit participation" (a bottom-line concept), the auditor also must have audited the entire income statement and make reference to the related audit report.

Sample Review Report on Financial Statements

Independent Accountant's Review Report

[Appropriate Addressee]

I (We) have reviewed the accompanying financial statements of XYZ Company, which comprise the balance sheets as of December 31, 20X2 and 20X1, and the related statements of income, changes in stockholders' equity, and cash flows for the years then ended, and the related notes to the financial statements. A review includes primarily applying analytical procedures to management's (owners') financial data and making inquiries of company management (owners). A review is substantially less in scope than an audit, the objective of which is the expression of an opinion regarding the financial statements as a whole. Accordingly, I (we) do not express such an opinion.

Management's Responsibility for the Financial Statements

Management (Owners) is (are) responsible for the preparation and fair presentation of these financial statements in accordance with accounting principles generally accepted in the United States of America; this includes the design, implementation, and maintenance of internal control relevant to the preparation and fair presentation of financial statements that are free from material misstatement whether due to fraud or error.

Accountant's Responsibility

My (Our) responsibility is to conduct the review engagements in accordance with Statements on Standards for Accounting and Review Services promulgated by the Accounting and Review Services Committee of the AICPA. Those standards require me (us) to perform procedures to obtain limited assurance as a basis for reporting whether I am (we are) aware of any material modifications that should be made to the financial statements for them to be in accordance with accounting principles generally accepted in the United States of America. I (We) believe that the results of my (our) procedures provide a reasonable basis for our conclusion.

Accountant's Conclusion

Based on my (our) reviews, I am (we are) not aware of any material modifications that should be made to the accompanying financial statements in order for them to be in accordance with accounting principles generally accepted in the United States of America.

[Signature of accounting firm or accountant, as appropriate]

[Accountant's city and state]

[Date of the accountant's report]

Sample Compilation Report on Financial Statements

Accountant's Compilation Report

Management is responsible for the accompanying financial statements of XYZ Company, which comprise the balance sheets as of December 31, 20X1 and 20X2 and the related statements of income, changes in stockholders' equity, and cash flows for the years then ended, and the related notes to the financial statements in accordance with accounting principles generally accepted in the United States of America. I (We) have performed compilation engagements in accordance with Statements on Standards for Accounting and Review Services promulgated by the Accounting and Review Services Committee of the AICPA. I (We) did not audit or review the financial statements nor was (were) I (we) required to perform any procedures to verify the accuracy or completeness of the information provided by management. Accordingly, I (we) do not express an opinion, a conclusion, nor provide any form of assurance on these financial statements.

(Signature of accounting firm or accountant, as appropriate)

(Accountant's city and state)

(Date of the accountant's report)

Individual Sentences:

1. Management is responsible for the accompanying financial statements of XYZ Company, which comprise the balance sheets as of December 31, 20X1 and 20X2 and the related statements of income, changers in stockholders' equity, and cash flows for the years then ended, and the related notes to the financial statements in accordance with accounting principles generally accepted in the United States of America.

2. I (We) have performed compilation engagements in accordance with Statements on Standards for Accounting and Review Services promulgated by the Accounting and Review Services Committee of the AICPA.

3. I (We) did not audit or review the financial statements nor was (were) I (we) required to perform any procedures to verify the accuracy or completeness of the information provided by management.

4. Accordingly, I (we) do not express an opinion, a conclusion, nor provide any form of assurance on these financial statements.

Separate Report on Compliance
(No Instances of Noncompliance)

Independent Auditor's Report

(Appropriate Addressee)

We have audited, in accordance with auditing standards generally accepted in the United States of America, the financial statements of XYZ Company, which comprise the balance sheet as of December 31, 20X2, and the related statements of income, changes in stockholders' equity, and cash flows for the year then ended, and the related notes to the financial statements, and have issued our report thereon dated February 16, 20X3.

In connection with our audit, nothing came to our attention that caused us to believe that XYZ Company failed to comply with the terms, covenants, provisions, or conditions of sections XX to YY, inclusive, of the Indenture dated July 21, 20X0, with ABC Bank, insofar as they relate to accounting matters. However, our audit was not directed primarily toward obtaining knowledge of such noncompliance. Accordingly, had we performed additional procedures, other matters may have come to our attention regarding the Company's noncompliance with the above-referenced terms, covenants, provisions, or conditions of the Indenture, insofar as they relate to accounting matters.

This report is intended solely for the information and use of the board of directors and management of XYZ Company and ABC Bank and is not intended to be and should not be used by anyone other than these specified parties.

(Auditor's signature)

(Auditor's city and state)

(Date of the auditor's report)

Separate Report on Compliance (with Noncompliance Identified)

> **Independent Auditor's Report**
>
> (Appropriate Addressee)
>
> We have audited, in accordance with auditing standards generally accepted in the United States of America, the financial statements of XYZ Company, which comprise the balance sheet as of December 31, 20X2, and the related statements of income, changes in stockholders' equity, and cash flows for the year then ended, and the related notes to the financial statements, and have issued our report thereon dated March 5, 20X3.
>
> In connection with our audit, we noted that XYZ Company failed to comply with the "Working Capital" provision of section XX of the Loan Agreement dated March 1, 20X2, with ABC Bank. Our audit was not directed primarily toward obtaining knowledge as to whether XYZ Company failed to comply with the terms, covenants, provisions, or conditions of sections XX to YY, inclusive, of the Loan Agreement, insofar as they relate to accounting matters. Accordingly, had we performed additional procedures, other matters may have come to our attention regarding noncompliance with the above-referenced terms, covenants, provisions, or conditions of the Loan Agreement, insofar as they relate to accounting matters.
>
> This report is intended solely for the information and use of the board of directors and management of XYZ Company and ABC Bank and is not intended to be and should not be used by anyone other than these specified parties.
>
> (Auditor's signature)
>
> (Auditor's city and state)
>
> (Date of the auditor's report)

Combined Report on Audited Financial Statements and Compliance Issues

Independent Auditor's Report

(Appropriate Addressee)

We have audited the accompanying financial statements of ABC Company, which comprise the balance sheet as of December 31, 20X1, and the related statements of income, changes in stockholders' equity, and cash flows for the year then ended, and the related notes to the financial statements.

Management's Responsibility for the Financial Statements

Management is responsible for the preparation and fair presentation of these financial statements in accordance with accounting principles generally accepted in the United States of America; this includes the design, implementation, and maintenance of internal control relevant to the preparation and fair presentation of financial statements that are free from material misstatement, whether due to fraud or error.

Auditor's Responsibility

Our responsibility is to express an opinion on these financial statements based on our audit. We conducted our audit in accordance with auditing standards generally accepted in the United States of America. Those standards require that we plan and perform the audit to obtain reasonable assurance about whether the financial statements are free from material misstatement.

An audit involves performing procedures to obtain audit evidence about the amounts and disclosures in the financial statements. The procedures selected depend on the auditor's judgment, including the assessment of the risks of material misstatement of the financial statements, whether due to fraud or error. In making those risk assessments, the auditor considers internal control relevant to the entity's preparation and fair presentation of the financial statements in order to design audit procedures that are appropriate in the circumstances, but not for the purpose of expressing an opinion on the effectiveness of the entity's internal control. Accordingly, we express no such opinion. An audit also includes evaluating the appropriateness of accounting policies used and the reasonableness of significant accounting estimates made by management, as well as evaluating the overall presentation of the financial statements.

We believe that the audit evidence we have obtained is sufficient and appropriate to provide a basis for our audit opinion.

Opinion

In our opinion, the financial statements referred to above present fairly, in all material respects, the financial position of ABC Company as of December 31, 20X1, and the results of its operations and its cash flows for the year then ended in accordance with accounting principles generally accepted in the United States of America.

Other Matter

In connection with our audit, nothing came to our attention that caused us to believe that ABC Company failed to comply with the terms, covenants, provisions, or conditions of sections XX to YY, inclusive, of the Indenture dated July 21, 20X0 with XYZ Bank, insofar as they relate to accounting matters. However, our audit was not directed primarily toward obtaining knowledge of such noncompliance. Accordingly, had we performed additional procedures, other matters may have come to our attention regarding the Company's noncompliance with the above-referenced terms, covenants, provisions, or conditions of the Indenture, insofar as they relate to accounting matters.

Restricted Use Relating to the Other Matter

The communication related to compliance with the aforementioned Indenture described in the Other Matter paragraph is intended solely for the information and use of the boards of directors and management of ABC Company and XYZ Bank and is not intended to be and should not be used by anyone other than these specified parties.

(Auditor's signature)

(Auditor's city and state)

(Date of the auditor's report)

Other Professional Services

PCAOB on Reporting on Internal Control in an Integrated Audit

In October 2015, the Statement on Auditing Standards (SAS) No. 130, *An Audit of Internal Control Over Financial Reporting That Is Integrated With an Audit of Financial Statements,* was issued. SAS 130 is effective for integrated audits for periods ending on or after December 15, 2016, at which point it replaced Statement on Standards for Attestation Engagements (SSAE) No. 15, *An Examination of an Entity's Internal Control Over Financial Reporting That Is Integrated With an Audit of Its Financial Statements.* SAS 130 is eligible for testing on or after January 1, 2017.

After studying this lesson, you should be able to:

1. Understand the auditor's responsibilities when reporting on internal control over financial reporting in an integrated audit of an issuer's financial statements in accordance with PCAOB Auditing Standards.

2. Familiarize yourself with the structure of the report on internal control over financial reporting for such an engagement, whether the report is issued separately or combined with the audit report on the entity's financial statements.

I. **"An Audit of Internal Control Over Financial Reporting That Is Integrated with an Audit of Financial Statements"**

II. **Applicability of Standard**—When engaged to "perform an audit of management's assessment of the effectiveness of internal control over financial reporting" (ICFR), the objective of such an engagement is to express an opinion on the effectiveness of ICFR.

III. **Some Important Definitions**

    A. **Control Deficiency**—When the design or operation of a control does not allow management or employees, in the normal course of performing their assigned functions, to prevent or detect misstatements on a timely basis.

        1. **Deficiency in design**—When a control necessary to meet the control objective is missing or when an existing control is not properly designed so that, even if the control operates as designed, the control objective is not always met.

        2. **Deficiency in operation**—When a properly designed control does not operate as designed or when the person performing the control does not possess the necessary authority or qualifications to perform the control effectively.

    B. **Material Weakness**—A deficiency, or a combination of deficiencies, in ICFR such that there is a reasonable possibility that a material misstatement of the company's annual or interim financial statements will not be prevented or detected on a timely basis. (If one or more material weaknesses exist, the company's ICFR is not considered to be effective.)

    C. **Significant Deficiency**—A deficiency, or a combination of deficiencies, in ICFR that is less severe than a material weakness, yet important enough to merit attention by those responsible for oversight of the company's financial reporting.

IV. **Planning the Audit**—The audit of ICFR should be integrated with the audit of the financial statements (i.e., the tests of controls should be designed to address both the objectives of the audit of ICFR and the audit of the financial statements).

A. Role of Risk Assessment—"Risk assessment underlies the entire audit process described by this standard, including the determination of significant accounts and disclosures and relevant assertions, the selection of controls to test, and the determination of the evidence necessary for a given control."

   1. There is a direct relationship between the risk of material weakness and the amount of audit attention that is needed.

   2. **Materiality**—Should use the same materiality considerations in planning the audit of ICFR as for the audit of the company's annual financial statements.

B. Using the Work of Others—The auditor may use the work of others to reduce the work the auditor might otherwise have to perform.

   1. Includes internal auditors, other company personnel, service auditors (when a service organization is involved), and third parties working under the direction of management or the audit committee; the auditor should assess the competence and objectivity of those whose work the auditor plans to use.

   2. As the risk associated with a control increases, the auditor should take increasing responsibility for performing the work instead of using the work of others.

V. Using a Top-Down Approach—Begins at the financial statement level and with the auditor's understanding of the overall risks to ICFR; the auditor then focuses on *entity-level* controls and works down to significant accounts and disclosures and their relevant assertions.

A. Identifying Entity-Level Controls—The auditor must test those entity-level controls that are important to the conclusion about the effectiveness of ICFR.

   1. **Entity-level controls**—Include controls related to the control environment, controls over management override, the company's risk assessment process, controls to monitor results of operations or other controls, controls over the period-end financial reporting process; and policies that address significant business control and risk management practices.

   2. **Control environment**—Because of its importance to ICFR, the auditor must evaluate the control environment at the company.

   3. **Period-end financial reporting process**—Because of its importance to ICFR, the auditor must evaluate the period-end financial reporting process.

B. Identifying Significant Accounts and Disclosures and their Relevant Assertions

   1. **Relevant assertions**—Those financial statement assertions that have a reasonable possibility of containing a material misstatement. (PCAOB auditing standards specifically refer to the following asertions (1) existence or occurrence; (2) completeness; (3) valuation or allocation; (4) rights and obligations; and (5) presentation and disclosure.)

   2. **Risk factors**—The auditor should consider risk factors relevant to the identification of significant accounts and disclosures and their relevant assertions, including the nature of the account or disclosure; size and composition of the account; susceptibility to misstatement, volume of activity and complexity of transactions; and changes from the prior period, among others.

C. Understanding Likely Sources of Misstatement

   1. **The auditor should achieve these control objectives**—(a) Understand the flow of transactions related to the relevant assertions; (b) verify that the auditor has identified the points within the company's processes at which a material misstatement could arise; (c) identify the controls that management has implemented to address these potential misstatements; and (d) identify the controls that management has implemented over the company's assets that could materially misstate the financial statements.

   2. **Performing walkthroughs**—Following a transaction from origination through the company's processes until reflected in the financial records is frequently the most effective way to achieve the objectives above. (Procedures usually include inquiry, observation, inspection of relevant documentation, and re-performance of controls.)

    D. **Selecting Controls to Test**—The auditor should test those controls that are important to the conclusion about whether the company's controls sufficiently address the assessed risk of misstatement to each relevant assertion.

VI. Testing Controls

    A. **Nature of Tests of Controls** (From least to most persuasive)—Inquiry, observation, inspection of relevant documentation, and re-performance of a control:

        1. **Testing design effectiveness**—Procedures include inquiry of appropriate personnel, observation of the company's operations, and inspection of relevant documentation (may be addressed by appropriate walkthroughs).

        2. **Testing operating effectiveness**—Procedures include inquiry of appropriate personnel, observation of the company's operations, inspection of relevant documentation, and re-performance of the control.

    B. **Timing of Tests of Controls**—Testing controls over a greater period of time provides more evidence than testing over a shorter period of time; testing closer to the date of management's assessment provides more evidence than testing performed earlier in the year.

    C. **Extent of Tests of Controls**—The more extensively a control is tested, the greater the evidence to evaluate the effectiveness of the control.

    D. **Roll-Forward Procedures**—When operating effectiveness has been tested at an interim date, the auditor should consider what additional testing for the remaining period may be necessary.

VII. Evaluating Identified Deficiencies

    A. **Basic Responsibility**—The auditor must evaluate identified control deficiencies to determine whether, individually or in combination, they constitute material weaknesses as of the date of management's assessment (based on whether there is a "reasonable possibility" that the controls will fail to prevent or detect a material misstatement, not whether a misstatement has actually occurred).

    B. **Indicators of Material Weaknesses**—Examples include (1) identification of fraud involving senior management (whether or not material); (2) restatement of previously issued financial statements; (3) identification by the auditor of a material misstatement of the financial statements in the current period; and (4) ineffective oversight of the company's external financial reporting and internal control by the company's audit committee.

    C. **Communicating Identified Deficiencies**

        1. The auditor must communicate (in writing) all **material weaknesses** identified to **management and the audit committee**.

        2. The auditor must also communicate (in writing) other **significant deficiencies** identified to the **audit committee**.

        3. The auditor should communicate (in writing) all other identified deficiencies in ICFR to **management** and inform the audit committee that such a communication has been made.

        4. If the auditor concludes that the audit committee's oversight of financial reporting and ICFR is ineffective, he or she must communicate that conclusion in writing to the board of directors.

VIII. Reporting on Internal Control over Financial Reporting

    A. **Separate or Combined Reports**—The auditor may choose to issue a combined report on the financial statements and on ICFR or separate reports.

    B. Title of report should include the word "independent" (e.g., "Report of Independent Registered Public Accounting Firm").

    C. **Combined Report**—An unqualified report on the financial statements and on ICFR consists of five paragraphs: (1) introduction; (2) scope; (3) definition; (4) inherent limitations; and (5) opinion.

    D. **Separate Reports**—The auditor should add an additional paragraph to the audit report on the financial statements that references the report on ICFR; and the auditor should add an additional paragraph to the report on ICFR that references the audit report on the financial statements.

E. **Report Date**—If separate reports are issued, they should be dated the same (the date as of which the auditor has obtained sufficient competent evidence).

F. **If One (or More) Material Weakness Exists**—The auditor must express an adverse opinion (unless there is a scope limitation).

    1. **When expressing an adverse opinion**—The auditor's report must include the definition of a material weakness and refer to management's assessment of the material weakness. (If not included in management's assessment, the auditor's report should state that fact.)

    2. Should determine the effect the adverse opinion on ICFR has on the opinion on the entity's financial statements.

G. **If There is a Scope Limitation**—The auditor should disclaim an opinion or withdraw from the engagement.

Sample Report on the Effectiveness of Internal Control Over Financial Reporting

Report of Independent Registered Public Accounting Firm

Separate Audit Report on ICFR

(Introductory paragraph)

We have audited ABC Company's internal control over financial reporting as of December 31, 20X2, based on (*Identify control criteria, e.g., "criteria established in Internal Control—Integrated Framework issued by the Committee of Sponsoring Organizations of the Treadway Commission (COSO)"*). ABC Company's management is responsible for maintaining effective internal control over financial reporting and for its assessment of the effectiveness of internal control over financial reporting, included in the accompanying (*title of management's report*). Our responsibility is to express an opinion on the company's internal control over financial reporting based on our audit.

(Scope paragraph)

We conducted our audit in accordance with the standards of the Public Company Accounting Oversight Board (United States). Those standards require that we plan and perform the audit to obtain reasonable assurance about whether effective internal control over financial reporting was maintained in all material respects. Our audit of internal control over financial reporting included obtaining an understanding of internal control over financial reporting, assessing the risk that a material weakness exists, and testing and evaluating the design and operating effectiveness of internal control based on the assessed risk. Our audit also included performing such other procedures as we considered necessary in the circumstances. We believe that our audit provides a reasonable basis for our opinion.

(Definition paragraph)

A company's internal control over financial reporting is a process designed to provide reasonable assurance regarding the reliability of financial reporting and the preparation of financial statements for external purposes in accordance with generally accepted accounting principles. A company's internal control over financial reporting includes those policies and procedures that (1) pertain to the maintenance of records that, in reasonable detail, accurately and fairly reflect the transactions and dispositions of the assets of the company; (2) provide reasonable assurance that transactions are recorded as necessary to permit preparation of financial statements in accordance with generally accepted accounting principles, and that receipts and expenditures of the company are being made only in accordance with authorizations of management and directors of the company; and (3) provide reasonable assurance regarding prevention or timely detection of unauthorized acquisition, use, or disposition of the company's assets that could have a material effect on the financial statements.

(Inherent limitations paragraph)

Because of its inherent limitations, internal control over financial reporting may not prevent or detect misstatements. Also, projections of any evaluation of effectiveness to future periods are subject to the risk that controls may become inadequate because of changes in conditions, or that the degree of compliance with the policies or procedures may deteriorate.

(Opinion paragraph)

In our opinion, ABC Company maintained, in all material respects, effective internal control over financial reporting as of December 31, 20X2, based on (*identify control criteria, e.g., "criteria established in Internal Control—Integrated Framework issued by the Committee of Sponsoring Organizations of the Treadway Commission (COSO)"*).

(Explanatory paragraph)

We have also audited, in accordance with the standards of the Public Company Accounting Oversight Board (United States), the (*identify financial statements*) of ABC Company and our report dated (*date of report, which should be the same as the date of the report on the effectiveness of internal control over financial reporting*) expressed (*include nature of opinion*).

(Signature)

(City and State or Country)

(Date)

Sample Combined Audit Report on Financial Statements and on the Effectiveness of Internal Control Over Financial Reporting

Report of Independent Registered Public Accounting Firm

(Introductory paragraph)

We have audited the accompanying balance sheets of ABC Company as of December 31, 20X2 and 20X1, and the related statements of income, stockholders' equity and comprehensive income, and cash flows for each of the years in the three-year period ended December 31, 20X2. We have also audited ABC Company's internal control over financial reporting as of December 31, 20X2, based on (*Identify control criteria, e.g., "criteria established in Internal Control—Integrated Framework issued by the Committee of Sponsoring Organizations of the Treadway Commission (COSO)"*). ABC Company's management is responsible for these financial statements, for maintaining effective internal control over financial reporting, and for its assessment of the effectiveness of internal control over financial reporting, included in the accompanying (*title of management's report*). Our responsibility is to express an opinion on these financial statements and an opinion on the company's internal control over financial reporting based on our audits.

(Scope paragraph)

We conducted our audits in accordance with the standards of the Public Company Accounting Oversight Board (United States). Those standards require that we plan and perform the audits to obtain reasonable assurance about whether the financial statements are free of material misstatement and whether effective internal control over financial reporting was maintained in all material respects. Our audits of the financial statements included examining, on a test basis, evidence supporting the amounts and disclosures in the financial statements, assessing the accounting principles used and significant estimates made by management, and evaluating the overall financial statement presentation. Our audit of internal control over financial reporting included obtaining an understanding of internal control over financial reporting, assessing the risk that a material weakness exists, and testing and evaluating the design and operating effectiveness of internal control based on the assessed risk. Our audits also included performing such other procedures as we considered necessary in the circumstances. We believe that our audits provide a reasonable basis for our opinions.

(Definition paragraph)

A company's internal control over financial reporting is a process designed to provide reasonable assurance regarding the reliability of financial reporting and the preparation of financial statements for external purposes in accordance with generally accepted accounting principles. A company's internal control over financial reporting includes those policies and procedures that (1) pertain to the maintenance of records that, in reasonable detail, accurately and fairly reflect the transactions and dispositions of the assets of the company; (2) provide reasonable assurance that transactions are recorded as necessary to permit preparation of financial statements in accordance with generally accepted accounting principles, and that receipts and expenditures of the company are being made only in accordance with authorizations of management and directors of the company; and (3) provide reasonable assurance regarding prevention or timely detection of unauthorized acquisition, use, or disposition of the company's assets that could have a material effect on the financial statements.

(Inherent limitations paragraph)

Because of its inherent limitations, internal control over financial reporting may not prevent or detect misstatements. Also, projections of any evaluation of effectiveness to future periods are subject to the risk that controls may become inadequate because of changes in conditions, or that the degree of compliance with the policies or procedures may deteriorate.

(Opinion paragraph)

In our opinion, the financial statements referred to above present fairly, in all material respects, the financial position of ABC Company as of December 31, 20X2 and 20X1, and the results of its operations and its cash flows for each of the years in the three-year period ended December 31, 20X2 in conformity with accounting principles generally accepted in the United States of America. Also in our opinion, ABC Company maintained, in all material respects, effective internal control over financial reporting as of December 31, 20X2, based on (*identify control criteria, for example, "criteria established in Internal Control—Integrated Framework issued by the Committee of Sponsoring Organizations of the Treadway Commission (COSO)"*).

(Signature)

(City and State or Country)

(Date)

PCAOB on Reporting Whether a Previously Reported Material Weakness Continues to Exist

After studying this lesson, you should be able to:

1. Know the PCAOB requirements, in general, when an auditor is engaged to report on whether a previously reported material weakness in internal control over financial reporting continues to exist under Auditing Standard No. 4.

2. Know management's specific responsibilities before an auditor can report on whether a previously reported material weakness in internal control over financial reporting continues to exist.

3. Understand the auditor's specific responsibilities when reporting on whether a previously reported material weakness in internal control over financial reporting continues to exist.

I. **"Reporting on Whether a Previously Reported Material Weakness Continues to Exist"**

II. **Applicability**—When engaged to report on whether a previously reported material weakness in internal control over financial reporting continues to exist as of a date specified by management. (The date specified by management must be a date after that of management's most recent annual assessment.) PCAOB standards do not require reporting on whether a previously reported material weakness continues to exist, so such an engagement is voluntary.

III. **The Auditor's Objective**—In an engagement to report on whether a previously reported material weakness continues to exist to express an opinion about the existence of a specifically identified material weakness as of a specified date (does not relate to the overall effectiveness of internal control over financial reporting); may report on more than one material weakness as part of the same engagement.

IV. **Conditions for Engagement Performance**—Cannot report on whether a previously reported material weakness continues to exist unless all of the following are met:

   A. Management accepts responsibility for the effectiveness of internal control over financial reporting.

   B. Management evaluates the effectiveness of the specific control(s) that it believes addresses the material weakness using the same control criteria that management used for its most recent annual assessment of internal control over financial reporting and management's stated control objective(s).

   C. Management asserts that the specific control(s) identified is (are) effective in achieving the stated control objective.

   D. Management supports its assertion with sufficient evidence, including documentation.

   E. Management presents a written report that will accompany the auditor's report that contains all the elements required by the PCAOB:

   1. Statement of management's responsibility for establishing and maintaining effective internal control over financial reporting;

   2. Statement identifying the control criteria used by management to conduct the required annual assessment of internal control;

   3. Identification of the material weakness that was identified as part of management's annual assessment (or by the auditor's report on it);

   4. Identification of the control objective(s) addressed by the specified controls and a statement that the specified controls achieve the stated control objective(s) as of a specified date; *and*

   5. Statement that the identified material weakness no longer exists as of the specified date because the specified controls address the material weakness.

V. Performing the Engagement

A. An individual material weakness may be associated with a single stated control objective (or more than one)—A *stated control objective* is the specific control objective identified by management that, if achieved, would result in the material weakness no longer existing.

B. Auditor uses materiality at the financial-statement level, rather than at the individual account-balance level, in evaluating whether a material weakness exists.

C. Obtaining an Understanding of Internal Control over Financial Reporting

    1. The extensiveness of the required understanding of internal control increases with the pervasiveness of the effects of the material weakness.

    2. Must perform a walkthrough for all major classes of transactions that are directly affected by controls specifically identified by management as addressing the material weakness—An auditor who has reported on internal control in accordance with PCAOB auditing standards for the most recent annual assessment is not required to perform a walkthrough for this engagement.

    3. Successor auditors may determine that they are unable to obtain a sufficient basis for reporting on whether a previously reported material weakness continues to exist without performing a complete audit of internal control over financial reporting in accordance with PCAOB auditing standards.

D. Testing and Evaluating Whether a Material Weakness Continues to Exist

    1. If management has not supported its assertion with sufficient evidence (a required condition) the auditor cannot complete this engagement.

    2. Auditor should evaluate the appropriateness of management's chosen date—for example, controls that operate daily and continuously can be as of almost any date of management's choosing; controls that operate over the company's period-end reporting process can usually only be tested in connection with a period-end.

    3. Auditor should obtain evidence about the effectiveness of all controls specifically identified in management's assertion (all controls that are necessary to achieve the stated control objective should be specifically identified and evaluated)—Determine whether the specified control operated as designed and whether the person performing the control possesses the authority and qualifications to perform the control effectively.

E. Using the Work of Others—The auditor may consider the work of others in deciding the nature, timing, or extent of the work that should be performed. (The auditor should perform any walkthroughs, however, because of the judgment involved.)

F. Obtain Written Representations from Management—About various matters (ranging from management's responsibility for establishing and maintaining internal control, management's evaluation of the effectiveness of the specified controls, describing any fraud issues, and stating whether there were material subsequent events, among other matters).

VI. Auditor's Report—On whether a previously reported material weakness continues to exist may only issue an **unqualified opinion** or a **disclaimer of opinion** (cannot issue a qualified opinion—any limitation on the scope precludes an expression of opinion).

A. See the sample below for a *continuing auditor* who has previously reported on the company's internal control over financial reporting in accordance with PCAOB auditing standards as of the company's most recent year-end.

B. Report Modifications—For any of the following conditions:

    1. Other material weaknesses that were reported previously by the company as part of the company's annual assessment of internal control are not addressed by the auditor's opinion.

    2. A significant subsequent event has occurred since the date reported on.

    3. Management's report contains additional information—express a disclaimer of opinion on the additional information.

Sample Auditor's Report for a Continuing Auditor Expressing an Opinion That a Previously Reported Material Weakness No Longer Exists

Report of Independent Registered Public Accounting Firm

We have previously audited and reported on management's annual assessment of XYZ Company's internal control over financial reporting as of December 31, 200X based on (identify control criteria, e.g., *"criteria established in Internal Control—Integrated Framework issued by the Committee of Sponsoring Organizations of the Treadway Commission (COSO)."*) Our report, dated (*date of report*), identified the following material weakness in the Company's internal control over financial reporting:

(Describe material weakness)

We have audited management's assertion, included in the accompanying (*title of management's report*), that the material weakness in internal control over financial reporting identified above no longer exists as of (*date of management's assertion*) because the following control(s) addresses the material weakness:

(Describe control(s))

Management has asserted that the control(s) identified above achieves the following stated control objective, which is consistent with the criteria established in (*identify control criteria used for management's annual assessment of internal control over financial reporting*): (*state control objective addressed*). Management also has asserted that it has tested the control(s) identified above and concluded that the control(s) was designed and operated effectively as of (*date of management's assertion*). XYZ Company's management is responsible for its assertion. Our responsibility is to express an opinion on whether the identified material weakness continues to exist as of (*date of management's assertion*) based on our auditing procedures.

Our engagement was conducted in accordance with the standards of the Public Company Accounting Oversight Board (United States). Those standards require that we plan and perform the engagement to obtain reasonable assurance about whether a previously reported material weakness continues to exist at the company. Our engagement included examining evidence supporting management's assertion and performing such other procedures as we considered necessary in the circumstances. We obtained an understanding of the company's internal control over financial reporting as part of our previous audit of management's annual assessment of XYZ Company's internal control over financial reporting as of December 31, 200X and updated that understanding as it specifically relates to changes in internal control over financial reporting associated with the material weakness described above. We believe that our auditing procedures provide a reasonable basis for our opinion.

In our opinion, the material weakness described above no longer exists as of (*date of management's assertion*).

We were not engaged to and did not conduct an audit of internal control over financial reporting as of (*date of management's assertion*), the objective of which would be the expression of an opinion on the effectiveness of internal control over financial reporting. Accordingly, we do not express such an opinion. This means that we have not applied auditing procedures sufficient to reach conclusions about the effectiveness of any controls of the company as of any date after December 31, 200X, other than the control(s) specifically identified in this report. Accordingly, we do not express an opinion that any other controls operated effectively after December 31, 200X.

Because of its inherent limitations, internal control over financial reporting may not prevent or detect misstatements. Also, projections of any evaluation of the effectiveness of specific controls or internal control over financial reporting overall to future periods are subject to the risk that controls may become inadequate because of changes in conditions or that the degree of compliance with the policies or procedures may deteriorate.

(Signature)

(City and State/or Country)

(Date)

Auditing Employee Benefit Plans

After studying this lesson, you should be able to:

1. Identify the two types of employee benefit plans that are associated with the Employee Retirement Income Security Act of 1974 (known as ERISA).

2. Identify the basic types of welfare plans and pension plans under ERISA.

3. Know when employee benefit plans are generally required to be audited under ERISA.

4. Know the circumstances that might permit a "limited-scope" (instead of a "full-scope") audit engagement for an employee benefit plan.

5. Know the structure of the auditor's report for a "limited-scope" audit engagement of a pension plan.

Employee benefit plans are a unique, technical subject matter for which extensive professional guidance is available, including the AICPA's Audit and Accounting Guide, Employee Benefit Plans, which exceeds 800 pages. The purpose of this lesson is to introduce the fundamental issues associated with auditing employee benefit plans.

The Employee Retirement Income Security Act of 1974 (ERISA) applies to most employee benefit plans. ERISA is comprised of four sections: Title I deals with the Department of Labor (DOL) responsibilities, including reporting and disclosure (and auditing) requirements; Title II specifies the tax law requirements; Title III identifies specific enforcement-related matters; and Title IV addresses multiemployer plan issues, including plan termination procedures. Additional resources are provided on the website of the Employee Benefits Security Administration (EBSA).

I. Basic Issues Related to Employee Benefit Plans Under ERISA

A. There are two fundamental types of employee benefit plans under ERISA:

1. **Welfare plans**—These provide benefits such as healthcare, disability, death, unemployment, job training, and vacation.

2. **Pension plans**—These provide benefits involving retirement income or deferral of income beyond an employee's period of employment.

B. **Eligibility Requirements**—The plan must specify the eligibility requirements.

1. ERISA specifies minimum eligibility requirements for pension plans. The minimum age to be eligible to enter the plan cannot be set above age 21, and the minimum employment to enter the plan is generally 12 months (2 years if the plan is fully vested); generally, an employee has to work at least 1000 hours for the year to count toward eligibility.

2. ERISA does not provide specific eligibility requirements for welfare plans.

C. **Nondiscrimination Requirements**—ERISA requirements promote the participation of a broad set of employees in an employee benefit plan; for example, the plan features dealing with contributions and vesting applicable to highly compensated employees usually must be the same for other participants.

D. **Vesting Requirements**—ERISA establishes specific minimum vesting standards for pension plans; pension plans may vest more quickly than these requirements, but they cannot vest less quickly. [Note: Benefits are "vested" when the employee has earned the rights to those benefits without any further performance requirements or conditions.]

E. **Funding Requirements**—"Qualified" pension plans (those having tax-exempt status) are subject to specific funding requirements; welfare plans are not required to be funded, although plan documents typically do address funding issues.

F. **Exemptions from ERISA**—ERISA provides certain specific exemptions from some or all of ERISA, but the auditor is not responsible for determining whether a plan is subject to ERISA requirements or whether the plan must be audited (although the auditor may, of course, assist in determining those matters); the plan sponsor's legal counsel should be involved in those determinations.

G. **GAAP classifies employee benefit plans into either of two categories:**

1. **Defined benefit plans**—The actual benefits are specified in the plan design; the plan's obligations are based on the determination of an actuary.

2. **Defined contribution plans**—The benefits are limited by the specified contributions to each participant's specific account.

3. ERISA requires that pension plans be funded whether they are viewed as defined benefit or defined contribution plans.

II. **Welfare Plans—Basic Terminology**

A. Welfare plans may be classified as defined benefit or defined contribution plans.

1. **Defined benefit plans**—These are common (e.g., a specific commitment to provide healthcare coverage) and usually do not create separate accounts for each participant.

2. **Defined contribution plans**—Individual accounts are maintained separately for each participant, and benefits are limited to the balance in the individual's account; an example that has grown in popularity is medical flexible spending accounts.

B. **Unfunded versus Funded Plans**

1. **Unfunded plans**—The benefits are either paid from the employer's assets or by insurance coverage (or a combination of those); ERISA exempts unfunded plans, which exempts most welfare plans. (The auditor is not responsible for determining whether the plan is "unfunded" or "funded"; the plan sponsor's legal counsel should be involved in determining that.)

2. **Funded plans**—If any portion of an ERISA benefit plan is deemed "funded," then all of the plan's activities are subject to the ERISA audit requirements; in this case, the plan assets are required to be held in trust.

III. **Pension Plans—Basic Terminology**

A. **Defined Contribution Plans**

1. **401(k) plans**—These permit employees to defer a portion of their income to the pension plan; taxes are deferred until a distribution is made at a future date.

   a. The employer may make a matching contribution, although employer contributions generally are not required.

   b. Roth 401(k) contributions—Subject to specific tax requirements, contributions are made with after-tax dollars so that neither the original contribution nor the investment earnings will be subject to taxes when distributed.

2. **403(b) plans**—Similar to 401(k) plans, these are associated with charitable organizations and public school entities; there are numerous technical requirements, including a "universal availability" requirement that nearly all employees are entitled to participate in the plan; also, plan assets may be held in a custodial account and need not be held in trust.

3. **Employee stock ownership plans**—ESOPs are stock incentive plans primarily invested in the employer's securities; these plans are subject to many complex technical issues that require auditors to study the underlying plan document in detail.

B. **Defined Benefit Plans**

1. **Traditional plans**—The benefits are based on the plan's benefit formula, and the accounting considerations are based on various actuarial concepts.

2. **Cash balance plans**—In such plans, participants may choose to take lump-sum cash distributions or to take distributions as annuities.

IV. **General Audit Considerations**

A. **ERISA Audit Requirements**—ERISA requires an annual audit by an "independent qualified public accountant" of the financial statements of employee benefit plans (i.e., those that are not exempt from such a requirement).

1. **Pension plans**—An audit normally is required for a pension plan covered by ERISA having at least 100 participants at the start of the plan year (considered a "large" plan); the number of "participants" is based on those eligible to participate regardless of the number actually participating.

2. **Welfare plans**—An audit is normally required for a welfare plan covered by ERISA having the following characteristics: (a) it is a "large" plan having at least 100 participants at the start of the plan year (based on those who have actually elected to participate), and (b) the plan is "funded" (meaning that assets are held in trust or an account is established in the plan's name).

3. **Additional exemptions**—There is a general exemption for pension plans of any number of participants when (1) the benefits are provided by an insurance contract for each participant, and (2) those insurance contracts are funded by premiums paid from the employer's general assets (perhaps paid in part by participants' contributions); there is a similar general exemption for welfare plans of any number of participants.

> **Note**
> Determining whether an audit is required for an employee benefit plan requires careful study of the underlying plan documents. The plan administrator may need to consult with an attorney knowledgeable about ERISA in making that determination.

B. **DOL Form 5500**—The DOL requires plan financial statements to be filed on Form 5500, *Annual Return/Report of Employee Benefit Plan*; the financial statements may be based on GAAP, the cash basis, or the modified cash basis of accounting; the DOL also requires the auditor to express an opinion on whether the financial statements and supplemental schedules comply with applicable DOL requirements.

C. **GAAS**—Audits of employee benefit plans should be conducted according to generally accepted auditing standards; the audit takes into consideration relevant compliance issues, but the audit is not designed to ensure compliance with applicable laws (such compliance is the responsibility of the plan administrator, not the auditor).

D. **Inquiries about the Plan's Tax Status**—The auditor should inquire of management (and obtain appropriate written representations) as to whether the plan complies with applicable laws and regulations affecting the plan's qualified tax status; the auditor should also read any correspondence with the IRS.

E. **Audit Areas in a "Full-Scope Audit" (the Alternative to a "Limited-Scope Audit")**—The auditor should address these eight areas: (1) plan investments and investment income, (2) employee and employer contributions, (3) payments of benefits, (4) participant demographic and payroll data, (5) loans to participants, (6) the allocation of investment income to individual participants, (7) liabilities and plan obligations, and (8) administrative expenses.

V. Limited-Scope Audit Engagements

A. DOL regulations allow the plan administrator to elect a "limited-scope audit engagement" involving specific assets that are held by a qualified, regulated financial institution (e.g., an insurance company, a bank, or a trust company that is subject to periodic state or federal examination); this election does not apply to assets held by a broker/dealer or an investment company.

B. **Required certification**—The qualified financial institution holding these plan assets must furnish a certification that the investments and related investment activity are "complete and accurate"; without an acceptable certification, a full-scope audit is required (a mere confirmation is not a substitute for such certification).

C. The plan administrator may then direct the auditor not to perform any audit procedures on the investment assets or activities that are the object of the qualified financial institution's certification; these investments normally represent the preponderance of the plan's assets.

D. Auditor Responsibilities Regarding the Certification—The auditor should (1) read the qualified financial institution's certification, (2) agree the certified information with that reported in the plan's financial statements, and (3) verify that the financial statement disclosures regarding the certified information are in accordance with the requirements of GAAP and in compliance with DOL requirements.

E. Audit Areas in a "Limited-Scope Audit"—The auditor should evaluate the noninvestment activity of the plan, including: (1) employee and employer contributions, (2) payments of benefits, (3) participant demographic and payroll data, (4) loans to participants, (5) the allocation of investment income to individual participants, (6) liabilities and plan obligations, and (7) administrative expenses.

F. Limited-Scope Audit Reports—See the AICPA sample report that follows.

   1. The audit report includes a disclaimer of opinion on the plan's financial statements (due to the scope limitation);

   2. The audit report includes an "Other Matter" paragraph that comments on supplemental schedules that are required by the DOL, along with a disclaimer of opinion on those supplemental schedules.

   3. The audit report includes an opinion that the information complies with applicable DOL rules and regulations.

Sample Standard Limited-Scope Audit Report

Independent Auditor's Report

[Appropriate Addressee]

Report on the Financial Statements

We were engaged to audit the accompanying financial statements of XYZ 401(k) Plan, which comprise the statements of net assets available for benefits as of December 31, 20X2 and 20X1, and the related statement of changes in net assets available for benefits for the year ended December 31, 20X2, and the related notes to the financial statements.

Management's Responsibility for the Financial Statements

Management is responsible for the preparation and fair presentation of these financial statements in accordance with accounting principles generally accepted in the United Statements of America; this includes the design, implementation, and maintenance of internal control relevant to the preparation and fair presentation of financial statements that are free from material misstatement, whether due to fraud or error.

Auditor's Responsibility

Our responsibility is to express an opinion on these financial statements based on conducting the audits in accordance with auditing standards generally accepted in the United States of America. Because of the matter described in the Basis for Disclaimer of Opinion paragraph, however, we were not able to obtain sufficient appropriate audit evidence to provide a basis for an audit opinion.

Basis for Disclaimer of Opinion

As permitted by 29 CFR 2520.103-8 of the Department of Labor's Rules and Regulations for Reporting and Disclosure under the Employee Retirement Income Security Act of 1974, the plan administrator instructed us not to perform, and we did not perform, any auditing procedures with respect to the information summarized in Note X, which was certified by ABC Bank, the trustee *[or custodian]* of the Plan, except for comparing such information with the related information included in the financial statements. We have been informed by the plan administrator that the trustee *[or custodian]* holds the Plan's investment assets and executes investment transactions. The plan administrator has obtained a certification from the trustee *[or custodian]* as of December 31, 20X2 and 20X1, and for the year ended December 31, 20X2, that the information provided to the plan administrator by the trustee *[or custodian]* is complete and accurate.

Disclaimer of Opinion

Because of the significance of the matter described in the Basis for Disclaimer of Opinion paragraph, we have not been able to obtain sufficient appropriate audit evidence to provide a basis for an audit opinion. Accordingly, we do not express an opinion on these financial statements.

Other Matter

The supplemental schedules *[identify schedules]* as of or for the year ended December 31, 20X2, are required by the Department of Labor's (DOL) Rules and Regulations for Reporting and Disclosure under the Employee Retirement Income Security Act of 1974 and are presented for the purpose of additional analysis and are not a required part of the financial statements. Because of the significance of the matter described in the Basis for Disclaimer of Opinion paragraph, we do not express an opinion on these supplemental schedules.

Report on Form and Content in Compliance with DOL Rules and Regulations

The form and content of the information included in the financial statements and supplemental schedules, other than that derived from the information certified by the trustee *[or custodian]*, have been audited by us in accordance with auditing standards generally accepted in the United States of America and, in our opinion, are presented in compliance with the Department of Labor's Rules and Regulations for Reporting and Disclosure under the Employee Retirement Income Security Act of 1974.

[Auditor's signature]

[Auditor's city and state]

[Date of the auditor's report]

Introduction to Attestation Standards

After studying this lesson, you should be able to:

1. State the definition of an "attestation engagement" and the three different kinds of attestation engagements identified in the definition of "attestation engagement."

2. Describe the non-authoritative principles associated with attestation engagements, consisting of (a) purpose and premise; (b) responsibilities; (c) performance; and (d) reporting.

Statements on Standards for Attestation Engagements (SSAEs) are issued by the AICPA's Auditing Standards Board (ASB) and are applicable to the preparation and issuance of attestation reports for nonissuers. In April 2016, the ASB replaced substantially all of the then-existing SSAEs with "clarified" SSAEs, similar to what the Auditing Standards Board previously did with the Statements on Auditing Standards and to what the Accounting and Review Services Committee did with the Statements on Standards for Accounting and Review Services. The main purpose of this project was to make the clarified SSAEs easier to read and understand and, therefore, to improve the application of these standards in practice; a further purpose was to more closely align U.S attestation-related professional standards with international standards.

Accordingly, the ASB adopted clarity drafting conventions, such as the following: (1) specified objectives for each of the clarified sections of the AT-C (i.e., the clarified SSAE sections); (2) included a section on definitions, as applicable, in each AT-C; (3) separated the professional "requirements" from the "application and other explanatory material" parts of each AT-C; and (4) adopted formatting techniques (e.g., using bullet lists) to improve the flow and readability of each AT-C.

The clarified SSARSs were issued as SSAE No. 18, *Attestation Standards: Clarification and Recodification*. It was comprised of the following primary sections:

- AT-C Preface, *Preface to the Attestation Standards*
- AT-C Section 105, *Concepts Common to All Attestation Engagements*
- AT-C Section 205, *Examination Engagements*
- AT-C Section 210, *Review Engagements*
- AT-C Section 215, *Agreed-Upon Procedures Engagements*
- AT-C Section 305, *Prospective Financial Information*
- AT-C Section 310, *Reporting on Pro Forma Financial Information*
- AT-C Section 315, *Compliance Attestation*
- AT-C Section 320, *Reporting on an Examination of Controls at a Service Organization…*
- AT-C Section 395, *Management's Discussion and Analysis*

The previously issued AT Section *701, Management's Discussion and Analysis*, was adopted as is without being issued in clarified format. The ASB concluded that practitioners rarely report on such MD&A presentations, so the existing guidance would be classified as AT-C Section 395 in unclarified format until further notice.

Compliance with the SSAEs is enforceable under the AICPA Code of Professional Conduct, specifically the *Compliance With Standards* rule (ET Sec. 1.310.001).

I. Definition

Definition
Attestation Engagement: "An examination, review, or agreed-upon procedures engagement performed under the attestation standards related to subject matter or an assertion that is the responsibility of another party."

II. Structure of the Attestation Standards

    A. Section 105—This section addresses the concepts that are common to any attestation engagement.

    B. Section 205, 210, and 215—These sections address the additional "level of service" requirements and guidance applicable to examination, review, and agreed-upon procedures engagements, respectively.

    C. 300-Level Sections—These sections address the additional "subject-matter" requirements and guidance associated with certain specific topics.

III. Principles for Understanding Attestation Engagements (Not Authoritative)

    A. Purpose and Premise

        1. Purpose—"The purpose of an attestation engagement is to provide users of information, generally third parties, with an opinion, conclusion, or findings regarding the reliability of subject matter or an assertion about the subject matter, as measured against suitable and available criteria."

        2. Premise—"An engagement in accordance with the attestation standards is conducted on the premise that the responsible party is responsible for:

            a. The subject matter (and, if applicable, the preparation and presentation of the subject matter) in accordance with (or based on) the criteria;

            b. Its assertion about the subject matter;

            c. Measuring, evaluating, and, when applicable, presenting subject matter that is free from material misstatement, whether due to fraud or error; *and*

            d. Providing the practitioner with:

                i. Access to all information of which the responsible party is aware that is relevant to the measurement, evaluation, or disclosure of the subject matter;

                ii. Access to additional information that the practitioner may request from the responsible party for the purpose of the engagement; *and*

                iii. Unrestricted access to persons within the appropriate party(ies) from whom the practitioner determines it is necessary to obtain evidence."

    B. Responsibilities—"Practitioners are responsible for complying with the relevant performance and reporting requirements established in the attestation standards."

    C. Performance

        1. Performance responsibilities—"In all services provided under the attestation standards, practitioners are responsible for

            a. Having the appropriate competence and capabilities to perform the engagement,

            b. Complying with relevant ethical requirements,

            c. Maintaining professional skepticism, *and*

            d. Exercising professional judgment throughout the planning and performance of the engagement."

        2. For an examination engagement—"To express an opinion in an examination, the practitioner obtains reasonable assurance about whether the subject matter, or an assertion about the subject matter, is free from material misstatements, whether due to fraud or error. To obtain reasonable assurance, which is a high but not absolute level of assurance, the practitioner

            a. Plans the work and properly supervises other members of the engagement team.

            b. Identifies and assesses the risks of material misstatement, whether due to fraud or error, based on an understanding of the subject matters, its measurement or evaluation, the criteria, and other engagement circumstances.

    c. Obtains sufficient appropriate evidence about whether material misstatements exist by designing and implementing appropriate responses to the assessed risks. Examination procedures may involve inspection, observation, analysis, inquiry, reperformance, recalculation, or confirmation with outside parties."

3. **For a review engagement**—"To express a conclusion in a review, the practitioner obtains limited assurance about whether any material modification should be made to the subject matter in order for it to be in accordance with (or based on) the criteria or to an assertion about the subject matter in order for it to be fairly stated. In a review, the nature and extent of the procedures are substantially less than in an examination. To obtain limited assurance in a review, the practitioner

    a. Plans the work and properly supervises other members of the engagement team.

    b. Focuses procedures in those areas in which the practitioner believes increased risks of misstatements exist, whether due to fraud or error, based on the practitioner's understanding of the subject matter, its measurement or evaluation, the criteria, and other engagement circumstances.

    c. Obtains review evidence, through the application of inquiry and analytical procedures or other procedures as appropriate, to obtain limited assurance that no material modifications should be made to the subject matter in order for it to be in accordance with (or based on) the criteria."

4. **For an agreed-upon procedures engagement**—"To report on the application of agreed-upon procedures, the practitioner applies procedures determined by the specified parties who are the intended users of the practitioner's report and who are responsible for the sufficiency of the procedures for their purposes. As a result of the engagement, the practitioner reports on the results of the engagement but does not provide an opinion or conclusion on the subject matter or assertion. In an agreed-upon procedures engagement, the practitioner

    a. Plans the work and properly supervises other members of the engagement team.

    b. Applies the procedures agreed to by the specified parties and reports on their results."

D. Reporting—"Based on evidence obtained, the practitioner expresses an opinion in an examination, expresses a conclusion in a review, or reports findings in an agreed-upon procedures engagement."

Attestation Standards—Common Concepts

After studying this lesson, you should be able to:

1. Describe the guidance that is applicable to attest engagements, including Statements on Standards for Attestation Engagements (SSAEs), interpretive publications, and other attestation publications.

2. Identify the two types of professional requirements ("unconditional requirements" and "presumptively mandatory requirements") and the language associated with each.

3. Describe the preconditions that are applicable to any attestation engagement.

I. General Comments

A. Written Assertion—A written assertion as to whether the subject matter is measured or evaluated according to suitable criteria is expected when performing an examination, review, or agreed-upon procedures engagement under the attestation standards.

1. **For an examination or a review engagement**

   a. **When the engaging party is the responsible party and refuses to provide a written assertion**—The practitioner should withdraw from the engagement when that is permitted.

   b. **When the engaging party is not the responsible party and the responsible party refuses to provide a written assertion**—That refusal should be disclosed in the practitioner's report, and the report's use should be restricted to the engaging party.

2. **For an agreed-upon procedures engagement**—When the responsible party refuses to provide a written assertion, that refusal should be disclosed in the practitioner's report.

B. Definitions

> **Definitions**
>
> *Engaging Party*: "The party(ies) that engages the practitioner to perform the attestation engagement."
>
> *Responsible Party*: "The party(ies) responsible for the subject matter. If the nature of the subject matter is such that no such party exists, a party who has a reasonable basis for making a written assertion about the subject matter may be deemed to be the responsible party."

1. The firm has a responsibility to establish and maintain a system of quality control over its attestation practice to provide reasonable assurance that: (a) personnel comply with professional standards and applicable legal and regulatory requirements; and (b) reports issued by the firm are appropriate in the circumstances.

2. Attestation standards apply to individual attestation engagements, whereas quality control standards apply to the firm's attestation practice as a whole.

II. Guidance Applicable to Attestation Engagements

A. Two Categories of Professional Requirements in the SSAEs

1. **Unconditional requirements**—Must be complied with in all relevant circumstances and are indicated by the word "must."

2. **Presumptively mandatory requirements**—Aallow for rare exceptions and are indicated by the word "should." For any such exceptions, the practitioner should perform alternative procedures to meet the requirement's intent.

B. "Application and Other Explanatory Material" (including appendices of SSAEs)—These are not "requirements" and are presented separately within the SSAEs. Indicated by the words "may," "might," or "could," they may explain what a requirement means or provide examples of appropriate procedures.

C. The Role of "Interpretive" and "Other" Publications

1. **Interpretive publications**—The accountant should consider the guidance of applicable interpretive publications in performing the engagement. These are recommendations, not requirements, on the application of SSAEs in particular circumstances after Auditing Standards Board members have had the opportunity to comment on the proposed interpretations.

2. **Other attestation publications**—The accountant may evaluate the relevance and appropriateness of such guidance to the engagement, but other attestation publications have no authoritative status.

III. Preconditions for an Attestation Engagement

A. Three Fundamental Preconditions Applicable to Any Attestation Engagement

1. The practitioner must be independent.

2. The responsible party must take responsibility for the subject matter.

3. The engagement must have the following four characteristics:

   a. The subject matter is appropriate.

> **Note**
>
> Subject matter is "appropriate" if it is (a) capable of consistent measurement or evaluation, and (b) can be subject to procedures to obtain sufficient appropriate evidence to support the opinion, conclusion, or findings, as applicable.
>
> If the subject matter is not appropriate for an examination, it is not appropriate for a review.

   b. The criteria to be used are suitable and available.

> **Note**
>
> Suitable criteria have these characteristics: (a) they are relevant to the subject matter; (b) they are free from bias; (c) they allow reasonably consistent measurements/evaluations; and (d) they do not omit relevant factors.
>
> Criteria established by a body designated by the AICPA are considered to be suitable.
>
> If criteria are "unsuitable" for an examination, they are also unsuitable for a review.
>
> When criteria are available only to specified parties, the use of the practitioner's report is required to be restricted to the specified parties.

   c. The practitioner expects to obtain the necessary evidence related to the opinion, conclusion or findings.

   d. The practitioner's opinion, conclusion, or findings is to be expressed in a written report.

B. If Any of These Preconditions Are Not Met—The practitioner should attempt to resolve the issue(s) with the engaging party. If the engagement has already been accepted, the practitioner should determine whether it is appropriate to continue with the engagement, and (if so) how to communicate the matter in the report.

IV. Other Considerations Common to Any Attestation Engagement

A. Acceptance and Continuance—Appropriate procedures related to acceptance and continuance of attestation engagements should be followed. The practitioner should not accept an attestation engagement unless he or she has reached an understanding with the engaging party as to the terms of the engagement.

B. Acceptance of a Change in the Terms of the Engagement—"Reasonable justification" is required to change the terms of an engagement to a lower level of service.

1. **If there is reasonable justification**—The practitioner's report should not reference the original engagement, any procedures that may have been performed, or scope limitations that caused the engagement to change.

2. A change in the nature of the engagement originally requested may not be considered reasonably justified if that change is motivated by an inability to obtain sufficient appropriate evidence regarding the subject matter.

C. Using the Work of Other Practitioner(s)

1. Obtain an understanding about the other practitioner's independence and competence.

2. Communicate with the other practitioner about the scope and timing of the other practitioner's work. Be involved with the work of the other practitioner when assuming responsibility for that work.

3. Evaluate the adequacy of other practitioner's work for purposes of the engagement.

4. Determine whether to reference the other practitioner in the report.

D. Engagement Documentation

1. **Documentation completion date**—The practitioner should assemble the final engagement file no later than 60 days following the report release date.

   a. **Deletions**—After the documentation completion date, the practitioner should not delete or discard any documentation prior to the end of the retention period.

   b. **Additions**—After the documentation completion date, additions may be made, but the practitioner must document the reasons for the additions as well as when and by whom the additions were made/reviewed.

2. **Retention**—The practitioner should adopt reasonable procedures to retain the documentation for a period sufficient to meet his or her needs and any legal/regulatory requirements.

3. **Confidentiality**—The practitioner should adopt reasonable procedures to protect the confidentiality of the documentation.

4. **Departures from presumptively mandatory requirements**—The practitioner should document the justification for such a departure and how alternative procedures met the intent of that requirement.

E. Engagement Quality Control Review

1. When such a review is required, the engagement partner should discuss with the quality control reviewer the significant findings; the engagement partner should not release the report until the engagement quality control review is completed.

2. The engagement quality control reviewer should evaluate the significant judgments and conclusions reached, including the following:

   a. Discussing significant findings with the engagement partner;

   b. Reading the written subject matter/assertion and proposed report;

   c. Reading selected documentation for significant judgments and conclusions reached; *and*

   d. Considering whether the proposed report is appropriate.

Examination Engagements

After studying this lesson, you should be able to:

1. Understand the practitioner's responsibility to obtain a written assertion for an examination engagement.

2. Understand the practitioner's responsibilities in performing an examination engagement, including obtaining written representations.

I. Definition

Definition

Examination Engagement: "An attestation engagement in which the practitioner obtains reasonable assurance by obtaining sufficient appropriate evidence about the measurement or evaluation of subject matter against criteria in order to be able to draw reasonable conclusions on which to base the practitioner's opinion about whether the subject matter is in accordance with (or based on) the criteria or the assertion is fairly stated, in all material respects."

Note

The guidance for examination engagements is provided in the Clarified SSAEs, specifically by AT-C 205, *Examination Engagements*. In addition, the practitioner is required to comply with AT-C 105 *(Concepts Common to All Attestation Engagements)* as well as any applicable subject-matter sections.

Compliance with these attestation standards is enforceable under the AICPA's Code of Professional Conduct (specifically, the *Compliance With Standards* rule*)*.

II. Agreeing on the Terms of the Engagement

A. The practitioner and the engaging party should agree on the terms of the engagement, which should be documented in an engagement letter (or other suitable form of written agreement).

B. The terms of the engagement should include the following:

1. The objective and scope of the engagement;

2. The responsibilities of the practitioner;

3. The responsibilities of the responsible party and the engaging party, if those are different;

4. A statement that the engagement will be conducted according to AICPA attestation standards;

5. A statement about the inherent limitations of an examination;

6. A statement identifying the criteria for measurement or evaluation of the subject matter; *and*

7. Acknowledgment by the engaging party to provide the practitioner with a representation letter at the conclusion of the engagement.

C. Such an agreement should be obtained for each engagement, but, if the terms of the preceding engagement have not changed, the practitioner may simply remind the engaging party of the terms of the engagement (and document that communication).

III. Request a Written Assertion about the Subject Matter

A. **If the Engaging Party Is the Responsible Party and Refuses to Provide a Written Assertion—** The practitioner should withdraw when that is permitted.

B. **If the Engaging Party Is Not the Responsible Party and the Responsible Party Refuses to Provide a Written Assertion—**The practitioner need not withdraw but should disclose that refusal in the practitioner's report and restrict the use of the report to the engaging party.

C. The responsible party is still responsible for the subject matter as a whole, and the practitioner should request a written assertion covering the entire relevant period(s), even when the responsible party was not present during some (or all) of the period covered by the practitioner's report.

IV. Planning and Performing the Engagement

A. Engagement Planning–Related Matters

1. The practitioner should establish an overall strategy that specifies the scope, timing, and direction of the engagement, including considering factors significant to the engagement team as well as the necessary resources.

2. The practitioner should develop an engagement plan that specifies the nature, timing, and extent of procedures to be performed.

3. The practitioner may need to revise the overall strategy and engagement plan due to unexpected events or changes in conditions.

4. The practitioner should perform risk assessment procedures to identify the risks of material misstatement and to design appropriate procedures in response to that assessment; he or she should also obtain an understanding of internal control over the preparation of the subject matter.

B. Engagement Performance–Related Matters

1. **Tests of control**—The practitioner should perform tests of control about the operating effectiveness of relevant controls when (a) intending to rely on controls for purposes of designing other procedures; (b) procedures other than tests of control cannot provide sufficient appropriate evidence; or (c) the subject matter is internal control.

2. **Procedures other than tests of control**—The practitioner should design and perform tests of details or analytical procedures, unless the subject matter is internal control.

3. **Analytical procedures performed in response to assessed risks**—The practitioner should (a) determine the suitability of specific analytical procedures; (b) evaluate the reliability of the data from which an expectation is developed; (c) develop an expectation that is sufficiently precise to identify material misstatements; and (d) investigate significant differences from the expectation by inquiry or other procedures.

4. **Procedures regarding estimates**—The practitioner should evaluate (a) whether the responsible party has appropriately applied the criteria to any estimates; and (b) whether the methods underlying estimates are appropriate and have been consistently applied (and that any changes in the estimates or methods used are appropriate).

5. **Fraud and noncompliance with laws and regulations**—The practitioner should (a) consider the risk of material misstatement due to fraud or noncompliance with laws or regulations, (b) make inquiries of appropriate parties about such matters, and (c) evaluate whether there are any unusual relationships that might indicate risks of material misstatement due to fraud or noncompliance with laws or regulations.

6. **Communication responsibilities**—The practitioner should communicate to the responsible party (and also to the engaging party, if different) (a) any known or suspected fraud, (b) any known or suspected noncompliance with laws or regulations, (c) uncorrected misstatements, and (d) identified internal control deficiencies.

7. **Using the work of a practitioner's specialist**

   a. When planning to use the work of a practitioner's specialist, the practitioner should (1) evaluate the specialist's competence and objectivity; (2) obtain an understanding of the specialist's expertise; (3) agree with the specialist regarding the scope of the work to be performed, the parties' roles, the need for communication, and the need to meet confidentiality requirements; and (4) evaluate the specialist's work for the practitioner's purposes.

    b. The practitioner's procedures when planning to use the work of a specialist will vary with the circumstances, including the risks of material misstatement and the practitioner's experience working with the specialist.

    c. An agreement between the practitioner and the practitioner's specialist often is obtained in the form of an engagement letter (but it is not technically required).

8. Using the work of internal auditors

    a. When planning to use the work of the internal audit function (either in obtaining evidence or in providing direct assistance), the practitioner should evaluate the **competence** and **objectivity** of the internal audit function;

    b. When planning to use the work of the internal audit function in obtaining evidence, the practitioner should also evaluate whether the work was subject to a **systematic and disciplined approach**.

    c. When planning to use the internal auditors to provide direct assistance, the practitioner should obtain written acknowledgment from the responsible party that the internal auditors will be allowed to follow the practitioner's directives without interference.

    d. The practitioner is responsible for all significant judgments and should appropriately supervise and review the work of the internal auditors.

9. Considering subsequent events and subsequently discovered facts

    a. The practitioner should inquire whether the responsible party (and the engaging party, if different) is aware of any subsequent events up to the date of the report that could have a significant effect; and if there are, the practitioner should perform appropriate procedures regarding those events.

    b. The practitioner has no responsibility to perform additional procedures after the report date; however, if there are subsequently discovered facts that may have caused revision of the report if known at the report date, the practitioner should respond appropriately to those facts.

V. Written Representations

A. The practitioner should request written representations from the responsible party, including the responsible party's assertion about the subject matter.

B. When the Engaging Party Is Not the Responsible Party—The practitioner should request additional written representations from the engaging party.

C. If the Responsible Party Refuses to Provide the Requested Written Representations

    1. When the engaging party is the responsible party—The practitioner should discuss the matters with the appropriate party (parties) and take appropriate action if the matters are not resolved satisfactorily.

    2. When the engaging party is not the responsible party—The practitioner should

        a. Make inquiries of the responsible party and seek oral responses.

        b. If satisfactory oral responses are obtained—The practitioner should restrict the use of the report to the engaging party.

        c. If one or more of the requested representations are not provided (either in writing or orally) —A scope limitation exists, and the practitioner should determine the effect on the report.

D. The representations should address the subject matter and periods covered by the practitioner's report.

E. The written representations letter should have the same date as the practitioner's report.

VI. Documentation

A. The documentation should permit an experienced practitioner without any connection to the engagement to understand the work performed and the basis for the primary decisions.

B. The practitioner should prepare documentation sufficient to comply with AICPA Professional Standards and applicable legal and regulatory requirements, including these six matters:

1. The identifying characteristics of the specific items tested;

2. Who performed the work and the date the work was completed;

3. The discussions with the responsible party (or others) about significant findings or issues, including the nature of the matters discussed (and when and with whom the discussions occurred);

4. The actions taken when the engaging party is the responsible party and will not provide one or more of the requested written representations (or when representations provided are not seen as reliable);

5. The oral responses provided when the engaging party is not the responsible party and the responsible party will not provide the requested written representations; *and*

6. Who reviewed the work performed and the date of that review.

C. The documentation normally addresses the following additional matters: (1) compliance with relevant ethical requirements, including applicable independence requirements; (2) conclusions about acceptance and continuance of client relationships and engagements; and (3) conclusions about any consultations that occurred during the engagement.

D. If information has been obtained that is inconsistent with the practitioner's final conclusion about a significant matter, the practitioner should document how he or she dealt with the inconsistency.

Examination Reports

After studying this lesson, you should be able to:

1. Recognize the elements that are required in a practitioner's unmodified examination report for an attestation engagement.

2. Identify the various types of modified reports that might be issued for an examination engagement and the circumstances that would result in each type of modification.

I. Focus of the Practitioner's Report

    A. May either report on the responsible party's written assertion or report directly on the subject matter.

    B. When reporting on the assertion, the assertion should accompany the practitioner's report (or the assertion may be clearly stated in the report).

II. Content of an Unmodified Examination Report

    A. A standardized format for the examination report is not required for all examination engagements—The report is to include the identified basic elements but may be tailored to the circumstances of the engagement.

    B. These 12 elements should be included in the unmodified report:

        1. A title that includes the word "independent"

        2. An appropriate addressee

        3. Identification of the applicable subject matter or assertion, including the point in time or period of time involved

        4. Identification of the criteria against which the subject matter was measured or evaluated

        5. A statement that identifies (a) the responsible party and its responsibility, and (b) the practitioner's responsibility to express an opinion

        6. A statement that (a) the examination was conducted in accordance with AICPA attestation standards, (b) those standards require the practitioner to plan and perform the engagement to obtain reasonable assurance (whether the subject matter is in accordance with the criteria in all material respects or whether the responsible party's assertion is fairly stated), and (c) the practitioner believes the evidence obtained is sufficient and appropriate to provide a reasonable basis for the opinion

        7. A description of the nature of an examination engagement

        8. A statement describing any significant inherent limitations associated with the engagement

        9. An opinion about whether the subject matter is in accordance with (or based on) the criteria in all material respects or whether the responsible party's assertion is fairly stated in all material respects

        10. The signature of the practitioner's firm (either manual or printed)

        11. The city and state where the practitioner practices

        12. The date of the report

    C. AT-C Section 205 provides several examples of unmodified examination reports.

Example 1
Practitioner's Unmodified Examination Report on the Subject Matter

The following is an illustrative practitioner's report for an examination engagement in which the practitioner has examined the subject matter and is reporting directly on the subject matter.

Independent Accountant's Report

[*Appropriate Addressee*]

We have examined [*identify the subject matter; e.g., the accompanying schedule of investment returns of XYZ Company for the year ended December 31, 20XX*]. XYZ Company's management is responsible for [*identify the subject matter; e.g., presenting the schedule of investment returns*] in accordance with (or based on) [*identify the criteria; e.g., the ABC criteria set forth in Note 1*]. Our responsibility is to express an opinion on [*identify the subject matter; e.g., the schedule of investment returns*] based on our examination.

Our examination was conducted in accordance with attestation standards established by the American Institute of Certified Public Accountants. Those standards require that we plan and perform the examination to obtain reasonable assurance about whether [*identify the subject matter; e.g., the schedule of investment returns*] is in accordance with (or based on) the criteria, in all material respects. An examination involves performing procedures to obtain evidence about [*identify the subject matter; e.g., the schedule of investment returns*]. The nature, timing, and extent of the procedures selected depend on our judgment, including an assessment of the risks of material misstatement of [*identify the subject matter; e.g., the schedule of investment returns*], whether due to fraud or error. We believe that the evidence we obtained is sufficient and appropriate to provide a reasonable basis for our opinion.

[*Include a description of significant inherent limitations, if any, associated with the measurement or evaluation of the subject matter against the criteria.*]

[*Additional paragraph(s) may be added to emphasize certain matters relating to the attestation engagement or the subject matter.*]

In our opinion, [*identify the subject matter; e.g., the schedule of investment returns of XYZ Company for the year ended December 31, 20XX or the schedule of investment returns referred to above*], is presented in accordance with (or based on) [*identify the criteria; e.g., the ABC criteria set forth in Note 1*], in all material respects.

[*Practitioner's signature*]
[*Practitioner's city and state*]
[*Date of practitioner's report*]

Example 2
Practitioner's Unmodified Examination Report on an Assertion

The following is an illustrative practitioner's report for an examination engagement in which the practitioner has examined the responsible party's assertion and is reporting on that assertion.

Independent Accountant's Report

[*Appropriate Addressee*]

We have examined management of XYZ Company's assertion that [*identify the assertion, including the subject matter and the criteria; e.g., the accompanying schedule of investment returns of XYZ Company for the year ended December 31, 20XX, is presented in accordance with [or based on] the ABC criteria set forth in Note 1*]. XYZ Company's management is responsible for its assertion. Our responsibility is to express an opinion on management's assertion based on our examination.

Our examination was conducted in accordance with attestation standards established by the American Institute of Certified Public Accountants. Those standards require that we plan and perform the examination to obtain reasonable assurance about whether management's assertion is fairly stated, in all material respects. An examination involves performing procedures to obtain evidence about management's assertion. The nature, timing, and extent of the procedures selected depend on our judgment, including an assessment of the risks of material misstatement of management's assertion, whether due to fraud or error. We believe that the evidence we obtained is sufficient and appropriate to provide a reasonable basis for our opinion.

[*Include a description of significant inherent limitations, if any, associated with the measurement or evaluation of the subject matter against the criteria.*]

[*Additional paragraph(s) may be added to emphasize certain matters relating to the attestation engagement or the subject matter.*]

In our opinion, management's assertion that [*identify the assertion, including the subject matter and the criteria; e.g., the accompanying schedule of investment returns of XYZ Company for the year ended December 31, 20XX, is presented in accordance with [or based on] the ABC criteria set forth in Note 1*] is fairly stated, in all material respects.

[*Practitioner's signature*]
[*Practitioner's city and state*]
[*Date of practitioner's report*]

III. Modified Opinions

A. Modify the Opinion

1. When sufficient appropriate evidence has not been obtained in all material respects (regarding the scope); *or*

2. When the subject matter is not in accordance with the criteria in all material respects (regarding the presentation).

B. When Modifying the Opinion—Include a separate paragraph in the report that describes the reason(s) for the modification.

C. Qualified Opinion—Express a qualified opinion when the possible effect of the scope limitation "could be material, but not pervasive" or when the misstatement of the subject matter "is material, but not pervasive" to the subject matter.

D. Adverse Opinion—Express an adverse opinion when the misstatement of the subject matter is both "material and pervasive" to the subject matter.

E. Disclaimer of Opinion—Express a disclaimer of opinion when the possible effect of the scope limitation could be both "material and pervasive."

F. When expressing either a qualified or an adverse opinion due to misstatement of the subject matter—Express the opinion directly on the *subject matter*, not on the assertion (even if the assertion acknowledges the misstatement).

G. Change the description of the practitioner's responsibility for modified opinions.

1. **When expressing a qualified or an adverse opinion**—Amend the description of the practitioner's responsibility to express the belief that the evidence obtained is sufficient and appropriate to provide a basis for the modified opinion.

2. **When expressing a disclaimer of opinion**—Amend the description of the practitioner's responsibility to say that the practitioner was engaged to examine the subject matter (or assertion).

IV. Other Examination Reporting Considerations

A. Restricted Use Paragraph—An alert to restrict the use of the report should be added in three circumstances:

1. When the criteria used to evaluate the subject matter are appropriate only for a limited number of parties;

2. When the criteria used to evaluate the subject matter are available only to specified parties; *or*

3. When the engaging party is not the responsible party and the responsible party does not provide the requested written representations but does provide appropriate oral responses—The practitioner's report should be restricted to the engaging party.

B. Reference to the Practitioner's Specialist

1. Should not refer to the work of the practitioner's specialist in a report having an unmodified opinion.

2. May refer to an external specialist when the opinion is modified and reference is relevant to understanding the modification.

C. Other Information

1. **If the practitioner's report is included in a document that contains the subject matter or assertion, along with other information**—Read the other information for material inconsistencies.

2. **If there is a material inconsistency (or if a material misstatement of fact exists in the other information)**—Discuss the matter with the responsible party and take appropriate action such as:

   a. Request that the appropriate party consult with a third party (such as legal counsel);

   b. Seek legal advice about possible actions;

   c. Communicate with third parties (such as a regulator);

   d. Describe the material inconsistency in the report; *or*

   e. Withdraw, when that is permissible.

3. "Other information" does not include information on the appropriate party's website.

D. If a Written Report Is Readily Available—The practitioner may also report orally or by using symbols (such as a web seal with a hyperlink to a written report).

Review Engagements

After studying this lesson, you should be able to:

1. Understand the practitioner's responsibility to obtain a written assertion for a review engagement.

2. Understand the practitioner's responsibilities in performing a review engagement, including obtaining written representations.

I. Definition

Definition

Review Engagement: "An attestation engagement in which the practitioner obtains limited assurance by obtaining sufficient appropriate review evidence about the measurement or evaluation of subject matter against criteria in order to express a conclusion about whether any material modification should be made to the subject matter in order for it to be in accordance with (or based on) the criteria or to the assertion in order for it to be fairly stated."

Note

The guidance for examination engagements is provided in the Clarified SSAEs, specifically by AT-C 210, *Review Engagements*. In addition, the practitioner is required to comply with AT-C 105, *Concepts Common* to *All Attestation Engagements,* as well as any applicable subject-matter sections.

Compliance with these attestation standards is enforceable under the AICPA's Code of Professional Conduct (specifically, the *Compliance With Standards* rule).

AT-C 210 specifically prohibits review engagements involving (a) prospective financial information; (b) internal control; or (c) compliance with the requirements of specified laws, regulations, rules, contracts, or grants.

II. Agreeing on the Terms of the Engagement

A. The practitioner and the engaging party should agree on the terms of the engagement, which should be documented in an engagement letter (or other suitable form of written agreement).

B. These terms should include the following:

1. The objective and scope of the engagement;

2. The responsibilities of the practitioner;

3. The responsibilities of the responsible party and the engaging party, if those are different;

4. A statement that the engagement will be conducted according to AICPA attestation standards;

5. A statement that a review is substantially less in scope than an examination and that, accordingly, no opinion will be expressed;

6. A statement identifying the criteria for measurement or evaluation of the subject matter; *and*

7. Acknowledgment by the engaging party to provide the practitioner with a representation letter at the conclusion of the engagement.

C. Such an agreement should be obtained for each engagement, but, if the terms of the preceding engagement have not changed, the practitioner may simply remind the engaging party of the terms of the engagement (and document that communication).

III. Request a Written Assertion about the Subject Matter

A. If the engaging party is the responsible party and refuses to provide a written assertion— The practitioner should withdraw when that is permitted.

B. **If the engaging party is not the responsible party and the responsible party refuses to provide a written assertion**—The practitioner need not withdraw but should disclose that refusal in the practitioner's report and restrict the use of the report to the engaging party.

C. The responsible party is still responsible for the subject matter as a whole and should request a written assertion covering the entire relevant period(s), even when the responsible party was not present during some (or all) of the period covered by the practitioner's report.

IV. Planning and Performing the Engagement

A. The practitioner should obtain a sufficient understanding of the subject matter and circumstances of the engagement to design and perform procedures to achieve the objectives of the engagement.

B. **Procedures to Be Performed**

   1. The practitioner should design and perform analytical procedures and make inquiries to obtain limited assurance.

   2. Analytical procedures may not be applicable when the subject matter is qualitative instead of quantitative. In that case, the practitioner may need to perform other appropriate procedures.

   3. The practitioner should increase the focus in the areas of the engagement that have increased risks of material misstatement.

C. **Analytical Procedures**

   1. The practitioner should: (a) determine the suitability of specific analytical procedures (considering the subject matter and assessed risks of material misstatement); (b) evaluate the reliability of data from which the expectation is developed; and (c) develop an expectation that is sufficiently precise to identify material misstatements.

   2. The practitioner should investigate significant differences from expectations by (a) inquiring of the responsible party and (b) performing any other procedures considered necessary.

D. **Inquiries and Other Review Procedures**—The practitioner should inquire of the responsible party about the following:

   1. Whether the subject matter has been prepared according to (or based on) the criteria;

   2. The practices used by the responsible party to measure and record the subject matter;

   3. Questions arising in connection with the other review procedures; *and*

   4. Communications from regulatory authorities or others, if any.

E. **Fraud, Laws, and Regulations**—The practitioner should make inquiries to determine whether the applicable parties have any knowledge of fraud (including suspected or alleged fraud) or noncompliance with laws or regulations affecting the subject matter.

F. **Incorrect, Incomplete, or Otherwise Unsatisfactory Information**—The practitioner should perform additional procedures to obtain limited assurance as to whether any material modifications should be made to the subject matter.

G. **Using the Work of a Practitioner's Specialist or Internal Auditors**—The practitioner should apply the same requirements stated in AT-C 205 (regarding examination engagements).

H. **Considering Subsequent Events and Subsequently Discovered Facts**

   1. The practitioner should inquire whether the responsible party (and the engaging party, if different) is aware of any subsequent events up to the date of the report that could have a significant effect; if there are, the practitioner should perform appropriate procedures applicable to those events.

   2. There is no responsibility to perform additional procedures after the report date. If there are subsequently discovered facts that may have caused revision of the report if known at the report date, the practitioner should respond appropriately to those facts.

V. Written Representations

    A. The practitioner should request written representations from the responsible party, including the responsible party's assertion about the subject matter.

    B. When the Engaging Party Is Not the Responsible Party—The practitioner should request additional written representations from the engaging party.

    C. When the Responsible Party Refuses to Provide the Requested Written Representations

        1. If the engaging party is the responsible party—The practitioner should withdraw from the engagement (when withdrawal is permitted under applicable law or regulation).

        2. When the engaging party is not the responsible party—The practitioner should

            a. Make inquiries of the responsible party and seek oral responses.

            b. If satisfactory oral responses are obtained—The practitioner should restrict the use of the report to the engaging party.

            c. If one or more of the requested representations are not provided (either in writing or orally) —A scope limitation exists, and the practitioner should withdraw from the engagement, if possible.

    D. The representations should address the subject matter and periods covered by the practitioner's report.

    E. The written representations letter should have the same date as the practitioner's report.

VI. Documentation

    A. The documentation should permit an experienced practitioner without any connection to the engagement to understand the work performed and the basis for the primary decisions.

    B. The practitioner should prepare documentation sufficient to comply with AICPA Professional Standards and applicable legal and regulatory requirements, including the following matters:

        1. The identifying characteristics of the specific items tested;

        2. Who performed the work and the date the work was completed;

        3. The discussions with the responsible party (or others) about significant findings or issues, including the nature of the matters discussed (and when and with whom the discussions occurred);

        4. The actions taken when the engaging party is the responsible party and will not provide one or more of the required written representations (or when representations provided are not seen as reliable);

        5. The oral responses provided when the engaging party is not the responsible party and the responsible party will not provide the required written representations; *and*

        6. Who reviewed the work performed and the date it was reviewed.

    C. The documentation normally addresses the following additional matters:

        1. Compliance with relevant ethical requirements, including applicable independence requirements;

        2. Conclusions about acceptance and continuance of client relationships and engagements; *and*

        3. Conclusions about any consultations that occurred during the engagement.

    D. If Information Has Been Obtained that Is Inconsistent with the Practitioner's Final Conclusion about a Significant Matter—The practitioner should document how the practitioner dealt with the inconsistency.

Review Reports

I. **Focus of the Practitioner's Report**

   A. May either report on the responsible party's written assertion or directly on the subject matter.

   B. When reporting on the assertion, the assertion should accompany the practitioner's report (or the assertion may be clearly stated in the report).

II. **Content of an Unmodified Review Report**

   A. A standardized format for the review report is not required for all review engagements. The report is to include the identified basic elements but may be tailored to the circumstances of the engagement.

   B. **The following elements should be included in the unmodified review report:**

      1. A title that includes the word "independent";

      2. An appropriate addressee;

      3. Identification of the applicable subject matter or assertion, including the point in time or period of time involved;

      4. Identification of the criteria against which the subject matter was measured or evaluated;

      5. Statement that identifies (a) the responsible party and its responsibility and (b) the practitioner's responsibility to express a conclusion;

      6. Statement that (a) the review was conducted in accordance with AICPA attestation standards, (b) those standards require the practitioner to plan and perform the engagement to obtain limited assurance whether any material modifications should be made (either to the subject matter or to the responsible party's assertion), (c) a review is substantially less in scope than an examination so disclaim an opinion, and (d) the practitioner believes the review provides a reasonable basis for the conclusion;

      7. Statement describing any significant inherent limitations associated with the engagement;

      8. The conclusion about whether any material modifications should be made to the subject matter or to the responsible party's assertion;

      9. The signature of the practitioner's firm (either manual or printed);

      10. The city and state where the practitioner practices; *and*

      11. The date of the report.

C. AT-C Section 210 provides several examples of review reports.

Example 1
Practitioner's Review Report on Subject Matter; Unmodified Conclusion

Note: The following is an illustrative practitioner's report for a review engagement in which the practitioner has reviewed the subject matter and is reporting directly on the subject matter.

Independent Accountant's Review Report

[*Appropriate Addressee*]

We have reviewed [*identify the subject matter; e.g., the accompanying schedule of investment returns of XYZ Company for the year ended December 31, 20XX*]. XYZ Company's management is responsible for [*identify the subject matter; e.g., presenting the schedule of investment returns*] in accordance with (or based on) [*identify the criteria; e.g., the ABC criteria set forth in Note 1*]. Our responsibility is to express a conclusion on [*identify the subject matter; e.g., the schedule of investment returns*] based on our review.

Our review was conducted in accordance with attestation standards established by the American Institute of Certified Public Accountants. Those standards require that we plan and perform the review to obtain limited assurance about whether any material modifications should be made to [*identify the subject matter; e.g., the schedule of investment returns*] in order for it to be in accordance with (or based on) the criteria. A review is substantially less in scope than an examination, the objective of which is to obtain reasonable assurance about whether [*identify the subject matter; e.g., the schedule of investment returns*] is in accordance with (or based on) the criteria, in all material respects, in order to express an opinion. Accordingly, we do not express such an opinion. We believe that our review provides a reasonable basis for our conclusion.

[*Include a description of significant inherent limitations, if any, associated with the measurement or evaluation of the subject matter against the criteria.*]

[*Additional paragraph(s) may be added to emphasize certain matters relating to the attestation engagement or the subject matter.*]

Based on our review, we are not aware of any material modifications that should be made to [*identify the subject matter; e.g., the accompanying schedule of investment returns of XYZ Company for the year ended December 31, 20XX*], in order for it be in accordance with (or based on) [*identify the criteria; e.g., the ABC criteria set forth in Note 1*].

[*Practitioner's signature*]
[*Practitioner's city and state*]
[*Date of practitioner's report*]

Example 2
Practitioner's Review Report on Subject Matter; Qualified Conclusion

Note: The following is an illustrative practitioner's report for a review engagement that expresses a qualified conclusion because the review identified conditions that, result in a material, but not pervasive, misstatement of the subject matter, based on the criteria. The practitioner has reviewed the subject matter and is also reporting on the subject matter.

Independent Accountant's Review Report

[*Appropriate Addressee*]

We have reviewed [*identify the subject matter; e.g., the accompanying schedule of investment returns of XYZ Company for the year ended December 31, 20XX*]. XYZ Company's management is responsible for [*identify the subject matter, for example, presenting the schedule of investment returns*] based on [*identify the criteria; e.g., the ABC criteria set forth in Note 1*]. Our responsibility is to express a conclusion on [*identify the subject matter; e.g., the schedule of investment returns*] based on our review.

Our review was conducted in accordance with attestation standards established by the American Institute of Certified Public Accountants. Those standards require that we plan and perform the review to obtain limited assurance about whether any material modifications should be made to [*identify the subject matter; e.g., the schedule of investment returns*] in order for it to be in accordance with (or based on) the criteria. A review is substantially less in scope than an examination, the objective of which is to obtain reasonable assurance about whether [*identify the subject matter; e.g., the schedule of investment returns*] is in accordance with (or based on) the criteria, in all material respects, in order to express an opinion. Accordingly, we do not express such an opinion. We believe that our review provides a reasonable basis for our conclusion.

[*Include a description of significant inherent limitations, if any, associated with the measurement or evaluation of the subject matter against the criteria.*]

[*Additional paragraph(s) may be added to emphasize certain matters relating to the attestation engagement or the subject matter.*]

Our review identified [*describe condition(s) that, individually or in the aggregate, resulted in a material misstatement, or deviation from, the criteria*].

Based on our review, except for the matter(s) described in the preceding paragraph, we are not aware of any material modifications that should be made to [*identify the subject matter; e.g., the accompanying schedule of investment returns of XYZ Company for the year ended December 31, 20XX*], in order for it to be in accordance with (or based on) [*identify the criteria; e.g., the ABC criteria set forth in Note 1*].

[*Practitioner's signature*]
[*Practitioner's city and state*]
[*Date of practitioner's report*]

III. Modified Conclusions

A. Misstatement of Subject Matter

1. The practitioner should consider whether qualification of the conclusion in the "standard practitioner's report" is an adequate way to disclose the misstatement of the subject matter. If that is not an adequate way to disclose the matter, then the practitioner should withdraw from the engagement.

2. The practitioner may express a qualified conclusion with the phrase "except for the effects of . . ." when the effects are material but not pervasive. In such a case, the practitioner should report directly on the subject matter, not on the assertion (even if the assertion acknowledges the misstatement).

3. If the effects of the misstatement are material and pervasive, the practitioner should withdraw from the engagement when that is permissible.

B. Scope Limitations—If sufficient appropriate review evidence is not obtained, a scope limitation exists, and the practitioner should withdraw when that is permissible.

IV. Other Review Reporting Considerations

A. Restricted-Use Paragraph—An alert to restrict the use of the report should be added in the following circumstances:

1. When the criteria used to evaluate the subject matter are appropriate only for a limited number of parties;

2. When the criteria used to evaluate the subject matter are available only to specified parties; *or*

3. When the engaging party is not the responsible party and the responsible party does not provide the requested written representations but does provide appropriate oral responses. In this case, the practitioner's report should be restricted to the engaging party.

B. Reference to the Practitioner's Specialist

1. The practitioner should not refer to the work of the practitioner's specialist in a report having an unmodified conclusion.

2. The practitioner may refer to an external specialist when the conclusion is modified and reference to the specialist is relevant to understanding the modification.

C. Other Information

1. **If the practitioner's report is included in a document that contains the subject matter or assertion, along with other information**—The practitioner should read the other information for material inconsistencies.

2. **If there is a material inconsistency (or if a material misstatement of fact exists in the other information)**—The practitioner should discuss the matter with the responsible party and take appropriate action [e.g., (a) request that the appropriate party consult with a third party (such as legal counsel); (b) seek legal advice about possible actions; (c) communicate with third parties (such as a regulator); (d) describe the material inconsistency in the report; or (e) withdraw, when that is permissible].

Agreed-Upon Procedures Engagements

After studying this lesson, you should be able to:

1. Understand the practitioner's responsibilities in performing an agreed-upon procedures engagement, including obtaining a written assertion and written representations.

2. Recognize the elements that are required in a practitioner's agreed-upon procedures report.

I. Definitions

Definitions

Agreed-Upon Procedures Engagement: "An attestation engagement in which a practitioner performs specific procedures on subject matter or an assertion and reports the findings without providing an opinion or a conclusion on it. The parties to the engagement … agree upon and are responsible for the sufficiency of the procedures for their purposes."

Nonparticipant Party: "An additional specified party the practitioner is requested to add as a user of the practitioner's report subsequent to the completion of the agreed-upon procedures engagement."

Specified Party: "The intended user(s) to whom use of the written practitioner's report is limited."

Note

The guidance for agreed-upon procedures engagements is provided in the Clarified SSAEs, specifically by AT-C 215, *Agreed-Upon Procedures Engagements*. In addition, the practitioner is required to comply with AT-C 105 (*Concepts Common to All Attestation Engagements*) as well as any applicable subject-matter sections.

Compliance with these attestation standards is enforceable under the AICPA's Code of Professional Conduct (specifically, the *Compliance With Standards* rule).

II. Agreeing on the Terms of the Engagement

A. The practitioner and the engaging party should agree on the terms of the engagement, which should be documented in an engagement letter (or other suitable form of written agreement).

B. The terms of the engagement should include the following:

1. The nature of the engagement;

2. Identification of the subject matter or assertion, the responsible party, and the criteria to be used;

3. Identification of the specified parties;

4. Acknowledgment by the specified parties of their responsibility for the sufficiency of the agreed-upon procedures for their purposes;

5. The responsibilities of the practitioner;

6. A statement that the engagement will be conducted according to AICPA attestation standards;

7. Enumeration of (or reference to) the procedures to be performed;

8. Identification of disclaimers expected to be in the report;

9. Identification of the restricted use of the practitioner's report;

10. Identification of any assistance to be provided to the practitioner;

11. Identification of any practitioner's external specialist to be used; *and*

12. Agreement about materiality limits to be applied, if applicable.

III. Requesting a Written Assertion

A. The practitioner should request a written assertion about the subject matter from the responsible party.

B. **If the Engaging Party is Not the Responsible Party and the Responsible Party Refuses to Provide a Written Assertion**—The written agreement (engagement letter) should state that no such assertion will be provided.

C. **When the Responsible Party Was Not Present during Some (or All) of the Period Covered by the Practitioner's Report**—The responsible party still is responsible for the subject matter as a whole, and the practitioner should request a written assertion covering the entire relevant period(s).

IV. Planning and Performing the Engagement

A. **Procedures to Be Performed**—The practitioner should not agree to perform procedures that are vague in meaning or otherwise open to varying interpretations.

1. Examples of *unacceptable* words (because they are too vague) to describe actions include the following: note, review, general review, limited review, evaluate, analyze, check, test, interpret, and verify.

2. Examples of *acceptable* words to describe actions include the following: inspect, confirm, compare, agree, trace, inquire, recalculate, observe, and mathematically check.

B. **Using the Work of a Practitioner's External Specialist**—Any involvement of a practitioner's external specialist should be agreed to by the specified parties; and the practitioner's report should describe any assistance provided by the practitioner's external specialist.

C. **Using the Work of Internal Auditors**—Only the engagement team (or other practitioners) should perform the agreed-upon procedures referenced in the practitioner's report.

D. **Communication Responsibilities**—The practitioner should communicate any known and suspected fraud and noncompliance with laws or regulations to the responsible party (and to the engaging party when the engaging party is not the responsible party).

V. Written Representations

A. The practitioner should request written representations from the responsible party, including the responsible party's assertion about the subject matter.

B. **When the Engaging Party Is Not the Responsible Party**—The practitioner should request additional written representations from the engaging party.

C. **If the Responsible Party Refuses to Provide the Requested Written Representations**

1. **If the engaging party is the responsible party**—The practitioner should discuss the matters with the appropriate party (parties) and, if the matters are not resolved satisfactorily, take appropriate action (such as withdrawing from the engagement or determining the effect of the matter on the report).

2. **When the engaging party is not the responsible party**—The practitioner should:

   a. Make inquiries of the responsible party and seek oral responses.

   b. **If satisfactory oral responses are not obtained**—The practitioner should take appropriate action (such as withdrawing from the engagement or determining the effect of the matter on the report).

D. The representations should address the subject matter and periods covered by the practitioner's report.

E. The written representations letter should have the same date as the practitioner's report.

VI. Documentation

A. The documentation should be sufficient to determine that the specified parties agreed on the procedures to be performed.

B. The documentation should be sufficient to determine that the practitioner complied with Professional Standards and applicable legal and regulatory requirements, including:

    1. The identifying characteristics of specific items tested;

    2. Who performed the work and the date the work was completed;

    3. The discussions with the responsible party (or others) about significant findings or issues, including the nature of the matters discussed (and when and with whom the discussions occurred);

    4. The actions taken when the engaging party is the responsible party and will not provide one or more of the requested written representations (or the representations provided are not seen as reliable);

    5. The oral responses provided when the engaging party is not the responsible party and the responsible party will not provide the requested written representations; *and*

    6. Who reviewed the work performed and the date it was reviewed.

C. The documentation should be sufficient to determine the results of the procedures performed and the evidence that was obtained.

VII. Reporting Issues for Agreed-Upon Procedures Engagements

A. **A standardized format for the report is not required for all agreed-upon procedures engagements**—The report should include the identified basic elements but may be tailored to the circumstances of the engagement.

B. **Content of the Practitioner's Agreed-Upon Procedures Report**

    1. A title that includes the word "independent";

    2. An appropriate addressee;

    3. Identification of the subject matter or assertion and the nature of the engagement;

    4. Identification of the specified parties;

    5. A statement that the procedures were agreed to by the specified parties;

    6. A statement that identifies the responsible party for the subject matter or assertion;

    7. A statement that the specified users are responsible for the sufficiency of the procedures performed;

    8. A list of the procedures performed and the related findings;

    9. A description of agreed-upon materiality limits, if applicable;

    10. A statement that the engagement was conducted in accordance with AICPA attestation standards, that the practitioner was not engaged to conduct an examination or a review, that the practitioner does not express an opinion or conclusion, and that other matters might have been reported had the practitioner performed additional procedures;

    11. A description of the assistance of practitioner's external specialist, if applicable;

    12. A statement regarding reservations concerning procedures or findings, if applicable;

13. An alert to restrict the use of the report to specified parties (when the engagement is also performed under Government Auditing Standards, the alert should describe the purpose of the report and state that it is not suitable for any other purpose);

14. A manual or printed signature of the practitioner's firm;

15. The city and state of the practitioner's office; *and*

16. The date of the report.

C. AT-C Section 215 provides several examples of review reports.

Example 1
Practitioner's Agreed-Upon Procedures Report Related to a Statement of Investment Performance Statistics

The following is an illustrative practitioner's report for an agreed-upon procedures engagement involving a statement of investment performance statistics.

Independent Accountant's Report on Applying Agreed-Upon Procedures

[*Appropriate Addressee*]

We have performed the procedures enumerated below, which were agreed to by [*identify the specified party(ies); e.g., the audit committees and managements of ABC Inc. and XYZ Fund*], on [*identify the subject matter; e.g., the accompanying Statement of Investment Performance Statistics of XYZ Fund for the year ended December 31, 20X1*]. XYZ Fund's management is responsible for [*identify the subject matter; e.g., the Statement of Investment Performance Statistics for the year ended December 31, 20X1*]. The sufficiency of these procedures is solely the responsibility of the parties specified in this report. Consequently, we make no representation regarding the sufficiency of the procedures enumerated below either for the purpose for which this report has been requested or for any other purpose.

[*Include paragraphs to enumerate procedures and findings.*]

This agreed-upon procedures engagement was conducted in accordance with attestation standards established by the American Institute of Certified Public Accountants. We were not engaged to and did not conduct an examination or review, the objective of which would be the expression of an opinion or conclusion, respectively, on [*identify the subject matter; e.g., the accompanying Statement of Investment Performance Statistics of XYZ Fund for the year ended December 31, 20X1*]. Accordingly, we do not express such an opinion or conclusion. Had we performed additional procedures, other matters might have come to our attention that would have been reported to you.

[*Additional paragraph(s) may be added to describe other matters.*]

This report is intended solely for the information and use of [*identify the specified party(ies); e.g., the audit committees and managements of ABC Inc. and XYZ Fund*] and is not intended to be, and should not be, used by anyone other than the specified parties.

[*Practitioner's signature*]
[*Practitioner's city and state*]
[*Date of practitioner's report*]

D. If the Responsible Party Refuses to Provide Written Assertion—The practitioner should disclose that refusal in the agreed-upon procedures report.

E. Restrictions on the Performance of Procedures

1. **When restrictions on the performance of agreed-upon procedures occur**— The practitioner should attempt to obtain agreement from the specified parties for modification of the agreed-upon procedures.

2. **When such agreement cannot be obtained**—The practitioner should describe any such restrictions in the practitioner's report or withdraw from the engagement.

F. **Adding Specified Parties (Nonparticipant Parties)**

1. **When agreeing to add a nonparticipant party**—The practitioner should obtain acknowledgment (normally in writing) that the nonparticipant party agrees to the procedures performed and takes responsibility for the sufficiency of those procedures.

2. **When adding a nonparticipant party**—The date of the report should not be changed.

3. **When providing written acknowledgment that the nonparticipant has been added**—The acknowledgment should normally state that no procedures have been performed after the date of the practitioner's report.

G. **When the Subject Matter Consists of Elements, Accounts, or Items of a Financial Statement**—The practitioner's report might add a statement that the agreed-upon procedures do not constitute an audit (or review) and include an appropriate disclaimer regarding an opinion (or conclusion).

H. **Reservations Concerning Procedures or Findings**—The practitioner may include "explanatory paragraph(s)" to comment on matters such as the following:

1. Disclosure of assumptions or interpretations used

2. Description of the condition of records, controls, or data involved

3. Explanation that the practitioner has no responsibility to update the practitioner's report

I. **When an Agreed-Upon Procedures Report May Be Publicly Available**—A restricted-use report filed with regulatory authorities or governmental entities may be made available to the public as required by law or regulation.

Prospective Financial Information

After studying this lesson, you should be able to:

1. Identify the two different types of prospective financial information.

2. Identify the two kinds of engagements for prospective financial information under the clarified attestation standards, and recognize the elements that are required in a practitioner's report for each of those kinds of engagements.

I. Definitions

Definitions

Financial Forecast: "Prospective financial statements that present, to the best of the responsible party's knowledge and belief, an entity's expected financial position, results of operations, and cash flows. A financial forecast is based on the responsible party's assumptions reflecting conditions it expects to exist and the course of action it expects to take."

Financial Projection: "Prospective financial statements that present, to the best of the responsible party's knowledge and belief, given one or more hypothetical assumptions, an entity's expected financial position, results of operations, and cash flows. A financial projection is sometimes prepared to present one or more hypothetical courses of actions for evaluation, as in response to a question such as 'What would happen if …?' A financial projection is based on the responsible party's assumptions reflecting conditions it expects would exist and the course of action it expects would be taken, given one or more hypothetical assumptions."

Partial Presentation: "A presentation of prospective financial information that excludes one or more of the applicable items required for prospective financial statements as described in chapter 8 of the [AICPA Guide]."

Applicability: AT-C 305, *Prospective Financial Information*, applies to **examination** or **agreed-upon procedures** engagements involving prospective financial information, specifically to such reports issued on or after May 1, 2017.

II. Examination Engagements on Prospective Financial Information

A. **Preconditions**—The practitioner should not accept an engagement to examine a:

1. Forecast or projection unless the responsible party has agreed to disclose the significant assumptions;

2. Projection unless the responsible party has agreed to identify which of the assumptions are hypothetical and to comment on the limitations of the projection's usefulness; *or*

3. Partial presentation that does not comment on the limitations of the presentation's usefulness.

B. **Requesting a Written Assertion**—The practitioner should request a written assertion from the responsible party; if that party refuses, the practitioner should withdraw when that is permitted by applicable law or regulation.

C. **Planning**—The practitioner should establish an overall engagement strategy that guides the development of the engagement plan to determine the scope and timing of the work and should obtain an appropriate level of knowledge about the entity's industry (and accounting principles used) and the key factors underlying the prospective financial information.

D. Examination Procedures

1. The practitioner should perform the procedures considered necessary to report on whether the assumptions underlying the forecast (or projection) are suitably supported and provide a reasonable basis for the forecast (or projection).

2. The practitioner should evaluate the support for significant assumptions individually and in the aggregate. They are viewed as suitably supported if each significant assumption is supported by the "preponderance" of the information.

3. **For a forecast**—The practitioner should evaluate whether there is a reasonably objective basis for the forecast and whether sufficiently objective assumptions can be developed for each key factor identified.

4. **For a projection**—The practitioner should evaluate whether the hypothetical assumptions are consistent with the purpose of the projection; the practitioner need not obtain support for the hypothetical assumptions, however.

5. **Evaluating the preparation and presentation of a forecast or projection**—The practitioner should obtain reasonable assurance that:

   a. The presentation reflects the identified assumptions;

   b. Any computations made are mathematically accurate;

   c. Assumptions are internally consistent;

   d. Accounting principles used are appropriate;

   e. Information is presented according to the AICPA Guide; *and*

   f. Assumptions have been adequately disclosed.

E. Written Representations in an Examination Engagement

1. **For a forecast**—In addition to the representations required by AT-C 205 (regarding examination engagements), the practitioner should request the following from the responsible party:

   a. The forecast presents the expected financial statements and reflects expected conditions;

   b. The underlying assumptions are reasonable and suitably supported; *and*

   c. If the forecast is expressed as a range, the range was not selected in a misleading manner.

2. **For a projection**—In addition to the representations required by AT-C 205, the practitioner should request representations from the responsible party that:

   a. Identify the hypothetical assumptions (and identify any of those that are considered to be "improbable");

   b. Describe the limitations of the usefulness of the presentation;

   c. The projection presents expected financial information based on present circumstances, expected conditions, and the occurrence of the hypothetical events;

   d. The assumptions (other than the hypothetical assumptions) are reasonable and suitably supported; *and*

   e. If the projection is expressed as a range, the range was not selected in a misleading manner.

3. **Regarding the requirement in AT-C 205 that the subject matter is presented in accordance with "the criteria"** —Specifically, the practitioner should reference the AICPA Guide.

4. The practitioner should request the required written representations from the responsible party (even if the engaging party is not the responsible party). There is no alternative to obtaining the requested representations, so the responsible party's refusal to furnish the representations is a scope limitation that may preclude an unmodified opinion and warrant withdrawal.

F. Content of a Report on an Examination of a Forecast

1. A title that includes the word "independent";

2. An appropriate addressee;

3. Identification of the prospective financial information involved;

4. Identification of the criteria as the AICPA Guide;

5. A statement that identifies the responsible party and its responsibility and that identifies the practitioner's responsibility;

6. A statement that identifies that the examination was performed in accordance with attestation standards established by the AICPA, that describes the role of those standards, and that expresses the belief that the evidence obtained provides a reasonable basis for the opinion;

7. A statement that describes the nature of the examination engagement;

8. An opinion whether the presentation is in accordance with the AICPA Guide, and whether the underlying assumptions are suitably supported and provide a reasonable basis for the forecast or projection;

9. A statement that the prospective results may not be achieved and identifying any other significant inherent limitations;

10. A statement that there is no responsibility to update the report for events occurring after the date of the report;

11. The signature of the practitioner's firm;

12. The city and state of the practitioner; *and*

13. The date of the report.

14. **When the prospective information is presented as a range**—The practitioner should include a separate paragraph stating that the responsible party has chosen to present the expected results (of one or more assumptions) as a range.

G. Additional Elements for a Report on an Examination of a Projection

1. Identification of the hypothetical assumptions;

2. Description of the purpose for which the projection was prepared; *and*

3. An alert to restrict the use of the report to the specified parties.

> **Note**
>
> Any type of prospective financial statements (either a forecast or a projection) would be appropriate for limited use; however, only a forecast is appropriate for general use.
>
> A forecast has to be based on a realistic premise that is supportable; however, the premise for a projection need not be supportable, although the hypothetical assumptions should be consistent with the presentation's purpose. In evaluating assumptions other than hypothetical assumptions, the practitioner can conclude that they are suitably supported if each significant assumption is supported by the "preponderance" of information.

H. Modified opinions should be expressed for the following circumstances:

1. **If the prospective financial information departs in a material way from AICPA presentation guidelines**—The practitioner should express a *qualified or adverse* opinion.

2. **If the prospective financial information fails to disclose any "significant assumptions" or if one or more of the significant assumptions are not suitably supported or do not provide a reasonable basis for the forecast or projection**—The practitioner should express an *adverse* opinion.

3. **If unable to obtain sufficient appropriate evidence as a basis for the opinion**—The practitioner should express a *disclaimer of opinion*.

I. **Partial Presentations**

1. The practitioner should consider whether key factors affecting elements, accounts, or items that are related to those in the partial presentation have been taken into consideration and whether all significant assumptions have been disclosed.

2. Partial presentations usually are appropriate only for limited use. The practitioner should include a description of any limitations on the usefulness of the presentation.

J. AT-C 305 provides examples of unmodified examination reports on a forecast and on a projection that do not contain a range.

Example 1
Practitioner's Examination Report on a Financial Forecast

Independent Accountant's Report

[*Appropriate Addressee*]

We have examined the accompanying forecast of XYZ Company, which comprises [*identify the statements; e.g., the forecasted balance sheet as of December 31, 20XX, and the related forecasted statements of income, stockholders' equity, and cash flows for the year then ending*], based on the guidelines for the presentation of a forecast established by the American Institute of Certified Public Accountants. XYZ Company's management is responsible for preparing and presenting the forecast in accordance with the guidelines for the presentation of a forecast established by the American Institute of Certified Public Accountants. Our responsibility is to express an opinion on the forecast based on our examination.

Our examination was conducted in accordance with attestation standards established by the American Institute of Certified Public Accountants. Those standards require that we plan and perform the examination to obtain reasonable assurance about whether the forecast is presented in accordance with the guidelines for the presentation of a forecast established by the American Institute of Certified Public Accountants, in all material respects. An examination involves performing procedures to obtain evidence about the forecast. The nature, timing, and extent of the procedures selected depend on our judgment, including an assessment of the risks of material misstatement of the forecast, whether due to fraud or error. We believe that the evidence we obtained is sufficient and appropriate to provide a reasonable basis for our opinion.

In our opinion, the accompanying forecast is presented, in all material respects, in accordance with the guidelines for the presentation of a forecast established by the American Institute of Certified Public Accountants, and the underlying assumptions are suitably supported and provide a reasonable basis for management's forecast.

There will usually be differences between the forecasted and actual results because events and circumstances frequently do not occur as expected, and those differences may be material. We have no responsibility to update this report for events and circumstances occurring after the date of this report.

[*Practitioner's signature*]
[*Practitioner's city and state*]
[*Date of practitioner's report*]

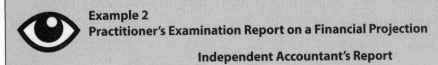

Example 2
Practitioner's Examination Report on a Financial Projection

Independent Accountant's Report

[*Appropriate Addressee*]

We have examined the accompanying projection of XYZ Company, which comprises [*identify the statements; e.g., the projected balance sheet as of December 31, 20XX, and the related projected statements of income, stockholders' equity, and cash flows for the year then ending*] based on the guidelines for the presentation of a projection established by the American Institute of Certified Public Accountants. XYZ Company's management is responsible for preparing and presenting the projection based on [*identify the hypothetical assumption; e.g., the granting of the requested loan as described in the summary of significant assumptions*] in accordance with the guidelines for the presentation of a projection established by the American Institute of Certified Public Accountants. The projection was prepared for [*describe the special purpose, for example, the purpose of negotiating a loan to expand XYZ Company's plant*]. Our responsibility is to express an opinion on the projection based on our examination.

Our examination was conducted in accordance with attestation standards established by the American Institute of Certified Public Accountants. Those standards require that we plan and perform the examination to obtain reasonable assurance about whether the projection is presented in accordance with the guidelines for the presentation of a projection established by the American Institute of Certified Public Accountants, in all material respects. An examination involves performing procedures to obtain evidence about the projection. The nature, timing, and extent of the procedures selected depend on our judgment, including an assessment of the risks of material misstatement of the projection, whether due to fraud or error. We believe that the evidence we obtained is sufficient and appropriate to provide a reasonable basis for our opinion.

In our opinion, [*describe the hypothetical assumption(s); e.g., assuming the granting of the requested loan for the purpose of expanding XYZ Company's plant as described in the summary of significant assumptions*] the projection referred to above is presented, in all material respects, in accordance with the guidelines for the presentation of a projection established by the American Institute of Certified Public Accountants, and the underlying assumptions are suitably supported and provide a reasonable basis for management's projection given the hypothetical assumption(s).

Even if [*identify the hypothetical assumption; e.g., the loan is granted and the plant is expanded*], there will usually be differences between the projected and actual results because events and circumstances frequently do not occur as expected, and those differences may be material. We have no responsibility to update this report for events and circumstances occurring after the date of this report.

The accompanying projection and this report are intended solely for the information and use of [*identify specified parties, for example, XYZ Company and DEF National Bank*] and are not intended to be and should not be used by anyone other than these specified parties.

[*Practitioner's signature*]
[*Practitioner's city and state*]
[*Date of practitioner's report*]

III. Agreed-Upon Procedures Engagements on Prospective Financial Information

    A. Preconditions for an Agreed-Upon Procedures Engagement—The practitioner should not perform such an engagement on a forecast or projection unless the prospective financial information includes a summary of significant assumptions.

    B. Content of the Practitioner's Agreed-Upon Procedures Report

        1. A title that includes the word "independent";

        2. An appropriate addressee;

3. Identification of the prospective financial information and the nature of the engagement;

4. Identification of the specified parties;

5. A statement that the procedures performed were agreed to by the specified parties;

6. A statement that identifies the responsible party and its responsibility for presenting the forecast or projection in accordance with AICPA guidelines;

7. A statement that the specified parties are responsible for the sufficiency of the procedures performed and that the practitioner makes no representation regarding the sufficiency of the procedures;

8. A list of the procedures performed (or reference to those procedures) and related findings. (The practitioner should not express a conclusion);

9. A description of any agreed-upon materiality limits, as applicable;

10. A statement that (a) the engagement was conducted in accordance with AICPA attestation standards; (b) did not conduct an examination or a review; (c) does not express such an opinion or conclusion; and (d) had additional procedures been performed, other matters might have been identified that would have been reported;

11. A description of any assistance provided by a practitioner's external specialist, as applicable;

12. A statement that the prospective results may not be achieved and identifying any other significant inherent limitations;

13. A statement that there is no responsibility to update the report for events occurring after the date of the report;

14. Any reservations concerning procedures or findings, as applicable;

15. An alert restricting the use of the report to the specified parties;

16. The signature of the practitioner's firm;

17. The city and state of the practitioner; *and*

18. The date of the report.

C. AT-C 305 provides an example of an agreed-upon procedures report on a forecast.

Example 3
Practitioner's Agreed-Upon Procedures Report Related to a Forecast

Independent Accountant's Agreed-Upon Procedures Report

[Appropriate Addressee]

We have performed the procedures enumerated below, which were agreed to by [*identify the specified parties; e.g., the boards of directors of XYZ Corporation and ABC Company*], on [*identify the statements; e.g., the forecasted balance sheet as of December 31, 20XX, and the related forecasted statements of income, stockholders' equity, and cash flows of DEF Company, a subsidiary of ABC Company, for the year then ending*]. DEF Company's management is responsible for preparing and presenting the forecast in accordance with the guidelines for the presentation of a forecast established by the American Institute of Certified Public Accountants. The sufficiency of these procedures is solely the responsibility of those parties specified in this report. Consequently, we make no representation regarding the sufficiency of the procedures enumerated below either for the purpose for which this report has been requested or for any other purpose.

[*Include paragraphs to enumerate procedures and findings*.]

This agreed-upon procedures engagement was conducted in accordance with attestation standards established by the American Institute of Certified Public Accountants. We were not engaged to and did not conduct an examination or review, the objective of which would be the expression of an opinion or conclusion, respectively, about whether the forecast is presented in accordance with the guidelines for the presentation of a forecast established by the American Institute of Certified Public Accountants or whether the underlying assumptions are suitably supported or provide a reasonable basis for management's forecast. Accordingly, we do not express such an opinion or conclusion. Had we performed additional procedures, other matters might have come to our attention that would have been reported to you.

There will usually be differences between the forecasted and actual results because events and circumstances frequently do not occur as expected, and those differences may be material. We have no responsibility to update this report for events and circumstances occurring after the date of this report.

This report is intended solely for the information and use of [*identify the specified parties; e.g., the boards of directors of ABC Company and XYZ Corporation*] and is not intended to be, and should not be, used by anyone other than these specified parties.

[*Practitioner's signature*]
[*Practitioner's city and state*]
[*Date of practitioner's report*]

Pro Forma Financial Information

After studying this lesson, you should be able to:

1. State what is meant by the term "pro forma" financial information.

2. Identify the two kinds of engagements associated with pro forma financial information under the clarified attestation standards.

3. Recognize the elements that are required in a practitioner's examination or review report on pro forma financial information.

I. Definitions

Definitions

Criteria for the Preparation of Pro Forma Financial Information: "The basis disclosed in the pro forma financial information that management used to develop the pro forma financial information, including the assumptions underlying the pro forma financial information."

Pro Forma Financial Information: "A presentation that shows what the significant effects on historical financial information might have been had a consummated or proposed transaction (or event) occurred at an earlier date."

Applicability: AT-C 310, *Reporting on Pro Forma Financial Information*, applies to **examination** or **review** engagements involving pro forma financial information.

It does not apply to agreed-upon procedures engagements involving pro forma financial information or when parties request a comfort letter on pro forma financial information in connection with a stock offering.

For example, pro forma financial information may be used to show the effects of (a) business combinations; (b) changes in capitalization; (c) dispositions of significant business segments; (d) changes in the form of business organizations; or (e) proposed sales of securities.

II. Examination or Review Engagements on Pro Forma Financial Information

A. **Preconditions** (in addition to those identified in other relevant AT-C sections)

1. The document containing the pro forma financial information must also include the historical financial statements (or the historical financial statements must be readily available);

2. For an examination, the historical financial statements must have been audited; for a review, the historical financial statements must have been either audited or reviewed—they cannot express a higher level of assurance on the pro forma information than on the historical financial statements;

3. The audit report or the review report, as applicable, must be included in the document containing the pro forma financial information (or it must be readily available); *and*

4. The practitioner should obtain an appropriate level of knowledge of the entity's accounting and financial reporting practices to perform the necessary procedures to report on the pro forma financial information.

B. **Requesting a Written Assertion**—The practitioner should request a written assertion from management; if management refuses, the practitioner should withdraw from the engagement (when that is permitted by law or regulation).

C. Assessing the Suitability of the Criteria—The criteria used by management are considered "suitable" when the criteria address the following matters:

1. That the financial information is extracted from the applicable historical financial statements;

2. That the pro forma adjustments are directly attributable to the transaction (event), are factually supportable, and consistent with the entity's applicable financial reporting framework and its accounting policies; *and*

3. That the pro forma financial information is appropriately presented, including adequate disclosures for users' understanding.

D. Examination and Review Procedures—The practitioner should apply the following procedures to the assumptions and pro forma adjustments for either an examination or a review engagement:

1. Obtain an understanding of the underlying transaction (event);

2. Obtain an understanding of the accounting and financial reporting practices of the entity (entities); if another practitioner performed the audit/review of the historical financial statements, the practitioner still should obtain this understanding;

3. Discuss with management their assumptions about the effects of the transaction/event;

4. Obtain sufficient evidence regarding the adjustments;

5. Evaluate whether pro forma adjustments are included for all significant effects;

6. Evaluate whether management's underlying assumptions are presented in a clear, comprehensive manner;

7. Evaluate whether the pro forma adjustments are consistent with each other and with the data used to make them;

8. Evaluate whether the computations of the adjustments are mathematically accurate and whether the pro forma column properly applies those adjustments to the historical financial statements; *and*

9. Read the pro forma financial information and evaluate whether (a) the transaction/event, the underlying assumptions, and the pro forma adjustments (and any significant uncertainties) have been adequately described; and (b) the source of the historical financial information involved has been properly identified.

E. Written Representation in an Examination and a Review Engagement

1. The practitioner should request the following written representations (in addition to those identified in other relevant AT-C sections):

   a. That management is responsible for the underlying assumptions used;

   b. That the assumptions are factually supportable (meaning that they are supported by the "preponderance" of the information);

   c. That the assumptions (a) provide a reasonable basis for presenting the significant effects, (b) the related adjustments properly reflect those assumptions, and (c) the pro forma amounts properly reflect those adjustments to the historical financial statements;

   d. That the pro forma adjustments are consistent with the entity's applicable financial reporting framework; *and*

   e. That the pro forma financial information is properly presented with proper disclosure of the significant effects directly attributable to the transaction/event involved.

2. Management's refusal to provide the requested written representations is a scope limitation sufficient to cause the practitioner to withdraw from the examination or review engagement. There is no alternative for obtaining the requested written representations from management for an engagement to examine or review pro forma financial information.

III. Content of the Practitioner's Report

A. Examination Report

1.   A title that includes the word "independent";

2.   An appropriate addressee;

3.   Reference to the pro forma adjustments included;

4.   Reference to management's description of the transaction (or event);

5.   Description of the pro forma financial information being reported on;

6.   Identification of the criteria used to evaluate the pro forma financial information;

7.   Reference to the financial statements from which the historical financial information is derived (refer to any modification of the auditor's report);

8.   A statement that the pro forma adjustments are based on management's assumptions;

9.   A statement to identify management's responsibility and to identify the practitioner's responsibility to express an opinion;

10. A statement that the examination was conducted in accordance with attestation standards established by the AICPA and other statements describing the examination engagement;

11. A statement describing the objectives and limitations of pro forma financial information;

12. An opinion whether management's assumptions provide a reasonable basis for presenting the significant effects and whether the pro forma adjustments give appropriate effect to those assumptions and the pro forma amounts reflect the proper adjustments to the historical financial statement amounts;

13. The signature of the practitioner's firm;

14. The city and state where the practitioner practices; *and*

15. The date of the report.

B. Review Report

1.   A title that includes the word "independent";

2.   An appropriate addressee;

3.   Reference to the pro forma adjustments included;

4.   Reference to management's description of the transaction (or event);

5.   A description of the pro forma financial information being reported on;

6.   Identification of the criteria used to evaluate the pro forma financial information;

7.   Reference to the financial statements from which the historical financial information is derived (the practitioner should state whether the financial statements were audited or reviewed and identify any modification of such report);

8.   A statement that the pro forma adjustments are based on management's assumptions;

9.   A statement to identify management's responsibility and to identify the practitioner's responsibility to express a conclusion;

10. A statement that the review was conducted in accordance with attestation standards established by the AICPA and other statements describing the review engagement;

11. A statement describing the objectives and limitations of pro forma financial information;

12. A conclusion whether the practitioner is aware of any material modifications that should be made to: (a) management's assumptions for them to provide a reasonable basis for presenting the significant effects, (b) the pro forma adjustments for them to give appropriate effect to those assumptions, and (c) the pro forma amounts for them to reflect the proper adjustments to the historical financial statement amounts;

13. The signature of the practitioner's firm;

14. The city and state where the practitioner practices; *and*

15. The date of the report.

C. AT-C 310 provides examples of an unmodified examination report and an unmodified review report on pro forma financial information.

 Example 1
Practitioner's Examination Report on Pro Forma Financial Information: Unmodified Opinion

Independent Accountant's Report

[Appropriate Addressee]

We have examined the pro forma adjustments giving effect to the underlying transaction (or event) described in Note 1 and the application of those adjustments to the historical amounts in the accompanying pro forma condensed balance sheet of X Company as of December 31, 20X1, and the related pro forma condensed statement of income for the year then ended (pro forma financial information), based on the criteria in Note 1. The historical condensed financial statements are derived from the historical financial statements of X Company, which were audited by us, and of Y Company, which were audited by other accountants, appearing elsewhere herein [*or "and are readily available"*]. The pro forma adjustments are based on management's assumptions described in Note 1. X Company's management is responsible for the pro forma financial information. Our responsibility is to express an opinion on the pro forma financial information based on our examination.

Our examination was conducted in accordance with attestation standards established by the American Institute of Certified Public Accountants. Those standards require that we plan and perform the examination to obtain reasonable assurance about whether, based on the criteria in Note 1, management's assumptions provide a reasonable basis for presenting the significant effects directly attributable to the underlying transaction (or event), and, in all material respects, the related pro forma adjustments give appropriate effect to those assumptions, and the pro forma amounts reflect the proper application of those adjustments to the historical financial statement amounts. An examination involves performing procedures to obtain evidence about management's assumptions, the related pro forma adjustments, and the pro forma amounts in the pro forma condensed balance sheet of X Company as of December 31, 20X1, and the related pro forma condensed statement of income for the year then ended. The nature, timing, and extent of the procedures selected depend on our judgment, including an assessment of the risks of material misstatement of the pro forma financial information, whether due to fraud or error. We believe that the evidence we obtained is sufficient and appropriate to provide a reasonable basis for our opinion.

The objective of this pro forma financial information is to show what the significant effects on the historical financial information might have been had the underlying transaction (or event) occurred at an earlier date. However, the pro forma condensed financial statements are not necessarily indicative of the results of operations or related effects on financial position that would have been attained had the above-mentioned transaction (or event) actually occurred at such earlier date.

In our opinion, based on the criteria in Note 1, management's assumptions provide a reasonable basis for presenting the significant effects directly attributable to the above-mentioned transaction (or event) described in Note 1, and, in all material respects, the related pro forma adjustments give appropriate effect to those assumptions, and the pro forma amounts reflect the proper application of those adjustments to the historical financial statement amounts in the pro forma condensed balance sheet of X Company as of December 31, 20X1, and the related pro forma condensed statement of income for the year then ended.

[Practitioner's signature]
[Practitioner's city and state]
[Date of practitioner's report]

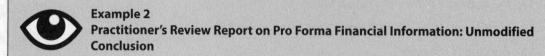

Example 2
Practitioner's Review Report on Pro Forma Financial Information: Unmodified Conclusion

Independent Accountant's Report

[Appropriate Addressee]

We have reviewed the pro forma adjustments giving effect to the transaction (or event) described in Note 1 and the application of those adjustments to the historical amounts in the accompanying pro forma condensed balance sheet of X Company as of March 31, 20X2, and the related pro forma condensed statement of income for the three months then ended (pro forma financial information), based on the criteria in Note 1. These historical condensed financial statements are derived from the historical unaudited financial statements of X Company, which were reviewed by us, and of Y Company, which were reviewed by other accountants, appearing elsewhere herein [*or "and are readily available"*]. The pro forma adjustments are based on management's assumptions as described in Note 1. X Company's management is responsible for the pro forma financial information. Our responsibility is to express a conclusion based on our review.

Our review was conducted in accordance with attestation standards established by the American Institute of Certified Public Accountants. Those standards require that we plan and perform our review to obtain limited assurance about whether, based on the criteria in Note 1, any material modifications should be made to management's assumptions in order for them to provide a reasonable basis for presenting the significant effects directly attributable to the underlying transaction (or event); the related pro forma adjustments, in order for them to give appropriate effect to those assumptions; or the pro forma amounts, in order for them to reflect the proper application of those adjustments to the historical financial statement amounts. A review is substantially less in scope than an examination, the objective of which is to obtain reasonable assurance about whether, based on the criteria, management's assumptions provide a reasonable basis for presenting the significant effects directly attributable to the underlying transaction (or event), and, in all material respects, the related pro forma adjustments give appropriate effect to those assumptions, and the pro forma amounts reflect the proper application of those adjustments to the historical financial statement amounts, in order to express an opinion. Accordingly, we do not express such an opinion. We believe that our review provides a reasonable basis for our conclusion.

The objective of this pro forma financial information is to show what the significant effects on the historical financial information might have been had the underlying transaction (or event) occurred at an earlier date. However, the pro forma condensed financial statements are not necessarily indicative of the results of operations or related effects on financial position that would have been attained had the above-mentioned transaction (or event) actually occurred at such earlier date.

Based on our review, we are not aware of any material modifications that should be made to management's assumptions in order for them to provide a reasonable basis for presenting the significant effects directly attributable to the above-mentioned transaction (or event) described in Note 1, the related pro forma adjustments in order for them to give appropriate effect to those assumptions, or the pro forma amounts, in order for them to reflect the proper application of those adjustments to the historical financial statement amounts in the pro forma condensed balance sheet of X Company as of March 31, 20X2, and the related pro forma condensed statement of income for the three months then ended, based on the criteria in Note 1.

[Practitioner's signature]
[Practitioner's city and state]
[Date of practitioner's report]

Compliance Attestation

After studying this lesson, you should be able to:

1. Identify the two kinds of engagements for compliance attestation under the clarified attestation standards.

2. Understand the practitioner's responsibilities in performing each of those types of engagements regarding compliance attestation, including recognizing the elements that are required in a practitioner's examination or agreed-upon procedures report on compliance.

I. Definitions

Definitions

Compliance with Specified Requirements: "An entity's compliance with specified laws, regulations, rules, contracts, or grants."

Material Noncompliance: "A failure to follow compliance requirements or a violation of prohibitions included in the specified requirements that results in noncompliance that is quantitatively or qualitatively material, either individually or when aggregated with other noncompliance."

Applicability: AT-C 315, *Compliance Attestation*, applies to **examination** or **agreed-upon procedures** reports dated on or after May 1, 2017, related to compliance with specified requirements (or agreed-upon procedures related to internal control over compliance).

The practitioner may be engaged to report directly on the subject matter (compliance), on management's assertion about compliance, or on internal control over compliance.

II. Examination Engagements

A. Preconditions (in addition to those identified in other relevant AT-C sections):

1. Management accepts responsibility for compliance with specified requirements and the entity's internal control over compliance; *and*

2. Management evaluates the entity's compliance with specified requirements.

B. Practitioner Should Request a Written Assertion from Management—If management refuses, the practitioner should withdraw from the engagement when that is permissible.

C. Examination Procedures

1. The practitioner should obtain an understanding of the specified requirements, including:

   a. Consideration of laws, regulations, rules, contracts, and grants relevant to the specified requirements;

   b. Consideration of knowledge obtained through prior engagements and regulatory reports; *and*

   c. Discussion with appropriate personnel within the entity.

2. **When the entity involved has operations in several components**—The practitioner should determine the nature, timing, and extent of testing at the individual components.

3. **Internal control over compliance**—The practitioner should obtain an understanding of internal control over compliance and assess the risks of material noncompliance; should consider the kinds of potential noncompliance and design appropriate tests of compliance.

4. **Compliance with regulatory requirements**—The practitioner should review reports and communications involving the regulatory agencies; may make inquiries of the regulatory agencies (e.g., about any examinations in progress).

D. **Written Representations in an Examination Engagement**

1. The practitioner should request written representations from management (in addition to those required by AT-C 205) that:

   a. Management takes responsibility for internal control over compliance;

   b. Management has performed an evaluation of the entity's compliance with specified requirements; *and*

   c. Management has provided its interpretation of any compliance requirements that are subject to different interpretations.

2. Management's refusal to furnish the required written representations is a scope limitation sufficient to preclude an unmodified opinion and may warrant withdrawal when that is permitted; there is no alternative to obtaining the required written representations (as discussed in AT-C 205).

E. **Content of the Practitioner's Examination Report**

1. A title that includes the word "independent";

2. An appropriate addressee;

3. Identification of the compliance matters being reported on (or the assertion involved);

4. Identification of the specified requirements; should also identify the criteria, if those criteria are not included in the compliance requirement;

5. A statement identifying management's responsibility for compliance and the practitioner's responsibility to express an opinion;

6. A statement that the examination was conducted in accordance with attestation standards established by the AICPA and other statements describing the examination engagement;

7. A statement describing the nature of an examination engagement;

8. A statement that describes any significant inherent limitations;

9. A statement that the examination does not provide a legal determination;

10. An opinion whether the entity complied with the specified requirements, in all material respects, or whether management's assertion is fairly stated;

11. The signature of the practitioner's firm;

12. The city and state where the practitioner practices; *and*

13. The date of the report.

F. AT-C 315 provides example of an unmodified examination report on compliance, which is presented below near the end of these materials.

III. **Agreed-Upon Procedures Engagements**

A. **Preconditions** (in addition to those identified in other relevant AT-C sections)

1. Management accepts responsibility for compliance with specified requirements and the entity's internal control over compliance; *and*

2. Management evaluates the entity's compliance with specified requirements.

B. **Written Representations in an Agreed-Upon Procedures Engagement**—The practitioner should request written representations from management (in addition to those required by AT-C 215) that:

1. Management takes responsibility for internal control over compliance;

2. Management has performed an evaluation of the entity's compliance with specified requirements or internal control over compliance;

3. Management has provided its interpretation of any compliance requirements that are subject to different interpretations; *and*

4. Management has disclosed any known noncompliance occurring subsequent to the period covered by the practitioner's report.

C. **Content of the Practitioner's Agreed-Upon Procedures Report**

1. A title that includes the word "independent";

2. An appropriate addressee;

3. Identification of the specified requirements being reported on;

4. Statement identifying management's responsibility for compliance with the specified requirements;

5. Identification of the specified parties;

6. A statement that the specified parties are responsible for the sufficiency of the procedures performed;

7. A list of the procedures performed (or reference to them) and the findings;

8. A description of any agreed-upon materiality limits, if applicable;

9. A statement that the agreed-upon procedures engagement was conducted in accordance with attestation standards established by the AICPA and other statements pointing out that it was not an examination or a review and include a disclaimer of opinion or any other conclusion;

10. A description of the assistance provided by a practitioner's external specialist, if applicable;

11. Any reservations about the procedures or findings, if applicable;

12. An alert that restricts the use of the report to specified users;

13. The signature of the practitioner's firm;

14. The city and state where the practitioner practices; *and*

15. The date of the report.

D. AT-C 315 provides examples of an unmodified examination report on compliance and an agreed-upon procedures report on compliance, which follow.

Example 1
Practitioner's Examination Report on Compliance; Unmodified Opinion

The following is an illustrative practitioner's examination report for an engagement in which the practitioner is reporting on subject matter (an entity's compliance with specified requirements during a period of time).

Independent Accountant's Report

[*Appropriate addressee*]

We have examined XYZ Company's compliance with [*identify the specified requirements, for example, the requirements listed in Attachment 1*] during the period January 1, 20X1, to December 31, 20X1. Management of XYZ Company is responsible for XYZ Company's compliance with the specified requirements. Our responsibility is to express an opinion on XYZ Company's compliance with the specified requirements based on our examination.

Our examination was conducted in accordance with attestation standards established by the American Institute of Certified Public Accountants. Those standards require that we plan and perform the examination to obtain reasonable assurance about whether XYZ Company complied, in all material respects, with the specified requirements referenced above. An examination involves performing procedures to obtain evidence about whether XYZ Company complied with the specified requirements. The nature, timing, and extent of the procedures selected depend on our judgment, including an assessment of the risks of material noncompliance, whether due to fraud or error. We believe that the evidence we obtained is sufficient and appropriate to provide a reasonable basis for our opinion.

Our examination does not provide a legal determination on XYZ Company's compliance with specified requirements.

In our opinion, XYZ Company complied, in all material respects, with [*identify the specified requirements; e.g., the requirements listed in Attachment 1*] during the period January 1, 20X1, to December 31, 20X1.

[*Practitioner's signature*]
[*Practitioner's city and state*]
[*Date of practitioner's report*]

Example 2
Practitioner's Agreed-Upon Procedures Report Related to Compliance

The following is an illustrative practitioner's agreed-upon procedures report related to an entity's compliance with specified requirements in which the procedures and findings are enumerated rather than referenced.

Independent Accountant's Report on Applying Agreed-Upon Procedures

[*Appropriate Addressee*]

We have performed the procedures enumerated below, which were agreed to by [*identify the specified parties; e.g., the management and board of directors of XYZ Company*], related to XYZ Company's compliance with [*identify the specified requirements; e.g., the requirements listed in Attachment 1*] during the period January 1, 20X1, to December 31, 20X1]. XYZ Company's management is responsible for its compliance with those requirements. The sufficiency of these procedures is solely the responsibility of those parties specified in this report. Consequently, we make no representations regarding the sufficiency of the procedures enumerated below either for the purpose for which this report has been requested or for any other purpose.

[*Include paragraphs to enumerate procedures and findings.*]

This agreed-upon procedures engagement was conducted in accordance with attestation standards established by the American Institute of Certified Public Accountants. We were not engaged to and did not conduct an examination or review, the objective of which would be the expression of an opinion or conclusion, respectively, on compliance with specified requirements. Accordingly, we do not express such an opinion or conclusion. Had we performed additional procedures, other matters might have come to our attention that would have been reported to you.

This report is intended solely for the information and use of [*identify the specified parties; e.g., the management and board of directors of XYZ Company*] and is not intended to be, and should not be, used by anyone other than the specified parties.

[*Practitioner's signature*]
[*Practitioner's city and state*]
[*Date of practitioner's report*]

Management's Discussion and Analysis (MD&A)

After studying this lesson, you should be able to:

1. Identify the two kinds of attestation engagements for MD&A presentations under the clarified attestation standards.

2. Identify the three specific matters addressed by the practitioner's opinion (for an examination) or conclusion (for a review) regarding MD&A presentations under the clarified attestation standards.

3. Identify the four assertions that are implicitly associated with MD&A presentations.

When the Auditing Standards Board issued the clarified attestation standards, the ASB decided to retain the "old" guidance with respect to attestation engagements involving MD&A presentations. Rather than issue "clarified" guidance applicable to MD&A presentations, the ASB simply designated the existing guidance as AT-C Section 395. The justification was provided in a note:

"The Auditing Standards Board (ASB) has not clarified AT section 701 because practitioners rarely perform attest engagements to report on management's discussion and analysis prepared pursuant to the rules and regulations adopted by the U.S. Securities and Exchange Commission. Therefore, the ASB decided that it would retain AT section 701 in its current unclarified format as section 395 until further notice."

I. Applicability

A. When attesting to MD&A that has been prepared according to the requirements of the SEC and that MD&A is presented in annual reports or in other documents.

B. Can even apply to a nonpublic entity that provides a written assertion that the SEC requirements were used as criteria for the presentation of the MD&A.

   1. **Precondition to accept an MD&A engagement**—Must have audited the annual financials for the latest period applicable to the MD&A presentation; any other financials involved must have been audited (or at least reviewed if interim/quarterly financials) by the practitioner or a predecessor auditor.

II. Examination of MD&A—Results in Positive Assurance

A. **Purpose**—To express an opinion on whether:

   1. **Required elements**—The presentation includes the elements required by the SEC:

      a. Discussion of **financial condition** (liquidity and capital resources);

      b. Discussion of **changes in financial condition**;

      c. Discussion of **results of operations.**

   2. **Historical amounts**—The historical financial amounts are accurately derived from the financials.

   3. **Basis for conclusions**—The underlying information, assumptions, etc., provide a reasonable basis for the disclosures within the MD&A.

B. **Four Assertions Implicitly Embodied in the MD&A Presentation**

   1. **Occurrence**—Whether reported events actually occurred during the period.

   2. **Consistency with the financials**—Whether historical amounts have been accurately derived from the financials.

   3. **Completeness of the explanation**—Whether the description of matters comprising the MD&A presentation is complete.

4. **Presentation and disclosure**—Whether information in the MD&A is properly classified, described, and disclosed.

C. **Primary Dimensions of an Examination of MD&A**

1. **Planning the examination** (similar to an audit engagement)—Develop an overall strategy that limits "attestation risk" to an acceptably low level.

    a. **Inherent risk**—Varies with the assertion involved.

    b. **Control risk** (same as previously discussed).

    c. **Detection risk** (same as previously discussed).

2. **Consideration of internal control applicable to MD&A** (similar to an audit)—Pertains to assessment of control risk, documenting the understanding, and communication of significant deficiencies.

3. **Obtain sufficient evidence**—Varies with the circumstances but includes reading the MD&A for consistency with the financials, examining related documents, reading minutes, reading communications from the SEC, and obtaining written representations from management, among other things.

4. **Consideration of subsequent events** (SEC expects MD&A to reflect events at or near the filing date)—Read minutes and available interim financials; make inquiries of management and obtain appropriate representations in writing.

D. **Reporting on MD&A**—Financial statements with the auditor's report should accompany the document containing the MD&A (or be incorporated by reference to documents filed with the SEC).

1. **Title**—"Independent Accountant's Report."

2. **Unmodified examination report**—Four paragraphs:

    a. Introductory paragraph (four sentences).

        i. Identify MD&A presentation;

        ii. Identify management's responsibility;

        iii. Identify accountant's responsibility; *and*

        iv. Refer to related audit report.

    b. **Scope paragraph**—Three sentences:

        i. Refer to attestation standards established by AICPA;

        ii. Describe scope of examination; *and*

        iii. Say that examination provides reasonable basis for opinion.

    c. **Explanatory paragraph**—Three sentences:

        i. Comment on the need for estimates and assumptions;

        ii. Comment on the role of future expectations; *and*

        iii. State that actual results may differ.

    d. **Opinion paragraph**—One long sentence. Indicate whether (1) the presentation includes elements required by SEC; (2) the historical amounts are accurately derived; and (3) the underlying information and assumptions provide a reasonable basis for the MD&A.

3. **Dating report**—As of completion of the examination procedures.

4. **Modifications of the examination report**

    a. **Reservations as to presentation**—Results in a *qualified* or *adverse* opinion.

b. **Reservations as to scope**—Results in a *qualified* opinion or a *disclaimer* of opinion.

c. **Division of responsibility**—May refer to another practitioner's report on MD&A for a specific component as a partial basis for one's own report.

d. **Emphasis of a matter**—Presented as a separate paragraph (e.g., information included beyond the SEC's requirements).

Sample Examination Report on (Annual) MD&A when Reporting Directly on the Subject Matter, Not on Management's Assertion

Independent Accountant's Report

(Introductory paragraph)

We have examined ABC Company's Management's Discussion and Analysis taken as a whole, included (incorporated by reference) in the Company's (insert description of registration statement or document). Management is responsible for the preparation of the Company's Management's Discussion and Analysis pursuant to the rules and regulations adopted by the Securities and Exchange Commission. Our responsibility is to express an opinion on the presentation based on our examination. We have audited, in accordance with auditing standards generally accepted in the United States of America, the financial statements of ABC Company as of December 31, 20X3 and 20X2, and for each of the years in the three-year period ended December 31, 20X3, and in our report dated [Month and day], 20X4, we expressed an unqualified opinion on those financial statements.

(Scope paragraph)

Our examination of Management's Discussion and Analysis was conducted in accordance with attestation standards established by the American Institute of Certified Public Accountants and, accordingly, included examining, on a test basis, evidence supporting the historical amounts and disclosures in the presentation. An examination also includes assessing the significant determinations made by management as to the relevancy of information to be included and the estimates and assumptions that affect reported information. We believe that our examination provides a reasonable basis for our opinion.

(Explanatory paragraph)

The preparation of Management's Discussion and Analysis requires management to interpret the criteria, make determinations as to the relevancy of information to be included, and make estimates and assumptions that affect reported information. Management's Discussion and Analysis includes information regarding the estimated future impact of transactions and events that have occurred or are expected to occur, expected sources of liquidity and capital resources, operating trends, commitments, and uncertainties. Actual results in the future may differ materially from management's present assessment of this information because events and circumstances frequently do not occur as expected.

(Opinion paragraph)

In our opinion, the Company's presentation of Management's Discussion and Analysis includes, in all material respects, the required elements of the rules and regulations adopted by the Securities and Exchange Commission; the historical financial amounts included therein have been accurately derived, in all material respects, from the Company's financial statements; and the underlying information, determinations, estimates, and assumptions of the Company provide a reasonable basis for the disclosures contained therein.

(Signature)

(Practitioner's city and state)

(Date)

III. Review of MD&A—Results in Negative Assurance

  A. Purpose—To report whether the practitioner has any reason to believe that:

    1. The presentation does *not* include the elements required by the SEC;

    2. The historical financial amounts are *not* accurately derived from the financials; *and*

    3. The underlying information, assumptions, etc., do *not* provide a reasonable basis for the disclosures within the MD&A.

  B. Primary Dimensions of a Review of MD&A

    1. Obtain an understanding of the SEC requirements regarding MD&A.

    2. Plan the engagement—Develop an overall strategy;

    3. Consider relevant portions of internal control affecting MD&A presentation;

    4. Apply *analytical procedures* and make *inquiries* of management (usually do not have to obtain corroboration);

    5. Consider subsequent events; *and*

    6. Obtain written representations from management.

  C. Unmodified Review Report—Usually consists of five paragraphs (if including a restricted-use paragraph at the end of the report); the accountantmay review the entity's annual MD&A presentation or an interim MD&A presentation.

    1. Title—"Independent Accountant's Report"

    2. Introductory paragraph—Three sentences. Delete the sentence on accountant's responsibility and

      a. Identify MD&A presentation;

      b. Identify management's responsibility; *and*

      c. Refer to related audit report.

    3. Scope paragraph—Four sentences. Add a disclaimer:

      a. Refer to attestation standards established by the AICPA;

      b. Describe a review engagement;

      c. Say that scope is less than that of an examination; *and*

      d. Disclaim an opinion.

    4. Explanatory paragraph—Three sentences. Same as for an examination report:

      a. Comment on the need for estimates and assumptions;

      b. Comment on the role of future expectations; *and*

      c. State that actual results may differ.

    5. Conclusions paragraph—One long sentence. Negative assurance as to whether presentation does not include elements required by SEC, historical amounts are not accurately derived, and underlying information and assumptions do not provide a reasonable basis for the MD&A.

    6. Restricted-use paragraph—One sentence. Restrict the distribution when the MD&A presentation and the practitioner's report are not intended to be filed with the SEC under the 1933 and 1934 Securities Acts.

    7. Dating report—As of completion of the review procedures.

    8. Changes to the usual review report—Reservations as to presentation resulting in a qualified review report; reference to other practitioners; or emphasis of a matter.

Sample Reports

Examination of Forecast

Independent Accountant's Report

To the Board of Directors and Stockholders

ABC Company

We have examined the accompanying forecasted balance sheet, statements of income, retained earnings, and cash flows of ABC Company as of December 31, 20X1, and for the year then ending. ABC Company's management is responsible for the forecast. Our responsibility is to express an opinion on the forecast based on our examination.

Our examination was conducted in accordance with attestation standards established by the American Institute of Certified Public Accountants and, accordingly, included such procedures as we considered necessary to evaluate both the assumptions used by management and the preparation and presentation of the forecast. We believe that our examination provides a reasonable basis for our opinion.

In our opinion, the accompanying forecast is presented in conformity with guidelines for presentation of a forecast established by the American Institute of Certified Public Accountants, and the underlying assumptions provide a reasonable basis for management's forecast. However, there usually will be differences between the forecasted and actual results, because events and circumstances frequently do not occur as expected, and those differences may be material. We have no responsibility to update this report for events and circumstances occurring after the date of this report.

/s/ CPA firm (signed by engagement partner)

Date (usually the last day of fieldwork)

AUP of Forecast

Sample Agreed-Upon Procedures Report on Forecast Financial Information

Independent Accountant's Report on Applying Agreed-Upon Procedures

Board of Directors—XYZ Corporation

Board of Directors—ABC Company

At your request, we have performed certain agreed-upon procedures, as enumerated below, with respect to the forecasted balance sheet and the related forecasted statements of income, retained earnings, and cash flows of DEF Company, a subsidiary of ABC Company, as of December 31, 20XX, and for the year then ending. These procedures, which were agreed to by the Boards of Directors of XYZ Corporation and ABC Company, were performed solely to assist you in evaluating the forecast in connection with the proposed sale of DEF Company to XYZ Corporation. DEF Company's management is responsible for the forecast.

This agreed-upon procedures engagement was conducted in accordance with attestation standards established by the American Institute of Certified Public Accountants. The sufficiency of these procedures is solely the responsibility of the specified parties. Consequently, we make no representation regarding the sufficiency of the procedures described below either for the purpose for which this report has been requested or for any other purpose.

[Include paragraphs to enumerate (or reference) procedures and findings]

We were not engaged to and did not conduct an examination, the objective of which would be the expression of an opinion on the accompanying prospective financial statements. Accordingly, we do not express an opinion on whether the prospective financial statements are presented in conformity with AICPA presentation guidelines or on whether the underlying assumptions provide a reasonable basis for the presentation. Had we performed additional procedures, other matters might have come to our attention that would have been reported to you. Furthermore, there will usually be differences between the forecasted and actual results, because events and circumstances frequently do not occur as expected, and those differences may be material. We have no responsibility to update this report for events and circumstances occurring after the date of this report.

This report is intended solely for the information and use of the Boards of Directors of ABC Company and XYZ Corporation and is not intended to be and should not be used by anyone other than these specified parties.

/s/ CPA firm (signed by engagement partner)

Date (usually the last day of fieldwork)

Compilation of Forecast

> ## Accountant's Compilation Report
>
> We have compiled the accompanying forecasted balance sheet, statements of income, retained earnings, and cash flows of ABC Company as of December 31, 20X1, and for the year then ending, in accordance with attestation standards established by the American Institute of Certified Public Accountants.
>
> A compilation is limited to presenting in the form of a forecast information that is the representation of management and does not include evaluation of the support for the assumptions underlying the forecast. We have not examined the forecast and, accordingly, do not express an opinion or any other form of assurance on the accompanying statements or assumptions. Furthermore, there usually will be differences between the forecasted and actual results, because events and circumstances frequently do not occur as expected, and those differences may be material. We have no responsibility to update this report for events and circumstances occurring after the date of this report.
>
> /s/ CPA firm (signed by engagement partner)
>
> Date

Examination of Pro Forma

Independent Accountant's Report

We have examined the pro forma adjustments reflecting the transactions [or event] described in Note 1 and the application of those adjustments to the historical amounts in the accompanying pro forma financial condensed balance sheet of ABC Company as of December 31, 20X1, and the pro forma condensed statement of income for the year then ended. The historical condensed financial statements are derived from the historical financial statements of ABC Company, which were audited by us, and of XYZ Company, which were audited by other accountants, appearing elsewhere herein. Such pro forma adjustments are based upon management's assumptions described in Note 2. ABC Company's management is responsible for the pro forma financial information. Our responsibility is to express an opinion on the pro forma financial information based on our examination.

Our examination was conducted in accordance with attestation standards established by the American Institute of Certified Public Accountants and, accordingly, included such procedures as we considered necessary in the circumstances. We believe that our examination provides a reasonable basis for our opinion.

The objective of this pro forma financial information is to show what the significant effects on the historical financial information might have been had the transaction [or event] occurred at an earlier date. However, the pro forma condensed financial statements are not necessarily indicative of the results of operations or related effects on financial position that would have been attained had the above-mentioned transaction [or event] actually occurred earlier.

In our opinion, management's assumptions provide a reasonable basis for presenting the significant effects directly attributable to the above-mentioned transaction [or event] described in Note 1, the related pro forma adjustments give appropriate effect to those assumptions, and the pro forma column reflects the proper application of those adjustments to the historical financial statement amounts in the pro forma condensed balance sheet as of December 31, 20X1, and the pro forma condensed statement of income for the year then ended.

/s/ CPA firm (signed by engagement partner)

Date

Note
Additional paragraph(s) may be added to emphasize certain matters relating to the attest engagement or the subject matter.

Review of Pro Forma

Independent Accountant's Report

We have reviewed the pro forma adjustments reflecting the transactions [or event] described in Note 1 and the application of those adjustments to the historical amounts in the accompanying pro forma financial condensed balance sheet of XYZ Company as of March 31, 20X2, and the pro forma condensed statement of income for the three months then ended. The historical condensed financial statements are derived from the historical unaudited financial statements of XYZ Company, which were reviewed by us, and of ABC Company, which were reviewed by other accountants, appearing elsewhere herein. Such pro forma adjustments are based upon management's assumptions described in Note 2. XYZ Company's management is responsible for the pro forma financial information.

Our review was conducted in accordance with attestation standards established by the American Institute of Certified Public Accountants. A review is substantially less in scope than an examination, the objective of which is the expression of an opinion on management's assumptions, the pro forma adjustments and the application of those adjustments to historical financial information. Accordingly, we do not express such an opinion.

The objective of this pro forma financial information is to show what the significant effects on the historical financial information might have been had the transaction [or event] occurred at an earlier date. However, the pro forma condensed financial statements are not necessarily indicative of the results of operations or related effects on financial position that would have been attained had the above-mentioned transaction [or event] actually occurred earlier.

Based on our review, nothing came to our attention that caused us to believe that management's assumptions do not provide a reasonable basis for presenting the significant effects directly attributable to the above-mentioned transaction [or event] described in Note 1, that the related pro forma adjustments do not give appropriate effect to those assumptions, or that the pro forma column does not reflect the proper application of those adjustments to the historical financial statement amounts in the pro forma condensed balance sheet as of March 31, 20X2, and the pro forma condensed statement of income for the three months then ended.

/s/ CPA firm (signed by engagement partner)

Date (usually the last day of fieldwork)

Note
Additional paragraph(s) may be added to emphasize certain matters relating to the attest engagement or the subject matter.

Examination for Compliance

Independent Accountant's Report

We have examined management's assertion about (*name of entity*)'s compliance with (*list specified compliance requirements*) during the (*period*) ended (*date*) included in the accompanying (*title of management report*). Management is responsible for (name of entity)'s compliance with those requirements. Our responsibility is to express an opinion on management's assertion about the Company's compliance based on our examination.

Our examination was made in accordance with standards established by the American Institute of Certified Public Accountants and, accordingly, included examining, on a test basis, evidence about (*name of entity*)'s compliance with those requirements and performing such other procedures as we considered necessary in the circumstances. We believe that our examination provides a reasonable basis for our opinion. Our examination does not provide a legal determination on (*name of entity*)'s compliance with specified requirements.

In our opinion, management's assertion (*identify management's assertion—for example that XYZ Company complied with the aforementioned requirements for the year ended December 31, 20X1*) is fairly stated, in all material respects.

/s/ CPA firm (signed by engagement partner)

Date (usually the last day of fieldwork)

AUP for Compliance

Independent Accountant's Report

To the Audit Committees and Managements of ABC Inc. and XYZ Fund

We have performed the procedures enumerated below, which were agreed to by the audit committees and managements of ABC Inc. and XYZ Fund, solely to assist you in evaluating the accompanying Statement of Investment Performance Statistics of XYZ Fund (prepared in accordance with the criteria specified therein) for the year ended December 31, 20X1. XYZ Fund's management is responsible for the statement of investment performance statistics. This agreed-upon procedures engagement was conducted in accordance with attestation standards established by the American Institute of Certified Public Accountants. The sufficiency of these procedures is solely the responsibility of those parties specified in this report. Consequently, we make no representation regarding the sufficiency of the procedures described below either for the purpose for which this report has been requested or for any other purpose.

We were not engaged to and did not conduct an examination, the objective of which would be the expression of an opinion on the accompanying Statement of Investment Performance Statistics of XYZ Fund. Accordingly, we do not express such an opinion. Had we performed additional procedures, other matters might have come to our attention that would have been reported to you.

This report is intended solely for the information and use of the audit committees and managements of ABC Inc. and XYZ Fund, and is not intended to be and should not be used by anyone other than these specified parties.

/signature/

[Date]

Note
Include paragraphs to enumerate *procedures* and *findings*—or reference appendix (appendices) where these procedures and findings are identified.

Example Management Report
(with No Material Weaknesses Reported)

Management's Report on Internal Control Over Financial Reporting

ABC Company's internal control over financial reporting is a process effected by those charged with governance, management, and other personnel, designed to provide reasonable assurance regarding the preparation of reliable financial statements in accordance with *[applicable financial reporting framework, such as accounting principles generally accepted in the United States of America]*. An entity's internal control over financial reporting includes those policies and procedures that (1) pertain to the maintenance of records that, in reasonable detail, accurately and fairly reflect the transactions and dispositions of the assets of the entity; (2) provide reasonable assurance that transactions are recorded as necessary to permit preparation of financial statements in accordance with *[applicable financial reporting framework, such as accounting principles generally accepted in the United States of America]*, and that receipts and expenditures of the entity are being made only in accordance with authorizations of management and those charged with governance; and (3) provide reasonable assurance regarding prevention, or timely detection and correction, of unauthorized acquisition, use, or disposition of the entity's assets that could have a material effect on the financial statements.

Management of ABC Company is responsible for designing, implementing, and maintaining effective internal control over financial reporting. Management assessed the effectiveness of ABC Company's internal control over financial reporting as of December 31, 20XX, based on *[identify criteria]*. Based on that assessment, management concluded that, as of December 31, 20XX, ABC Company's internal control over financial reporting is effective, based on *[identify criteria]*.

Internal control over financial reporting has inherent limitations. Internal control over financial reporting is a process that involves human diligence and compliance and is subject to lapses in judgment and breakdowns resulting from human failures. Internal control over financial reporting also can be circumvented by collusion or improper management override. Because of its inherent limitations, internal control over financial reporting may not prevent, or detect and correct, misstatements. Also, projections of any assessment of effectiveness to future periods are subject to the risk that controls may become inadequate because of changes in conditions, or that the degree of compliance with the policies or procedures may deteriorate.

ABC Company

[Report signers, if applicable]

[Date]

Unmodified Opinions on Financial Statements and ICFR (Combined Report)

[*Appropriate Addressee*]

Report on Internal Control Over Financial Reporting

We have audited the accompanying financial statements of ABC Company, which comprise the balance sheet as of December 31, 20XX, and the related statements of income, changes in stockholders' equity, and cash flows for the year then ended, and the related notes to the financial statements. We have also audited ABC Company's internal control over financial reporting as of December 31, 20XX, based on [*identify criteria*].

Management's Responsibility for the Financial Statements and Internal Control Over Financial Reporting

Management is responsible for the preparation and fair presentation of these financial statements in accordance with accounting principles generally accepted in the United States of America; this includes the design, implementation, and maintenance of effective internal control over financial reporting relevant to the preparation and fair presentation of financial statements that are free from material misstatement, whether due to fraud or error. Management is also responsible for its assessment about the effectiveness of internal control over financial reporting, included in the accompanying [*title of management's report*].

Auditor's Responsibility

Our responsibility is to express an opinion on these financial statements and an opinion on the entity's internal control over financial reporting based on our audits. We conducted our audits in accordance with auditing standards generally accepted in the United States of America. Those standards require that we plan and perform the audits to obtain reasonable assurance about whether the financial statements are free from material misstatement and whether effective internal control over financial reporting was maintained in all material respects.

An audit of financial statements involves performing procedures to obtain audit evidence about the amounts and disclosures in the financial statements. The procedures selected depend on the auditor's judgment, including the assessment of the risks of material misstatement of the financial statements, whether due to fraud or error. In making those risk assessments, the auditor considers internal control relevant to the entity's preparation and fair presentation of the financial statements in order to design audit procedures that are appropriate in the circumstances. An audit of financial statements also includes evaluating the appropriateness of accounting policies used and the reasonableness of significant accounting estimates made by management, as well as evaluating the overall presentation of the financial statements.

An audit of internal control over financial reporting involves performing procedures to obtain audit evidence about whether a material weakness exists. The procedures selected depend on the auditor's judgment, including the assessment of the risks that a material weakness exists. An audit includes obtaining an understanding of internal control over financial reporting and testing and evaluating the design and operating effectiveness of internal control over financial reporting based on the assessed risk.

We believe that the audit evidence we have obtained is sufficient and appropriate to provide a basis for our audit opinions.

Definition and Inherent Limitations of Internal Control Over Financial Reporting

An entity's internal control over financial reporting is a process effected by those charged with governance, management, and other personnel, designed to provide reasonable assurance regarding the preparation of reliable financial statements in accordance with [*applicable financial reporting framework, such as accounting principles generally accepted in the United States of America*]. An entity's internal control over financial reporting includes those policies and procedures that (1) pertain to the maintenance of records that, in reasonable detail, accurately and fairly reflect the transactions and dispositions of the assets of the entity; (2) provide reasonable assurance that transactions are recorded as necessary to permit preparation of financial statements in accordance with [*applicable financial reporting framework, such as accounting principles generally accepted in the United States of America*], and that receipts and expenditures of the entity are being made only in accordance with authorizations of management and those charged with governance; and (3) provide reasonable assurance regarding prevention, or timely detection and correction of unauthorized acquisition, use, or disposition of the entity's assets that could have a material effect on the financial statements.

Because of its inherent limitations, internal control over financial reporting may not prevent, or detect and correct, misstatements. Also, projections of any assessment of effectiveness to future periods are subject to the risk that controls may become inadequate because of changes in conditions, or that the degree of compliance with the policies or procedures may deteriorate.

Opinions

In our opinion, the financial statements referred to above present fairly, in all material respects, the financial position of ABC Company as of December 31, 20XX, and the results of its operations and its cash flows for the year then ended in accordance with [*applicable financial reporting framework, such as accounting principles generally accepted in the United States of America*]. Also, in our opinion, ABC Company maintained, in all material respects, effective internal control over financial reporting as of December 31, 20XX, based on [*identify criteria*].

Report on Other Legal and Regulatory Requirements

[*Form and content of this section of the auditor's report will vary depending on the nature of the auditor's other reporting responsibilities.*]

[*Auditor's signature*]

[*Auditor's city and state*]

[*Date of the auditor's report*]

Unmodified Opinion on ICFR (Separate Report on ICFR)

[*Appropriate Addressee*]

Report on Internal Control Over Financial Reporting

We have audited ABC Company's internal control over financial reporting as of December 31, 20XX, based on [*identify criteria*].

Management's Responsibility for Internal Control Over Financial Reporting

Management is responsible for designing, implementing, and maintaining effective internal control over financial reporting, and for its assessment about the effectiveness of internal control over financial reporting, included in the accompanying [*title of management's report*].

Auditor's Responsibility

Our responsibility is to express an opinion on the entity's internal control over financial reporting based on our audit. We conducted our audit in accordance with auditing standards generally accepted in the United States of America. Those standards require that we plan and perform the audit to obtain reasonable assurance about whether effective internal control over financial reporting was maintained in all material respects.

An audit of internal control over financial reporting involves performing procedures to obtain audit evidence about whether a material weakness exists. The procedures selected depend on the auditor's judgment, including the assessment of the risks that a material weakness exists. An audit includes obtaining an understanding of internal control over financial reporting and testing and evaluating the design and operating effectiveness of internal control over financial reporting based on the assessed risk.

We believe that the audit evidence we have obtained is sufficient and appropriate to provide a basis for our audit opinion.

Definition and Inherent Limitations of Internal Control Over Financial Reporting

An entity's internal control over financial reporting is a process effected by those charged with governance, management, and other personnel, designed to provide reasonable assurance regarding the preparation of reliable financial statements in accordance with [*applicable financial reporting framework, such as accounting principles generally accepted in the United States of America*]. An entity's internal control over financial reporting includes those policies and procedures that (1) pertain to the maintenance of records that, in reasonable detail, accurately and fairly reflect the transactions and dispositions of the assets of the entity; (2) provide reasonable assurance that transactions are recorded as necessary to permit preparation of financial statements in accordance with [*applicable financial reporting framework, such as accounting principles generally accepted in the United States of America*], and that receipts and expenditures of the entity are being made only in accordance with authorizations of management and those charged with governance; and (3) provide reasonable assurance regarding prevention, or timely detection and correction of unauthorized acquisition, use, or disposition of the entity's assets that could have a material effect on the financial statements.

Because of its inherent limitations, internal control over financial reporting may not prevent, or detect and correct, misstatements. Also, projections of any assessment of effectiveness to future periods are subject to the risk that controls may become inadequate because of changes in conditions, or that the degree of compliance with the policies or procedures may deteriorate.

Opinion

In our opinion, ABC Company maintained, in all material respects, effective internal control over financial reporting as of December 31, 20XX, based on [*identify criteria*].

Report on Financial Statements

We also have audited, in accordance with auditing standards generally accepted in the United States of America, the [*identify financial statements*] of ABC Company, and our report dated [*date of report, which should be the same as the date of the report on the audit of ICFR*] expressed [*include nature of opinion*].

Report on Other Legal and Regulatory Requirements

[*Form and content of this section of the auditor's report will vary depending on the nature of the auditor's other reporting responsibilities.*]

[*Auditor's signature*]

[*Auditor's city and state*]

[*Date of the auditor's report*]

Adverse Opinion on ICFR (Separate Report on ICFR)

[*Appropriate Addressee*]

Report on Internal Control Over Financial Reporting

We have audited ABC Company's internal control over financial reporting as of December 31, 20XX, based on [*identify criteria*].

Management's Responsibility for Internal Control Over Financial Reporting

Management is responsible for designing, implementing, and maintaining effective internal control over financial reporting, and for its assessment about the effectiveness of internal control over financial reporting, included in the accompanying [*title of management's report*].

Auditor's Responsibility

Our responsibility is to express an opinion on the entity's internal control over financial reporting based on our audit. We conducted our audit in accordance with auditing standards generally accepted in the United States of America. Those standards require that we plan and perform the audit to obtain reasonable assurance about whether effective internal control over financial reporting was maintained in all material respects.

An audit of internal control over financial reporting involves performing procedures to obtain audit evidence about whether a material weakness exists. The procedures selected depend on the auditor's judgment, including the assessment of the risks that a material weakness exists. An audit includes obtaining an understanding of internal control over financial reporting and testing and evaluating the design and operating effectiveness of internal control over financial reporting based on the assessed risk.

We believe that the audit evidence we have obtained is sufficient and appropriate to provide a basis for our adverse audit opinion.

Definition and Inherent Limitations of Internal Control Over Financial Reporting

An entity's internal control over financial reporting is a process effected by those charged with governance, management, and other personnel, designed to provide reasonable assurance regarding the preparation of reliable financial statements in accordance with [*applicable financial reporting framework, such as accounting principles generally accepted in the United States of America*]. An entity's internal control over financial reporting includes those policies and procedures that (1) pertain to the maintenance of records that, in reasonable detail, accurately and fairly reflect the transactions and dispositions of the assets of the entity; (2) provide reasonable assurance that transactions are recorded as necessary to permit preparation of financial statements in accordance with [*applicable financial reporting framework, such as accounting principles generally accepted in the United States of America*], and that receipts and expenditures of the entity are being made only in accordance with authorizations of management and those charged with governance; and (3) provide reasonable assurance regarding prevention, or timely detection and correction of unauthorized acquisition, use, or disposition of the entity's assets that could have a material effect on the financial statements.

Because of its inherent limitations, internal control over financial reporting may not prevent, or detect and correct, misstatements. Also, projections of any assessment of effectiveness to future periods are subject to the risk that controls may become inadequate because of changes in conditions, or that the degree of compliance with the policies or procedures may deteriorate.

Basis for Adverse Opinion

A material weakness is a deficiency, or a combination of deficiencies, in internal control over financial reporting, such that there is a reasonable possibility that a material misstatement of the entity's financial statements will not be prevented, or detected and corrected, on a timely basis. The following material weakness has been identified and included in the accompanying [*title of management's report*].

[*Identify the material weakness described in management's report.*]

Adverse Opinion

In our opinion, because of the effect of the material weakness described in the Basos for Adverse Opinion paragraph on the achievement of the objectives of [identify criteria], ABC Company has not maintained effective internal control over financial reporting as of December 31, 20XX, based on [*identify criteria*].

Report on Financial Statements

We also have audited, in accordance with auditing standards generally accepted in the United States of America, the [*identify financial statements*] of ABC Company, and our report dated [*date of report, which should be the same as the date of the report on the audit of ICFR*] expressed [*include nature of opinion*]. We considered the material weakness identified above in determining the nature, timing, and extent of audit procedures applied in our audit of the 20XX financial statements, and this report does not affect such report on the financial statements.

Report on Other Legal and Regulatory Requirements

[*Form and content of this section of the auditor's report will vary depending on the nature of the auditor's other reporting responsibilities.*]

[*Auditor's signature*]

[*Auditor's city and state*]

[*Date of the auditor's report*]

Examination of MD&A

Review of MD&A

Sample Review Report on (Interim) MD&A When Reporting Directly on the Subject Matter, Not an Assertion

Independent Accountant's Report

We have reviewed ABC Company's Management's Discussion and Analysis taken as a whole, included in the Company's [insert description of registration statement or document]. Management is responsible for the preparation of the Company's Management's Discussion and Analysis pursuant to the rules and regulations adopted by the Securities and Exchange Commission. We have reviewed, in accordance with standards established by the American Institute of Certified Public Accountants, the interim financial information of ABC Company as of June 30, 20X2 and 20X1, and for the three-month and six-month periods then ended, and have issued our report thereon dated July XX, 20X6.

We conducted our review of Management's Discussion and Analysis in accordance with attestation standards established by the American Institute of Certified Public Accountants. A review of Management's Discussion and Analysis consists principally of applying analytical procedures and making inquiries of persons responsible for financial, accounting, and operational matters. It is substantially less in scope than an examination, the objective of which is the expression of an opinion on the presentation. Accordingly, we do not express such an opinion.

The preparation of Management's Discussion and Analysis requires management to interpret the criteria, make determinations as to the relevancy of information to be included, and make estimates and assumptions that affect reported information. Management's Discussion and Analysis includes information regarding the estimated future impact of transactions and events that have occurred or are expected to occur, expected sources of liquidity and capital resources, operating trends, commitments, and uncertainties. Actual results in the future may differ materially from management's present assessment of this information because events and circumstances frequently do not occur as expected.

Based on our review, nothing came to our attention that caused us to believe that the Company's presentation of Management's Discussion and Analysis does not include, in all material respects, the required elements of the rules and regulations adopted by the Securities and Exchange Commission, that the historical financial amounts included therein have not been accurately derived, in all material respects, from the Company's financial statements, or that the underlying information, determinations, estimates, and assumptions of the Company do not provide a reasonable basis for the disclosures contained therein.

This report is intended solely for the information and use of (list or refer to specified parties) and is not intended to be and should not be used by anyone other than the specified parties.

/s/ CPA firm (signed by engagement partner)

Date (usually the last day of fieldwork)

Multiple Choice Questions

I. Ethics, Professional Responsibilities, and General Principles

AICPA Code of Professional Conduct

Introduction and Preface

AICPA.940502REG-BL

1. Which of the following statements best explains why the CPA profession has found it essential to promulgate ethical standards and to establish means for ensuring their observance?

    A. A distinguishing mark of a profession is its acceptance of responsibility to the public.
    B. A requirement for a profession is to establish ethical standards that stress primary responsibility to clients and colleagues.
    C. Ethical standards that emphasize excellence in performance over material rewards establish a reputation for competence and character.
    D. Vigorous enforcement of an established code of ethics is the best way to prevent unscrupulous acts.

AICPA.141052AUD-SIM

2. Which of the following is true regarding the Principles of Professional Conduct?

    A. To live up to the Code of Professional Conduct, members may have to work hard, but they do not have to sacrifice their own best interests.
    B. Members must not only be competent in the provision of professional services; they must also cooperate with other members to improve the art of accounting.
    C. Due care in the audit area is satisfied if a member knows generally accepted accounting principles and generally accepted accounting standards inside and out.
    D. Because the Code of Professional Conduct does not expressly prohibit a member from moonlighting as a circus trapese performer, a member could perform at a local bar as "Sam the Flying CPA."

Members in Public Practice

MIPPs Introduction and Conceptual Framework

AICPA.141017AUD-SIM

3. Which of the following are sources of safeguards that might reduce a threat of noncompliance with the code to an acceptable level?

    A. Safeguards created by the profession.
    B. Safeguards implemented by the client.
    C. Safeguards implemented by the firm.
    D. All three choices provided.

AICPA.141015AUD-SIM

4. Which of the following is **not** a key concept in the code's Conceptual Framework?

    A. Threats.
    B. Safeguards.
    C. Unusual danger.
    D. Acceptable level.

AICPA.080937REG-1B

5. A CPA acting as an auditor must honor professional rules regarding:

    A. Integrity.
    B. Objectivity.
    C. Independence.
    D. All of the above.

MIPPs Nonindependence Rules

Conflicts of Interest, Directorships, and Gifts

AICPA.141010AUD-SIM

6. Which of the following would constitute a conflict of interest that poses a threat to objectivity?

    A. The ABC Accounting Firm is hired by Bozo Co. to provide litigation support services in its lawsuit against Bebop Corp., which is a tax client of ABC.
    B. Quan suggests that his tax client Linda invest her tax refund in Blitz Corporation without disclosing that he owns a large stake in Blitz.

C. Tibble recommends that his tax client Borton hire a financial planner named Tilden without disclosing that Tilden has agreed in exchange to refer all his clients who need an accountant to Tibble.

D. All three of the choices provided.

AICPA.141011AUD-SIM

7. If Maria has ABC for an attest client, from which of the following should she be wary of accepting gifts that might threaten her objectivity?

A. ABC.

B. ABC's officers.

C. ABC's major (> 10%) shareholders.

D. All three of the choices provided.

Reporting Income and Subordination of Judgment

AICPA.080940REG-1B

8. Son is a junior auditor from ABC Accounting Firm's audit team at client Mammoth Corporation. Son believes that Mammoth's CFO is mischaracterizing some important transactions. Mammoth's CFO is adamant about the treatment of these transactions. After doing substantial research and consulting with his supervisor, who supports Mammoth's view, Son believes that following Mammoth's preferred treatment would produce inaccurate financial statements that would materially mislead investors. What should Son do at this stage?

A. Make his concerns known to higher levels of his firm and/or the client.

B. Resign from ABC.

C. Inform the SEC.

D. Make his concerns known to higher levels of his firm and/or the client, resign from ABC, and inform the SEC.

AICPA.141009AUD-SIM

9. Which of the following would violate the Code of Professional Conduct?

A. Auditor Sam instructed an underling, Todd, to make a materially false entry in an audit client's financial statements.

B. Sam's superior, Sarah, knew what Sam had done and did not correct it.

C. Sarah signed the firm's audit report, knowing that the error had not been corrected.

D. All of the choices provided.

AICPA.141008AUD-SIM

10. Which of the following is (are) true regarding auditors who disagree with their supervisors regarding the proper handling of an important transaction for financial statement purposes?

A. The auditor should always defer to the superior who, after all, has superior experience.

B. The auditor should always quit on the spot rather than compromise her integrity.

C. The auditor should always discuss the matter with the superior if it appears that there is a significant threat that the financial statements will be inaccurate.

D. All of the choices provided.

Advocacy, Third-Party Service Providers (TSPs), General Standards, and Accounting Principles

AICPA.080942REG-1B

11. Sally has her own small accounting firm. Due to some personal connections with a top officer of Mediumsize Corporation, Sally landed an interview with Mediumsize as a potential tax client. Mediumsize has some complicated tax issues of a type that Sally has not handled before. Which of the following is true?

I. Because Sally has not handled these complicated issues before, she cannot take this engagement.

II. Sally can take this engagement if she believes in good faith that she can research these tax issues and handle them competently.

III. Sally can take this engagement if she believes in good faith that she can consult with experts in the area and thereby handle these tax issues competently.

A. I only.

B. II only.

C. I and II.

D. II and III.

AICPA.141014AUD-SIM

12. Members may properly:

I. Advocate on behalf of audit clients.

II. Advocate on behalf of tax clients.

A. I only.

B. II only.

C. I and II.

D. Neither I nor II.

AICPA.080943REG-1B

13. Dena prepared personal income tax returns for 100 clients last year. Two of her clients have come to her with valid complaints about errors she made in their returns, causing them to pay more than they should have in taxes. Which of the following is true?

I. Dena's CPA license should be revoked, because she obviously cannot exercise due professional care.

II. While it is certainly possible that Dena has acted without due professional care in these two instances, the AICPA does not demand perfection.

A. I only.
B. II only.
C. I and II.
D. Neither I nor II.

AICPA.080951REG-1B

14. Dain would violate the Code of Professional Responsibility if, during an audit, he:

I. Stated that he was not aware of any material modifications that should be made to the audited financial statements in order for them to be in conformity with GAAP if he was, in fact, aware of needed material modifications.

II. Stated that he was not aware of any material modifications that should be made to the audited financial statements in order for them to be in conformity with GAAP if he was aware of immaterial modifications that would be desirable.

A. I only.
B. II only.
C. I and II.
D. Neither I nor I.

AICPA.941102REG-BL

15. According to the profession's ethical standards, which of the following events may justify a departure from a Statement of Financial Accounting Standards?

	New legislation	Evolution of a new form of business transaction
A.	No	Yes
B.	Yes	No
C.	Yes	Yes
D.	No	No

Discreditable Acts

AICPA.940501REG-BL

16. Which of the following actions by a CPA most likely violates the profession's ethical standards?

A. Arranging with a financial institution to collect notes issued by a client in payment of fees due.
B. Compiling the financial statements of a client that employed the CPA's spouse as a bookkeeper.
C. Retaining client records after the client has demanded their return.

D. Purchasing a segment of an insurance company's business that performs actuarial services for employee benefit plans.

AICPA.080955REG-1B

17. Which of the following actions by a CPA most likely does not constitute an act discreditable to the profession?

A. Sexually harassing an employee.
B. Providing for a right of contribution from the client in an audit engagement letter.
C. Providing for a right of indemnification from the client in an audit engagement letter.
D. All of the above.

AICPA.111160AUD

18. According to the AICPA Code of Professional Conduct, which of the following actions by a CPA most likely involves an act discreditable to the profession?

A. Refusing to provide the client with copies of the CPA's audit documentation.
B. Auditing financial statements according to governmental standards despite the client's preferences.
C. Accepting a commission from a nonattest function client.
D. Retaining client records after the client demands their return.

AICPA.080923REG-1B

19. Which of the following actions by a CPA most likely constitutes an act discreditable to the profession?

A. Discriminating on the basis of race in employment.
B. Negligently making false journal entries.
C. Failing to pay one's own personal income tax.
D. All three of the choices provided.

AICPA.090603REG-I-B

20. Spinner, CPA, had audited Lasco Corp's financial statements for the past several years. Prior to the current year's engagement, a disagreement arose that caused Lasco to change auditing firms. Lasco has demanded that Spinner provide Lasco with Spinner's audit documentation so that Lasco may show them to prospective auditors to help them prepare their bids for Lasco's audit engagement. Spinner refused and Lasco commenced litigation. Under the ethical standards of the profession, will Spinner be successful in refusing to turn over the documentation?

A. Yes, because Spinner is the owner of the audit documentation.
B. Yes, because Lasco is required to direct prospective auditors to contact Spinner

to make arrangements to view the audit documentation in Spinner's office.

C. No, because Lasco has a legitimate business reason for demanding that Spinner surrender the audit documentation.

D. No, because it was Lasco's financial statements that were audited.

Fees

AICPA.090604REG-I-B

21. Assuming appropriate disclosure is made, which of the following fee arrangements generally would be permitted under the ethical standards of the profession?

   A. A fee paid to the client's audit firm for recommending investment advisory services to the client.

   B. A fee paid to the client's tax accountant for recommending a computer system to the client.

   C. A contingent fee paid to the CPA for preparing the client's amended income tax return.

   D. A contingent fee paid to the CPA for reviewing the client's financial statements.

AICPA.120602AUD

22. According to the Code of Professional Conduct of the AICPA, for which type of service may a CPA receive a contingent fee?

   A. Performing an audit of a financial statement.

   B. Performing a review of a financial statement.

   C. Performing an examination of a prospective financial statement.

   D. Seeking a private letter ruling.

assess.AICPA.AUD.code.prof.con-0022

23. Considering only the provisions of the AICPA Code of Professional Conduct, which of the following services may a CPA perform for a commission or contingent fee?

   A. Preparation of an original income tax return.

   B. Representation of a nonattest client in an IRS examination.

   C. Preparation of an amended income tax return to claim a deduction that was inadvertently omitted on an originally filed return.

   D. Performance of consulting services for an audit client.

AICPA.080961REG-1B

24. In which of the following scenarios has Ed, a CPA, **not** committed an ethical violation in relation to a tax client, Harriett, who asked Ed

what she should do with a $12,000 tax refund she received from the IRS?

   A. Ed referred Harriett to investment adviser Sue, without disclosing to Harriett that Sue was Ed's sister-in-law.

   B. Ed referred Harriett to the investment advising firm of Stuart, Scott & Barney, without disclosing that he (Ed) was an unnamed partner in that firm.

   C. Ed recommended that Harriett purchase certain investment instruments from Mathwell Kilby & Co., without disclosing that Mathwell Kilby paid Ed a 5% commission on each transaction.

   D. Ed sold Harriett an investment instrument, disclosing that he was earning a 5% commission on the transaction.

AICPA.080963REG-1B

25. Tammy is looking to increase the revenue stream for her accounting firm. She is thinking of using commissions and referral fees to do so. Which of the following is true regarding commissions and referral fees?

   I. Neither is permitted when the client is an audit client.

   II. Both are permitted when the client is not an audit client, if they are properly disclosed.

   A. I only.
   B. II only.
   C. I and II.
   D. Neither I nor II.

Advertising and Confidentiality

AICPA.060651REG

26. Page, CPA, has T Corp. and W Corp. as audit clients. T Corp. is a significant supplier of raw materials to W Corp. Page also prepares individual tax returns for Time, the owner of T Corp., and West, the owner of W Corp. When preparing West's return, Page finds information that raises going-concern issues with respect to W Corp.

May Page disclose this information to Time?

   A. Yes, because Page has a fiduciary relationship with Time.

   B. Yes, because there is **no** accountant-client privilege between Page and West.

   C. No, because the information is confidential and may **not** be disclosed without West's consent.

   D. No, because the information should only be disclosed in Page's audit report on W Corp.'s financial statements.

AICPA.941114REG-BL

27. Which of the following statements concerning an accountant's disclosure of confidential client data is generally correct?

    A. Disclosure may be made to any state agency without a subpoena.
    B. Disclosure may be made to any party on consent of the client.
    C. Disclosure may be made to comply with an IRS audit request.
    D. Disclosure may be made just for the heck of it.

AICPA.931110REG-BL

28. A CPA's audit documentation

    A. Need not be disclosed under a federal court subpoena.
    B. Must be disclosed under an IRS administrative subpoena.
    C. Must be disclosed to another accountant purchasing the CPA's practice even if the client hasn't given permission.
    D. Need not be disclosed to a state CPA society quality review team.

AICPA.090602REG-I-B

29. A CPA in public practice may not disclose confidential client information regarding auditing situations without the client's consent in response to which of the following situations?

    A. A review of the CPA's professional practice by a state CPA society.
    B. A letter to the client from the IRS.
    C. An inquiry from the professional ethics division of the AICPA.
    D. A court-ordered subpoena or summons.

AICPA.082100REG-I.B

30. Which of the following acts by a CPA is a violation of professional standards regarding the confidentiality of client information?

    A. Releasing financial information to a local bank with the approval of the client's mail clerk.
    B. Allowing a review of professional practice without client authorization.
    C. Responding to an enforceable subpoena.
    D. Faxing a tax return to a loan officer at the request of the client.

Form of Organization and Names

AICPA.080964REG-1B

31. Maisy wishes to start her own accounting firm and wonders what restrictions there are on names of such firms. Which of the following is accurate?

    A. An accounting firm's name may not be misleading.
    B. An accounting firm's name may include the names of past owners.
    C. An accounting firm's name may (if not misleading) include a fictitious name.
    D. All three choices provided.

AICPA.080966REG-1B

32. Which firms must have a majority of their financial interests owned by CPAs?

    I. Attest firms.
    II. Firms that identify themselves as "Members of the AICPA."

    A. I only.
    B. II only.
    C. I and II.
    D. Neither I nor II.

AICPA.080965REG-1B

33. Allen wishes to start his own audit firm. In which form may he practice, assuming the form is permitted in his state?

    A. Sole proprietorship.
    B. General partnership.
    C. LLP.
    D. All three answer choices provided.

MIPPs Independence Rules

Introduction to MIPPs Independence Rules

AICPA.101057AUD-SIM

34. The Melancon accounting firm audits XYZ Co. out of its Boston office. Who, among the following Melancon employees, is a "covered member" regarding XYZ?

    A. Sim, the receptionist who handles many administrative tasks for the XYZ audit team.
    B. Tim, the records guy who lugs around many, many boxes of records that the audit team must review.
    C. Bit, the new college accounting graduate, who was added to the XYZ audit team on his first day at Melancon.
    D. None of the three choices provided.

AICPA.101055AUD-SIM

35. Which of the following is an example of the type of threat to independence that the AICPA's conceptual framework anticipates in its rules?

    A. ABC Auditing prepared source documents for client XYZ Co. that were ultimately audited by ABC.
    B. ABC Auditing acted as a promoter of audit client XYZ Co.'s stock in an initial public offering.

C. ABC Auditing's audit partner in charge of the XYZ Co. audit learned that her spouse had been promoted from a nonmanagerial role to CFO at XYZ.

D. All three choices provided.

Network Firms and Affiliates

AICPA.141027AUD-SIM

36. Which of the following is (are) true?

A. If Firm A and Firm B are in the same network, A must be independent of B's attest clients if use of the audit or review reports is unrestricted.

B. If Firm A and Firm B are in the same network, A must be independent of B's attest clients if use of the audit or review reports is restricted.

C. Firms may never use partners or professional employees of other firms on their audit teams.

D. All three answer choices provided are true.

AICPA.141028AUD-SIM

37. Which of the following are "affiliates" of clients so that a member in public practice might have to worry about its relationships with the entity in order to preserve independence?

A. The Dawes accounting firm is auditing ABC Co., which owns 61% of the stock of DEF Mfg. Co. (from which Dawes has borrowed quite a bit of money).

B. The Dawes accounting firm is auditing DEF Co., which is owned substantially by ABC Mfg. Co. (from which Dawes has borrowed quite a bit of money).

C. The Dawes accounting firm is auditing ABC Co. and has borrowed quite a bit of money from DEF Mfg. Co. while the Pensive Hedge Fund owns a majority control of both ABC and DEF.

D. All three answer choices provided.

Reissues, Engagement Letters, ADR, and Unpaid Fees

AICPA.141020AUD-SIM

38. The Cheng Accounting Firm is concerned with litigation costs, so it is inserting provisions in all its engagement letters that require arbitration rather than litigation of disputes between Cheng and its attest clients. Which of the following is true?

I. Such a provision is simply not allowed by the code.

II. Such a provision is allowed, but if it is invoked, Cheng should apply the Conceptual

Framework to determine whether independence is impaired by the fact that it and its client have potentially been placed in positions of material adverse interests.

A. I only.

B. II only.

C. Both I and II.

D. Neither I nor II.

AICPA.141021AUD-SIM

39. The Espinoza Accounting Firm is set to certify the financial statements of client ABC Co. on May 15, 2020. However, ABC did not pay Espinoza's bill for doing the previous audit that was signed on May 15, 2019. Which of the following is true?

A. Because ABC has not paid Espinoza in more than a year, Espinoza's independence would be impaired if it signed this new report in 2020.

B. Espinoza can avoid any independence problems by simply not billing ABC, which cannot be behind on its bills if it has not received any bills.

C. Espinoza's independence would not be impaired if ABC would issue to it a signed note, promising to pay within six months.

D. ABC's independence considerations should prevent it from signing the May 15, 2020, report even if ABC is in bankruptcy.

Financial Interests

Overview and Unsolicited Financial Interests

AICPA.111159AUD

40. A CPA purchased stock in a client corporation and placed it in a trust as an educational fund for the CPA's minor child. The trust securities are not material to the CPA's wealth but are material to the child's personal net worth. According to the AICPA Code of Professional Conduct, would this action impair the CPA's independence with the client?

A. No, because the CPA would not have a direct financial interest in the client.

B. Yes, because the stock would be a direct financial interest and materiality is a factor.

C. Yes, because the stock would be an indirect financial interest and materiality is not a factor.

D. Yes, because the stock would be a direct financial interest and materiality is not a factor.

AICPA.141025AUD-SIM

41. Which of the following create(s) an independence problem?

    A. Sam is on the attest team for client ABC Co. While he does not currently own any ABC stock, he has signed a commitment to purchase a small amount but not until a month after the audit report will issue.

    B. Sam is on the attest team for client ABC Co. While he does not currently own any ABC stock in his own name. He is beneficiary of a trust that holds a significant amount of ABC stock. Sam does not control the trust's investments.

    C. Sam is not a "covered member" for purposes of his firm's audit of ABC Co., but he is a partner in a different office and does own 7% of ABC's shares.

    D. All three answer choices provided.

Mutual Funds and Retirement Plans

AICPA.141029AUD-SIM

42. Jo is a member in public practice who is very wealthy and has no individual investments that are material to her. Which of the following investments would impair Jo's independence?

    A. Jo owns 3% of a diversified mutual fund and is on her firm's attest team for that fund.

    B. Jo owns 4% of a diversified mutual fund and is on her firm's attest team for ABC Co., whose shares are in the mutual fund's portfolio of stocks.

    C. Jo owns 2% of an undiversified mutual fund that has ABC Co. stock in its portfolio (and Jo is on her firm's attest team for ABC).

    D. All three of the choices provided.

AICPA.141031AUD-SIM

43. Which of the following creates an independence problem?

    I. Sally participates in her firm's retirement plan, which allows her to select which companies' stocks go into her portfolio. Sally selects a small amount of ABC Co. stock, even though she is on her firm's audit team for ABC.

    II. Although Sally has not selected ABC Co. stock for her retirement plan's portfolio, her spouse, Joe, has done so.

    A. I only.
    B. II only.
    C. Both I and II.
    D. Neither I nor II.

Partnerships, 529s, Trust and Estates, Employee Benefit Plans

AICPA.141023AUD-SIM

44. The Lox Accounting Firm audits ABC Co. Pim is a Lox tax partner in the office that runs the ABC audit. Pim has been asked to be a trustee of an estate that has ABC stock in its portfolio. In which of the following situations would there be an independence problem for Lox?

    A. Pim has authority to make investment decisions for the estate.

    B. The estate owns more than 10% of ABC stock.

    C. More than 10% of the estate's assets are invested in ABC stock.

    D. All three choices provided.

AICPA.141022AUD-SIM

45. Art is on his firm's audit team for client ABC Co. Which of the following is an indirect financial interest?

    A. Art is a general partner in a partnership that owns stock in ABC.

    B. Art is a limited partner in a partnership that owns stock in ABC and is on the partnership's investments committee.

    C. Art is a member in a member-managed limited liability corporation that owns stock in ABC.

    D. Art is a member in an agent-managed limited liability corporation that owns stock in ABC.

Depository Accounts, Brokerage Accounts, and Insurance Policies

AICPA.141037AUD-SIM

46. Which of the following situations creates an independence problem for Kim?

    I. Kim owns an insurance policy that does not contain an investment option and was issued under normal terms, procedures, and requirements.

    II. Kim owns an insurance policy with an investment option, and she invested a small amount in the ABC Mutual Fund, even though Kim is a covered member for purposes of ABC, which is an audit client of her firm.

    A. I only.
    B. II only.
    C. Both I and II.
    D. Neither I nor II.

AICPA.141035AUD-SIM

47. The Patton Accounting Firm and one of its partners, Tilly, have depository accounts at the ABC Bank. ABC has just approached Patton about becoming the bank's auditor. In which of the following situations would there be an independence problem if Patton became ABC's auditor?

    A. ABC is in robust financial health.
    B. Tilly's account is fully insured.
    C. Tilly's account is not fully insured, but the uninsured amount is not material to her financial situation.
    D. None of the three choices provided.

Loans, Leases, and Business Relationships

AICPA.080967REG-1B

48. Tondry is a CPA working for a Big Four firm as an auditor. Tondry has purchased a small minority interest in XYZ Co., which provides technical computer support and other nonaudit services for businesses. At least one of the businesses that receives technical support from XYZ (and purchases software on XYZ's recommendation for which XYZ received a commission), is an audit client for which Tondry is on the audit engagement team. Given these facts, which of the following is true?

    I. Tondry's actions have created an independence problem.
    II. The employees and agents of XYZ must follow independence rules just as Tondry must.

    A. I only.
    B. II only.
    C. I and II.
    D. Neither I nor II.

AICPA.141033AUD-SIM

49. The Bilton Accounting Firm needs office space, and ABC Co. has office space to lease out. ABC is an attest client of Bilton. Which of the following would **not** create an independence problem?

    A. ABC signs a capital lease agreement with Bilton on terms and conditions that are comparable with other leases in the area.
    B. ABC signs an operating lease with Bilton on terms and conditions that are comparable with other leases in the area, and Bilton is always on time with its payments.
    C. ABC signs an operating lease with Bilton that gives it a 10% discount from what ABC charges its other tenants.
    D. All three of the choices provided.

AICPA.141034AUD-SIM

50. Which of the following situations does not create an independence problem for the Brixton Accounting Firm relative to its attest client ABC Co.

    A. Both Brixton and ABC Co. own Microsoft stock.
    B. Both Brixton and ABC Co. purchase major stakes in a local technology start-up company.
    C. One of Brixton's covered members is friends with ABC's chief executive officer, and they pursue their passion for skiing by jointly purchasing a ski chalet in Vail.
    D. None of the above create an independence problem.

Family Relationships

AICPA.080925REG-1B

51. Anchorage Alltime Dairy (AAD) is an audit client of Thorn Granton's Juneau office. Al is on the audit team. Betsy evaluates Al's work and determines his pay. Carol is a tax professional in the Juneau office, who provided 20 hours of tax advice to AAD during the last audit cycle. Dave is a tax partner in the Juneau office, who has never provided any services to AAD. Which of the following situations would create an independence problem under the new AICPA rules?

    A. Al's brother Sam is in charge of manure disposal for AAD.
    B. Betsy's live-in lover owns enough AAD stock that it is material to him, but it does not allow him to exert significant influence over AAD.
    C. Carol's mother is a receptionist for AAD and, via its pension plan, indirectly owns a small amount of AAD stock.
    D. None of the choices provided.

AICPA.141006AUD-SIM

52. Which of the following is *not* an immediate family member?

    A. A covered member's spouse.
    B. A covered member's spousal equivalent.
    C. A covered member's nondependent child.
    D. A covered member's dependent stepson.

AICPA.141007AUD-SIM

53. Which of the following is *not* a close relative?

    A. A parent.
    B. A spousal equivalent.
    C. A sister.
    D. A nondependent child.

Employment Relationships

Current Employment

AICPA.080930REG-1B

54. Manny is a well-respected CPA in his hometown of Cut & Shoot, TX, which has a population of slightly over 5,000. Manny currently audits a nonprofit organization and has recently been approached by this organization to join its board. The board is currently made up of many influential figures in the community and they would like to add Manny's name to that list for increased recognition. Manny would love to help out the community but is afraid that this might affect his independence. Which of the following situations would cause Manny's involvement with the board to result in a lack of independence?

   A. Manny's position is purely honorary.
   B. Manny has been asked to only contribute his name.
   C. Manny is only required to vote in critical management affairs, which do not arise frequently.
   D. Manny's position is identified as honorary on external materials.

AICPA.060648REG

55. Under the ethical standards of the profession, which of the following business relationships would generally **not** impair an auditor's independence?

   A. Promoter of a client's securities.
   B. Member of a client's board of directors.
   C. Client's general counsel.
   D. Advisor to a client's board of trustees.

Subsequent Employment

AICPA.111157AUD

56. An issuer may hire an employee of a registered public accounting firm who served on the audit engagement team within the previous year for which of the following positions?

   A. Controller.
   B. CFO.
   C. CEO.
   D. Staff accountant.

AICPA.120604AUD

57. A cooling-off period of how many years is required before a member of an issuer's audit engagement team may begin working for the registrant in a key position?

   A. One year.
   B. Two years.
   C. Three years.
   D. Four years.

Other Associations and Relationships

AICPA.141039AUD-SIM

58. Which of the following safeguards must be met for Sam, who is a member of his condominium association, to be able to serve as a covered member of his firm, which audits the condominium association, without impairing independence?

   A. Sam's annual assessment must not be material to him or to the association.
   B. If the condominium association were liquidated, Sam would not receive a distribution.
   C. The condominium association's creditors would not be able to successfully sue Sam to recover his personal assets if the association became insolvent.
   D. All of the three choices provided.

AICPA.141040AUD-SIM

59. Which categories of covered members must be concerned with independence problems that might arise from gifts they receive from attest clients?

   I. Team members.
   II. Other partners in the office.

   A. I only.
   B. II only.
   C. Both I and II.
   D. Neither I nor II.

Nonaudit Services

Code Provisions

AICPA.141004AUD-SIM

60. The Flakel Accounting Firm audits ABC Co., a public company. ABC would like to fire its current tax consultant and replace it with Flakel. Which of the following is true?

   I. This action would necessarily violate the Code.
   II. This action would violate Sarbanes-Oxley rules, unless ABC's audit committee preapproved the hiring.

III. This action would violate Sarbanes-Oxley rules even if ABC's audit committee preapproved the hiring.

A. I only.
B. II only.
C. III only.
D. I and II.

AICPA.141001AUD-SIM

61. Which of the following would be deemed by the code "management responsibilities" that would likely impair independence if a covered member performed them for an attest client?

A. Setting policy or strategic direction for the attest client.
B. Taking custody of client assets.
C. Preparing source documents that evidence the occurrence of a transaction.
D. All of the choices provided.

AICPA.141002AUD-SIM

62. Which of the following are considered by the code to be nonaudit services that could impair independence if performed by a covered member for an attest client?

A. Discussing with the client selection and application of accounting standards or policies.
B. Discussing with the client the appropriateness of the client's methods used to determine accounting and financial reporting.
C. Discussing with the client the form or content of the financial statements.
D. None of the choices provided.

Specific Services

AICPA.141051AUD-SIM

63. Which of the following internal audit functions may be performed by an auditor for a private company attest client?

A. Reporting to the board on behalf of management regarding internal audit affairs.
B. Identifying opportunities for improvement.
C. Determining which, if any, recommendations for improving internal control systems should be implemented.
D. Performing ongoing monitoring activities that affect execution of transactions.

AICPA.141049AUD-SIM

64. Which of the following benefit plan administration services may not be provided by an auditor to a private company attest client?

A. Communicate summary plan data to plan trustee.

B. Advice client management regarding impact of plan provisions.
C. Prepare account valuations.
D. Make disbursements on plan's behalf.

Members in Business

AICPA.141044AUD-SIM

65. Which of the following is **not** true regarding application of the Conceptual Framework for members in business?

A. An adverse interest threat arises when a member in business sues her employer.
B. A familiarity threat arises when a member in business hires a relative to work for his employer.
C. A self-review threat arises when a member in business reviews some internal audit work that she herself performed before she was promoted to her current position.
D. A familiarity threat arises when a member in business has a long association with an employer.

Other Members

AICPA.141046AUD-SIM

66. Who of the following is an "other member" for code purposes?

A. Tim, who is a retired CPA.
B. Tom, who is an unemployed CPA.
C. Bill, who is a CPA currently working as a rodeo clown.
D. All of the choices provided.

AICPA.141048AUD-SIM

67. Which of the following is a duty owed by an "other member"?

I. Duty to be independent in fact and appearance.
II. Duty to avoid committing discreditable acts.

A. I only.
B. II only.
C. I and II.
D. Neither I nor II.

AICPA.141047AUD-SIM

68. Which of the following are discreditable acts that should not be performed by other members?

A. Sexual harassment in employment.
B. Soliciting disclosure of CPA exam questions.
C. Failure to file a tax return.
D. All of the listed answer choices.

Requirements of SEC and PCAOB

Securities and Exchange Commission (SEC)

aq.sec.exch.com.001_2017

69. Which of the following are "covered persons" for purposes of the SEC's independence rules?

   A. Sarah, a tax partner at her firm. She gave 15 hours of advice to her firm's audit team regarding the audit of ABC Co.
   B. Tory, the chairman and senior partner at Sarah's firm.
   C. Burt, the lead partner for the ABC Co. audit at Sarah's firm.
   D. All of the options.

aq.sec.exch.com.002_2017

70. Which of the following persons are "close family members" for purposes of SEC independence rules?

   A. Tina, a 14-year-old whose mother is on her firm's audit engagement team for the ABC Co. audit.
   B. Tip, whose cousin Fred is the lead partner on the ABC Co. audit.
   C. Merlin, whose granddaughter just joined an accounting firm and is providing technical advice to the audit team doing the ABC Co. audit.
   D. Sam, whose best friend since childhood is Muhammad, who is on the audit team for the ABC Co. audit.

aq.sec.exch.com.003_2017

71. Which of the following financial investments is **not** likely to create an independence problem for Kim, who is a "covered person" at her accounting firm for purposes of the audit of ABC Co.?

   A. Kim owns 0.1% of ABC's outstanding shares.
   B. Kim owns 1% of XYZ Co., which in turn owns 40% of ABC's shares.
   C. Kim owns 5% of an undiversified mutual fund that has a significant investment in ABC.
   D. Kim is a trustee of the Melon Trust. The trust owns a few shares of ABC, but Kim had nothing to do with that acquisition and, indeed, has no authority to make investment decisions for the trust.

aq.sec.exch.com.004_2017

72. Which of the following transactions impairs independence under the SEC rules?

   A. The Lark audit firm audits ABC Co., a Fortune 100 company that manufactures widgets. Pam, who is on Lark's audit team, borrows money from ABC to buy a car. The loan is collateralized by the automobile.
   B. The Wren audit firm audits XYZ Co., a publicly traded financial institution. Pim, who is on Wren's audit team, has a credit card issued by XYZ and currently owes $20,000 on the card.
   C. The Meadowlark audit firm audits LMN Co., a publicly traded insurance company, which is teetering on the brink of bankruptcy. Pom is on Meadowlark's audit team for the LMN audit and owns a life insurance policy issued by Pom that she bought before she became a covered person.
   D. All of the options.

Public Company Accounting Oversight Board (PCAOB)

aq.aud.pcaob.001_2017

73. The Niblock accounting firm audited JFK, Inc., a public company. Niblock also provided tax services to JFK, receiving as its fee 20% of any tax savings JFK enjoyed because of Niblock's advice. Which of the following is true?

   A. Tax advice to a public company audit client is automatically forbidden and impairs independence.
   B. This tax advice impairs independence because of the nature of the tax advice given.
   C. This tax advice impairs independence because it was provided on a contingent fee basis.
   D. If the contingent fee had been only 10%, it would have been fine.

aq.aud.pcaob.002_2017

74. Whether seeking an audit committee's permission to provide permissible tax services or other non-audit services to a public company audit client or when preparing to take a public company on as a new audit client, three important steps are:

   A. Describe, discuss, and document.
   B. Request, explain, and record.
   C. Seek, document, and reconsider.
   D. Describe, examine, and reexamine.

aq.aud.pcaob.003_2017

75. The Single accounting firm audits Double, Inc., a public company. Which of the following people may **not** receive any tax service consulting from Single?

   A. Bill, who is an outside director on Double's board.
   B. Omar, Double's head of internal audit.
   C. Kelly, Double's controller, who was hired away from a competitor in the middle of an audit cycle when the former controller died suddenly and the contract to provide the tax advice was assigned before Kelly joined Double and the services were terminated 39 days after Kelly began work.
   D. Sally, assistant CFO of a Double subsidiary that is audited by Triple accounting firm.

Requirements of GAO and DOL

Government Accounting Office (GAO)

AICPA.101019AUD-SIM

76. The City of Fairluth's internal auditor became ill, which created some difficult situations. Chiang typically audited Fairluth on behalf of his accounting firm. When the mayor prevailed upon Chiang to temporarily help prepare the city's basic financial records, he did so. Later, he and his team audited those records and pronounced them fair and accurate. And they probably were. Nonetheless, is it possible that we have an independence problem here under GAO guidelines regarding nonaudit services?

   A. No, this was an emergency situation and Chiang acted sensibly in a manner that does not implicate independence rules so that supplemental safeguards need even be considered.
   B. No, this activity did raise independence issues, but they are easily remedied by resort to supplemental safeguards such as ensuring that extent of the audit work was not reduced below that which is normal.
   C. Yes, this activity raises independence problems that are so severe that they cannot be remedied by application of supplemental safeguards.
   D. None of the above.

AICPA.101136AUD-SIM

77. The GAO's independence rules for auditing apply when Sam audits which of the following:

   A. IBM.
   B. The Corner Store, a small business opened by two recent immigrants.
   C. Maricopa County, Arizona.
   D. All of the above.

AICPA.101018AUD-SIM

78. Sue's firm was hired to audit a Reno County project that used federal grant money to attempt to create jobs for people on welfare. Sue was in charge of the audit, and her team found many questionable practices. When the chief administrator of Reno County's government heard about Sue's preliminary findings, he called her into his office and told her that her firm would lose every single audit contract it had with every single unit of Reno County government if he was not pleased with Sue's audit report. This is an example of:

   A. A potential personal impairment of independence.
   B. A potential external impairment of independence.
   C. A potential organizational impairment of independence.
   D. None of the above.

Department of Labor (DOL)

AICPA.101015AUD-SIM

79. Tim is an auditor helping to audit an employee benefit plan. Which of the following roles connected to the plan would create independence problems for Tim if performed by a partner in his office?

   A. Promoter.
   B. Underwriter.
   C. Voting Trustee.
   D. All of the above.

AICPA.101016AUD-SIM

80. Wang is an auditor helping to audit an employee benefit plan. Which of the following services would create independence problems for Wang if performed by members of his office for the plan?

   A. Maintaining financial records.
   B. Performing actuarial services.
   C. Advising on tax issues.
   D. All of the above.

assess.AICPA.AUD.dol-0023

81. According to the U.S. Department of Labor, an auditor of an employee benefit plan would be considered independent if

   A. The auditor is committed to acquire a material indirect financial interest in the plan sponsor.
   B. An actuary associated with the auditor's firm renders services to the plan.
   C. A member of the auditor's firm is an investment advisor to the plan.
   D. The auditor's firm maintains financial records for the plan.

AICPA.101014AUD-SIM

82. The ABC Accounting firm is auditing an employee benefit plan. Which of the following parties cannot have any direct or material indirect financial interest in the plan to prevent an independence violation?

   A. A member of the engagement team.
   B. A partner in an office in another city.
   C. ABC itself.
   D. A, B, and C.

II. Assessing Risk and Developing a Planned Response

Financial Statement Audits

Accounting vs. Auditing

aq.acct.aud.001_2017

83. Which of the following is not a primary responsibility of an auditor:

   A. Provide regulators with an opinion on whether the financial statements are presented fairly, in all material respects, in accordance with the applicable financial reporting framework.
   B. Provide creditors with an opinion on whether the financial statements are presented fairly, in all material respects, in accordance with the applicable financial reporting framework.
   C. Provide management with an opinion on whether the financial statements are presented fairly, in all material respects, in accordance with the applicable financial reporting framework.
   D. Provide investors with an opinion by the auditor on whether the financial statements are presented fairly, in all material respects, in accordance with the applicable financial reporting framework.

GAAS and Principles

AICPA.900547AUD-AU

84. The exercise of due professional care requires that an auditor

   A. Examine all available corroborating evidence.
   B. Critically review the judgment exercised at every level of supervision.
   C. Reduce control risk below the maximum.
   D. Attain the proper balance of professional experience and formal education.

AICPA.090780.AUD-AU

85. According to GAAS, which of the following terms identifies a requirement for audit evidence?

   A. Appropriate.
   B. Adequate.
   C. Reasonable.
   D. Disconfirming.

AICPA.101119AUD

86. An independent auditor must have which of the following?

   A. A pre-existing and well-informed point of view with respect to the audit.
   B. Technical training that is adequate to meet the requirements of a professional.
   C. A background in many different disciplines.
   D. Experience in taxation that is sufficient to comply with generally accepted auditing standards.

Professional Standards

AICPA.130506AUD-SIM

87. Interpretive publications include all of the following, except for

   A. Appendices to Statements on Auditing Standards.
   B. Articles in the AICPA's *Journal of Accountancy*.
   C. Auditing guidance included in AICPA Audit and Accounting Guides.
   D. Auditing interpretations of the Statements on Auditing Standards.

AICPA.130507AUD-SIM

88. In AICPA professional standards, the word *should* indicates an (a)

   A. Interpretive suggestion that does not constitute a professional requirement.
   B. Unconditional requirement with which the auditor is obligated to comply.
   C. Presumptively mandatory requirement from which the CPA may depart in rare circumstances.
   D. Recommendation that has no authoritative status.

Quality Control Standards (SQCS)

assess.AICPA.AUD.sqcs-0032

89. Which of the following activities would be most helpful to a CPA in deciding whether to accept a new audit client?

   A. Reviewing industry benchmarking data.
   B. Considering the client's compensation methods.
   C. Evaluating the CPA's ability to properly service the client.
   D. Evaluating the most recent peer review of the client's previous auditor.

AICPA.941124AUD-AU

90. The primary purpose of establishing quality control policies and procedures for deciding whether to accept a new client is to

   A. Enable the CPA firm to attest to the reliability of the client.

B. Satisfy the CPA firm's duty to the public concerning the acceptance of new clients.

C. Minimize the likelihood of association with clients whose management lacks integrity.

D. Anticipate before performing any field work whether an unqualified opinion can be expressed.

AICPA.911101AUD-AU

91. A CPA firm would be reasonably assured of meeting its responsibility to provide services that conform with professional standards by

A. Adhering to generally accepted auditing standards.

B. Having an appropriate system of quality control.

C. Joining professional societies that enforce ethical conduct.

D. Maintaining an attitude of independence in its engagements.

AICPA.921103AUD-AU

92. One of a CPA's firm's basic objectives is to provide professional services that conform with professional standards.

Reasonable assurance of achieving this basic objective is provided through

A. A system of quality control.

B. A system of peer review.

C. Continuing professional education.

D. Compliance with generally accepted reporting standards.

AICPA.111173AUD

93. Which of the following actions should a CPA firm take to comply with the AICPA's quality control standards?

A. Establish procedures that comply with the standards of the Sarbanes-Oxley Act.

B. Use attributes sampling techniques in testing internal controls.

C. Consider inherent risk and control risk before determining detection risk.

D. Establish policies to ensure that the audit work meets applicable professional standards.

Overview of Audit Process

AICPA.940503AUD-AU

94. The audit work performed by each assistant should be reviewed to determine whether it was adequately performed and to evaluate whether the

A. Auditor's system of quality control has been maintained at a high level.

B. Results are consistent with the conclusions to be presented in the auditor's report.

C. Audit procedures performed are approved in the professional standards.

D. Audit has been performed by persons having adequate technical training and proficiency as auditors.

AICPA.901116AUD-AU-SIM

95. Principles Underlying an Audit Conducted in Accordance with GAAS state that sufficient appropriate audit evidence is to be obtained through designing and implementing appropriate responses, i.e., by performing audit procedures, to afford a reasonable basis for an opinion regarding the financial statements under audit. The substantive evidential matter required by this standard may be obtained, in part, through

A. Flowcharting the internal control structure.

B. Proper planning of the audit engagement.

C. Analytical procedures.

D. Audit documentation.

Overview of Auditor's Report

AICPA.901107AUD-AU-SIM

96. GAAS require the auditor's report to contain either an expression of opinion regarding the financial statements or an assertion to the effect that an opinion cannot be expressed. The objective of this requirement is to prevent

A. Misinterpretations regarding the degree of responsibility the auditor is assuming.

B. An auditor from reporting on one basic financial statement and not the others.

C. An auditor from expressing different opinions on each of the basic financial statements.

D. Restrictions on the scope of the examination, whether imposed by the client, or by the inability to obtain evidence.

AICPA.920511AUD-AU-SIM

97. An auditor's responsibility to express an opinion on the financial statements is

A. Implicitly represented in the auditor's unmodified report.

B. Explicitly represented in the responsibility paragraphs of the auditor's unmodified report.

C. Explicitly represented in the opening paragraph of the auditor's unmodified report.

D. Explicitly represented in the opinion paragraph of the auditor's unmodified report.

AICPA.100984AUD-AU-SIM

98. The auditor makes explicit reference to "auditing standards generally accepted in the United States of America" in which paragraph of the standard unmodified audit report?

   A. Opening.
   B. Auditor's Responsibility.
   C. Opinion.
   D. Both B and C.

AICPA.911121AUD-AU

99. How does an auditor make the following representations when issuing the standard auditor's report on comparative financial statements?

	Examination of evidence	Consistent application of accounting principles
A.	Explicitly	Explicitly
B.	Implicitly	Implicitly
C.	Implicitly	Explicitly
D.	Explicitly	Implicitly

Different Types of Engagements

AICPA.990403AUD-AU

100. An entity engaged a CPA to determine whether the client's web sites meet defined criteria for standard business practices and controls over transaction integrity and information protection.

   In performing this engagement, the CPA should comply with the provisions of

   A. Statements on Assurance Standards.
   B. Statements on Standards for Attestation Engagements.
   C. Statements on Standards for Management Consulting Services.
   D. Statements on Auditing Standards.

AICPA.920560AUD-AU

101. An attestation engagement is one in which a CPA is engaged to

   A. Issue a written communication expressing a conclusion about the reliability of a written assertion that is the responsibility of another party.
   B. Provide tax advice or prepare a tax return based on financial information the CPA has not audited or reviewed.
   C. Testify as an expert witness in accounting, auditing, or tax matters, given certain stipulated facts.

   D. Assemble pro forma financial statements based on the representations of the entity's management without expressing any assurance.

PCAOB Responsibilities

assess.AICPA.AUD.pcaob.resp-0043

102. At least how often should the PCAOB inspect a registered public accounting firm that regularly issues audit reports to 50 issuers?

   A. Annually.
   B. Every two years.
   C. Every three years.
   D. As requested by the firm.

AICPA.040214FAR-SIM

103. The Public Company Accounting Oversight Board (PCAOB) is charged with all of the following responsibilities except:

   A. Establishing accounting standards for public companies.
   B. Establishing auditing standards.
   C. Registering accounting firms that will audit public companies.
   D. Inspecting accounting firms that will audit public companies.

AICPA.101150AUD

104. The Sarbanes-Oxley Act of 2002 imposes a mandatory rotation applicable to both the audit engagement partner and the quality control (also called review) partner. How long in total is the partner allowed to serve as the engagement partner or review partner before someone else must serve in that capacity?

   A. 3 years.
   B. 5 years.
   C. 7 years.
   D. 10 years.

AICPA.101149AUD

105. Under the Sarbanes-Oxley Act of 2002, which of the following is **not** a stated responsibility of the Public Company Accounting Oversight Board?

   A. Conducting inspections of registered public accounting firms.
   B. Overseeing the registration of public accounting firms.
   C. Issuing accounting standards that must be followed by issuers in financial reporting.
   D. Issuing auditing standards that must be followed by registered public accounting firms in auditing the financial statements of issuers.

PCAOB on Engagement Quality Review

AICPA.100980AUD-SIM

106. Which of the following is **not** a correct statement regarding differences between PCAOB auditing standards on engagement quality review and AICPA Statements on Quality Control Standards (SQCS)?

   A. PCAOB auditing standards require a concurring approval of issuance before the engagement report is released, whereas the SQCS have no such requirement.
   B. PCAOB auditing standards require a cooling-off period of at least two years before an engagement partner can serve as an engagement quality reviewer, whereas the SQCS have no such requirement.
   C. PCAOB auditing standards require engagement quality review documentation to be retained separately from the related engagement documentation for 10 years, whereas SQCS only require that the engagement quality review documentation be retained for 5 years with the other related engagement documentation.
   D. PCAOB auditing standards require an engagement quality review before an audit report is released, whereas SQCS do not require an engagement quality review.

AICPA.100981AUD-SIM

107. Which of the following statements is correct regarding characteristics required of an engagement quality reviewer under PCAOB auditing standards?

   A. Only a partner of the registered public accounting firm conducting the audit can serve as an engagement quality reviewer.
   B. An individual outside of the registered public accounting firm becomes an "associated person" of the registered public accounting firm when receiving compensation from the firm for performing the engagement quality review.
   C. There is no requirement that the engagement quality reviewer must be independent from the client involved, since the engagement quality reviewer cannot make engagement team decisions or otherwise assume any responsibilities of the engagement team.
   D. The engagement quality reviewer is required to be a partner in a public accounting firm, regardless of whether the reviewer is from within the firm or outside the firm responsible for the audit engagement subject to the engagement quality review.

AICPA.100979AUD-SIM

108. PCAOB standards applicable to an engagement quality review identify each of the following as examples of a "significant engagement deficiency," except for when

   A. The engagement team concluded that management's accounting estimates were unreasonable.
   B. The engagement team reached an inappropriate conclusion.
   C. The firm is not independent of its client.
   D. The engagement report is inappropriate.

Planning Activities

Pre-Engagement Planning Issues

AICPA.941103AUD-AU

109. Hill, CPA, has been retained to audit the financial statements of Monday Co. Monday's predecessor auditor was Post, CPA, who has been notified by Monday that Post's services have been terminated.

   Under these circumstances, which party should initiate the communications between Hill and Post?

   A. Hill, the successor auditor.
   B. Post, the predecessor auditor.
   C. Monday's controller or CFO.
   D. The chairman of Monday's board of directors.

AICPA.010502AUD-AU

110. Which of the following factors most likely would cause a CPA to not accept a new audit engagement?

   A. The prospective client has already completed its physical inventory count.
   B. The CPA lacks an understanding of the prospective client's operations and industry.
   C. The CPA is unable to review the predecessor auditor's documentation.
   D. The prospective client is unwilling to make all financial records available to the CPA.

AICPA.020403AUD-AU

111. An auditor's engagement letter most likely would include

   A. Management's acknowledgment of its responsibility for maintaining effective internal control.
   B. The auditor's preliminary assessment of the risk factors relating to misstatements arising from fraudulent financial reporting.
   C. A reminder that management is responsible for illegal acts committed by employees.
   D. A request for permission to contact the client's lawyer for assistance in identifying litigation, claims, and assessments.

AICPA.940502AUD-AU

112. Which of the following factors most likely would cause an auditor not to accept a new audit engagement?

   A. An inadequate understanding of the entity's internal control structure.
   B. The close proximity to the end of the entity's fiscal year.
   C. Concluding that the entity's management probably lacks integrity.
   D. An inability to perform preliminary analytical procedures before assessing control risk.

AICPA.130712AUD

113. Which of the following matters does an auditor usually include in the engagement letter?

   A. Arrangements regarding fees and billing.
   B. Analytical procedures that the auditor plans to perform.
   C. Indications of negative cash flows from operating activities.
   D. Identification of working capital deficiencies.

Planning and Supervision

AICPA.911112AUD-AU

114. Which of the following circumstances most likely would cause an auditor to consider whether material misstatements exist in an entity's financial statements?

   A. Supporting records that should be readily available are frequently not produced when requested.
   B. Significant deficiencies previously communicated have not been corrected.
   C. Clerical errors are listed on a monthly computer-generated exception report.
   D. Differences are discovered during the client's annual physical inventory count.

AICPA.930502AUD-AU

115. Which of the following procedures would an auditor least likely perform in planning a financial statement audit?

   A. Coordinating the assistance of entity personnel in data preparation.
   B. Discussing matters that may affect the audit with firm personnel responsible for non-audit services to the entity.
   C. Selecting a sample of vendors' invoices for comparison to receiving reports.
   D. Reading the current year's interim financial statements.

AICPA.120712AUD

116. Which of the following procedures would an auditor most likely perform in the planning stage of an audit?

   A. Make a preliminary judgment about materiality.
   B. Confirm a sample of the entity's accounts payable with known creditors.
   C. Obtain written representations from management that there are NO unrecorded transactions.
   D. Communicate management's initial selection of accounting policies to the audit committee.

AICPA.101116AUD

117. Which of the following conditions most likely would pose the greatest risk in accepting a new audit engagement?

   A. Staff will need to be rescheduled to cover this new client.
   B. There will be a client-imposed scope limitation.
   C. The firm will have to hire a specialist in one audit area.
   D. The client's financial reporting system has been in place for 10 years.

AICPA.980518AUD-AU

118. Which of the following procedures would an auditor most likely include in the planning phase of a financial statement audit?

   A. Obtain an understanding of the entity's risk assessment process.
   B. Identify specific internal control activities designed to prevent fraud.
   C. Evaluate the reasonableness of the entity's accounting estimates.
   D. Perform cutoff tests of the entity's sales and purchases.

Materiality

AICPA.970510AUD-AU

119. Which of the following would an auditor most likely use in determining the auditor's preliminary judgment about materiality?

   A. The results of the initial assessment of control risk.
   B. The anticipated sample size for planned substantive tests.
   C. The entity's financial statements of the prior year.
   D. The assertions that are embodied in the financial statements.

AICPA.980521AUD-AU

120. When issuing an unqualified opinion, the auditor who evaluates the audit findings should be satisfied that the

   A. Amount of known misstatement is documented in the management representation letter.
   B. Estimate of the total likely misstatement is less than a material amount.
   C. Amount of known misstatement is acknowledged and recorded by the client.
   D. Estimate of the total likely misstatement includes the adjusting entries already recorded by the client.

AICPA.900551AUD-AU

121. When planning a sample for a substantive test of details, an auditor should consider tolerable misstatement for the sample. This consideration should

   A. Be related to the auditor's business risk.
   B. Not be adjusted for qualitative factors.
   C. Be related to preliminary judgments about materiality levels.
   D. Not be changed during the audit process.

AICPA.931106AUD-AU

122. In considering materiality for planning purposes, an auditor believes that misstatements aggregating $10,000 would have a material effect on an entity's income statement, but that misstatements would have to aggregate $20,000 to materially affect the balance sheet.

   Ordinarily, it would be appropriate to design auditing procedures that would be expected to detect misstatements that aggregate

   A. $10,000
   B. $15,000
   C. $20,000
   D. $30,000

AICPA.101115AUD

123. An auditor finds several errors in the financial statements that the client prefers not to correct. The auditor determines that the errors are not material in the aggregate. Which of the following actions by the auditor is most appropriate?

   A. Document the errors in the summary of uncorrected errors, and document the conclusion that the errors do **not** cause the financial statements to be misstated.
   B. Document the conclusion that the errors do **not** cause the financial statements to be misstated, but do **not** summarize uncorrected errors in the audit documentation.
   C. Summarize the uncorrected errors in the audit documentation, but do **not** document whether the errors cause the financial statements to be misstated.
   D. Do **not** summarize the uncorrected errors in the audit documentation, and do **not** document a conclusion about whether the uncorrected errors cause the financial statements to be misstated.

Audit Risk

AICPA.921110AUD-AU

124. As the acceptable level of detection risk increases, an auditor may change the

   A. Assessed level of control risk from below the maximum to the maximum level.
   B. Assurance provided by tests of controls by using a larger sample size than planned.
   C. Timing of substantive tests from year end to an interim date.
   D. Nature of substantive tests from a less effective to a more effective procedure.

AICPA.941108AUD-AU

125. Inherent risk and control risk differ from detection risk in that they

   A. Arise from the misapplication of auditing procedures.
   B. May be assessed in either quantitative or nonquantitative terms.
   C. Exist independently of the financial statement audit.
   D. Can be changed at the auditor's discretion.

AICPA.910526AUD-AU

126. The acceptable level of detection risk is inversely related to the

   A. Assurance provided by substantive tests.
   B. Risk of misapplying auditing procedures.
   C. Preliminary judgment about materiality levels.
   D. Risk of failing to discover material misstatements.

AICPA.970511AUD-AU

127. Holding other planning considerations equal, a decrease in the number of misstatements in a class of transactions that an auditor could tolerate most likely would cause the auditor to

   A. Apply the planned substantive tests prior to the balance sheet date.
   B. Perform the planned auditing procedures closer to the balance sheet date.

C. Increase the assessed level of control risk for relevant financial statement assertions.

D. Decrease the extent of auditing procedures to be applied to the class of transactions.

AICPA.940523AUD-AU

128. When an auditor increases the assessed level of control risk because certain control procedures were determined to be ineffective, the auditor would most likely increase the

A. Extent of tests of controls.
B. Level of detection risk.
C. Extent of tests of details.
D. Level of inherent risk.

Analytical Procedures

AICPA.931138AUD-AU

129. For audits of financial statements made in accordance with generally accepted auditing standards, the use of analytical procedures is required to some extent

	As a substantive test	In the final review stage
A.	Yes	Yes
B.	Yes	No
C.	No	Yes
D.	No	No

AICPA.950547AUD-AU

130. Analytical procedures used in the overall review stage of an audit generally include

A. Gathering evidence concerning account balances that have not changed from the prior year.
B. Retesting control procedures that appeared to be ineffective during the assessment of control risk.
C. Considering unusual or unexpected account balances that were not previously identified.
D. Performing tests of transactions to corroborate management's financial statement assertions.

AICPA.920558AUD-AU

131. Analytical procedures used in planning an audit should focus on

A. Identifying possible scope limitations and gathering evidence in assessing control risk environmental factors.
B. Enhancing the understanding of the entity's business and the transactions and events that have occurred since the last audit.
C. Aggregating data at a low level and substantiating management's assertions that are embodied in the financial statements.

D. Discovering material weaknesses in the internal control structure and reporting them to the entity's management for corrective action.

AICPA.950548AUD-AU

132. Which of the following would not be considered an analytical procedure?

A. Estimating payroll expense by multiplying the number of employees by the average hourly wage rate and the total hours worked.
B. Projecting an error rate by comparing the results of a statistical sample with the actual population characteristics.
C. Computing accounts receivable turnover by dividing credit sales by the average net receivables.
D. Developing the expected current-year sales based on the sales trend of the prior five years.

AICPA.910504AUD-AU

133. A basic premise underlying the application of analytical procedures is that

A. The study of financial ratios is an acceptable alternative to the investigation of unusual fluctuations.
B. Statistical tests of financial information may lead to the discovery of material errors in the financial statements.
C. Plausible relationships among data may reasonably be expected to exist and continue in the absence of known conditions to the contrary.
D. These procedures cannot replace tests of balances and transactions.

Detecting Fraud

AICPA.950515AUD-AU

134. Which of the following statements reflects an auditor's responsibility for detecting errors and irregularities?

A. An auditor is responsible for detecting employee errors and simple fraud, but not for discovering irregularities involving employee collusion or management override.
B. An auditor should plan the audit to detect errors and irregularities that are caused by departures from GAAP.
C. An auditor is not responsible for detecting errors and irregularities unless the application of GAAS would result in such detection.
D. An auditor should design the audit to provide reasonable assurance of detecting errors and irregularities that are material to the financial statements.

AICPA.111178AUD

135. Prior to, or in conjunction with, the information-gathering procedures for an audit, audit team members should discuss the potential for material misstatement due to fraud. Which of the following best characterizes the mindset that the audit team should maintain during this discussion?

A. Presumptive.
B. Judgmental.
C. Criticizing.
D. Questioning.

AICPA.130717AUD

136. While performing an audit of the financial statements of a company for the year ended December 31, year 1, the auditor notes that the company's sales increased substantially in December, year 1, with a corresponding decrease in January, year 2. In assessing the risk of fraudulent financial reporting or misappropriation of assets, what should be the auditor's initial indication about the potential for fraud in sales revenue?

A. There is a broad indication of misappropriation of assets.
B. There is an indication of theft of the entity's assets.
C. There is an indication of embezzling receipts.
D. There is a broad indication of financial reporting fraud.

AICPA.120711AUD

137. Which of the following situations most likely represents the highest risk of a misstatement arising from misappropriations of assets?

A. A large number of bearer bonds on hand.
B. A large number of inventory items with low sales prices.
C. A large number of transactions processed in a short period of time.
D. A large number of fixed assets with easily identifiable serial numbers.

AICPA.010503AUD-AU

138. Which of the following factors would be most likely to heighten an auditor's concern about the risk of fraudulent financial reporting?

A. Large amounts of liquid assets that are easily convertible into cash.
B. Low growth and profitability as compared to other entities in the same industry.
C. Financial management's participation in the initial selection of accounting principles.
D. An overly complex organizational structure involving unusual lines of authority.

Fraud: Evaluation and Communication

AICPA.900555AUD-AU

139. Disclosure of irregularities to parties other than a client's senior management and its audit committee or board of directors ordinarily is not part of an auditor's responsibility.

However, to which of the following outside parties may a duty to disclose irregularities exist?

	To the SEC when the client reports an auditor change	To a successor auditor when the successor makes appropriate inquiries	To a government funding agency from which the client receives financial assistance
A.	Yes	Yes	No
B.	Yes	No	Yes
C.	No	Yes	Yes
D.	Yes	Yes	Yes

Detecting Illegal Acts

AICPA.101118AUD

140. Which of the following information that comes to an auditor's attention would be most likely to raise a question about the occurrence of illegal acts?

A. The exchange of property for similar property in a nonmonetary transaction.
B. The discovery of unexplained payments made to government employees.
C. The presence of several difficult-to-audit transactions affecting expense accounts.
D. The failure to develop adequate procedures that detect unauthorized purchases.

AICPA.101093AUD

141. During the audit of a new client, the auditor determined that management had given illegal bribes to municipal officials during the year under audit and for several prior years. The auditor notified the client's board of directors, but the board decided to take no action because the amounts involved were immaterial to the financial statements. Under these circumstances, the auditor should

A. Add an explanatory paragraph emphasizing that certain matters, while not affecting the unqualified opinion, require disclosure.
B. Report the illegal bribes to the municipal official at least one level above those persons who received the bribes.
C. Consider withdrawing from the audit engagement and disassociating from future relationships with the client.
D. Issue an "except for" qualified opinion or an adverse opinion with a separate paragraph that explains the circumstances.

AICPA.970513AUD-AU

142. Which of the following information discovered during an audit most likely would raise a question concerning possible illegal acts?

   A. Related party transactions, although properly disclosed, were pervasive during the year.
   B. The entity prepared several large checks payable to cash during the year.
   C. Material internal control weaknesses previously reported to management were not corrected.
   D. The entity was a campaign contributor to several local political candidates during the year.

Using the Work of a "Specialist"

AICPA.930533AUD-AU

143. An auditor who uses the work of a specialist may refer to the specialist in the auditor's report if the

   A. Specialist's findings provide the auditor greater assurance of reliability about management's representations.
   B. Auditor issues a modified opinion because of a matter related to the specialist's findings.
   C. Auditor's use of the specialist's findings is different from that of prior years.
   D. Specialist is a related party whose findings fully corroborate management's financial statement assertions.

AICPA.941165AUD-AU

144. Which of the following statements is correct about the auditor's use of the work of a specialist?

   A. The specialist should not have an understanding of the auditor's corroborative use of the specialist's findings.
   B. The auditor is required to perform substantive procedures to verify the specialist's assumptions and findings.
   C. The client should not have an understanding of the nature of the work to be performed by the specialist.
   D. The auditor should obtain an understanding of the methods and assumptions used by the specialist.

AICPA.090751.AUD.AU

145. Which of the following statements is correct concerning an auditor's use of the work of an actuary in assessing a client's pension obligations?

   A. The auditor is required to understand the objectives and scope of the actuary's work.
   B. The reasonableness of the actuary's assumptions is strictly the auditor's responsibility.
   C. The client is required to consent to the auditor's use of the actuary's work.
   D. If the actuary has a relationship with the client, the auditor may not use the actuary's work.

AICPA.090795.AUD-AU

146. An auditor who uses the work of a specialist may refer to the specialist in the auditor's report if the

   A. Auditor believes that the specialist's findings are reasonable in the circumstances.
   B. Specialist's findings support the related assertions in the financial statements.
   C. Auditor modifies the report because of the difference between the client's and the specialist's valuations of an asset.
   D. Specialist's findings provide the auditor with greater assurance of reliability about management's representations.

AICPA.070614AUD

147. An auditor intends to use the work of an actuary who has a relationship with the client. Under these circumstances, the auditor

   A. Is required to disclose the contractual relationship in the auditor's report.
   B. Should assess the risk that the actuary's objectivity might be impaired.
   C. Is not permitted to rely on the actuary because of a lack of independence.
   D. Should communicate this matter to the audit committee as a significant deficiency.

Required Communications with those Charged with Governance

AICPA.910555AUD-AU

148. Which of the following matters is an auditor required to communicate to an entity's audit committee (or those charged with governance)?

	Significant audit adjustments	Changes in significant accounting policies
A.	Yes	Yes
B.	Yes	No
C.	No	Yes
D.	No	No

AICPA.930559AUD-AU

149. Which of the following statements is correct concerning an auditor's required communication with an entity's audit committee?

    A. This communication should include disagreements with management about significant audit adjustments, whether satisfactorily resolved or unresolved.

    B. If matters are communicated orally, it is necessary to repeat the communication of recurring matters each year.

    C. If matters are communicated in writing, the report is required to be distributed to both the audit committee and management.

    D. This communication is required to occur before the auditor's report on the financial statements is issued.

AICPA.921160AUD-AU

150. Which of the following matters is an auditor required to communicate to an entity's audit committee (or those charged with governance)?

    I. Disagreements with management about matters significant to the entity's financial statements that have been satisfactorily resolved.

    II. The auditor's views about qualitative aspects of the entity's significant accounting practices, including accounting policies, accounting estimates, and financial statement disclosures.

    A. I only.

    B. II only.

    C. Both I and II.

    D. Neither I nor II.

AICPA.951184AUD-AU

151. Which of the following statements is correct about an auditor's required communication with an entity's audit committee (or those charged with governance)?

    A. Any matters communicated to the entity's audit committee (or those charged with governance) also are required to be communicated to the entity's management.

    B. The auditor is required to inform the entity's audit committee (or those charged with governance) about errors discovered by the auditor and subsequently corrected by management.

    C. Disagreements with management about the application of significant accounting principles are required to be communicated to the entity's audit committee (or those charged with governance).

    D. All deficiencies or weaknesses in the internal control structure are required to be communicated to the audit committee.

AICPA.950519AUD-AU

152. An auditor would be least likely to initiate a discussion with a client's audit committee concerning

    A. The methods used to account for significant unusual transactions.

    B. The maximum dollar amount of misstatements that could exist without causing the financial statements to be materially misstated.

    C. Indications of fraud and illegal acts committed by a corporate officer that were discovered by the auditor.

    D. Disagreements with management as to accounting principles that were resolved during the current year's audit.

PCAOB on Communications with Audit Committees

AICPA.130503AUD-SIM

153. The objectives of Auditing Standard No. 16, "Communications with Audit Committees," include all of the following, except for

    A. Enhancing communications between the audit committee and the entity's internal audit function.

    B. Obtaining information from the audit committee that is relevant to the audit.

    C. Providing the audit committee with timely information about significant audit issues.

    D. Communicating to the audit committee the auditor's responsibilities and establish an understanding of the terms of the engagement.

AICPA.130504AUD-SIM

154. Under PCAOB auditing standards, the auditor should communicate all of the following matters to an issuer's audit committee at the beginning of the audit engagement except for

    A. Significant issues that the auditor discussed with management in connection with the auditor's appointment/retention.

    B. The terms of the engagement, including the objectives of the audit and the parties' respective responsibilities.

    C. The qualitative aspects of the entity's significant accounting policies, including any indications of management bias.

    D. An overview of the audit strategy and timing of the audit, along with any significant risks identified by the auditor.

AICPA.130505AUD-SIM

155. The format and timing of the auditor's required communication with an issuer's audit committee is best characterized by the following:

	Format of the communication	Timing of the communication
A.	Must be in writing	Must be by the date of the auditor's report
B.	Must be in writing	Must be prior to issuing the auditor's report
C.	May be written or oral (unless otherwise specified)	Must be by the date of the auditor's report
D.	May be written or oral (unless otherwise specified)	Must be prior to issuing the auditor's report

Internal Control—Concepts & Standards

Internal Control Concepts 1

AICPA.901144AUD-AU

156. In planning an audit of certain accounts, an auditor may conclude that specific procedures used to obtain an understanding of an entity's internal control structure need not be included because of the auditor's judgments about materiality and assessments of

A. Control risk.
B. Detection risk.
C. Sampling risk.
D. Inherent risk.

AICPA.940518AUD-AU

157. An auditor's flowchart of a client's accounting system is a diagrammatic representation that depicts the auditor's

A. Assessment of control risk.
B. Identification of weaknesses in the system.
C. Assessment of the control environment's effectiveness.
D. Understanding of the system.

AICPA.120707AUD

158. Obtaining an understanding of an internal control involves evaluating the design of the control and determining whether the control has been

A. Authorized.
B. Implemented.
C. Tested.
D. Monitored.

AICPA.940521AUD-AU

159. When obtaining an understanding of an entity's internal control procedures, an auditor should concentrate on the substance of the procedures, rather than their form, because

A. The procedures may be operating effectively but may not be documented.
B. Management may establish appropriate procedures but not enforce compliance with them.
C. The procedures may be so inappropriate that no reliance is contemplated by the auditor.
D. Management may implement procedures whose costs exceed their benefits.

Internal Control Concepts 2

AICPA.901143AUD-AU

160. An auditor's primary consideration regarding an entity's internal control structure policies and procedures is whether they

A. Prevent management override.
B. Relate to the control environment.
C. Reflect management's philosophy and operating style.
D. Affect the financial statement assertions.

AICPA.951104AUD-AU

161. Which of the following auditor concerns could most likely be so serious that the auditor concludes that a financial statement audit cannot be conducted?

A. The entity has no formal written code of conduct.
B. The integrity of the entity's management is suspect.
C. Procedures requiring segregation of duties are subject to management override.
D. Management fails to modify prescribed controls for changes in conditions.

AICPA.950533AUD-AU

162. After obtaining an understanding of the internal control structure and assessing control risk, an auditor decided to perform tests of controls. The auditor most likely decided that

A. It would be efficient to perform tests of controls that would result in a reduction in planned substantive tests.
B. Additional evidence to support a further reduction in control risk is not available.
C. An increase in the assessed level of control risk is justified for certain financial statement assertions.

D. There were many internal control structure weaknesses that could allow errors to enter the accounting system.

AICPA.020511AUD-AU

163. An auditor observed that a client mails monthly statements to customers. Subsequently, the auditor reviewed evidence of follow-up on the errors reported by the customers.

This test of controls most likely was performed to support management's financial statement assertion(s) of

	Presentation and disclosure	Rights and obligations
A.	Yes	Yes
B.	Yes	No
C.	No	Yes
D.	No	No

AICPA.940524AUD-AU

164. An auditor uses the assessed level of control risk to

A. Evaluate the effectiveness of the entity's internal control policies and procedures.
B. Identify transactions and account balances where inherent risk is at the maximum.
C. Indicate whether materiality thresholds for planning and evaluation purposes are sufficiently high.
D. Determine the acceptable level of detection risk for financial statement assertions.

Internal Control Standards 1

AICPA.900529AUD-AU

165. Which of the following elements of an entity's internal control structure includes the development of personnel manuals documenting employee promotion and training policies?

A. Control activities.
B. Control environment.
C. Accounting system.
D. Quality control system.

AICPA.920538AUD-AU

166. For certain controls, such as segregation of duties, documentary evidence may not exist. An auditor would most likely test the procedures by

A. Reperformance and corroboration.
B. Observation and inquiry.
C. Inspection and vouching.
D. Confirmation and recomputation.

AICPA.900531AUD-AU

167. After obtaining an understanding of an entity's internal control structure, an auditor may assess control risk at the maximum level for some assertions because the auditor

A. Believes the internal control policies and procedures are unlikely to be effective.
B. Determines that the pertinent internal control structure elements are not well documented.
C. Performs tests of controls to restrict detection risk to an acceptable level.
D. Identifies internal control policies and procedures that are likely to prevent material misstatements.

AICPA.120710AUD

168. Which of the following is the best way to compensate for the lack of adequate segregation of duties in a small organization?

A. Disclosing lack of segregation of duties to the external auditors during the annual review.
B. Replacing personnel every three or four years.
C. Requiring accountants to pass a yearly background check.
D. Allowing for greater management oversight of incompatible activities.

AICPA.111177AUD

169. Which of the following is not a component of internal control?

A. Control environment.
B. Control activities.
C. Inherent risk.
D. Monitoring.

Internal Control Standards 2

AICPA.070604AUD

170. When companies use information technology (IT) extensively, evidence may be available only in electronic form. What is an auditor's best course of action in such situations?

A. Assess the control risk as high.
B. Use audit software to perform analytical procedures.
C. Use generalized audit software to extract evidence from client databases.
D. Perform limited tests of controls over electronic data.

AICPA.020409AUD-AU

171. Which of the following auditor concerns most likely could be so serious that the auditor concludes that a financial statement audit cannot be performed?

A. Management fails to modify prescribed internal controls for changes in information technology.
B. Internal control activities requiring segregation of duties are rarely monitored by management.
C. Management is dominated by one person who is also the majority stockholder.
D. There is a substantial risk of intentional misapplication of accounting principles.

AICPA.941142AUD-AU

172. The objective of tests of details of transactions performed as tests of controls is to

A. Monitor the design and use of entity documents such as prenumbered shipping forms.
B. Determine whether internal control structure policies and procedures have been placed in operation.
C. Detect material misstatements in the account balances of the financial statements.
D. Evaluate whether internal control structure procedures operated effectively.

AICPA.130709AUD

173. When the operating effectiveness of a control is **not** evidenced by written documentation, an auditor should obtain evidence about the control's effectiveness by

A. Mailing confirmations.
B. Inquiry and other procedures such as observation.
C. Analytical procedures.
D. Recalculating the balance in related accounts.

AICPA.930509AUD-AU

174. When an auditor assesses control risk below the maximum level, the auditor is required to document the auditor's

	Basis for concluding that control risk is below the maximum level	Understanding of the entity's internal control structure elements
A.	No	No
B.	Yes	Yes
C.	Yes	No
D.	No	Yes

Required Communications

AICPA.911143AUD-AU

175. Which of the following statements is correct concerning significant deficiencies noted in an audit?

A. Significant deficiencies are material weaknesses in the design or operation of specific internal control structure elements.
B. The auditor is obligated to search for significant deficiencies that could adversely affect the entity's ability to record and report financial data.
C. Significant deficiencies should not be recommunicated each year unless management has failed to acknowledge its understanding of such deficiencies.
D. The auditor should separately identify and communicate significant deficiencies and material weaknesses.

AICPA.930523AUD-AU

176. A letter issued regarding significant deficiencies relating to an entity's internal control observed during an audit of financial statements should include a

A. Restriction on the distribution of the report.
B. Description of tests performed to search for material weaknesses.
C. Statement of compliance with applicable laws and regulations.
D. Paragraph describing management's evaluation of the effectiveness of the control structure.

AICPA.941144AUD-AU

177. Significant deficiencies are matters that come to an auditor's attention that should be communicated to an entity's audit committee (or those charged with governance) because they represent

A. Disclosures of information that significantly contradict the auditor's going concern assumption.
B. Material irregularities or illegal acts perpetrated by high-level management.
C. Significant deficiencies in the design or operation of internal control.
D. Manipulation or falsification of accounting records or documents from which financial statements are prepared.

AICPA.010414AUD-AU

178. Which of the following matters would an auditor most likely consider to be a significant deficiency to be communicated to the audit committee (or otherwise those charged with governance)?

A. Management's failure to renegotiate unfavorable long-term purchase commitments.
B. Recurring operating losses that may indicate going concern problems.
C. Evidence of a lack of objectivity by those responsible for accounting decisions.
D. Management's current plans to reduce its ownership equity in the entity.

AICPA.921123AUD-AU

179. Which of the following representations should not be included in a report on internal control related matters noted in an audit?

A. Significant deficiencies related to internal control design exist, but none is deemed to be a material weakness.
B. There are no significant deficiencies in the design or operation of the internal control structure.
C. Corrective follow-up action is recommended due to the relative significance of material weaknesses discovered during the audit.
D. The auditor's consideration of internal control would not necessarily disclose all significant deficiencies that exist.

Using the Work of an Internal Audit Function

AICPA.900528AUD-AU

180. Miller Retailing, Inc. maintains a staff of three full-time internal auditors who report directly to the controller. In planning to use the internal auditors to provide assistance in performing the audit, the independent auditor will most likely

A. Place limited reliance on the work performed by the internal auditors.
B. Decrease the extent of the tests of controls needed to support the assessed level of detection risk.
C. Increase the extent of the procedures needed to reduce control risk to an acceptable level.
D. Avoid using the work performed by the internal auditors.

AICPA.090791.AUD-AU

181. When assessing the competence of the internal auditors, an independent CPA should obtain information about the

A. Organizational level to which the internal auditors report.
B. Quality of the internal auditors' working paper documentation.
C. Policies prohibiting internal auditors from auditing sensitive matters.
D. Internal auditors' preliminary assessed level of control risk.

AICPA.950559AUD-AU

182. An internal auditor's work would most likely affect the nature, timing, and extent of an independent CPA's auditing procedures when the internal auditor's work relates to assertions about the

A. Existence of contingencies.
B. Valuation of intangible assets.
C. Existence of fixed asset additions.
D. Valuation of related party transactions.

AICPA.941168AUD-AU

183. In assessing the competence and objectivity of an entity's internal auditor, an independent auditor would be least likely to consider information obtained from

A. Discussions with management personnel.
B. External quality reviews of the internal auditor's activities.
C. Previous experience with the internal auditor.
D. The results of analytical procedures.

AICPA.931117AUD-AU

184. For which of the following judgments may an independent auditor share responsibility with an entity's internal auditor who is assessed to be both competent and objective?

	Materiality of misstatements	Evaluation of accounting estimates
A.	Yes	No
B.	No	Yes
C.	No	No
D.	Yes	Yes

III. Performing Further Procedures and Obtaining Evidence

Internal Control: Transaction Cycles

Specific Transaction Cycles

AICPA.010504AUD-AU

185. An auditor suspects that certain client employees are ordering merchandise for themselves over the Internet without recording the purchase or receipt of the merchandise. When vendors' invoices arrive, one of the employees approves the invoices for payment. After the invoices are paid, the employee destroys the invoices and the related vouchers.

In gathering evidence regarding the fraud, the auditor would most likely select items for testing from the file of all

A. Cash disbursements.
B. Approved vouchers.
C. Receiving reports.
D. Vendors' invoices.

AICPA.941126AUD-AU

186. Proper segregation of duties reduces the opportunities to allow persons to be in positions to both

A. Journalize entries and prepare financial statements.
B. Record cash receipts and cash disbursements.
C. Establish internal controls and authorize transactions.
D. Perpetrate and conceal errors and irregularities.

Revenue/Receipts—Sales

AICPA.940528AUD-AU

187. Which of the following internal control procedures would most likely assure that all billed sales are correctly posted to the accounts receivable ledger?

A. Daily sales summaries are compared to daily postings to the accounts receivable ledger.
B. Each sales invoice is supported by a prenumbered shipping document.
C. The accounts receivable ledger is reconciled daily to the control account in the general ledger.
D. Each shipment on credit is supported by a prenumbered sales invoice.

AICPA.941136AUD-AU

188. Which of the following procedures would most likely not be an internal control procedure designed to reduce the risk of errors in the billing process?

A. Comparing control totals for shipping documents with corresponding totals for sales invoices.
B. Using computer programmed controls on the pricing and mathematical accuracy of sales invoices.
C. Matching shipping documents with approved sales orders before invoice preparation.
D. Reconciling the control totals for sales invoices with the accounts receivable subsidiary ledger.

AICPA.900534AUD-AU

189. Tracing bills of lading to sales invoices provides evidence that

A. Shipments to customers were invoiced.
B. Shipments to customers were recorded as sales.
C. Recorded sales were shipped.
D. Invoiced sales were shipped.

AICPA.970414AUD-AU

190. Which of the following fraudulent activities could most likely be perpetrated due to the lack of effective internal controls in the revenue cycle?

A. Fictitious transactions may be recorded that cause an understatement of revenues and an overstatement of receivables.
B. Claims received from customers for goods returned may be intentionally recorded in other customers' accounts.
C. Authorization of credit memos by personnel who receive cash may permit the misappropriation of cash.
D. The failure to prepare shipping documents may cause an overstatement of inventory balances.

AICPA.930520AUD-AU

191. Sound internal control procedures dictate that defective merchandise returned by customers should be presented initially to the

   A. Accounts receivable supervisor.
   B. Receiving clerk.
   C. Shipping department supervisor.
   D. Sales clerk.

Revenue/Receipts—Cash

AICPA.910528AUD-AU

192. An auditor would consider a cashier's job description to contain compatible duties if the cashier receives remittances from the mailroom and also prepares the

   A. Prelist of individual checks.
   B. Monthly bank reconciliation.
   C. Daily deposit slip.
   D. Remittance advices.

AICPA.950530AUD-AU

193. Sound internal control procedures dictate that, immediately upon receiving checks from customers by mail, a responsible employee should

   A. Add the checks to the daily cash summary.
   B. Verify that each check is supported by a prenumbered sales invoice.
   C. Prepare a duplicate listing of checks received.
   D. Record the checks in the cash receipts journal.

AICPA.930514AUD-AU

194. Which of the following internal control procedures would most likely deter lapping of collections from customers?

   A. Independent internal verification of dates of entry in the cash receipts journal with dates of daily cash summaries.
   B. Authorization of write-offs of uncollectible accounts by a supervisor independent of credit approval.
   C. Segregation of duties between receiving cash and posting the accounts receivable ledger.
   D. Supervisory comparison of the daily cash summary with the sum of the cash receipts journal entries.

AICPA.020507AUD-AU

195. Which of the following circumstances would most likely cause an auditor to suspect that material misstatements exist in a client's financial statements?

   A. The assumptions used in developing the prior year's accounting estimates have changed.
   B. Differences between reconciliations of control accounts and subsidiary records are not investigated.
   C. Negative confirmation requests yield fewer responses than in the prior year's audit.
   D. Management consults with another CPA firm about complex accounting matters.

AICPA.900535AUD-AU

196. Employers bond employees who handle cash receipts because fidelity bonds reduce the possibility of employing dishonest individuals and

   A. Protect employees who make unintentional errors from possible monetary damages resulting from their errors.
   B. Deter dishonesty by making employees aware that insurance companies may investigate and prosecute dishonest acts.
   C. Facilitate an independent monitoring of the receiving and depositing of cash receipts.
   D. Force employees in positions of trust to take periodic vacations and rotate their assigned duties.

Expenditures/Disbursements

AICPA.911138AUD-AU

197. Mailing disbursement checks and remittance advices should be controlled by the employee who

   A. Approves the vouchers for payment.
   B. Matches the receiving reports, purchase orders, and vendors' invoices.
   C. Maintains possession of the mechanical check-signing device.
   D. Signs the checks last.

AICPA.120727AUD

198. Which of the following controls should prevent an invoice for the purchase of merchandise from being paid twice?

   A. The check signer accounts for the numerical sequence of receiving reports used in support of each payment.
   B. An individual independent of cash operations prepares a bank reconciliation.
   C. The check signer reviews and cancels the voucher packets.
   D. Two check signers are required for all checks over a specified amount.

AICPA.921116AUD-AU

199. When the shipping department returns nonconforming goods to a vendor, the purchasing department should send to the accounting department the

   A. Unpaid voucher.
   B. Debit memo.
   C. Vendor invoice.
   D. Credit memo.

AICPA.931129AUD-AU

200. In a well-designed internal control structure, employees in the same department most likely would approve purchase orders, and also

   A. Reconcile the open invoice file.
   B. Inspect goods upon receipt.
   C. Authorize requisitions of goods.
   D. Negotiate terms with vendors.

AICPA.090755.AUD.AU

201. Which of the following situations could most likely lead to an embezzlement scheme?

   A. The accounts receivable bookkeeper receives a list of payments prepared by the cashier and personally makes entries in the customers' accounts receivable subsidiary ledger.
   B. Each vendor invoice is matched with the related purchase order and receiving report by the vouchers payable bookkeeper who personally approves the voucher for payment.
   C. Access to blank checks and signature plates is restricted to the cash disbursements bookkeeper who personally reconciles the monthly bank statement.
   D. Vouchers and supporting documentation are examined and then canceled by the treasurer who personally mails the checks to vendors.

Payroll Cycle

AICPA.101095AUD

202. Which of the following activities performed by a department supervisor would most likely help in the prevention or detection of a payroll fraud?

   A. Distributing paychecks directly to department employees.
   B. Setting the pay rate for departmental employees.
   C. Hiring employees and authorizing them to be added to payroll.
   D. Approving a summary of hours each employee worked during the pay period.

AICPA.101121AUD

203. Which of the following payroll control activities would most effectively ensure that payment is made only for work performed?

   A. Require all employees to record arrival and departure by using the time clock.
   B. Have a payroll clerk recalculate all time cards.
   C. Require all employees to sign their time cards.
   D. Require employees to have their direct supervisors approve their time cards.

Miscellaneous Cycles

AICPA.921119AUD-AU

204. In obtaining an understanding of a manufacturing entity's internal control structure concerning inventory balances, an auditor would most likely

   A. Review the entity's descriptions of inventory policies and procedures.
   B. Perform test counts of inventory during the entity's physical count.
   C. Analyze inventory turnover statistics to identify slow-moving and obsolete items.
   D. Analyze monthly production reports to identify variances and unusual transactions.

AICPA.911139AUD-AU

205. The safeguarding of inventory most likely includes

   A. Comparison of the information contained on the purchase requisitions, purchase orders, receiving reports, and vendors' invoices.
   B. Periodic reconciliation of detailed inventory records with the actual inventory on hand by taking a physical count.
   C. Analytical procedures for raw materials, goods in process, and finished goods that identify unusual transactions, theft, and obsolescence.
   D. Application of established overhead rates on the basis of direct labor hours or direct labor costs.

AICPA.931128AUD-AU

206. The objectives of the internal control structure for a production cycle are to provide assurance that transactions are properly executed and recorded, and that

   A. Production orders are prenumbered and signed by a supervisor.
   B. Custody of work in process and of finished goods is properly maintained.

C. Independent internal verification of activity reports is established.

D. Transfers to finished goods are documented by a completed production report and a quality control report.

AICPA.931134AUD-AU

207. Equipment acquisitions that are misclassified as maintenance expense would most likely be detected by an internal control procedure that provides for

A. Segregation of duties of employees in the accounts payable department.

B. Independent verification of invoices for disbursements recorded as equipment acquisitions.

C. Investigation of variances within a formal budgeting system.

D. Authorization by the board of directors of significant equipment acquisitions.

AICPA.951127AUD-AU

208. When there are numerous property and equipment transactions during the year, an auditor who plans to assess control risk at a low level usually performs

A. Tests of controls and extensive tests of property and equipment balances at the end of the year.

B. Analytical procedures for current year property and equipment transactions.

C. Tests of controls and limited tests of current year property and equipment transactions.

D. Analytical procedures for property and equipment balances at the end of the year.

Audit Evidence: Concepts & Standards

Overview of Substantive Procedures

assess.AICPA.AUD.sub.proc-0030

209. Which of the following is an analytical procedure?

A. Comparing current-year balances to prior-year balances.

B. Matching sales invoices to shipping documents.

C. Confirming accounts receivable.

D. Making inquiries of client management.

AICPA.070643AUD

210. At the conclusion of an audit, an auditor is reviewing the evidence gathered in support of the financial statements. With regard to the valuation of inventory, the auditor concludes that the evidence obtained is not sufficient to support management's representations. Which of the following actions is the auditor most likely to take?

A. Consult with the audit committee and issue a disclaimer of opinion.

B. Consult with the audit committee and issue a qualified opinion.

C. Obtain additional evidence regarding the valuation of inventory.

D. Obtain a statement from management supporting their inventory valuation.

AICPA.090796.AUD-AU

211. Which of the following ratios would an engagement partner most likely consider in the overall review stage of an audit?

A. Total liabilities/net sales.

B. Accounts receivable/inventory.

C. Cost of goods sold/average inventory.

D. Current assets/quick assets.

AICPA.941102AUD-AU

212. Which of the following factors would most likely influence an auditor's determination of the auditability of an entity's financial statements?

A. The complexity of the accounting system.

B. The existence of related party transactions.

C. The adequacy of the accounting records.

D. The operating effectiveness of control procedures.

assess.AICPA.AUD.sub.proc-0029

213. Which of the following best identifies the effect of an increase in the risk of material misstatement on detection risk and the extent of substantive procedures?

A. The acceptable level of detection risk decreases, and the extent of substantive procedures increases.

B. The acceptable level of detection risk increases, and the extent of substantive procedures increases.

C. The acceptable level of detection risk decreases, and the extent of substantive procedures decreases.

D. The acceptable level of detection risk increases, and the extent of substantive procedures decreases.

Nature of Evidence 1

AICPA.020411AUD-AU

214. An auditor observed that a client mails monthly statements to customers. Subsequently, the auditor reviewed evidence of follow-up on the errors reported by the customers.

This test of controls most likely was performed to support management's financial statement assertion(s) of

	Presentation and disclosure	Rights and obligations
A.	Yes	Yes
B.	Yes	No
C.	No	Yes
D.	No	No

AICPA.130731AUD

215. Which of the following is a management assertion regarding account balances at the period end?

A. Transactions and events that have been recorded have occurred and pertain to the entity.
B. Transactions and events have been recorded in the proper accounts.
C. The entity holds or controls the rights to assets, and liabilities are obligations of the entity.
D. Amounts and other data related to transactions and events have been recorded appropriately.

AICPA.930526AUD-AU

216. Which of the following procedures would provide the most reliable audit evidence?

A. Inquiries of the client's internal audit staff held in private.
B. Inspection of prenumbered client purchase orders filed in the vouchers payable department.
C. Analytical procedures performed by the auditor on the entity's trial balance.
D. Inspection of bank statements obtained directly from the client's financial institution.

AICPA.931133AUD-AU

217. Which of the following internal control procedures would an entity be most likely to use to assist in satisfying the completeness assertion related to long-term investments?

A. Senior management verifies that securities in the bank safe deposit box are registered in the entity's name.
B. The internal auditor compares the securities in the bank safe deposit box with recorded investments.
C. The treasurer vouches the acquisition of securities by comparing brokers' advices with canceled checks.
D. The controller compares the current market prices of recorded investments with the brokers' advices on file.

AICPA.950539AUD-AU

218. Which of the following types of audit evidence is the most persuasive?

A. Prenumbered client purchase order forms.
B. Client work sheets supporting cost allocations.
C. Bank statements obtained from the client.
D. Client representation letter.

Nature of Evidence 2

AICPA.101123AUD

219. Which of the following procedures is considered a test of controls?

A. An auditor reviews the entity's check register for unrecorded liabilities.
B. An auditor evaluates whether a general journal entry was recorded at the proper amount.
C. An auditor interviews and observes appropriate personnel to determine segregation of duties.
D. An auditor reviews the audit documentation to ensure proper sign-off.

AICPA.130737AUD

220. An auditor of a nonissuer should design tests of details to ensure that sufficient audit evidence supports which of the following?

A. The planned level of control risk.
B. Management's assertions that internal controls exist and are operating efficiently.
C. The effectiveness of internal controls.
D. The planned level of assurance at the relevant assertion level.

AICPA.130713AUD

221. Which of the following is an important consideration when deciding the nature of tests to use in a financial statement audit?

A. Tests of details typically provide a low level of assurance.
B. Analytical procedures are an inefficient means of obtaining assurance.
C. The procedures to be applied on a particular engagement are a matter of the auditor's professional judgment.
D. The use of tests of controls should be considered without regard to the level of assurance required.

AICPA.970415AUD-AU

222. Which of the following procedures would an auditor most likely perform to test controls relating to management's assertion about the

completeness of cash receipts for cash sales at a retail outlet?

A. Observe the consistency of the employees' use of cash registers and tapes.
B. Inquire about employees' access to recorded but undeposited cash.
C. Trace the deposits in the cash receipts journal to the cash balance in the general ledger.
D. Compare the cash balance in the general ledger with the bank confirmation request.

AICPA.010512AUD-AU

223. Which of the following procedures would an auditor most likely perform during an audit engagement's overall review stage in formulating an opinion on an entity's financial statements?

A. Obtain assurance from the entity's attorney that all material litigation has been disclosed in the financial statements.
B. Verify the clerical accuracy of the entity's proof of cash and its bank cutoff statement.
C. Determine whether inadequate provisions for the safeguarding of assets have been corrected.
D. Consider whether the results of audit procedures affect the assessment of the risk of material misstatement due to fraud.

PCAOB Risk Assessment Standards

AICPA.111151AUD-SIM

224. The PCAOB identifies each of the following as a financial statement assertion to be addressed by the auditor except for

A. Existence or occurrence.
B. Completeness.
C. Cutoff.
D. Presentation and disclosure.

AICPA.130718AUD

225. When a PCAOB auditing standard indicates that an auditor "could" perform a specific procedure, how should the auditor decide whether and how to perform the procedure?

A. By comparing the PCAOB standard with related AICPA auditing standards.
B. By exercising professional judgment in the circumstances.
C. By soliciting input from the issuer's audit committee.
D. By evaluating whether the audit is likely to be subject to inspection by the PCAOB.

AICPA.111153AUD-SIM

226. In PCAOB AS Section 2110, "Identifying and Assessing Risks of Material Misstatement," the PCAOB states that the auditor should perform all of the following as risk assessment procedures except for

A. Incorporating a degree of unpredictability in planned audit procedures.
B. Obtaining an understanding of the company and its environment.
C. Performing analytical procedures.
D. Inquiring of the audit committee, management, and others within the company about the risks of material misstatement.

Evaluation of Misstatements Identified During the Audit

AICPA.130511AUD-SIM

227. An auditor is not required to document

A. Identified material misstatements that have been corrected by management.
B. The basis for the auditor's determination of materiality levels used.
C. Senior management's awareness of (and agreement with) the tolerable misstatement specified by the auditor for material elements of the financial statements.
D. The auditor's conclusion as to whether any misstatements that management chose not to correct are, in fact, material.

assess.AICPA.AUD.eval.miss-0038

228. In a financial statement audit of a nonissuer, an auditor would consider a judgmental misstatement to be a misstatement that

A. Involves an estimate.
B. Exists because of nonstatistical sampling performed by the auditor.
C. Arises from a flaw in the accounting system.
D. Arises from a routine calculation.

AICPA.101135AUD-SIM

229. For all (non-trivial) factual misstatements identified by the auditor, the auditor should

A. Request management to review their assumptions and methods used to develop a more appropriate accounting estimate.
B. Communicate the matters to the appropriate level of management to request correction.
C. Obtain an understanding of management's justification and modify the audit report to express an adverse opinion.
D. Make the appropriate adjusting journal entries to correct the identified misstatements.

AICPA.130512AUD-SIM

230. The term *judgmental misstatement* would best apply to

A. Management's unreasonable accounting estimates for uncollectible receivables.
B. Sales transactions that were recorded but not yet shipped as of year-end.
C. Unrecorded payables associated with goods received in the last month of the entity's fiscal year.
D. The auditor's estimate of a misstatement in a population suggested by audit sampling techniques.

AICPA.120717AUD

231. Each of the following might be considered as a type of factual misstatement, EXCEPT

A. An inaccuracy in accounting processing data.
B. The misapplication of accounting principles.
C. Differences between management and the auditor's judgment regarding accounting estimates.
D. A difference between the classification of a reported financial statement element and the classification according to generally accepted accounting principles.

Audit Documentation

AICPA.941117AUD-AU

232. The permanent file of an auditor's documentation generally would not include

A. Bond indenture agreements.
B. Lease agreements.
C. Working trial balance.
D. Flowchart of internal control structure.

AICPA.940551AUD-AU

233. Which of the following is required documentation in an audit, in accordance with generally accepted auditing standards?

A. A flowchart or narrative of the accounting system describing the recording and classification of transactions for financial reporting.
B. An audit program setting forth in detail the procedures necessary to accomplish the engagement's objectives.
C. A letter signed by the client acknowledging responsibility for preparing requested audit scheduled by specific due dates.
D. An internal control questionnaire identifying policies and procedures that assure specific objectives will be achieved.

AICPA.921135AUD-AU

234. Which of the following factors most likely would affect an auditor's judgment about the quantity, type, and content of the auditor's documentation?

A. The assessed level of control risk.
B. The likelihood of a review by a concurring (second) partner.
C. The number of personnel assigned to the audit.
D. The content of the management representation letter.

AICPA.950570AUD-AU

235. Which of the following pairs of accounts would an auditor most likely analyze on the same audit documentation?

A. Notes receivable and interest income.
B. Accrued interest receivable and accrued interest payable.
C. Notes payable and notes receivable.
D. Interest income and interest expense.

AICPA.950571AUD-AU

236. An auditor's documentation serves mainly to

A. Provide the principal support for the auditor's report.
B. Satisfy the auditor's responsibilities concerning the Code of Professional Conduct.
C. Monitor the effectiveness of the CPA firm's quality control procedures.
D. Document the level of independence maintained by the auditor.

PCAOB on Audit Documentation

AICPA08115001.AUD.SOA.3

237. Audit documentation associated with public companies must be retained for at least

A. 3 years.
B. 5 years.
C. 7 years.
D. 10 years.

AICPA08115001.AUD.SOA.4

238. For audits of public companies, audit documentation must be assembled within how many days of the report release date?

A. 30 days.
B. 45 days.
C. 60 days.
D. 90 days.

AICPA08115001.AUD.SOA.5

239. According to PCAOB auditing standards, after the documentation completion date,

   A. Documentation can be added or deleted as deemed appropriate.
   B. Documentation can be added but not deleted.
   C. Documentation cannot be added but can be deleted.
   D. Documentation cannot be added or deleted.

Confirmation

AICPA.980523AUD-AU

240. Under which of the following circumstances would the use of the blank form of confirmations of accounts receivable most likely be preferable to positive confirmations?

   A. The recipients are likely to sign the confirmations without devoting proper attention to them.
   B. Subsequent cash receipts are unusually difficult to verify.
   C. Analytical procedures indicate that few exceptions are expected.
   D. The combined assessed level of inherent risk and control risk is low.

AICPA.931140AUD-AU

241. In which of the following circumstances would the use of the negative form of accounts receivable confirmation most likely be justified?

   A. A substantial number of accounts may be in dispute and the accounts receivable balance arises from sales to a few major customers.
   B. A substantial number of accounts may be in dispute and the accounts receivable balance arises from sales to many customers with small balances.
   C. A small number of accounts may be in dispute and the accounts receivable balance arises from sales to a few major customers.
   D. A small number of accounts may be in dispute and the accounts receivable balance arises from sales to many customers with small balances.

AICPA.950545AUD-AU

242. Which of the following statements is correct concerning the use of negative confirmation requests?

   A. Unreturned negative confirmation requests rarely provide significant explicit evidence.
   B. Negative confirmation requests are effective when detection risk is low.
   C. Unreturned negative confirmation requests indicate that alternative procedures are necessary.
   D. Negative confirmation requests are effective when understatements of account balances are suspected.

AICPA.090742.AUD.AU

243. The blank form of accounts receivable confirmations may be less efficient than the positive form because

   A. Shipping documents need to be inspected.
   B. Recipients may sign the forms without proper investigation.
   C. More nonresponses to the requests are likely to occur.
   D. Subsequent cash receipts need to be verified.

AICPA.120714AUD

244. Under which of the following circumstances should an auditor consider confirming the terms of a large complex sale?

   A. When the assessed level of control risk over the sale is low.
   B. When the assessed level of detection risk over the sale is high.
   C. When the combined assessed level of inherent and control risk over the sale is moderate.
   D. When the combined assessed level of inherent and control risk over the sale is high.

Accounting Estimates

AICPA.090314AUD-SIM

245. In evaluating the reasonableness of an entity's accounting estimates, an auditor normally would be concerned about assumptions that are

   A. Susceptible to bias.
   B. Consistent with prior periods.
   C. Insensitive to variations.
   D. Similar to industry guidelines.

AICPA.950569AUD-AU

246. Which of the following procedures would an auditor ordinarily perform first in evaluating management's accounting estimates for reasonableness?

   A. Develop independent expectations of management's estimates.
   B. Consider the appropriateness of the key factors or assumptions used in preparing the estimates.

C. Test the calculations used by management in developing the estimates.

D. Obtain an understanding of how management developed its estimates.

AICPA.090747.AUD.AU

247. Which of the following statements is correct regarding accounting estimates?

A. The auditor's objective is to evaluate whether accounting estimates are reasonable in the circumstances.

B. Accounting estimates should be used when data concerning past events can be accumulated in a timely, cost-effective manner.

C. An important accounting estimate is management's listing of accounts receivable greater than 90 days past due.

D. Accounting estimates should not be used when the outcome of future events related to the estimated item is unknown.

AICPA.941157AUD-AU

248. In evaluating the reasonableness of an accounting estimate, an auditor most likely would concentrate on key factors and assumptions that are

A. Consistent with prior periods.

B. Similar to industry guidelines.

C. Objective and not susceptible to bias.

D. Deviations from historical patterns.

AICPA.940545AUD-AU

249. In evaluating an entity's accounting estimates, one of an auditor's objectives is to determine whether the estimates are

A. Not subject to bias.

B. Consistent with industry guidelines.

C. Based on objective assumptions.

D. Reasonable in the circumstances.

Fair Value Estimates

AICPA.101142AUD

250. Which of the following statements describing the auditor's responsibilities when evaluating an entity's fair value measurements and disclosures is incorrect?

A. The auditor is responsible for obtaining an understanding of relevant controls related to fair value measurement and disclosures.

B. The auditor is responsible for determining that the entity's fair value measurements and methods used meet the requirements of GAAP and are consistently applied.

C. The auditor is responsible for engaging a specialist to evaluate the reasonableness of the fair value measurements and disclosures whenever those fair value measurements are material to an entity's financial statements.

D. The auditor is responsible for obtaining sufficient appropriate evidence to provide reasonable assurance that fair value measurements and disclosures meet the requirements of GAAP.

AICPA.101141AUD

251. The auditor's responsibility to communicate with those charged with governance about fair value measurements and disclosure issues is best described by the following statement:

A. The auditor should determine whether those charged with governance are informed about management's processes in developing material fair value estimates, including significant assumptions used by management.

B. The auditor should determine whether those charged with governance are actively involved in designing and taking responsibility for the adequacy of internal controls over fair value measurements and disclosures.

C. The auditor should determine whether those charged with governance were consulted by management and had adequate input in forming the entity's estimates for fair value measurement and disclosures.

D. The auditor should determine whether those charged with governance take responsibility for the reasonableness of the entity's fair value measurements and disclosures.

AICPA.101143AUD

252. When there are no observable market prices, the auditor is not obligated to consider whether

A. Management's valuation method is appropriate in the circumstances.

B. Management's selection of a specialist is appropriate for the audit engagement.

C. Management's valuation method is appropriate relative to the industry and environment of the entity.

D. Management has appropriately applied criteria provided by GAAP.

Lawyer's Letters

AICPA.950563AUD-AU

253. The refusal of a client's attorney to provide information requested in an inquiry letter generally is considered

  A. Grounds for an adverse opinion.
  B. A limitation on the scope of the audit.
  C. Reason to withdraw from the engagement.
  D. Equivalent to a significant deficiency.

AICPA.911160AUD-AU

254. Which of the following is not an audit procedure that the independent auditor would perform concerning litigation, claims, and assessments?

  A. Obtain assurance from management that it has disclosed all unasserted claims that the lawyer has advised are probable of assertion and must be disclosed.
  B. Confirm directly with the client's lawyer that all claims have been recorded in the financial statements.
  C. Inquire about and discuss with management the policies and procedures adopted for identifying, evaluating, and accounting for litigation, claims, and assessments.
  D. Obtain from management a description and evaluation of litigation, claims, and assessments existing at the balance sheet date.

AICPA.931139AUD-AU

255. The primary source of information to be reported about litigation, claims, and assessments is the

  A. Client's lawyer.
  B. Court records.
  C. Client's management.
  D. Independent auditor.

AICPA.090789.AUD-AU

256. Which of the following procedures would be most likely to assist an auditor in identifying litigation, claims, and assessments?

  A. Inspect checks included with the client's cut-off bank statement.
  B. Obtain a letter of representations from the client's underwriter of securities.
  C. Apply ratio analysis on the current-year's liability accounts.
  D. Read the file of correspondence from taxing authorities.

AICPA.990524AUD-AU

257. A lawyer's response to an auditor's inquiry concerning litigation, claims, and assessments may be limited to matters that are considered individually or collectively material to the client's financial statements. Which parties should reach an understanding on the limits of materiality for this purpose?

  A. The auditor and the client's management.
  B. The client's audit committee and the lawyer.
  C. The client's management and the lawyer.
  D. The lawyer and the auditor.

Management Representations Letters

AICPA.990526AUD-AU

258. Key Co. plans to present comparative financial statements for the years ended December 31, 2005, and 2006, respectively. Smith, CPA, audited Key's financial statements for both years and plans to report on the comparative financial statements on May 1, 2007. Key's current management team was not present until January 1, 2006. What period of time should be covered by Key's management representation letter?

  A. January l, 2005, through December 31, 2006.
  B. January 1, 2005, through May 1, 2007.
  C. January 1, 2006, through December 31, 2006.
  D. January 1, 2006, through May 1, 2007.

AICPA.951157AUD-AU

259. Which of the following matters would an auditor most likely include in a management representations letter?

  A. Communications with the audit committee concerning weaknesses in internal control structure.
  B. The completeness and availability of minutes of stockholders' and directors' meetings.
  C. Plans to acquire or merge with other entities in the subsequent year.
  D. Management's acknowledgment of its responsibility for the detection of all employee fraud.

AICPA.101130AUD

260. Which of the following management roles would typically be acknowledged in a management representation letter?

  A. Management has the responsibility for the design of controls to detect fraud.
  B. Management communicates its views on ethical behavior to its employees.

C. Management's knowledge of fraud is communicated to the audit committee.

D. Management's compensation is contingent upon operating results.

AICPA.930532AUD-AU

261. One purpose of a management representation letter is to reduce

A. Audit risk to an aggregate level of misstatement that could be considered material.

B. An auditor's responsibility to detect material misstatements only to the extent that the letter is relied upon.

C. The possibility of a misunderstanding concerning management's responsibility for the financial statements.

D. The scope of an auditor's procedures concerning related party transactions and subsequent events.

AICPA.950567AUD-AU

262. The date of the management representation letter should coincide with the date of the

A. Balance sheet.

B. Latest interim financial information.

C. Auditor's report.

D. Latest related party transaction.

Related Party Issues

AICPA.120705AUD

263. In auditing related party transactions, an auditor ordinarily places primary emphasis on

A. The probability that related party transactions will recur.

B. Confirming the existence of the related parties.

C. Verifying the valuation of the related party transactions.

D. The adequacy of the disclosure of the related party transactions.

AICPA.941169AUD-AU

264. After determining that a related party transaction has, in fact, occurred, an auditor should

A. Add a separate paragraph to the auditor's standard report to explain the transaction.

B. Perform analytical procedures to verify whether similar transactions occurred, but were not recorded.

C. Obtain an understanding of the business purpose of the transaction.

D. Substantiate that the transaction was consummated on terms equivalent to an arm's-length transaction.

AICPA.951158AUD-AU

265. Which of the following auditing procedures would be most likely to assist an auditor in identifying related party transactions?

A. Inspecting correspondence with lawyers for evidence of unreported contingent liabilities.

B. Vouching accounting records for recurring transactions recorded just after the balance sheet date.

C. Reviewing confirmations of loans receivable and payable for indications of guarantees.

D. Performing analytical procedures to seek indications of possible financial difficulties.

AICPA.901132AUD-AU

266. Which of the following events most likely indicates the existence of related parties?

A. Borrowing a large sum of money at a variable rate of interest.

B. Selling real estate at a price that differs significantly from its book value.

C. Making a loan without scheduled terms for repayment of the funds.

D. Discussing merger terms with a company that is a major competitor.

AICPA.911156AUD-AU

267. After identifying related party transactions, an auditor most likely would

A. Substantiate that the transactions were consummated on terms equivalent to those prevailing in arms-length transactions.

B. Discuss the implications of the transactions with third parties, such as the entity's attorneys and bankers.

C. Determine whether the transactions were approved by the board of directors or other appropriate officials.

D. Ascertain whether the transactions would have occurred if the parties had not been related.

PCAOB on Related Parties

AICPA.151010AUD-SIM

268. Suppose that management of an issuer makes an assertion in a footnote to the company's financial statements that material transactions with related parties were conducted on terms equivalent to those prevailing in arm's-length transactions. If evidence cannot be obtained to support this assertion and management

declines to alter that footnote, what type of audit opinion would be appropriate?

A. Unqualified with an explanatory paragraph.
B. Qualified for a scope limitation.
C. Qualified or adverse for a material misstatement.
D. Disclaimer of opinion.

AICPA.151007AUD-SIM

269. PCAOB auditing standards dealing with related-party issues specifically require an auditor of an issuer to obtain an understanding of the company's process for each of the following except for

A. Identifying related parties and transactions with related parties.
B. Authorizing and approving transactions with related parties.
C. Determining that the terms of related-party transactions are substantially equivalent to those prevailing in arm's-length transactions with unrelated parties.
D. Accounting for and disclosing relationships and transactions with related parties in the financial statements.

AICPA.151009AUD-SIM

270. PCAOB auditing standards require an auditor of a public company to communicate with the audit committee about a variety of related-party matters. Each of the following is required to be communicated with the audit committee except

A. The auditor's evaluation of the company's identification and financial reporting treatment of related-party relationships and transactions.
B. Management's justification for engaging in transactions with a related party instead of arm's-length transactions with unrelated parties.
C. Related-party relationships or transactions with parties discovered by the auditor that were previously undisclosed to the auditor.
D. Related-party transactions identified by the auditor that appear to lack an appropriate business purpose.

Subsequent Events and Related Issues

AICPA.941167AUD-AU

271. An auditor issued an audit report that was dual dated for a subsequent event occurring after the audit report date but before release of the auditor's report.

The auditor's responsibility for events occurring subsequent to the audit report date was

A. Limited to include only events occurring up to the date of the last subsequent event referenced.
B. Limited to the specific event referenced.
C. Extended to subsequent events occurring through the date of release of the report.
D. Extended to include all events occurring since the audit report date.

AICPA.950565AUD-AU

272. Which of the following procedures would an auditor be most likely to perform in obtaining evidence about subsequent events?

A. Determine that changes in employee pay rates after year end were properly authorized.
B. Recompute depreciation charges for plant assets sold after year end.
C. Inquire about payroll checks that were recorded before year end but cashed after year end.
D. Investigate changes in long-term debt occurring after year end.

AICPA.130701AUD

273. An auditor is considering whether the omission of the confirmation of investments impairs the auditor's ability to support a previously expressed unmodified opinion. The auditor need not perform this omitted procedure if

A. The results of alternative procedures that were performed compensate for the omission.
B. The auditor's assessed level of detection risk is low.
C. The omission is documented in a communication with the audit committee.
D. No individual investment is material to the financial statements taken as a whole.

AICPA.951156AUD-AU

274. Which of the following procedures would an auditor be most likely to perform to obtain evidence about the occurrence of subsequent events?

A. Confirming a sample of material accounts receivable established after year end.
B. Comparing the financial statements being reported on with those of the prior period.
C. Investigating personnel changes in the accounting department occurring after year end.
D. Inquiring as to whether any unusual adjustments were made after year end.

AICPA.940553AUD-AU

275. Zero Corp. suffered a loss that would have a material effect on its financial statements on an uncollectible trade account receivable due to a customer's bankruptcy.

This occurred suddenly, due to a natural disaster ten days after Zero's balance sheet date, but one month before the issuance of the financial statements and the auditor's report. Under these circumstances,

	The financial statements should be adjusted	The event requires financial statement disclosure, but no adjustment	The auditor's report should be modified for a lack of consistency
A.	Yes	No	No
B.	Yes	No	Yes
C.	No	Yes	Yes
D.	No	Yes	No

Going Concern Issues

AICPA.120709AUD

276. An auditor should consider which of the following when evaluating the ability of a company to continue as a going concern?

   A. Audit fees.
   B. Future assurance services.
   C. Management's plans for disposal of assets.
   D. A lawsuit for which judgment is NOT anticipated for 18 months.

AICPA.940555AUD-AU

277. Which of the following auditing procedures most likely would assist an auditor in identifying conditions and events that may indicate substantial doubt about an entity's ability to continue as a going concern?

   A. Inspecting title documents to verify whether any assets are pledged as collateral.
   B. Confirming with third parties the details of arrangements to maintain financial support.
   C. Reconciling the cash balance per books with the cut-off bank statement and the bank confirmation.
   D. Comparing the entity's depreciation and asset capitalization policies to other entities in the industry.

AICPA.120702AUD

278. Which of the following audit procedures most likely would assist an auditor in identifying conditions and events that may indicate there could be substantial doubt about an entity's ability to continue as a going concern?

   A. Confirmation of accounts receivable from principal customers.
   B. Reconciliation of interest expense with debt outstanding.
   C. Confirmation of bank balances.
   D. Review of compliance with terms of debt agreements.

AICPA.940562AUD-AU

279. When an auditor concludes there is substantial doubt about a continuing audit client's ability to continue as a going concern for a reasonable period of time, the auditor's responsibility is to

   A. Issue a qualified or adverse opinion, depending upon materiality, due to the possible effects on the financial statements.
   B. Consider the adequacy of disclosure about the client's possible inability to continue as a going concern.
   C. Report to the client's audit committee that management's accounting estimates may need to be adjusted.
   D. Reissue the prior year's auditor's report and add an emphasis-of-matter paragraph that specifically refers to "substantial doubt" and "going concern."

AICPA.111193AUD-SIM

280. An auditor concludes that there is substantial doubt about an entity's ability to continue as a going concern for a reasonable period of time. The entity's financial statements adequately disclose its financial difficulties. Under these circumstances, the auditor's report is required to include an emphasis-of-matter paragraph that specifically uses the phrase(s)

	"Except for the effects of such adjustments"	"Possible discontinuance of the entity's operations"
A.	Yes	Yes
B.	Yes	No
C.	No	Yes
D.	No	No

Audit Evidence: Specific Audit Areas

Introduction to Auditing Individual Areas

AICPA.101145AUD

281. Confirmation procedures applicable to assets (e.g., accounts receivable) fundamentally address which assertion associated with account balances at the end of the period?

   A. Existence.
   B. Completeness.
   C. Presentation and disclosure.
   D. Valuation and allocation.

AICPA.101147AUD

282. There are certain substantive auditing procedures that might appropriately be performed when auditing any element of the financial statements, particularly balance-sheet elements. Which of the following is **not** a substantive procedure potentially applicable to every balance-sheet element?

A. Reviewing the accounting records for anything that appears to be unusual.
B. Performing tests of control to evaluate the effectiveness of relevant controls.
C. Making appropriate inquiries of management or other client personnel about matters related to the particular balance-sheet element.
D. Agreeing the financial statement elements to the underlying accounting records, such as the entity's general ledger.

AICPA.101146AUD

283. Which of the following is **not** an assertion associated with account balances at the end of the period?

A. Valuation and allocation.
B. Rights and obligations.
C. Classification.
D. Existence.

Cash

AICPA.020417AUD-AU

284. Which of the following characteristics most likely would be indicative of check kiting?

A. High turnover of employees who have access to cash.
B. Many large checks that are recorded on Mondays.
C. Low average balance compared to high level of deposits.
D. Frequent ATM checking account withdrawals.

AICPA.111175AUD

285. An auditor has identified the controller's review of the bank reconciliation as a control to test. In connection with this test, the auditor interviews the controller to understand the specific data reviewed on the reconciliation. In addition, the auditor verifies that the bank reconciliation is properly prepared by the accountant and reviewed by the controller, as evidenced by their respective sign-offs. Which of the following types of audit procedures do these actions illustrate?

A. Observation and inspection of records.
B. Confirmation and re-performance.

C. Inquiry and inspection of records.
D. Analytical procedures and re-performance.

AICPA.930534AUD-AU

286. The primary purpose of sending a standard confirmation request to financial institutions with which the client has done business during the year is to

A. Detect kiting activities that may otherwise not be discovered.
B. Corroborate information regarding deposit and loan balances.
C. Provide the data necessary to prepare a proof of cash.
D. Request information about contingent liabilities and secured transactions.

AICPA.101125AUD

287. Which of the following would be a consideration in planning a sample for a test of subsequent cash receipts?

A. Preliminary judgments about materiality levels.
B. The amount of bad debt write-offs in the prior year.
C. The size of the intercompany receivable balance.
D. The auditor's allowable risk of assessing control risk is too low.

AICPA.020408AUD-AU

288. On receiving a client's bank cut-off statement, an auditor most likely would trace

A. Prior-year checks listed in the cut-off statement to the year-end outstanding checklist.
B. Deposits in transit listed in the cut-off statement to the year-end bank reconciliation.
C. Checks dated after year end listed in the cut-off statement to the year-end outstanding checklist.
D. Deposits recorded in the cash receipts journal after year end to the cut-off statement.

Accounts Receivable

AICPA.070610AUD

289. Which of the following strategies would be most likely to improve the response rate of the confirmations of accounts receivable?

A. Restrict the selection of accounts to be confirmed to those customers with large balances.
B. Include a list of items or invoices that constitute the customers' account balances.

C. Explain to customers that discrepancies will be investigated by an independent third party.

D. Ask customers to respond to the confirmation requests directly to the auditor by fax.

AICPA.120713AUD

290. An auditor is required to confirm accounts receivable if the accounts receivable balances are

A. Older than the prior year.

B. Material to the financial statements.

C. Smaller than expected.

D. Subject to valuation estimates.

AICPA.920525AUD-AU

291. Which of the following most likely would be detected by an auditor's review of a client's sales cut-off?

A. Shipments lacking sales invoices and shipping documents.

B. Excessive write-offs of accounts receivable.

C. Unrecorded sales at year end.

D. Lapping of year-end accounts receivable.

AICPA.901121AUD-AU

292. Two assertions for which confirmation of accounts receivable balances provides primary evidence are

A. Completeness and valuation.

B. Valuation and rights and obligations.

C. Rights and obligations and existence.

D. Existence and completeness.

AICPA.090787.AUD-AU

293. An auditor's tests of controls for completeness for the revenue cycle usually include determining whether

A. Each receivable is collected subsequent to the year end.

B. An invoice is prepared for each shipping document.

C. Each invoice is supported by a customer purchase order.

D. Each credit memo is properly approved.

Inventory

AICPA.950540AUD-AU

294. An auditor most likely would inspect loan agreements under which an entity's inventories are pledged to support management's financial statement assertion of

A. Rights and obligations.

B. Valuation or allocation.

C. Existence or occurrence.

D. Completeness.

AICPA.111171AUD

295. The purpose of tracing a sample of inventory tags to a client's computerized listing of inventory items is to determine whether the inventory items

A. Represented by tags were included on the listing.

B. Included on the listing were properly counted.

C. Represented by tags were reduced to lower of cost or market.

D. Included in the listing were properly valued.

AICPA.120731AUD

296. Which of the following management assertions is an auditor most likely testing if the audit objective states that all inventory on hand is reflected in the ending inventory balance?

A. The entity has rights to the inventory.

B. Inventory is properly valued.

C. Inventory is valid and exists.

D. Inventory is complete.

AICPA.950543AUD-AU

297. An auditor most likely would make inquiries of production and sales personnel concerning possible obsolete or slow-moving inventory to support management's financial statement assertion of

A. Valuation or allocation.

B. Rights and obligations.

C. Existence or occurrence.

D. Cut-off.

AICPA.111195AUD

298. A portion of a client's inventory is in public warehouses. Evidence of the existence of this merchandise can most efficiently be acquired through which of the following methods?

A. Observation.

B. Confirmation.

C. Calculation.

D. Inspection.

Investments in Securities and Derivative Instruments

AICPA.090792.AUD-AU

299. An auditor is testing the reasonableness of dividend income from investments in publicly held companies. The auditor most likely would compute the amount that should have been received and recorded by the client by

A. Reading the details of the board of directors' meetings.

B. Confirming the details with the investee companies' registrars.

C. Electronically accessing the details of dividend records on the Internet.

D. Examining the details of the client's most recent cut-off bank statement.

AICPA.070612AUD

300. In establishing the existence and ownership of long-term investments in the form of publicly traded stock, an auditor most likely would inspect the securities or

A. Correspond with the investee company to verify the number of shares owned.

B. Confirm the number of shares owned that are held by an independent custodian.

C. Apply analytical procedures to the dividend income and investments accounts.

D. Inspect the cash receipts journal for amounts that could represent the sale of securities.

AICPA.930531AUD-AU

301. In testing long-term investments, an auditor ordinarily would use analytical procedures to ascertain the reasonableness of the

A. Completeness of recorded investment income.

B. Classification between current and noncurrent portfolios.

C. Valuation of marketable equity securities.

D. Existence of unrealized gains or losses in the portfolio.

AICPA.950544AUD-AU

302. In confirming with an outside agent, such as a financial institution, that the agent is holding investment securities in the client's name, an auditor would most likely gather evidence in support of management's financial statement assertions of existence or occurrence and

A. Valuation or allocation.

B. Rights and obligations.

C. Completeness.

D. Presentation and disclosure.

AICPA.911144AUD-AU

303. To satisfy the valuation assertion when auditing an investment accounted for by the equity method, an auditor most likely would

A. Inspect the stock certificates evidencing the investment.

B. Examine the audited financial statements of the investee company.

C. Review the broker's advice or canceled check for the investment's acquisition.

D. Obtain market quotations from financial newspapers or periodicals.

Fixed Assets

AICPA.950555AUD-AU

304. In performing a search for unrecorded retirements of fixed assets, an auditor most likely would

A. Inspect the property ledger and the insurance and tax records, and then tour the client's facilities.

B. Tour the client's facilities and then inspect the property ledger and the insurance and tax records.

C. Analyze the repair and maintenance account and then tour the client's facilities.

D. Tour the client's facilities and then analyze the repair and maintenance account.

AICPA.130714AUD

305. Which of the following procedures would an auditor most likely complete to test the existence assertion of property, plant and equipment?

A. Obtaining a listing of all current-year additions, vouching significant additions to original invoices, and determining that they have been placed in service.

B. Obtaining a detailed fixed-asset register and ensuring items are appropriately capitalized.

C. Obtaining a listing of current-year additions and verifying that items are recorded in the proper period.

D. Obtaining a detailed fixed-asset register and ensuring depreciation methods are applied consistently.

AICPA.941162AUD-AU

306. An auditor analyzes repairs and maintenance accounts primarily to obtain evidence in support of the audit assertion that all

A. Noncapitalizable expenditures for repairs and maintenance have been recorded in the proper period.

B. Expenditures for property and equipment have been recorded in the proper period.

C. Noncapitalizable expenditures for repairs and maintenance have been properly charged to expense.

D. Expenditures for property and equipment have not been charged to expense.

AICPA.070603AUD

307. An analysis of which of the following accounts would best aid in verifying that all fixed assets have been capitalized?

A. Cash.

B. Depreciation expense.

C. Property tax expense.

D. Repairs and maintenance.

AICPA.951149AUD-AU

308. Which of the following explanations most likely would satisfy an auditor who questions management about significant debits to the accumulated depreciation accounts?

   A. The estimated remaining useful lives of plant assets were revised upward.
   B. Plant assets were retired during the year.
   C. The prior year's depreciation expense was erroneously understated.
   D. Overhead allocations were revised at year end.

Current Liabilities

AICPA.951147AUD-AU

309. Which of the following procedures would an auditor most likely perform in searching for unrecorded liabilities?

   A. Trace a sample of accounts payable entries recorded just before year end to the unmatched receiving report file.
   B. Compare a sample of purchase orders issued just after year end with the year-end accounts payable trial balance.
   C. Vouch a sample of cash disbursements recorded just after year end to receiving reports and vendor invoices.
   D. Scan the cash disbursements entries recorded just before year end for indications of unusual transactions.

AICPA.910503AUD-AU

310. An auditor's purpose in reviewing the renewal of a note payable shortly after the balance sheet date most likely is to obtain evidence concerning management's assertions about

   A. Existence or occurrence.
   B. Presentation and disclosure.
   C. Completeness.
   D. Valuation or allocation.

AICPA.950573AUD-AU

311. Which of the following procedures would an auditor least likely perform before the balance sheet date?

   A. Confirmation of accounts payable.
   B. Observation of merchandise inventory.
   C. Assessment of control risk.
   D. Identification of related parties.

AICPA.951148AUD-AU

312. An auditor traced a sample of purchase orders and the related receiving reports to the purchases journal and the cash disbursements journal. The purpose of this substantive audit procedure most likely was to

   A. Identify unusually large purchases that should be investigated further.
   B. Verify that cash disbursements were for goods actually received.
   C. Determine that purchases were properly recorded.
   D. Test whether payments were for goods actually ordered.

AICPA.931137AUD-AU

313. In auditing accounts payable, an auditor's procedures most likely would focus primarily on management's assertion of

   A. Existence or occurrence.
   B. Presentation and disclosure.
   C. Completeness.
   D. Valuation or allocation.

Long-term Liabilities

AICPA.941160AUD-AU

314. In auditing long-term bonds payable, an auditor most likely would

   A. Perform analytical procedures on the bond premium and discount accounts.
   B. Examine documentation of assets purchased with bond proceeds for liens.
   C. Compare interest expense with the bond payable amount for reasonableness.
   D. Confirm the existence of individual bondholders at year end.

AICPA.090317AUD-SIM

315. In the following schedule of analysis related to accrued interest payable associated with long-term liabilities, the tickmark ¥ most likely is associated with which particular auditing procedure?

Wrigleyville Company

Schedule of Accrued Interest Payable

As of 12/31/X1

Payee	Due Date	Beginning Balance	20X1 Expense	Payments	Ending Balance
Second City Bank— Line of Credit	11/4/X7	$2,500 Ψ	$10,250 ¥	$11,500 €	$1,250
4% bonds payable	10/28/X5	$7,500 Ψ	$22,500 ¥	$25,000 €	$5,000
5 % bonds payable	2/12/X8	$22,500 Ψ	$100,750 ¥	$120,000 €	$3,250
Total		$32,500	$133,500	$156,500	$9,500 G

A. Agreed to the cash disbursements journal and traced to the applicable bank statement.
B. Agreed to the general ledger.
C. Recomputed interest expense.
D. Agreed to the prior year's audit documentation.

AICPA.090316AUD-SIM

316. In the following schedule of analysis related to long-term liabilities, the tickmark € most likely is associated with which particular auditing procedure?

Wrigleyville Company

Schedule of Long-Term Debt

As of 12/31/X1

Payee	Due Date	Face Amount	Beginning Balance	Additions	Payments	Ending Balance
Second City Bank—Line of Credit	11/4/X7	$10,000,000	$500,000 ø	$800,000 Δ	$400,000 €	$900,000
4% bonds payable	10/28/X5	$3,000,000	$750,000 ø		$250,000 €	$500,000
5% bonds payable	2/12/X8	$9,000,000	$3,250,000 ø		$250,000 €	$3,000,000
Total			$4,500,000	$800,000	$900,000	$4,400,000
				Less: current portion of long-term debt		500,000 ©
						$3,900,000 G

A. Agreed to the cash disbursements journal and traced to the applicable bank statement.
B. Agreed to the general ledger.
C. Recomputed interest expense.
D. Agreed the current portion of long-term debt to the loan agreement's payment schedule.

D. Inspecting the accounts payable subsidiary ledger for unrecorded long-term debt.

AICPA.090315AUD-SIM

317. The permanent file section of the audit documentation that is kept for a continuing audit engagement most likely would contain

A. The most recent lawyer's letter applicable to unresolved litigation.
B. The most recent time budget for the audit engagement.
C. Copies (or abstracts) of the entity's lease agreements.
D. Copies of the entity's most recent tax returns.

AICPA.910508AUD-AU

318. An auditor's program to examine long-term debt most likely would include steps that require

A. Comparing the original issuance value of the debt to its year-end market value.
B. Correlating interest expense recorded for the period with outstanding debt.
C. Verifying the existence of the debt by re-examining documentation related to the original issuance of the debt in a prior year.

Stockholders' Equity

AICPA.990421AUD-AU

319. An auditor usually obtains evidence of stockholders' equity transactions by reviewing the entity's

A. Minutes of board of directors' meetings.
B. Transfer agent's records.
C. Cancelled stock certificates.
D. Treasury stock certificate book.

AICPA.920518AUD-AU

320. During an audit of an entity's stockholders' equity accounts, the auditor determines whether there are restrictions on retained earnings resulting from loans, agreements, or state law.

This audit procedure most likely is intended to verify management's assertion of or about

A. Existence or occurrence.
B. Completeness.
C. Valuation or allocation.
D. Presentation and disclosure.

AICPA.900510AUD-AU

321. When a client company does not maintain its own stock records, the auditor should obtain written confirmation from the transfer agent and registrar concerning

   A. Restrictions on the payment of dividends.
   B. The number of shares issued and outstanding.
   C. Guarantees of preferred stock liquidation value.
   D. The number of shares subject to agreements to repurchase.

AICPA.980522AUD-AU

322. In auditing a client's retained earnings account, an auditor should determine whether there are any restrictions on retained earnings that result from loans, agreements, or state law.

   This procedure is designed to corroborate management's financial statement assertion of

   A. Valuation or allocation.
   B. Existence or occurrence.
   C. Completeness.
   D. Rights and obligations.

AICPA.941161AUD-AU

323. In performing tests concerning the granting of stock options, an auditor should

   A. Confirm the transaction with the Secretary of State in the state of incorporation.
   B. Verify the existence of option holders in the entity's payroll records or stock ledgers.
   C. Determine that sufficient treasury stock is available to cover any new stock issued.
   D. Trace the authorization for the transaction to a vote of the board of directors.

Payroll

AICPA.940549AUD-AU

324. An auditor most likely would extend substantive tests of payroll when

   A. Payroll is extensively audited by the state government.
   B. Payroll expense is substantially higher than in the prior year.
   C. Overpayments are discovered in performing tests of details.
   D. Employees complain to management about too much overtime.

AICPA.941159AUD-AU

325. In auditing payroll, an auditor most likely would

   A. Verify that checks representing unclaimed wages are mailed.
   B. Trace individual employee deductions to entity journal entries.
   C. Observe entity employees during a payroll distribution.
   D. Compare payroll costs with entity standards or budgets.

AICPA.950554AUD-AU

326. When control risk is assessed as low for assertions related to payroll, substantive tests of payroll balances most likely would be limited to applying analytical procedures and

   A. Observing the distribution of paychecks.
   B. Footing and crossfooting the payroll register.
   C. Inspecting payroll tax returns.
   D. Recalculating payroll accruals.

AICPA.020414AUD-AU

327. An auditor reviews the reconciliation of payroll tax forms that a client is responsible for filing in order to

   A. Verify that payroll taxes are deducted from employees' gross pay.
   B. Determine whether internal control activities are operating effectively.
   C. Uncover fictitious employees who are receiving payroll checks.
   D. Identify potential liabilities for unpaid payroll taxes.

AICPA.951150AUD-AU

328. Which of the following circumstances most likely would cause an auditor to suspect an employee payroll fraud scheme?

   A. There are significant unexplained variances between standard and actual labor costs.
   B. Payroll checks are disbursed by the same employee each payday.
   C. Employee time cards are approved by individual departmental supervisors.
   D. A separate payroll bank account is maintained on an imprest basis.

Audit Sampling

Introduction to Sampling

AICPA.941156AUD-AU

329. Which of the following sample planning factors would influence the sample size for a substantive test of details for a specific account?

	Expected amount of misstatements	Measure of tolerable misstatement
A.	No	No
B.	Yes	Yes
C.	No	Yes
D.	Yes	No

AICPA.101131AUD

330. When performing a substantive test of a random sample of cash disbursements, an auditor is supplied with a photocopy of vendor invoices supporting the disbursements for one particular vendor, rather than the original invoices. The auditor is told that the vendor's original invoices have been misplaced. What should the auditor do in response to this situation?

A. Randomly increase the number of items in the substantive test to increase the reliance that may be placed on the overall test.

B. Reevaluate the risk of fraud and design alternate tests for the related transactions.

C. Increase testing by agreeing more of the payments to this particular vendor to the photocopies of its invoices.

D. Count the missing original documents as misstatements and project the total amount of the error based on the size of the population and the dollar amount of the errors.

AICPA.130736AUD

331. Which of the following statements about audit sampling risks is correct for a nonissuer?

A. Nonsampling risk arises from the possibility that, when a substantive test is restricted to a sample, conclusions might be different than if the auditor had tested each item in the population.

B. Nonsampling risk can arise because an auditor failed to recognize misstatements.

C. Sampling risk is derived from the uncertainty in applying audit procedures to specific risks.

D. Sampling risk includes the possibility of selecting audit procedures that are not appropriate to achieve the specific objective.

AICPA.940543AUD-AU

332. While performing a test of details during an audit, an auditor determined that the sample results supported the conclusion that the recorded account balance was materially misstated. It was, in fact, not materially misstated.

This situation illustrates the risk of

A. Assessing control risk too high.
B. Assessing control risk too low.
C. Incorrect rejection.
D. Incorrect acceptance.

AICPA.950536AUD-AU

333. An advantage that using statistical sampling methods have over nonstatistical sampling methods in tests of controls is that the statistical methods

A. Can more easily convert the sample into a dual-purpose test useful for substantive testing.

B. Eliminate the need to use judgment in determining appropriate sample sizes.

C. Afford greater assurance than a nonstatistical sample of equal size.

D. Provide an objective basis for quantitatively evaluating sample risk.

Attributes Sampling

AICPA.901158AUD-AU

334. To determine the sample size for a test of controls, an auditor should consider the tolerable deviation rate, the allowable risk of assessing control risk too low, and the

A. Expected deviation rate.
B. Upper precision limit.
C. Risk of incorrect acceptance.
D. Risk of incorrect rejection.

AICPA.920554AUD-AU

335. What is an auditor's evaluation of a statistical sample for attributes when a test of 50 documents results in 3 deviations, if tolerable rate is 7%, the expected population deviation rate is 5%, and the allowance for sampling risk is 2%?

A. Modify the planned assessed level of control risk because the tolerable rate plus the allowance for sampling risk exceeds the expected population deviation rate.

B. Accept the sample results as support for the planned assessed level of control risk because the sample deviation rate plus the allowance for sampling risk exceeds the tolerable rate.

C. Accept the sample results as support for the planned assessed level of control risk because the tolerable rate less the allowance for sampling risk equals the expected population deviation rate.

D. Modify the planned assessed level of control risk because the sample deviation rate plus the allowance for sampling risk exceeds the tolerable rate.

AICPA.940544AUD-AU

336. The sample size of a test of controls varies inversely with

	Expected population deviation rate	Tolerable rate
A.	Yes	Yes
B.	No	No
C.	Yes	No
D.	No	Yes

AICPA.120726AUD

337. For which of the following audit tests would an auditor most likely use attribute sampling?

A. Inspecting purchase orders for proper approval by supervisors.

B. Making an independent estimate of recorded payroll expense.

C. Determining that all payables are recorded at year end.

D. Selecting accounts receivable for confirmation of account balances.

AICPA.931120AUD-AU

338. As a result of sampling procedures applied as tests of controls, an auditor incorrectly assesses control risk lower than appropriate.

The most likely explanation for this situation is that

A. The deviation rates of both the auditor's sample and the population exceed the tolerable rate.

B. The deviation rates of both the auditor's sample and the population is less than the tolerable rate.

C. The deviation rate in the auditor's sample is less than the tolerable rate, but the deviation rate in the population exceeds the tolerable rate.

D. The deviation rate in the auditor's sample exceeds the tolerable rate, but the deviation rate in the population is less than the tolerable rate.

Variables Sampling

AICPA.111199AUD

339. An auditor discovers that an account balance believed not to be materially misstated based on an audit sample was materially misstated based on the total population of the account balance. This is an example of which of the following types of sampling risks?

A. Incorrect rejection.

B. Incorrect acceptance.

C. Assessing control risk too low.

D. Assessing control risk too high.

AICPA.941154AUD-AU

340. Which of the following sampling methods would be used to estimate a numerical measurement of a population, such as a dollar value?

A. Attributes sampling.

B. Stop-or-go sampling.

C. Variables sampling.

D. Random number sampling.

AICPA.930543AUD-AU

341. Which of the following most likely would be an advantage in using classical variables sampling rather than probability-proportional-to-size (PPS) sampling?

A. An estimate of the standard deviation of the population's recorded amounts is not required.

B. The auditor rarely needs the assistance of a computer program to design an efficient sample.

C. Inclusion of zero and negative balances generally does not require special design considerations.

D. Any amount that is individually significant is automatically identified and selected.

AICPA.951143AUD-AU

342. How would increases in tolerable misstatement and assessed level of control risk affect the sample size in a substantive test of details?

	Increase in tolerable misstatement	Increase in assessed level of control risk
A.	Increase sample size	Increase sample size
B.	Increase sample size	Decrease sample size
C.	Decrease sample size	Increase sample size
D.	Decrease sample size	Decrease sample size

AICPA.901130AUD-AU

343. Stratified mean per unit (MPU) sampling is a statistical technique that may be more efficient than unstratified MPU because it usually

 A. May be applied to populations where many monetary errors are expected to occur.
 B. Produces an estimate that has a desired level of precision with a smaller sample size.
 C. Increases the variability among items in a stratum by grouping sampling units with similar characteristics.
 D. Yields a weighted sum of the strata standard deviations that is greater than the standard deviation of the population.

Probability-Proportional-to-Size (PPS) Sampling

AICPA.910517AUD-AU

344. Which of the following statements is correct concerning probability-proportional-to-size (PPS) sampling, also known as dollar unit sampling?

 A. The sampling distribution should approximate the normal distribution.
 B. Overstated units have a lower probability of sample selection than units that are understated.
 C. The auditor controls the risk of incorrect acceptance by specifying this risk level for the sampling plan.
 D. The sampling interval is calculated by dividing the number of physical units in the population by the sample size.

AICPA.140405AUD-SIM

345. Hill has decided to use (PPS) sampling, sometimes called dollar-unit sampling, in the audit of a client's accounts receivable balances. Hill plans to use the following PPS sampling table:

Reliability Factors for Errors of Overstatement

Number of Overstatements	Risk of Incorrect Acceptance				
	1%	5%	10%	15%	20%
0	4.61	3.00	2.31	1.90	1.61
1	6.64	4.75	3.89	3.38	3.00
2	8.41	6.30	5.33	4.72	4.28
3	10.05	7.76	6.69	6.02	5.52
4	11.61	9.16	8.00	7.27	6.73

ADDITIONAL INFORMATION

Tolerable misstatement (net of the effect of expected misstatements)	$24,000
Risk of incorrect acceptance	20%
Number of misstatements allowed	1
Recorded amount of accounts receivable	$240,000
Number of accounts	360

What sample size should Hill use?

 A. 120
 B. 108
 C. 60
 D. 30

AICPA.920530AUD-AU

346. In a probability-proportional-to-size sample with a sampling interval of $5,000, an auditor discovered that a selected account receivable with a recorded amount of $10,000 had an audit amount of $8,000.

If this were the only error discovered by the auditor, the projected error of this sample would be

 A. $1,000.
 B. $2,000.
 C. $4,000.
 D. $5,000.

AICPA.090790.AUD-AU

347. Which of the following is the primary objective of probability proportional to sample size?

 A. To identify overstatement errors.
 B. To increase the proportion of smaller-value items in the sample.
 C. To identify items where controls were not properly applied.
 D. To identify zero and negative balances.

AICPA.140404AUD-SIM

348. In a PPS sampling application, the sampling interval was $6,000. The auditor discovered that a selected account receivable having a recorded amount of $5,000 had an audit amount of $1,000. What was the projected error associated with this sample?

 A. $ 4,000
 B. $ 1,200
 C. $ 4,800
 D. $ 3,200

IT (Computer) Auditing

IT Controls—General Controls

AICPA.911124AUD-AU

349. Which of the following is not a major reason for maintaining an audit trail for a computer system?

A. Deterrent to irregularities.
B. Monitoring purposes.
C. Analytical procedures.
D. Query answering.

AICPA.910516AUD-AU

350. An auditor would most likely be concerned with which of the following controls in a distributed data processing system?

A. Hardware controls.
B. Systems documentation controls.
C. Access controls.
D. Disaster recovery controls.

AICPA.940516AUD-AU

351. Which of the following statements most likely represents a disadvantage for an entity that keeps microcomputer-prepared data files rather than manually prepared files?

A. Attention is focused on the accuracy of the programming process, rather than on errors in individual transactions.
B. It is usually easier for unauthorized persons to access and alter the files.
C. Random error associated with processing similar transactions in different ways is usually greater.
D. It is usually more difficult to compare recorded accountability with physical count of assets.

AICPA.910514AUD-AU

352. An auditor would least likely use computer software to

A. Access client data files.
B. Prepare spreadsheets.
C. Assess EDP control risk.
D. Construct parallel simulations.

AICPA.070605AUD

353. The ultimate purpose of assessing control risk is to contribute to the auditor's evaluation of the risk that

A. Specific internal control activities are not operating as designed.
B. The collective effect of the control environment may not achieve the control objectives.

C. Tests of controls may fail to identify activities relevant to assertions.
D. Material misstatements may exist in the financial statements.

IT Controls—Application Controls

AICPA.951110AUD-AU

354. Which of the following is an example of a validity check?

A. The computer ensures that a numerical amount in a record does not exceed some predetermined amount.
B. As the computer corrects errors and data are successfully resubmitted to the system, the causes of the errors are printed out.
C. The computer flags any transmission for which the control field value did not match that of an existing file record.
D. After data for a transaction are entered, the computer sends certain data back to the terminal for comparison with data originally sent.

AICPA.940531AUD-AU

355. An auditor most likely would introduce test data into a computerized payroll system to test internal controls related to the

A. Existence of unclaimed payroll checks held by supervisors.
B. Early cashing of payroll checks by employees.
C. Discovery of invalid employee I.D. numbers.
D. Proper approval of overtime by supervisors.

AICPA.910531AUD-AU

356. In a computerized payroll system environment, an auditor would be least likely to use test data to test controls related to

A. Missing employee numbers.
B. Proper approval of overtime by supervisors.
C. Time tickets with invalid job numbers.
D. Agreement of hours per clock cards with hours on time tickets.

AICPA.951103AUD-AU

357. Able Co. uses an online sales order processing system to process its sales transactions. Able's sales data are electronically sorted and subjected to edit checks.

A direct output of the edit checks most likely would be a

A. Report of all missing sales invoices.
B. File of all rejected sales transactions.
C. Printout of all user code numbers and passwords.
D. List of all voided shipping documents.

AICPA.941138AUD-AU

358. Which of the following controls is a processing control designed to ensure the reliability and accuracy of data processing?

	Limit test	Validity check test
A.	Yes	Yes
B.	No	No
C.	No	Yes
D.	Yes	No

IT Evidence–Gathering Procedures

AICPA.951152AUD-AU

359. A primary advantage of using generalized audit software packages to audit the financial statements of a client that uses an EDP system is that the auditor may

A. Access information stored on computer files while having a limited understanding of the client's hardware and software features.

B. Consider increasing the use of substantive tests of transactions in place of analytical procedures.

C. Substantiate the accuracy of data through self-checking digits and hash totals.

D. Reduce the level of required tests of controls to a relatively small amount.

AICPA.900508AUD-AU

360. Processing data through the use of simulated files provides an auditor with information about the operating effectiveness of control policies and procedures.

One of the techniques involved in this approach makes use of

A. Input validation.

B. Program code checking.

C. Controlled re-processing.

D. Integrated test facility.

AICPA.950572AUD-AU

361. When an auditor tests a computerized accounting system, which of the following is true of the test data approach?

A. Several transactions of each type must be tested.

B. Test data are processed by the client's computer programs under the auditor's control.

C. Test data must consist of all possible valid and invalid conditions.

D. The program tested is different from the program used throughout the year by the client.

AICPA.010415AUD-AU

362. An auditor who wishes to capture an entity's data as transactions are processed and continuously test the entity's computerized information system most likely would use which of the following techniques?

A. Snapshot application.

B. Embedded audit module.

C. Integrated data check.

D. Test data generator.

AICPA.010517AUD-AU

363. Which of the following computer-assisted auditing techniques processes client input data on a controlled program under the auditor's control to test controls in the computer system?

A. Test data.

B. Review of program logic.

C. Integrated test facility.

D. Parallel simulation.

Other IT Considerations

AICPA.010407AUD-AU

364. Which of the following characteristics distinguishes electronic data interchange (EDI) from other forms of electronic commerce?

A. EDI transactions are formatted using standards that are uniform worldwide.

B. EDI transactions need not comply with generally accepted accounting principles.

C. EDI transactions are ordinarily processed without the Internet.

D. EDI transactions are usually recorded without security or privacy concerns.

AICPA.990423AUD-AU

365. Which of the following strategies would a CPA most likely consider in auditing an entity that processes most of its financial data only in electronic form, such as a paperless system?

A. Continuous monitoring and analysis of transaction processing with an embedded audit module.

B. Increased reliance on internal control activities that emphasize the segregation of duties.

C. Verification of encrypted digital certificates used to monitor the authorization of transactions.

D. Extensive testing of firewall boundaries that restrict the recording of outside network traffic.

AICPA.990511AUD-AU

366. Which of the following statements is correct concerning internal control in an electronic data interchange (EDI) system?

A. Preventive controls are generally more important than detective controls in EDI systems.
B. Control objectives for EDI systems are generally different from the objectives for other information systems.
C. Internal controls in EDI systems rarely permit control risk to be assessed at below the maximum.
D. Internal controls related to the segregation of duties are generally the most important controls in EDI systems.

AICPA.990508AUD-AU

367. Which of the following is usually a benefit of using electronic funds transfer for international cash transactions?

A. Improvement of the audit trail for cash receipts and disbursements.
B. Creation of self-monitoring access controls.
C. Reduction of the frequency of data entry errors.
D. Off-site storage of source documents for cash transactions.

AICPA.990413AUD-AU

368. Which of the following is an essential element of the audit trail in an electronic data interchange (EDI) system?

A. Disaster recovery plans that ensure proper backup of files.
B. Encrypted hash totals that authenticate messages.
C. Activity logs that indicate failed transactions.
D. Hardware security modules that store sensitive data.

IV. Forming Conclusions and Reporting

Audit Reports

Introduction to Audit Reports

AICPA.951168AUD-AU

369. GAAS require the auditor's report to contain either an expression of opinion regarding the financial statements or an assertion to the effect that an opinion cannot be expressed.

The objective of this requirement is to prevent

A. An auditor from expressing different opinions on each of the basic financial statements.
B. Restrictions on the scope of the audit, whether imposed by the client or by the inability to obtain evidence.
C. Misinterpretations regarding the degree of responsibility the auditor is assuming.
D. An auditor from reporting on one basic financial statement and not the others.

AICPA.940575AUD-AU

370. When financial statements contain a departure from GAAP because, due to unusual circumstances, the statements would otherwise be misleading, the auditor should explain the unusual circumstances in a separate paragraph and express an opinion that is

A. Unmodified.
B. Qualified.
C. Adverse.
D. Qualified or adverse, depending on materiality.

AICPA.910544AUD-AU

371. If an auditor is satisfied that there is only a remote likelihood of a loss resulting from the resolution of a matter involving an uncertainty, the auditor should express a(n)

A. Unmodified opinion.
B. Unmodified opinion with a separate emphasis-of-matter paragraph.
C. Qualified opinion or disclaimer of opinion, depending upon the materiality of the loss.
D. Qualified opinion or disclaimer of opinion, depending on whether the uncertainty is adequately disclosed.

AICPA.980421AUD-AU

372. When issuing an unmodified opinion, the auditor who evaluates the audit findings should be satisfied that the

A. Amount of known misstatement is documented in the management representation letter.

B. Estimate of the total likely misstatement is less than a material amount.

C. Amount of known misstatement is acknowledged and recorded by the client.

D. Estimate of the total likely misstatement includes the adjusting entries already recorded by the client.

AICPA.911123AUD-AU

373. For an entity's financial statements to be presented fairly in conformity with generally accepted accounting principles, the principles selected should

A. Be applied on a basis consistent with those followed in the prior year.

B. Be approved by the Auditing Standards Board or the appropriate industry subcommittee.

C. Reflect transactions in a manner that presents the financial statements within a range of acceptable limits.

D. Match the principles used by most other entities within the entity's particular industry.

PCAOB on Audit Reports

AICPA08115001.AUD.SOA.1

374. The PCAOB issued an auditing standard that specified the reporting language to be used in audit reports applicable to issuers relative to the AICPA standards that the PCAOB adopted on an interim basis in April 2003. The PCAOB audit report modifications included all of the following except for

A. Changed the title of the report from "Independent Auditor's Report" to "Report of the Independent Registered Public Accounting Firm."

B. Changed the date of the auditor's report to the date that the issuer's financial statements have been filed with the Securities and Exchange Commission.

C. Replaced the reference to "auditing standards generally accepted in the United States of America" with reference to "the standards of the Public Company Accounting Oversight Board (United States)."

D. Added a requirement that registered public accounting firms specify their city and state (or country, as applicable) along with their signature and date of the audit report.

Audits of Group Financial Statements

AICPA.990415AUD-AU

375. Which of the following procedures would the group auditor most likely perform after deciding to make reference to a component auditor who audited a subsidiary of the reporting entity?

A. Review the audit documentation and the audit programs of the component auditor.

B. Visit the other CPA and discuss the results of the component auditor's procedures.

C. Make inquiries about the professional reputation and independence of the component auditor.

D. Determine that the component auditor has a sufficient understanding of the subsidiary's internal control.

AICPA.951177AUD-AU

376. The auditor's report contains the following sentences:

We did not audit the financial statements of EZ Inc., a wholly-owned subsidiary, whose statements reflect total assets and revenues constituting 27 percent and 29 percent, respectively, of the related consolidated totals. Those statements were audited by other auditors whose report has been furnished to us and our opinion, insofar as it relates to the amounts included for EZ Inc., is based solely on the report of the other auditors.

These sentences

A. Indicate a division of responsibility.

B. Assume responsibility for the other auditor.

C. Require a departure from an unmodified opinion.

D. Are an improper form of reporting.

AICPA.930555AUD-AU

377. In the group auditor's report, the group engagement partner decides not to make reference to a component auditor who audited a client's subsidiary. The group auditor could justify this decision if, among other requirements, the group engagement partner

A. Issues an unmodified opinion on the consolidated financial statements.

B. Learns that the component auditor issued an unmodified opinion on the subsidiary's financial statements.

C. Is unable to review the audit programs and audit documentation of the component auditor.

D. Is satisfied as to the independence and professional reputation of the component auditor.

AICPA.950577AUD-AU

378. The group engagement partner decides not to refer to the audit of a component auditor who audited a subsidiary of the group auditor's client. After making inquiries about the component auditor's professional reputation and independence, the group engagement partner most likely would

A. Add an emphasis-of-matter paragraph to the auditor's report indicating that the subsidiary's financial statements are not material to the consolidated financial statements.

B. In the engagement letter that the group auditor assumes no responsibility for the component auditor's work and opinion.

C. Obtain written permission from the component auditor to omit the reference in the group engagement partner's audit report.

D. Contact the component auditor and review the audit programs and documentation pertaining to the subsidiary.

AICPA.911130AUD-AU

379. In which of the following situations would a group engagement partner least likely make reference to a component auditor who audited a subsidiary of the entity?

A. The component auditor was retained by the group auditor and the work was performed under the group auditor's guidance and control.

B. The group auditor finds it impracticable to review the component auditor's work or otherwise be satisfied as to the component auditor's work.

C. The group engagement partner is unable to be satisfied as to the independence and professional reputation of the component auditor.

D. The principal auditor is unable to be satisfied as to the independence and professional reputation of the other auditor.

Emphasis-of-Matter Paragraphs and Other-Matter Paragraphs

AICPA.951164AUD-AU

380. An auditor most likely would express an unmodified opinion and would not add an emphasis-of-matter or other-matter paragraph to the report if the auditor

A. Wishes to emphasize that the entity had significant transactions with related parties.

B. Concurs with the entity's change in its method of accounting for inventories.

C. Discovers that supplementary information required by FASB has been omitted.

D. Believes that there is a remote likelihood of a material loss resulting from an uncertainty.

AICPA.900512AUD-AU

381. An separate paragraph following the opinion paragraph of an auditor's report describes an uncertainty as follows:

As discussed in Note X to the financial statements, the Company is a defendant in a lawsuit alleging infringement of certain patent rights and claiming damages. Discovery proceedings are in progress. The ultimate outcome of the litigation cannot presently be determined. Accordingly, no provision for any liability that may result upon adjudication has been made in the accompanying financial statements.

What type of audit report should the auditor issue under these circumstances?

A. Unmodified.

B. "Subject to" qualified.

C. "Except for" qualified.

D. Disclaimer.

AICPA.921149AUD-AU

382. Green, CPA, concludes that there is substantial doubt about JKL Co.'s ability to continue as a going concern.

If JKL's financial statements adequately disclose its financial difficulties, Green's auditor's report should

	Include a separate paragraph following the opinion paragraph	Specifically use the words "going concern"	Specifically use the words "substantial doubt"
A.	Yes	Yes	Yes
B.	Yes	Yes	No
C.	Yes	No	Yes
D.	No	Yes	Yes

Qualified for Scope Limitation

AICPA.901105AUD-AU

383. Tech Company has disclosed an uncertainty due to pending litigation. The auditor's decision to issue a qualified opinion rather than an unmodified opinion with an emphasis-of-matter paragraph most likely would be determined by the

A. Lack of sufficient evidence.

B. Inability to estimate the amount of loss.

C. Entity's lack of experience with such litigation.

D. Lack of insurance coverage for possible losses from such litigation.

AICPA.070639AUD

384. Under which of the following circumstances would an auditor's expression of an unmodified opinion be inappropriate?

A. The auditor is unable to obtain the audited financial statements of a significant subsidiary.

B. The financial statements are prepared on the entity's income tax basis.

C. There are significant deficiencies in the design and operation of the entity's internal control.

D. Analytical procedures indicate that many year-end account balances are not comparable with the prior year's balances.

AICPA.101132AUD

385. When qualifying an opinion because of an insufficiency of audit evidence, an auditor should modify the situation in the

	Auditor's Responsibility section	Notes to the financial statements
A.	Yes	Yes
B.	Yes	No
C.	No	Yes
D.	No	No

AICPA.930544AUD-AU

386. An auditor most likely would modify the audit report if the entity's financial statements include a footnote on related party transactions

A. Disclosing loans to related parties at interest rates significantly below prevailing market rates.

B. Describing an exchange of real estate for similar property in a non-monetary related party transaction.

C. Stating that a particular related party transaction occurred on terms equivalent to those that would have prevailed in an arm's-length transaction.

D. Presenting the dollar volume of related party transactions and the effects of any change in the method of establishing terms from prior periods.

AICPA.910542AUD-AU

387. An auditor was unable to obtain audited financial statements or other evidence supporting an entity's investment in a foreign subsidiary.

Between which of the following opinions should the entity's auditor choose?

A. Adverse and unmodified, with an emphasis-of-matter paragraph added.

B. Disclaimer and unmodified with an emphasis-of-matter paragraph added.

C. Qualified and adverse.

D. Qualified and disclaimer.

Qualified for Misstatement

AICPA.900509AUD-AU

388. An auditor would be most likely to consider modifying an otherwise unmodified opinion if the client's financial statements include a footnote on related party transactions

A. Representing that certain related party transactions were consummated on terms equivalent to those obtainable in transactions with unrelated parties.

B. Presenting the dollar volume of related party transactions and the effects of any change in the method of establishing terms from that used in the prior period.

C. Explaining the business purpose of the sale of real property to a related party.

D. Disclosing compensating balance arrangements maintained for the benefit of related parties.

AICPA.931151AUD-AU

389. When an auditor qualifies an opinion because of inadequate disclosure, the auditor should describe the nature of the omission in a separate basis for qualified opinion paragraph and modify the

	Introductory paragraph	Management responsibility paragraph
A.	Yes	Yes
B.	Yes	No
C.	No	Yes
D.	No	No

AICPA.120723AUD

390. Zag Co. issues financial statements that present financial position and results of operations but Zag omits the related statement of cash flows. Zag would like to engage Brown, CPA, to audit its financial statements without the statement of cash flows although Brown's access to all of the information underlying the basic financial statements will not be limited. Under these circumstances, Brown most likely would

A. Add an emphasis-of-matter paragraph to the standard auditor's report that justifies the reason for the omission.

B. Refuse to accept the engagement as proposed because of the client-imposed scope limitation.

C. Explain to Zag that the omission requires a qualification of the auditor's opinion.

D. Prepare the statement of cash flows as an accommodation to Zag and express an unmodified opinion.

AICPA.930546AUD-AU

391. If a privately held company issues financial statements that purport to present its financial position and results of operations, but omits the statement of cash flows, the auditor ordinarily will express a(n)

A. Disclaimer of opinion.

B. Qualified opinion.

C. Review report.

D. Unmodified opinion with a separate emphasis-of-matter paragraph.

AICPA.910546AUD-AU

392. When an auditor qualifies an opinion because of inadequate disclosure, the auditor should describe the nature of the omission in a separate basis of opnion paragraph and modify the

	Introductory paragraph	Management responsibility paragraph	Opinion paragraph
A.	Yes	No	No
B.	Yes	Yes	No
C.	No	Yes	Yes
D.	No	No	Yes

Adverse Opinion

AICPA.951165AUD-AU

393. An auditor would express an unmodified opinion with an emphasis-of-matter paragraph added to the auditor's report for

	An unjustified accounting change	A material weakness in the internal control structure
A.	Yes	Yes
B.	Yes	No
C.	No	Yes
D.	No	No

AICPA.901114AUD-AU

394. Tread Corp. accounts for the effect of a material accounting change prospectively when the inclusion of the cumulative effect of the change is required in the current year.

The auditor would choose between expressing a(n)

A. Qualified opinion or a disclaimer of opinion.

B. Disclaimer of opinion or an unmodified opinion with an emphasis-of-paragraph.

C. Unmodified opinion with an emphasis-of-matter paragraph and an adverse opinion.

D. Adverse opinion and a qualified opinion.

AICPA.940587AUD-AU

395. In which of the following circumstances would an auditor be most likely to express an adverse opinion?

A. The chief executive officer refuses the auditor access to minutes of board of directors' meetings.

B. Tests of controls show that the entity's internal control structure is so ineffective that it cannot be relied upon.

C. The financial statements are not in conformity with the FASB Statements regarding the capitalization of leases.

D. Information comes to the auditor's attention that raises substantial doubt about the entity's ability to continue as a going concern.

AICPA.120728AUD

396. A client has capitalizable leases but refuses to capitalize them in the financial statements. Which of the following reporting options does an auditor have if the amounts pervasively distort the financial statements?

A. Qualified opinion.

B. Unmodified opinion.

C. Disclaimer opinion.

D. Adverse opinion.

Disclaimer of Opinion

AICPA.900518AUD-AU

397. Under which of the following circumstances would a disclaimer of opinion not be appropriate?

A. The auditor is engaged after fiscal year-end and is unable to observe physical inventories or apply alternative procedures to verify their balances.

B. The auditor is unable to determine the amounts associated with illegal acts committed by the client's management.

C. The financial statements fail to contain adequate disclosure concerning related party transactions.

D. The client refuses to permit its attorney to furnish information requested in a letter of audit inquiry.

AICPA.931146AUD-AU

398. When disclaiming an opinion due to a client-imposed scope limitation, an auditor should indicate in a separate paragraph why the

audit did not comply with generally accepted auditing standards. The auditor should also

	Modify the Auditor's Responsibility Section	Omit the opinion paragraph
A.	No	Yes
B.	Yes	Yes
C.	No	No
D.	Yes	No

AICPA.900557AUD-AU

399. Morris, CPA, suspects that a pervasive scheme of illegal bribes exists throughout the operations of Worldwide Import-Export, Inc., a new audit client. Morris notified the audit committee and Worldwide's legal counsel, but neither could assist Morris in determining whether the amounts involved were material to the financial statements or whether senior management was involved in the scheme.

Under these circumstances, Morris should

A. Express an unmodified opinion with a separate emphasis-of-matter paragraph.
B. Disclaim an opinion on the financial statements.
C. Express an adverse opinion on the financial statements.
D. Express an unmodified opinion with a separate other-matter paragraph.

Consistency of Financial Statements

AICPA.901108AUD-AU

400. When there has been a change in accounting principle that materially affects the comparability of the comparative financial statements presented and the auditor concurs with the change, the auditor should

	Concur explicitly with the change	Issue an "except for" qualified opinion	Refer to the change in an emphasis-of-matter paragraph
A.	No	No	Yes
B.	Yes	No	Yes
C.	Yes	Yes	No
D.	No	Yes	No

AICPA.951174AUD-AU

401. In the first audit of a new client, an auditor was able to extend auditing procedures to gather sufficient evidence about consistency. Under these circumstances, the auditor should

A. Not report on the client's income statement.

B. Not refer to consistency in the auditor's report.
C. State that the consistency standard does not apply.
D. State that the accounting principles have been applied consistently.

AICPA.140701AUD-SIM

402. An entity changed from the straight-line method to the declining balance method of depreciation for all newly acquired assets. This change has no material effect on the current year's financial statements, but is reasonably certain to have a substantial effect in later years. If the change is disclosed in the notes to the financial statements, the auditor should issue a report with a(n)

A. Qualified opinion.
B. Required "other-matter" paragraph.
C. Unmodified opinion.
D. Disclaimer of opinion.

AICPA.130721AUD

403. When there has been a change in accounting principles, but the effect of the change on the comparability of the financial statements is **not** material, the auditor should

A. Not refer to the change in the auditor's report.
B. Refer to the note in the financial statements that discusses the change.
C. Refer to the change in an emphasis-of-matter paragraph.
D. Explicitly state whether the change conforms with GAAP.

PCAOB on Evaluating Consistency

AICPA.090651.AUD.SOA.6

404. An auditor should ordinarily add an explanatory paragraph to the auditor's report to identify a material matter related to

A. A change in reporting entity resulting from a specific transaction or event.
B. A change in accounting principle caused by the issuance of a new authoritative accounting standard that rendered the principle previously used no longer generally accepted.
C. A change in classification in previously issued financial statements.
D. All of the above.

AICPA.090650.AUD.SOA.6

405. If management has not justified that the alternative accounting principle is preferable to an accounting principle previously used and

the effect of the change in accounting principle is material to a company's financial statements, the auditor should

A. Decide between a qualified opinion and an adverse opinion.
B. Decide between a qualified opinion and a disclaimer of opinion.
C. Issue an unqualified opinion with an explanatory paragraph.
D. Decide between a disclaimer of opinion and an adverse opinion.

AICPA.090647.AUD.SOA.6

406. When there is a change in accounting principle, the auditor should evaluate whether all of the following criteria have been met, except for whether

A. The change has been authorized by those charged with governance.
B. The method of accounting for the effect of the change conforms to GAAP.
C. The disclosures related to the change are adequate.
D. Management has justified that the alternative accounting principle selected is preferable to the previously used accounting principle.

Opening Balances—Initial Audits

AICPA.940576AUD-AU

407. Park, CPA, was engaged to audit the financial statements of Tech Co., a new client, for the year ended December 31, 20x1. Park obtained sufficient audit evidence for all of Tech's financial statement items except Tech's opening inventory. Due to inadequate financial records, Park could not verify Tech's January 1, 20x1, inventory balances.

Park's opinion on Tech's 20x1 financial statements most likely will be on the

	Balance sheet	Income statement
A.	Disclaimer	Disclaimer
B.	Unmodified	Disclaimer
C.	Disclaimer	Adverse
D.	Unmodified	Adverse

AICPA.130729AUD

408. Which of the following would a successor auditor ask the predecessor auditor to provide after accepting an audit engagement?

A. Disagreements between the predecessor auditor and management as to significant accounting policies and principles.
B. The predecessor auditor's understanding of the reasons for the change of auditors.

C. Facts known to the predecessor auditor that might bear on the integrity of management.
D. Matters that may facilitate the evaluation of financial reporting consistency between the current and prior years.

Other Information Along with Financial Statements

AICPA.921157AUD-AU

409. When audited financial statements are presented in a client's document containing other information, the auditor should

A. Perform inquiry and analytical procedures to ascertain whether the other information is reasonable.
B. Add an emphasis-of-matter paragraph to the auditor's report without changing the opinion on the financial statements.
C. Perform the appropriate substantive auditing procedures to corroborate the other information.
D. Read the other information to determine that it is consistent with the audited financial statements.

Supplementary Information Related to Financial Statements

AICPA.940563AUD-AU

410. Investment and property schedules are presented for purposes of additional analysis in an auditor-submitted document. The schedules are not required parts of the basic financial statements, but accompany the financial statements.

When reporting on such supplementary information in relation to the financial statements as a whole, the measurement of materiality is the

A. Same as that used in forming an opinion on the basic financial statements taken as a whole.
B. Lesser of the individual schedule of investments or schedule of property, taken by itself.
C. Greater of the individual schedule of investments or schedule of property, taken by itself.
D. Combined total of both the individual schedules of investments and property, taken as a whole.

assess.AICPA.AUD.sup.info-0044

411. When an accountant compiles a client's financial statements accompanied by supplemental

information, which of the following is a required element of the accountant's separate report on the supplemental information?

A. A statement that the information has been compiled from information that is the representation of management without audit or review.
B. A list of the procedures performed by the accountant during the compilation.
C. A statement that the accountant did **not** become aware of any material modifications that should be made to the information.
D. A confirmation of the independence of the accountant with respect to the information presented.

AICPA.950587AUD-AU

412. If supplementary information in a document accompanying the basic financial statements has been subjected to auditing procedures, the auditor may include in the auditor's report on the financial statements an opinion that the accompanying information is fairly stated in

A. Accordance with generally accepted auditing standards.
B. Conformity with generally accepted accounting principles.
C. All material respects in relation to the financial statements as a whole.
D. Accordance with attestation standards expressing a conclusion about management's assertions.

Required Supplementary Information

AICPA.940582AUD-AU

413. What is an auditor's responsibility for supplementary information, which is outside the basic financial statements, but which is required by the FASB?

A. The auditor has no responsibility for required supplementary information, as long as it is outside the basic financial statements.
B. The auditor's only responsibility for required supplementary information is to determine that such information has not been omitted.
C. The auditor should apply certain limited procedures to the required supplementary information and report deficiencies in, or omissions of, such information.
D. The auditor should apply tests of details of transactions and balances to the required supplementary information and report any material misstatements in such information.

AICPA.070635AUD

414. An auditor determines that the entity is presenting certain supplementary financial disclosures of pension information that are required by the GASB. Under these circumstances, the auditor should

A. Add an other-matter paragraph to the auditor's report preceding the opinion paragraph that explicitly identifies the required supplementary information as unaudited.
B. State that the audit is not being performed in accordance with generally accepted auditing standards.
C. Document in the audit documentation that the required supplementary information is presented, but should not apply any procedures to the information.
D. Compare the required supplementary information for consistency with the audited financial statements.

AICPA.090799.AUD-AU

415. What is an auditor's responsibility for supplementary information, such as disclosure of pension information, which is outside the basic financial statements, but required by the GASB?

A. The auditor should engage a specialist, such as an actuary, to verify that management's assertions are reasonable.
B. The auditor's only responsibility for supplementary information is to determine that such information has not been omitted.
C. The auditor should perform tests of transactions to the supplementary information to verify that it is reasonably comparable to the prior year information.
D. The auditor should apply certain limited procedures to the supplementary information and report deficiencies in, or omissions of, such information.

AICPA.900525AUD-AU

416. If management declines to present supplementary information required by the Governmental Accounting Standards Board (GASB), the auditor should issue a(n)

A. Adverse opinion.
B. Qualified opinion with an other-matter paragraph.
C. Unmodified opinion.
D. Unmodified opinion with an additional explanatory paragraph.

PCAOB on Auditing Supplemental Information

AICPA.140402AUD-SIM

417. In reporting on supplemental information under PCAOB auditing standards, the auditor's procedures should include each of the following except for

    A. Obtain an understanding of the purpose of the supplemental information and the criteria used by management for its preparation.
    B. Inquire of management about any significant assumptions or interpretations underlying the presentation of the supplemental information.
    C. Obtain written confirmation from the regulatory authorities that the supplemental information complies with regulatory requirements.
    D. Verify that the supplemental information reconciles to the underlying accounting or other records of the entity.

AICPA.140401AUD-SIM

418. The definition of "supplemental information" under PCAOB auditing standards includes all of the following except for

    A. A public company's sustainability report consisting of a variety of financial and nonfinancial measures of performance, which is made available to readers on the entity's web site.
    B. Supporting schedules that brokers and dealers are required to file with the Securities and Exchange Commission.
    C. Information outside of the financial statements that is derived from the entity's accounting records, which is covered by the auditor's report in relation to financial statements audited under PCAOB auditing standards.
    D. Information that is required to be presented under the rules of a regulatory authority, which is covered by the auditor's report in relation to financial statements audited under PCAOB auditing standards.

AICPA.140403AUD-SIM

419. The auditor's report on supplemental information under PCAOB auditing standards should include a statement about each of the following except for

    A. A statement that the supplemental information is management's responsibility.
    B. A statement that the methods of measurement and presentation have not changed from those used in the prior period.
    C. A statement that the supplemental information complies with the applicable regulatory requirements.
    D. An opinion (or disclaimer) as to whether the supplemental information is fairly stated in relation to the financial statements as a whole.

Alert to Restrict Report

AICPA.130501AUD-SIM

420. When adding an alert to restrict the auditor's report, the auditor should place the alert

    A. In the introductory paragraph of the auditor's report.
    B. In the Auditor's Responsibility section of the auditor's report.
    C. In a paragraph preceding the opinion paragraph.
    D. In a paragraph at the end of the auditor's report.

Financial Statements Using Another Country's Framework

AICPA.941188AUD-AU

421. Before reporting on the financial statements of a U.S. entity that have been prepared in conformity with another country's accounting principles, an auditor practicing in the U.S. should

    A. Understand the accounting principles generally accepted in the other country.
    B. Be certified by the appropriate auditing or accountancy board of the other country.
    C. Notify management that the auditor is required to disclaim an opinion on the financial statements.
    D. Receive a waiver from the auditor's state board of accountancy to perform the engagement.

AICPA.910549AUD-AU

422. The financial statements of KCP America, a U.S. entity, are prepared for inclusion in the consolidated financial statements of its non-U.S. parent. These financial statements are prepared in conformity with the accounting principles generally accepted in the parent's country and are for use only in that country.

    How may KCP America's auditor report on these financial statements?

    I. A U.S.-style report (without revision).
    II. A U.S.-style report revised to reference the accounting principles of the parent's country.
    III. The report form of the parent's country.

	I	II	III
A.	Yes	No	No
B.	No	Yes	No
C.	Yes	No	Yes
D.	No	Yes	Yes

Reporting on Summary Financial Statements

AICPA.911129AUD-AU

423. An auditor may report on condensed financial statements that are derived from complete audited financial statements if the

   A. Auditor indicates whether the information in the condensed financial statements is consistent in all material respects.
   B. Condensed financial statements are presented in comparative form with the prior year's condensed financial statements.
   C. Auditor describes the additional review procedures performed on the condensed financial statements.
   D. Condensed financial statements are distributed only to management and the board of directors.

Interim Financial Information

AICPA.090860AUD-SIM

424. Which of the following statements is correct regarding a review of interim financial information under AICPA Professional Standards?

   A. The independent accountant should establish an understanding with the client regarding the engagement, but documenting that understanding through a written communication with the client is optional.
   B. An engagement to review the entity's interim financial information can only be accepted if the independent accountant has already audited the entity's most recent annual financial statements.
   C. The independent accountant should make appropriate inquiries of persons responsible for financial and accounting matters, but need not obtain written representations from management.
   D. The independent accountant is required to obtain sufficient knowledge of the entity's business and its internal control related to the interim financial information.

AICPA.111200AUD

425. When planning a review of an audit client's interim financial statements, which of the following procedures should the accountant perform to update the accountant's knowledge about the entity's business and its internal control?

   A. Perform analytical procedures on selected accounts by comparing the interim amounts to the amounts for the previous audited fiscal year end.
   B. Inquire of the entity's outside legal counsel about the status of any previous pending litigation and any new litigation involving the entity.
   C. Select a sample of material revenue transactions occurring during the interim period and examine supporting documentation.
   D. Consider the results of audit procedures performed with respect to the current year's financial statements.

AICPA.940564AUD-AU

426. An independent accountant's report is based on a review of interim financial information. If this report is presented in a registration statement, a prospectus should include a statement clarifying that the

   A. Accountant's review report is not a part of the registration statement within the meaning of the Securities Act of 1933.
   B. Accountant assumes no responsibility to update the report for events and circumstances occurring after the date of the report.
   C. Accountant's review was performed in accordance with standards established by the Financial Accounting Standards Board.
   D. Accountant obtained corroborating evidence to determine whether material modifications are needed for such information to conform with GAAP.

AICPA.111180AUD

427. Which of the following statements would not normally be included in a representation letter for a review of interim financial information?

   A. To the best of our knowledge and belief, no events have occurred subsequent to the balance sheet and through the date of this letter that would require adjustment to or disclosure in the interim financial information.
   B. We acknowledge our responsibility for the design and implementation of programs and controls to prevent and detect fraud.

C. We understand that a review consists principally of performing analytical procedures and making inquiries about the interim financial information.

D. We have made available to you all financial records and related data.

AICPA.921151AUD-AU

428. Which of the following procedures ordinarily should be performed when an independent accountant conducts a review of interim financial information under AICPA Professional Standards?

A. Verify changes in key account balances.

B. Read the minutes of meetings of those charged with governance.

C. Inspect the open purchase order file.

D. Perform cutoff tests for cash receipts and disbursements.

Other Types of Reports

Reports on Application of Requirements of Framework

AICPA.940567AUD-AU

429. In connection with a proposal to obtain a new client, an accountant in public practice is asked to prepare a written report on the application of accounting principles to a specific transaction. The accountant's report should include a statement that

A. Any difference in the facts, circumstances, or assumptions presented may change the report.

B. The engagement was performed in accordance with Statements on Standards for Consulting Services.

C. The guidance provided is for management use only and may not be communicated to the prior or continuing auditors.

D. Nothing came to the accountant's attention that caused the accountant to believe that the accounting principles violated GAAP.

F/S with Special Purpose Frameworks

AICPA.130722AUD

430. An entity prepares its financial statements on its income tax basis. A description of how that basis differs from GAAP should be included in the

A. Notes to the financial statements.

B. Auditor's engagement letter.

C. Management representation letter.

D. Introductory paragraph of the auditor's report.

AICPA.950582AUD-AU

431. An auditor's report on financial statements prepared on the cash receipts and disbursements basis of accounting should include all of the following except

A. A reference to the note to the financial statements that describes the cash receipts and disbursements basis of accounting.

B. A statement that the cash receipts and disbursements basis of accounting is not a comprehensive basis of accounting.

C. An opinion as to whether the financial statements are presented fairly in conformity with the cash receipts and disbursements basis of accounting.

D. A statement that the audit was conducted in accordance with generally accepted auditing standards.

AICPA.900521AUD-AU

432. When reporting on financial statements prepared on the same basis of accounting used for income tax purposes, the auditor should include in the report a paragraph that

A. Emphasizes that the financial statements are not intended to have been examined in accordance with generally accepted auditing standards.

B. Refers to the authoritative pronouncements that explain the income tax basis of accounting being used.

C. States that the income tax basis of accounting is a basis of accounting other than generally accepted accounting principles.

D. Justifies the use of the income tax basis of accounting.

AICPA.090752.AUD.AU

433. Which of the following titles would be considered suitable for financial statements that are prepared on a cash basis?

A. Income statement.

B. Statement of operations.

C. Statement of revenues collected and expenses paid.

D. Statement of cash flows.

AICPA.921154AUD-AU

434. An auditor's special report on financial statements prepared in conformity with the cash basis of accounting should include a separate explanatory paragraph after the opinion paragraph that

A. Justifies the reasons for departing from generally accepted accounting principles.

B. States whether the financial statements are fairly presented in conformity with another basis of accounting.

C. Refers to the note to the financial statements that describes the basis of accounting.

D. Explains how the results of operations differ from financial statements prepared in conformity with generally accepted accounting principles.

Audits of Single F/S and Specific Elements, Accounts, or Items

AICPA.951187AUD-AU-SIM

435. An auditor is engaged to report on selected financial data that are included in a client-prepared document containing audited financial statements. Under these circumstances, the report on the selected data should

A. Refer to the report issued on the audited financial statements.

B. Be distributed only to senior management and the board of directors.

C. State that the presentation is a comprehensive basis of accounting other than GAAP.

D. Indicate that the data are not fairly stated in all material respects.

AICPA.120725AUD-SIM

436. An auditor is engaged to report on selected financial data that are included in a client-prepared document containing audited financial statements. Under these circumstances, the report on the selected data should

A. State that the presentation is based on a special-purpose framework.

B. Restrict the use of the report to those specified users within the entity.

C. Refer to the report issued on the entity's audited financial statements.

D. Indicate that the data are subject to prospective results that may NOT be achieved.

AICPA.111184AUD

437. As a condition of obtaining a loan from First National Bank, Maxim Co. is required to submit an audited balance sheet, but not the related statements of income, retained earnings, or cash flows. Maxim would like to engage a CPA to audit only its balance sheet. Under these circumstances, the CPA

A. May not audit only Maxim's balance sheet if the amount of the loan is material to the financial statements taken as a whole.

B. May not audit only Maxim's balance sheet if Maxim is a non-issuer.

C. May audit only Maxim's balance sheet if the CPA disclaims an opinion on the other financial statements.

D. May audit only Maxim's balance sheet if access to the information underlying the basic financial statements is not limited.

Reporting on Compliance with Requirements in a F/S Audit

AICPA.101088AUD

438. Reports are considered special reports when issued in conjunction with

A. Interim financial information reviewed to determine whether material modifications should be made to conform with GAAP.

B. Feasibility studies presented to illustrate an entity's results of operations.

C. Compliance with aspects of regulatory requirements related to audited financial statements.

D. Pro forma financial presentations designed to demonstrate the effects of hypothetical transactions.

AICPA.900511AUD-AU

439. An auditor's report would be designated a special report when it is issued in connection with

A. Interim financial information of a publicly held company that is subject to a limited review.

B. Compliance with aspects of regulatory requirements related to audited financial statements.

C. Application of accounting principles to specified transactions.

D. Limited use prospective financial statements such as a financial projection.

Service Organizations—User Auditors

AICPA.120725AUD-SIM

440. An auditor is engaged to report on selected financial data that are included in a client-prepared document containing audited financial statements. Under these circumstances, the report on the selected data should

A. State that the presentation is based on a special-purpose framework.

B. Restrict the use of the report to those specified users within the entity.

C. Refer to the report issued on the entity's audited financial statements.

D. Indicate that the data are subject to prospective results that may NOT be achieved.

AICPA.111184AUD

441. As a condition of obtaining a loan from First National Bank, Maxim Co. is required to submit an audited balance sheet, but not the related statements of income, retained earnings, or cash flows. Maxim would like to engage a CPA to audit only its balance sheet. Under these circumstances, the CPA

A. May not audit only Maxim's balance sheet if the amount of the loan is material to the financial statements taken as a whole.

B. May not audit only Maxim's balance sheet if Maxim is a non-issuer.

C. May audit only Maxim's balance sheet if the CPA disclaims an opinion on the other financial statements.

D. May audit only Maxim's balance sheet if access to the information underlying the basic financial statements is not limited.

AICPA.951187AUD-AU-SIM

442. An auditor is engaged to report on selected financial data that are included in a client-prepared document containing audited financial statements. Under these circumstances, the report on the selected data should

A. Refer to the report issued on the audited financial statements.

B. Be distributed only to senior management and the board of directors.

C. State that the presentation is a comprehensive basis of accounting other than GAAP.

D. Indicate that the data are not fairly stated in all material respects.

Service Organizations—Service Auditors

AICPA.990530AUD-AU

443. Payroll Data Co. (PDC) processes payroll transactions for a retailer.

Cook, CPA, is engaged to express an opinion on a description of PDC's internal controls placed in operation as of a specific date. These controls are relevant to the retailer's internal control, so Cook's report may be useful in providing the retailer's independent auditor with information necessary to plan a financial statement audit.

Cook's report should

A. Contain a disclaimer of opinion on the operating effectiveness of PDC's controls.

B. State whether PDC's controls were suitably designed to achieve the retailer's objectives.

C. Identify PDC's controls relevant to specific financial statement assertions.

D. Disclose Cook's assessed level of control risk for PDC.

AICPA.951137AUD-AU

444. Computer Services Company (CSC) processes payroll transactions for schools.

Drake, CPA, is engaged to report on CSC's policies and procedures placed in operation as of a specific date. These policies and procedures are relevant to the schools' internal control structure, so Drake's report will be useful in providing the schools' independent auditors with information necessary to plan their audits.

Drake's report expressing an opinion on CSC's policies and procedures placed in operation as of a specific date should contain a(an)

A. Description of the scope and nature of Drake's procedures.

B. Statement that CSC's management has disclosed to Drake all design deficiencies of which it is aware.

C. Opinion on the operating effectiveness of CSC's policies and procedures.

D. Paragraph indicating the basis for Drake's assessment of control risk.

Comfort Letters

AICPA.070636AUD

445. Comfort letters ordinarily are

	Addressed to the entity's	Signed by the entity's
A.	Audit committee	Independent auditor
B.	Underwriter of securities	Senior management
C.	Audit committee	Senior management
D.	Underwriter of securities	Independent auditor

AICPA.921158AUD-AU

446. Comfort letters ordinarily are signed by the entity's

A. Independent auditor.

B. Underwriter of securities.

C. Audit committee.

D. Senior management.

Government Auditing Standards

AICPA.921156AUD-AU

447. Hill, CPA, is auditing the financial statements of Helping Hand, a not-for-profit organization that receives financial assistance from governmental agencies.

    To detect misstatements in Helping Hand's financial statements resulting from violations of laws and regulations, Hill should focus on violations that

    A. Could result in criminal prosecution against the organization.
    B. Involve significant deficiencies to be communicated to the organization's trustees and the funding agencies.
    C. Have a direct and material effect on the amounts in the organization's financial statements.
    D. Demonstrate the existence of material weaknesses in the organization's internal control structure.

AICPA.940571AUD-AU

448. For an entity that does not receive governmental financial assistance, an auditor's standard report on financial statements generally would not refer to

    A. Significant estimates made by management.
    B. An assessment of the entity's accounting principles.
    C. Management's responsibility for the financial statements.
    D. The entity's internal control structure.

AICPA.910547AUD-AU

449. The GAO standards of reporting for governmental financial audits incorporate the AICPA standards of reporting and prescribe supplemental standards to satisfy the unique needs of governmental audits.

    Which of the following is a supplemental reporting standard for government financial audits?

    A. A written report on the auditor's understanding of the entity's internal control structure and assessment of control risk should be prepared.
    B. Material indications of illegal acts should be reported in a document with distribution restricted to senior officials of the entity audited.
    C. Instances of abuse, fraud, mismanagement, and waste should be reported to the organization with legal oversight authority over the entity audited.

D. All privileged and confidential information discovered should be reported to the senior officials of the organization that arranged for the audit.

AICPA.930524AUD-AU

450. Reporting on internal control structure under Government Auditing Standards differs from reporting under generally accepted auditing standards in that Government Auditing Standards require a

    A. Written report describing the entity's internal control structure procedures specifically designed to prevent fraud, abuse, and illegal acts.
    B. Description of the scope of the auditors' testing of internal control over financial reporting.
    C. Statement of negative assurance that the internal control structure procedures not tested have an immaterial effect on the entity's financial statements.
    D. Statement of positive assurance that internal control structure procedures designed to detect material errors and irregularities were tested.

AICPA.101114AUD

451. Which of the following is correct about reporting on compliance with laws and regulations in a financial audit under Government Auditing Standards (the Yellow Book)?

    A. Auditors are **not** required to report fraud, illegal acts, and other material noncompliance in the audit report.
    B. In some circumstances, auditors are required to report fraud and illegal acts directly to parties external to the audited entity.
    C. The auditor's key findings of the audit of the financial statements should be communicated in a separate report.
    D. The reporting standards in a governmental audit are identical to the auditor's responsibilities under generally accepted auditing standards.

Compliance Audits

AICPA.931158AUD-AU

452. In performing a financial statement audit in accordance with Government Auditing Standards, an auditor is required to report on the entity's compliance with laws and regulations. This report should

    A. State that compliance with laws and regulations is the responsibility of the entity's management.

B. Describe the laws and regulations that the entity should comply with.

C. Provide an opinion on overall compliance with laws and regulations.

D. Indicate that the auditor does not possess legal skills and cannot make legal judgments.

AICPA.910560AUD-AU

453. Kent is auditing an entity's compliance with requirements governing a major federal financial assistance program in accordance with the Single Audit Act. Kent detected noncompliance with requirements that have a material effect on that program.

Kent's report on compliance should express a(an)

A. Unqualified opinion with a separate explanatory paragraph.

B. Qualified opinion or an adverse opinion.

C. Adverse opinion or disclaimer of opinion.

D. Limited assurance on the items tested.

AICPA.951189AUD-AU

454. In auditing compliance with requirements governing major federal financial assistance programs under the Single Audit Act, the auditor's consideration of materiality differs from materiality under generally accepted auditing standards.

Under the Single Audit Act, materiality is

A. Calculated in relation to the financial statements taken as a whole.

B. Determined separately for each major federal financial assistance program.

C. Decided in conjunction with the auditor's risk assessment.

D. Ignored, because all account balances, regardless of size, are fully tested.

AICPA.930560AUD-AU

455. Tell, CPA, is auditing the financial statements of Youth Services Co. (YSC), a not-for-profit organization, in accordance with Government Auditing Standards. Tell's report on YSC's compliance with laws and regulations is required to contain statements of

	Positive assurance	Negative assurance
A.	Yes	Yes
B.	Yes	No
C.	No	Yes
D.	No	No

SSARSs—General Principles

AICPA.151002AUD-SIM

456. Unconditional requirements in the clarified Statements on Standards for Accounting and Review Services are indicated by the word

A. Should.

B. Must.

C. May.

D. Could.

AICPA.931112AUD-AU

457. A CPA is required to comply with the provisions of Statements on Standards for Accounting and Review Services when

	Processing financial data for clients of other CPA firms	Consulting on accounting matters
A.	Yes	Yes
B.	Yes	No
C.	No	Yes
D.	No	No

AICPA.901140AUD-AU

458. The authoritative body designated to promulgate standards concerning an accountant's association with unaudited financial statements of an entity that is not required to file financial statements with an agency regulating the issuance of the entity's securities is the

A. Financial Accounting Standards Board.

B. General Accounting Office.

C. Accounting and Review Services Committee.

D. Auditing Standards Board.

SSARSs—Preparation of Financial Statements

AICPA.151005AUD-SIM

459. The clarified SSARSs applicable to preparation engagements (AR-C 70) do not apply to the following engagements, except for

A. Preparing financial statements to be presented alongside a personal financial plan.

B. Preparing financial statements for submission to taxing authorities.

C. Preparing financial statement in connection with litigation services.

D. Assisting with preparing financial statements by performing bookkeeping services.

SSARSs—Compilation Engagements

AICPA.920505AUD-AU

460. Which of the following statements should **not** be included in an accountant's standard report based on the compilation of an entity's financial statements?

   A. A statement that the compilation was performed in accordance with standards promulgated by the American Institute of CPAs.
   B. A statement that the accountant has not audited or reviewed the financial statements.
   C. A statement that the accountant does not express an opinion but expresses only limited assurance on the financial statements.
   D. A statement that no procedures were performed to verify the accuracy or completeness of the information provided by management.

AICPA.120718AUD

461. An accountant was asked by a potential client to perform a compilation of its financial statements. The accountant is not familiar with the industry in which the client operates. In this situation, which of the following actions is the accountant most likely to take?

   A. Request that management engage an independent industry expert to consult with the accountant.
   B. Accept the engagement and obtain an adequate level of knowledge about the industry.
   C. Decline the engagement.
   D. Postpone accepting the engagement until the accountant has obtained an adequate level of knowledge about the industry.

AICPA.101110AUD

462. Which of the following services, if any, may an accountant who is **not** independent provide?

   A. Compilations, but **not** reviews.
   B. Reviews, but **not** compilations.
   C. Both compilations and reviews.
   D. No services.

AICPA.101086AUD

463. An accountant compiled the financial statements of a nonissuer in accordance with Statements on Standards for Accounting and Review Services (SSARS). If the accountant has an ownership interest in the entity, which of the following statements is correct?

   A. The accountant should refuse the compilation engagement.
   B. A report need **not** be issued for a compilation of a nonissuer.
   C. The accountant is required to include the disclaimer "I am an owner of the entity" in the report.
   D. The accountant is required to include the statement "I am **not** independent with respect to the entity" in the compilation report.

AICPA.951180AUD-AU

464. Financial statements of a nonpublic entity subject to a compilation engagement should be accompanied by the accountant's report stating that

   A. The scope of the accountant's procedures has not been restricted in testing the financial information that is the representation of management.
   B. The accountant assessed the accounting principles used and significant estimates made by management.
   C. The accountant does not express an opinion or any other form of assurance on the financial statements.
   D. A compilation consists principally of inquiries of entity personnel and analytical procedures applied to financial data.

SSARSs—Review Engagements

AICPA.921145AUD-AU

465. Which of the following procedures is **not** usually performed by the accountant during a review engagement of a nonpublic entity?

   A. Inquiring about actions taken at meetings of the board of directors that may affect the financial statements.
   B. Issuing a report stating that the review was performed in accordance with standards established by the AICPA.
   C. Reading the financial statements to consider whether they conform with generally accepted accounting principles.
   D. Communicating any material weaknesses discovered during the consideration of the internal control structure.

AICPA.900504AUD-AU

466. Inquiry and analytical procedures ordinarily performed during a review of a nonpublic entity's financial statements include

   A. Inquiries concerning actions taken at meetings of the owners and those charged with governance.

B. Analytical procedures designed to test the accounting records by obtaining corroborating evidential matter.

C. Inquiries designed to identify significant deficiencies in the internal control structure.

D. Analytical procedures concerning management's assertions regarding continued existence.

AICPA.101105AUD

467. Which of the following is required of an accountant in reviewing a company's financial statements under Statements on Standards for Accounting and Review Services (SSARS)?

A. Obtain knowledge of the client's industry.
B. Send bank confirmations.
C. Assess the operating effectiveness of the entity's internal control over financial reporting.
D. Observe client's physical inventory.

AICPA.120736AUD

468. Which of the following procedures would be generally performed when evaluating the accounts receivable balance in an engagement to review financial statements in accordance with *Statements on Standards for Accounting and Review Services*?

A. Perform a reasonableness test of the balance by computing days' sales in receivables.
B. Vouch a sample of subsequent cash receipts from customers.
C. Confirm individually significant receivable balances with customers.
D. Review subsequent bank statements for evidence of cash deposits.

AICPA.090762.AUD.AU

469. Which of the following statements is correct regarding a review of a nonpublic entity's financial statements in accordance with Statements on Standards for Accounting and Review Services (SSARS)?

A. The accountant is required to assess the risk of fraud.
B. It is **not** necessary for the accountant to obtain a management representation letter.
C. An opinion is expressed in the review report.
D. The accountant must be independent to issue the review report.

SSARSs—Other Topics

AICPA.941179AUD-AU

470. Gole, CPA, is engaged to review the 20x2 financial statements of North Co., a nonpublic entity. Previously, Gole audited North's 20x1 financial statements and expressed an unmodified opinion. Gole decides to include a separate paragraph in the 20x2 review report because North plans to present comparative financial statements for 20x2 and 20x1.

This separate paragraph should indicate that

A. The 20x2 review report is intended solely for the information of management and the board of directors.
B. The 20x1 auditor's report may no longer be relied on.
C. No auditing procedures were performed after the date of the 20x1 auditor's report.
D. There are justifiable reasons for changing the level of service from an audit to a review.

AICPA.111201AUD

471. An accountant has been engaged to compile pro forma financial statements. During the accountant's acceptance procedures, it is discovered that the accountant is not independent with respect to the company. What action should the accountant take with regard to the compilation?

A. The accountant should discuss the lack of independence with legal counsel to determine whether it is appropriate to accept the engagement.
B. The accountant should disclose the lack of independence in the accountant's compilation report.
C. The accountant should withdraw from the engagement.
D. The accountant should compile the pro forma financial statements but should not provide a compilation report.

AICPA.111168AUD

472. A CPA is reporting on comparative financial statements of a nonissuer. The CPA audited the prior year's financial statements and reviewed those of the current year in accordance with *Statements on Standards for Accounting and Review Services* (SSARS). The CPA has added a separate paragraph to the review report to describe the responsibility assumed for the prior year's audited financial statements. This separate paragraph should indicate

A. The type of opinion expressed previously.
B. That the CPA did **not** update the assessment of control risk.

C. The reasons for the change from an audit to a review.

D. That the audit report should **no** longer be relied on.

Other Professional Services

PCAOB on Reporting on Internal Control in an Integrated Audit

AICPA.111179AUD

473. Each of the following types of controls is considered to be an entity-level control, except those

A. Relating to the control environment.
B. Pertaining to the company's risk assessment process.
C. Regarding the company's annual stockholder meeting.
D. Addressing policies over significant risk management practices.

AICPA08115013.AUD.SOA.5

474. PCAOB Auditing Standard No. 5 directs auditors to begin their study of internal control at the financial statement level and the overall risks to internal control over financial reporting, then consider "entity-level" controls, followed by focusing on the relevant assertions for significant accounts and disclosures. This approach is best described as a

A. Bottom-up approach.
B. Top-down approach.
C. Center-out approach.
D. Risk-centric approach.

AICPA08115017.AUD.SOA.5

475. According to PCAOB auditing standards, when the auditor issues separate reports on the financial statements and on internal control over financial reporting,

A. The reports will normally have different dates, depending upon when audit fieldwork is completed for the financial statements and when the tests of control are completed.
B. Each report should be entitled "Report of Independent Auditor."
C. Each report should include a separate paragraph that discusses the "inherent limitations" of any audit engagement.
D. Each report should include a paragraph that references the other related report.

assess.AICPA.AUD.aud.stand5-0042

476. According to the PCAOB, each of the following statements is true with respect to the auditor's

responsibility to communicate material weaknesses in internal control over financial reporting **except**

A. All such weaknesses must be communicated in writing to the audit committee.
B. All such weaknesses must be communicated in writing to management.
C. All such weaknesses must be communicated prior to the issuance of the auditor's report on internal control over financial reporting.
D. All such weaknesses must be communicated in writing to all stockholders.

AICPA08115014.AUD.SOA.5

477. An auditing procedure that is applicable to "testing operating effectiveness" that is not associated with "testing design effectiveness" is

A. Inquiry.
B. Observation.
C. Inspection of relevant documentation.
D. Reperformance of the control procedure.

PCAOB on Whether Previously Reported Material Weakness Continues to Exist

AICPA08115001.AUD.SOA.7

478. According to PCAOB auditing standards, a "stated control objective" is best described as

A. The specific control objective that management has failed to identify and that, therefore, constitutes a material weakness.
B. The specific control objective identified by management that, if achieved, would result in the material weakness no longer existing.
C. A strategic objective of those charged with governance.
D. The related internal control activities that make it probable that the auditor can assess control risk as low.

AICPA08115001.AUD.SOA.8

479. According to PCAOB auditing standards, in evaluating whether a material weakness exists, an auditor should focus on materiality at the

A. Individual account-balance level.
B. Financial statement level.
C. Planning-stage level.
D. Quantitative level without regard to the qualitative circumstances.

AICPA08115001.AUD.SOA.6

480. PCAOB auditing standards apply when an issuer's auditor is engaged to report on whether a previously reported material weakness in internal control over financial reporting continues to exist as of a date specified by management. Which of the following statements is correct?

   A. Whenever an auditor's report on internal control over financial reporting identifies a material weakness, the auditor must also be engaged to issue a subsequent report within three months to indicate whether the previously reported material weakness continues to exist.

   B. Whenever an auditor's report on internal control over financial reporting identifies a material weakness, the auditor must also be engaged to issue a subsequent report within six months to indicate whether the previously reported material weakness continues to exist.

   C. Whenever an auditor's report on internal control over financial reporting identifies a material weakness, the auditor must also be engaged to issue a subsequent report within nine months to indicate whether the previously reported material weakness continues to exist.

   D. PCAOB auditing standards do not require an auditor to report whether a previously reported material weakness continues to exist, so such an engagement is voluntary.

Attestation Standards

AICPA.130708AUD

481. Which of the following should a practitioner perform as part of an engagement for agreed-upon procedures in accordance with *Statements on Standards for Attestation Engagements*?

   A. Issue a report on findings based on specified procedures performed.

   B. Assess whether the procedures meet the needs of the parties.

   C. Express negative assurance on findings of work performed.

   D. Report the differences between agreed-upon and audit procedures.

AICPA.120737AUD

482. According to the AICPA *Statements on Standards for Attestation Engagements*, a public accounting firm should establish quality control policies to provide assurance about which of the following matters related to agreed-upon procedures engagements?

   A. Use of the report is NOT restricted.

   B. The public accounting firm takes responsibility for the sufficiency of procedures.

   C. The practitioner is independent from the client and other specified parties.

   D. The practitioner sets the criteria to be used in the determination of findings.

AICPA.090748.AUD.AU

483. A practitioner has been engaged to apply agreed-upon procedures in accordance with *Statements on Standards for Attestation Engagements* (SSAE) to prospective financial statements. Which of the following conditions must be met for the practitioner to perform the engagement?

   A. The prospective financial statement includes a summary of significant accounting policies.

   B. The practitioner takes responsibility for the sufficiency of the agreed-upon procedures.

   C. The practitioner and specified parties agree upon the procedures to be performed by the practitioner.

   D. The practitioner reports on the criteria to be used in the determination of findings.

AICPA.070617AUD

484. A CPA is engaged to examine management's assertion that the entity's schedule of investment returns is presented in accordance with specific criteria. In performing this engagement, the CPA should comply with the provisions of

   A. Statements on Standards for Accounting and Review Services (SSARS).

   B. Statements on Auditing Standards (SAS).

   C. Statements on Standards for Consulting Services (SSCS).

   D. Statements on Standards for Attestation Engagements (SSAE).

Financial Forecasts and Projections

AICPA.090785.AUD-AU

485. A CPA is engaged to examine an entity's financial forecast. The CPA believes that several significant assumptions do not provide a reasonable basis for the forecast. Under these circumstances, the CPA should issue a(an)

   A. Adverse opinion.

   B. Pro forma opinion.

   C. Qualified opinion.

   D. Unqualified opinion with an explanatory paragraph.

AICPA.130723AUD

486. When an accountant compiles projected financial statements, the accountant's report should include a separate paragraph that

A. Disclaims any form of assurance on the historical financial statements.
B. Expresses limited assurance that the results will be within the projected range.
C. Describes the limitations on the usefulness of the projection.
D. Evaluates the hypothetical assumptions used to prepare the projection.

AICPA.090757.AUD.AU

487. An accountant's compilation report on a financial forecast should include a statement that

A. The hypothetical assumptions used in the forecast are reasonable in the circumstances.
B. The forecast should be read only in conjunction with the audited historical financial statements.
C. The accountant expresses only limited assurance on the forecasted statements and their assumptions.
D. There will usually be differences between the forecasted and actual results.

AICPA.901109AUD-AU

488. Accepting an engagement to compile a financial projection for a publicly held company most likely would be inappropriate if the projection were to be distributed to

A. A bank with which the entity is negotiating for a loan.
B. A labor union with which the entity is negotiating a contract.
C. The principal stockholder, to the exclusion of the other stockholders.
D. All stockholders of record as of the report date.

Pro Forma Financial Information

assess.AICPA.AUD.pro.forma.fin-0034

489. Each of the following items should be included in a presentation of pro forma financial statements **except**

A. The significant assumptions used in developing the pro forma information.
B. The source of the historical information on which the pro forma information is based.
C. An indication that the pro forma information is **not** necessarily indicative of results.
D. All direct and indirect effects attributed to the related transaction.

assess.AICPA.AUD.pro.forma.fin-0006

490. Which of the following standards should a CPA firm apply in a review of pro forma financial information?

A. *Statements on Standards for Attestation Engagements*
B. *Statements on Standards for Consulting Services*
C. *Statements on Standards for Accounting and Review Services*
D. Generally accepted auditing standards

assess.AICPA.AUD.pro.forma.fin-0003

491. A practitioner reporting on pro forma financial information does **not** possess an understanding of the client's business and the industry in which the client operates. The practitioner should take which of the following actions?

A. Issue a disclaimer, because the scope of work was **not** sufficient to express an opinion.
B. Review industry trade journals.
C. Refer a substantial portion of the audit to another CPA who will act as the principal. practitioner.
D. Perform ratio analysis of the financial data of comparable prior periods.

Compliance Attestation

AICPA.951181AUD-AU

492. A CPA's report on agreed-upon procedures related to management's assertion about an entity's compliance with specified requirements should contain

A. A statement of limitations on the use of the report.
B. An opinion about whether management's assertion is fairly stated.
C. Negative assurance that control risk has not been assessed.
D. An acknowledgment of responsibility for the sufficiency of the procedures.

AICPA.910551AUD-AU-SIM

493. Which of the following professional services would be subject to the Statements on Standards for Attestation Engagements (SSAEs)?

A. A management consulting engagement to provide IT-related advice to a client.
B. An engagement to report on an entity's compliance with statutory requirements.
C. An income tax engagement to prepare federal and state tax returns.
D. The compilation of financial statements from a nonissuer's accounting records.

Reporting on Internal Control in an Integrated Audit

assess.AICPA.900541AUD-AU

494. When engaged to express an opinion on an entity's internal accounting control over financial reporting in an integrated audit of a nonissuer, an auditor should

    A. Obtain management's written representations acknowledging responsibility for establishing and maintaining the system of internal control.
    B. Qualify any opinion concerning management's assertion that the cost of correcting any weaknesses exceeds the benefits.
    C. Keep informed of events subsequent to the date of the report that might have affected the auditor's opinion.
    D. Disclaim an opinion on whether the system taken as a whole is sufficient to prevent or detect material errors or fraud.

assess.AICPA.901156AUD-AU

495. An auditor's report expressing an unmodified opinion on an entity's internal control over financial reporting in an integrated audit of a nonissuer should state that the

    A. Engagement is different in purpose and scope from obtaining an understanding of the internal control and assessing control risk as part of the audit of the financial statements.
    B. Auditor's opinion does not necessarily increase the reliability of the entity's financial statements unless they are audited.
    C. Entity maintained effective internal control over financial reporting as of a specific date.
    D. Auditor did not apply procedures in the engagement that duplicate those procedures previously applied in assessing control risk as part of the audit of the financial statements.

assess.AICPA.910537AUD-AU

496. An audit of a nonissuer's internal control over financial reporting in an integrated audit will generally

    A. Require procedures that duplicate those already applied in assessing control risk during a financial statement audit.
    B. Increase the reliability of the financial statements that have already been audited.
    C. Be more extensive in scope than the assessment of control risk made during the financial statement audit.
    D. Be more limited in scope than the assessment of control risk made during a financial statement audit.

assess.AICPA.941146AUD-AU

497. Snow, CPA, was engaged by Master Co., a nonpublic company, to audit and report on the effectiveness of Master's internal control over financial reporting in an integrated audit.

    Snow's report should state that
    A. Because of the inherent limitations of internal control over financial reporting, misstatements may occur and not be detected.
    B. Management's assessment is based on criteria established by the American Institute of Certified Public Accountants.
    C. The results of Snow's tests of internal control over financial reporting will form the basis for Snow's opinion on the fairness of Master's financial statements in conformity with GAAP.
    D. The purpose of the audit of internal control over financial reporting is to enable Snow to plan the audit of Master's financial statements and determine the nature, timing, and extent of tests to be performed.

assess.AICPA.941118AUD-AU

498. Which of the following conditions is necessary for an auditor to accept an engagement to audit and report on an entity's internal control over financial reporting in an integrated audit for a nonissuer?

    A. The auditor anticipates relying on the entity's internal control in a financial statement audit.
    B. Management presents its written assessment about the effectiveness of the entity's internal control over financial reporting.
    C. The auditor is the continuing auditor who previously has audited the entity's financial statements.
    D. Management agrees to restrict the distributor of the auditor's report on internal control over financial reporting to specified users.

Management's Discussion and Analysis (MD&A)

AICPA.020413AUD-AU

499. A CPA is required to comply with the provisions of Statements on Standards for Attestation Engagements (SSAE) when engaged to

A. Report on financial statements that the CPA generated through the use of computer software.
B. Review management's discussion and analysis (MD&A) prepared pursuant to rules and regulations adopted by the SEC.
C. Provide the client with a financial statement format that does not include dollar amounts.
D. Audit financial statements that the client prepared for use in another country.

Assurance Services

assess.AICPA.990402AUD-AU

500. Which of the following is a term for an attest engagement in which a CPA assesses a client's commercial Internet site for predefined criteria that are designed to measure transaction integrity, information protection, and disclosure of business practices?

A. ElectroNet.
B. EDIFACT.
C. TechSafe.
D. WebTrust.

Answers and Explanations

1. **Answer: A**

   Ethical standards are not legally required, and so the goal in creating them lies in showing a willingness to go above and beyond minimum requirements. Observing ethical standards shows the public that CPAs are more concerned than are most professions with working in an ethical and trustworthy fashion.

2. **Answer: B**

   The code requires members to cooperate with each other to improve the art of accounting (and to maintain the public's confidence in the profession, and to carry out the profession's special responsibilities).

3. **Answer: D**

   Because the three chocies provided are all examples of sources of safeguards, this is the best answer.

4. **Answer: C**

   Unusual danger is not part of the Conceptual Framework.

5. **Answer: D**

   Because the first three choices are all correct, D is the best answer.

6. **Answer: D**

   Because the three choices provided are all examples of conflicts of interest, this is the best answer.

7. **Answer: D**

   Because all three answer choices provided are correct, this is the best answer. Maria should also be very concerned about gifts from ABC's directors.

8. **Answer: A**

   At this stage, Son should keep things in-house. The AICPA rules recommend that he go to the "appropriate level of management," such as his supervisor's superior, the client's audit committee, etc. However, if that does not produce satisfaction and Son is convinced that the financials are about to be materially misstated, he should consider resigning and contacting regulatory authorities.

9. **Answer: D**

   Because the answers provided are all correct, this is the best answer.

10. **Answer: C**

    Communication is critical in determining the responsibilities of auditors when they have disagreements with their superiors over serious matters.

11. **Answer: D**

    Because choices II and III are both accurate, this is the best answer.

12. **Answer: B**

    Members may advocate on behalf of tax and advisory service clients, although they should never stretch the bounds of performance standards, go beyond sound and reasonable professional practice, or compromise their credibility.

13. **Answer: B**

    The AICPA and state accountancy boards do not expect CPAs to be "Ms. or Mr. Super Accountant."

14. **Answer: A**

    Material departures from GAAP, which require material modifications, violate the Code of Professional Conduct.

15. **Answer: C**

    There is a strong presumption that established accounting principles must always be followed. However, the AICPA cannot always anticipate all circumstances in which such principles might be applied and recognizes that there may be occasional situations where literal application of pronouncements on accounting principles would render financial statements misleading. In those situations, departure from the accounting principles is justified under the Code of Ethics.

16. **Answer: C**

    Only audit documentation may be retained indefinitely by a CPA. Such documentation may be necessary for defending against a malpractice suit. Client records, however, must be returned to a client upon request.

17. **Answer: B**

While the SEC and most government agencies oppose full indemnification of wrongdoers, contribution is typically allowed and, therefore, would not violate the Code.

18. **Answer: D**

Client records belong to the client and should be returned to the client upon demand (even if there is an ongoing fee dispute).

19. **Answer: D**

All of these are listed as discreditable acts according to the Acts Discreditable Rule. This is the best answer.

20. **Answer: A**

Spinner may, under proper circumstances, have to convey to Lasco (a) client-provided records, (b) client records prepared by Spinner, and (c) supporting records. However, it should not have to convey its audit documentation, which it owns.

21. **Answer: B**

Tax accountants can accept referral fees and commissions. However, they should be disclosed to the client (and the question instructs us to assume appropriate disclosure).

22. **Answer: D**

While auditors may not receive contingent fees for performing attest-related services, seeking a private letter ruling is not an attest-related service. Unless the auditor is also providing attest services for the client, a contingent fee for seeking a private letter ruling is allowed.

23. **Answer: B**

Because during an examination the IRS will almost certainly look at the merits of the tax return, there is no temptation to play the "audit lottery," so contingent fees are allowed under the Code. Of course, in regard to attest clients, PCAOB rules say that an auditor of a public company may not provide to it *any* tax services on a contingent fee basis and remain independent

24. **Answer: D**

Assuming that Harriett is not also an audit client, then commissions and referral fees are permitted, if properly disclosed.

25. **Answer: C**

Because both I and II are accurate, this is the best answer.

26. **Answer: C**

This is the best answer, as this question emphasizes the importance of the confidentiality duty that accountants have vis-a-vis all their clients.

27. **Answer: B**

Disclosure may not be made to any party without either a court order or the consent of the client, unless the requesting party is a state CPA regulatory body. If the client consents, then the information may be released to anyone that the client has approved.

28. **Answer: B**

There are only a few circumstances in which information may be disclosed without the consent of the client. These include when a valid court order demanding release of the information is issued, when a quality review board of a state's CPA society requests the information, when a client consents to disclosure, and whenever professional obligations otherwise require it.

29. **Answer: B**

A CPA should refuse to produce confidential client records in response to a mere request from the IRS or SEC.

30. **Answer: A**

It is extremely unlikely that a client's mail clerk would have authority to approve the release of confidential financial information. The CPA, therefore, should not release it.

31. **Answer: D**

Because the three choices provided are all accurate, this is the best answer. Accounting firms have substantial leeway in choosing names, so long as they do not mislead.

32. **Answer: A**

Attest firms must be majority owned by CPAs.

33. **Answer: D**

Because all three choices are all permitted, this is the best answer.

34. Answer: C

As a staff member who works on the engagement, Bit is a "covered member."

35. Answer: D

Because the three choices are all accurate, this is the best answer.

36. Answer: A

Independence is required if use of such reports is unrestricted.

37. Answer: D

Because all three answer choices are correct, this is the best answer.

38. Answer: B

The code does note that entering into binding arbitration potentially creates independence problems by placing the firm and the client in positions of material adverse interests, creating a self-interest threat.

39. Answer: A

A member in public practice may not sign a current-year audit report if it has unpaid fees from the client for services provided more than one year prior.

40. Answer: D

This is a direct financial interest. Therefore, materiality is not a factor. A direct financial interest impairs independence even if it is immaterial.

41. Answer: D

Because all three answer choices are correct, this is the best answer.

42. Answer: A

There would be an impairment here, for Jo owns a direct though immaterial interest in the audit client: the mutual fund.

43. Answer: C

Both of these situations create an independence problem. The ability of Sally and Joe to self-direct their investments makes their interests in ABC direct. Therefore, there is an independence problem even if the investments are immaterial.

44. Answer: D

Because all three situations create independence problems, this is the best answer.

45. Answer: D

Unless Art participates in the investment decisions of his limited liability corporation, which is not indicated in the facts, his interests in its underlying investments are indirect if the LLC is agent managed.

46. Answer: B

Under these facts, Kim's interest in ABC is a direct financial interest, which creates an independence problem.

47. Answer: D

Because the three answer choices provided are all incorrect, this is the best answer.

48. Answer: D

Because Tondry only has a minority share in the business, even though the business provides services to an attest client, there is no independence violation and no need for the business' employees to follow independence requirements.

49. Answer: B

If an operating lease is on normal terms and all amounts are paid in accordance with the terms of the lease, there are no independence problems.

50. Answer: A

Because Microsoft is a public company, this situation creates no independence problem, although it might be considered a joint investment.

51. Answer: B

Betsy is in a position to influence the attest engagement team. Her live-in lover is a spousal equivalent, which qualifies him as an immediate family member. He is therefore covered by the independence rules. Although he could hold a non-key position, if he owns enough AAD stock that it is material to him, there is clearly a significant independence problem.

52. Answer: C

Immediate family members include spouses, spousal equivalents, and dependents but not nondependent children.

53. Answer: B

Close relatives include parents, siblings, and nondependent children but not spousal equivalents, who are immediate family members.

54. Answer: C

A CPA serving on a charitable board can never vote or participate in management affairs and, therefore, this choice would impair independence.

55. Answer: D

The role of advisor to a client's board is not forbidden by AICPA independence rules.

56. Answer: D

This is the best answer. The SOX provision addresses CEOs, controllers, CFOs, CAOs, or persons serving in equivalent positions.

57. Answer: A

The cooling-off period is one year, so this answer is correct.

58. Answer: D

Because the three answer choices provided are all correct, this is the best answer.

59. Answer: A

Regarding independence, the firm, team members, and those in a position to influence may not accept gifts from attest clients unless the value of those gifts is clearly insignificant to the recipient.

60. Answer: B

Sarbanes-Oxley requires audit committee preapproval.

61. Answer: D

Because the other three answer choices are all examples of "management responsibilities," this is the best answer.

62. Answer: D

Because the other three answer choices are all examples of communications that are not deemed nonaudit services, this is the best answer.

63. Answer: B

This is merely an advisory function and is permissible.

64. Answer: D

This is a management responsibility that goes too far to avoid an independence problem.

65. Answer: D

This is not true—this is a problem for members in public practice who may not be able to be adequate watchdogs of attest clients if they become too familiar with them. But no compliance threat arises for a member in business who works for an employer for a long time.

66. Answer: D

Because the three choices provided are all examples of "other members," this is the best answer.

67. Answer: B

Even other members must avoid discreditable acts.

68. Answer: D

Because the three choices provided are all examples of discreditable acts, this is the best answer.

69. Answer: D

All three of these people are "covered persons" for SEC purposes.

70. Answer: A

Tina is both a CFM and an Immediate Family Member (IFM) if we assume that she is dependent on her mother, which she probably is.

71. Answer: D

This relationship is permissible so long as Kim has no authority to make investment decisions for the trust.

72. Answer: D

All answer choices impair independence under SEC rules.

73. Answer: C

Auditors of public companies cannot provide any services to an audit client on a contingent fee basis.

74. Answer: A

In each of these three cases, the accounting firm is to describe in writing important issues surrounding the relationship, discuss those specifically with the audit committee, and document the discussion for posterity.

75. **Answer: B**

Because Omar is in a Financial Reporting Oversight Role and none of the exceptions appears to apply, he may not receive any tax services from Single.

76. **Answer: C**

Under GAGAS, auditors should never audit their own work, which is what is happening here. This creates an independence problem so severe that it cannot be remedied by application of supplemental safeguards.

77. **Answer: C**

This is a government entity, and no doubt an entity that receives federal funds, so in addition to the AICPA's Code of Professional Conduct, GAGAS and attendant independence rules will apply.

78. **Answer: B**

The potential impairment threat is external, stemming from the threatened firing.

79. **Answer: D**

Because all three of the initial choices (A, B, and C) are correct, the best answer is D.

80. **Answer: A**

Under DOL guidelines, many consulting services are permitted, but one cannot maintain independence while auditing records that one maintained in the first place.

81. **Answer: B**

Department of Labor rules allow audit firms to provide actuarial services to a plan without impairing independence.

82. **Answer: D**

Choices A and C would both be correct under the current AICPA Code of Professional Conduct as well, although B would not. But B is correct under DOL standards.

83. **Answer: C**

The auditor's primary role is to provide an impartial (independent) report on the reliability of management's financial statements. These financial statements are distributed to interested parties outside of the reporting entity itself, such as actual or potential shareholders and creditors, major customers

and suppliers, employees, regulators, and others for their decision-making (resource allocation) needs. Management prepares the financial statements and represents that they are in fact fairly presented while the auditor is auditing such representations.

84. **Answer: B**

The exercise of due professional care requires that a critical review of the work completed and the judgments made be performed at every level of supervision.

85. **Answer: A**

GAAS requires the auditor to obtain "sufficient appropriate audit evidence…"

86. **Answer: B**

GAAS requires auditors to have adequate technical training and proficiency in auditing.

87. **Answer: B**

Articles in the *Journal of Accountancy* have no authoritative status, and would be classified as *other auditing publications*.

88. **Answer: C**

The word *should* indicates a presumptively mandatory requirement.

89. **Answer: C**

The AICPA's *Statements on Quality Control Standards* emphasize four specific issues in making client acceptance/continuance decisions: (1) the integrity of management and those charged with governance; (2) the competence of the engagement team (including time and resources); (3) compliance with relevant ethical requirements (such as independence); and (4) significant issues from prior engagements that affect the continuing relationship. Evaluating the CPA's ability to properly service the client is associated with the competence of the engagement team, which is identified as an important consideration.

90. **Answer: C**

Quality control policies and procedures governing new client acceptance are established to minimize the likelihood of association with a client whose management lacks integrity. A firm should be selective in determining its professional relationships.

91. **Answer: B**

A firm is required to establish an appropriate system of quality control to provide reasonable assurance of conforming with professional standards.

92. **Answer: A**

A firm establishes a system of internal control in order to provide reasonable assurance that the professional services provided will conform to professional standards.

93. **Answer: D**

The AICPA's quality control standards are applicable to the CPA firm's portfolio of audit (and other financial statement related) services, which is consistent with this answer.

94. **Answer: B**

The audit work performed by each assistant should be reviewed for adequacy and to ensure that it supports the conclusions reached.

95. **Answer: C**

Substantive evidential matter required by the Principles may include evidence obtained through the performance of substantive analytical procedures (as well as that obtained through inspection, observation, inquiries, and confirmation). Analytical procedures performed as substantive tests can be used to provide substantive evidential matter.

96. **Answer: A**

The objective of the requirement is to prevent misinterpretations regarding the degree of responsibility the auditor is assuming when his name is associated with financial statements.

97. **Answer: B**

GAAS require an auditor to express an opinion on the financial statements. That responsibility is EXPLICITLY represented in the Auditor's Responsibility paragraphs of the auditor's unmodified report which states that the auditor's responsibility is to express an opinion.

98. **Answer: B**

The second sentence of the Auditor's Responsibility section states as follows: "We conducted our audits in accordance with auditing standards generally accepted in the United States of America."

99. **Answer: D**

The standard auditor's report on comparative financial statements states explicitly that evidence is obtained (and therefore examined) and implies that accounting principles have been consistently applied. Such application is assumed unless the report indicates otherwise.

100. **Answer: B**

The type of engagement described is a WebTrust assurance engagement. It is performed in accordance with the Statements on Standards for Attestation Engagements.

101. **Answer: A**

An attestation engagement is one in which the practitioner is engaged to issue an examination, a review, or an agreed-upon procedures report on subject matter or an assertion about subject matter that is the responsibility of another party.

102. **Answer: C**

Registered public accounting firms that audit more than 100 issuers must be inspected annually; those that audit 100 or fewer issuers must be inspected every three years. In this case, a registered public accounting firm that issues audit report to 50 issuers would be inspected every three years.

103. **Answer: A**

The FASB establishes accounting standards. PCAOB establishes auditing standards.

104. **Answer: B**

Title II of the Sarbanes-Oxley Act of 2002 establishes 5 years as the upper limit for how long someone can serve as the engagement partner or review partner before mandatory rotation is required.

105. **Answer: C**

The PCAOB is a standard-setting body for certain matters related to registered public accounting firms (including auditing and quality control, among other matters). However, the PCAOB is not an accounting standard-setting body and does not promulgate GAAP affecting the financial statements of issuers.

106. **Answer: C**

The PCAOB (specifically, AS Section 1220) identifies a number of differences relative to the AICPA's quality control standards, including those stated in the first, second, and last choices. However, the PCAOB requires the engagement quality review documentation to be retained along with (not separately from!) the related engagement documentation; and PCAOB auditing standards require such audit documentation to be retained for 7 years, not 10. Moreover, the AICPA's SQCS do not require that the engagement quality review documentation be retained along with the related audit documentation. Hence, C is correct.

107. **Answer: B**

The PCAOB (specifically, AS Section 1220) states: "An outside reviewer who is not already associated with a registered public accounting firm would become associated with the firm issuing the report if he or she . . . (1) receives compensation from the firm issuing the report for performing the review or (2) performs the review as agent for the firm issuing the report."

108. **Answer: A**

The PCAOB (specifically, AS Section 1220) identifies the following as "significant engagement deficiencies": when (1) the engagement team failed to obtain sufficient appropriate evidence; (2) the engagement team reached an inappropriate overall conclusion; (3) the engagement report is not appropriate; or (4) the firm is not independent of its client. Since B, C, and D are specifically identified as significant engagement deficiencies, A is the correct answer. If management's accounting estimates are unreasonable, it constitutes a GAAP departure, not a deficiency in the performance of the audit engagement.

109. **Answer: A**

The initiative belongs to Hill, the successor auditor. When an auditor has been retained to audit the financial statements of an entity, the auditor contacts the predecessor auditor to obtain information about matters that may affect the conduct of the audit and to review the prior year audit documentation. The successor auditor should contact the predecessor auditor prior to final acceptance of the engagement.

110. **Answer: D**

A CPA would not accept a client who was unwilling to make all financial records available. Access to all financial records would be a minimum requirement for the audit, and management is required to state in the management representation letter that all financial records and data have been made available to the auditors.

111. **Answer: A**

The engagement letter would typically refer to:

1. the objective of the audit;
2. management's responsibilities for the financial statements, for internal control over financial reporting, and for compliance with laws and regulations;
3. availability of financial records;
4. representation letter;
5. auditor's responsibilities;
6. components of an audit; and
7. correction of misstatements.

112. **Answer: C**

Management integrity via the control environment sets the tone of an organization and provides the foundation for all other components of internal control. An inherent limitation of an internal control structure is the possibility of management override. Thus, the lack of management integrity can impact the audit in terms of the occurrence of both employee and management errors and irregularities. If the auditor believes that management lacks integrity, the risk that material misstatements might not be discovered becomes unacceptably high. As a result, the auditor would probably decide not to accept the engagement.

113. **Answer: A**

The engagement letter identifies the respective responsibilities of the entity and the auditor, and essentially constitutes the contract between the parties. It is customary for the engagement letter to address fee-related issues.

114. **Answer: A**

An auditor would consider whether material misstatements exist if supporting records that should be readily available are frequently not produced when requested. This could indicate a lack of internal control and the possibility of management misrepresentation which, in turn, could indicate an opportunity for material misstatements to be present.

115. **Answer: C**

In planning an audit, an auditor would coordinate client assistance to be rendered, discuss matters that may affect the audit with consulting and tax staff, and read the current year's interim financial statements. The auditor would not select a sample of vendors' invoices for comparison to receiving reports as this is a substantive evidence-gathering procedure, not a planning procedure.

116. **Answer: A**

In planning the overall audit strategy and designing the written audit plan, the auditor should consider materiality for the financial statements taken as a whole.

117. **Answer: B**

ANY client-imposed scope limitation is a problem. When you add that problem to the greater risk arising from a new client, you have greatly increased the risk related to the new engagement. A new client, by definition, is a client that will require more time to study and understand in order to perform the audit. If the client is also telling the auditors that certain audit procedures will not be allowed, the risk of missing a material misstatement becomes very high.

118. **Answer: A**

The auditor is required to obtain an understanding of the entity's environment, including internal control sufficient to plan the audit. Risk assessment is one of the five components of the internal control structure. Obtaining an understanding of the entity's risk assessment process would be part of obtaining an understanding of internal control.

119. **Answer: C**

Materiality refers to a cutoff amount for a misstatement over which the financial statements would be unfairly presented. In determining this amount, out of the choices given, the most likely source is the prior year financial statements. The statements would provide the auditor with the most information to use in setting materiality.

120. **Answer: B**

In order to issue an unqualified opinion, the auditor must be confident that no material misstatements exist in the financial statements. While misstatements may exist, in total they must be believed to be less than a material amount.

121. **Answer: C**

When planning a sample for a substantive test of details, the auditor's consideration of tolerable misstatement for the sample would be related to the preliminary judgment of materiality. The auditor determines the nature, timing, and extent of auditing procedures to be applied in order to obtain reasonable assurance of detecting material misstatements in the financial statements.

122. **Answer: A**

$10,000.

123. **Answer: A**

The auditor is allowed to "pass" on aggregated errors that are not material. This analysis and conclusion must be documented in the audit documentation.

124. **Answer: C**

Performing substantive tests at an interim date increases the risk that misstatements that exist at the balance sheet date will not be detected by the auditor. Evidence collected at an interim date is therefore less strong than evidence collected at year end. Increasing detection risk means that the auditor can obtain less or weaker evidence. As a result, the auditor may be able to push the timing of substantive tests from year end to an interim date.

125. **Answer: C**

Inherent risk and control risk are environmental risks pertaining to the client. They are assessed by the auditor and exist independently of the financial statement audit. Detection risk is the only risk controllable by the auditor. It relates to the auditor's procedures and can be changed by the auditor.

126. **Answer: A**

Detection risk is inversely related to the assurance provided by substantive tests. The lower the detection risk, the more assurance needed from substantive testing.

127. **Answer: B**

When the level of tolerable misstatements decreases, the auditor will have to increase substantive testing to ensure that all material misstatements are detected. Performing the planned auditing procedures closer to the balance sheet date increases the effectiveness of substantive procedures and thus increases substantive testing.

128. **Answer: C**

An increase in the assessed level of control risk means that the risk of a material misstatement occurring and not being detected has increased. To offset that increased risk, the auditor should make decisions that decrease the level of detection risk. Increasing the emphasis on tests of details would decrease detection risk.

129. **Answer: C**

Analytical procedures are required during planning and in the final review stage. They may be, but are not required to be, used as substantive tests.

130. **Answer: C**

Analytical procedures are used in the overall review stage to assess the audit conclusions reached and to evaluate the overall financial statement presentation. Such procedures generally may include considering the adequacy of the evidence gathered to address unusual or unexpected balances identified during planning, and considering unusual or unexpected balances not previously identified.

131. **Answer: B**

Analytical procedures used in planning the audit should focus on:
1) enhancing the auditor's understanding of the client's business and the transactions and events that have occurred since the last audit; and
2) identifying areas of specific risk to the audit.

132. **Answer: B**

This answer can be selected by a process of elimination. Analytical procedures involve the comparison of recorded amounts, or ratios developed from recorded amounts, to expectations developed by the auditor. Projecting an error rate by comparing the results of a statistical sample with the actual population characteristics does NOT involve a comparison between an auditor expectation and a recorded balance, and would not be considered an analytical procedure. If you considered the error rate to be part of a test of control effort, then clearly it is not an analytical procedure. If you considered the error rate to be part of a substantive procedure intended to verify the validity of an account balance then it would be classified as a substantive test of details, not an analytical procedure.

133. **Answer: C**

Analytical procedures assume that plausible relationships among data may reasonably be expected to exist and continue in the absence of known conditions to the contrary. For this reason, data can be used to predict future balances against which recorded balances may be compared.

134. **Answer: D**

The auditor is required to design the audit to provide reasonable assurance of detecting material misstatements in the financial statements. This is done by first assessing the risk that errors and irregularities resulting in material misstatements in the financial statements may occur and then identifying the auditing procedures to be performed that will provide reasonable assurance that such misstatements have been identified.

135. **Answer: D**

Professional Standards emphasize the importance of "professional skepticism" when considering fraud-related risks. Professional skepticism is described as "... an attitude that includes a questioning mind and a critical assessment of audit evidence."

136. **Answer: D**

The substantial increase in sales in year 1 and substantial decrease in sales in year 2 is consistent with earnings management that might be associated with financial reporting fraud.

137. **Answer: A**

Risk factors associated with opportunities to misappropriate assets include easily convertible assets, such as bearer bonds.

138. **Answer: D**

The risk of fraudulent financial reporting is heightened by the existence of an overly complex organizational structure involving unusual lines of authority. This type of structure would make it easier to override internal controls to materially misstate the financial statements.

139. Answer: D

The existence of irregularities (fraud) is considered to be a severe problem in an audit due to potential ramifications for other areas of the audit. As a result, the auditor has a duty to disclose irregularities to the SEC when the client reports an auditor change, to a successor auditor when the successor makes appropriate inquiries, and to a government funding agency from which the client receives financial assistance.

140. Answer: B

Doesn't this immediately raise questions?! Why would payments be made to government employees, especially unexplained payments? They sound like bribes.

141. Answer: C

The auditor may decide that withdrawal is necessary when the client fails to take the remedial action considered necessary. This failure may indicate a greater problem with the control environment and overall governance. As a result, it may affect the auditor's ability to rely on management representations as well as the relationship with the client going forward.

142. Answer: B

Large checks payable to cash would be most likely to raise questions regarding possible illegal acts. Valid company disbursements are typically made by check and controlled through accounts payable. Cash payments are unusual and difficult to control. As a result, large checks payable to cash would present a red flag during the audit.

143. Answer: B

The auditor's report may refer to the specialist if the opinion is modified as a result of the specialist's findings by adding a separate paragraph to explain the reason(s) for the modified opinion. Reference, otherwise, is not allowed as it may imply that a more thorough audit was performed than an audit that did not result in such a reference.

144. Answer: D

The auditor should obtain an understanding of the specialist's field of expertise sufficient to enable determination of the nature, objectives, and scope of the specialist's work and evaluation of the adequacy of that work. This includes obtaining an understanding of the significant assumptions and methods used by the specialist.

145. Answer: A

When using a specialist, in general, the auditor is obligated to obtain an understanding of the work to be performed by the specialist, including the nature, objectives, and scope of the specialist's work.

146. Answer: C

AICPA Professional Standards indicate that reference to the work of a specialist may be made in the auditor's report if the auditor believes such reference will facilitate an understanding of the reason for a modified opinion.

147. Answer: B

The auditor is required to gain an understanding of the relationship and assess the risk that the actuary's objectivity might be impaired. Impairment might occur when the client has the ability to directly, or indirectly, control or significantly influence the actuary.

148. Answer: A

The auditor is required to communicate both significant audit adjustments and changes in significant accounting policies to the audit committee (or those charged with governance). Both would be included under significant findings from the audit.

149. Answer: A

The auditor is required to communicate with the audit committee about the following: the auditor's responsibilities under GAAS, significant accounting policies, management judgments and accounting estimates, significant audit adjustments (resolved and unresolved, other information in documents containing audited financial statements, disagreements with management, consultation with other accountants, and difficulties encountered in performing the audit.

150. Answer: C

The auditor is required to report to the audit committee on both disagreements with management about matters significant to the entity's financial statements that have been satisfactorily resolved and "significant findings from the audit," including the auditor's views about qualitative aspects of the entity's significant accounting practices, including accounting policies, accounting estimates, and financial statement disclosures.

151. **Answer: C**

The auditor is required to communicate disagreements with management to those charged with governance that arose during the audit about matters that are individually or in the aggregate significant to the financial statements or the auditor's report.

152. **Answer: B**

The maximum dollar amount of misstatements, that could exist without causing the financial statements to be materially misstated, is an auditor judgment. The auditor's determination of materiality levels is generally NOT discussed with the audit committee.

153. **Answer: A**

PCAOB AS Section 1301 identifies the following four objectives: (1) communicate to the audit committee the auditor's responsibilities and establish an understanding of the terms of the engagement; (2) obtain information from the audit committee relevant to the audit; (3) communicate to the audit committee information about the strategy and timing of the audit; and (4) provide the audit committee with timely observations about significant audit matters. These objectives do not include enhancing communications between the audit committee and the entity's internal audit function.

154. **Answer: C**

Although the auditor would discuss with the audit committee the qualitative aspects of the entity's significant accounting policies (and any indications of management bias), those matters would be discussed at the end of the audit.

155. **Answer: D**

Unless otherwise specified, the communication may be written or oral. (For example, an engagement letter obviously must be in writing.) The PCAOB requires that the communication be timely and prior to the issuance of the auditor's report.

156. **Answer: D**

If the auditor has concluded that an account is immaterial and that inherent risk is low, the auditor might decide to skip the procedures used to obtain an understanding of the related internal controls because the risk of a material misstatement occurring is low. This is really a rather tricky question because GAAS require the auditor to obtain an understanding of the internal control structure sufficient to plan the audit. In the case of immateriality combined with low inherent risk, the auditor does not need to understand the internal controls specifically related to the account in order to plan the audit.

157. **Answer: D**

A flowchart is a pictorial representation that utilizes a standard set of symbols to demonstrate the transaction processing procedures and accompanying data flow in an information system. It enables the auditor to summarize his/her understanding of the system in a clear, concise, and logical manner.

158. **Answer: B**

Obtaining an understanding of an entity's internal controls over financial reporting involves evaluating the design of relevant controls and determining whether they have been implemented (sometimes referred to as "placed into operation").

159. **Answer: B**

Internal controls may have been placed in operation, yet may not be effective because they are not properly acted upon. The auditor is concerned about the effectiveness of the control and its ability to prevent or detect material misstatements in the financial statements. As a result, the auditor must focus on the substance of the control rather than the form.

160. **Answer: D**

The auditor is primarily interested in whether an entity's internal controls affect the financial statement assertions. Specifically, the auditor is interested in the policies and procedures that pertain to an entity's ability to record, process, summarize, and report financial data consistent with the assertions embodied in the financial statements.

161. **Answer: B**

The auditor would decide that an audit could not be conducted if management integrity were questioned. Management integrity is such a critical component of an effective internal control environment that the suspected lack thereof would be cause for the auditor to withdraw from the engagement.

162. **Answer: A**

After obtaining an understanding of internal control and assessing control risk, an auditor will perform tests of controls, if it is believed that such performance will result in a reduction in planned substantive tests. If the performance of tests of controls would not result in a reduction in substantive testing, completing tests of controls would be inefficient and therefore should not be performed.

163. **Answer: C**

Follow-up on errors reported by customers provides evidence that the customers exist and that the receivables are valid; i.e., that the client has the rights to the assets. The auditor's test of controls thus provides evidence to support the assertion of rights and obligations. It does not address presentation and disclosure.

164. **Answer: D**

The auditor assesses control risk (the risk that the internal control structure will not prevent or detect a material misstatement) and inherent risk (the risk of a material misstatement occurring) in order to determine the acceptable level of detection risk.

165. **Answer: B**

The control environment sets the tone of an organization, influencing the control consciousness of its people. It includes the following factors: integrity and ethical values, commitment to competence, board of directors or audit committee participation, management's philosophy and operating style, organizational structure, assignment of authority and responsibility, and human resource policies and practices. The development of personnel manuals documenting employee promotion and training policies is a component of human resource policies and practices.

166. **Answer: B**

Segregation of duties and similar controls which lack documentation of their functioning are best tested through observation and inquiry.

167. **Answer: A**

The auditor may assess control risk at maximum for some assertions if he/she believes that the internal controls are not effective. If they are not effective, they cannot be relied upon to reduce substantive testing. Control risk, therefore, may be assessed at maximum and more emphasis placed on substantive testing.

168. **Answer: D**

Closer management oversight directed specifically at such incompatible activities would be an effective approach in mitigating the risks involved.

169. **Answer: C**

COSO's Internal Control Integrated Framework identifies five components of an internal control system: (1) control environment; (2) risk assessment; (3) control activities; (4) information and communication system; and (5) monitoring. Accordingly, inherent risk is not one of those components.

170. **Answer: C**

When evidence is available only in electronic form, the auditor may find that generalized audit software is the best and most efficient means of extracting evidence from client databases. Generalized audit software consists of programs that enable an auditor to perform tests on client computer files and databases.

171. **Answer: D**

The auditor would conclude that a financial audit could not be performed if he/she determined that a substantial risk of intentional misapplication of accounting principles existed. The key word is "intentional" as the risk of management override is an inherent limitation of any internal control system. Management can override the system to make material misstatements in the financial statements and the auditors may not be able to detect such entries. If management is believed to be intentionally misapplying accounting principles, the financial statements are likely to contain material misstatements that may be extremely difficult, if not impossible, to detect. Thus, the auditors would withdraw from the engagement.

172. **Answer: D**

The objective of tests of details of transactions performed as tests of controls is to evaluate whether internal controls operated effectively. A test of details of transactions performed as a test of control will enable the auditor to detect a control failure.

173. **Answer: B**

Inquiry and observation may be useful in evaluating the effectiveness of internal controls, including those that are undocumented.

174. Answer: B

The auditor must always document his/her understanding of the entity's internal control components as well as the basis for assessing control risk below maximum.

175. Answer: D

Professional standards define "material weaknesses" and "significant deficiencies," and provide a sample written communication about internal control matters noted in an audit that separately reports material weaknesses and significant deficiencies if both categories of deficiencies have been identified in an audit of an entity's financial statements.

176. Answer: A

Letters on significant deficiencies are restricted as to distribution. The letters are intended solely for the use of the audit committee (or those charged with governance), management, and others within the organization.

177. Answer: C

Significant deficiencies should be reported to the audit committee because they are significant deficiencies in the design or operation of internal control that could adversely affect the entity's financial reporting process.

178. Answer: C

A significant deficiency is a control deficiency in the design or operation of internal control that can adversely affect the financial statements. If those responsible for accounting decisions appear to lack objectivity, the resultant accounting decisions may result in material misstatements of the financial statements. For example, revenue recognition decisions might be made to increase current period net income (and managerial bonuses).

179. Answer: B

An auditor is not allowed to issue a report indicating that no significant deficiencies were found. Such a report might be misinterpreted.

180. Answer: A

The independent auditor will place only limited reliance on the work performed by the internal auditors because of their lack of independence. While internal auditors can never be fully independent, a greater level of relative independence is obtained when they report to the board of directors or the audit committee.

181. Answer: B

AICPA Professional Standards indicate that the auditor should assess the competence and objectivity of the internal audit function if the internal auditors' work is considered relevant to planning the audit. The independent auditor would consider the quality of the internal auditor's work products, including documentation, among other matters, in evaluating the internal auditor's competence.

182. Answer: C

Some of the work performed by internal auditors may provide direct evidence about material misstatements in assertions. As a result, the auditor may be able to rely upon such work and reduce the nature, timing, or extent of the auditing procedures to be performed related to those assertions. Internal audit work pertaining to the existence of fixed asset additions would provide direct evidence which could be used to restrict other audit work to be performed.

183. Answer: D

Analytical procedures are performed to aid in the detection of unusual transactions, as substantive procedures, and to aid in the overall review of the financial statements. The results of such procedures would not provide evidence which would aid the independent auditor in assessing the competence and objectivity of the internal auditors.

184. Answer: C

An independent auditor may NOT share responsibility with an internal auditor in any audit judgment area, regardless of the internal auditor's competence and objectivity. The internal auditor's work may be considered by the independent auditor in obtaining an understanding of the internal control structure or as evidence about material misstatements. Final judgments, however, must always be made by the independent auditor.

185. Answer: A

If the auditor is concerned that invoices and vouchers are being paid and destroyed, the most appropriate population for testing is cash disbursements. The auditor would select a sample of inventory disbursements and trace to the vendor invoice, approved voucher, and receiving report.

186. Answer: D

Segregation of duties involves the separation of the responsibilities of authorizing transactions, recording transactions, and maintaining custody of assets. It is intended to reduce the opportunities for any person to be in a position to both perpetrate and conceal errors or irregularities in the normal course of his/her duties.

187. Answer: A

To assure that all billed sales are correctly posted to the accounts receivable ledger, the auditor should start with the population of billed sales. The daily sales summaries will provide evidence of the population of billed sales. A comparison then of the daily sales summaries to the daily postings to the accounts receivable ledger will provide assurance that all billed sales are correctly posted to the accounts receivable ledger.

188. Answer: D

The procedure most UNlikely to be an internal control designed to reduce the risk of errors in the billing process is reconciling the control totals for sales invoices with the accounts receivable subsidiary ledger. This reconciliation ensures that sales invoices are completely and accurately posted to the accounts receivable subsidiary ledger. It would not minimize errors in the billing process.

189. Answer: A

Tracing bills of lading to sales invoices provides evidence that shipments to customers were invoiced. It is a test of the completeness assertion.

190. Answer: C

Effective internal controls include adequate segregation of duties. The failure to separate authorization of credit memos from cash handling is a segregation of duties failure in the revenue cycle.

191. Answer: B

Defective merchandise returned by customers should be presented initially to the receiving clerk. The function of the receiving department is to receive and inspect goods and to document the receipt in the form of a receiving report.

192. Answer: C

Adequate segregation of duties provides for the separation of authorizing, recording, and custodial duties. Receiving remittances from the mailroom is a custodial duty. It may properly be combined with preparation of the daily deposit slip which would also require custody of the asset.

193. Answer: C

The greatest risk for checks received in the mail is the risk of such checks being lost or misappropriated. Sound internal control, therefore, dictates the preparation of a listing of checks received as soon as possible.

194. Answer: C

Lapping occurs when a remittance received from one customer is stolen and the shortage is hidden by crediting the first customer's account with the cash received from a second customer. Lapping is best prevented by separating custody from recording. The person responsible for receiving cash should not also be responsible for posting the amounts to the accounts receivable subsidiary ledger.

195. Answer: B

An auditor would suspect material misstatements to be present if differences between reconciliations of control accounts and subsidiary records were not investigated. Such differences should be investigated and corrected to ensure that control accounts and subsidiary records agree. Without this control procedure material misstatements may exist in the form of differences between the control accounts and subsidiary records.

196. Answer: B

Fidelity bonding insures the company against loss from illegal acts by employees. Bonded employees must be approved by the bonding company and claims filed against the bonding company are investigated before settlement occurs. As a result, fidelity bonding reduces the possibility of employing dishonest individuals and deters dishonesty by making employees aware that insurance companies may investigate and prosecute dishonest acts.

197. **Answer: D**

Adequate segregation of duties requires that authorization, custodial, and recordkeeping functions be separated. An employee who mails disbursement checks and remittance advices has custodial responsibilities. That same employee should not approve vouchers for payment (authorization); match the receiving reports, purchase orders, and vendors' invoices (authorization); or maintain possession of the check-signing device (conflicting custodial). The checks should be mailed by the employee who signs the checks last to prevent tampering with the signed checks.

198. **Answer: C**

An effective procedure to prevent duplicate payments is to cancel the documentation supporting the payment request at the time payment is made. For example, by stamping the documents as "paid."

199. **Answer: B**

A debit memo advises accounting that the vendor invoice should not be paid in full due to returned goods. When the shipping department returns nonconforming goods to a vendor, purchasing should send accounting a debit memo.

200. **Answer: D**

Approval of purchase orders and negotiation of terms with vendors are both authorization functions which are properly performed by employees in the purchasing department.

201. **Answer: C**

Allowing the bookkeeper to have access to the accounting records and to the signature plates, which effectively enables the bookkeeper to initiate unauthorized transactions, while also having responsibility for preparing the monthly bank reconciliations is an improper segregation of duties.

202. **Answer: D**

The approval of employee hours by the departmental supervisor is a control which helps to ensure that only hours worked are paid. This reduces the chance that employees will submit hours that were not actually worked or were unauthorized.

203. **Answer: D**

The approval of time cards by supervisors helps to ensure that payment is made only for work performed. The supervisor's approval indicates that the employee has indeed worked the hours indicated on the time card. The approved hours per the time card will then be paid. Thus, payment is made only for work performed.

204. **Answer: A**

An understanding of the internal control structure is usually obtained by performing such procedures as inquiries of management and staff, inspection of documents and records, and observation of activities and operations. In obtaining an understanding of internal controls pertaining to inventory, an auditor most likely would review the entity's descriptions of inventory policies and procedures.

205. **Answer: B**

The safeguarding of inventory most likely includes periodic reconciliation of detailed inventory records with the actual inventory on hand by taking a physical count. In order to safeguard inventory, you need to check periodically to ascertain whether you have physical possession of the inventory you have recorded.

206. **Answer: B**

Management's objectives in establishing and maintaining an internal control structure are to ensure that: 1) transactions are executed in accordance with management's general or specific authorization; 2) transactions are recorded as necessary to permit preparation of the financial statements in accordance with GAAP and to maintain accountability for assets; 3) access to assets is permitted only in accordance with management's authorization; and 4) the recorded accountability for assets is compared with the existing assets at reasonable intervals and differences are investigated and resolved. Ensuring that custody of work in process and of finished goods is properly maintained is an example of the third objective.

207. **Answer: C**

Misclassification of equipment acquisitions as maintenance expenses would most likely be detected through investigation of variances. Equipment acquisitions tend to be large dollar purchases which would distort normal maintenance expenses and thus create variances. Investigation of the variances would then reveal the misclassification.

208. **Answer: C**

The assessment of control risk at a low level requires that the auditor provide the basis for reducing the assessment. The basis is provided by performing tests of controls and documenting the results which support a lowered control risk assessment. In turn, the low control risk assessment enables the auditor to reduce the amount of substantive testing in that area, thus limiting the testing of current year property and equipment transactions.

209. **Answer: A**

Analytical procedures are defined as "evaluations of financial information through analysis of plausible relationships among both financial and nonfinancial data." That definition encompasses evaluating the current-year balances by comparing them to prior-year balances for reasonableness.

210. **Answer: C**

The auditor would seek to obtain the additional evidence needed to support the valuation of inventory.

211. **Answer: C**

This ratio is called "inventory turnover," which is a traditional ratio that is useful in evaluating whether inventory might be slow-moving. In that event, inventory might need to be written down to better reflect the estimated future benefits. This might be appropriately considered in the partner's review.

212. **Answer: C**

The factor most likely to influence an auditor's determination of the auditability of an entity's financial statements is the adequacy of the accounting records. The lack of adequate accounting records is a scope limitation which could prevent the auditor from obtaining sufficient evidence to render an opinion.

213. **Answer: A**

As the risk of material misstatement increases, the auditor should decrease detection risk accordingly. The auditor may lower detection risk by increasing the extent of substantive procedures (e.g., by increasing sample sizes).

214. **Answer: C**

Follow-up on errors reported by customers provides evidence that the customers exist and

that the receivables are valid; i.e., that the client has the rights to the assets. The auditor's test of controls thus provides evidence to support the assertion of rights and obligations. It does not address presentation and disclosure.

215. **Answer: C**

There are 4 assertions applicable to account balances at the period end: (1) existence; (2) completeness; (3) rights or obligations; and (4) valuation and allocation.

216. **Answer: D**

Bank statements obtained directly from the financial institution would provide the most reliable evidence as they were obtained from an independent source outside the client.

217. **Answer: B**

The completeness assertion for long-term investments addresses the proper inclusion of all long-term investments. An internal control satisfying the completeness assertion would compare the securities on hand with those recorded to ensure that all recorded securities held were actually held.

218. **Answer: C**

Greater reliability (and thus, persuasiveness) is achieved from evidence obtained from sources outside the entity, even when that evidence is obtained from the client.

219. **Answer: C**

This is a test of controls. The auditor is verifying that segregation of duties exists and is operating effectively.

220. **Answer: D**

The auditor should consider whether the assessments of the risks of material misstatement at the relevant assertion level in engagement planning are appropriate in light of the auditor's substantive procedures.

221. **Answer: C**

Audit procedures should be responsive to the auditor's assessment of the risks of material misstatement. The specific procedures that are appropriate in the circumstances is a matter of professional judgment.

222. **Answer: A**

The cardinal rule regarding cash receipts is to ensure that they are recorded. By requiring employees to record all sales in the cash register and to give customers the cash register tape evidencing the sale, companies can ensure that all cash sales are recorded (the completeness of cash receipts for cash sales.) The auditor can test controls by observing employees' use of cash registers and tapes.

223. **Answer: D**

During the overall review stage, the auditor assesses the conclusions reached and the evaluation of the overall financial statement presentation. As part of that evaluation, he/she would consider whether the results of the audit procedures performed affect the risk of material misstatement due to fraud. The overall review would include considering the adequacy of the evidence gathered in response to unusual or unexpected balances and whether such balances reflected a misstatement due to fraud.

224. **Answer: C**

"Cutoff" was not identified as one of five financial assertions discussed by the PCAOB. The AICPA's risk assessment standards identify 13 assertions across three categories of assertions. And one of those is "cutoff," which is included among the assertions associated with "transactions or events during the period."

225. **Answer: B**

The word "could" does not indicate a professional requirement. Instead, it indicates an audit consideration that is based on the auditor's professional judgment.

226. **Answer: A**

The auditor should incorporate a degree of unpredictability in planning audit procedures, but this is considered an "overall response" to the risks of material misstatement, not a "risk assessment procedure."

227. **Answer: C**

The auditor should not divulge to management the specific levels of materiality used or the materiality levels allocated to individual elements of the financial statements. So obtaining such agreement would not be appropriate.

228. **Answer: A**

AICPA Professional Standards describe the term "judgmental misstatement" as follows: "differences in estimates, such as a difference in a fair value estimate" (AU-C 450. A11).

229. **Answer: B**

The auditor should request management to correct (non-trivial) identified factual misstatements.

230. **Answer: A**

The definition of judgmental misstatements includes unreasonable accounting estimates (as well as the selection of inappropriate accounting policies).

231. **Answer: C**

Differences between management and the auditor in making judgments about accounting estimates are included in the definition of judgmental misstatements and would not normally be included among known misstatements.

232. **Answer: C**

The working trial balance would NOT appear in the permanent file. It is normally included in the current year audit documentation.

233. **Answer: B**

GAAS require that a written audit program be prepared that details the audit procedures considered necessary to achieve the objectives of the audit.

234. **Answer: A**

As the assessed level of control risk increases (decreases), the acceptable level of detection risk decreases (increases) and the nature, timing, and extent of the audit work performed and the related documentation are altered.

235. **Answer: A**

Notes receivable and interest income would most likely be analyzed on the same working paper as they are directly related to each other. Interest income is earned on notes receivable and is a function of the interest rate and the principal balances on the notes.

236. **Answer: A**

Audit documentation serves mainly to provide the principal support for the opinion rendered in the auditor's report. It also aids the auditor in the conduct and supervision of the audit.

237. Answer: C

PCAOB auditing standards specify a 7-year retention period for audit documentation.

238. Answer: B

PCAOB auditing standards specify a documentation completion date of no more than 45 days following the report release date.

239. Answer: B

PCAOB Auditing Standards state that additional documentation can be added after the documentation completion date (which requires further documentation of the reasons why, etc.), but nothing can be deleted after that date.

240. Answer: A

Using the blank form of confirmation of accounts receivable provides greater assurance that the recipient of the confirmation has verified that the information is correct. It is more likely to be used when the auditor is concerned that recipients will not devote proper attention to the confirmations.

241. Answer: D

The use of negative accounts receivable confirmations requires: 1) a low risk of material misstatement; 2) a large number of small balances; and 3) an expected very low exception rate; 4) no reason to believe that the recipients of the confirmations would not review them properly. Having a small number of accounts in dispute and an accounts receivable balance arising from sales to many customers with small balances meets two of the fourthree criteria and would be more likely to justify the use of negative confirmations.

242. Answer: A

When negative confirmations are used, the respondent is asked to return the request only if there is a problem or error in the balance. Thus, it is assumed that the balances are correct unless the confirmation is returned. Unreturned negative confirmation requests, therefore, are considered to be evidence. This evidence is implied, it is not explicit.

243. Answer: C

AICPA Professional Standards indicate that using blank confirmation requests may provide a greater degree of assurance about the information confirmed because of the need to fill in the amount. However, blank forms might also result in lower response rates because additional effort is required of the recipients. When lower response rates occur, the auditor may have to perform more alternative procedures making the confirmation effort less efficient.

244. Answer: D

The auditor would be more likely to confirm certain relevant contract terms as the risk of material misstatement increases. In this case, the risk of material misstatement is said to be "high," which is consistent with the need to perform additional procedures to address revenue-recognition issues.

245. Answer: A

This question focuses on something that would be a "concern" to the auditor about an accounting estimate. To the extent that the estimate is potentially biased (e.g., perhaps management has a lot of latitude in determining the resulting estimate), the auditor would be concerned about the reasonableness of that estimate.

246. Answer: D

In evaluating management's accounting estimates for reasonableness, the auditor must first obtain an understanding of how management developed the estimate. While this approach is cited in the Standards, common sense should also tell you that you must first understand how the estimate was created.

247. Answer: A

AICPA Professional Standards indicate that the auditor is responsible for evaluating the reasonableness of accounting estimates made by management in the context of the applicable financial reporting framework.

248. Answer: D

In evaluating the reasonableness of an accounting estimate, an auditor concentrates on key factors and assumptions that are:

1. significant to the accounting estimate;
2. sensitive to variations;
3. deviations from historical patterns; and
4. subjective and susceptible to misstatement and bias.

249. **Answer: D**

The auditor must evaluate the reasonableness of the accounting estimates made by management. Because of their nature, such estimates are subject to bias, even when the estimation process involves the use of relevant and reliable data and competent personnel.

250. **Answer: C**

This is not an accurate characterization of the auditor's responsibilities. The decision to engage a specialist is a matter of professional judgment. The auditor may have the necessary skill and knowledge to audit fair values or may decide to use a specialist.

251. **Answer: A**

The auditor will consider whether or not the nature of significant assumptions used in fair value measurements, the degree of subjectivity involved in the development of the assumptions, and the relative materiality of the items being measured at fair value need to be communicated to those charged with governance.

252. **Answer: B**

The decision to engage a specialist is an auditor judgment, not a management decision.

253. **Answer: B**

The refusal of a client's attorney to provide information requested in an inquiry letter is considered a limitation on the scope of the audit. It would result in a disclaimer or a qualified opinion.

254. **Answer: B**

The auditor would NOT confirm with the attorney that ALL claims have been recorded in the financial statements. All claims do not require recording and the attorney would not have knowledge of what had been recorded in the financial statements.

255. **Answer: C**

Management is the primary source of information about litigation, claims, and assessments. The information provided by management is corroborated by the client's lawyer.

256. **Answer: D**

A taxing authority could impose an assessment on an entity related to tax matters. The auditor might then identify the existence of such an assessment by reviewing correspondence between the entity and the taxing authority.

257. **Answer: A**

The client and the auditor should reach an understanding about materiality. This understanding is then communicated to the attorney who will limit his/her response accordingly.

258. **Answer: B**

The management representation letter should address all periods covered by the auditor's report. Key's management representation letter, therefore, should cover the two periods being audited up through the date of the report, i.e., from January 1, 2005, through May 1, 2007. This requirement exists even if management was not present during all periods covered by the auditor's report.

259. **Answer: B**

The management representations letter typically includes a comment along the following lines: "We have provided you with access to all information, of which we are aware that is relevant to the preparation and fair presentation of the financial statements such as records, documentation and other matters, and additional information that you have requested from us for the purpose of the audit." The foregoing passage encompasses the completeness and availability of all minutes of any meetings of stockholders and the board of directors.

260. **Answer: A**

This is a required item in the management representation letter. Management must acknowledge its responsibility for the design and implementation of programs and controls to prevent and detect fraud.

261. **Answer: C**

A management representation letter is obtained by the auditor to reduce the possibility of a misunderstanding concerning management's responsibility for the financial statements and to document the representations made by management during the course of the audit.

262. **Answer: C**

The auditor is concerned with events occurring through the date of the report that might impact the financial statements. Therefore, the management representation letter should be dated with the date of the auditor's report.

263. **Answer: D**

   GAAP focuses on providing full disclosure of related party issues, so the auditor places primary emphasis on evaluating the adequacy of disclosure of such transactions.

264. **Answer: C**

   After determining that a related party transaction has occurred, the auditor should obtain an understanding of the business purpose of the transaction. The auditor should apply the procedures considered necessary to determine the purpose, nature, and extent of the related party transactions and their effects on the financial statements.

265. **Answer: C**

   Reviewing confirmation of loans receivable and payable for indications of guarantees is one of the auditing procedures that will assist the auditor in identifying related party transactions.

266. **Answer: C**

   Transactions considered to indicate the existence of related parties include making loans with no scheduled terms for repayment of the funds. Such terms, or the lack thereof, appear more favorable than loans made independently between unrelated parties.

267. **Answer: C**

   The auditor's primary concern with regard to related party transactions is disclosure. After identifying related party transactions, the auditor should examine the transactions in order to determine the purpose, nature, and extent of the transactions and their effects on the financial statements. In that process, the auditor would look to see if the transactions were properly authorized by the board of directors.

268. **Answer: C**

   PCAOB auditing standards (specifically, AS Section 2410) state that the auditor should consider a qualified or adverse opinion under such circumstances.

269. **Answer: C**

   The PCAOB requires the auditor to obtain an understanding of the company's process for the following: (1) identifying related parties and transactions with related parties; (2) authorizing and approving transactions with related parties; and (3) accounting for and disclosing relationships and transactions with related parties

in the financial statements. There is no reason to expect that related-party transactions will have terms substantially equivalent to those associated with transactions with unrelated parties.

270. **Answer: B**

   The PCAOB does not require the auditor to communicate with the audit committee about management's justification for engaging in transactions with a related party instead of with an unrelated party. Indeed, the company should have an appropriate process established to authorize and approve transactions with related parties, which presumably informs the audit committee as necessary.

271. **Answer: B**

   When a subsequent event disclosed in the financial statements occurs after audit report date but before release of the report, the auditor may elect to dual date his/her report. In doing so, the auditor is limiting responsibility for events occurring subsequent to the audit report date to the specific event referenced.

272. **Answer: D**

   The auditor should inquire with management as to whether there was any significant change in capital stock, long-term debt, or working capital after year end.

273. **Answer: A**

   The auditor may not have to perform the omitted confirmation procedures if alternative (redundant) procedures compensate for the omission and limit audit risk to an acceptably low level.

274. **Answer: D**

   To obtain evidence about the occurrence of subsequent events, the auditor most likely would inquire as to whether any unusual adjustments were made after year end.

275. **Answer: D**

   The occurrence of a natural disaster ten days after the balance sheet date which results in a material loss is an example of a Type II subsequent event. A Type II event pertains to conditions that arose subsequent to the balance sheet date and therefore do not require adjustment of the financial statements. Such events must, however, be disclosed if they are of such a nature that disclosure is necessary in order to keep the financial statements from being misleading. No report modification is necessary.

276. Answer: C

In evaluating management's plans to deal with the adverse effects of conditions and events, the auditor may appropriately consider the feasibility of management's plans for disposal of certain assets.

277. Answer: B

GAAS indicate that it is not necessary to design procedures solely directed toward an entity's going concern capabilities. Auditing procedures designed for other purposes may also be used to investigate potential going concern issues. Suggested procedures include the confirmation of financial support arrangements with third parties.

278. Answer: D

The normal effect of violating the terms of debt agreements (including debt covenants) is to render the associated debt immediately due, which may cause significant financial stress on the entity and cause the auditor to have substantial doubt about the entity's ability to continue as a going concern.

279. Answer: B

In a situation in which the auditor has substantial doubt about an entity's ability to continue as a going concern, the auditor is responsible for considering the possible effects on the financial statements and the adequacy of related disclosure in the financial statements. Such disclosures might include conditions that give rise to the assessment of substantial doubt, as well as management's plans. The auditor should include an emphasis-of-matter paragraph in the report (following the opinion paragraph) stating the auditor's conclusion that "substantial doubt about the entity's ability to continue as a going concern" exists.

280. Answer: D

Neither of those phrases is appropriate. "Except for..." is language used to identify a qualification for a departure from the applicable accounting framework. Since the entity's financial statements adequately disclose the uncertainties surrounding the going concern issue, a qualification is not appropriate. The phrase "possible discontinuance of the entity's operations" is not consistent with language suggested in AICPA Professional Standards, which, instead, offer the phrase "substantial doubt about the entity's ability to continue as a going concern."

281. Answer: A

GAAS indicate that external confirmations are frequently used to verify account balances. In doing so, they provide stronger evidence for the existence assertion than for the other assertions identified.

282. Answer: B

Tests of control are not a "substantive" procedure.

283. Answer: C

"Classification" is included among the five assertions associated with "classes of transactions and events for the period under audit," as identified by GAAS.

284. Answer: C

Check kiting occurs when cash is fraudulently created through the transfer of money between banks. Insufficient funds checks are written and deposited among a series of banks and the float is used to "create" cash. Kiting would be evidenced by a low average balance compared to a high level of deposits because, although deposits are being made, checks are immediately written to remove the funds, resulting in a low average balance.

285. Answer: C

The interview of the controller is "inquiry"; the review of the bank reconciliation for evidence that the control procedure of interest was performed (and initialed as performed) is "inspection of records."

286. Answer: B

The primary purpose of standard bank confirmations is to corroborate information regarding deposit and loan balances.

287. Answer: A

In planning the sample, the auditor must determine how many and how much, i.e., how many cash receipts and what dollar cut-off. Both are affected by materiality levels.

288. Answer: A

A cut-off bank statement is a regular bank statement that is prepared by the bank for a shorter period than normal. It is sent directly to (or picked up by) the auditors.

289. **Answer: B**

A difficulty commonly encountered by recipients of a confirmation request is the inability to determine what has been included in a given accounts receivable balance. Providing a list of the items or invoices making up the balance will facilitate the customer's reconciliation efforts and make it easier to respond to a confirmation request.

290. **Answer: B**

There is a presumption that the auditor will confirm selected receivables when they are material.

291. **Answer: C**

An auditor's review of sales cut-off would reveal unrecorded sales at year end, as well as subsequent year sales that were improperly included in the current year.

292. **Answer: C**

Confirmations of accounts receivable balances provide primary evidence for rights and obligations and existence. Direct responses from third parties provide proof that the accounts receivable are valid (that they exist) and that the amounts are properly owed to the entity.

293. **Answer: B**

In testing the completeness assertion (regarding omissions) related to sales and receivables, the auditor starts with a source document and agrees the item to the accounting records. Starting with a shipping document and tracing it to the sales journal (that is, to a sales invoice recorded in the sales journal) would be an appropriate test for unrecorded sales and receivables.

294. **Answer: A**

Inspection of loan agreements to determine whether inventories are pledged is a test for rights and obligations.

295. **Answer: A**

The direction of the test is critical to the resulting inference. This test involves tracing from a type of source document (the count "tags") to the accounting records (since the computerized listing of inventory items is, in effect, the subsidiary ledger that supports the inventory-adjusted general ledger balance). Hence, this test addresses the "completeness" assertion by dealing with the risk of omission.

296. **Answer: D**

Whether the inventory on hand is properly included in the reported ending inventory balance deals with the risk of omission, which involves the completeness assertion.

297. **Answer: A**

Inquiries of production and sales personnel to identify possible obsolete or slow-moving inventory will enable the auditor to determine if the inventory is correctly valued. This procedure is a test for the valuation or allocation assertion.

298. **Answer: B**

When inventory is held in a public warehouse, the auditor would ordinarily obtain direct confirmation from the custodian.

299. **Answer: C**

To establish the "reasonableness" of dividends on investments in public companies, the auditor might find relevant corroborating information using the Internet, such as visiting the SEC's website for information about dividends pertaining to investee companies.

300. **Answer: B**

Publicly traded stock is commonly held by a custodian on behalf of the investor. It would be most efficient and effective to confirm the number of shares owned with the independent custodian.

301. **Answer: A**

Analytical procedures could be used to ascertain the reasonableness of the completeness of recorded investment income. The auditor uses analytical procedures to develop an expectation of investment income. This figure is then compared to recorded investment income and significant differences are investigated further.

302. **Answer: B**

The rights and obligations assertion deals with whether the entity has the rights to or is obligated for the assets and liabilities in the financial statements. Confirming with an outside agent that the agent is holding securities in the client's name would address the existence of, and the client's rights to, such assets.

303. **Answer: B**

The equity method requires that the investment be valued by reflecting changes in the investee's equity. As a result, the auditor must examine copies of the audited financial statements of the investee company.

304. **Answer: A**

Inspecting the property ledger and the insurance and tax records would allow the auditor to identify old assets likely to have been retired. Touring the client's facilities would then allow the auditor to determine whether the assets are still present.

305. **Answer: A**

Agreeing the recorded additions of fixed assets to the underlying invoices and verifying that the assets have actually been placed in service (perhaps by inspecting the assets) establishes that the recorded assets are properly recorded, which is the essence of the existence assertion.

306. **Answer: D**

Analysis of repairs and maintenance accounts is primarily performed to identify capitalizable expenditures erroneously charged to expense.

307. **Answer: D**

Debits that appear in repairs and maintenance expense have not been capitalized. A careful analysis of those charges will enable the auditor to identify major repairs and other expenditures that should have been capitalized.

308. **Answer: B**

Significant debits to the accumulated depreciation accounts occur when plant assets are retired. The other choices are incorrect, as the impact on accumulated depreciation would be a credit or represent no effect.

309. **Answer: C**

Vouching a sample of cash disbursements recorded just after year end to receiving reports and vendor invoices would enable the auditor to determine if the goods were actually received or owned before year end. As a result, the amounts paid after year end would need to be accrued as year-end liabilities.

310. **Answer: B**

A note payable that is renewed after the balance sheet date would be examined by the auditor in order to ensure that it was properly presented at the balance sheet date and that

related disclosures were adequate. This would provide the auditor with evidence for the presentation and disclosure assertions.

311. **Answer: A**

Performing substantive tests before the balance sheet date increases the risk that the auditor will not detect material misstatements in the balances at the balance sheet date. In selecting procedures to perform before the balance sheet date, the auditor must consider the problems involved in controlling this increase in risk. The auditor's primary concern with accounts payable is completeness. Confirmation efforts in this area would, therefore, be directed toward zero or low-balance accounts and would be least likely to be performed before the balance sheet date, as it would have to be re-performed as of the balance sheet date.

312. **Answer: C**

Tracing a sample of purchase orders and the related receiving reports to the purchases journal and the cash disbursements journal will enable the auditor to determine that the purchases were properly recorded. Going from the detail into the records tests for the proper inclusion and recording of the items.

313. **Answer: C**

In auditing accounts payable, the auditor is more concerned that the balance may be understated. As a result, the primary assertion of interest is completeness.

314. **Answer: C**

In auditing long-term bonds payable, an auditor would compare interest expense with the bond payable amount for reasonableness. This procedure would provide evidence supporting the completeness and proper statement of interest expense, including limited evidence related to the amortization of bond premium and discounts. It would also provide evidence supporting the completeness and proper statement of the bonds payable balance.

315. **Answer: C**

The tickmark ¥ is consistently used with respect to 20X1 "expense." Calculating the interest expense (presumably using the effective interest method) is a relevant audit procedure to gather evidence as to the reasonableness of such recorded expense.

316. **Answer: A**

The tickmark € is consistently used with respect to payments. Tracing those payments to the cash disbursements journal and then to the relevant bank statement is a relevant audit procedure to gather evidence as to the validity of identified payments of this debt.

317. **Answer: C**

The permanent file would usually include copies or abstracts of significant contracts that affect multiple years. Lease agreements have financial statement effects and frequently involve multiple years, so the auditor would keep those copies or abstracts of key provisions in the permanent file.

318. **Answer: B**

The audit program for long-term debt would include an analysis of related interest expense. The auditor would thus correlate current interest expense with outstanding debt to ascertain the reasonableness of recorded interest expense.

319. **Answer: A**

To verify stockholders' equity transactions, the auditor would review minutes of board of directors' meetings. The minutes would document changes such as the issuance of new capital stock, the purchase of treasury shares, or merger through an exchange of stock.

320. **Answer: D**

Determination as to whether restrictions on retained earnings exist addresses assertions about presentation and disclosure. Restrictions on retained earnings impact the amount of retained earnings available for dividends and, thus, require disclosure.

321. **Answer: B**

The stock transfer agent is responsible for controlling the number of shares issued, for issuing new shares, and for canceling shares. The registrar maintains stockholder records. The confirmation would include the number of shares issued and outstanding.

322. **Answer: D**

Frequently, procedures that address presentation and disclosure also address rights and obligations. The rights and obligations

assertion would relate to whether the entity had the rights to the reported retained earnings.

323. **Answer: D**

An auditor would trace the authorization for stock options to a vote of the board of directors. This procedure would provide evidence supporting the existence of the stock options.

324. **Answer: C**

If overpayments are discovered, the auditor would likely extend substantive tests of payroll in order to ascertain whether such overpayments materially impact the financial statements.

325. **Answer: D**

In auditing payroll, an auditor would be likely to compare payroll costs with entity standards or budgets. This comparison would enable the auditor to detect unusual fluctuations or amounts that might indicate a material misstatement is present.

326. **Answer: D**

When control risk is assessed as low, substantive procedures in this area are typically limited to analytical procedures and recalculating year-end accruals.

327. **Answer: D**

The review of payroll tax reconciliations is performed to identify potential liabilities for unpaid payroll taxes. The salaries and wages on which the payroll taxes are based are typically reconciled to gross salaries and wages per the general ledger. If the amounts differ, it may indicate additional payroll tax liabilities.

328. **Answer: A**

The presence of significant unexplained variances between standard and actual labor costs might cause an auditor to suspect an employee payroll fraud scheme. The other choices provided represent internal control strengths in the payroll area.

329. **Answer: B**

Both the expected amount of misstatements and the measure of tolerable misstatement are factors that would influence sample size for a substantive test of details for a specific account.

330. **Answer: B**

Fraud risk increases when copies of documents are provided instead of originals and more so when they are related to a single vendor, rather than multiple vendors. The auditor will need to obtain other evidence to support the transactions in question.

331. **Answer: B**

Nonsampling risk refers to any error unrelated to sampling risk that the auditor might commit when performing an audit sampling task, such as failing to recognize a misstatement or otherwise misinterpreting the audit evidence.

332. **Answer: C**

Deciding that the sample results support the conclusion that the balance is materially misstated when it is not is an illustration of the risk of incorrect rejection. As a result, the auditor will perform additional and unnecessary work.

333. **Answer: D**

The use of statistical methods assists the auditor in designing an efficient sample, measuring the sufficiency of the evidence, and evaluating the sample results. Thus, this provides an objective basis for quantitatively evaluating sample risk.

334. **Answer: A**

To determine the sample size for a test of controls, the auditor considers the tolerable deviation rate, the allowable risk of assessing control risk too low, and the expected deviation rate. The auditor also considers the relationship of the sample to the objective of the test of controls.

335. **Answer: D**

If a test of 50 documents results in 3 deviations, the upper error limit will be 8%, which exceeds the tolerable rate of 7%. The upper error limit consists of the sample error rate of 6% (3/50) plus the allowance for sampling risk of 2%. If the upper error limit exceeds the tolerable rate, the auditor will modify the planned assessed level of control risk because the results indicate that the control cannot be relied upon.

336. **Answer: D**

The sample size of a test of controls varies inversely with the tolerable deviation rate. It varies directly with the expected population rate.

337. **Answer: A**

The term "attributes sampling" is used in the context of testing internal control issues, such as evaluating the appropriate authorization of purchase transactions.

338. **Answer: C**

If the auditor has incorrectly assessed control risk lower than appropriate, the sample deviation rate must have been less than the actual rate and the actual population rate exceeds the tolerable rate. This would cause the auditor to accept the control as effective when it really was not and, thus, to assess control risk lower than appropriate.

339. **Answer: B**

Incorrect acceptance involves concluding that a financial statement element was fairly stated, based on an audit sampling application, when, in fact, the element was materially misstated. This is consistent with the circumstances described in this question.

340. **Answer: C**

Variables sampling, or classical variables sampling, is used to calculate a best estimate of a population value with confidence intervals around the estimate. Commonly used variables sampling methods are mean-per-unit, difference estimation, and ratio estimation.

341. **Answer: C**

Because PPS sampling utilizes dollar units for sampling, the inclusion of zero and negative balances requires special design considerations. This would be an advantage for classical variables sampling, rather than PPS sampling.

342. **Answer: C**

Increasing tolerable misstatement decreases sample size, while increasing the assessed level of control risk increases sample size.

343. **Answer: B**

Stratification of the population enables the auditor to separate the population into size-related classes. For example, all transactions over $50,000 may be grouped into a class. Applying MPU sampling to these strata or classes will then result in a higher level of precision for a smaller sample size.

344. Answer: C

PPS sampling enables the auditor to directly control for the risk of incorrect acceptance by requiring the auditor to specify the desired level of that risk.

345. Answer: D

$$n = \frac{\text{Reliability factor (from tables)} \times \text{Book value}}{\text{Tolerable misstatement, net of expected misstatements}} \quad \frac{3 \times \$240,000}{\$24,000} = 30$$

346. Answer: B

In a probability-proportional-to-size application, the projected error of the sample is the amount of the difference between the book value and the audit value when the amount of the account examined is greater than the sampling interval.

347. Answer: A

PPS sampling is most effective in detecting overstatements, since the likelihood of an item's selection increases with the recorded magnitude of the item.

348. Answer: C

When the recorded balance of the account involved is less than the sampling interval, the auditor must determine the "tainting" percentage and apply that percentage to the sampling interval. In this case the tainting percentage = [($5,000 − $1,000)/$5,000] = 80%. Accordingly, the projected misstatement is $6,000 × 80% = $4,800.

349. Answer: C

Maintaining an audit trail for a computer system provides a deterrent to irregularities, facilitates monitoring, and enables queries to be answered. It does NOT enable analytical procedures to be performed.

350. Answer: C

A distributed data processing system links minicomputers in remote locations with a centralized computer. The controls of greatest concern to the auditor are access controls because each minicomputer will be able to access the central computer and it will be more difficult to control access to minicomputers in remote locations.

351. Answer: B

A disadvantage of microcomputer-prepared data files is that the files are compact and in a single location. It is also more difficult to secure

microcomputers. As a result, it is easier for unauthorized persons to access and alter the files.

352. Answer: C

Computer software would not be used to assess EDP control risk. Assessments of control risk are a matter of auditor judgment; the use of computer software will not facilitate that judgment.

353. Answer: D

The auditor's objective is to collect sufficient evidence to express an opinion on the financial statements and to provide reasonable assurance that the financial statements are not materially misstated. Thus, the auditor's objective in assessing control risk is to determine how internal controls affect the risk that the financial statements will be materially misstated. Remember that control risk is the risk that internal controls will fail to prevent or detect a material misstatement.

354. Answer: C

A validity check is a check to see if the data carry valid values. Of the items listed, this item is the only validity check. The computer matches a control field value to an existing file record and highlights those which do not match.

355. Answer: C

Test data are used by auditors to test the controls over data processing. In this case, test data would most likely be used to test the internal controls that prevent invalid employee I.D. numbers from being input.

356. Answer: B

Test data involve the use of fictitious transactions to test whether application controls are functioning properly. They would be used to test controls related to missing employee numbers, time tickets with invalid job numbers, and agreement of hours per clock cards with hours on time tickets. They would be LEAST likely to be used to test controls related to proper approval of overtime by supervisors, which are more likely to occur outside the application.

357. Answer: B

Edit checks ensure that only valid transactions are processed. The direct output of edit checks for a sales order processing system would most likely be a file of all rejected sales transactions. These transactions would need to be researched and corrected so that they could be re-entered into processing.

358. **Answer: A**

Limit tests and validity check tests are both processing controls designed to ensure the reliability and accuracy of data processing. While the Study Text has included both as examples of input controls, they can also be utilized as processing controls.

359. **Answer: A**

Generalized audit software programs perform common audit tasks, such as footing a file, sorting, extracting, and summarizing. They allow an auditor to access information stored on computer files even with only a limited understanding of the client's hardware and software.

360. **Answer: D**

An integrated test facility is a concurrent audit technique that processes data through the use of simulated files. It involves the creation of a dummy company against which transactions are submitted for processing concurrently with "live" transactions. The auditor is able to determine whether controls are working properly and whether processing is correct.

361. **Answer: B**

Test data are dummy transactions developed by the auditor to test processing by client programs. The auditor will not test every control, but will focus on those important to the application being evaluated.

362. **Answer: B**

An embedded audit module is a program inserted into the client's system to capture designated transactions, such as large or unusual transactions, for later review by the auditor. It enables the auditor to continuously test the client's computerized information system.

363. **Answer: D**

Parallel simulation is a computer-assisted auditing technique in which an auditor-written or auditor-controlled program is used to process client data. The results are then compared to those obtained using the client's program and differences are investigated. This technique enables the auditor to test controls in and processing performed by a client program.

364. **Answer: A**

Electronic data interchange (EDI) utilizes standardized formats for electronically transferring information. By adopting EDI, a company can electronically transfer information from one system into another. The elimination of manual re-entry of data and paperwork reduces costs and increases accuracy.

365. **Answer: A**

An audit of an entity with primarily electronic data systems would be more likely to include continuous monitoring and analysis via an embedded audit module because, in such environments, transactions or accounting records may be available on a temporary basis and in machine-readable form only.

366. **Answer: A**

Preventive controls are controls that attempt to deter problems before they occur. Detective controls are controls that discover problems after they occur. In an EDI system, the emphasis would be on preventive controls rather than on detective controls, due to the volume and speed of processing. Waiting to discover problems could result in an unacceptable loss of millions of dollars.

367. **Answer: C**

Using electronic funds transfer for international cash transactions reduces the manual handling and data entry related to such transfers. As a result, the frequency of data entry errors is reduced. As a general rule, whenever the data must be "touched" by human hands, the opportunity for error is introduced. The less the data are touched, the fewer the opportunities for error.

368. **Answer: C**

The audit trail is the means by which an accounting transaction can be traced through an accounting information system. In an EDI system, the audit trail would include activity logs that indicate failed transactions, as they identify the disposition of those transactions.

369. **Answer: C**

The objective is to prevent users of audited financial statements from misinterpreting the degree of responsibility the auditor is assuming when the auditor's name is associated with financial statements.

370. **Answer: A**

When strict adherence to GAAP would result in misleading financial statements, the auditor may issue an unmodified opinion accompanied by an emphasis-of-matter paragraph describing the GAAP departure.

371. **Answer: A**

If there is only a remote likelihood of a loss resulting from an uncertainty, GAAP does not require adjustment or disclosure. The auditor should express an unmodified opinion.

372. **Answer: B**

In order to issue an unmodified opinion, the auditor must be confident that no material misstatements exist in the financial statements. While misstatements may exist, in total they must be believed to be less than a material amount.

373. **Answer: C**

The accounting principles utilized in the preparation of the financial statements should: 1) be prepared in accordance with the identified financial reporting framework; 2) be appropriate in the circumstances; 3) provide information about matters that may affect the use, understanding, and interpretation of the financial statements; 4) classify and summarize information in a reasonable manner; and 5) reflect transactions in a manner that presents the financial position, results of operations, and cash flows stated within a range of reasonable and practicable limits.

374. **Answer: B**

The PCAOB did not change how the auditor's report is dated. That date is determined by when the auditor has gathered sufficient appropriate audit evidence as a reasonable basis for the opinion, not by the date of any filings with the SEC. Answers A, C, and D were changes in the auditor's report as a result of the PCAOB's auditing standards.

375. **Answer: C**

When part of the audit is performed by a component auditor, the group auditor is required to make inquiries concerning the professional reputation, independence, and competence of the component auditor.

376. **Answer: A**

The language used indicates a division of responsibility. When the group engagement partner decides not to accept responsibility for the work performed by a component auditor, the group engagement partner must disclose this fact in the audit report.

377. **Answer: D**

The group engagement partner can elect to take full responsibility for the financial statements, so long as satisfaction with the independence, and professional reputation, and competence of the component auditor is obtained and the additional requirements for assuming responsibility have been met.

378. **Answer: D**

The group engagement partner may decide not to make reference to the audit of a component auditor after obtaining satisfaction as to the professional reputation, independence, and competence of the component auditor and the work performed. Satisfaction with the work performed might be obtained by visiting the component auditor and discussing the procedures performed and the related results, reviewing the audit programs, and/or reviewing the documentation of the component auditor, including the internal control work performed.

379. **Answer: A**

group engagement partner is not as likely to refer to a component auditor when the component auditor was retained by the group auditor and the work was performed under the group auditor's guidance and control.

380. **Answer: D**

An unmodified audit report would be appropriate, since there is no need for disclosure if the likelihood of a material loss is indeed remote.

381. **Answer: A**

The auditor should express an unmodified opinion. The disclosure of the contingent liability has been made and is considered adequate by the auditor.
An emphasis-of-matter paragraph may be added after the opinion paragraph to bring attention to the uncertainty.

382. **Answer: A**

Green's audit report should include an emphasis-of-matter paragraph following the opinion paragraph to bring attention to the existence of the going concern issue. The paragraph should include the phrases "substantial doubt" and "going concern."

383. **Answer: A**

A qualified opinion is rendered when a GAAP departure or a scope limitation exists. The lack of sufficient evidence represents a scope limitation, which could result in a qualified opinion.

384. Answer: A

If the auditor is unable to obtain the audited financial statements of a significant subsidiary, the auditor has a scope limitation. As a result, a qualified or disclaimer opinion would be expressed (and an unmodified opinion would be inappropriate).

385. Answer: B

The last sentence in the Auditor's Responsibility section would be modified to state, "We believe that the audit evidence we have obtained is sufficient and appropriate to provide a basis for our qualified audit opinion." A qualified opinion resulting from a scope limitation (an insufficiency of audit evidence) also results in the addition of a separate paragraph (Basis for Qualified Opinion, which describes the circumstances involved) and a modified opinion paragraph. No mention would be made in the notes to the financial statements.

386. Answer: C

Material related party transactions must be disclosed. In general, it is not possible to determine whether or not such transactions were conducted on terms equivalent to those in an arm's-length transaction. If the entity's financial statements include a footnote on related party transactions that states that a particular related party transaction occurred on terms equivalent to those that would have prevailed in an arm's-length transaction, should obtain sufficient appropriate evidence to verify arm's-length equivalence (which is unlikely in view of the rather hypothetical nature of that statement).

387. Answer: D

The auditor's inability to obtain audited financial statements or other evidence supporting an entity's investment in a foreign subsidiary represents a scope limitation. Either a qualified opinion or a disclaimer would be issued.

388. Answer: A

A footnote stating that certain related party transactions were consummated on terms equivalent to those obtainable in transactions with unrelated parties would not be acceptable to the auditor unless the auditor verified that the representations were correct. If no verification occurred (or this perhaps were not possible), the opinion might be modified as a result.

389. Answer: D

An opinion qualified because of inadequate disclosure would include a separate basis for qualified opinion paragraph describing the nature of the omission and modifications in the opinion paragraph. There would be no modifications in the introductory or management responsibility paragraphs.

390. Answer: C

When an entity omits a statement of cash flows, the auditor may accept an engagement to audit the other financial statements, but should qualify the opinion, since a statement of cash flows is required when general-purpose financial statements present financial position and results of operation.

391. Answer: B

Omission of the statement of cash flows results in a qualified opinion due to a GAAP departure.

392. Answer: D

An opinion qualified because of inadequate disclosure would include a separate basis for qualified opinion paragraph and a modification of the opinion paragraph. No modification of the introductory or management responsibility paragraphs would be required.

393. Answer: D

An unjustified change in accounting principles is a GAAP departure that would result in a qualified or adverse opinion. A material weakness in internal control should be reported to those charged with governance, but would not be reported in an unmodified audit report.

394. Answer: D

Accounting for the effect of a material accounting change prospectively, when GAAP require inclusion of the cumulative effect of the change in the current year, is a GAAP departure. A material GAAP departure results in either an adverse or a qualified opinion.

395. Answer: C

An adverse opinion is issued when a material and pervasive GAAP departure is present in the financial statements. If the financial statements do not conform with FASB requirements for the capitalization of leases, a GAAP departure is present. If considered to be of sufficient magnitude to cause the financial statements to be misleading, the auditor would issue an adverse opinion.

396. Answer: D

When a misstatement is material and the effect on the financial statements is pervasive, the auditor should express an adverse opinion indicating that the financial statements are not fairly stated.

397. Answer: C

A disclaimer is issued when the scope limitations pertaining to the audit are so pervasive that the auditor in unable to express an opinion. Lack of adequate disclosures in the financial statements is a GAAP departure, not a scope limitation. Thus, a disclaimer of opinion would not be appropriate.

398. Answer: D

A disclaimer report omits the scope paragraph (the second paragraph in the auditor's responsibility section that describes an audit) and adds a separate paragraph explaining why the audit did not comply with generally accepted auditing standards (Basis for Disclaimer of Opinion). The scope paragraph is omitted because any descriptions of procedures performed could be misunderstood. If a disclaimer is issued, the auditor does not feel that the audit work performed was sufficient to render an opinion. The opinion paragraph remains but it indicates that the scope of work was insufficient to support an opinion.

399. Answer: B

Morris should disclaim an opinion because of the pervasiveness of the scheme and the nature of the items involved. Although the auditor was not precluded by the client from obtaining sufficient evidence to evaluate the impact of the illegal bribes on the financial statements, the fact that they could not ascertain whether senior management was involved is a critical deficiency.

400. Answer: A

If a change in accounting principle has occurred and the auditor concurs with the change, the only requirement that must be met is to refer to the change in an emphasis-of-matter paragraph following an otherwise unmodified opinion. It is not necessary for the auditor to concur explicitly with the change nor is it appropriate for the opinion to be qualified as a result of the change.

401. Answer: B

GAAS require that the auditor identify occasions in which the accounting principles have not been applied consistently. No mention is to be made in the report if the consistency requirement is met. If the auditor was able to obtain sufficient evidence about consistency, the auditor's report should not refer to consistency.

402. Answer: C

A change in depreciation method applicable to existing assets would be viewed as a change in estimate, not a change in accounting principle. (In this case, the different depreciation method is only applicable to new assets, which would not even be considered a change in estimate.) In any case, since the effect on the current period's financial statements is specified to be immaterial, an unmodified opinion should be expressed.

403. Answer: A

The auditor's report should not mention a change in accounting principle that has an immaterial effect on comparability. Only material matters are relevant to the auditor's report.

404. Answer: B

PCAOB auditing standards (specifically, AS Section 2820) identify two specific matters that affect the auditor's evaluation of consistency of financial statements: (1) a change in accounting principle; and (2) an adjustment to correct a misstatement in previously issued financial statements (i.e., a "restatement"). A change in accounting principle may be at management's discretion or it may be mandated by a change in accounting standards that eliminates an accounting alternative that was previously accepted but no longer is.

405. Answer: A

When there is a change in accounting principle, the auditor should evaluate whether: (1) the newly adopted principle is GAAP; (2) the method of accounting for the effect of the change conforms to GAAP; (3) the disclosures related to the change are adequate; and (4) the company has justified that the alternative accounting principle is preferable. If one (or more) of the above criteria is (are) not met, the auditor should treat the matter, if material, as a GAAP departure, which involves a choice between a qualified opinion and an adverse opinion.

406. **Answer: A**

When there is a change in accounting principle, the auditor is required to evaluate four matters: (1) whether the newly adopted principle is GAAP; (2) whether the method of accounting for the effect of the change conforms to GAAP; (3) whether the disclosures related to the change are adequate; and (4) whether the company has justified that the alternative accounting principle is GAAP. Hence, it is not true to suggest that the change must be authorized by those charged with governance.

407. **Answer: B**

The inability to verify the beginning inventory makes the auditor unable to express an opinion on any financial statement in which inventory is a material component. Beginning inventory is material to cost of goods sold and net income. As a result, the auditor is unable to express an opinion and must disclaim on the income and retained earnings statements and the statement of cash flows. The auditor will, however, be able to render an unmodified opinion on the balance sheet.

408. **Answer: D**

The auditor may inquire of the predecessor auditor about issues related to the consistency of financial reporting over time, but that is not something that the auditor is required to inquire about prior to accepting the audit engagement. The other answer options should be conducted prior to acceptance.

AICPA Professional Standards require an auditor (the successor) to make several inquiries of the predecessor auditor before accepting the audit engagement. These matters include:(1) information bearing on the integrity of management; (2) disagreements with management about accounting or auditing issues; (3) communications to those charged with governance about fraud and noncompliance with laws and regulations; (4) communications to management and those charged with governance about internal control issues; and (5) the predecessor's understanding for the reasons the entity changed auditors.

409. **Answer: D**

When the audited financial statements are presented in a client's document containing other information, the auditor is required to read the other information to determine whether it is consistent with the audited financial statements.

410. **Answer: A**

The audit of supplementary information in relation to the financial statements as a whole measures materiality just like that used in forming an opinion on the basic financial statements.

411. **Answer: A**

The accountant's separate report on the supplementary information should include a statement that the supplementary information is the responsibility of management and was derived from and relates directly to the underlying records used to prepare the financial statements. The report should further state that the supplementary information was not audited or reviewed (since it was compiled) and that no assurance of any type is provided.

412. **Answer: C**

When an auditor has been engaged to determine whether supplementary information is fairly stated in relation to the financial statements, the auditor may include in the auditor's report on the financial statements an opinion that the accompanying information is fairly stated in all material respects in relation to the financial statements as a whole.

413. **Answer: C**

Supplementary information, which is required by the FASB, differs from other information presented outside the basic financial statements because authoritative guidelines have been established for the measurement and presentation of such information. As a result, an auditor's responsibility for required supplementary information is to apply certain limited procedures to ascertain whether the information has been presented in accordance with the prescribed guidelines.

414. **Answer: D**

When required supplementary information is included with the financial statements, the auditor is required to perform the following: 1) inquire OF management about methods of preparing the information and whether such methods have changed; 2) ask about significant assumptions; 3) compare the information for consistency with management's responses, the audited financial statements, and other knowledge obtained during the audit; and 4) obtain additional representations in the management representation letter.

415. **Answer: D**

AICPA Professional Standards describe the limited procedures that the auditor is to perform to address required supplementary information. The auditor is further required to report deficiencies in or the omission of such information.

416. **Answer: D**

Failure Failure to include supplementary information required by the Governmental Accounting Standards Board would result in an unmodified opinion with an other-matter paragraph.

417. **Answer: C**

The auditor should obtain management's representation that the supplemental information complies with the applicable regulatory (or other) criteria, and the auditor should evaluate whether the information is presented in conformity with the regulatory criteria. However, a written confirmation from the regulatory authority would not be obtained.

418. **Answer: A**

Information that a company voluntarily presents on its web site is outside the PCAOB's definition of "supplemental information." As a practical matter, sustainability reports are not required, nor is third-party assurance on sustainability required.

419. **Answer: B**

The auditor should obtain management's representation that the methods of measurement or presentation have not changed from those used in the prior period. However, the auditor's report does not include such a statement.

420. **Answer: D**

The alert to restrict the distribution of the auditor's report is presented at the end of the auditor's report.

421. **Answer: A**

When reporting on financial statements prepared in conformity with another country's accounting principles, an auditor practicing in the U.S. must perform the procedures necessary to comply with the professional standards of U.S. generally accepted auditing standards. The auditor must understand the accounting principles generally accepted in the other country.

422. **Answer: D**

Provided that the financial statements prepared in conformity with another country's GAAP are for use only outside the United States, KCP America's auditor may issue either a U.S.-style report revised to reference the accounting principles (financial reporting framework) of the parent's country or the report form of the parent's country.

423. **Answer: A**

An auditor's report on condensed financial statements should indicate: 1) the auditor has audited and expressed an opinion on the complete financial statements; 2) the date of the auditor's report on such statements; 3) the type of opinion expressed; and 4) whether the information in the condensed financial statements is consistent, in all material respects, with the audited financial statements.

424. **Answer: D**

The professional standards indicate that in order to perform a review of interim financial information, the accountant should have an understanding of the entity's business and its internal control as they relate to the preparation of both annual and interim financial information sufficient to identify potential material misstatements and to select appropriate inquiry and analytical procedures.

425. **Answer: D**

AICPA Professional Standards specifically identify that the accountant should consider the results of any audit procedures performed with respect to the current year's financial statements as a procedure that would be applicable to planning a review of interim financial information with respect to updating the auditor's knowledge of the entity's business and its internal control.

426. **Answer: A**

The SEC requires that, when an auditor's review report on interim financial information is included in a registration statement, the prospectus must include a statement indicating that the accountant's review report is not a part of the registration statement within the meaning of the Securities Act of 1933.

427. **Answer: C**

The AICPA's sample management representation letter for interim financial information does not include a representation about understanding the meaning of a "review" of interim financial information. The nature of such an engagement would be clearly communicated in the required engagement letter, but it would not be a statement of fact by management in response to the auditor's inquiries.

428. **Answer: B**

A review of interim financial information requires that the accountant read the minutes of meetings of those charged with governance and perform a limited number of other procedures.

429. **Answer: A**

An accountant's report on the application of accounting principles to a specific transaction should include: 1) a statement that the engagement was conducted in accordance with applicable AICPA standards, 2) a description of the transaction and the accounting principles to be applied, 3) a statement indicating that responsibility for proper accounting treatment rests with the preparers of the financial statements, and 4) a statement that any difference in the facts, circumstances, or assumptions may change the report. (AU 625)

430. **Answer: A**

The financial statements would contain a footnote that describes the basis of the financial statement presentation and how it differs from GAAP.

431. **Answer: B**

This is a negatively worded request. They are looking for the statement that should NOT be made. An auditor's report on financial statements prepared on the cash receipts and disbursements basis of accounting should include a statement that the cash receipts and disbursements basis of accounting is a basis of accounting that is not GAAP.

432. **Answer: C**

A report on financial statements prepared on the income tax basis of accounting must include a paragraph that states that the income tax basis of accounting is a basis of accounting other than generally accepted accounting principles.

433. **Answer: C**

AICPA Professional Standards indicate that use of titles such as balance sheet, statement of financial position, statement of income, statement of operations, and statement of cash flows, or similar titles are usually interpreted as GAAP financial statements. As a result, they should not be used for financial statements prepared in accordance with a special purpose framework. Statement of revenues collected and expenses paid would be considered a suitable title for a cash basis financial statement.

434. **Answer: C**

The separate explanatory paragraph should refer to the note that describes the basis of accounting.

435. **Answer: A**

In an engagement to report on selected financial data included in a client-prepared document containing audited financial statements, the report on such data should refer to the audit report on the financial statements.

436. **Answer: C**

When an auditor is engaged to audit a specific element of the financial statements, i.e., selected financial data, in conjunction with an engagement to audit the financial statements, the report on the specific element should include the date of the audit report on the financial statements and the type of opinion expressed.

437. **Answer: D**

The auditor may express an opinion on a single financial statement (such as the balance sheet) and this is consistent with the meaning of the phrase "taken as a whole." Of course, the auditor must still obtain sufficient appropriate evidence as a reasonable basis for that opinion.

438. **Answer: C**

Special reports apply to engagements that involve compliance with contracts or regulatory requirements related to financial statements.

439. **Answer: B**

Auditors' reports issued in connection with requirements to comply with contractual agreements or regulatory requirements other than GAAP are designated as special reports.

440. **Answer: C**

When an auditor is engaged to audit a specific element of the financial statements, i.e., selected financial data, in conjunction with an engagement to audit the financial statements, the report on the specific element should include the date of the audit report on the financial statements and the type of opinion expressed.

441. **Answer: D**

The auditor may express an opinion on a single financial statement (such as the balance sheet) and this is consistent with the meaning of the phrase "taken as a whole." Of course, the auditor must still obtain sufficient appropriate evidence as a reasonable basis for that opinion.

442. **Answer: A**

In an engagement to report on selected financial data included in a client-prepared document containing audited financial statements, the report on such data should refer to the audit report on the financial statements.

443. **Answer: A**

A report on controls placed in operation should include a disclaimer on operating effectiveness as this type of engagement does not include any tests of controls. It is not intended to provide a user auditor with a basis for reducing control risk below maximum.

444. **Answer: A**

The service auditor's report expressing an opinion on the description of CSC's internal controls as of a specific date would include a scope paragraph describing the scope and nature of the procedures employed.

445. **Answer: D**

Comfort letters are requested by and addressed to underwriters and other parties. They provide the underwriter with "reasonable grounds to believe there are no material omissions or misstatements in financial statements related to a 1933 Act securities offering." They are addressed to the underwriter (or other requesting parties) and signed by the auditor.

446. **Answer: A**

Comfort letters are issued (and signed) by an entity's independent auditor for the purpose of providing a "due diligence" defense to underwriters and certain other requesting parties in connection with a securities offering.

447. **Answer: C**

The auditor is responsible for planning the audit to detect material misstatements in the financial statements. The auditor therefore focuses on violations of laws and regulations with a direct and material effect on the financial statements.

448. **Answer: D**

If an entity is receiving governmental financial assistance, it is subject to audits conducted under Government Auditing Standards (the Yellow Book) in addition to GAAS. Government standards require specific consideration of the internal control structure established to ensure compliance with the laws and regulations applicable to the financial assistance and issuance of a separate report on internal control. Thus, an entity which is not receiving governmental assistance would not refer to internal control in the auditor's standard report.

449. **Answer: A**

GAO reporting standards require a written report on the auditor's understanding of the entity's internal control (which, in turn, is used to assess control risk).

450. **Answer: B**

Government Auditing Standards require that the scope of the auditors' testing of internal control over financial reporting be described. It can be included as a separate report or in a combined report with the report on compliance with laws and regulations. Generally accepted auditing standards do not require this report.

451. **Answer: B**

Auditors are required to report known or likely fraud, illegal acts, violations of contracts or grants, or abuse directly to outside parties when: 1) management fails to report such information as required by law or regulation; or 2) when management fails to take timely and appropriate action to respond to fraud, illegal acts, violations, or abuse that is likely to be material to the financial statements and involves government agency funding.

452. **Answer: A**

The report on the entity's compliance with laws and regulations should include a statement indicating that compliance with laws and regulations is the responsibility of the entity's management.

453. Answer: B

If the auditor detects noncompliance with requirements that have a material effect on the program being audited, the auditor should issue a qualified or adverse opinion on compliance.

454. Answer: B

The Single Audit Act requires entities receiving federal financial assistance of at least $750,000 to have a single, organization-wide financial and compliance audit. The audit, however, should examine compliance with the general and specific requirements applicable to each program. As a result, materiality is determined separately for each major federal financial assistance program.

455. Answer: A

The auditor is required to give positive assurance on the items tested as to compliance with laws and regulations. The auditor provides negative assurance on the items not tested.

456. Answer: B

"Must" indicates an unconditional requirement in the SSARSs.

457. Answer: D

The Statements on Standards for Accounting and Review Services are not applicable when: 1) preparing a working trial balance; 2) assisting in adjusting the books of account; 3) consulting on accounting, tax, and similar matters; 4) preparing tax returns; 5) providing bookkeeping or data processing services, and 6) processing financial data for clients of other accounting firms.

458. Answer: C

The standards that address unaudited financial statements are the Statements on Standards for Accounting and Review Services.

459. Answer: A

AR-C 70 does, in fact, apply to engagements to prepare financial statements to be presented; alongside a personal financial plan. However, AR-C 70 does not apply to an engagement to prepare financial statements as part of a written personal financial plan prepared by the accountant. The key word here is "alongside" a personal financial plan.

460. Answer: C

A compilation report should include the following statement: "Accordingly, I (we) do not express an opinion, a conclusion, nor provide any form of assurance on these financial statements." There is no reference to "limited assurance" in the compilation report.

461. Answer: B

The accountant may accept a compilation for an entity in an industry with which the accountant is unfamiliar providing that the accountant obtains the required level of knowledge before completing the engagement.

462. Answer: A

An accountant may perform a compilation even if not independent. An accountant may not perform a review unless he/she is independent.

463. Answer: D

The accountant is required to issue a compilation report which discloses the lack of independence by including the statement "I am not independent with respect to the entity" (or similar words to that effect).

464. Answer: C

Financial statements of a nonpublic entity which have been compiled by an accountant should be accompanied by a report stating that the accountant does not express an opinion or any other form of assurance on the financial statements.

465. Answer: D

In a review engagement, the accountant would **not** obtain an understanding of internal control for purposes of assessing control risk and, thus, would **not** identify or communicate any material weaknesses in internal control.

466. Answer: A

Procedures performed during a review consist primarily of inquiries of management and the performance of analytical procedures. Inquiries concerning actions taken at meetings of the owners and those charged with governance would commonly be performed during a review.

467. Answer: A

In a review engagement, the accountant is required to obtain an understanding of the entity's industry, its business activities, and the accounting principles and practices used by the entity.

468. **Answer: A**

The basis for conclusions in a review engagement consists primarily of inquiries and analytical procedures. An analytical procedure such as this might be performed.

469. **Answer: D**

A review provides "negative assurance" for which the accountant is required to be independent.

470. **Answer: C**

When the current-period financial statements have been reviewed and the prior period financial statements were audited, the accountant's review report on the current period should indicate the degree of responsibility assumed for the prior financials. The current report would include a separate (other-matter) paragraph indicating, among other things, that no auditing procedures were performed after the date of the 20x1 auditor's report.

471. **Answer: B**

AICPA Professional Standards related to compilation of pro forma financial information point out that the accountant is not prohibited from issuing a compilation report under those circumstances, but the compilation report should disclose the lack of independence.

472. **Answer: A**

In these circumstances, AICPA standards require the accountant to add a separate paragraph to the review report stating (1) that the prior period's financial statements were audited; (2) the date of the previous report; (3) the type of opinion expressed; (4) the reasons for any modification of the report; and (5) that no auditing procedures were performed after the date of the previous report.

473. **Answer: C**

The term "entity-level control" refers to those policies and procedures that have very broad implications to the achievement of an entity's control-related objectives related to operating activities, financial reporting, and compliance. However, the entity's control objectives would not generally be applicable to a company's annual stockholder meeting.

474. **Answer: B**

This approach is labeled a "top-down approach" by PCAOB auditing standards (specifically, AS Section 2201).

475. **Answer: D**

When issuing a separate audit report on the financial statements and on internal control over financial reporting, the separate reports should each contain an additional paragraph that references the other report.

476. **Answer: D**

The distribution of the auditor's written communication about identified material weaknesses to management and the audit committee should be restricted to those parties. It should not be issued for general distribution to other parties, such as the entity's stockholders.

477. **Answer: D**

PCAOB auditing standards (specifically, AS Section 2201) identify the following procedures as applicable to "testing design effectiveness": inquiry, observation and inspection of relevant documentation. In addition to those procedures, the PCAOB adds reperformance of the control for "testing operating effectiveness."

478. **Answer: B**

AS Section 6115 (para. 16) states: "A stated control objective in the context of an engagement to report on whether a material weakness continues to exist is the specific control objective identified by management that, if achieved, would result in the material weakness no longer existing."

479. **Answer: B**

AS Section 6115 (para. 16) states: "A stated control objective in the context of an engagement to report on whether a material weakness continues to exist is the specific control objective identified by management that, if achieved, would result in the material weakness no longer existing."

480. **Answer: D**

AS Section 6115 states that such an engagement is voluntary.

481. **Answer: A**

An agreed-upon procedures report expresses assurance in the form of procedures and findings with respect to the procedures performed.

482. **Answer: C**

Independence is an important quality control consideration for engagements that involve assurance, including agreed-upon procedures engagements (which express assurance in the form of "procedures" and "findings").

483. **Answer: C**

The specified parties and the practitioner must agree upon the procedures to be performed by the practitioner that the specified parties believe are appropriate.

484. **Answer: D**

The clue here is that the CPA was engaged to examine management's assertion. An engagement of this nature is addressed by the Statements on Standards for Attestation Engagements. Attestation engagements are "engagement is defined as follows: "An examination, review, or agreed-upon procedures engagement performed under the attestation standards related to subject matter or an assertion that is the responsibility of another party.""

485. **Answer: A**

Regarding an examination of a forecast, AICPA Professional Standards (AT 301.41) state, "In an adverse opinion the practitioner should ... state that the presentation is not in conformity with presentation guidelines and should refer to the explanatory paragraph. When applicable, his or her opinion paragraph should also state that, in the practitioner's opinion, the assumptions do not provide a reasonable basis for the prospective financial statements."

486. **Answer: C**

The accountant's compilation report on a projection should include a description of the special purpose for which the projection was prepared, along with a separate paragraph to restrict the use of the report to the specified parties.

487. **Answer: D**

The compilation report applicable to a forecast includes a statement such as: "Furthermore, there will usually be differences between the forecasted and actual results, because events and circumstances frequently do not occur as expected, and those differences may be material".

488. **Answer: D**

Financial projections are based on one or more hypothetical assumptions which must be clearly understood by the reader of the projection. As a result, the distribution of financial projections is limited to the responsible party and third parties with whom the responsible party is negotiating directly. It would not be appropriate for the projection to be distributed to all stockholders of record as of the report date.

489. **Answer: D**

The practitioner's report on pro form financial information does not include commentary regarding all direct and indirect effects attributed to the event or transaction involved.

490. **Answer: A**

The AICPA's guidance on reporting on pro forma financial information is included in the *Statements on Standards for Attestation Engagements*.

491. **Answer: B**

When a practitioner does not have the necessary understanding of the client's business and industry for purposes of reporting on pro forma financial information, the practitioner should consider whether sufficient knowledge of these matters can be obtained. It is possible that industry-related knowledge might be obtained by reviewing applicable industry trade journals.

492. **Answer: A**

The report on agreed-upon procedures related to management's assertion about an entity's compliance with specified requirements should include a statement of limitations on the use of the report. The report is intended to be used solely by the specified users and, as a result, restrictions on distribution need to be clearly stated.

493. **Answer: B**

Such an engagement is subject to the SSAEs. Specifically, AT-C Section 315, "Compliance Attestation" applies to engagements related to an entity's compliance with requirements of applicable laws, regulations, or contracts.

494. **Answer: A**

In an audit of on an entity's internal control over financial reporting, in an integrated audit, the auditor must obtain management's written representations acknowledging responsibility for establishing and maintaining internal control over financial reporting. Management must provide a written assessment about the effectiveness of the internal control over financial reporting using suitable and available criteria.

495. **Answer: C**

An auditor's unmodified report on internal control over financial reporting would provide the opinion that the company maintained, in all material respects, effective internal control over financial reporting as of a specific date (usually year end), based on the identified control criteria.

496. **Answer: C**

In a financial statement audit, consideration is given to internal control in terms of its impact on the fair presentation of the financial statements. In an examination of internal control over financial reporting, the purpose of the engagement is to express an opinion on the operating effectiveness of internal control over financial reporting. As a result, the work performed in an audit on internal control over financial reporting is more extensive in scope than that performed during the control risk assessment in a financial statement audit.

497. **Answer: A**

An audit report on internal control over financial reporting should include a paragraph describing the inherent limitations of internal control over financial reporting and the fact that misstatements may occur and not be detected and corrected as a result.

498. **Answer: B**

In order for an auditor to accept an engagement to audit and report on a nonissuer's internal control over financial reporting, management must provide a written assessment about the effectiveness of internal control in a report that accompanies the auditor's report.

499. **Answer: B**

The attestation standards must be followed when reviewing MD&A prepared pursuant to SEC requirements. The standards apply to both an examination and a review of MD&A.

500. **Answer: D**

In a WebTrust assurance engagement, the practitioner expresses an opinion on management's assertions regarding business practices, transaction integrity, and information protection. The engagement is conducted in accordance with the attestation standards. A WebTrust Seal of Assurance can be displayed for a limited period of time on the websites of entities who receive unqualified opinions in WebTrust engagements.

Task-Based Simulations

Ethics, Professional Responsibilities, and General Principles

AICPA Code of Professional Conduct

MIPPs Nonindependence Rules: Fees

Task-Based Simulation 1

Code of Professional Conduct

Assume that you are employed by DFW, CPAs. One of the partners has asked you to research the Professional Standards for the section that identifies the requirements regarding the acceptance of contingent fees for engagements.

Title choices

A. AU-C
B. PCAOB
C. AT
D. AR
E. ET
F. BL
G. CS
H. QC

	(A)	(B)	(C)	(D)	(E)	(F)	(G)	(H)
1. Which title of the Professional Standards addresses this issue and will be helpful in responding to the partner?	○	○	○	○	○	○	○	○
2. Enter the exact section and paragraphs with helpful information.								

Task-Based Simulation 1 Solution

Research		
	Authoritative Literature	
		Help

		(A)	(B)	(C)	(D)	(E)	(F)	(G)	(H)
1.	Which title of the Professional Standards addresses this issue and will be helpful in responding to the partner?	○	○	○	○	●	○	○	○

2. Enter the exact section and paragraphs with helpful information.	1.510.001	01

Financial Interests: Overview and Unsolicited Financial Interests

Task-Based Simulation 2

Research		
	Authoritative Literature	
		Help

Covered Member

You work with a CPA firm as an assistant. The senior on the XYZ audit has asked you to determine whether you are eligible to work on the XYZ audit since he knows that you own 100 shares of XYZ worth $700 in total. He has asked you to research the following:

Title choices

A. AU-C
B. PCAOB
C. AT
D. AR
E. ET
F. BL
G. CS
H. QC

		(A)	(B)	(C)	(D)	(E)	(F)	(G)	(H)
1.	He thinks that he recalls the issue relates to whether you are or are not a "covered member." He would like you to find the definition of a covered member in the professional standards. Which title of the Professional Standards addresses this issue and will be helpful in responding to the senior?	○	○	○	○	○	○	○	○

2. Enter the exact section and paragraphs with helpful information.

3. Regardless of what you find, he would like you to determine whether a covered member may have such an immaterial financial investment in an audit client. What title, section, and paragraph addresses this issue?

Task-Based Simulation 2 Solution

Research

Authoritative Literature

Help

	(A)	(B)	(C)	(D)	(E)	(F)	(G)	(H)
1. He thinks that he recalls the issue relates to whether you are or are not a "covered member." He would like you to find the definition of a covered member in the professional standards. Which title of the Professional Standards addresses this issue and will be helpful in responding to the senior?	○	○	○	○	●	○	○	○

2. Enter the exact section and paragraphs with helpful information.

ET 0.400.02

3. Regardless of what you find, he would like you to determine whether a covered member may have such an immaterial financial investment in an audit client. What title, section, and paragraph addresses this issue?

ET   1.240.010   02

Employment Relationships: Other Associations and Relationships

Task-Based Simulation 3

Independence Issues

Authoritative Literature

Help

Assume that you are analyzing relationships for your firm to identify situations in which an auditor's independence may be impaired. For each of the following numbered situations, determine whether the auditor (a covered member in the situation) is considered to be independent. If the auditor's independence would **not** be impaired select No. If the auditor's independence would be impaired select Yes.

	Yes	No
1. The auditor is a cosigner of a client's checks.	○	○
2. The auditor is a member of a country club that is a client.	○	○
3. The auditor owns a large block of stock in a client but has placed it in a blind trust.	○	○
4. The auditor placed her checking account in a bank that is her client. The account is fully insured by a federal agency.	○	○
5. The client has not paid the auditor for services for the past two years.	○	○
6. The auditor is leasing part of his building to a client.	○	○
7. The auditor joins, as an ordinary member, a trade association that is also a client.	○	○
8. The auditor has an immaterial, indirect financial interest in the client.	○	○

Task-Based Simulation 3 Solution

Independence Issues		
	Authoritative Literature	
		Help

		Yes	No
1.	The auditor is a cosigner of a client's checks.	●	○
2.	The auditor is a member of a country club that is a client.	○	●
3.	The auditor owns a large block of stock in a client but has placed it in a blind trust.	●	○
4.	The auditor placed her checking account in a bank that is her client. The account is fully insured by a federal agency.	○	●
5.	The client has not paid the auditor for services for the past two years.	●	○
6.	The auditor is leasing part of his building to a client.	●	○
7.	The auditor joins, as an ordinary member, a trade association that is also a client.	○	●
8.	The auditor has an immaterial, indirect financial interest in the client.	○	●

Explanations

1. **(Y)** Since the auditor is a cosigner on a client's check, the auditor could become liable if the client defaults. This relationship impairs the auditor's independence.
2. **(N)** Independence is not impaired because membership in the country club is essentially a social matter.
3. **(Y)** An auditor may not hold a direct financial interest in a client. Putting it in a blind trust does not solve the impairment of independence.
4. **(N)** If the auditor places his/her account in a client bank, this does not impair independence if the accounts are state or federally insured. If the accounts are not insured, independence is not impaired if the amounts are immaterial.
5. **(Y)** The auditor's independence is impaired when prior years' fees for professional services remain unpaid for more than one year.
6. **(Y)** The auditor's independence is impaired when s/he leases space out of a building s/he owns to a client.
7. **(N)** When the auditor does not serve in management, s/he may join a trade association who is a client.
8. **(N)** Independence is impaired for direct financial interests and material, indirect financial interests but not for immaterial, indirect financial interests.

Nonaudit Services: Specific Services

Task-Based Simulation 4

Providing Various Services		
	Authoritative Literature	
		Help

The firm of Willingham and Whiting (WW), CPAs, has had requests from a number of clients and prospective clients as to providing various types of services. Please reply as to whether the appropriate independence rules (AICPA and/or PCAOB) allow the following engagements with:

A—Allowable, given these facts.

N—Not allowable, given these facts.

(If both AICPA and PCAOB rules apply and one of them does not allow the services, answer N.)

Case	Request	Public or nonpublic client	Allowable (A) or not allowable (N)?
1.	Provide internal audit outsourcing as well as perform the audit.	Public	
2.	Prepare the corporate tax return as well as perform the audit.	Public	
3.	Prepare the corporate tax return as well as perform the audit.	Nonpublic	
4.	Provide bookkeeping services as well as perform the audit; WW will not determine journal entries, authorize transactions, prepare or modify source documents.	Nonpublic	
5.	Provide financial information systems design and implementation assistance; WW provides no attest services for that company.	Public	
6.	Serve on the board of directors of the company; WW provides no attest services for that company.	Public	
7.	Implement an off-the-shelf accounting package as well as perform the audit.	Nonpublic	
8.	Provide actuarial services related to certain liabilities as well as perform the audit; the subjectively determined liabilities relate to a material portion of the financial statements.	Nonpublic	
9.	Provide actuarial services related to certain liabilities as well as perform the audit; the subjectively determined liabilities relate to material portion of the financial statements.	Public	
10.	Corporate executives of an audit client want to have WW provide tax planning for themselves (not the company).	Public	

Task-Based Simulation 4 Solution

Providing Various Services			
	Authoritative Literature		
		Help	

Case	Request	Public or nonpublic client	Allowable (A) or not allowable (N)?
1.	Provide internal audit outsourcing as well as perform the audit.	Public	N
2.	Prepare the corporate tax return as well as perform the audit.	Public	A
3.	Prepare the corporate tax return as well as perform the audit.	Nonpublic	A
4.	Provide bookkeeping services as well as perform the audit; WW will not determine journal entries, authorize transactions, prepare or modify source documents.	Nonpublic	A
5.	Provide financial information systems design and implementation assistance; WW provides no attest services for that company.	Public	A
6.	Serve on the board of directors of the company; WW provides no attest services for that company.	Public	N
7.	Implement an off-the-shelf accounting package as well as perform the audit.	Nonpublic	A
8.	Provide actuarial services related to certain liabilities as well as perform the audit; the subjectively determined liabilities relate to a material portion of the financial statements.	Nonpublic	N
9.	Provide actuarial services related to certain liabilities as well as perform the audit; the subjectively determined liabilities relate to material portion of the financial statements.	Public	N
10.	Corporate executives of an audit client want to have WW provide tax planning for themselves (not the company).	Public	N

Explanations

1. Not allowable (PCAOB requirements prohibit)
2. Allowable (PCAOB permits preparation of corporate tax return for audit client)
3. Allowable (AICPA permits preparation of corporate tax return for audit client)
4. Allowable (AICPA permits bookkeeping, given the auditor does not perform the services listed as being excluded from auditor responsibility. PCAOB prohibits bookkeeping services.)
5. Allowable (Because no attest services are provided)
6. Not allowable (PCAOB prohibits performing such responsibilities for audit client.)
7. Allowable (AICPA permits if it is an off-the-shelf system, meaning not designed by the firm)
8. Not allowable (Prohibited when amounts are subjectively determined and material)
9. Not allowable (Prohibited when amounts are subjectively determined and material)
10. Not allowable (Tax planning is prohibited for the audit client—corporate executives are in a key position with respect to the audit.)

Task-Based Simulation 5

Research		
	Authoritative Literature	
		Help

Payroll System Engagement

Michael Edlinger is president of Edlinger Corporation, a nonpublic manufacturer of kitchen cabinets. He has been approached by Marla Wong, a partner with Wong and Co., CPAs, who suggests that her firm can design a payroll system for Edlinger that will either save his corporation money or be free. More specifically, Ms. Wong proposes to design a payroll system for Edlinger on a contingent fee basis. She suggests that her firm's fee will be 25% of the savings in payroll for each of the next four years. After four years Edlinger will be able to keep all future savings. Edlinger Corporation's payroll system costs currently are approximately $200,000 annually, and the corporation has not previously been a client of Wong. Edlinger Corporation is audited by another CPA firm and Wong & Co. provides no other services to Edlinger Corporation. Select one of the following topics to answer question 1.

Selections

A. AU-C
B. PCAOB
C. AT
D. AR
E. ET
F. BL
G. CS
H. QC

	(A)	(B)	(C)	(D)	(E)	(F)	(G)	(H)
1. Which topic of the Professional Standards addresses this issue and will be helpful in determining whether Wong & Co. may perform this engagement under these terms without violating professional requirements?	○	○	○	○	○	○	○	○

2. Provide the appropriate paragraph citation that addresses this issue.

3. Interpret your findings in parts 1 and 2 and conclude whether Wong & Co. may perform this service without violating professional standards.

Yes, this service may be performed without violating professional standards.

No, this service may not be performed without violating professional standards.

Task-Based Simulation 5 Solution

Research

Authoritative Literature

Help

	(A)	(B)	(C)	(D)	(E)	(F)	(G)	(H)
1. Which topic of the Professional Standards addresses this issue and will be helpful in determining whether Wong & Co. may perform this engagement under these terms without violating professional requirements?	○	○	○	○	●	○	○	○

2. Provide the appropriate paragraph citation that addresses this issue.

1.510.001	01

3. Interpret your findings in parts 1 and 2 and conclude on whether Wong & Co. may perform this service without violating professional standards.

X   Yes, this service may be performed without violating professional standards.

   No, this service may not be performed without violating professional standards.

Assessing Risk and Developing a Planned Response

Planning Activities

Pre-Engagement Planning Issues

Task-Based Simulation 6

Research Topics		
	Authoritative Literature	
		Help

Assume that you have been hired to perform the audit of Hanmei's financial statements. When planning such an audit, you often may need to refer to various of the profession's auditing standards. For each of the following circumstances in Column A, select the topic that is likely to provide the most guidance in the planning of the audit. A topic may be selected once, more than once, or not at all.

Topic

A. Analytical Procedures
B. Materiality
C. Communications between Predecessor and Successor Auditors
D. Consideration of Fraud in a Financial Statement Audit
E. Understanding the Entity and Its Environment and Assessing the Risks of Material Misstatement

F. Consideration of Laws and Regulations
G. Management Representations
H. Part of the Audit Performed by Other Independent Auditors
I. Related Parties

Transactions	(A)	(B)	(C)	(D)	(E)	(F)	(G)	(H)	(I)
1. Possible risk factors related to misappropriation of assets.	O	O	O	O	O	O	O	O	O
2. The relationship between materiality used for planning versus evaluation purposes.	O	O	O	O	O	O	O	O	O
3. Hanmei Corp. has transactions with the corporation president's brother.	O	O	O	O	O	O	O	O	O
4. Comparing a client's unaudited results for the year with last year's audited results.	O	O	O	O	O	O	O	O	O
5. Auditing and reporting guidance on the possible need to reaudit previous year results due to the disbanding of the firm that performed last year's audit.	O	O	O	O	O	O	O	O	O
6. Requirements relating to identifying violations of occupational safety and health regulations.	O	O	O	O	O	O	O	O	O
7. Audit report considerations when audit of a subsidiary of the client will be performed by Williams & Co., CPAs.	O	O	O	O	O	O	O	O	O
8. The need to brainstorm among audit team members about how accounts could be intentionally misstated.	O	O	O	O	O	O	O	O	O
9. Details on considering design effectiveness of controls.	O	O	O	O	O	O	O	O	O
10. The importance of considering the possibility of overstated revenues (for example, through premature revenue recognition).	O	O	O	O	O	O	O	O	O

Task-Based Simulation 6 Solution

Research Topics		
	Authoritative Literature	
		Help

Topic

A. Analytical Procedures
B. Materiality
C. Communications between Predecessor and Successor Auditors
D. Consideration of Fraud in a Financial Statement Audit
E. Understanding the Entity and Its Environment and Assessing the Risks of Material Misstatement

F. Consideration of Laws and Regulations
G. Management Representations
H. Part of the Audit Performed by Other Independent Auditors
I. Related Parties

Transactions	(A)	(B)	(C)	(D)	(E)	(F)	(G)	(H)	(I)
1. Possible risk factors related to misappropriation of assets.	○	○	○	●	○	○	○	○	○
2. The relationship between materiality used for planning versus evaluation purposes.	○	●	○	○	○	○	○	○	○
3. Hanmei Corp. has transactions with the corporation president's brother.	○	○	○	○	○	○	○	○	●
4. Comparing a client's unaudited results for the year with last year's audited results.	●	○	○	○	○	○	○	○	○
5. Auditing and reporting guidance on the possible need to reaudit previous year results due to the disbanding of the firm that performed last year's audit.	○	○	●	○	○	○	○	○	○
6. Requirements relating to identifying violations of occupational safety and health regulations.	○	○	○	○	○	●	○	○	○
7. Audit report considerations when audit of a subsidiary of the client will be performed by Williams & Co., CPAs.	○	○	○	○	○	○	○	●	○
8. The need to brainstorm among audit team members about how accounts could be intentionally misstated.	○	○	○	●	○	○	○	○	○
9. Details on considering design effectiveness of controls.	○	○	○	○	●	○	○	○	○
10. The importance of considering the possibility of overstated revenues (for example, through premature revenue recognition).	○	○	○	●	○	○	○	○	○

Audit Risk

Task-Based Simulation 7

Effects on Audit Risk Components		
	Authoritative Literature	
		Help

Bestwood Furniture, Inc., a private company that produces wood furniture, is undergoing a year 2 audit. The situations in the following table describe changes Bestwood made during year 2 that may or may not contribute to audit risk. For each situation, select from the list provided the impact, if any, that the situation has on a specific component of audit risk for the year 2 audit. A selection may be used once, more than once, or not at all.

Impact on component of audit risk

A. Decreases control risk
B. Decreases detection risk
C. Decreases inherent risk
D. Increases control risk
E. Increases detection risk
F. Increases inherent risk
G. No impact on audit risk

Situation	(A)	(B)	(C)	(D)	(E)	(F)	(G)
1. During year 2, the company instituted a new procedure whereby the internal audit department distributes payroll checks to employees for selected payroll cycles.	O	O	O	O	O	O	O
2. During year 2, the company centralized authority for changes in accounting software programs by placing sole responsibility for such changes with the programmer who makes the changes, replacing a system in which an individual other than the programmer reviews such changes.	O	O	O	O	O	O	O
3. Early in year 2, the company extended its existing warranty program on certain of its major products in an effort to increase revenue.	O	O	O	O	O	O	O

Task-Based Simulation 7 Solution

Effects on Audit Risk Components		
	Authoritative Literature	
		Help

Situation	(A)	(B)	(C)	(D)	(E)	(F)	(G)
1. During year 2, the company instituted a new procedure whereby the internal audit department distributes payroll checks to employees for selected payroll cycles.	●	O	O	O	O	O	O
2. In year 2, the auditor noted that the company's newly hired purchasing agent was **not** obtaining competitive bids for all major purchase requisitions.	O	O	O	●	O	O	O
3. Early in year 2, the company extended its existing warranty program on certain of its major products in an effort to increase revenue.	O	O	O	O	O	●	O

Task-Based Simulation 8

Risk of Material Misstatement Analysis		
	Authoritative Literature	
		Help

You are working with William Bond, CPA, and you are considering the risk of material misstatement in planning the audit of Toxic Waste Disposal (TWD) Company's financial statements for the year ended

December 31, 20X1. TWD is a privately owned entity that contracts with municipal governments to remove environmental waste. Based only on the following information, indicate whether each of the following factors would **most** likely increase (I), decrease (D), or have no effect on the risk of material misstatement (N).

	(I)	(D)	(N)
1. Because municipalities have received increased federal and state funding for environmental purposes, TWD returned to profitability for the first year following three years with losses.	O	O	O
2. TWD's Board of Directors is controlled by Mead, the majority stockholder, who also acts as the chief executive officer.	O	O	O
3. The internal auditor reports to the controller and the controller reports to Mead.	O	O	O
4. The accounting department has experienced a high rate of turnover of key personnel.	O	O	O
5. TWD's bank has a loan officer who meets regularly with TWD's CEO and controller to monitor TWD's financial performance.	O	O	O
6. TWD's employees are paid biweekly.	O	O	O
7. TWD has such a strong financial presence in its history so as to allow it often to dictate the terms or conditions of transactions with its suppliers.	O	O	O
8. During 20X1, TWD changed its method of preparing its financial statements from the cash basis to generally accepted accounting principles.	O	O	O
9. During 20X1, TWD sold one-half of its controlling interest in United Equipment Leasing (UEL) Co. TWD retained significant influence over UEL.	O	O	O
10. During 20X1, litigation filed against TWD from an action 10 years ago that alleged that TWD discharged pollutants into state waterways was dropped by the state. Loss contingency disclosures that TWD included in prior years' financial statements are being removed from the 20X1 financial statements.	O	O	O
11. During December 20X1, TWD signed a contract to lease disposal equipment from an entity owned by Mead's parents. This related-party transaction is not disclosed in TWD's notes to the 20X1 financial statements.	O	O	O
12. During December 20X1, TWD completed a barter transaction with a municipality. TWD removed waste from the municipally owned site and acquired title to another contaminated site at below market price. TWD intends to service this new site in 20X2.	O	O	O
13. During December 20X1, TWD increased its casualty insurance coverage on several pieces of sophisticated machinery from historical cost to replacement cost.	O	O	O
14. Inquiries about the substantial increase in revenue TWD recorded in the fourth quarter of 20X1 disclosed a new policy. TWD guaranteed to several municipalities that it would refund the federal and state funding paid to TWD if any municipality fails a federal or state site clean-up inspection in 20X2.	O	O	O
15. An initial public offering of TWD's stock is planned for late 20X2.	O	O	O

Task-Based Simulation 8 Solution

Risk of Material Misstatement Analysis		
	Authoritative Literature	
		Help

AU-C 200, 240, and 320 all require that auditors consider factors influencing the risk of material misstatement and that the risk of material misstatement be considered during the planning phase of an audit engagement.

1. (**D**) Since TWD returned to profitable operation, its healthier financial condition leads to a decrease in the risk of material misstatement.
2. (**I**) The risk of material misstatement increases when management is dominated by a single person. Since Mead controls the Board of Directors, is a majority stockholder, and is the CEO, it would appear that Mead dominates management.
3. (**I**) The risk of material misstatement increases when the internal auditor reports to top management rather than to the audit committee because it is less likely that the internal auditor will be able to objectively perform the function.
4. (**I**) The risk of material misstatement increases when the key management positions (particularly senior accounting personnel) encounter turnover.
5. (**D**) The loan officer's continual monitoring of TWD decreases the risk of material misstatement.
6. (**N**) Timing of payroll cycles would normally have no impact on the risk of material misstatement.
7. (**I**) A strong financial presence or ability to dominate a certain industry sector that allows a company to dictate terms or conditions to suppliers or customers may result in inappropriate or non-arm's-length transactions.
8. (**I**) A change to generally accepted accounting principles will increase the risk of material misstatement because the change in basis requires management to prepare a number of entries that have not been made in the past; these entries may be made improperly. Also, difficulties in determining beginning accrual basis balances increases the risk of misstatement.
9. (**I**) The sale of one-half of the company's controlling interest in United Equipment Leasing is an entry that is out of the ordinary course of business, and accordingly, increases the risk of material misstatement.
10. (**D**) Litigation results in contentious and difficult accounting valuation issues because an accountant must attempt to determine the likelihood of loss and the amount.
11. (**I**) The risk of material misstatement increases when significant related-party transactions occur and management has an aggressive attitude towards reporting of the transactions.
12. (**I**) The risk of material misstatement increases in situations where there are unusual and difficult accounting issues present. It would appear that the barter transaction with a below-market purchase would be considered an unusual transaction.
13. (**N**) The amount of insurance coverage would have little impact on the risk of material misstatement.
14. (**I**) The risk of material misstatement increases as it appears that management has taken an aggressive attitude toward reporting this transaction. In addition, this appears to be an unusual and difficult accounting issue involving revenue recognition.
15. (**I**) Experience has shown that a number of entities have intentionally misstated reported financial condition and operating results in situations in which a public (or private) placement of securities is planned. Accordingly, an initial public offering of stock increases the risk of material misstatement.

Fraud: Evaluation and Communication

Task-Based Simulation 9

Risk Analysis		
	Authoritative Literature	
		Help

DietWeb Inc. (hereafter DietWeb) was incorporated and began business in March of 20X1, seven years ago. You are working on the 20X8 audit—your CPA firm's fifth audit of DietWeb.

The company's mission is to provide solutions that help individuals to realize their full potential through better eating habits and lifestyles. Much of 20X1 and 20X2 was spent in developing a unique software platform that facilitates the production of individualized meal plans and shopping lists using a specific mathematical algorithm, which considers the user's physical condition, proclivity to exercise, food preferences, cooking preferences, desire to use prepackaged meals or dine out, among others. DietWeb sold its first online diet program in 20X2 and has continued to market memberships through increasing online advertising arrangements through the years. The company has continued to develop this program throughout the years and finally became profitable in 20X6.

DietWeb is executing a strategy to be a leading online provider of services, information, and products related to nutrition, fitness and motivation. In 20X8, the company derived approximately 86% of its total revenues from the sale of approximately 203,000 personalized subscription-based online nutrition plans related to weight management, to dietary regimens such as vegetarianism and to specific medical conditions such as Type 2 diabetes. Given the personal nature of dieting, DietWeb assures customers of complete privacy of the information they provide. To this point DietWeb's management is proud of its success in assuring the privacy of information supplied by its customers—this is a constant battle given the variety of intrusion attempts by various Internet hackers.

DietWeb nutrition plans are paid in advance by customers and offered in increments of 13 weeks with the customers having the ability to cancel and receive a refund of the unused portion of the subscription— this results in a significant level of "deferred revenue" each period. Although some DietWeb members are billed through use of the postal system, most DietWeb members currently purchase programs and products using credit cards, with renewals billed automatically, until cancellation. One week of a basic DietWeb membership costs less than one-half the cost of a weekly visit to the leading classroom-based diet program. The president, Mr. William Readings, suggests that in addition to its superior cost-effectiveness, the DietWeb online diet program is successful relative to classroom-based programs due to its customization, ease of use, expert support, privacy, constant availability, and breadth of choice. The basic DietWeb membership includes:

- Customized meal plans and workout schedules and related tools such as shopping lists, journals, and weight and exercise tracking.
- Interactive online support and education including approximately 100 message boards on various topics of interest to members and a library of dozens of multimedia educational segments presented by experts including psychologists, mental health counselors, dietitians, fitness trainers, a spiritual advisor, and a physician.
- 24/7/365 telephone support from a staff of approximately 30 customer service representatives, nutritionists, and fitness personnel.

Throughout its nine-year history, Mr. William Readings has served as chief executive officer. The other three founders of the company are also officers. A fifth individual, Willingsley Williamson, also a founder, served as Chief Financial Officer until mid-20X8 when he left the company due to a difference of opinion with Mr. Readings. The four founders purchased Mr. Williamson's stock and invested an additional approximately $1.2 million in common stock during 20X8 so as to limit the use of long-term debt.

The company's board of directors is currently composed of the four individuals who remain active in the company; these four individuals also serve as the company's audit committee; Mr. Readings chairs both the board and the audit committee. Previously, Mr. Readings had also served on the board and the audit committee. With Mr. Williamson's departure, Ms. Jane Jennings, another of the founders, became the company's CFO.

The nutrition and diet industry in many ways thrives because individuals are becoming more aware of the negative health and financial consequences of being overweight, and consider important both weight loss and healthy weight maintenance. A study by two respected researchers concluded that obesity was linked to higher rates of chronic illness than living in poverty, than smoking, or than drinking. In addition, the American Cancer Society reported that as many as 14% of cancer deaths in men and 20% of cancer deaths in women could be related to being overweight.

The financial costs of excess weight are also high. A 20X8 study based on data from a major automobile manufacturer's health-care plan showed that an overweight adult has annual health-care costs that are 7.3% higher than a person in a healthy weight range, while obese individuals have annual health-care costs that are 69% higher than a person of a healthy weight. With health-care cost inflation running in the double digits in the United States since 20X4, supporters of the industry believe that the implementation of effective weight management tools will attract more attention from insurers, employers, consumers, and the government. As of January 20X9 five nutrition- or fitness-related bills were being considered in Congress, and several states had enacted or were considering enacting legislation relating to the sale of "junk" food in public schools. In addition, the U.S. Food and Drug Administration, Department of Health and Human Services, and Federal Trade Commission are contemplating new labeling requirements for packaged food and restaurant food, new educational and motivational programs related to healthy eating and exercise, and increased regulation of advertising claims for food.

In response to consumers' growing demand for more healthful eating options, quick-service and full-service restaurants have introduced new offerings including salads, sandwiches, burgers, and other food items designed for the weight-conscious person. At the retail level, sales of natural and organic foods have been growing more rapidly than the overall food and over-the-counter drug market for the last several years. Nutritional supplement sales in the United States, for instance, are estimated to have grown 34% between 20X4 and 20X8, while natural and organic foods are estimated to be growing at a rate of approximately 15% annually. Also, the industry has a tendency to change quickly as dieting fads regularly are introduced; some remain popular for years, some for only months.

Approximately 60% of the U.S. adult population, or 120 million adults, are overweight and, of those, the Calorie Control Council estimates only about 50 million are dieting in a given year. About 15% of these dieters are using a commercial weight loss center, generating revenues of approximately $1.5 billion annually. DietWeb targets dieters who are online, which represents about two-thirds of the total universe at current Internet penetration rates, or 34 million adults, about 5 million of whom are spending approximately $1 billion at weight loss centers.

At the same time, the online dieting segment of the market is growing rapidly. The online diet industry in the United States generated in excess of $100 million in 20X8, compared to revenues of approximately $75 million in 20X2. The industry includes other online nutrition and diet-oriented websites.

Another group of competitors to DietWeb are commercial weight loss centers, an industry that has shown marked decline in the last decade. According to Market Analysis Enterprises, the number of commercial weight loss centers in the United States declined approximately 50% between 20X2 and 20X8, from over 8,600 to approximately 4,400. DietWeb competes against this segment on the basis of lower price, superior value, convenience, availability, the ability to personalize a meal plan on an ongoing basis, its extensive support capabilities, and the breadth of its meal plan options.

	(A)	(B)	(C)	(D)
1. Of the following, which is likely to be one of DietWeb's major risks of doing business on the Internet in the future?	○	○	○	○

    A. Maintaining privacy of customer information.
    B. Maintaining the ability to pay Federal Communication Commission Internet use fees.
    C. Inability to provide 24/7/365 support.
    D. Inability to reach customers beyond the United States.

	(A)	(B)	(C)	(D)
2. Which of the following is likely to be the most significant business risk for DietWeb?	○	○	○	○

    A. Internal control limitations due to the small size of the company.
    B. Inability of the Internet to provide adequate support for such a business due to its instability.
    C. Entrance of new competitors onto the Internet.
    D. Misstatements of revenues due to difficulties in determining appropriate year-end cutoffs.

	(A)	(B)	(C)	(D)
3. Which of the following is most accurate concerning DietWeb's audit committee?	○	○	○	○

    A. It should be considered very independent in that the company's founders serve on it.
    B. Mr. Readings' chairmanship of the audit committee creates a situation in which the audit committee serves a strong independent role due to his closeness to company operations.
    C. Because all committee members are members of management, the audit committee lacks independence.
    D. The audit committee does not have enough members in that the size of the board of directors should be less than that of the audit committee.

<table>
<tr><td></td><td>(A)</td><td>(B)</td><td>(C)</td><td>(D)</td></tr>
</table>

4. Which of the following indicates an increased risk of misstatement due to fraud?

    A. Resignation of Mr. Williamson.
    B. Domination of management by company founders.
    C. Issuance of debt during 20X8.
    D. Competition with non-Internet weight loss organizations.

5. Which of the following is the most significant risk facing DietWeb that might cause it to not be able to continue increasing sales?

    A. A decreasing market in the United States for dietary products.
    B. DietWeb must respond to dieting fads on a timely basis.
    C. The constantly decreasing number of individuals in the United States.
    D. Obsolescence of the Internet.

Task-Based Simulation 9 Solution

Risk Analysis
Authoritative Literature
Help

	(A)	(B)	(C)	(D)

1. Of the following, which is likely to be one of DietWeb's major risks of doing business on the Internet in the future?   **● (A)**

    A. Maintaining privacy of customer information.
    B. Maintaining the ability to pay Federal Communication Commission Internet use fees.
    C. Inability to provide 24/7/365 support.
    D. Inability to reach customers beyond the United States.

2. Which of the following is likely to be the most significant business risk for DietWeb?   **● (C)**

    A. Maintaining privacy of customer information.
    B. Maintaining the ability to pay Federal Communication Commission Internet use fees.
    C. Inability to provide 24/7/365 support.
    D. Inability to reach customers beyond the United States.

3. Which of the following is most accurate concerning DietWeb's audit committee?   **● (C)**

    A. It should be considered very independent in that the company's founders serve on it.
    B. Mr. Readings' chairmanship of the audit committee creates a situation in which the audit committee serves a strong independent role due to his closeness to company operations.
    C. Because all committee members are members of management, the audit committee lacks independence.
    D. The audit committee does not have enough members in that the size of the board of directors should be less than that of the audit committee.

	(A)	(B)	(C)	(D)
4. Which of the following indicates an increased risk of misstatement due to fraud?	●	○	○	○

   A.   Resignation of Mr. Williamson.
   B.   Domination of management by company founders.
   C.   Issuance of debt during 20X8.
   D.   Competition with non-Internet weight loss organizations.

	(A)	(B)	(C)	(D)
5. Which of the following is the most significant risk facing DietWeb that might cause it to not be able to continue increasing sales?	○	●	○	○

   A.   A decreasing market in the United States for dietary products.
   B.   DietWeb must respond to dieting fads on a timely basis.
   C.   The constantly decreasing number of individuals in the United States.
   D.   Obsolescence of the Internet.

Explanations

1. **(A)** The requirement is to identify DietWeb's major listed risk of doing business on the Internet. Answer (A) is correct because DietWeb must carefully maintain the privacy of their customers' information—both due to law and due to DietWeb's assurance provided to its customers. Answer (B) is incorrect because there are no major Federal Communications Commission Internet use fees. Answer (C) is incorrect because the case indicates no particular problem in providing 24/7/365 support. Answer (D) is incorrect because the Internet is able to reach customers beyond the United States.

2. **(C)** The requirement is to identify the most significant business risk listed for DietWeb. Answer (C) is correct because barriers to entrance on the Internet are ordinarily not high. Another organization might develop similar (or more accepted) software, and/or charge lower prices than those charged by DietWeb. Answer (A) is incorrect because internal control limitations need not necessarily be a major problem, and because internal control relates to control risk more directly than to the company's business risk. Answer (B) is incorrect because while Internet instability may cause difficulties, few would consider it as significant a problem as new competitors. Answer (D) is incorrect because determining appropriate year-end cutoffs is **not** likely to create major difficulties.

3. **(C)** The requirement is to identify the most accurate statement concerning DietWeb's audit committee. Answer (C) is correct because the audit committee has no members who are independent of management. Answer (A) is incorrect because the audit committee has no members who are independent of management. Answer (A) is incorrect because the company founders are not independent. Answer (B) is incorrect because Mr. Readings' chairmanship of the audit committee is likely to result in a weak, not a strong audit committee. Answer (D) is incorrect because the size of the board of directors virtually always exceeds that of the audit committee—it is not equal to or less than in size.

4. **(A)** The requirement is to identify a factor that indicates an increased risk of misstatement due to fraud. Answer (A) is correct because the simulation provides no explanation of the nature of the disagreement that led to Mr. Williamson's resignation from an apparently very desirable job. Answer (B) is incorrect because many small companies are dominated by company founders and those companies do not generally misstate earnings due to fraud. Answer (C) is incorrect because the issuance of debt need not indicate fraud. Answer (D) is incorrect because competition itself need not lead to an increased risk of misstatement due to fraud.

5. **(B)** The requirement is to identify the most significant risk facing DietWeb that might cause it not to be able to continue increasing sales. Answer (B) is correct because the industry information makes clear that the market changes rapidly—only companies that can respond in a timely basis are likely to be able to maintain and improve sales. Answers (A) and (C) are incorrect because there is no indication that the United States will face a decreasing market for dietary products or that the population is decreasing. Answer (D) is incorrect because at this point there is no indication of obsolescence of the Internet.

Task-Based Simulation 10

Audit Risk Application		
	Authoritative Literature	
		Help

Green, CPA, is considering audit risk, including fraud risk, at the financial statement level in planning the audit of National Federal Bank (NFB) Company's financial statements for the year ended December 31, 20X5. Audit risk at the financial statement level is influenced by the risk of material misstatements, which may be indicated by a combination of factors related to management, the industry, and the entity. In assessing such factors Green has gathered the following information concerning NFB's environment.

Company Profile

NFB is a federally insured bank that has been consistently more profitable than the industry average by marketing mortgages on properties in a prosperous rural area, which has experienced considerable growth in recent years. NFB packages its mortgages and sells them to large mortgage investment trusts. Despite recent volatility of interest rates, NFB has been able to continue selling its mortgages as a source of new lendable funds.

NFB's board of directors is controlled by Smith, the majority stockholder, who also acts as the chief executive officer. Management at the bank's branch offices has authority for directing and controlling NFB's operations and is compensated based on branch profitability. The internal auditor reports directly to Harris, a minority shareholder, who also acts as chairman of the board's audit committee.

The accounting department has experienced little turnover in personnel during the five years Green has audited NFB. NFB's formula consistently underestimates the allowance for loan losses, but its controller has always been receptive to Green's suggestions to increase the allowance during each engagement.

Recent Developments

During 20X5, NFB opened a branch office in a suburban town 30 miles from its principal place of business. Although this branch is not yet profitable due to competition from several well-established regional banks, management believes that the branch will be profitable by 20X7. Also, during 20X5, NFB increased the efficiency of its accounting operations by installing a new, sophisticated computer system.

Based only on the information above, indicate whether the following factors indicate an increased or decreased audit risk. Also, indicate whether the factor is a fraud risk factor.

Factor	Increased audit risk	Decreased audit risk	Fraud risk factor
1. Branch management authority	○	○	○
2. Government regulation	○	○	○
3. Company profitability	○	○	○
4. Demand for product	○	○	○
5. Interest rates	○	○	○
6. Availability of mortgage funds	○	○	○
7. Involvement of principal shareholder in management	○	○	○
8. Branch manager compensation	○	○	○
9. Internal audit reporting relationship	○	○	○
10. Accounting department turnover	○	○	○

(Continued)

Factor	Increased audit risk	Decreased audit risk	Fraud risk factor
11. Continuing audit relationship	○	○	○
12. Internal controls over accounting estimates	○	○	○
13. Response to proposed accounting adjustments	○	○	○
14. New unprofitable branch	○	○	○
15. New computer system	○	○	○

Task-Based Simulation 10 Solution

Audit Risk Application

Authoritative Literature

Help

Factor	Increased audit risk	Decreased audit risk	Fraud risk factor
1. Branch management authority	●	○	●
2. Government regulation	○	●	○
3. Company profitability	○	●	○
4. Demand for product	○	●	○
5. Interest rates	●	○	○
6. Availability of mortgage funds	○	●	○
7. Involvement of principal shareholder in management	○	●	○
8. Branch manager compensation	●	○	●
9. Internal audit reporting relationship	○	●	○
10. Accounting department turnover	○	●	○
11. Continuing audit relationship	○	●	○
12. Internal controls over accounting estimates	●	○	●
13. Response to proposed accounting adjustments	○	●	○
14. New unprofitable branch	●	○	●
15. New computer system	●	○	○

Internal Control—Concepts and Standards

Internal Control Concepts 2

Task-Based Simulation 11

```
┌─────────────────┐
│ Research        │
│        ┌────────────────────────┐
│        │ Authoritative Literature │
│        │            ┌──────────────────┐
│        │            │ Help             │
└────────┴────────────┴──────────────────┘
```

Internal Control Limitations

In a discussion with the controller of Gemcon, a nonpublic company, the topic of limitations of internal control arose. Relatedly, the Professional Standards acknowledge that internal control has certain limitations that affect financial statement audits. Search the Professional Standards to find the location at which a number of limitations are discussed together.

Selections

A. AU-C
B. PCAOB
C. AT
D. AR
E. ET
F. BL
G. CS
H. QC

	(A)	(B)	(C)	(D)	(E)	(F)	(G)	(H)
1. Which title of the Professional Standards addresses this issue?	○	○	○	○	○	○	○	○

2. Enter the exact section and paragraph number(s) that indicate that internal control has limitations.

Task-Based Simulation 11 Solution

```
┌─────────────────┐
│ Research        │
│        ┌────────────────────────┐
│        │ Authoritative Literature │
│        │            ┌──────────────────┐
│        │            │ Help             │
└────────┴────────────┴──────────────────┘
```

	(A)	(B)	(C)	(D)	(E)	(F)	(G)	(H)
1. Which title of the Professional Standards addresses this issue?	●	○	○	○	○	○	○	○

2. Enter the exact section and paragraph number(s) that indicate that internal control has limitations.

315	A46-A48

Internal Control—Required Communications

Task-Based Simulation 12

Internal Control–Related Matters Communication		
	Authoritative Literature	
		Help

You have been asked by the audit partner to draft a letter to the client on internal control related matters. You were informed that the written communication regarding significant deficiencies and material weaknesses indentified during an audit of financial statements should include certain statements.

For each of the significant deficiencies and material weaknesses reflected in the table below, select from the list provided the appropriate disposition of each statement in regard to the letter to the client on internal control–related matters. Each selection may be used once, more than once, or not at all.

Selection List

Included

Excluded

Included, but only with client management's approval

Communicated orally with no need to document the communication

Internal controls	Related matters
State that the purpose of the audit was to express an opinion on the financial statements, and to express an opinion on the effectiveness of the entity's internal control over financial reporting.	_____
Identify, if applicable, items that are considered to be material weaknesses.	_____
State that the author is not expressing an opinion on the effectiveness of internal control.	_____
Include the definition of the term *significant deficiency*.	_____
Include the definition of the term *material weakness*, where relevant.	_____
State that the author is expressing an unqualified opinion on the effectiveness of internal control.	_____
State that the communication is intended solely for management and external parties.	_____
Identify the matters that are considered to be significant deficiencies.	_____

Task-Based Simulation 12 Solution

Internal Control Related Matters Communication		
	Authoritative Literature	
		Help

AU-C 265 includes the matters required to be included in the written communication regarding significant deficiencies and material weaknesses indentified during an audit as

- State that the purpose of the audit was to express an opinion on the financial statements, but not to express an opinion on the effectiveness of the entity's internal control over financial reporting.
- State that the auditor is not expressing an opinion on the effectiveness of internal control.
- Include the definition of the terms *significant deficiency* and, where relevant, *material weakness*.
- Identify the matters that are considered to be significant deficiencies and, if applicable, those that are considered to be material weaknesses.
- State that the communication is intended solely for the information and use of management, those charged with governance, and others within the organization and is not intended to be and should not be used by anyone other than those specified parties. If an entity is required to furnish such auditor communications to a governmental authority, specific reference to such governmental authorities may be made.

Internal controls	Related matters	Explanation
State that the purpose of the audit was to express an opinion on the financial statements, and to express an opinion on the effectiveness of the entity's internal control over financial reporting.	Excluded	The latter part of the sentence is incorrect since no opinion on internal control effectiveness is issued.
Identify, if applicable, items that are considered to be material weaknesses.	Included	Required
State that the author is not expressing an opinion on the effectiveness of internal control.	Included	Required
Include the definition of the term *significant deficiency*.	Included	Required
Include the definition of the term *material weakness*, where relevant.	Included	Required
State that the author is expressing an unqualified opinion on the effectiveness of internal control.	Excluded	The auditor expresses no opinion on internal control.
State that the communication is intended solely for management and external parties.	Excluded	The communication is not intended for external parties.
Identify the matters that are considered to be significant deficiencies.	Included	Required

Performing Further Procedures and Obtaining Evidence

Internal Control: Transaction Cycles

Revenue/Receipts—Sales

Task-Based Simulation 13

Sales/Shipping Process		
	Authoritative Literature	
		Help

You are working for Smith & Co. CPAs. The partially completed flowchart on the following page depicts part of Welcore Inc., your client's revenue cycle. Some of the flowchart symbols are labeled to indicate controls and records. For each symbol numbered 1 through 13, select one response from the answer lists below. Each response in the lists may be selected once or not at all.

Operations and controls	**Documents, journals, ledgers, and files**
A. Enter shipping data	P. Shipping document
B. Verify agreement of sales order and shipping document	Q. General ledger master file
C. Write off accounts receivable	R. General journal
D. To warehouse and shipping department	S. Master price file
E. Authorize account receivable write-off	T. Sales journal
F. Prepare aged trial balance	U. Sales invoice
G. To sales department	V. Cash receipts journal
H. Release goods for shipment	W. Uncollectible accounts file
I. To accounts receivable department	X. Shipping file
J. Enter price data	Y. Aged trial balance
K. Determine that customer exists	Z. Open order file
L. Match customer purchase order with sales order	
M. Perform customer credit check	
N. Prepare sales journal	
O. Prepare sales invoice	

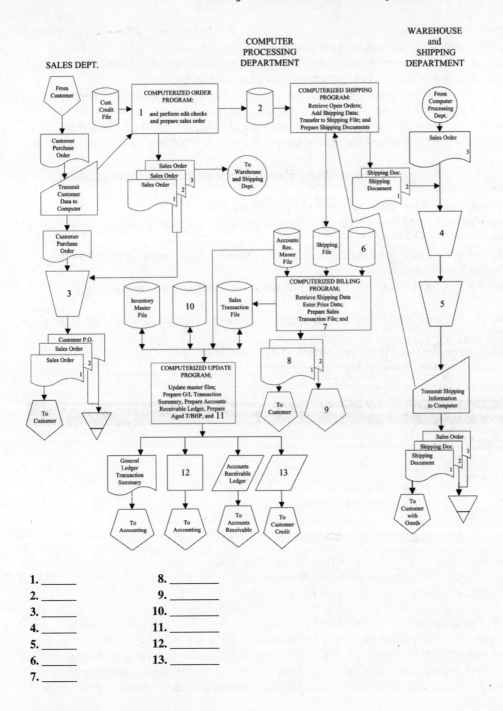

1. _____
2. _____
3. _____
4. _____
5. _____
6. _____
7. _____

8. _____
9. _____
10. _____
11. _____
12. _____
13. _____

Task-Based Simulation 13 Solution

Sales/Shipping Process

Authoritative Literature

Help

1. **(M)** *Perform customer credit check*—The customer credit file is being accessed, making it likely that a credit check is occurring.
2. **(Z)** *Open order file*—The processing to the right of #2 begins with "open orders," making this an open order file.

3. (L) *Match customer purchase order with sales order*—Two copies of the sales order are being combined with the customer purchase order through a manual operation (the trapezoid).

4. (B) *Verify agreement of sales order and shipping document*—This manual operation (trapezoid) includes two copies of the shipping document being combined with the sales order.

5. (H) *Release goods for shipment*—The department is the warehouse and shipping department, and out of this operation is "shipping information"; accordingly goods are being released for shipment.

6. (S) *Master price file*—The operation below #6 includes entering price data; since the first two files being accessed are the accounts receivable master file and the shipping file, this third file must include prices.

7. (O) *Prepare sales invoice*—Since a document is being prepared through this computerized billing program, it is the sales invoice.

8. (U) *Sales invoice*—A sales invoice is normally sent to the customer.

9. (I) *To accounts receivable department*—This copy of the sales invoice informs accounts receivable that the sale has been both processed and shipped.

10. (Q) *General ledger master file*—Because the processing step below includes updating of master files, this is the general ledger master file.

11. (N) *Prepare sales journal*—Sales transactions are being processed; accordingly a sales journal is prepared.

12. (T) *Sales journal*—From above, a sales journal was prepared; the accounting department will receive the sales journal.

13. (Y) *Aged trial balance*—In the processing step above, an aged trial balance of accounts receivable is prepared; the credit department will receive such a report.

Revenue/Receipts—Cash

Task-Based Simulation 14

Cash Receipts and Billing		
	Authoritative Literature	
		Help

An auditor's working papers include the narrative description of the cash receipts and billing portions of Southwest Medical Center's internal control. Evaluate the information in the situation as being either (1) a strength, (2) a weakness, or (3) not a strength or a weakness.

Southwest is a health-care provider that is owned by a partnership of five physicians. It employs eleven physicians, including the five owners, twenty nurses, five laboratory and X-ray technicians, and four clerical workers. The clerical workers perform such tasks as reception, correspondence, cash receipts, billing, accounts receivable, bank deposits, and appointment scheduling. These clerical workers are referred to in the situation as office manager, clerk #1, clerk #2, and clerk #3. Assume that the narrative is a complete description of the system.

About two-thirds of Southwest's patients receive medical services only after insurance coverage is verified by the office manager and communicated to the clerks. Most of the other patients pay for services by cash or check when services are rendered, although the office manager extends credit on a case-by-case basis to about 5% of the patients.

When services are rendered, the attending physician prepares a prenumbered service slip for each patient and gives the slip to clerk #1 for pricing. Clerk #1 completes the slip and gives the completed slip to clerk #2 and a copy to the patient.

Using the information on the completed slip, clerk #2 performs one of the following three procedures for each patient:

- Clerk #2 files an insurance claim and records a receivable from the insurance company if the office manager has verified the patient's coverage, or
- Clerk #2 posts a receivable from the patient on clerk #2's PC if the office manager has approved the patient's credit, or
- Clerk #2 receives cash or a check from the patient as the patient leaves the medical center, and clerk #2 records the cash receipt.

At the end of each day, clerk #2 prepares a revenue summary.

Clerk #1 performs correspondence functions and opens the incoming mail. Clerk #1 gives checks from insurance companies and patients to clerk #2 for deposit. Clerk #2 posts the receipt of patients' checks on clerk #2's PC patient receivable records and insurance companies' checks to the receivables from the applicable insurance companies. Clerk #1 gives mail requiring correspondence to clerk #3.

Clerk #2 stamps all checks "for deposit only" and each day prepares a list of checks and cash to be deposited in the bank. (This list also includes the cash and checks personally given to clerk #2 by patients.) Clerk #2 keeps a copy of the deposit list and gives the original to clerk #3.

Clerk #3 personally makes the daily bank deposit and maintains a file of the daily bank deposits. Clerk #3 also performs appointment scheduling for all of the doctors and various correspondence functions. Clerk #3 also maintains a list of patients whose insurance coverage the office manager has verified.

When insurance claims or patient receivables are not settled within 60 days, clerk #2 notifies the office manager. The office manager personally inspects the details of each instance of nonpayment. The office manager converts insurance claims that have been rejected by insurance companies into patient receivables. Clerk #2 records these patient receivables on clerk #2's PC and deletes these receivables from the applicable insurance companies. Clerk #2 deletes the patient receivables that appear to be uncollectible from clerk #2's PC when authorized by the office manager. Clerk #2 prepares a list of patients with uncollectible balances and gives a copy of the list to clerk #3, who will not allow these patients to make appointments for future services.

Once a month an outside accountant posts clerk #2's daily revenue summaries to the general ledger, prepares a monthly trial balance and monthly financial statements, accounts for prenumbered service slips, files payroll forms and tax returns, and reconciles the monthly bank statements to the general ledger. This accountant reports directly to the physician who is the managing partner.

All four clerical employees perform their tasks on PCs that are connected through a local area network. Each PC is accessible with a password that is known only to the individual employee and the managing partner. Southwest uses a standard software package that was acquired from a software company and that cannot be modified by Southwest's employees. None of the clerical employees have access to Southwest's check-writing abilities.

For each of the following conditions indicate whether it is a strength, weakness, or neither.

Condition	Strength	Weakness	Neither
1. Southwest is involved only in medical services and has not diversified its operations.	○	○	○
2. Insurance coverage for patients is verified and communicated to the clerks by the office manager before medical services are rendered.	○	○	○
3. The physician who renders the medical services documents the services on a prenumbered slip that is used for recording revenue and as a receipt for the patient.	○	○	○
4. Cash collection is centralized in that clerk #2 receives the cash (checks) from patients and records the cash receipt.	○	○	○

(Continued)

Condition	Strength	Weakness	Neither
5. Southwest extends credit rather than requiring cash or insurance in all cases.	○	○	○
6. The office manager extends credit on a case-by-case basis rather than using a formal credit search and established credit limits.	○	○	○
7. The office manager approves the extension of credit to patients and also approves the write-offs of uncollectible patient receivables.	○	○	○
8. Clerk #2 receives cash and checks and prepares the daily bank deposit.	○	○	○
9. Clerk #2 maintains the accounts receivable records and can add or delete information on the PC.	○	○	○
10. Prenumbered service slips are accounted for on a monthly basis by the outside accountant, who is independent of the revenue generating and revenue recording functions.	○	○	○
11. The bank reconciliation is prepared monthly by the outside accountant, who is independent of the revenue generating and revenue recording functions.	○	○	○
12. Computer passwords are only known to the individual employees and the managing partner, who has no duties in the revenue recording functions.	○	○	○
13. Computer software cannot be modified by Southwest's employees.	○	○	○
14. None of the employees who perform duties in the revenue generating and revenue recording are able to write checks.	○	○	○

Task-Based Simulation 14 Solution

Cash Receipts and Billing		
	Authoritative Literature	
		Help

Condition	Strength	Weakness	Neither
1. Southwest is involved only in medical services and has not diversified its operations.	○	○	●
2. Insurance coverage for patients is verified and communicated to the clerks by the office manager before medical services are rendered.	●	○	○
3. The physician who renders the medical services documents the services on a prenumbered slip that is used for recording revenue and as a receipt for the patient.	●	○	○
4. Cash collection is centralized in that clerk #2 receives the cash (checks) from patients and records the cash receipt.	○	●	○
5. Southwest extends credit rather than requiring cash or insurance in all cases.	○	○	●
6. The office manager extends credit on a case-by-case basis rather than using a formal credit search and established credit limits.	○	●	○
7. The office manager approves the extension of credit to patients and also approves the write-offs of uncollectible patient receivables.	○	●	○
8. Clerk #2 receives cash and checks and prepares the daily bank deposit.	○	●	○

Condition	Strength	Weakness	Neither
9. Clerk #2 maintains the accounts receivable records and can add or delete information on the PC.	○	●	○
10. Prenumbered service slips are accounted for on a monthly basis by the outside accountant, who is independent of the revenue generating and revenue recording functions.	●	○	○
11. The bank reconciliation is prepared monthly by the outside accountant, who is independent of the revenue generating and revenue recording functions.	●	○	○
12. Computer passwords are only known to the individual employees and the managing partner, who has no duties in the revenue recording functions.	●	○	○
13. Computer software cannot be modified by Southwest's employees.	●	○	○
14. None of the employees who perform duties in the revenue generating and revenue recording are able to write checks.	●	○	○

Task-Based Simulation 15

Purchases and Disbursements

Authoritative Literature

Help

The flowchart on the following page depicts part of a client's purchases and cash disbursements cycle. Some of the flowchart symbols are labeled to indicate operations, controls, and records. For each symbol numbered 1 through 12, select one response from the answer lists below. Each response in the lists may be selected once or not at all.

Operations and controls	Connectors, documents, departments, and files	
A. Approve receiving report	J. Accounts payable	O. Purchase order No. 5
B. Prepare and approve voucher	K. Canceled voucher package	P. Receiving report No. 1
C. Prepare purchase order	L. From purchasing	Q. Stores
D. Prepare purchase requisition	M. From receiving	R. To vendor
E. Prepare purchases journal	N. From vouchers payable	S. Treasurer
F. Prepare receiving report		T. Unpaid voucher file, filed by due date
G. Prepare sales journal		
H. Prepare voucher		
I. Sign checks and cancel voucher package documents		

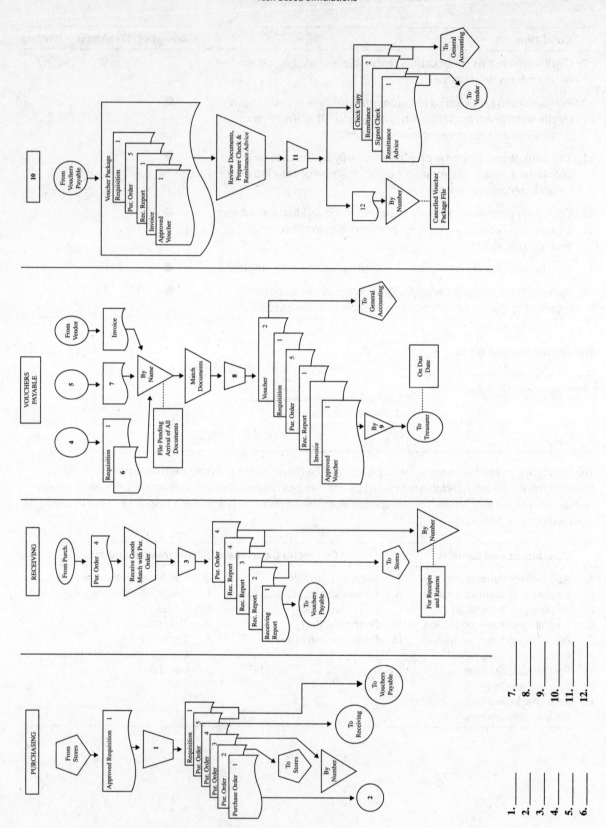

Task-Based Simulation 15 Solution

Purchases and Disbursements		
	Authoritative Literature	
		Help

1. (**C**) *Prepare purchase order*—A trapezoid represents a manual operation. Here, a purchase order enters the flowchart after this step; accordingly, a purchase order is being prepared.

2. (**R**) *To vendor*—A circle represents a connector, a symbol indicating that a document is entering or leaving that portion of the flowchart. Here a copy of the purchase order is sent to the vendor to order the goods. This must be the case, because otherwise the vendor would not be informed of the order.

3. (**F**) *Prepare receiving report*—A trapezoid represents a manual operation. Here, a receiving report enters the flowchart after this step; accordingly, a receiving report is being prepared. Also, note above this step that goods are received, the point at which one would expect preparation of a receiving report.

4. (**L**) *From purchasing*—A circle represents a connector, a symbol indicating that a document is entering or leaving that portion of the flowchart. The document here is from purchasing because below the connector is requisition No. 1, which purchasing has sent with the purchase order No. 5 to vouchers payable, as evidenced by the connector in the bottom far right under purchasing.

5. (**M**) *From receiving*—A circle represents a connector, a symbol indicating that a document is entering or leaving that portion of the flowchart. The document here is from receiving because under the receiving portion of the flowchart, approximately 3/4 of the way down, we see a connector indicating that receiving report No. 1 is being sent to vouchers payable. Also, toward the bottom under the vouchers payable portion of the flowchart, we see that receiving report No. 1 is indeed in the system.

6. (**O**) *Purchase order No. 5*—We know from item 4 that this document was sent from purchasing, and we know that purchasing has sent to vouchers payable requisition No. 1 and purchase order No. 5. Since requisition No. 1 is labeled on the flowchart, this must be purchase order No. 5.

7. (**P**) *Receiving report No. 1*—We know from item 5 that this document was sent from receiving, and since we know that receiving has sent receiving report No. 1 to vouchers payable this must be that document.

8. (**B**) *Prepare and approve voucher*—A trapezoid represents a manual operation. Here, an approved voucher enters the flowchart after this step; accordingly, a voucher is being prepared and approved in this step.

9. (**T**) *Unpaid voucher file, filed by due date*—The triangle symbol represents a file. Entering this file are the approved but unpaid vouchers with the support of their invoices, receiving reports, purchase orders and purchase requisitions. Because these vouchers are sent to the treasurer in order of due date (the bottom, right symbol under vouchers payable) this file is the unpaid voucher file, filed by due date.

10. (**S**) *Treasurer*—Because the unpaid vouchers (the "voucher package") was sent from vouchers payable to the treasurer, this is the treasurer.

11. (**I**) *Sign checks and cancel voucher package documents*—A trapezoid represents a manual operation. Here, the operation prior to 11 involves a review of documents and preparation of a check and a remittance advice. After this operation the documents changed are a "canceled voucher package file" and a "signed check;" accordingly, checks are being signed and the voucher package is being canceled.

12. (**K**) *Canceled voucher package*—After step 11, the check copy, remittance advice No. 1, the signed check, and remittance advice No. 2 exit on the far right. Accordingly, item 12 is the voucher package, now canceled as evidenced by the description below the triangular file symbol.

Audit Evidence: Concepts and Standards

Overview of Substantive Procedures

Task-Based Simulation 16

Observed Ratio Changes		
	Authoritative Literature	
		Help

Items 1 through 6 represent an auditor's observed changes in certain financial statement ratios or amounts from the prior year's ratios or amounts. For each observed change, select the **most** likely explanation or explanations from List B. Select only the number of explanations as indicated. Answers on the list may be selected once, more than once, or not at all.

List B

A. Items shipped on consignment during the last month of the year were recorded as sales.

B. A significant number of credit memos for returned merchandise that were issued during the last month of the year were not recorded.

C. Year-end purchases of inventory were overstated by incorrectly including items received in the first month of the subsequent year.

D. Year-end purchases of inventory were understated by incorrectly excluding items received before the year-end.

E. A larger percentage of sales occurred during the last month of the year, as compared to the prior year.

F. A smaller percentage of sales occurred during the last month of the year, as compared to the prior year.

G. The same percentage of sales occurred during the last month of the year, as compared to the prior year.

H. Sales increased at the same percentage as cost of goods sold, as compared to the prior year.

I. Sales increased at a greater percentage than cost of goods sold increased, as compared to the prior year.

J. Sales increased at a lower percentage than cost of goods sold increased, as compared to the prior year.

K. Interest expense decreased, as compared to the prior year.

L. The effective income tax rate increased, as compared to the prior year.

M. The effective income tax rate decreased, as compared to the prior year.

N. Short-term borrowing was refinanced on a long-term basis at the same interest rate.

O. Short-term borrowing was refinanced on a long-term basis at lower interest rates.

P. Short-term borrowing was refinanced on a long-term basis at higher interest rates.

Auditor's observed changes	(A)	(B)	(C)	(D)	(E)	(F)	(G)	(H)	(I)	(J)	(K)	(L)	(M)	(N)	(O)	(P)
1. Inventory turnover increased substantially from the prior year. (Select four explanations)	○	○	○	○	○	○	○	○	○	○	○	○	○	○	○	○
2. Accounts receivable turnover decreased substantially from the prior year. (Select three explanations)	○	○	○	○	○	○	○	○	○	○	○	○	○	○	○	○
3. Allowance for doubtful accounts increased from the prior year, but allowance for doubtful accounts as a percentage of accounts receivable decreased from the prior year. (Select three explanations)	○	○	○	○	○	○	○	○	○	○	○	○	○	○	○	○
4. Long-term debt increased from the prior year, but interest expense increased a larger-than-proportionate amount than long-term debt. (Select one explanation)	○	○	○	○	○	○	○	○	○	○	○	○	○	○	○	○
5. Operating income increased from the prior year although the entity was less profitable than in the prior year. (Select two explanations)	○	○	○	○	○	○	○	○	○	○	○	○	○	○	○	○
5. Gross margin percentage was unchanged from the prior year although gross margin increased from the prior year. (Select one explanation)	○	○	○	○	○	○	○	○	○	○	○	○	○	○	○	○

Task-Based Simulation 16 Solution

Observed Ratio Changes		
	Authoritative Literature	
		Help

Auditor's observed changes	(A)	(B)	(C)	(D)	(E)	(F)	(G)	(H)	(I)	(J)	(K)	(L)	(M)	(N)	(O)	(P)
1. Inventory turnover increased substantially from the prior year. (Select four explanations)	●	●	○	●	●	○	○	○	○	○	○	○	○	○	○	○
2. Accounts receivable turnover decreased substantially from the prior year. (Select three explanations)	●	●	○	○	●	○	○	○	○	○	○	○	○	○	○	○
3. Allowance for doubtful accounts increased from the prior year, but allowance for doubtful accounts as a percentage of accounts receivable decreased from the prior year. (Select three explanations)	●	●	○	○	●	○	○	○	○	○	○	○	○	○	○	○
4. Long-term debt increased from the prior year, but interest expense increased a larger-than-proportionate amount than long-term debt. (Select one explanation)	○	○	○	○	○	○	○	○	○	○	○	○	○	○	○	●
5. Operating income increased from the prior year although the entity was less profitable than in the prior year. (Select two explanations)	○	○	○	○	○	○	○	○	○	○	○	●	○	○	○	●
6. Gross margin percentage was unchanged from the prior year although gross margin increased from the prior year. (Select one explanation)	○	○	○	○	○	○	○	●	○	○	○	○	○	○	○	○

Explanations

1. (**A, B, D, E**) The requirement is to identify three explanations for an increase in the inventory turnover when compared to the prior year. The inventory turnover is calculated by dividing the cost of goods sold by the inventory. An increase may occur either through (1) an overstatement of the cost of goods sold (the numerator), (2) an understatement of inventory (the denominator), or (3) a combination of changes. Answer (A) is correct because the recording of the consignment shipment as a sale will overstate cost of goods sold and understate the ending inventory. Answer (B) is correct because not recording the credit memos will result in understatement of inventory. Answer (D) is correct because the understatement of purchases of inventory will understate the ending inventory. Answer (E) is correct because a larger percentage of sales in the last month of the year is likely to result in a lower ending inventory.

Answer (C) is incorrect because overstating the year-end purchases will result in overstatement of inventory, and thereby decrease the inventory turnover. Answers (F) through (J) are all incorrect because such changes in sales will not affect the inventory turnover ratio. Answers (K) through (P) are all incorrect because the interest expense, income tax rate, and the short-term borrowing do not affect the inventory turnover. Note that this question relies upon an unstated assumption that the year-end inventory is not adjusted to a year-end physical count.

2. **(A, B, E)** The requirement is to identify three explanations for a decrease in the accounts receivable turnover when compared to the prior year. The accounts receivable turnover is calculated by dividing sales by accounts receivable. A decrease may occur through (1) an understatement of sales (the numerator), (2) an overstatement of accounts receivable (the denominator), or (3) a combination of misstatements of sales and accounts receivable that decrease the ratio. Answer (A) is correct because recording the consignment as sales overstates both sales and accounts receivable by an identical amount, thus decreasing the ratio; the decrease is due to the entry debiting accounts receivable and crediting sales for the same amount. Answer (B) is correct because not recording the credit memo overstates both sales and accounts receivable by an identical amount, thus decreasing the ratio; this identical amount of decrease is due to the lack of a debit to sales returns and allowances and a credit to accounts receivable. Note that answers (A) and (B) are correct in any situation in which the ratio is greater than 1.0; when the ratio is less than 1.0 they result in an increase in the ratio. Answer (E) is correct because while the sales for the year remain at the expected level, accounts receivable at year-end will be at a higher than average level due to the year-end sales.

Answers (C) and (D) are incorrect because the level of inventory does not affect the ratio. Answers (F) and (G) are incorrect because a larger, not a smaller or the same, percentage of sales near year-end decreases the ratio. Answers (H), (I) and (J) are incorrect because one would expect accounts receivable to increase at the same rate as the increase in sales. Answers (K) through (P) are all incorrect because interest expense, income tax rate, and the short-term borrowing do not affect the accounts receivable turnover.

3. **(A, B, E)** The requirement is to identify three explanations for an increase in the allowance for doubtful accounts but a decrease in the allowance for doubtful accounts as a percentage of accounts receivable. The allowance for doubtful accounts as a percentage of accounts receivable is calculated by dividing the allowance for doubtful accounts by accounts receivable. The percentage may decrease due to (1) a decrease in the allowance for doubtful accounts, (2) an increase in the accounts receivable, or (3) a combination of misstatements that decrease the ratio; here, however, we are told that reason (1), a decrease in the allowance, has not occurred. Answer (A) is correct because recording the consignment as a sale results in an increase in accounts receivable, which decreases the ratio. Answer (B) is correct because not recording the credit memos overstates accounts receivable, thereby decreasing the ratio. Answer (E) is correct because the larger percentage of sales occurring during the last month of the year results in accounts receivable at year-end that will be at a higher than average level due to the year-end sales.

Answers (C) and (D) are incorrect because the level of inventory does not affect the ratio. Answers (F) and (G) are incorrect because a larger, not a smaller or the same, percentage of sales near year-end decreases the ratio. Answers (H), (I), and (J) are incorrect because one would expect accounts receivable and the allowance for doubtful accounts to increase at approximately the same rate as the increase in sales. Answers (K) through (P) are all incorrect because interest expense, income tax rate, and the short-term borrowing do not affect the accounts receivable turnover.

4. **(P)** The requirement is to identify a reason why long-term debt increased, but interest expense increased a larger-than-proportionate amount than long-term debt. Answer (P) is correct because the higher interest rates on long-term debt will result in higher interest expense. Answers (A) through (M) are all incorrect because they relate neither to long-term debt nor interest expense. Answers (N) and (O) are incorrect because refinancing at the same or a lower interest rate will result in smaller-than-proportionate amounts of interest expense.

5. **(L, P)** The requirement is to identify two reasons why operating income might increase, yet the company would be less profitable. Since operating income increased and net income decreased, the explanation must be items that are listed on the income statement between operating income and net income—interest expense and federal income taxes. The net of these two expenses must have increased to result in a situation in which the entity was less profitable. Answer (L) is correct because an increase in the effective income tax rate could decrease the profit when compared to the prior year. Answer (P) is correct because higher interest rates decrease profits. Answers (A) through (J) are

all incorrect because they pertain to details of operating income. Answers (K) and (M) are incorrect because a decrease in interest expense or the income tax rate would increase net income. Answer (N) is incorrect because refinancing at the same rate will not affect net income. Answer (O) is incorrect because refinancing at a lower interest rate will increase profits.

6. **(H)** The requirement is to identify one reason why the gross margin percentage may remain unchanged, despite an increase in gross margin from the prior year. Answer (H) is correct because when sales increase at the same percentage as cost of goods sold, the gross margin percentage remains unchanged, and yet the increased sales will result in an increase in the gross margin. Answers (A) through (D) are all incorrect because they will result in a change in the gross margin percentage. Answers (E), (F), and (G) are all incorrect because no increase in sales is indicated and no information on the gross margin is provided. Answers (I) and (J) are incorrect because they suggest a decrease and an increase in the gross margin, respectively. Answers (K) through (P) are all incorrect because interest expense, income tax rate, and debt do not affect gross margin.

Task-Based Simulation 17

Spreadsheet Completion		
	Authoritative Literature	
		Help

Analytical procedures are evaluations of financial information made by a study of plausible relationships among financial and nonfinancial data. Understanding and evaluating such relationships are essential to the audit process.

The following spreadsheet with the financial statements were prepared by Holiday Manufacturing Co. for the year ended December 31, 20X1. Also presented are various financial statement ratios for Holiday as calculated from the prior year's financial statements. Sales represent net credit sales. The total assets and the receivables and inventory balances at December 31, 20X1, were the same as at December 31, 20X0.

Holiday Manufacturing Co.
BALANCE SHEET
December 31, 20X1

	A	B	C	D	E	F	G
1.	Cash		$240,000		Accounts payable		$160,000
2.	Receivables		400,000		Notes payable		100,000
3.	Inventory		600,000		Other current liabilities		140,000
4.	Total current assets		$1,240,000		Total current liabilities		400,000
5.							
6.	Plant and equipment—net		760,000		Long-term debt		350,000
7.					Common stock		750,000
8.					Retained earnings		500,000
9.	Total assets		$2,000,000		Total liabilities and capital		$2,000,000
10.							
11.							
12.	Income Statement						
13.	Year ended December 31, 20X1						
14.							
15.	Sales				$3,000,000		
16.	Cost of goods sold						
17.	Materials		800,000				
18.	Labor		700,000				

(Continued)

	A	B	C	D	E	F	G
19.	Overhead		300,000		1,800,000		
20.	Gross margin				1,200,000		
21.							
22.	Selling expenses		240,000				
23.	General and admin. exp.		300,000		540,000		
24.	Operating income				660,000		
25.	Less: interest expense				40,000		
26.	Income before taxes				620,000		
27.	Less: federal income taxes				220,000		
28.	Net income				$400,000		
29.							
30.							
31.							
32.	Ratios		**12/31/X1**		**12/31/X0**		
33.	Current ratio		**(1)**		2.5		
34.	Quick ratio		**(2)**		1.3		
35.	Accounts receivable turnover		**(3)**		5.5		
36.	Inventory turnover		**(4)**		2.5		
37	Total asset turnover		**(5)**		1.2		
38.	Gross margin %		**(6)**		35%		
39.	Net operating margin %		**(7)**		25%		
40.	Times interest earned		**(8)**		10.3		
41.	Total debt to equity %		**(9)**		50%		

Insert spreadsheet formulas into the worksheet to allow the direction calculation of each ratio (1 through 9). Use cell location rather than amounts.

Task-Based Simulation 17 Solution

Spreadsheet Completion

Authoritative Literature

Help

Holiday Manufacturing Co.
BALANCE SHEET
December 31, 20X1

	A	B	C	D	E	F	G
1.	Cash		$240,000		Accounts payable		$160,000
2.	Receivables		400,000		Notes payable		100,000
3.	Inventory		600,000		Other current liabilities		140,000
4.	Total current assets		$1,240,000		Total current liabilities		400,000
5.							
6.	Plant and equipment—net		760,000		Long-term debt		350,000
7.					Common stock		750,000
8.					Retained earnings		500,000
9.	Total assets		$2,000,000		Total liabilities and capital		$2,000,000
10.							
11.							
12.	Income Statement						
13.	Year ended December 31, 20X1						
14.							
15.	Sales				$3,000,000		
16.	Cost of goods sold						
17.	Materials		800,000				
18.	Labor		700,000				
19.	Overhead		300,000		1,800,000		
20.	Gross margin				1,200,000		
21.							
22.	Selling expenses		240,000				
23.	General and admin. exp.		300,000		540,000		
24.	Operating income				660,000		
25.	Less: interest expense				40,000		
26.	Income before taxes				620,000		
27.	Less: federal income taxes				220,000		
28.	Net income				$400,000		
29.							
30.							
31.							
32.	Ratios		12/31/X1		12/31/X0		
33.	Current ratio		(1)		2.5		
34.	Quick ratio		(2)		1.3		
35.	Accounts receivable turnover		(3)		5.5		
36.	Inventory turnover		(4)		2.5		
37	Total asset turnover		(5)		1.2		
38.	Gross margin %		(6)		35%		
39.	Net operating margin %		(7)		25%		
40.	Times interest earned		(8)		10.3		
41.	Total debt to equity %		(9)		50%		

	Ratio	Spreadsheet Formula	Calculation		
1. **(H)**	Current ratio = $\dfrac{\text{Current assets}}{\text{Current liabilities}}$	= C8/G8			
2. **(E)**	Quick ratio = $\dfrac{\text{Quick assets}^*}{\text{Current liabilities}}$	= (C5+C6)/G8	$\dfrac{\$240{,}000 + \$400{,}000}{\$400{,}000}$	$= \dfrac{\$640{,}000}{\$400{,}000}$	$= 1.6$

Cash + Accounts receivable. Also marketable securities would be included if the company owned any.

$$\frac{\text{Sales}}{\text{Accounts receivable}}$$

3. **(K)** Accounts receivable turnover =   = E19/C6

$$\frac{\$3{,}000{,}000}{\$400{,}000} = 7.5$$

$$\frac{\$1{,}800{,}000}{\$600{,}000} = 3.0$$

$$\frac{\$3{,}000{,}000}{\$2{,}000{,}000} = 1.5$$

$$\frac{\$1{,}200{,}000}{\$3{,}000{,}000} = 40\%$$

4. **(G)** Inventory turnover = $\dfrac{\text{Cost of goods sold}}{\text{Inventory}}$ = E23/C7

5. **(D)** Total asset turnover = $\dfrac{\text{Sales}}{\text{Total assets}}$ = E19/C13

6. **(T)** Gross margin percentage = $\dfrac{\text{Gross margin}}{\text{Sales}}$ = E24/E19

7. **(P)** Net operating margin % = $\dfrac{\text{Operating income}}{\text{Sales}}$ = E28/E19

8. **(N)** Times interest earned = $\dfrac{\text{Operating income}}{\text{Interest expense}}$ = E28/E29

| 9. **(U)** | Total debt to equity percentage = | $\dfrac{\text{Total debt}^*}{\text{Owners' equity}^{**}}$ | = (G8+G10)/ (G11+G12) | $\dfrac{\$400{,}000 + \$350{,}000}{\$750{,}000 + \$500{,}000}$ | $= \dfrac{\$750{,}000}{\$1{,}250{,}000}$ | 60% |

*Total current liabilities + Long-term debt
**Common stock + Retained earnings

Nature of Evidence 2

Task-Based Simulation 18

Assertions and Audit Procedures

Authoritative Literature

Help

You are a staff auditor with Williams and Co. CPAs. Bill Jones, a new hire, has come to you with questions concerning "assertions" and "audit procedures." For **items 1 through 6,** match each assertion with the statement that most closely approximates its meaning. Each statement may be used only once.

Statement

A. There is such an asset
B. The company legally owns the assets
C. All assets have been recorded
D. Transactions are recorded in the correct accounting period
E. Assets are recorded at proper amounts
F. Assets are properly classified

Assertion	(A)	(B)	(C)	(D)	(E)	(F)
1. Completeness	O	O	O	O	O	O
2. Cutoff	O	O	O	O	O	O
3. Existence and occurrence	O	O	O	O	O	O
4. Presentation and disclosure	O	O	O	O	O	O
5. Rights and obligations	O	O	O	O	O	O
6. Valuation	O	O	O	O	O	O

Auditors perform audit procedures to obtain audit evidence that will allow them to draw reasonable conclusions as to whether the client's financial statements follow generally accepted accounting principles. Match each audit procedure with its type. Each type of audit procedure is used, one of them twice.

Type of audit procedure

A. Analytical procedures
B. Tests of controls
C. Risk assessment procedures (other than analytical procedures)
D. Test of details of account balances, transactions, or disclosures

Audit procedures	(A)	(B)	(C)	(D)
1. Prepare a flowchart of internal control over sales.	O	O	O	O
2. Calculate the ratio of bad debt expense to credit sales.	O	O	O	O
3. Determine whether disbursements are properly approved.	O	O	O	O
4. Confirm accounts receivable.	O	O	O	O
5. Compare current financial information with comparable prior periods.	O	O	O	O

Task-Based Simulation 18 Solution

Assertions and Audit Procedures		
	Authoritative Literature	
		Help

Assertion	(A)	(B)	(C)	(D)	(E)	(F)
1. Completeness	○	○	●	○	○	○
2. Cutoff	○	○	○	●	○	○
3. Existence and occurrence	●	○	○	○	○	○
4. Presentation and disclosure	○	○	○	○	○	●
5. Rights and obligations	○	●	○	○	○	○
6. Valuation	○	○	○	○	●	○

Audit procedures	(A)	(B)	(C)	(D)
1. Prepare a flowchart of internal control over sales.	○	○	●	○
2. Calculate the ratio of bad debt expense to credit sales.	●	○	○	○
3. Determine whether disbursements are properly approved.	○	●	○	○
4. Confirm accounts receivable.	○	○	○	●
5. Compare current financial information with comparable prior periods.	●	○	○	○

Audit Evidence: Specific Audit Areas

Cash

Task-Based Simulation 19

Bank Reconciliation		
	Authoritative Literature	
		Help

Items 1 through 6 represent the items that an auditor ordinarily would find on a client-prepared bank reconciliation. The accompanying **List of Auditing Procedures** represents substantive auditing procedures. For each item, select one or more procedures, as indicated, that the auditor **most** likely would perform to gather evidence in support of that item. The procedures on the **List** may be selected once, more than once, or not at all.

Assume

- The client prepared the bank reconciliation on 10/2/X5.
- The bank reconciliation is mathematically accurate.
- The auditor received a cutoff bank statement dated 10/7/X5 directly from the bank on 10/11/X5.
- The 9/30/X5 deposit in transit, outstanding checks #1281, #1285, #1289, and #1292, and the correction of the error regarding check #1282 appeared on the cutoff bank statement.
- The auditor assessed control risk concerning the financial statement assertions related to cash at the maximum.

General Company
BANK RECONCILIATION
1ST NATIONAL BANK OF U.S. BANK ACCOUNT
September 30, 20X5

1. Select two procedures	Balance per bank		$28,375
2. Select five procedures	Deposits in transit		
	9/29/X5	$4,500	
	9/30/X5	1,525	6,025
			34,400
3. Select five procedures	Outstanding checks		
	# 988 8/31/X5	2,200	
	#1281 9/26/X5	675	
	#1285 9/27/X5	850	
	#1289 9/29/X5	2,500	
	#1292 9/30/X5	7,225	(13,450)
			20,950
4. Select one procedure	Customer note collected by bank		(3,000)
5. Select two procedures	Error: Check #1282, written on 9/26/X5		
	for $270 was erroneously charged by bank as $720; bank was notified on 10/2/X5		450
6. Select one procedure	Balance per books		$18,400

List of Auditing Procedures

A. Trace to cash receipts journal.
B. Trace to cash disbursements journal.
C. Compare to 9/30/X1 general ledger.
D. Confirm directly with bank.
E. Inspect bank credit memo.

F. Inspect bank debit memo.
G. Ascertain reason for unusual delay.
H. Inspect supporting documents for reconciling item not appearing on cutoff statement.
I. Trace items on the bank reconciliation to cutoff statement.
J. Trace items on the cutoff statement to bank reconciliation.

Task-Based Simulation 19 Solution

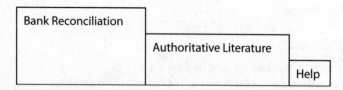

1. **(D, I)** The balance per bank may be traced to a standard form used to confirm account balance information with financial institutions and to the cutoff statement (on which will appear the beginning balance).

2. **(A, G, H, I, J)** One of the deposits in transit does not appear on the cutoff bank statement (the 9/29/X5 deposit for $4,500). Accordingly, that deposit should be traced to the cash receipts journal (procedure A), the reason for the delay should be investigated (procedure G), and supporting documents should be inspected (procedure H). Both deposits should be traced to and from the bank reconciliation and the cutoff statement (procedures I and J).

3. (**B, G, H, I, J**) One of the checks does not appear on the cutoff statement (check #988 dated 8/31/X5 for $2,200). Accordingly, that check should be traced to the cash disbursements journal (procedure B), the reason for the delay should be investigated (procedure G), and supporting documents should be inspected (procedure H). All checks should be traced to and from the bank reconciliation and cutoff statement (procedures I and J).

4. (**E**) The credit memo from the bank for the note collected should be investigated.

5. (**E, I**) The credit for the check that was charged by the bank for an incorrect amount should be investigated on both the bank credit memo and on the cutoff statement.

6. (**C**) The only source of the balance per books is the cash general ledger account as of 9/30/05.

Accounts Receivable

Task-Based Simulation 20

```
┌─────────────────────────────────────┐
│ Accounts Receivable Confirmations    │
│         ┌───────────────────────────┐│
│         │ Authoritative Literature  ││
│         │            ┌──────┐       ││
│         │            │ Help │       ││
└─────────┴────────────┴──────┴───────┘
```

An auditor may use confirmations of accounts receivable. Reply as to whether the following statements are correct or incorrect with respect to the confirmation process when applied to accounts receivable.

Statement	Correct	Incorrect
1. The confirmation requests should be mailed to respondents by the CPAs.	○	○
2. A combination of positive and negative request forms must be used if receivables are significant.	○	○
3. Second requests are ordinarily sent for positive form confirmations requests when the first request is not returned.	○	○
4. Confirmations address existence more than they address completeness.	○	○
5. Confirmation of accounts receivable is a generally accepted auditing standard.	○	○
6. Absent a few circumstances, there is a presumption that the auditor will confirm accounts receivable.	○	○
7. Auditors should always confirm the total balances of accounts rather than individual portions (e.g., if the balance is made up of three sales, all three should be confirmed).	○	○
8. Auditors may ignore individually immaterial accounts when confirming accounts receivable.	○	○
9. The best way to evaluate the results of the confirmation process is to total the misstatements identified and to compare that total to the account's tolerable error amounts.	○	○
10. Accounts receivable are ordinarily confirmed on a standard form developed by the American Institute of Certified Public Accountants and the Financial Executives Institute.	○	○

Task-Based Simulation 20 Solution

Accounts Receivable Confirmations		
	Authoritative Literature	
		Help

Statement	Correct	Incorrect
1. The confirmation requests should be mailed to respondents by the CPAs.	●	○
2. A combination of positive and negative request forms must be used if receivables are significant.	○	●
3. Second requests are ordinarily sent for positive form confirmations requests when the first request is not returned.	●	○
4. Confirmations address existence more than they address completeness.	●	○
5. Confirmation of accounts receivable is a generally accepted auditing standard.	○	●
6. Absent a few circumstances, there is a presumption that the auditor will confirm accounts receivable.	●	○
7. Auditors should always confirm the total balances of accounts rather than individual portions (e.g., if the balance is made up of three sales, all three should be confirmed).	○	●
8. Auditors may ignore individually immaterial accounts when confirming accounts receivable.	○	●
9. The best way to evaluate the results of the confirmation process is to total the misstatements identified and to compare that total to the account's tolerable error amounts.	○	●
10. Accounts receivable are ordinarily confirmed on a standard form developed by the American Institute of Certified Public Accountants and the Financial Executives Institute.	○	●

Task-Based Simulation 21

Research		
	Authoritative Literature	
		Help

Confirmation of Accounts Receivable

Bill Smith, the president of Alex Inc., a nonpublic audit client, has suggested to you that his previous auditor did **not** confirm accounts receivable and he sees no reason why you should do so.

Selections

A. AU-C
B. PCAOB
C. AT
D. AR
E. ET
F. BL
G. CS
H. QC

	(A)	(B)	(C)	(D)	(E)	(F)	(G)	(H)
1. Which title of the Professional Standards addresses this issue and will be helpful in responding to him?	○	○	○	○	○	○	○	○
2. Enter the exact section and paragraph(s) with helpful information.								

Task-Based Simulation 21 Solution

Research		
	Authoritative Literature	
		Help

Confirmation of Accounts Receivable	(A)	(B)	(C)	(D)	(E)	(F)	(G)	(H)
1. Which title of the Professional Standards addresses this issue and will be helpful in responding to him?	●	○	○	○	○	○	○	○
2. Enter the exact section and paragraph(s) with helpful information.				330		20, A54–A56		

Inventory

Task-Based Simulation 22

Inventory Audit Objectives and Procedures		
	Authoritative Literature	
		Help

The auditor determines that each of the following objectives will be part of the audit of Enright Corporation. For each audit objective, select a substantive procedure that would help to achieve the audit objectives. Each of the procedures may be used once, more than once, or not at all.

Substantive procedure

A. Review minutes of board of directors meetings and contracts, and make inquiries of management.
B. Test inventory transactions between a preliminary physical inventory date and the balance sheet date.
C. Obtain confirmation of inventories pledged under loan agreement.
D. Review perpetual inventory records, production records, and purchasing records for indication of current activity.
E. Reconcile physical counts to perpetual records and general ledger balances and investigate significant fluctuation.
F. Examine sales after year-end and open purchase order commitments.
G. Examine paid vendors' invoices, consignment agreements, and contracts.
H. Analytically review and compare the relationship of inventory balance to recent purchasing, production, and sales activity.

	(A)	(B)	(C)	(D)	(E)	(F)	(G)	(H)
1. Identify inventory transactions involving related parties.	○	○	○	○	○	○	○	○
2. Determine that items counted are included in the inventory listing.	○	○	○	○	○	○	○	○
3. Determine that a proper cutoff of purchases has occurred at year-end.	○	○	○	○	○	○	○	○
4. Determine that financial statements include proper disclosures relating to inventory.	○	○	○	○	○	○	○	○
5. Determine that recorded inventory is owned.	○	○	○	○	○	○	○	○

Task-Based Simulation 22 Solution

Inventory Audit Objectives and Procedures

Authoritative Literature

Help

	(A)	(B)	(C)	(D)	(E)	(F)	(G)	(H)
1. Identify inventory transactions involving related parties.	●	○	○	○	○	○	○	○
2. Determine that items counted are included in the inventory listing.	○	○	○	○	●	○	○	○
3. Determine that a proper cutoff of purchases has occurred at year-end.	○	○	○	○	○	●	○	○
4. Determine that financial statements include proper disclosures relating to inventory.	○	○	●	○	○	○	○	○
5. Determine that recorded inventory is owned.	○	○	○	○	○	○	●	○

Explanations

1. **(A)** The requirement is to identify a procedure for identifying inventory transactions involving related parties. The best procedure listed is review minutes of Board of Directors' meeting and contracts, and to make inquiries of management; these are all procedures used to identify related-party transactions.
2. **(E)** The requirements is to identify a procedure for determining that items counted are included in the count sheet. The best procedure is to reconcile physical counts to perpetual records and general ledger balances and investigate significant fluctuations. This will allow the auditor to identify items not included.
3. **(F)** The requirement is to determine that a proper cutoff of purchases has occurred at year end. The best procedure listed is to review sales after year-end and open purchase order commitments—this will help determine whether transactions recorded after year-end should have been recorded prior to year-end. Another procedure, not listed, is to perform the procedure on transactions recorded right before year-end.
4. **(C)** The requirement is to determine that the financial statements include proper disclosures relating to inventory. Answer C is correct because inventories pledged under loan agreement should be disclosed.
5. **(G)** The requirement is to determine that recorded inventory is owned. Examining invoices is best because invoice will present information on the purchase.

Task-Based Simulation 23

Audit Objectives and Procedures

Authoritative Literature

Help

For each audit objective listed below select the most appropriate audit procedure for raw materials inventory (**Items 1–3**) and for Accounts Receivable (**Items 4–6**). Audit procedures may be used once, more than once, or not at all.

List of audit procedures for raw materials inventory

A. Compare standard costs of inventories with standardized market values.
B. Determine that all direct labor and overhead has been expensed and not included in inventory valuation.
C. Examine vendors' invoices.
D. Perform analytical procedures comparing inventory to various industry averages.

E. Review drafts of financial statement note disclosures.

F. Select a sample of items during the physical count and determine that the client has included items on inventory count sheets.

G. Select a sample of recorded items on count sheets and determine that the items are on hand.

	(A)	(B)	(C)	(D)	(E)	(F)	(G)
1. Determine that company legally owns inventories.	O	O	O	O	O	O	O
2. Establish the completeness of inventories.	O	O	O	O	O	O	O
3. Determine that the cost of inventories is proper.	O	O	O	O	O	O	O

List of audit procedures for accounts receivable

A. Analyze relationships between accounts receivable balances and changes in the current portion of long-term debt.

B. Compare accounts receivable on the accounts receivable lead schedule with those on supporting audit schedules.

C. Compare total 20X8 annual sales with those of 20X7.

D. Examine December 20X8 sales journal and determine that sales are properly recorded in December.

E. Examine January 20X9 sales journal and determine that sales are properly recorded in January.

F. Inquire of credit manager about the collectability of various receivables.

G. Review disclosure checklist for recommended and required accounts receivable disclosures.

	(A)	(B)	(C)	(D)	(E)	(F)	(G)
4. Determine that all accounts receivable are properly recorded as of year-end.	O	O	O	O	O	O	O
5. Determine that accounts receivable are properly valued at net realizable value.	O	O	O	O	O	O	O
6. Note disclosures related to accounts receivable are proper.	O	O	O	O	O	O	O

Task-Based Simulation 23 Solution

Audit Objectives and Procedures
Authoritative Literature
Help

	(A)	(B)	(C)	(D)	(E)	(F)	(G)
1. Determine that company legally owns inventories.	O	O	●	O	O	O	O
2. Establish the completeness of inventories.	O	O	O	O	O	●	O
3. Determine that the cost of inventories is proper.	O	O	●	O	O	O	O

Explanations

1. (**C**) Because ownership information is included on invoices, examining vendors' invoices will provide evidence that the company legally owns inventory raw material items.

2. (**F**) Selecting a sample of items and agreeing to the physical count sheet will establish that those items have been included in the count, and this will address completeness of inventories.

3. (**C**) Examining vendors' invoices will provide evidence as to the cost of the inventory items.

	(A)	(B)	(C)	(D)	(E)	(F)	(G)
4. Determine that all accounts receivable are properly recorded as of year-end.	○	○	○	○	●	○	○
5. Determine that accounts receivable are properly valued at net realizable value.	○	○	○	○	○	●	○
6. Note disclosures related to accounts receivable are proper.	·○	○	○	○	○	○	●

Explanations

4. **(E)** When examining the January 20X9 sales journal the auditor may identify sales that should have been recorded in December of 20X8.
5. **(F)** Auditors will generally inquire of the credit manager as to his or her beliefs concerning the collectability of various receivables, and thereby obtain evidence on the net realizable value of accounts receivable. Often one would expect an answer such as "analyze aging of receivables." Since that was not present here, (F) is the best reply.
6. **(G)** A disclosure checklist is used to determine that the disclosure requirements of generally accepted accounting principles have been met.

Task-Based Simulation 24

Auditing Inventory
Authoritative Literature
Help

Auditors often observe the counting of their clients' inventories. Reply as to whether the following statements are correct or incorrect with respect to the inventory observation.

Statement	Correct	Incorrect
1. With strong internal control, the inventory count may be at the end of the year or at other times.	○	○
2. When a client has many inventory locations, auditors ordinarily need not be present at each location.	○	○
3. All auditor test counts must be documented in the working papers.	○	○
4. Auditors' observation of the counting of their clients' inventories addresses the existence of inventory, and not the completeness of the count.	○	○
5. When the client manufactures a product, direct labor and overhead ordinarily become a part of inventory item costs.	○	○
6. Inventory is ordinarily valued at the lower of standard cost or market.	○	○
7. Inventory items present as "consigned in" should not be included in the clients' inventory value.	○	○
8. Auditor recording of test counts ordinarily replaces the need for client "tagging" of inventory.	○	○
9. Ordinarily, an auditor need not count all items in the inventory.	○	○
10. At the completion of the count, an auditor will ordinarily provide the client with copies of his or her inventory test counts to help assure inventory accuracy.	○	○

Task-Based Simulation 24 Solution

Auditing Inventory		
	Authoritative Literature	
		Help

Statement	Correct	Incorrect
1. With strong internal control, the inventory count may be at the end of the year or at other times.	●	○
2. When a client has many inventory locations, auditors ordinarily need not be present at each location.	●	○
3. All auditor test counts must be documented in the working papers.	○	●
4. Auditors' observation of the counting of their clients' inventories addresses the existence of inventory, and not the completeness of the count.	○	●
5. When the client manufactures a product, direct labor and overhead ordinarily become a part of inventory item costs.	●	○
6. Inventory is ordinarily valued at the lower of standard cost or market.	○	●
7. Inventory items present as "consigned in" should not be included in the clients' inventory value.	●	○
8. Auditor recording of test counts ordinarily replaces the need for client "tagging" of inventory.	○	●
9. Ordinarily, an auditor need not count all items in the inventory.	●	○
10. At the completion of the count, an auditor will ordinarily provide the client with copies of his or her inventory test counts to help assure inventory accuracy.	○	●

Investments in Securities and Derivative Instruments

Task-Based Simulation 25

Audit Investments and Accounts Receivable		
	Authoritative Literature	
		Help

Items 1 through 7 represent audit objectives for the investments and accounts receivable. To the right of each set of audit objectives is a listing of possible audit procedures for that account. For each audit objective, select the audit procedure that would primarily respond to the objective. Select only one procedure for each audit objective. A procedure may be selected only once, or not at all.

Audit procedures for investments

A. Trace opening balances in the subsidiary ledger to prior year's audit working papers.
B. Determine that employees who are authorized to sell investments do not have access to cash.
C. Examine supporting documents for a sample of investment transactions to verify that prenumbered documents are used.
D. Determine that any impairments in the price of investments have been properly recorded.
E. Verify that transfers from the current to the noncurrent investment portfolio have been properly recorded.
F. Obtain positive confirmations as of the balance sheet date of investments held by independent custodians.
G. Trace investment transactions to minutes of the Board of Directors meetings to determine that transactions were properly authorized.

Audit objectives for investments	(A)	(B)	(C)	(D)	(E)	(F)	(G)
1. Investments are properly described and classified in the financial statements.	○	○	○	○	○	○	○
2. Recorded investments represent investments actually owned at the balance sheet date.	○	○	○	○	○	○	○
3. Trading investments are properly valued at fair market value at the balance sheet date.	○	○	○	○	○	○	○

Audit procedures for accounts receivable

A. Analyze the relationship of accounts receivable and sales and compare it with relationships for preceding periods.
B. Perform sales cutoff tests to obtain assurance that sales transactions and corresponding entries for inventories and cost of goods sold are recorded in the same and proper period.
C. Review the aged trial balance for significant past due accounts.
D. Obtain an understanding of the business purpose of transactions that resulted in accounts receivable balances.
E. Review loan agreements for indications of whether accounts receivable have been factored or pledged.
F. Review the accounts receivable trial balance for amounts due from officers and employees.
G. Analyze unusual relationships between monthly accounts receivable balances and monthly accounts payable balances.

Audit objectives for accounts receivable	(A)	(B)	(C)	(D)	(E)	(F)	(G)
4. Accounts receivable represent all amounts owed to the entity at the balance sheet date.	○	○	○	○	○	○	○
5. The entity has legal rights to all accounts receivable at the balance sheet date.	○	○	○	○	○	○	○
6. Accounts receivable are stated at net realizable value.	○	○	○	○	○	○	○
7. Accounts receivable are properly described and presented in the financial statements.	○	○	○	○	○	○	○

Task-Based Simulation 25 Solution

Inventory Audit Objectives and Procedures	Authoritative Literature	Help

	(A)	(B)	(C)	(D)	(E)	(F)	(G)
1. Determine that company legally owns inventories.	○	○	○	○	●	○	○
2. Establish the completeness of inventories.	○	○	○	○	○	●	○
3. Determine that the cost of inventories is proper.	○	○	○	●	○	○	○

Explanations

1. (E) The verification of transfers from the current to the noncurrent investment portfolio will provide assurance that the investments are properly classified in the financial statements.
2. (F) Positive confirmation replies as of the balance sheet date for investments held by independent custodians will provide assurance that the recorded investments are in fact owned by the audit client.
3. (D) Because trading investments should be valued at fair market value, determining whether any impairments in the price of investments have been recorded will provide assurance that investments are properly valued.

Audit objectives for accounts receivable	(A)	(B)	(C)	(D)	(E)	(F)	(G)
4. Accounts receivable represent all amounts owed to the entity at the balance sheet date.	○	●	○	○	○	○	○
5. The entity has legal rights to all accounts receivable at the balance sheet date.	○	○	○	○	●	○	○
6. Accounts receivable are stated at net realizable value.	○	○	●	○	○	○	○
7. Accounts receivable are properly described and presented in the financial statements.	○	○	○	○	○	●	○

Explanations

4. (B) Performance of sales cutoff tests will provide assurance that sales transactions and the related receivables are recorded in the proper period. Thus, sales cutoff tests will provide assurance that all amounts owed to the entity at the balance sheet date are recorded in that period.
5. (E) A review of loan agreements, paying special attention to accounts receivable that have been factored, will provide assurance as to whether the entity has a legal right to all accounts receivable at the balance sheet date.
6. (C) An analysis of the aged trial balance for significant past due accounts will provide evidence with respect to accounts that may be uncollectible. Accordingly, the procedure will address the net realizable value of accounts receivable.
7. (F) Because material amounts due from officers and employees should be segregated from other receivables, a review of the trial balance for amounts due from officers and employees will provide assurance that accounts receivable are properly described and presented in the financial statements.

Task-Based Simulation 26

Research		
	Authoritative Literature	
		Help

Auditing Derivatives

The partner in charge of the nonpublic company audit you are currently working on is concerned about overall audit requirements relating to derivatives that are measured based on fair value. More specifically, she has asked you to find the section and paragraph that addresses an auditor's overall responsibilities in that area.

Selections

A. AU-C
B. PCAOB
C. AT
D. AR
E. ET
F. BL
G. CS
H. QC

	(A)	(B)	(C)	(D)	(E)	(F)	(G)	(H)
1. Which title of the Professional Standards addresses this issue and will be helpful in responding to her?	○	○	○	○	○	○	○	○
2. Enter the exact section and paragraph(s) with helpful information.								

Task-Based Simulation 26 Solution

Research		
	Authoritative Literature	
		Help

	(A)	(B)	(C)	(D)	(E)	(F)	(G)	(H)
1. Which title of the Professional Standards addresses this issue and will be helpful in responding to her?	●	○	○	○	○	○	○	○
2. Enter the exact section and paragraph(s) with helpful information.		501		06, A11–A18*				

*All of the paragraphs above not required, simply the overall location.

Fixed Assets

Task-Based Simulation 27

Substantive Procedures for Property, Plant, and Equipment		
	Authoritative Literature	
		Help

DietWeb Inc. (hereafter DietWeb) was incorporated and began business in March of 20X1, seven years ago. You are working on the 20X8 audit—your CPA firm's fifth audit of DietWeb. For each audit objective, select a substantive procedure that would help to achieve that objective. Each of the procedures may be used once, more than once, or not at all.

Substantive procedure

A. Trace opening balances in the summary schedules to the prior year's audit working papers.
B. Review the provision for depreciation expense and determine that depreciable lives and methods used in the current year are consistent with those used in the prior year.
C. Determine that responsibility for maintaining the property and equipment records is segregated from the responsibility for custody of property and equipment.
D. Examine deeds and title insurance certificates.
E. Perform cutoff test to verify that property and equipment additions are recorded in the proper period.
F. Determine that property and equipment is adequately insured.
G. Physically examine all recorded major property and equipment additions.
H. Analyze repairs and maintenance expense.

Audit objectives	(A)	(B)	(C)	(D)	(E)	(F)	(G)	(H)
1. DietWeb has legal rights to property and equipment acquired during the year.	○	○	○	○	○	○	○	○
2. DietWeb recorded property and equipment acquired during the year that did not actually exist at the balance sheet date.	○	○	○	○	○	○	○	○
3. DietWeb's property and equipment was properly valued at the balance sheet date.	○	○	○	○	○	○	○	○
4. DietWeb recorded all property and equipment assets that were purchased near year-end.	○	○	○	○	○	○	○	○
5. DietWeb recorded all property retirements that occurred during the year.	○	○	○	○	○	○	○	○
6. DietWeb capitalized all acquisitions that occurred during the period.	○	○	○	○	○	○	○	○

Task-Based Simulation 27 Solution

```
┌─────────────────────────┐
│ Substantive Procedures for │
│ Property, Plant, and Equipment │
│         ┌──────────────────────────┐
│         │ Authoritative Literature │
│         │         ┌──────────┐
│         │         │   Help   │
└─────────┴─────────┴──────────┘
```

Audit objectives	(A)	(B)	(C)	(D)	(E)	(F)	(G)	(H)
1. DietWeb has legal rights to property and equipment acquired during the year.	○	○	○	●	○	○	○	○
2. DietWeb recorded property and equipment acquired during the year that did not actually exist at the balance sheet date.	○	○	○	○	○	○	●	○
3. DietWeb's property and equipment was properly valued at the balance sheet date.	○	●	○	○	○	○	○	○
4. DietWeb recorded all property and equipment assets that were purchased near year-end.	○	○	○	○	●	○	○	○
5. DietWeb recorded all property retirements that occurred during the year.	○	○	○	○	○	○	●	○
6. DietWeb capitalized all acquisitions that occurred during the period.	○	○	○	○	○	○	○	●

Explanations

1. **(D)** The requirement is to identify the best substantive procedure to determine that DietWeb has legal rights to the property and equipment acquired during the year. Answer (D) is correct because the deeds and title insurance certificates will provide evidence that the company owns the property and equipment.

2. **(G)** The requirement is to identify the best substantive procedure to determine that DietWeb recorded property and equipment actually exists. Answer (G) is correct because physically examining the items will provide this evidence.

3. **(B)** The requirement is to identify a substantive procedure to test whether DietWeb's net property and equipment was properly valued at the balance sheet date. Answer (B) is correct because reviewing depreciation expense (and the related allowance for doubtful accounts) will indicate whether the net value is proper.

4. **(E)** The requirement is to identify how an auditor may test whether DietWeb recorded all property and equipment assets that were purchased during the year. Answer (E) is correct because performance of a cutoff test will indicate whether additions made during the year were properly recorded.

5. **(G)** The requirement is to identify a substantive procedure to test whether DietWeb recorded all property retirements that occurred during the year. Answer (G) is correct because examining the major recorded property and equipment items may identify situations in which an item has been retired (often due to its replacement) and is no longer available for physical examination.

6. **(H)** The requirement is to identify a substantive procedure to test whether DietWeb capitalized acquisitions. Answer (H) is correct because an analysis of repairs and maintenance accounts will reveal a situation in which such an acquisition has inappropriately been recorded as an expense and not capitalized.

Task-Based Simulation 28

Risk Analysis		
	Authoritative Literature	
		Help

You are working with William Bond, CPA, and you are considering the risk of material misstatement in planning the audit of Toxic Waste Disposal (TWD) Company's financial statements for the year ended December 31, 20X0.

Assume that you have identified the following risks at the account level relating to TWD's property and equipment. Identify the most closely related financial statement assertion and the audit procedure that might be planned to **most** likely address the risk. Financial statement assertions and audit procedures may be used once, more than once, or not used at all.

Related financial statement assertion	Audit procedures
A. Existence or occurrence	H. Determine that the responsibility for maintaining the property and equipment records is segregated from the responsibility for custody of property and equipment.
B. Completeness	
C. Rights and obligations	
D. Valuation or allocation	
E. Presentation and disclosure	I. Examine deeds and title insurance certificates.
F. Trace opening balances in the summary schedules to the prior year's audit working papers.	J. Perform cutoffs tests to verify that property and equipment additions are recorded in the proper period.
G. Review the provision for depreciation expense and determine that depreciable lives and methods used in the current year are consistent with those used in the prior year.	K. Determine that property and equipment are adequately insured.
	L. Physically examine all major property and equipment additions.

	Related financial statement assertion							Audit procedures				
Risk identified	(A)	(B)	(C)	(D)	(E)	(F)	(G)	(H)	(I)	(J)	(K)	(L)
1. TWD may not have legal title to certain property and equipment recorded as acquired during the year.	O	O	O	O	O	O	O	O	O	O	O	O
2. Recorded property and equipment acquisitions may include nonexistent assets.	O	O	O	O	O	O	O	O	O	O	O	O
3. Recorded net property and equipment are for proper amounts.	O	O	O	O	O	O	O	O	O	O	O	O

Task-Based Simulations 28 Solution

Risk Analysis

Authoritative Literature

Help

Risk identified	Related financial statement assertion							Audit procedures				
	(A)	**(B)**	**(C)**	**(D)**	**(E)**	**(F)**	**(G)**	**(H)**	**(I)**	**(J)**	**(K)**	**(L)**
1. TWD may not have legal title to certain property and equipment recorded as acquired during the year.	○	○	●	○	○	○	○	○	●	○	○	○
2. Recorded property and equipment acquisitions may include nonexistent assets.	●	○	○	○	○	○	○	○	○	○	○	●
3. Recorded net property and equipment are for proper amounts.	○	○	○	●	○	○	●	○	○	○	○	○

Explanations

1. **(C, I)** Legal titles relates most directly to the client having rights over the assets; an examination of deeds and title insurance certificates will provide assurance that the client has a legal right to the property and equipment acquired during the year.
2. **(A, L)** The recording of nonexistent assets relates most directly to existence of assets; physical examination of the major additions will address whether they exist.
3. **(D, G)** The proper recording of the net of property and equipment relates most directly to the valuation or allocation of the accounts; reviewing the provision for depreciation expense will address whether accumulated depreciation has been properly updated.

Payroll

Task-Based Simulation 29

Audit Procedures

Authoritative Literature

Help

Items 1 through 12 represent possible errors and fraud that you suspect may be present at General Company. The accompanying List of Auditing Procedures represents procedures that the auditor would consider performing to gather evidence concerning possible errors and fraud. For each item, select one or two procedures, as indicated, that the auditor **most** likely would perform to gather evidence in support of that item. The procedures on the list may be selected once, more than once, or not at all.

List of Auditing Procedures

A. Compare the details of the cash receipts journal entries with the details of the corresponding daily deposit slips.

B. Scan the debits to the fixed asset accounts and vouch selected amounts to vendors' invoices and management's authorization.

C. Perform analytical procedures that compare documented authorized pay rates to the entity's budget and forecast.

D. Obtain the cutoff bank statement and compare the cleared checks to the year-end bank reconciliation.

E. Prepare a bank transfer schedule.

F. Inspect the entity's deeds to its real estate.

G. Make inquiries of the entity's attorney concerning the details of real estate transactions.

H. Confirm the terms of borrowing arrangements with the lender.

I. Examine selected equipment repair orders and supporting documentation to determine the propriety of the charges.

J. Send requests to confirm the entity's accounts receivable on a surprise basis at an interim date.

K. Send a second request for confirmation of the receivable to the customer and make inquiries of a reputable credit agency concerning the customer's creditworthiness.

L. Examine the entity's shipping documents to verify that the merchandise that produced the receivable was actually sent to the customer.

M. Inspect the entity's correspondence files for indications of customer disputes for evidence that certain shipments were on consignment.

N. Perform edit checks of data on the payroll transaction tapes.

O. Inspect payroll check endorsements for similar handwriting.

P. Observe payroll check distribution on a surprise basis.

Q. Vouch data in the payroll register to documented authorized pay rates in the human resources department's files.

R. Reconcile the payroll checking account and determine if there were unusual time lags between the issuance and payment of payroll checks.

S. Inspect the file of prenumbered vouchers for consecutive numbering and proper approval by an appropriate employee.

T. Determine that the details of selected prenumbered vouchers match the related vendors' invoices.

U. Examine the supporting purchase orders and receiving reports for selected paid vouchers.

Possible misstatements due to errors and fraud

1. The auditor suspects that a kiting scheme exists because an accounting department employee who can issue and record checks seems to be leading an unusually luxurious lifestyle. (**Select only one procedure**)

2. An auditor suspects that the controller wrote several checks and recorded the cash disbursements just before year-end but did not mail the checks until after the first week of the subsequent year. (**Select only one procedure**)

3. The entity borrowed funds from a financial institution. Although the transaction was properly recorded, the auditor suspects that the loan created a lien on the entity's real estate that is not disclosed in its financial statements. (**Select only one procedure**)

4. The auditor discovered an unusually large receivable from one of the entity's new customers. The auditor suspects that the receivable may be fictitious because the auditor has never heard of the customer and because the auditor's initial attempt to confirm the receivable has been ignored by the customer. (**Select only two procedures**)

5. The auditor suspects that fictitious employees have been placed on the payroll by the entity's payroll supervisor, who has access to payroll records and to the paychecks. (**Select only one procedure**)

6. The auditor suspects that selected employees of the entity received unauthorized raises from the entity's payroll supervisor, who has access to payroll records. (**Select only one procedure**)

7. The entity's cash receipts of the first few days of the subsequent year were properly deposited in its general operating account after the year-end. However, the auditor suspects that the entity recorded the cash receipts in its books during the last week of the year under audit. (**Select only one procedure**)

8. The auditor suspects that vouchers were prepared and processed by an accounting department employee for merchandise that was neither ordered nor received by the entity. (**Select only one procedure**)

9. The details of invoices for equipment repairs were not clearly identified or explained to the accounting department employees. The auditor suspects that the bookkeeper incorrectly recorded the repairs as fixed assets. (**Select only one procedure**)

10. The auditor suspects that a lapping scheme exists because an accounting department employee who has access to cash receipts also maintains the accounts receivable ledger and refuses to take any vacation or sick days. (**Select only two procedures**)

11. The auditor suspects that the entity is inappropriately increasing the cash reported on its balance sheet by drawing a check on one account and not recording it as an outstanding check on that account and simultaneously recording it as a deposit in a second account. (**Select only one procedure**)

12. The auditor suspects that the entity's controller has overstated sales and accounts receivable by recording fictitious sales to regular customers in the entity's books. (**Select only two procedures**)

Task-Based Simulation 29 Solution

Audit Procedures		
	Authoritative Literature	
		Help

1. (**E**) Kiting involves manipulations causing an amount of cash to be included simultaneously in the balance of two or more bank accounts. Kiting schemes are based on the float period—the time necessary for a check deposited in one bank to clear the bank on which it was drawn. To detect kiting, a bank transfer schedule is prepared to determine whether cash is improperly included in two accounts.

2. (**D**) A comparison of the cleared checks to the year-end bank reconciliation will identify checks that were not mailed until after the first week of the subsequent year because most of those checks will not be returned with the cutoff statement and will appear to remain outstanding an abnormally long period of time.

3. (**H**) Among the terms confirmed for such a borrowing arrangement will be information on liens.

4. (**K, L**) A reply to the second request, or information from the credit agency, may confirm the existence of the new customer. Also, examination of shipping documents will reveal where the goods were shipped, and ordinarily to which party.

5. (**P**) Observing the payroll check distribution on a surprise basis will assist in detection since the auditor will examine details related to any paychecks not picked up by employees.

6. (**Q**) Vouching data in the payroll register to document authorized pay rates will reveal situations in which an employee is earning income at a rate that differs from the authorized rate.

7. (**A**) A comparison of the details of the cash receipts journal to the details on the daily deposit slips will reveal a circumstance since the details will have been posted to accounts during the last week of the year under audit.

8. (**U**) When vouchers are processed for merchandise not ordered or received, there will be no supporting purchase orders and receiving reports and this will alert the auditor to the problem.

9. (**B**) Scanning the debits to the fixed asset accounts and vouching selected amounts will reveal repairs that have improperly been capitalized.

10. (**A, J**) Lapping involves concealing a cash shortage by delaying the recording of journal entries for cash receipts. Since lapping includes differences between the details of postings to the cash receipts journal and corresponding deposit slips, comparing these records will reveal it. Also, confirmation requests may identify lapping when payments of receivables (as indicated by confirmation replies) appear to have taken too much time to be processed.

11. **(E)** Increasing cash by drawing a check in this manner is a form of kiting (see answer 1). Preparation of a bank transfer schedule will assist the auditor in identifying such transactions.

12. **(J, L)** Confirmations will identify overstated accounts receivable when customers disagree with the recorded balance due. Also, the related overstated sales will not have shipping documents indicating that a shipment has occurred.

Task-Based Simulation 30

Financial Statement Analysis		
	Authoritative Literature	
		Help

DietWeb Inc. (hereafter DietWeb) was incorporated and began business in March of 20X1, seven years ago. You are working on the 20X8 audit—your CPA firm's fifth audit of DietWeb. Analyze the following financial statements and reply to each of the questions that follow.

DietWeb, Inc.
BALANCE SHEET
December 31, 20X8 and 20X7
(in thousands)

Assets	20X8	20X7
Current assets		
Cash and cash equivalents	$3,032	$1,072
Trade receivables	485	450
Prepaid advertising expenses	59	609
Prepaid expenses and other current assets	175	230
Total current assets	3,751	2,361
Fixed assets, net	3,321	3,926
Total assets	$7,072	$6,287
Liabilities and shareholders' equity		
Current liabilities		
Accounts payable	$1,070	$909
Current maturities of notes payable	42	316
Deferred revenue	1,973	1,396
Other current liabilities	171	12
Total current liabilities	3,256	2,633
Long-term debt, less current maturity	34	176
Accrued liabilities	792	690
Deferred tax liability	15	145
Total liabilities	4,097	3,644

(Continued)

Assets	20X8	20X7
Shareholders' equity		
Common stock	6,040	4,854
Retained earnings	(3,065)	(2,211)
Total shareholders' equity	2,975	2,643
Total liabilities plus shareholders' equity	$7,072	$6,287

DietWeb, Inc.
INCOME STATEMENT
Two Years Ended December 31, 20X8 and 20X7
(in thousands)

Revenue	20X8	20X7
Costs and expenses	$19,166	$14,814
Cost of revenue	2,326	1,528
Product development	725	653
Sales and marketing	13,903	8,710
General and administrative	2,531	2,575
Depreciation and amortization	629	661
Impairment of intangible assets	35	–
Total costs and expenses	20,149	14,127
Net income before taxes	(983)	687
Income tax benefit	129	125
Net income (loss)	$(854)	$ 812

DietWeb, Inc.
STATEMENT OF CASH FLOWS
Year Ended December 31, 20X8

	20X8	20X7
Cash flows from operations		
Net income (loss)	$(854)	812
Adjustments to net income		
Depreciation	629	660
Increase in receivables	(35)	(47)
Decrease (Increase) in prepaid advertising	550	(650)
Decrease in other current assets	55	74
Increase (Decrease) in accounts payable	161	(540)
Increase in accrued liabilities	102	43
Increase (Decrease) in deferred revenue	432	(665)
Increase in common stock issued	1,186	–
Increase in other current liabilities	159	43

	20X8	20X7
Net cash provided (used) by operations	2,385	(270)
Cash flows from investing activities		
Purchase of property and equipment	(320)	2,016
Cash flows from financing activities		
New debt	613	40
Debt payments	(718)	(918)
Net cash provided (used) by financing activities	(105)	(878)
Net increase in cash and cash equivalents	$1,960	868
Cash and equivalents at beginning of year	$1,072	204
Cash and equivalents at end of year	$3,032	1,072

	(A)	(B)	(C)	(D)
1. The **most** likely misstatement in the financial statements is	O	O	O	O

   A. The increase in cash in 20X8.
   B. Treatment of impaired intangible assets as an expense in 20X8.
   C. Treatment of common stock issued as an adjustment to net income (loss) under cash flow from operations.
   D. An income tax benefit on the income statement as contrasted to income tax expense.

	(A)	(B)	(C)	(D)
2. Which of the following is the **most** unexpected change on the balance sheet, if one assumes the revenue increase in 20X8 is correct?	O	O	O	O

   A. Decrease in prepaid advertising expenses.
   B. Increase in accounts payable.
   C. Decrease in deferred revenues.
   D. Increase in common stock.

	(A)	(B)	(C)	(D)
3. Which of the following is **most** likely to lead the auditors to question whether DietWeb has the ability to continue as a going concern?	O	O	O	O

   A. The net loss incurred in 20X8.
   B. The decrease in cash that occurred in 20X8.
   C. Increases in fixed assets during 20X8.
   D. Mr. Readings serving as both CEO and chairman of the board of directors.

	(A)	(B)	(C)	(D)
4. Which of the following classifications is likely to be incorrect?	O	O	O	O

   A. Classification of prepaid expenses as assets.
   B. Classification of accrued liabilities as a noncurrent liability.
   C. A deferred tax liability with a positive balance.
   D. Retained earnings including a negative balance.

	(A)	(B)	(C)	(D)
5. Which of the following changes that have been recorded seems **most** unexpected?	O	O	O	O

   A. The decrease in fixed assets.
   B. The decrease in prepaid expenses and other current assets.
   C. An increase in cash during a year in which there is a net loss.
   D. An increase in accrued liabilities, given the large increase in sales.

Task-Based Simulation 30 Solution

```
┌─────────────────────────────────┐
│ Financial Statement Analysis    │
│   ┌───────────────────────────┐ │
│   │ Authoritative Literature  │ │
│   │    ┌──────┐               │ │
│   │    │ Help │               │ │
│   └────┴──────┴───────────────┘ │
└─────────────────────────────────┘
```

	(A)	(B)	(C)	(D)
1. The **most** likely misstatement in the financial statements is	○	○	●	○

    A. The increase in cash in 20X8.
    B. Treatment of impaired intangible assets as an expense in 20X8.
    C. Treatment of common stock issued as an adjustment to net income (loss) under cash flow from operations.
    D. An income tax benefit on the income statement as contrasted to income tax expense.

	(A)	(B)	(C)	(D)
2. Which of the following is the **most** unexpected change on the balance sheet, if one assumes the revenue increase in 20X8 is correct?	●	○	○	○

    A. Decrease in prepaid advertising expenses.
    B. Increase in accounts payable.
    C. Decrease in deferred revenues.
    D. Increase in common stock.

	(A)	(B)	(C)	(D)
3. Which of the following is **most** likely to lead the auditors to question whether DietWeb has the ability to continue as a going concern?	●	○	○	○

    A. The net loss incurred in 20X8.
    B. The decrease in cash that occurred in 20X8.
    C. Increases in fixed assets during 20X8.
    D. Mr. Readings serving as both CEO and chairman of the board of directors.

	(A)	(B)	(C)	(D)
4. Which of the following classifications is likely to be incorrect?	○	●	○	○

    A. Classification of prepaid expenses as assets.
    B. Classification of accrued liabilities as a noncurrent liability.
    C. A deferred tax liability with a positive balance.
    D. Retained earnings including a negative balance.

	(A)	(B)	(C)	(D)
5. Which of the following changes that have been recorded seems **most** unexpected?	●	○	○	○

    A. The decrease in fixed assets.
    B. The decrease in prepaid expenses and other current assets.
    C. An increase in cash during a year in which there is a net loss.
    D. An increase in accrued liabilities, given the large increase in sales.

Explanations

1. (**C**) The requirement is to identify a likely misstatement in the financial statements. Answer (C) is correct because common stock issued should be treated under financing rather than operations. Answer (A) is incorrect because an increase in cash may well occur—even during a year in which the company encounters a loss. Answer (B) is incorrect because there is no indication that the impairment expense is inappropriate. Answer (D) is incorrect because previous years' pattern of income and losses may create a situation in which a net income tax benefit occurs.

2. **(A)** The requirement is to identify, of the balance sheet changes listed, the most unexpected one. Answer (A) is unexpected in that prepaid advertising expenses decreased by more than 90%—at a time when the company increased its sales and marketing expenses so significantly. Answer (B) is incorrect because the relatively small increase in accounts payable may be expected given the increase in revenues. Answer (C) is incorrect because one would expect such an increase in deferred revenues as revenues increase. Answer (D) is incorrect since the company simply issued more stock—as indicated in the company profile.

3. **(A)** The requirement is to identify the factor that might lead the auditors to question whether DietWeb has the ability to continue as a going concern. Answer (A) is correct because the current net loss may raise a question as to future profitability. Answer (B) is incorrect because there was an increase in cash, not a decrease. Answer (C) is incorrect because fixed assets decreased rather than increased during 20X8. Answer (D) is incorrect because Mr. Reading's serving as CEO indicates no particular problem.

4. **(B)** The requirement is to identify an incorrect classification in the financial statements. Answer (B) is correct because accrued liabilities are in general current, not noncurrent, liabilities. Answer (A) is incorrect because prepaid expenses are ordinarily assets. Answer (C) is incorrect because one would expect the deferred tax liability to have a positive balance. Answer D is incorrect because the retained earnings negative balance may be explained by early year losses.

5. **(A)** The requirement is to identify the most unexpected change. Answer (A) is most unexpected because the expanded scale of operations would lead one to expect an increase in fixed assets, not a decrease. Answer (B) is incorrect because small changes in prepaid expense and other current assets are expected. Answer (C) is incorrect because it is not surprising that cash may increase when there is a net loss—particularly in a year when common stock has been issued. Answer (D) is incorrect because an increase in accrued liabilities is consistent with an increase in the scale of operations as indicated by a large increase in sales.

Introduction to Sampling

Task-Based Simulation 31

Sampling versus nonsampling risk

As a new assistant with Webber & Co. CPAs, you have been asked to perform research on the nature of sampling risk versus nonsampling risk.

Selections

A. AU-C
B. PCAOB
C. AT
D. AR
E. ET
F. BL
G. CS
H. QC

	(A)	(B)	(C)	(D)	(E)	(F)	(G)	(H)
1. Which title of the Professional Standards addresses this issue?	○	○	○	○	○	○	○	○

2. Enter the exact section and paragraph(s) which define sampling risk and nonsampling risk.

Task-Based Simulation 31 Solution

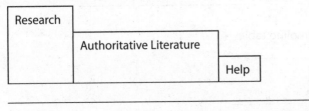

	(A)	(B)	(C)	(D)	(E)	(F)	(G)	(H)
1. Which title of the Professional Standards addresses this issue?	●	○	○	○	○	○	○	○

2. Enter the exact section and paragraph(s) which define sampling and nonsampling risk.

530	05

Probability-Proportional-to-Size (PPS) Sampling

Task-Based Simulation 32

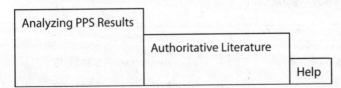

The following is a computer printout generated by audit software using probability-proportional-to-size (PPS) sampling:

Winz Corporation
Receivable Sampling Evaluation Results
December 31, 20X2

Population book value = $2,400,000; Tolerable misstatement = $280,000

Projected Misstatement

Book value	Audited value	Misstatement	Tainting percentage	Sampling interval	Projected misstatement
$1,000	$0	$1,000	100%	$80,000	$80,000
750	600	150	20%	$80,000	16,000
85,000	60,000	25,000	NA	NA	25,000
					$121,000

Basic Precision = 3.0 * $80,000 $240,000

Incremental Allowance

Reliability factor	Increment	(Increment −1)	Projected misstatement	Incremental allowance
3.00				
4.75	1.75	.75	$80,000	$60,000
6.30	1.55	.55	16,000	8,800
				$68,800

The software uses factors from the following PPS sampling table:

TABLE

Reliability Factors for Overstatements

Number of overstatements	Risk of incorrect acceptance				
	1%	5%	10%	15%	20%
0	4.61	3.00	2.31	1.90	1.61
1	6.64	4.75	3.89	3.38	3.00
2	8.41	6.30	5.33	4.72	4.28
3	10.05	7.76	6.69	6.02	5.52
4	11.61	9.16	8.00	7.27	6.73

Answer the following questions relating to the above worksheet:

Answers

1. What was the planned sample size?

2. What is the total misstatement in the sample?

3. What is the most likely total misstatement in the population?

4. Calculate the upper limit on misstatement.

5. Calculate the allowance for sampling risk.

6. Would one "accept" or "reject" the population as being materially correct?

7. What is the risk of incorrect acceptance?

A.	30 items	K.	$240,000
B.	60 items	L.	$308,800
C.	76 items	M.	$361,000
D.	90 items	N.	$429,800
E.	0	O.	Accept
F.	$26,150	P.	Reject
G.	$68,800	Q.	5%
H.	$80,000	R.	20%
I.	$121,000	S.	100%
J.	$189,800		

Task-Based Simulation 32 Solution

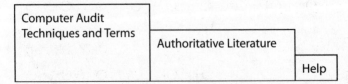

1. **(A)** Thirty items. Calculated by dividing the population book value ($2,400,000) by the sampling interval size ($80,000). Accordingly $2,400,000/80,000 = 30 items.
2. **(G)** $26,150. Calculated by summing the misstatements ($1,000 + $150 + $25,000 = $26,150).
3. **(I)** $121,000. Projected misstatement represents the most likely total misstatement in the population ($121,000).
4. **(N)** $429,800. The upper limit on misstatement is the sum of projected misstatement, basic precision, and the incremental allowance ($121,000 + $240,000 + $68,800 = $429,800).
5. **(L)** $308,800. The allowance for sampling risk is the sum of basic precision and the incremental allowance ($240,000 + $68,800 = $308,800).
6. **(P)** Reject because the upper limit on misstatement ($429,800) exceeds the tolerable misstatement ($280,000).
7. **(5%)** Because basic precision uses a 3.0 factor, the test is being performed at 5%.

IT (Computer) Auditing

IT Controls—General Controls

Task-Based Simulation 33

Computer processing has become the primary means used to process financial accounting information in most businesses. Consistent with this situation, CPAs must have knowledge of audit techniques using computers and of computer terminology.

Select the type of audit technique being described in **items 1 through 5**. Computer audit techniques may be used once, more than once, or not at all.

Computer audit technique

A. Auditing "around" the computer
B. Integrated test facility
C. Parallel simulation
D. Test data

Description	(A)	(B)	(C)	(D)
1. Auditing by manually testing the input and output of a computer system.	○	○	○	○
2. Dummy transactions developed by the auditor and processed by the client's computer programs, generally for a batch processing system.	○	○	○	○
3. Fictitious and real transactions are processed together without the client's operating personnel knowing of the testing process.	○	○	○	○
4. May include a simulated division or subsidiary into the accounting system with the purpose of running fictitious transactions through it.	○	○	○	○
5. Uses a generalized audit software package prepared by the auditors.	○	○	○	○

For **items 6 through 10** select the type of computer control that is described in the definition that is presented. Each control may be used once, more than once, or not at all.

Control

E. Backup and recovery	J. Hash total
F. Boundary protection	K. Missing data check
G. Check digit	L. Personal identification codes
H. Control digit	M. Visitor entry logs
I. File protection ring	

Description	(E)	(F)	(G)	(H)	(I)	(J)	(K)	(L)	(M)
6. A control that will detect blanks existing in input data when they should not.	○	○	○	○	○	○	○	○	○
7. A control to ensure that jobs run simultaneously in a multiprogramming environment cannot change the allocated memory of another job.	○	○	○	○	○	○	○	○	○
8. A digit added to an identification number to detect certain types of data transmission or transposition errors.	○	○	○	○	○	○	○	○	○
9. A terminal control to limit access to programs or files to authorized users.	○	○	○	○	○	○	○	○	○
10. A total of one field for all the records of a batch where the total is meaningless for financial purposes.	○	○	○	○	○	○	○	○	○

Task-Based Simulation 33 Solution

Computer Audit Techniques and Terms
Authoritative Literature
Help

Description	(A)	(B)	(C)	(D)
1. Auditing by manually testing the input and output of a computer system.	●	○	○	○
2. Dummy transactions developed by the auditor and processed by the client's computer programs, generally for a batch processing system.	○	○	○	●
3. Fictitious and real transactions are processed together without the client's operating personnel knowing of the testing process.	○	●	○	○
4. May include a simulated division or subsidiary into the accounting system with the purpose of running fictitious transactions through it.	○	●	○	○
5. Uses a generalized audit software package prepared by the auditors.	○	○	●	○

Explanations

1. **(A)** Auditing "around" the computer involves examining inputs into and outputs from the computer while ignoring processing, as contrasted to auditing "through" the computer, which in some manner directly utilizes the computer's processing ability.
2. **(D)** Test data is a set of dummy transactions developed by the auditor and processed by the client's computer programs to determine whether the controls that the auditor intends to rely upon are functioning as expected.
3. **(B)** An integrated test facility introduces dummy transactions into a system in the midst of live transactions and is often built into the system during the original design.
4. **(B)** An integrated test facility approach may incorporate a simulated division or subsidiary into the accounting system with the sole purpose of running test data through it.
5. **(C)** Parallel simulation involves processing actual client data through an auditor's software program to determine whether the output equals that obtained when the client processed the data.

Description	(E)	(F)	(G)	(H)	(I)	(J)	(K)	(L)	(M)
6. A control that will detect blanks existing in input data when they should not.	○	○	○	○	○	○	●	○	○
7. A control to ensure that jobs run simultaneously in a multiprogramming environment cannot change the allocated memory of another job.	○	●	○	○	○	○	○	○	○
8. A digit added to an identification number to detect certain types of data transmission or transposition errors.	○	○	●	○	○	○	○	○	○
9. A terminal control to limit access to programs or files to authorized users.	○	○	○	○	○	○	○	●	○
10. A total of one field for all the records of a batch where the total is meaningless for financial purposes.	○	○	○	○	○	●	○	○	○

Explanations

6. **(K)** A missing data check tests whether blanks exist in input data where they should not (e.g., an employee's division number). When the data is missing, an error message is output.
7. **(F)** Boundary protection is necessary because most large computers have more than one job running simultaneously (a multiprogramming environment). To ensure that these simultaneous jobs cannot destroy or change the allocated memory of another job, the systems software contains boundary protection controls.
8. **(G)** A check digit is an extra digit added to an identification number to detect certain types of data transmission or transposition errors. It is used to verify that the number was entered into the computer system correctly; one approach is using a check digit that is calculated as a mathematical combination of the other digits.
9. **(L)** Personal identification codes require individuals to in some manner identify themselves to determine that only authorized users access programs or files.
10. **(J)** A hash total is the total of one field for all the records of a batch where the total is a meaningless total for financial purposes, such as a mathematical sum of employee social security numbers to determine that all employees have been processed.

Forming Conclusions and Reporting

Audit Reports

Introduction to Audit Reports

Task-Based Simulation 34

Standard Report Elements

The senior auditor on your job has pointed out to you that the CPA firm always signs the audit report both for nonpublic companies with its signature and its location (Yuma, Arizona) and she suggests that she thinks it isn't necessary to provide the location.

1. Identify the title, section, and paragraph of the auditing standards that provide the basic elements that must be included in the auditor's standard report.

	Yes	No
2. Is she correct or incorrect concerning inclusion of the location?	○	○

Task-Based Simulation 34 Solution

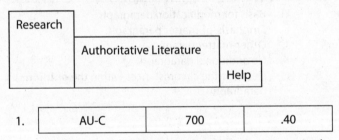

1.	AU-C	700	.40

2. She is not correct; including the location is required.

Disclaimer of Opinion

Task-Based Simulation 35

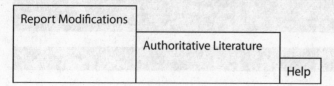

Report Modifications

Authoritative Literature

Help

Assume that **items 1 through 8** are situations that Jones, CPA, has encountered during his audit of Welles Incorporated, a nonpublic company. List A represents the types of opinions the auditor ordinarily would issue and List B represents a portion of the needed report modifications—whether an additional paragraph will be included. For each situation, select one response from List A and one from List B. Select as the best answers for each item the action the auditor would normally take. The types of opinions in List A and the report modifications in List B may be selected once, more than once, or not at all.

Assume

- The auditor is independent.
- The auditor previously expressed an unmodified opinion on the prior year's financial statements.
- Only single-year (not comparative) statements are presented for the current year.
- The conditions for an unmodified opinion exist unless contradicted by the facts.
- The conditions stated in the items to be answered are material, unless otherwise indicated.
- Each item to be answered is independent of the others.
- No report modifications are to be made except in response to the factual situation.
- The auditor will not treat a situation as an "emphasis of a matter" in what remains an unmodified audit report unless it is one of those circumstances specifically illustrated in the Professional Standards as an example of a matter an auditor may wish to emphasize.

List A	List B
Types of opinions	**Report modifications**
A. Either an "except for" qualified opinion or an adverse opinion	H. Basis for modification paragraph.
B. Either a disclaimer of opinion or an "except for" qualified opinion	I. Emphasis-of-matter paragraph.
C. Either an adverse opinion or a disclaimer of opinion	J. Other-matter paragraph
D. An "except for" qualified opinion	K. No additional paragraph.
E. An unmodified opinion	L. Describe the circumstances within the **opinion** paragraph
F. An adverse opinion	
G. A disclaimer of opinion	

	Types of Opinions (A–G)	Additional Paragraph (H–L)

1. Jones hired an actuary to assist in corroborating Welles' complex pension calculations concerning accrued pension liabilities that account for 35% of the client's total liabilities. The actuary's findings are reasonably close to Welles' calculations and support the financial statements.

2. Welles holds a note receivable consisting of principal and accrued interest payable in 20X4. The note's maker recently filed a voluntary bankruptcy petition, but Welles failed to reduce the recorded value of the note to its net realizable value, which is approximately 20% of the recorded amount.

	Types of Opinions (A–G)	Additional Paragraph (H–L)

3. Jones was engaged to audit a client's financial statements after the annual physical inventory count. The accounting records were not sufficiently reliable to enable him to become satisfied as to the year-end inventory balances.

4. Jones found an immaterial adjustment relating to inventory. Welles has refused to adjust the financial statements to reflect this immaterial item.

5. Welles' financial statements do not disclose certain long-term lease obligations. Jones determined that the omitted disclosures are required by FASB.

6. Jones decided not to take responsibility for the work of another CPA who audited a wholly owned subsidiary of Welles. The total assets and revenues of the subsidiary represent 27% and 28%, respectively, of the related consolidated totals.

7. Welles changed its method of accounting for the cost of inventories from FIFO to LIFO. Jones concurs with the change although it has a material effect on the comparability of the financial statements.

8. Due to losses and adverse key financial ratios, Jones has substantial doubt about Welles' ability to continue as a going concern for a reasonable period of time. The client has adequately disclosed its financial difficulties in a note to its financial statements. Also, Jones has ruled out the use of a disclaimer of opinion.

Task-Based Simulation 35 Solution

Report Modifications		
	Authoritative Literature	
		Help

1. **(E, K)** When an auditor hires a specialist to assist in corroborating a client estimate (here, complex pension calculations), and that specialist's findings are reasonably close to those of the client, no report modification is required or permitted. Since the specialist's findings support the financial statements in this situation, a standard unmodified audit report is appropriate. When major unresolved differences between the findings of management and the specialist exist, report modification is appropriate.

2. **(A, I)** When the client's financial statements materially depart from generally accepted accounting principles, either a qualified opinion or an adverse opinion is appropriate, depending on the magnitude of the misstatement. The value of the client's note receivable has been impaired and therefore the client should write the note receivable down to its net realizable value. The auditor will consider the pervasiveness of the misstatement to determine whether to issue a qualified opinion or an adverse opinion on the basis of the materiality of the misstatement. A basis for modification paragraph will be included.

3. **(B, H)** A situation where the auditor is unable to obtain sufficient appropriate audit evidence is referred to as a scope limitation. A scope limitation may require the auditor to either qualify his or her opinion or to disclaim an opinion altogether. Since the auditor was unable to observe the inventory count or to obtain evidence through alternative procedures, the auditor will have to decide whether to issue a qualified opinion or a disclaimer of opinion. The decision will be based on the auditor's judgment as to the nature and magnitude of the potential effects of the matters in question and by their significance to the financial statements. A basis for modification paragraph will be added to the report.

4. **(E, K)** An auditor need not modify a report for an immaterial item that the client declines to reflect.

5. **(A, I)** Since the client's financial statements omitted required disclosures on certain long-term lease obligations, they are not prepared in accordance with generally accepted accounting principles. As a result, the auditor should express either a qualified opinion or an adverse opinion. The decision to express either a qualified or adverse opinion is based on the pervasiveness of the misstatement. The audit report, for either opinion, will include a basis for modification paragraph to describe the substantive reasons for the modification.

6. **(E, K)** When a principal auditor decides not to take responsibility for the work of another auditor, the principal auditor should make reference to the work of the other auditor in the audit report, but no additional paragraph is added to the report. The opinion remains unmodified.

7. **(E, H)** When an auditor agrees with a change in accounting principles, a lack of consistency results in an unmodified opinion with an emphasis-of-matter paragraph.

8. **(E, H)** The auditor has substantial doubt about the client's ability to remain a going concern for a reasonable period of time. The audit report should emphasize this concern to the financial statement users. As a result, the auditor's report will include an unmodified opinion with an emphasis-of-matter paragraph following the opinion paragraph.

Consistency of Financial Statements

Task-Based Simulation 36

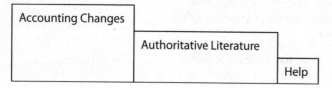

The audit of a nonpublic client, Park Publishing Co. for the year ended September 30, 20X2, is near completion. Your senior, Dave Moore, at Tyler & Tyler CPAs, has asked you to draft the audit report, considering the following:

- During fiscal year 20X2, Park changed its depreciation method. The engagement partner concurred with this change in accounting principle and its justification, and Moore wants it properly reflected in the auditors' report; the change is discussed in Note 7 to the financial statements.
- The 20X2 financial statements are affected by an uncertainty concerning a lawsuit over patent infringement, the outcome of which cannot presently be estimated. Moore has suggested the need for an emphasis-of-matter paragraph in the auditors' report related to this matter, which is discussed in Note 4 to the financial statements.
- The financial statements for the year ended September 30, 20X1, are to be presented for comparative purposes. Wilson & Wilson previously audited these statements and expressed a standard unmodified opinion.

1. Identify the paragraphs in the Professional Standards that provide guidance regarding the periods included in the auditor's evaluation of consistency. First present the paragraph(s) for the actual requirement and then the related application and other explanatory material *guidance*.
2. Identify the paragraph in Professional Standards that provides an example report of an auditor's report with an emphasis-of-matter paragraph because of pending *litigation*.
3. Wilson & Wilson's audit report will not be reissued. Identify the paragraphs in the Professional Standards that provide the requirements as to what the auditor should include in an other-matter paragraph concerning the 20X1 audit of Wilson & Wilson.

Task-Based Simulation 36 Solution

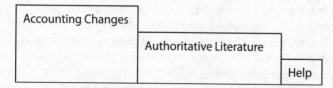

1. The appropriate guidance regarding reporting on the periods covered is AU-C 708.06 with interpretative guidance at AU-C 708.A2–.A3.

2. The appropriate guidance regarding emphasis of a matter is found in AU-C 706.A13.
3. The appropriate guidance regarding reporting on comparative financial statements is found in AU-C 700.54.

Other Types of Reports

SSARSs—Review Engagements

Task-Based Simulation 37

Research

Authoritative Literature

Help

Review Reports

The president of Enright Corporation, a nonpublic client, asked you to perform a review of the financial statements for the current year only. You have now completed your inquiry and other review procedures and find that you can issue a standard review report.

Selections

A. AU-C
B. PCAOB
C. AT
D. AR-C
E. ET
F. BL
G. CS
H. QC

	(A)	(B)	(C)	(D)	(E)	(F)	(G)	(H)
1. Which title of the Professional Standards presents a standard review report on one year?	○	○	○	○	○	○	○	○
2. Enter the exact section and paragraph that lists the basic elements of such a review report.								

Task-Based Simulation 37 Solution

Research

Authoritative Literature

Help

	(A)	(B)	(C)	(D)	(E)	(F)	(G)	(H)
1. Which title of the Professional Standards presents a standard review report on one year?	○	○	○	●	○	○	○	○
2. Enter the exact section and paragraph that lists the basic elements of such a review report.			90		39			

Other Professional Services

PCAOB on Reporting on Internal Control in an Integrated Audit

Task-Based Simulation 38

Integrated Audits

Assume that you are assigned to the audit of Regis Corporation, an issuer company. Your firm is performing its first integrated audit for the company, and the partner on the engagement has asked you to research professional standards to identify the controls that address the risk of fraud.

Selections

A. AU-C
B. PCAOB
C. AT
D. AR
E. ET
F. BL
G. CS
H. QC

	(A)	(B)	(C)	(D)	(E)	(F)	(G)	(H)
1. Which title of the Professional Standards addresses this issue?	○	○	○	○	○	○	○	○
2. Enter the exact Auditing Standard Number or section and paragraph with helpful information.								

Task-Based Simulation 38 Solution

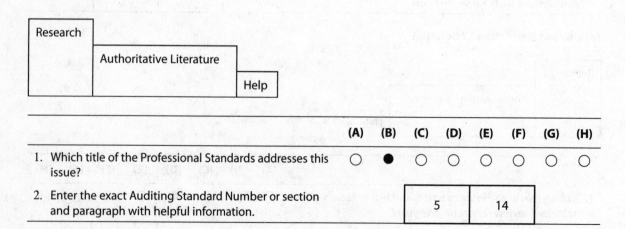

	(A)	(B)	(C)	(D)	(E)	(F)	(G)	(H)
1. Which title of the Professional Standards addresses this issue?	○	●	○	○	○	○	○	○
2. Enter the exact Auditing Standard Number or section and paragraph with helpful information.			5		14			

Index